The Founding of the Roman Catholic Church in Oceania

1825 to 1850

Princeton Theological Monograph Series

K. C. Hanson, Charles M. Collier, and D. Christopher Spinks, Series Editors

Other volumes in the series:

Ralph M. Wiltgen
The Founding of the Roman Catholic Church in Melanesia and Micronesia, 1850–1875

Richard Valantasis et al., editors
The Subjective Eye: Essays in Honor of Margaret Miles

Philip E. Harrold
A Place Somewhat Apart

S. Donald Fortson, III
Colonial Presbyterianism

David Hein
Geoffrey Fisher: Archbishop of Canterbury, 1945–1961

Estrelda Alexander and Amos Yong, editors
Philip's Daughters: Women in Pentecostal-Charismatic Leadership

Bernie A. Van De Walle
The Heart of the Gospel

Rod Janzen
Paul Tschetter

Brett H. Smith
Labor's Millenium

The Founding of the Roman Catholic Church in Oceania

1825 to 1850

RALPH M. WILTGEN

FOREWORD BY WILLIAM R. BURROWS

PICKWICK *Publications* · Eugene, Oregon

THE FOUNDING OF THE ROMAN CATHOLIC CHURCH IN OCEANIA, 1825 TO 1850

Princeton Theological Monograph Series 143

Pickwick Publications
A Division of Wipf and Stock Publishers
199 W. 8th Ave., Suite 3
Eugene, OR 97401

ISBN 13: 978-1-60899-536-3

Cataloging-in-Publication data:

Wiltgen, Ralph M., 1921–2007.

The founding of the Roman Catholic Church in Oceania, 1825 to 1850 / Ralph M. Wiltgen, with a Foreword by William R. Burrows.

Princeton Theological Monograph Series 143

xxiv + 602 p.; 25 cm.

ISBN 13: 978-1-60899-536-3 (alk. paper)

Includes bibliographical references (p. 551–56) and index

1. Catholic Church—Oceania—History. 2. Catholic church—Missions. 3. Missions—Oceania. I. Burrows, William R. II. Title. III. Series.

BV3640 .W5 2010

Manufactured in the U.S.A.

To
my nieces and nephews,
Kenny, Len, Don, Pat, Michael, Janet, Carol
Bill, Jim, Nancy, Susan
Tom, Ann, Larry, Barbara, Michael, Julie, Carolyn

CORRIGENDA

'Our missions here in Oceania
are difficult, but also possible,
and much good has already been done.
We also have reason to believe
that with time and with patience
more good will still be done.'

Bishop Pierre Bataillon, S.M.
Vicar Apostolic of Central Oceania
15 June 1852

Foreword to the 2010 Edition

WILLIAM R. BURROWS

ALL THOSE INTERESTED IN THE HISTORY OF THE VAST EXPANSE OF OCEANIA BETWEEN Hawaii and the western tip of New Guinea and of the rise of Catholicism in it will welcome this new edition of *The Founding of the Catholic Church in Oceania 1825 – 1850* by Father Ralph M. Wiltgen, SVD. Originally published by the Australian National University Press in 1979 in a cloth edition, it has been out of print for a number of years. It is in print again, thanks to Wipf & Stock Publisher's digitizing program, which uses the latest technology to make available for scholars important books covering the full range of Christian biblical, historical, and theological topics.

In a review of this book in the April 1981 issue of *American Historical Review*, Colin Newbury of Oxford University notes the detail in which Wiltgen recounts the origins of the Vatican's division of the Pacific, the marshalling of French and Italian resources, and even the existence of "official intrigue," "divided jurisdiction," and the "clash of personalities and policies" among the founding generation of missionaries. That same month, writing in *Missiology: An International Review*, Charles Forman says that, "This book confirms Wiltgen's reputation of being a "master of a narrative style of historical writing…based on meticulous examination of the archives of [the Congregation for the Evangelization of Peoples] and of the missionary Orders which worked in the Pacific." And he notes with dismay the fact documented so well by Wiltgen, "how little preparation was provided for the missionaries themselves," including their relative lack of interest in indigenous cultures. Forman also calls attention to their refusal to countenance "any revenge when they suffered at the hands of the local peoples."

Father Wiltgen, a member of the Society of the Divine Word—known popularly as the Divine Word Missionaries or the "SVD" (after the initials of its official Latin name, *Societas Verbi Divini*)—worked off and on for twenty years on this book. The narrative begins in 1825 in Hawaii, 71 years before the SVD began work on the northern coast of the country now called Papua New Guinea. The assignment to write the history of the SVD's work there, which was to tell the story from the mission's origins down to the post-World War II reconstruction era, was given Wiltgen in 1959, the year after Johannes Schütte took office as the sixth superior general of the Society.

The primary task that Wiltgen had been brought to Rome to accomplish, however, was to establish a professional news service and public relations department for his international missionary congregation. He was chosen for that work because superiors judged that his academic preparation as a scholar of mission and his abilities as a journalist and publicist would foster one of Father Schütte's chief goals: helping American and European Catholics understand the work of mission and grasp that the missionary vocation was intrinsic to Christian identity, not an add-on.

Founded in 1875, the Society of the Divine undertook its first missions in 1879 in China. It began work in West Africa in 1892 and northeast New Guinea in 1896. Born in 1921, Wiltgen was a Chicagoan who began training to become an SVD missionary in 1938, going through a twelve-year training period culminating in ordination to the priesthood in 1950. Imbibing the work ethic of the German SVDs who directed the Order's work in the United States from its foundation in 1897 through the 1940's, Wiltgen was legendary for intelligence, diligence, and the ability to carry on what we today call multi-tasking. Throughout his working life he always wore several hats and took on tasks that would challenge three normal men to do. From the beginning of his career till its end, he was simultaneously a priest who relished work in parishes, a journalist, a publicist, and an historian.

Instead of being assigned to missionary work overseas, as he had requested, Wiltgen went to the Gregorian University in Rome for doctoral studies in missiology (the history, theology, and theory of Christian mission) after ordination. The year he arrived at SVD headquarters in Rome, there were seventeen "student fathers" in residence in the Collegio del Verbo Divino. They came from around the world and introduced Wiltgen to the Society's internationality, an aspect of its identity that the SVD was emphasizing as it struggled to rebuild missions damaged and halted by the Second World War.

There were at least two important results of Wiltgen's assignment to doctoral studies in Rome. First, he developed an orientation that regarded missiology as primarily a study of mission history. Although, in the persons of such giants as Wilhelm Schmidt and Paul Schebesta, the SVD rightly lays claim to its members being among the principal founders of missionary anthropology, Wiltgen's bent was not toward the social anthropological nor to the theological dimensions of mission studies that became especially prominent during and after the Second Vatican Council. Having studied in Rome, he learned German (then the language of the house and of the Society as a whole) and Italian (the language of Church officialdom). And he came to the attention of superiors who needed native English-speakers in public positions to keep the Society from appearing to be a German-only organization. He would spend the rest of his life as a key person in the SVD generalate's ministry of helping members of many diverse nationalities work together harmoniously in the service of the gospel.

Wiltgen's dissertation on the history of West African Catholic missions was published in 1956 as *Gold Coast Mission History 1471–1880* (Techny, Illinois: Mission Press).

This is significant if one is to understand the grand plan for his New Guinea history. His research into African Catholic history spanned the four hundred years before the SVD began working in Togo. It showed him both how rich the archival resources were and how events recorded in them influenced what his relatively young Society's confreres met, how they adapted to it, and what they did.

When Father Schütte and the New Guinea SVDs said yes to Wiltgen's proposal that he tell the story of their work, it was in his mind, necessary to follow the path laid down in his dissertation research by beginning at the beginning with the tale of the SVD's missionary forebears in the Pacific. Thus what he projected to be a five-volume work begins in 1825, starting with the background story in France, Italy, and the Vatican of how the Picpus Fathers (Missionaries of the Sacred Hearts of Jesus and Mary) began work in the Sandwich Islands (Hawaii). He continues with the advent of the Marists in the South Pacific in 1836, and the foundation of the Church in New Zealand and Australia. This book, accordingly, centers on the beginnings of Catholicism in the far-flung islands of Micronesia, Polynesia, and eastern Melanesia, and includes Catholic beginnings in Australia and New Zealand.

The second book of Wiltgen's projected series narrows his focus to Melanesia and Micronesia. It was published by Wipf and Stock in January 2008, just after Father Wiltgen died (on 6 December 2007), as *The Founding of the Roman Catholic Church in Melanesia and Micronesia, 1850–1875*. You will note that Wiltgen ends the second book still twenty-one years short of 13 August 1896, the day when Divine Word Fathers Joseph Erdweg (1870–1925) and Franz Vormann (1868–1929) arrived in Friederich Wilhelmshafen, now known as Madang, as the first Divine Word Missionaries in Northeast New Guinea, which was then known as Kaiser Wilhelmsland.

In the SVD archives in Rome one finds evidence that Wiltgen intended to write at least three more volumes to tell the story of the founding of the church in Melanesia (i.e., the New Guinea main island and outlying islands to the east that run from the Bismarck Archipelago in the north through the Solomon Islands, which stretch hundreds of miles south). The center of his work would be the history of the SVD, on the northeast coast and the highlands. Nevertheless, whatever the understanding of his New Guinea confreres or Roman superiors, Wiltgen was committed to recounting the work of the Missionaries of the Sacred Heart in the Bismarck Archipelago and Papua, as well as the Marist missionaries in the Solomons and elsewhere from the 1870s through the post-World War II period. Although he was a publicist for his own order, he was also an admirer of the work of other communities.

Wiltgen, as I observe above, appears not to have had a great deal of interest in the anthropological or theological dimensions of mission studies. In addition, he pays scant attention to Protestant missions, although their work is just as significant, and in many areas virtually the only Christian presence. This book would have been far more valuable, for instance, if it had compared Catholic methods with the way in which Protestant missionaries nurtured churches in Polynesia in the 1820s that sent hundreds of missionaries to Papua in the 1870s. Instead, this is Roman Catholic ecclesiastical and mission history, the story of what European missionaries did — mostly priests, brothers, and bishops. Alongside this band of ecclesiastical personae, however, appears a motley cast of sailors, traders, burgeoning convict colonies, administrators, and colorful, often alcoholic layabouts. They are all portrayed in detail, including the details that reveal some as scoundrels and scalawags, others as legalistic careerists, and many who, though often heroic, even saintly in their lives, are not the sort of person one would want to take on a long trip.

Above all, Wiltgen's book introduces us to the manners and mores of a bye-gone era, and he brings it alive with direct quotes of its principals from primary documents he has located in archives spread across three continents. His book is a treasure trove with pointers for future researchers to pursue leads that go in dozens of different directions, including the intercultural encounter of missionaries and indigenous peoples that is, unfortunately, missing from this volume. On the terms set by Ralph Wiltgen, nevertheless, there is great value in this book, primarily because it shows the way in which nineteenth-century Catholic leaders responded to and took part in shaping an intercultural network that extended across the largest geographical area on the planet. Through the work these pioneers initiated, Christianity became the primary social network that joined the peoples of a vast Pacific Island world that had been physically and systematically linked for the first time in the nineteen century through improved navigation and ship-building technologies. Anyone who has worked in the Pacific for even a short time realizes that their Christian faith today forms a bond like no other among these far-flung peoples.

I first met Ralph Wiltgen in 1958 and thereafter on numerous occasions. The most memorable was during a period of three years in Rome from 1969 through 1972 when we lived in the same house on via dei Verbiti near the Pyramid of Caius Celsius. I was then a member of the SVD and studying theology at the Gregorian University. He was working on the book you hold in your hands. When Ralph heard I was assigned to New Guinea, he came to my room, and gave me a warm *abbrazzo Romano*, despite the fact that we were on opposite ends of the theological spectrum in those years so soon after Vatican Council II. I still remember his words, "Bill, you will never work with better men than those you'll be with in New Guinea." He was right.

May this new edition of Ralph Wiltgen's contribution to telling their story bring the lives and work of the predecessors of yesterday's and today's Divine Word Missionaries to the attention of a new generation.

Most of all, may it help Melanesian Christians understand better the lives of their European forebears in faith as they proceed with the work of translating the Gospel into their cultures.

Cortlandt Manor, New York
Holy Week 2010

Foreword

This is a book that many of us have been hoping for since the days when mission history progressed from the level of apologetics and works intended for the edification of adherents to that of objective historiography, a transition affirmed by the opening to researchers of the archives of Catholic Church bodies, including the religious orders, in Rome.

The new dispensation in ecclesiastical literature has enabled Father Wiltgen to give us a definitive study of the inception and early development of the Catholic Church in Oceania, from the founding of a Prefecture Apostolic for Hawaii in 1825, to its successful establishment throughout most of Polynesia and Australia by 1850.

It is a work of major scholarship, written with a sympathetic understanding of the difficulties encountered, born of his personal knowledge of the region, but nonetheless pointing out without fear or favour where errors were made or statements show less than candour. There can be few indeed who possess the training, dedication, patience and linguistic equipment needed to locate the pertinent records and translate them from their original Latin, French, Spanish and Italian, let alone to incorporate the gist of these authoritative primary sources, connected by his own erudite commentary, into a convincing and eminently readable history.

I write readable deliberately, for one might be pardoned for thinking that the story of missionary progress from a single prefecture apostolic to an archdiocese and no less than sixteen dioceses and vicariates apostolic might make for tedious reading. This is emphatically not the case, however, for through these pages pass a procession of diverse and often colourful characters: visionaries, adventurers, bureaucrats, martyrs—the whole range of human nature from saints to sinners. All have their parts in a dramatic chronicle of dedicated striving to save souls in the ultimate frontier of missionary endeavour. The result is a book which I found to be completely absorbing.

Admittedly the locale of Father Wiltgen's narrative possesses a fascination of its own to add to the interest of the events portrayed, for to the Pacific Ocean and its islands, including New Zealand, comprising a third of the earth's surface, he has combined for good measure the continent of Australia, in itself a third larger than all Europe. Thus the setting includes not only the romantic and salubrious islands of eastern Polynesia, where the main adversary was the would-be monopolistic Protestant missionary, but also inhospitable and unhealthy Melanesia, where missionary zeal alone proved unavailing against human intransigence and environmental dangers, as it did in the case of the peripatetic Australian Aborigine.

It is to be devoutly hoped that the success of this volume, which seems assured, will encourage Father Wiltgen to continue his story of the Catholic Church in the Pacific islands in a further study.

Research School of Pacific Studies   H. E. Maude
Australian National University
Canberra, Australia

Preface

Twenty-five years ago in my university studies of the historical method I was impressed by the words of the Greek historian Polybius: 'What does it profit the reader to wade through wars and battles and sieges of towns, and enslavements of peoples, if he is not to penetrate to the knowledge of the causes which have made one party succeed and the other fail in their respective situations?' Up to that time history seemed to me a mere collection of uninteresting names and dates, but penetrating to the knowledge of the causes did make it come alive. This I have tried to do, recounting events in such a way as to make the founders of the Roman Catholic Church in Oceania come alive. By their words and by their actions they should win your admiration, your pity, your scorn.

Seeking out the causes which made some men succeed and others fail required this researcher to wade through thousands of pages of handwritten documents in many different scripts 125 to 150 years old, some almost indecipherable, and most in Italian, Latin, French and Spanish. There were some printed sources in German and pitifully few in English, the language in which I had to tell my story. This research and study, supplemented by interviews and correspondence initiated by the author, led to the accumulation of additional information and uncovered further original documentation, including maps and photographs. From the ensemble it was possible to obtain new insights and to detect hidden causes that otherwise might have gone unnoticed. At this point it became possible to re-create the circumstances of time and place, so necessary to understand and to envision the often slow and always painful progress which took place in Oceania from 1825 to 1850.

Why did I begin with the year 1825? There were indeed numerous missionary efforts made in Oceania prior to that time, but these were sporadic and their unconnected histories are better adapted for a review than for a book. From the founding of the Prefecture Apostolic of the Sandwich Islands in 1825, however, Oceania saw continued and interrelated development expanding to one archdiocese, eight dioceses and eight vicariates apostolic by 1850. Telling how this came about, introducing you to the men responsible for founding them, showing you the friction, the suffering, the success and also the failure that accompanied their efforts, all this is the scope of my book.

In conclusion I must give thanks to all those who have assisted me in numberless ways to transform the writing up of this history from a dream to a reality. I thank especially my family and my friends for their prayers, support and encouragement. Thanks to the Very Reverend John Musinsky, S.V.D., superior general of the Divine Word Missionaries, for freeing me for this task. Thanks to all archivists and librarians as well as so many others who have supplied me with information upon request. My very special thanks go to Father Josef Metzler, archivist of the Sacred Congregation for the Evangelisation of Nations, to Father Amerigo Cools for his precision on matters concerning the Picpus Missions, and to Father Jean Coste, ever ready to locate Marist documents for me. I thank my publisher for his confidence in my work. My deepest thanks go to my faithful, efficient and self-sacrificing secretaries: Rosemarie Barto, Rose Marie Brown and Patricia O'Connell. I also wish to thank Ann Lahey for her thorough editing of the manuscript. And above all, thanks be to God for the health and the patience needed to bring this book to completion.

Special acknowledgment is due to the Sacred Congregation for the Evangelisation of Nations, to the Generalates of the Society of Mary (S.M.), Congregation of the Sacred Hearts of Jesus and Mary (SS.CC.), and the Pontifical Institute for Foreign Missions (P.I.M.E.), as also to the *Catholic Weekly* (Sydney), for permission to reproduce in this book materials found in their files. The maps were drawn by the Cartographic Office, Department of Human Geography, Australian National University, based on sketches prepared by me from information in the archives consulted.

Generous subsidies to publication were given by the Catholic Bishops Conference of Papua New Guinea and the Solomon Islands; De Rance, Inc., Milwaukee, U.S.A.; MISSIO, International Catholic Missionary Organisation, Aachen, Federal Republic of Germany; Miss Rose Marie Brown; Mrs Emil J. Kochton; Mr and Mrs Jack M. Reich; Mrs Lucie Stock; Mrs Ellen M. Wayne; Mrs Martha Wiltgen; and the Society of the Divine Word in Rome, Australia, Papua New Guinea and the United States of America.

Ralph M. Wiltgen, S.V.D.
11 July 1979

Collegio del Verbo Divino
Cas. Post. 5080
00153 Rome, Italy

Contents

Illustrations

Introduction

Readers unacquainted with hierarchical structure will need the following explanation in order better to understand this history.

The pope, in governing the Roman Catholic Church, is assisted by Sacred Congregations composed of cardinals with a cardinal prefect as head. The Sacred Congregation *de Propaganda Fide* founded in 1622 and since 15 August 1967 also called the Sacred Congregation for the Evangelisation of Nations, supervises and directs missionary activity around the world. Mission territories under its jurisdiction in their ascending order of rank are Prefectures Apostolic headed by Prefects Apostolic (priests), Vicariates Apostolic headed by Vicars Apostolic (bishops), Dioceses headed by Diocesan Bishops, and Archdioceses headed by Archbishops. Some few missions, like Sydney, pass through all four stages. An Ecclesiastical Province, the highest form of hierarchical development, is made up of one Archdiocese and one or more Dioceses, Vicariates Apostolic and Prefectures Apostolic.

Although the personnel needed to staff these mission territories may be drawn from the secular (or diocesan) clergy anywhere in the world, the personnel for the most part comes from religious communities known as orders, societies, or congregations. Before individuals or groups may take up missionary work in a specific territory, however, they need authorisation from the pope and this is obtained through the Sacred Congregation for the Evangelisation of Nations. Subsequently these individuals or groups are accountable for their missionary activity to this Sacred Congregation and through it to the pope. As mission territories develop, they are nearly always divided thus allowing for the creation of new mission territories. At times the new territory is offered to the missionary group already in charge of the parent mission, but it is not obliged to accept. This process of dividing territories and reassigning them goes on indefinitely.

The official Latin title for the Sacred Congregation referred to above is 'Sacra Congregatio pro Gentium Evangelizatione seu de Propaganda Fide', that is, 'The Sacred Congregation for the Evangelisation of Nations or *de Propaganda Fide*'. ('De Propaganda Fide' means 'for Propagating the Faith'.) From the time Pope Gregory XV founded the Sacred Congregation on 6 January 1622, it has never translated into any vernacular the words, 'de Propaganda Fide', considering them equivalent to a proper name. The author respects this position and tradition and will not use the title in translation.

But this creates a problem for the author because the name, 'Sacred

Congregation *de Propaganda Fide*', as well as the shorter forms, 'Propaganda Fide' and 'Propaganda', which occur often in quotations, would be meaningless, confusing and even misleading for an English language reader if left untranslated. Consequently the author has taken the liberty of using, even in quotations, the modern name of this Sacred Congregation as a substitute, namely, the Sacred Congregation for the Evangelisation of Nations, shortening it to 'Evangelisation Congregation' in those quotations where 'Propaganda Fide' or 'Propaganda' is used. Such substitutions are not called to the reader's attention in notes, since the references would be so frequent as to be annoying. Apparently the Sacred Congregation appreciated the difficulty in which writers of modern languages find themselves and therefore gave itself an additional name. Because of the above considerations the author feels justified in using this anachronism and hopes that his readers will agree to its necessity, or at least to its practicality.

The author has taken still another liberty. 'Monsignore' is the honorary title in Italian for an ecclesiastical superior, no matter whether his rank be priest, bishop or archbishop. This title cannot be translated into English as 'Monsignor', because in English language usage 'Monsignor' is an honorary title only for a priest and is never used for a bishop or archbishop. Since Vatican correspondence repeatedly uses 'Monsignore' when referring to bishops and archbishops, and since a literal translation would be misleading, I have designated the persons in question, even in quotations, as priests, bishops or archbishops. One is called bishop from the date of his nomination by the pope, and not only from the date of his episcopal ordination (formerly called consecration).

I

The Prefecture Apostolic of the Sandwich Islands

24 OCTOBER 1825

Jean-Baptiste Rives (1793–1833), a French cabin boy from Bordeaux who arrived in Honolulu between 1803 and 1806, fell in love with the Sandwich (now Hawaiian) Islands and decided to settle there. He succeeded in winning the confidence of the royal family about 1810 and became their factotum, serving as interpreter, teacher, secretary and doctor of medicine. He likewise fell in love with a local maiden, took her to wife, and began raising a family. Eventually he received an invitation to accompany twenty-six-year-old King Kamehameha II (also known as Liholiho) and Queen Kamamalu on their voyage to London. He readily accepted the invitation and with them and their suite of chiefs and servants boarded the chartered British whaler *Aigle* on 27 November 1823. The London *Times* reported on 19 May 1824 that their ship had been sighted at Portsmouth. A formal audience with King George IV was arranged for 21 June; but it never took place because by then the royal couple had the measles. The queen died from them on 8 July and six days later the king died too.

Instead of returning directly to Honolulu, Rives sailed for France, hoping to realise his dream of becoming the first French consul for the Sandwich Islands. He was aged thirty-one and dwarfish, but did not allow this to deter him from approaching the highest officials. In Paris in December 1824 he presented the French Minister of Foreign Affairs, Baron Anne-Hyacinthe-Maxence de Damas (1785-1862), with a memorandum outlining his proposals which included a commercial and religious expedition to the Pacific. He solicited additional support from the Minister of the Navy and the Minister of the Interior. In Le Havre he managed to persuade some businessmen to charter him a ship and he was promised a second ship by the French government.[1]

To obtain priests for the religious part of his program he called upon Father Charles-François Langlois (1767–1851), superior of the well-known Paris Foreign Mission Seminary founded in 1660, which later became the Paris Foreign Mission Society (M.E.P.). Rives told Langlois of the great possibilities for Catholicism in the Sandwich Islands. He was convinced that many of the islanders would readily become Catholics, if only there were priests to bring them the faith. The first missionaries could accompany him on his return voyage, he said, and in the islands none of the necessities of life would be lacking for them since he personally would look after them. There were no Methodists or Anabaptists in the islands, he added, but there were '40 or more Calvinist ministers who have been sent there from North America'. In all of the islands these missionaries had only three churches, he said, but they did have a school on each island for teaching the children reading and writing. When Langlois asked if the Protestant missionaries might prove hostile to incoming Catholic missionaries, Rives assured him that the Catholics would be able to work in peace.

Rives also had a personal request. Since his wife had never been baptised, he wondered if Langlois could obtain for him a dispensation from the pope so that his marriage could be put in order.[2]

The Protestant missionaries referred to by Rives were actually Congregationalists sent out by the American Board of Commissioners for Foreign Missions, which had been founded in 1810 at Bradford, Massachusetts. Its first missionaries to the Sandwich Islands arrived there in 1820 and numbered two ordained missionaries, two teachers, a physician, a printer, a farmer, their wives and children, and three young men from the Sandwich Islands who had been trained at the foreign mission school in Cornwall, Connecticut. By the end of 1824 according to their own statistics they had erected nine churches, had in their employ at least fifty indigene teachers on the various islands, and had 2,000 pupils who had learned to read.[3]

Langlois promised to write to Rome without delay for the marriage dispensation so earnestly desired by Rives. But he had no priests to offer for the Sandwich Islands. The French Revolution of 1789 and subsequently the Napoleonic era (1799–1815) had been disastrous for French missionary vocations, which had already been at a low ebb throughout the 1700s. The Paris Foreign Mission Seminary headed by Langlois had sent out only sixty missionaries from 1700 to 1822, and from 1792 onwards the seminary had been closed until the fall of Napoleon in 1815. In fact, Langlois had only six seminarians and a year would have to pass before any of them could be ordained. Besides, his seminary's missions in the Far East and in southern India were all suffering from a shortage of personnel and so it was impossible for him to think of taking up new work.

Nevertheless he assured Rives that he would contact mission authorities in Rome and would highly recommend the proposal that a Catholic mission be opened soon in the Sandwich Islands. He then drew up a list of twenty-nine questions for Rives to answer in writing, saying that Rome would surely want some detailed information on the area. He argued that submitting such a memorandum would save time by anticipating questions that Rome might otherwise ask. His questionnaire covered topics like the ancestral religion of the inhabitants, their customs, their attitudes toward Christianity, and the methods, successes and behaviour of the Protestant missionaries.

Langlois lost no time in contacting Rome. While Rives was still in Paris he wrote on 23 March 1825 to eighty-year-old Giulio Maria Cardinal della Somaglia (1744–1830) who, in addition to being the secretary of state to Pope Leo XII (1823–9), was serving provisionally as pro-prefect of the Sacred Congregation 'de Propaganda Fide'. This sacred congregation or commission

1 Page one of a seven-page questionnaire drawn up by Father Charles-François Langlois, superior of the Paris Foreign Mission Seminary, containing twenty-nine questions on the religion and customs of the Sandwich Islands inhabitants and answered by Jean-Baptiste Rives. Langlois sent the completed questionnaire to Rome on 23 March 1825. *Source: PF: SC Oceania vol. 1 (1816–41) f. 25r. (Chapter 1).*

of cardinals, today called also the Sacred Congregation for the Evangelisation of Nations (or the Evangelisation Congregation), had been founded by Pope Gregory XV on 6 January 1622. Its purpose and duty were to organise and direct the missionary activity of the Catholic Church throughout the world under the immediate supervision of the pope.

After giving what background he could about Rives, Langlois said that 'he holds strongly to the Catholic faith'. It was this attachment that now made him want to take along to the Sandwich Islands some Catholic missionaries, since he was convinced that very many of the people there could easily be won over to the Catholic faith. Langlois gave some details on the Protestant missionary work there and referred to the seven-page questionnaire filled out by Rives. The Sacred Congregation would surely be pleased with the information it contained, he said, and the cardinals would rejoice, because it showed 'how well disposed these people are for receiving the true faith'. But at the same time the report would deeply sadden the cardinals, because they would see how numerous and how ready to make every sacrifice in spreading their creed the Protestant missionaries were, whereas in fact Catholic missionaries were so few in number and none could be found who were 'animated with truly apostolic zeal'.

He wished that his own seminarians were numerous enough to take care of these needs, Langlois said, but he had so very few and the mission fields already entrusted to his society by Rome were suffering from a great shortage of personnel. 'So there is nothing else that we can do at the moment, but to make known to the Sacred Congregation what has become known to us, and to ask the Lord of the harvest earnestly to send forth labourers into his harvest, and to bewail vehemently the stubborn resistance of certain bishops who refuse to consent to the wishes of those in their dioceses who yearn to devote themselves to the missions.'

He also requested della Somaglia to obtain a disparity of cult dispensation from Pope Leo XII for Rives so that his marriage could be validated.[4]

The Rives-Langlois proposal on a new mission for the Sandwich Islands was handed over for action to Archbishop Pietro Caprano, secretary of the Evangelisation Congregation since 1823. He personally approached seventy-six-year-old Father Luigi Fortis, superior general of the Society of Jesus (S.J.), called also Company of Jesus or Jesuits, and offered him the mission. But Fortis said he needed more time and more information before making his decision. Caprano then on 19 May 1825 sent him the reports supplied earlier by Rives and Langlois and said in an accompanying letter that after Fortis had studied the reports, he and Fortis could meet again to settle the matter. He praised the Jesuit superior general for his 'ardent zeal', known far and wide, which guaranteed that he would make 'every effort to see the plan realised'. Fortis, however, returned the documentation by September and said that he could not accept the mission.[5]

The next one approached was fifty-seven-year-old Father Marie-Joseph-Pierre Coudrin (1768–1837). This priest had left Paris for Rome on 19 May, which curiously was the very day on which Caprano had sent the Rives-Langlois

2 The Very Reverend Marie-Joseph-Pierre Coudrin (1768–1837), founder of the Congregation of the Sacred Hearts of Jesus and Mary (SS.CC.), known also as the Picpus Fathers. *Source: SSCC. (Chapter 1).*

report to Fortis. Coudrin was the founder and superior general of the Congregation of the Sacred Hearts of Jesus and Mary (SS.CC.), known also as the Picpus Fathers, because their main house was on rue de Picpus in Paris.[6] This religious community was founded in 1800 and received papal approbation in 1817. Coudrin's chief aim in Rome, where he arrived on 8 June, was to obtain papal approbation for the rule which his community had perfected at its General Chapters of 1819 and 1824. During his six weeks in Rome he had a private audience with Pope Leo XII on 18 June, to whom he presented the new rule. Later he was received with great kindness by Cardinals della Somaglia, Pacca, Morozzo (who promised to expedite approbation of the rule), de Gregorio and Testaferrata.

On 15 July, six days before his return to France, Coudrin presented to Archbishop Caprano, secretary of the Evangelisation Congregation, a memorandum expressing his community's readiness and eagerness to serve in Oriental Rite missions in Europe or in foreign missions of the Latin Rite. It would be impossible to send men at once, however, because his members had had no missionary experience and there was no one to train them. But if the Evangelisation Congregation were interested, he said, he would send three members in vows to Rome 'as soon as permission is granted. The Sacred Congregation can then send them at once to whatever mission it considers best. We ask only that they be under no one but the Sacred Congregation for the Evangelisation of Nations and that their superior be named by the superior general of our community in accord with the wishes of the Sacred Congregation.'[7]

It was this memorandum which now prompted della Somaglia and Caprano to see if they could interest Coudrin in accepting the Sandwich Islands. But before approaching Coudrin they sought clearance from Pope Leo XII, since the Picpus Fathers up to this time had never been engaged in foreign missionary work.[8]

The pope had meanwhile reached a decision on 'the very complicated marriage case' of Rives and on 4 June the pertinent document had been sent by della Somaglia to Langlois. The pope had also given his approval to the Picpus rule on 26 August after it had been examined and approved by the Sacred Congregation for Bishops and Religious. News of this approbation reached Paris on 9 September and the very next day in Rome della Somaglia wrote to Coudrin inviting him to accept the Sandwich Islands. The timing was calculated to ensure acceptance by Coudrin, since he could hardly say no to a Vatican request coming hot on the heels of the approbation of his rule.[9]

Della Somaglia's letter said that 'a new evangelical harvest seems to be springing up which could well be entrusted for cultivation to the sacred labourers' of Coudrin's religious community. The cardinal mentioned how he had learned through Langlois of 'a certain Frenchman . . . based for about 20 years on the Sandwich Islands in the Pacific Ocean' who had been secretary to the king of those islands, was now in France, and wanted to take along some priests on his return. Prospects were good, he said, even though in the same islands there were 'forty and more ministers of the Calvinist sect sent there from

North America', who had persuaded a large majority of the islanders to give up their pagan superstition, destroy their temples, and embrace the Christian religion. 'But such is their inexperience, so reprehensible their way of life, and so great their concern for gain and for business, that they are held in contempt by many. And they make little progress with their disciples because they teach them the Christian religion according to the false principles of their sect.'[10]

This harsh judgment on the missionaries who had been sent to the Sandwich Islands by the American Board of Commissioners for Foreign Missions was based on the report of Rives. He as a Frenchman and a Catholic had precious little to say in favour of American Protestants. Unfortunately the animosity and prejudice already existing between Protestants and Catholics in America and Europe was being propagated at this early date throughout the Pacific islands where it would have a long and painful history. And although it would not colour every phase of missionary work, it would play a dominant role in determining where and when Catholic and Protestant missionary work would begin or end and how it would spread.

Della Somaglia near the end of his letter said that what he really needed were 'holy workers animated with true apostolic zeal'. It was this need that had prompted the Evangelisation Congregation when searching for personnel 'to fix its eyes and its thoughts' on Coudrin and on the members of his community. 'If in your ranks you have some members who are fit to launch this new mission, then let me know so that we can make the necessary arrangements.' It was Coudrin's 'ardent zeal for the propagation of the faith', the cardinal added, that *forced* him to hope for an affirmative answer.[11]

This letter reached Paris on 29 September and Coudrin set to work immediately reading books and contacting people. He wanted to find out all that he could about the Sandwich Islands and how his missionaries might get there. From Langlois, mentioned in the cardinal's letter, he learned that the 'certain Frenchman' so interested in getting priests was Rives, and he obtained a copy of the Langlois-Rives questionnaire that had been sent to Rome. From Rives in turn he learned that the bankers and shipowners Javal and Lafitte would be sending a ship to the Sandwich Islands in mid-November and that two or three of his priests could go along.[12]

Ten months earlier Rives, who wanted the French government to name him consul in the Sandwich Islands, had given a glowing report to Baron de Damas, Minister of Foreign Affairs, on how advantageous for French commerce it would be to have a trade route in the north Pacific from the west coast of North America via the Sandwich Islands to Canton, China. Rives then on his own initiative, but with approval from de Damas, had succeeded in stirring up the interest of Javal and Lafitte in this proposed French north Pacific trade route. Until this time it had been monopolised by British and American firms. Rives had also said in his report to the Minister of Foreign Affairs that French influence in the Sandwich Islands would be more lasting if French priests were to establish a mission there. This explains why he approached Langlois for personnel.[13]

Coudrin wrote back to della Somaglia on 6 October 1825, exactly one week

J.S.C.J.   26

33

Eminentissime Domine,

Summâ cum animi gratitudine perlegi Epistolam quam Eminentia Vestra ad me dirigere dignata est, circa novam missionem, quae tradi nobis posset in insulis dictis Sandwich excolenda. Semper pro jussis habebimus quaecumque videretur sancta Sedes Apostolica exoptare, iderio libenter hujusce missionis curam suscipiemus. Jam de insulis praedictis multa inquisivi. Mihi dictum fuit, Parisiis, navem disponi, quae, circa medium mensis novembris proxime futuri, ex Galliis ad insulas Sandwichianas est profectura. Spes datur duos ex nostris sacerdotibus et forsan tres hac in navi fore suscipiendos, qui ad praedictas plagas transvehantur. sic tres simul missioni evangelicae operam dare valebunt.

Valde exoptassem ut mihi possibile fuisset statim transmittere ad Eminentiam Vestram nomina fratrum nostra Congregationis qui tam sancto operi incipiendo primi destinabuntur; sed quantumvis certus sim omnes mandato meo obsequium promptum fore praestituros, mihi visum fuit magis expedire ut, prius illorum mente interrogata, inter illos seligerem eos qui, Missioni Sandwichianae libentius sese devoventes, magis idonei viderentur. cum vero in provinciis sint dispersi, et aliunde tempus urgeat, judicavi necessarium fore ut statim ad Eminentiam Vestram responsum dirigeretur, ne deperet occasio opportuna.

Quapropter pie enixeque rogo ut, si possibile sit, Eminentia Vestra quamprimum ad me transmittere dignetur omnes facultates necessarias illi quem designabo hujusce missionis Superiorem, ut sit praedicta missionis profectus apostolicus, et duobus sacerdotibus, qui ipsum comitabuntur, cum omnibus privilegiis quae talibus in circumstantiis conceduntur, praesertim quoad impedimenta instruendi et ... statim ... designatus fuerit, illius nomen indehcenter

3   The Latin letter of Superior General Coudrin of the Picpus Fathers addressed to Cardinal della Somaglia, pro-prefect of the Evangelisation Congregation, accepting responsibility for the Prefecture Apostolic of the Sandwich Islands. (This reply to della Somaglia's letter of 10 September was inadvertently dated 6 September for 6 October 1825.) *Source: PF: SC Oceania vol. 1 (1816–41) f. 33r. (Chapter 1).*

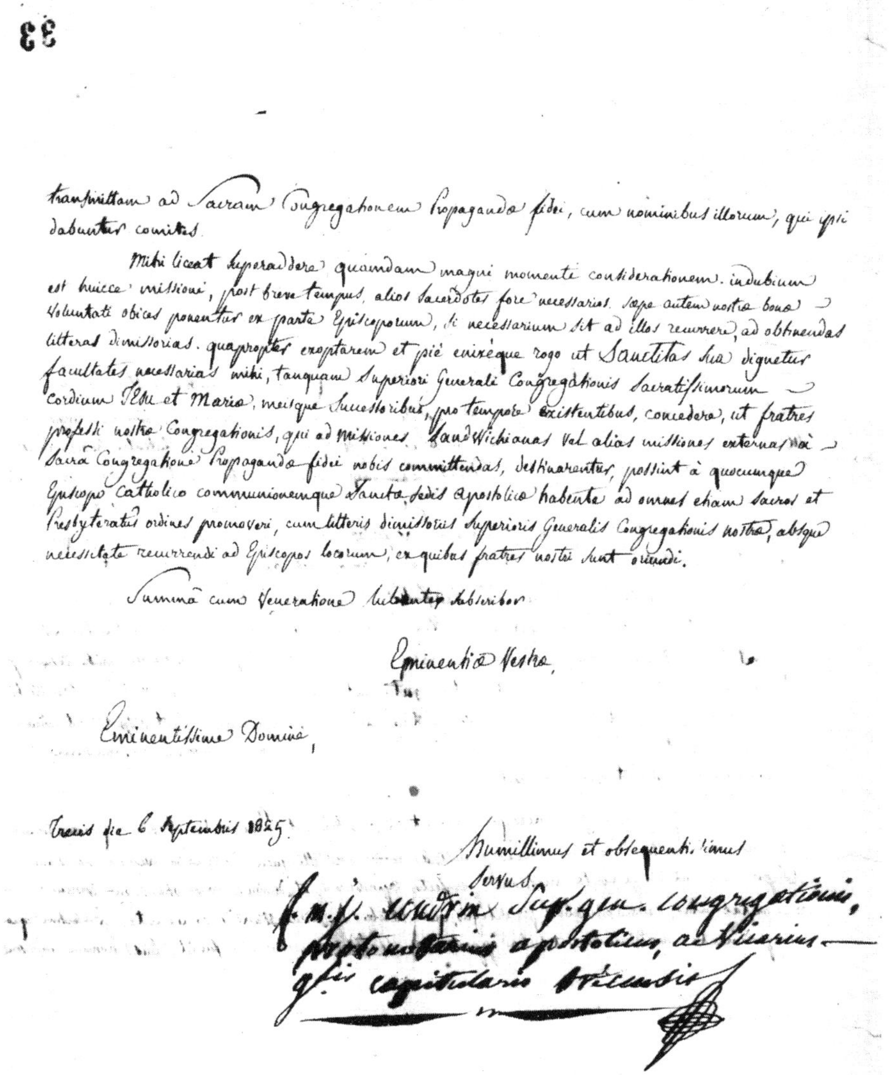

33

transmittam ad Sacram Congregationem Propaganda fidei, cum nominibus illorum, qui ipsi dabuntur comites.

Mihi liceat superaddere quamdam magni momenti considerationem. indubium est huicce missioni, post breve tempus, alios sacerdotes fore necessarios. saepe autem nostrae bonae voluntati obices ponentur ex parte Episcoporum, si necessarium sit ad illos recurrere, ad obtinendas litteras dimissorias. quapropter exoptarem et pie enixeque rogo ut Sanctitas sua dignetur facultates necessarias mihi, tanquam Superiori Generali Congregationis Sacratissimorum Cordium Jesu et Mariae, meisque successoribus, pro tempore existentibus, concedere, ut fratres professi nostrae Congregationis, qui ad missiones SandWichianas vel alias missiones externas a Sacra Congregatione Propaganda fidei nobis committendas, destinarentur, possint à quocumque Episcopo Catholico communionemque Sanctae Sedis apostolicae habente ad omnes etiam sacros et Presbyteratus ordines promoveri, cum litteris dimissoriis Superioris Generalis Congregationis nostrae, absque necessitate recurrendi ad Episcopos locorum, ex quibus fratres nostri sunt oriundi.

Summâ cum veneratione libenter subscribor

Eminentiae Vestrae,

Eminentissime Domine,

Trecis die 6 Septembris 1825.

humillimus et obsequentissimus servus.

f. m. j. coudrin Sup. gen. congregationis, protonotarius apostolicus, ac Vicarius g[ener]alis capitularis trecensis

4 Page two of Father Coudrin's letter dated 6 September 1825, as figure 3. *Source: PF: SC Oceania vol. 1 (1816–41) f. 33v. (Chapter 1).*

after the cardinal's letter had reached Paris. (In his haste and excitement he wrote September instead of October.)[14] 'We shall always consider as a command whatever seems to be the wish of the Holy Apostolic See,' he said, 'and therefore we shall gladly take charge of this mission.' Without going into details he pointed out that he had 'already done much research' on the Sandwich Islands and was told in Paris that a ship would be leaving for those islands in mid-November and that he could expect to get two and perhaps even three of his priests aboard. Since so few French ships sailed to those islands, it was necessary to act quickly in order not to lose this opportunity.

It was this very urgency of the matter, he explained, that made it impossible for him to submit with his letter the name of a candidate for the office of prefect apostolic and the names of the two priests who would accompany him. For although he was certain that his members 'would all give prompt obedience' to his orders, he considered it 'more expedient' to ask for volunteers. From among them he would then choose 'those who more willingly would want to devote themselves to the Sandwich mission and who would seem more suited for it'. But his priests were scattered throughout the various provinces of France and by the time he could get the names, send them on to Rome and get back the necessary faculties, the ship would already have sailed. Consequently he 'piously and earnestly' begged the cardinal, if at all possible, to send the faculties on to him at once and in such a way that he himself could give his missionaries their faculties and designate one of them as prefect apostolic. He would then forward their names without delay to Rome.

Was Coudrin asking for too much here? Designating the prefect apostolic of a mission was a long-standing prerogative of the cardinal prefect of the Evangelisation Congregation, and he might not want to surrender this right.

Coudrin went on to say that the mission without a doubt would soon need more priests. He therefore 'piously and earnestly' asked that the cardinal obtain for him as superior general and for his successors special faculties from the pope which would help remove 'the obstacles that are often placed in the way of our good will by bishops'. According to existing church law every member of his congregation wishing to be ordained to any of the seven minor or major orders—this included the priesthood—was obliged in each case to obtain beforehand from the bishop of his home diocese dimissorial letters, that is, official testimony of his suitability for ordination. The 'obstacles' created by bishops on these occasions would be eliminated completely, Coudrin declared, if the pope were to authorise 'any Catholic bishop in communion with the Holy Apostolic See to ordain . . . the professed members of our congregation who are assigned to the Sandwich missions or to other foreign missions that may be entrusted to us. . . .' At the same time he wished the pope to make it no longer necessary for these members to have recourse to the bishops of their home dioceses, 'provided only that they have dimissorial letters from the superior general of our congregation'.[15]

After posting his letter to della Somaglia on 6 October, Coudrin lost no time. He had Father Felix Cummins, Irish prior of his house in Paris, visit Baron de

Damas, Minister of Foreign Affairs, on 7 October in order to request free passage for his missionaries aboard a ship of the Royal Navy. On the following day Cummins formally submitted this request to the government in writing. Then Coudrin on 17 October wrote to Father Alexis-Jean-Augustin Bachelot, head of the major seminary at Tours, inviting him to become one of the three missionaries. 'Reflect on this before God,' he said, 'and answer me very promptly. These islands, which number about 500,000 souls, have not yet seen a Catholic priest. The Evangelisation Congregation is offering us this mission as if it were to be our congregation's very own. . . .'[16]

Cummins on 19 October was received at the Ministry of Foreign Affairs to discuss transportation and financial subsidies for the new mission. Comte Alexandre-Maurice d'Hauterive (1754–1830), who represented Baron de Damas at this meeting, told Cummins that France was interested in the north Pacific route and that it would be necessary for France to spread out from the Sandwich Islands and find suitable harbours in California and China.

On learning that Marquis Eugene de Montmorency was leaving for Rome, Coudrin penned a letter to Bartolomeo Cardinal Pacca (1756–1844) on 21 October, hoping that the cardinal's influence would make matters move more quickly in Rome. The French government ultimately promised free passage for the missionaries, and 4,000 francs as a subsidy for their first foundation, but stated that official government protection for the missionaries could not be guaranteed, because a liberal faction in the government was opposed to religious congregations like that of Father Coudrin, which had not been legally recognised. Giving such protection was also hampered by the fact that France had no political bonds with the Sandwich Islands.[17]

Coudrin's concern for a speedy decision was shared by Cardinal della Somaglia who took action in Rome long before the letter for Cardinal Pacca had arrived. Della Somaglia asked Archbishop Pietro Caprano, secretary of the Evangelisation Congregation, to see Pope Leo XII on 24 October 1825. At this audience Caprano requested the desired ecclesiastical privileges and powers—technically called faculties—for the new prefect apostolic and for the missionaries still to be chosen by Coudrin for the Sandwich Islands. The pope instructed Caprano 'to grant all the faculties that he would consider opportune, no matter how ample they might be'.[18] By granting these faculties the pope also created the Prefecture Apostolic of the Sandwich Islands.

Coudrin's haste, however, kept preying on Caprano's mind. Under normal circumstances the secretary would have considered this haste as zeal, but now it filled him with fear and suspicion because of a traumatic experience to which he had been subjected the year before. It had all begun with a series of fifteen letters coming to the Evangelisation Congregation in rapid succession in March and April 1824. They were from Mohamed Ali, Vice Regent of Egypt, and other personalities, and all insisted that the Catholic Coptic Patriarchate of Alexandria should be established, that Vicar Apostolic Massimo Giuaid of Egypt should be made Patriarch, and that Abramo Chasciur, a Coptic student from Egypt in Rome, should be made Archbishop of Memphis. This was all to happen within fifty-five days and Chasciur was to be sent to Egypt to ordain Giuaid a bishop and patriarch. The result was to be reunion between the Coptic Church and Rome, something greatly hoped for by Caprano.

Chasciur, however, was only twenty years old and had not yet begun his theological studies. When Caprano wanted to confer with ecclesiastical authorities in Egypt, another letter came from the Vice Regent insisting that Chasciur had to be ordained a bishop 'within 24 days' of receipt of the letter, or the breach with Rome would continue. Caprano as secretary bore almost full responsibility for the direction of the Evangelisation Congregation at this time because della Somaglia, its pro-prefect, was also secretary of state for Pope Leo XII. In his haste not to lose this opportunity for bringing about reunion, Caprano convoked an extraordinary meeting of the Evangelisation Congregation on 13 July and it unanimously decided to carry out all requests contained in the various letters. He then obtained the necessary dispensations from the pope on 18 July and himself ordained Chasciur a subdeacon, deacon and priest on 18, 25 and 26 July. In the Sistine Chapel on Sunday, 1 August, in the presence of all the students of the Evangelisation Congregation's college and with Caprano as his assisting prelate, Pope Leo XII with much pomp ordained Chasciur a bishop and named him Archbishop of Memphis, handing over to him the pallium, which had been brought in procession from Saint Peter's tomb in the adjoining basilica.

But upon arrival in Alexandria on 28 September, the priest sent along with Chasciur to teach him theology was appalled to learn that all the letters had been forged. Enraged over what had happened, the Vice Regent on 14 October sent the archbishop-impostor back to Rome. Chasciur had done all the forging—or nearly all of it—himself! Tried by the Holy Office, he was found guilty, was degraded, laicised and sentenced to lifelong imprisonment. Prefect Apostolic Daniele di Procida of Egypt on 30 October that same year sent a blistering letter to Rome expressing surprise and indignation over the Evangelisation Congregation's having acted 'with such great speed', whereas in conducting its business and in making decisions 'it has always moved and still moves as if it had lead in its feet'.

Caprano's health and also his policies were understandably affected by this experience, in spite of the comfort and understanding that he received from the pope. Fearing that Coudrin because of his haste might be foisting on the Sandwich Islands some additional 'Chasciurs', he persuaded della Somaglia to postpone drawing up the faculties and forwarding them to Coudrin, even though they had been granted by the pope. Before taking further action Caprano wanted to have more specific information on the project in general and on the missionaries in particular.

To obtain the desired information della Somaglia on 29 October wrote to Coudrin, saying that he was most grateful for his acceptance of the mission. But he pointed out at the same time that 'this is a serious affair and must be given due consideration before it can be carried out'. In order that Coudrin might become better acquainted with the true state of religion in the Sandwich Islands, a copy of the Langlois-Rives questionnaire was enclosed for his personal study.

'Afterwards you will indicate to us,' the cardinal said, 'what you believe is needed, so that the proposed missionary expedition may be launched in a very mature and advantageous way.'[19]

The cardinal wrote a second letter that same day to Archbishop Vincenzo Macchi, nuncio apostolic in Paris, and explained that he was writing confidentially. After acquainting him in some detail with the new project that was destined 'to provide for the needs of religion in the Sandwich Islands', and after praising Coudrin for his 'piety, zeal and virtuous conduct', the cardinal asked the nuncio for his 'most wise view on the whole affair in general'. He also wanted to have his judgment in particular 'on the qualities of the subjects whom Father Coudrin intends to present as missionaries'. But the nuncio was 'to keep secret the present commission', and was to send his reply to Rome 'with all possible haste'.[20]

A speedy reply dated 12 November did come, not from the nuncio, but from a rather indignant Coudrin. 'While we were anxiously awaiting word from the Apostolic See on the Sandwich missions', he said, 'Your Eminence's letter of 29 October arrived. But after the arrival of your first letter we had already given serious consideration to what would be necessary and advantageous for this mission. And as for the *Report* which Your Eminence so kindly sent us, we had already received a copy of it.'

At first sight it might seem more expedient for us, he continued, simply 'to wait for the commands of the Sacred Congregation', prepare two or three priests, and then send them 'at the time and in the manner designated'. But a French ship was being readied for sailing to those shores, he said, and it would be most advantageous if the missionaries could make use of it. This was especially true since Rives would be travelling aboard the very same ship, and it was Rives according to the cardinal's own words who could assure them of a peaceful ministry. A further reason for not neglecting this opportunity, Coudrin insisted, was that Rives would be staying in the Sandwich Islands only a short time and then was to return permanently to France.

Coudrin explained further that after getting the first letter from the cardinal he had visited the Minister of Foreign Affairs of the king of France. This official had promised free passage for his missionaries aboard a French ship which had delayed its departure and was now scheduled to leave for the Sandwich Islands in December. His own congregation, he said, would take upon itself the burden of all other expenses.

Then Coudrin listed the names, birthplaces and birthdays of the three missionaries chosen for the Sandwich Islands. And he requested that Father Alexis-Jean-Augustin Bachelot, born 22 February 1796 at Saint Cyr-Orne, France, be named the prefect apostolic with the faculty of subdelegating a vice-prefect, if circumstances should require it. He also asked that the three missionaries 'be given all faculties and privileges that were given to the Jesuits when they were first assigned to the Indian missions in America, since the circumstances are the same'.

This long Latin letter was so eloquent and convincing a piece of writing that della Somaglia decided to have Caprano make its entire contents known to Leo XII at the next weekly audience on Sunday, 27 November.

'Your Holiness certainly recalls', Caprano began, 'that it was with Your Beatitude's consent that an inquiry was made as to whether the Reverend Coudrin, superior and founder of the new Congregation of the Sacred Hearts of Jesus and Mary, and Vicar General of Troyes, would be prepared to take charge of the Sandwich Islands mission in the Pacific Ocean, a mission for which the Fathers of the Company of Jesus did not believe they could offer themselves. The response was even beyond what we desired! Not only did the Reverend Coudrin accept the offer, but he showed himself impatient to have some priests of his congregation depart for those islands, asking that they be furnished with suitable faculties, and insisting that haste be made in sending on to him everything that was needed.' This great haste, the archbishop explained, was due to the fact that a ship was about to leave for those islands, and a long period of time might elapse before a similar opportunity would present itself.

'In spite of all this pressure', he continued, 'it was thought best to delay the project. And so by letter of 29 October a *Report* describing with much accuracy the religious state of those islands was sent to the Reverend Coudrin; it had been sent to the Sacred Congregation by the Reverend Langlois, Superior of the [Paris] Foreign Mission Seminary.'

At this point Caprano read Coudrin's long Latin letter of 12 November to the pope, and then continued: 'This is the situation as it is at present, but it creates two difficulties for me. First I am reminded of what happened last year with regard to the Coptic Patriarch, and this makes me fear these affairs that are carried out with great haste. Secondly, the request that the missionaries be furnished with all the faculties and privileges received by the Jesuits when they undertook missions among the savages of America seems too indefinite, since these were granted at diverse times and under various popes.

'Nevertheless, it seems that my first difficulty ought to be silenced by the piety of the Reverend Coudrin, since all speak of him with the highest praise and since there is no reason for him to be deceitful in this matter. My second difficulty could easily disappear if one were to decide specifically what faculties should be given to the missionaries. Some norm could be established for determining this, like current practice and the most ample Briefs of the Supreme Pontiffs, principally those of Benedict XIV and Clement XIII, and also the Decrees of the Holy Office and of the Evangelisation Congregation.'

After hearing the above report Pope Leo XII once again gave his approval for the Sandwich Islands mission, and ordered that as quickly as possible the most ample faculties should be conferred on the priests of the Congregation of the Sacred Hearts of Jesus and Mary, so that they could properly exercise the ministry that they were being sent to perform.[21]

The audience with the pope took place on 27 November, a Sunday. All week long Caprano watched the mail for a reply from the nuncio apostolic in Paris, but no answer came. So on Saturday, 3 December, feast of the Jesuit missionary Saint Francis Xavier, he ordered that all official documents should be drawn up and signed. Bachelot was named the first Prefect Apostolic of the Sandwich Islands and letters patent were issued to his priest companions, Fathers Abraham Armand and Patrice Peter Short. Extraordinary faculties were also granted to the three missionaries in accord with the wishes previously expressed by the pope.[22]

That same day, 3 December, della Somaglia acknowledged the receipt of Coudrin's letter of 12 November, saying that 'the matter had been immediately referred to His Holiness, who highly approved of this expedition and graciously granted the faculties which you will find in the enclosed documents for the new workers going to this new harvest'. He wished the missionaries a good voyage and told Coudrin that it was his responsibility to inform the prefect apostolic that he should send a letter to the Sacred Congregation as quickly as possible after his arrival in the islands. It was to be a report on conditions affecting him and his fellow missionaries, as well as on other important matters touching the mission, 'so that by pooling our knowledge the Catholic cause may more easily be promoted'.[23]

Della Somaglia also wrote that same day to Macchi in Paris, complaining that his earlier request for information had not been answered. After telling the nuncio the latest developments, he said, 'It was thought well to conform without delay to the urgent requests of the excellent and zealous Reverend Coudrin in an affair of such great importance.' He enclosed his letter of 3 December for Coudrin together with a number of documents and asked the nuncio to pass these on to Coudrin 'immediately'. But if the 'accurate inquiries' made by the nuncio had meanwhile uncovered something of importance that was unfavourable to the mission in general or to the missionaries destined for it, the nuncio was to retain the documents in his possession and inform the cardinal of the reasons that had induced him not to pass them on to Coudrin. 'The delicacy of the charge entrusted to you is extreme', the cardinal said, 'but precisely for this reason we have confided in your well-known wisdom and prudence.'[24]

Actually the nuncio had sent a letter to della Somaglia dated 30 November, but this letter and the cardinal's second letter of 3 December crossed in the mail. The nuncio explained that he could have replied much sooner, and also at much more length, if he had not been instructed to keep his commission confidential. 'But the secret investigations, which I have not failed to make, did provide me with some definite information,' he said, 'and I hasten to send it on to you.'

In three large pages the nuncio attempted to show how inopportune it would be to start a Catholic mission in the Sandwich Islands at this time. 'The people still adore idols, and only a short while ago stopped sacrificing human blood', he said. In the entire population of 500,000 'there was not a single Catholic', although two men without being well instructed had been baptised by a French priest aboard a ship which had stopped there. He mentioned the Protestant mission from the United States, but said its ministers were 'little esteemed, being very ignorant and occupied with trade'.

Macchi said that Rives of Bordeaux was the only one behind the entire project and was stressing how urgent it was to have missionaries. 'While he was in the service of the king, Rives certainly could have used his influence with the king in order to obtain protection and backing for the missionaries.' But since the king was now dead, Macchi pointed out, and since no one knew whether his son had succeeded him to the throne, or perhaps some new dynasty, Rives was unable to provide the missionaries with guarantees. They might well run the risk of not being admitted, or of being expelled, or of not finding there the necessities of life. 'This last reflection merits all the more attention', Macchi said, 'because we are here concerned with such a very distant place. And although the French government would not oppose the departure of the missionaries, neither would it provide them with the usual subsidies, since their missionary congregation is not incorporated in the Paris Foreign Mission Seminary and is not legally recognised here.'

The nuncio was of the opinion that the missionaries should not be sent at this time for several reasons. First, more information was needed on the attitude of those now governing the Sandwich Islands. Secondly, 'more guarantees were required than those of only one private individual' like Rives. And thirdly, more factual data were needed before there would be good reason to hope that the missionaries could subsist there. Rives after all was returning with other Frenchmen 'for commercial reasons and without any title', and so there was little guarantee that he could do what he had promised.

As for the personnel to be provided by Coudrin, he did not yet know who they were. 'It is difficult for me to have secret advance knowledge of them,' he said, 'since Father Coudrin resides in Troyes.[25] But I do know in general that the ecclesiastics of that congregation are furnished with profound doctrine, have sufficient instruction and are of praiseworthy conduct. I have already taken opportune steps to learn the names of the candidates and I shall make haste in procuring for myself and passing on to Your Eminence precise information about them.'[26]

Cardinal della Somaglia was impressed with the reasoning of Macchi, and so was Secretary Caprano perhaps because it confirmed his own fears. Caprano then hastily drafted a letter, had it signed by della Somaglia, and sent it off on 15 December by return mail. It instructed Macchi 'to make use of all means in order to suspend for the present the expedition in question'. As the cardinal explained to the nuncio, he had sent the faculties because Coudrin had stressed so much how necessary it was for the missionaries to get aboard the ship leaving France in December. And yet on the other hand the Evangelisation Congregation 'did not want to make its decision final regarding the expedition' before having from the nuncio the information that it had requested as early as 29 October.

It was precisely this dilemma which had prompted della Somaglia to send all documents for Coudrin directly to the nuncio. 'And since your attitude toward the whole affair is so clear from your precious letter of 30 November', the cardinal said, 'I am certain that the packet addressed to the Reverend Coudrin has not been forwarded to him. Nor will you hand it over to him until you have received further word from this Sacred Congregation.'[27]

Coudrin while in Paris on 26 December 1825 received from the Holy See the decree approving the rule submitted by him for his religious community. Impatient with Rome's apparent delay in sending the necessary authorisation for the Sandwich Islands mission, Coudrin on the following day visited Nuncio Apostolic Macchi. It is not difficult to imagine that his enthusiasm made Macchi see many reasons which guaranteed the success of the Sandwich Islands mission.[28]

Three days later, on 30 December, Macchi wrote Cardinal della Somaglia that he had continued his investigations throughout the month of December and now had such good and certain news that it seemed the Sacred Congregation could 'confidently decide to go ahead as planned with the new mission for the Sandwich Islands'. He had learned that the prime minister of the government in those islands was a Catholic and that the missionaries could expect to receive protection and support from him. As for Rives, he was a most upright man and an excellent Catholic, enjoying not only the highest esteem and consideration in the islands, but also possessing there certain goods, all of which he had promised to hand over to the missionaries in order to assist them in their needs.

Macchi now also had information on the three priests chosen for the mission. Two were from France and one from Ireland; they spoke English well and had the necessary zeal and capacity for the ministry. Further, all three were skilled in mathematics, a talent that they could put to use in the schools that they would found. A highly skilled carpenter, one of the Brothers of the community, was also joining them. And Baron de Damas, the Minister of Foreign Affairs, had promised to provide the mission with sacred vessels and other furnishings by way of substitutes for the financial help which the French government could not grant because Coudrin's religious community was not legally recognised. Also, the Archbishop of Paris fully approved of the new mission and even encouraged it. As for funds, Coudrin had promised to provide his missionaries with a certain amount of money. And the French ship, which was to bring the missionaries to the Sandwich Islands free of charge, would also bring them back again, if for some unforeseen reason they should not succeed in establishing themselves there.

Consequently there was nothing more 'to fear', Macchi said, 'but on the contrary there was much to hope for'. The sailing date had once again been changed, however, and the ship was now to depart 'without fail on this coming 15 February'. He therefore asked Cardinal della Somaglia to let him know by return mail if the papers meant for Coudrin should now be turned over to him.[29]

The cardinal replied quickly and briefly on 17 January 1826, saying that this latest information 'gives us promise that the pious undertaking for the welfare of souls will happily succeed. I therefore hasten to ask you to consign without delay to the Reverend Coudrin the corresponding documents which I entrusted to your prudence on 3 December. Thus the priests chosen for the mission in question will be able to profit from the ship which very soon is to leave for the Sandwich Islands.'[30]

Coudrin, expecting the faculties for the Sandwich Islands mission to arrive in the offices of the nuncio apostolic at any time, paid him another visit on 1 February. As Macchi informed della Somaglia, the letter of 17 January from

Rome, authorising him to hand over the official documents to Coudrin, had arrived just prior to this visit. And so 'I gave him all those documents, which he was most happy to receive . . . , and he assured me that he would busy himself immediately with the necessary arrangements so that the missionaries can take advantage of the ship which will be sailing shortly to those islands.' When telling della Somaglia all of this on 8 February, Macchi ended his letter asking heaven to assist the missionaries with blessings on their long voyage, 'and crown their holy enterprise with happy success'.[31]

Returning to his house on rue de Picpus after seeing the nuncio, Coudrin had the community sing the Veni Creator in praise of the Holy Spirit and on that same day handed over to Bachelot his official appointment as Prefect Apostolic of the Sandwich Islands. Then on 11 February he sent a circular letter 'to all Brothers and Sisters of the congregation', announcing that the rule and community prayerbooks had been approved by Rome. At the same time he informed them that the Holy See had entrusted the Sandwich Islands to them as a mission field.[32]

Now that Coudrin had the official documents, the Minister of Foreign Affairs, Baron de Damas, was approached again and on 13 February he renewed his promises to help the Sandwich Islands missionaries. But 15 February came and went and their ship still did not sail.[33]

Father Cummins, prior of the Picpus house in Paris, went on 1 March to see the shipowners with whom Rives was dealing, and was horrified to learn that Rives had not even mentioned the missionaries! So on that same day Cummins went to see the Jewish bankers, Messrs. Javal, who had the chief investment in the venture. They received him coolly at first and showed surprise when it was suggested that they should take aboard Catholic missionaries. But when he pointed out that a successful Catholic mission in the Sandwich Islands would also facilitate their commercial relations, they paid closer attention to what he had to say. They were not in contact with the Minister of Foreign Affairs, they said, but with the Minister of the Navy, whom Cummins would have to see. Whatever he should decide would be agreeable to them, they said. Their ship, *Héros*, was now expected to arrive at Le Havre on 4 March and would leave for the Sandwich Islands about Easter (26 March).

This gave Cummins little time and so on 4 March he had an audience with Comte André-Jean de Chabrol (1771–1836), Minister of the Navy and of the Colonies. He made many promises, assuring the priest that he would request Messrs. Javal to grant passage aboard their ship for three missionaries and one catechist. On the following day Cummins went back to see Messrs. Javal, and once again they gave assurance that they would do whatever was the good pleasure of the Minister of the Navy.

Then under date of 23 March the Minister of the Navy and of the Colonies sent startling news to the Picpus Fathers, informing them that 'these businessmen would very gladly like to go along with your wishes in this matter, but they know for certain that English missionaries have been established in the Sandwich Islands for a long time. It seems as though they have even been well received, and it is feared that the steps which they might take to oppose a foundation of Catholic missionaries could endanger at the same time the very purpose for which their ship is being sent.' De Chabrol added that Messrs. Javal would later be sending other ships to the islands. Consequently the captain of their ship, *Héros*, had been ordered to obtain information on the advantages or difficulties that French missionaries might find there. 'If this information is favourable, as I hope, these businessmen would then be only too glad to provide passage. . . .'

Messrs. Lafitte, who together with Messrs. Javal were investing money in this venture, were the ones who most strongly opposed granting passage to the missionaries. Prefect Apostolic Bachelot then volunteered to go alone, feeling that it should be easier for one man to get passage aboard the ship. He would reconnoitre the place and make preparations for the others who would come after him. These ideas he sent to Coudrin on 25 March, but Coudrin did not like the idea of his going alone. Meanwhile Rives left for the Sandwich Islands aboard the *Héros* and the Picpus Fathers sought other means of getting to their mission.

Some days later they received word that a transport ship mounted with sixteen cannon was to leave Brest around the middle of May for the Pacific Ocean. It was a government ship and the missionaries felt that once aboard they could easily get to California; from there they would find their own way to the Sandwich Islands. They requested passage, but it was refused.

'We had almost lost hope of getting to the Sandwich Archipelago on a French vessel,' Coudrin's secretary later wrote, 'and were already thinking of going via England, when on 2 May 1826 M. Catineau de Laroche, department head in the Bureau of Commerce and of the Colonies, offered to send not only our [priest] missionaries, but also together with them a certain number of lay Brothers who could teach various crafts to the people living in the Sandwich Islands.'

De Laroche confirmed this in a letter to Cummins on 28 June. 'Recently I made an arrangement in the name of M. Rives,' he said, 'whereby it is possible for me to grant passage to a certain number of persons as far as the Sandwich Islands aboard a ship which will be sent from Bordeaux to China next October . . . I have particularly in mind providing this passage for the members of your community, without cost, so that they can preach the Catholic religion in these distant regions.'

But the letter was hardly posted when the Ministry of Foreign Affairs sent de Laroche an article on the Sandwich Islands published in *La revue britannique*. He was shocked on reading that the Protestant ministers there had gained the complete confidence of the people and enjoyed among them the greatest authority. He forwarded this article on 30 June to Cummins with some observations of his own, saying that he feared a confrontation would take place between the Catholic and Protestant missionaries. He therefore suggested that the French missionaries postpone going to the Sandwich Islands until the king of France was able to establish an agent there, who could then protect them. Meanwhile he would be at their service.

Anxious to destroy the unfavourable impression made on the Ministry of

Foreign Affairs and on de Laroche, Cummins on 15 July wrote a lengthy rebuttal and gave de Laroche and the Minister of Foreign Affairs each a copy. Far from discouraging the Picpus missionaries, he said, the detailed reports 'on the Anglo-American missions' only stimulated them the more. And Rives, who had been a companion of the late king from his youth, had gained his confidence and had almost won him over to Christianity. Even the prime minister currently in office in the islands had been baptised by a Catholic priest. 'Unless I am very much deceived', Cummins wrote, this official 'is an extraordinary man and is perhaps destined to play a great role in Oceania.'

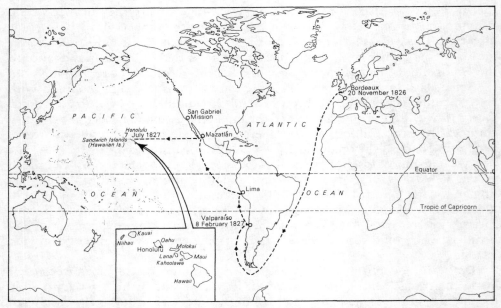

5   The Prefecture Apostolic of the Sandwich Islands was founded on 24 October 1825. The map shows the route taken by the Picpus missionaries who arrived in Honolulu on 7 July 1827. *(Chapter 1)*.

The rebuttal had its desired effect and two days later, 17 July, de Laroche saw Cummins and assured him that passage would be provided aboard the *Comète*, a commercial ship, for three priests and three Brothers as had been agreed upon earlier.[34]

.Meanwhile Coudrin had been informed that the Archbishop of Rouen wished to have him as his first vicar general. Coudrin accepted the offer and the king of France approved the nomination on 27 August. Two days later Coudrin consulted with Baron de Damas on the Sandwich mission. There seemed to be no further difficulties and so on 8 September he named Bachelot, already prefect apostolic, to be also the religious superior over the missionaries, and gave him the power to name an assistant superior. On 13 September the three priests and three Brothers now assigned to the Sandwich Islands received their religious habit and renewed their vows.

The six missionaries left Paris on 25 September for Bordeaux where their ship was to sail in October. Brother Eustache Hurel fell ill at Bordeaux on 30 October and was replaced ten days later by Brother Leonard Portal. The missionaries finally embarked on 16 November 1826, which was exactly one full year after the original sailing date mentioned by Coudrin in his first letter. A good wind finally took them out to the open sea on 20 November 1826. Aboard were Fathers Alexis Bachelot, the prefect apostolic, Abraham Armand, and Patrice Short; Brothers Melchior Bondu and Leonard; and seminarian Théodose Boissier.[35]

Coudrin wrote to della Somaglia again on 3 December 1826, saying 'a complete year' had elapsed since the cardinal's important letter of 3 December 1825 entrusting to his community the Sandwich Islands. But he could now report that his six men had finally boarded a ship 'which, God willing, will bring them to the desired mission'.[36]

Their ship reached Valparaíso (Chile) on 8 February 1827 and made stopovers at Quilca and Lima (Peru) and also at Mazatlán (Mexico) before reaching Honolulu.[37] Father Patrice Short wrote from Honolulu on 27 July 1827, saying, 'We arrived here in good health on the 7th of this month, which was the 20th day after our departure from Mazatlán and the 230th day after our departure from the mouth of the Garonne at Bordeaux. We were under sail for 150 days and spent 80 days in the various ports. . . .' The difficulties initially caused for them by the Protestant missionaries there, he said, were overcome under God 'by the joint efforts of the American and English consuls'. He said that the English consul had been particularly civil toward him, 'promising me from the very beginning complete protection as an English subject, saying that it was his duty to protect me, no matter what religion I might have'.[38]

On 14 July the missionaries said Mass for the first time in the Sandwich Islands.[39]

Bachelot, the prefect apostolic, wrote to della Somaglia on 20 July saying that 'the Frenchman [Jean-Baptiste Rives], who from his youth lived in these islands and became powerful, and under whose wings we were to be protected, is not here. He has not yet been able to reach these islands, although he began his voyage seven months before we began ours. And so we are quite forsaken. Like orphans, though, we trust that God will be our helper and we have cast our cares upon him.'[40]

He also wrote to Coudrin and said that 'the Protestant Methodists' had known in advance of his coming and tried to prevent his group from disembarking, but without success. They then tried to chase away the newly arrived missionaries from the islands, he said, but this effort also failed.[41]

By this time the Sacred Congregation for the Evangelisation of Nations had a new cardinal prefect, the learned Mauro Cappellari, who since the age of eighteen had been a Camaldolese monk. Cappellari wrote to Bachelot on 26 April 1828, expressing happiness over his safe arrival and urging him to send further reports. 'In this way', he said, 'we can rejoice in the Lord over the fruitfulness of your labours and we can provide those things, whatever they might be, which would seem conducive to the good of your mission.'[42]

What happened to Jean-Baptiste Rives, the man responsible for the first Roman Catholic missionaries being sent to the Sandwich Islands? He had left France for the Sandwich Islands aboard the *Héros*. But on reaching the Pacific coast of North America he became sidetracked, eager to win for himself a fortune by trading off part of the *Héros* cargo. After transferring to the Hawaiian schooner *Waverley*, he sailed up and down the California coast from Monterey as far as Mexico. But everywhere he was plagued by squandering and mismanagement, eventually losing all that he had. When the *Waverley* returned from Mexico in August 1828 to Monterey, where the *Héros* was to pick up Rives, he was not on board. He never did return to the Sandwich Islands, but died in Mexico on 18 August 1833 at the age of forty.[43]

2

The Prefecture Apostolic of the South Sea Islands

10 JANUARY 1830

Peter Dillon (1785?–1847), an Irishman and a Catholic born under the French flag, was in contact with the South Sea Islands, that is, those in the south Pacific, for twenty consecutive years, from 1809 to 1828. 'I speak numerous languages of these peoples fluently,' he could boast, 'and I have obtained more influence over their kings and princes than any other European who has yet visited these shores.' As captain of a ship he was in the service of England's East India Company.

In his travels he had noticed that in some islands the people were all becoming Methodists.[1] When asked by local leaders what he thought of the Methodist doctrines, he replied that he belonged to a different and much older religion, one that had been established by the apostles who had preached the word of God and converted the nations. He explained that 'all the sects established in the past three centuries are but branches separated from the trunk to which I belong'. His answer gave rise to other questions: 'Then why not send us some members of your religion to teach us what is right?' He promised to do so after he returned to Europe.[2]

Captain Dillon returned to Europe in 1828 as a famous man. The year before he had discovered the wreckage of the two ships, *Boussole* and *Astrolabe*, of the French navigator Jean-François De Galaup, Comte de La Pérouse (1741–88), who had disappeared in the South Seas on a scientific expedition around the world. D'Entrecasteaux, after whom some islands of New Guinea were later named, was commissioned in 1791 to search for the missing navigator but had no success. Nothing further was heard of La Pérouse until 1826 when Dillon at Tikopia in the Santa Cruz Islands north of New Hebrides discovered the silver hilt of a sword with semi-effaced initials, a definite clue. The next year he found the two ships on the reefs of Vanikoro Island nearby and brought parts of the wreckage to France where they were placed on exhibit in the Louvre maritime museum. On this occasion he was received in audience by King Charles X (2 March 1829). Dillon also published a two-volume work in London in 1829, his *Narrative and Successful Result of a Voyage in the South Seas . . . to Ascertain the Actual Fate of La Pérouse's Expedition.*

About the beginning of September that year Dillon visited the Séminaire des Irlandais in Paris, where young men had studied for the priesthood ever since the outbreak of religious persecution in Ireland. He sought out Father Patrick McSweeny (?–1865) of the diocese of Cork, Ireland, who the previous year had been appointed rector and administrator of the Irish seminary. He explained to him the great need for priests in the South Sea Islands, and said that he would place himself at the service of any priests willing to go there. McSweeny expressed his regrets, saying that he had no priests to spare. But he added that coincidentally a French priest had come to see him just a few days earlier, also asking for missionaries for the South Sea Islands. You are just the man he needs, the superior told Dillon, and then introduced him to this priest who was residing at the nearby Holy Ghost Seminary conducted by the Holy Ghost Fathers (S.Sp.S.).[3]

The priest was Father Gabriel-Henri-Jérôme de Solages (1786–1832), born on 21 August 1786 at Rabastens near Albi in southern France, in the same general area where La Pérouse had been born. His father was the powerful Marquis de Solages; his mother was Dame Elisabeth Thompson, born in England. During the French Revolution (1789–99) his parents had emigrated to England and Henri lived there until he was nineteen. He spoke French and English equally well. Back in France in 1806 he decided to enter the Seminary of Saint-Sulpice and was ordained a priest in Carcassonne on 17 December 1814.

Besides belonging to a noble family, he had wealth and a strong temperament. He was handsome, holy, and 'filled with zeal for the glory of God and the salvation of souls', according to the testimony of a friend. Because of his part-English background and because his birthplace was so near to that of La Pérouse, his eyes and heart early turned toward that immense tract of islands stretched across the Pacific Ocean known as Oceania. 'I can say that one of the chief reasons why I became a priest', he said, 'was that I wanted to work among the savages of the South Sea Islands.'

After his ordination de Solages served as a parish priest at Saint Benoît de Carmaux until 1823 when he became Vicar General of the Diocese of Pamiers below Toulouse in southern France. But his mind gave him no rest. He knew that English merchants were sweeping through the Pacific islands south of the equator (known then as the South Sea Islands), and that Methodist ministers were accompanying them. But there were no Catholic missionaries, except in the Sandwich Islands.[4] Towards the end of May 1829 he put down his ideas in writing about a mission to the South Sea Islands, and sent the letter to the Reverend Pieau, a friend who was secretary general to the Grand Almonry of France at its Paris headquarters.

Pieau was asked to use his influence with the Association for the Propagation of the Faith so that funds and personnel might by allocated to de Solages for the realisation of his project. This organisation, called nowadays in the English-speaking world the Society for the Propagation of the Faith, had been founded at Lyon in France in 1819 by Marie-Pauline Jaricot who quickly established groups of 10, 100, and 1,000, whose members each contributed one sou a week for the missions. The organisation grew so quickly that by 1829 there was a Southern Central Council for Lyon and a Northern Central Council for Paris and these two central councils were under a Superior Council whose president was the Cardinal-Archbishop of Rouen, Prince de Croÿ, who at the same time was Grand Almoner of France. Pieau, as secretary general to the Grand Almoner, consequently found no difficulty in bringing the letter of de Solages to the attention of the Association for the Propagation of the Faith.

The letter was read at a meeting of the Paris Central Council which happened to be attended also by Baron de Verna, president of the Lyon Central Council. Pieau informed de Solages on 6 June 1829 that the association had approved his plan and would give him whatever money he needed. But he himself would have to get the missionaries. And a preliminary condition for his receiving the money was that he obtain from Rome the spiritual jurisdiction over the countries which he wished 'to conquer for Jesus Christ', or that he join a missionary congregation. Upon the completion of this formality, he was to inform Pieau of the number of missionaries whom he had assembled and the association would then send him financial help.

The Paris Central Council on the following day officially informed the Lyon Central Council that de Solages had volunteered for mission work in the South Sea Islands.[5]

These plans were already in progress when de Solages in July was offered the position vacant for some months of Prefect Apostolic of Bourbon (now La Réunion), an island and French colony in the Indian Ocean, 21° south of the equator and 684 kilometres east of Madagascar. 'I hesitated a long time before accepting this office,' he said, 'fearing that it would prove to be an obstacle for the realisation of my plans.' But there were those who told him that the two missions were not incompatible, that in fact they could benefit one another, and so he decided to accept. It was at this stage that he left Pamiers for Paris and took up residence at the Holy Ghost Seminary. Rome quickly supplied him with spiritual faculties for Bourbon and the French government supplied letters patent entitling him to a salary and entrance to the colony. The royal ordinance naming him prefect apostolic was dated 17 August 1829.[6]

Father de Solages was already Prefect Apostolic of Bourbon when Captain Dillon was introduced to him by the superior of the Irish seminary. 'What was our surprise', de Solages wrote, 'when we learned that our ideas were identical, both for the plan to be followed as well as for the places where the missions were to be established.' Even the ages of the two men were practically the same; de Solages was forty-three years old and Dillon was hardly a year older.

Dillon too was struck by the coincidence. 'I find it impossible to express what I experienced upon seeing you for the first time', he told de Solages. This meeting with 'someone who had meditated for many years like myself on the same project' made it seem to me 'as if Divine Providence itself was at work'.[7]

One of the questions that they discussed in detail was the costly item of transportation for the missionaries. After several days of conversations, Dillon at the suggestion of de Solages put his ideas in writing on 7 September 1829. The most convenient and least expensive solution according to Dillon was to use the ship sent every year by the French government to bring provisions to its South American fleet based at Brazil, Valparaíso (Chile) and Lima (Peru). 'This ship after unloading its cargo at Peru or Chile returns empty', he said. 'Now if it were to have missionaries aboard, it could sail to Pitcairn Island, let the missionaries destined for this island disembark, and then head for the Marquesas Islands, or some other place, and from there to Tahiti and other nearby islands.'

Dillon said he had lived for fourteen months on the island of Tahiti and had been adopted by one of the local chiefs. The young daughter of this chief was now queen and also head of the royal family, and Dillon was convinced that he could persuade the Tahitians 'to cast off the yoke of the Methodists . . . and declare themselves in favour of a French missionary'.

From Tahiti in the Society Islands the ship could then sail to the Friendly or Tonga Islands. 'Many of the inhabitants here are completely devoted to me', Dillon said, 'and have even sailed with me. The great chief of the Ma'ufanga District on Tongatapu Island is a particular friend of mine. Recently two of his sons and one of his nephews made a five-month sea voyage with me. They would be pleased to see me once again, and to learn that I was bringing them pious missionaries to teach them religion, arts and crafts.

'From the Friendly Islands', he continued, 'one goes to the Fiji Islands which are the principal and most fertile islands in the South Seas. The people living on these islands are the most civilised in the Pacific Ocean . . . Europeans up until now have had very little contact with these islands. I visited them for the first time in the year 1809, again in 1813, and also in the years 1824 and 1825. For a considerable amount of time I lived on the shore at Bou and I have had frequent dealings with Vallon, king of the largest of these islands.'

Chiefs of nearly all neighbouring islands paid an annual tribute to Vallon, who once told Dillon that if he had a hundred whites to help him, he could train his subjects to be just as skilful as the whites. 'He offered me his own daughter in marriage', Dillon said. 'Although I could not accept his offer, I did let him know that I would like to own some land in his country, since I planned to return there one day. The king and his brothers then gave me an island with its inhabitants and produce. It is there that I would like to see the missionaries become established. Not only would I conduct them there, but I would also see to it that they receive an excellent reception from the natives.'

From the Fiji Islands the ship could then continue on its course to New Zealand, 'going to the Schoracaï River where the Protestant ministers have not yet penetrated'. The chief in this area had a young son, Prince Brian Boru, evidently named (by Dillon?) after an Irish hero, who Dillon said was aboard his ship with a fellow nobleman on a voyage to Calcutta and then accompanied him on his search for La Pérouse. 'I brought this young prince back to his family in December 1827', said Dillon, 'and I would suggest that we leave some missionaries also at this place. As for the needs of the missionaries, I shall be able to obtain for them from the chief whatever they might want.'[8]

The ship could next cross the Indian Ocean, stop at Bourbon, round the Cape of Good Hope on the southern tip of Africa, and then return to France. 'I would also recommend', Dillon added, 'that a certain number of the most outstanding natives on each of the islands where the ship drops anchor should be taken either to France or to Bourbon. There they could be instructed more thoroughly in that kind of knowledge which one feels would be most useful for advancing the work of civilisation in their respective countries.'

Although no more than seventy-four kilometres long, the oval-shaped island of Bourbon in the Indian Ocean was an important and well-developed French colony. It had been discovered in 1528, the French flag was hoisted over it in 1642, and colonisation began in 1654. Like the islands of the south Pacific it too lay in the torrid zone, and so the climate would prove agreeable for 'the most outstanding natives' who might be given special training there.

Dillon was personally convinced that there had never been 'a more favourable moment than the present for founding Catholic establishments in these countries'. Nor had the urgency to do so ever been as great. Delay in taking action, he said, would mean that the South Sea Islands 'later will be found to be completely overrun by the Protestant societies from England'.[9]

The letter by Pieau informing de Solages of the conditions that he had to fulfil in order to obtain financial aid for his project had been authorised by the Reverend L. Perreau. This priest was vicar general of the Grand Almoner, chaplain to the king, and simultaneously secretary and treasurer for the Superior Council of the Association for the Propagation of the Faith. De Solages had meanwhile established personal contact with Perreau and informed him that he had already found some priests who wished to accompany him to Oceania. He gave Perreau a copy of Dillon's letter of 7 September and asked that he send it to Rome to the cardinal prefect in charge of missions together with a request for jurisdiction and special spiritual faculties for the South Sea Islands.[10]

Perreau then wrote to Mauro Cardinal Cappellari, prefect of the Sacred Congregation for the Evangelisation of Nations, on 18 September. He said that Father de Solages, Vicar General of Pamiers, wanted 'another grace' in addition to the powers and title of Prefect Apostolic of Bourbon that he had received from the pope a short time before. He wanted to bring the Catholic faith to the south Pacific. 'Divine Providence seems to open the way to him through the acquaintance that he made of the Irish Captain Dillon, a very good Catholic . . . He has already found many French missionary priests whom he intends to take with him.'

Perreau told Cappellari that Cardinal Prince de Croÿ, the Grand Almoner of France, was away and so he was taking the liberty of writing in the cardinal's name. One of the ten special faculties that he requested was that 'the title of prefect apostolic with all the usual powers' be conferred by the pope on Father de Solages 'for the islands of the Pacific Ocean from Easter Island to New Zealand inclusive and from the equator on the north to the Antarctic Pole on the south'. This new office, Perreau suggested, was to be independent of the office of Prefect Apostolic of Bourbon, 'in such a way, that if he should come to renounce this latter title, he would still keep jurisdiction over the other islands designated in his request'.

He asked the cardinal to reply as quickly as possible if the proposal should prove pleasing to the pope. 'I wish to affirm again', he concluded, 'that the

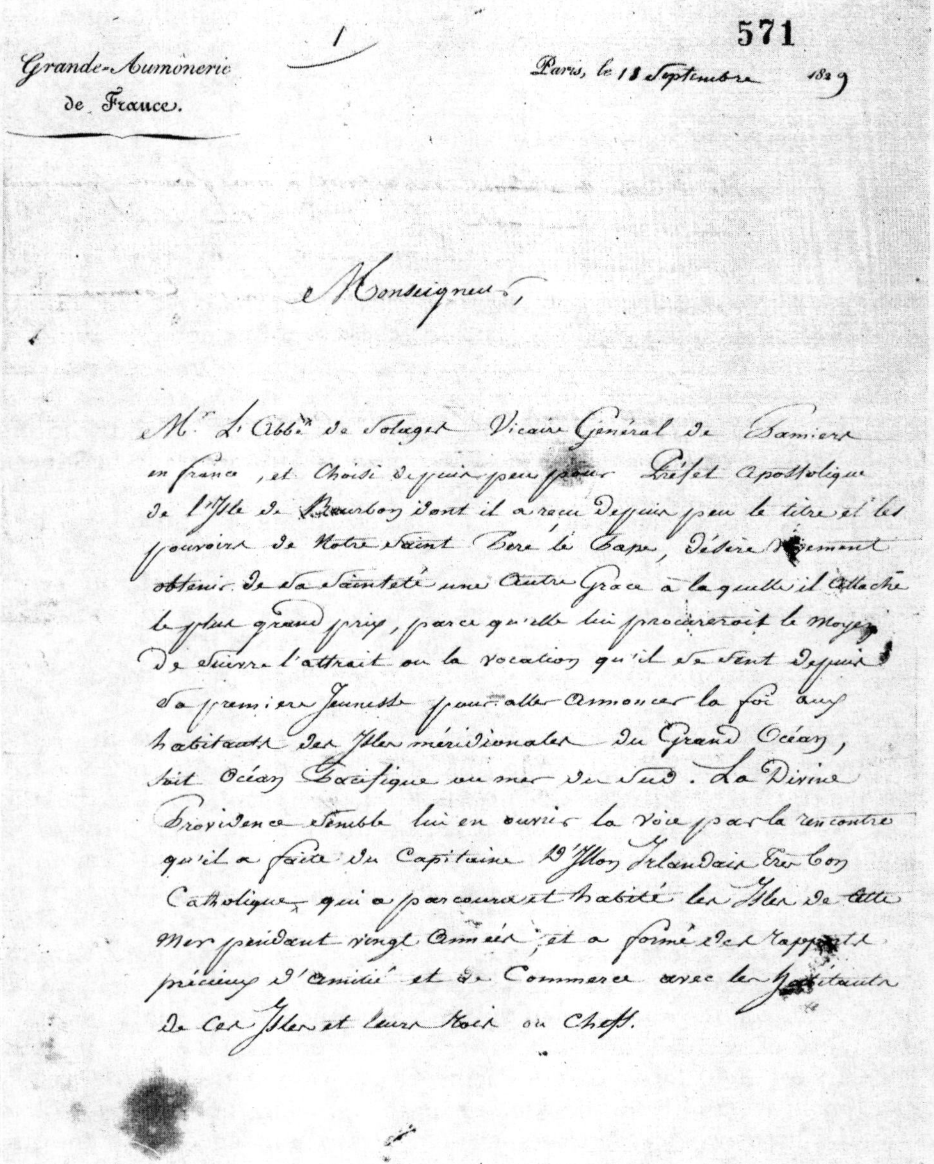

Grande-Aumônerie de France.

571

Paris, le 18 Septembre 1829

Monseigneur,

[handwritten letter text]

6   Letter of Vicar General L. Perreau of 18 September 1829 addressed to Cardinal Prefect Cappellari leading to the foundation of the Prefecture Apostolic of the South Sea Islands. *Source: PF: SOCG vol. 944 (1829) f. 571r. (Chapter 2).*

7 Sixth and last page of Vicar General Perreau's
letter, as figure 6. *Source: PF: SOCG vol. 944 (1829)
f. 573v. (Chapter 2).*

confidence of the Holy See could not be placed in a person more prudent, more zealous and more worthy on all scores for this task of saving souls.'[11]

Father Perreau certainly did not pause to calculate that he was requesting spiritual jurisdiction for Father de Solages over one-fourth of the Southern Hemisphere, that is, over nearly 65 million square kilometres. Added to this was his jurisdictional area in the Indian Ocean.

De Solages was anxious to take with him to Oceania as many priests as possible. It may well have been Perreau who suggested to him that he approach Father Marie-Joseph-Pierre Coudrin, founder of the Congregation of the Sacred Hearts of Jesus and Mary, better known at this time as the Picpus Fathers. This congregation already had one mission in the north Pacific Ocean, the Prefecture Apostolic of the Sandwich Islands.

Perreau knew Coudrin very well and if necessary could act as intermediary. In fact, it had been Perreau who wrote to Coudrin as early as 2 July 1826 to inform him that the Cardinal-Archbishop of Rouen, Prince de Croÿ, wanted to have him as his first vicar general, an office that Coudrin immediately accepted. Since Cardinal Prince de Croÿ was also president of the Superior Council of the Association for the Propagation of the Faith and likewise Grand Almoner of France, this appointment placed Coudrin in a most enviable position for obtaining financial assistance for his foreign missions.[12]

Father de Solages and Captain Dillon in the first half of October paid a visit to Coudrin at the house on rue de Picpus to inform him of their plan and to ask for personnel. Coudrin had recently been absent from Paris for seven months because Cardinal Prince de Croÿ had taken him along to Rome in February as his conclavist for the conclave which on 31 March elected Pius VIII as successor to the late Leo XII. Like de Solages and Dillon, Coudrin too had some connection with the Irish seminary in Paris. He had been ordained a priest clandestinely in the library there on 4 March 1792 during the French Revolution. It now seemed as if this seminary was destined to become a symbolical link binding these three men together in a sacred pact on behalf of the Southern Hemisphere.

But Father Hilarion Lucas, the secretary general of the congregation, present at the meeting, was quite noncommittal about what happened. 'Our Very Reverend Father applauded their zeal', he said, 'and there the matter rested. . . .'[13]

Without government support de Solages knew that his south Pacific mission could never be realised. He knew too that the purely spiritual arguments that he had used for Rome would not suffice with officials of state. And so in approaching them for ship passage and other favours he had to use arguments which told of definite economical and political benefits that would accrue to France from the enterprise.

Through a relative in parliament de Solages presented the 7 September 1829 letter of Dillon to Baron Charles Lemercier de Longpré d'Haussez (1778–1854), Minister of the Navy and of the Colonies, and subsequently both Dillon and de Solages had a conference with the minister. Dillon pointed out that Fiji would make a safe port for French ships in case of war with the British. De Solages added that in time of war it would be a simple matter for the French to take New Holland (now Australia) from the British, provided that there were French forces in New Zealand and in Fiji, since the many Irish settlers in New Holland 'are longing for the moment when they can shake off England's yoke'. After their conference de Solages wrote the minister on 5 October that he feared Dillon 'might offer his services to Russia, which doubtless will accept them', if the French government were not interested in the project, 'and then these beautiful countries of Oceania will be forever lost to France and the Catholic religion'.[14]

Later he had Captain Dillon write another letter, telling how the whaling and other industries in the Pacific were bringing great wealth to England and to the United States, wealth that could also be shared by France. Dillon explained in his letter that the same ship which transported the missionaries to their South Sea posts could furnish him the means of procuring territories and ports for France at the most important points in Oceania. It was this letter of Dillon that de Solages submitted to Prince Auguste-Jules-Armand-Marie de Polignac (1780–1847) when he requested free passage for himself and his missionaries aboard a government ship.[15]

De Polignac had become King Charles X's Minister of Foreign Affairs on 8 August 1829 and on 17 November that year would become President of the Council of Ministers. He had been ambassador to London from 1823 to 1829 and currently was one of the members of the Superior Council of the Association for the Propagation of the Faith. The association's 'Special Protector' was King Charles X himself. De Polignac answered de Solages on 16 October, saying that he had passed on the request to the Minister of the Navy and of the Colonies, who meanwhile had agreed to provide a ship for the venture. De Solages then went in person to confirm this offer with Baron d'Haussez and was advised to lose no time in making his preparations so that the ship could take advantage of the favourable season for rounding Cape Horn at the southern tip of South America.[16]

In a letter dated 25 October 1829, perhaps submitted during their meeting, the details of the missionary voyage were spelled out for Baron d'Haussez by de Solages. The ship would travel west from Valparaíso, he said, and go first to Pitcairn. This island of about five square kilometres had been uninhabited until 1790 when nine English mutineers of the *Bounty* fled there with six men and twelve women from Tahiti. The children of these first colonists spoke both English and Tahitian, and had been brought up as Christians by mutineer John Adams. Since there were no Protestant ministers on the island, de Solages believed that Catholic priests would be welcome.[17]

Since there were also some Europeans in the Marquesas Islands, he said, a priest would be dropped off there too.

Tahiti in the Society Islands would be the next stop, since Dillon was well known there. Some presents for the princes on the island, Dillon had said, were all that the Catholic missionaries needed in order to win the favour of the people and to get them to send away the Methodists. The Catholic mission would not be founded on Tahiti itself—lest the Catholic missionaries upon arrival immediately came in contact with the preachers—but rather on a nearby island. It was on this island that Captain Dillon possessed property, and here too the Protestant ministers had been expelled by the indigenes who had joined Captain Dillon and had asked him to get them some Catholic priests.

Then from Tahiti the ship would go to the Tonga or Friendly Islands, visiting Vava'u, Tongatapu, etc. From there it would sail to the Fiji Islands and then on to New Zealand where the remaining missionaries would settle at the Schoracaï River. It was here that the chief was indebted to Captain Dillon for saving the life of his son when a neighbouring tribe attempted to kill him.

From New Zealand the ship would bring de Solages to Bourbon in the Indian Ocean, then round the Cape of Good Hope, and so return to France, thus completing its voyage around the world.

'If this enterprise is to be perfect', de Solages pointed out, 'we shall need a dozen missionary priests and in addition at least an equal number of pious laymen. These laymen must know those arts and crafts which will prove most useful for the islands that we are to visit, and they must have with them an assortment of tools and instruments so they can practise their individual professions. We should also take along from Europe various kinds of grain, grape-vine seedlings, as well as other types of plants and bushes in order to enrich the countries which we pass. Above all, we would like to plant these in the places where the missionaries will establish themselves.

'It is also my intention', he continued, 'to take along with me to Bourbon some of the most outstanding individuals from the islands visited by our ship, so that they can obtain a more thorough education. As catechists they will later be returned to their countries where with the help of the missionaries they will extend more and more the domain of the faith in these regions. There is no need for me to mention to Your Excellency how important it is that the ship's officers chosen for this enterprise as well as their subordinates should all be men highly regarded for their principles and their good conduct.'[18]

As a direct result of this diplomacy de Solages received three magnanimous promises from the French government. He had asked only for passage aboard a sailing vessel bringing supplies to French depots in South America; he received instead a sailing vessel which was to be at his complete disposal for the duration of the voyage. Further, some thirty persons destined for the mission—priests, catechists and craftsmen—were to receive free passage. And finally, the government agreed to purchase at its own expense the lands needed by the missionaries for establishing mission stations, and also agreed to furnish the missionaries from its own supply depots with the tools and other items needed for these foundations. Father de Solages had a perfect right to be pleased.[19]

Since the government had placed a ship at his disposal, he no longer had to go to the South Sea Islands first, as he originally intended. He now drew up a revised plan and submitted it to Perreau for approval. His Prefecture of Bourbon, besides including Île Sainte Marie, a small French colony off the east coast of Madagascar, also included Madagascar itself, the fourth largest island in the world, almost 240 times larger than Bourbon. Father Jean-Louis Pastre, Prefect

Apostolic of Bourbon before de Solages, had requested Pope Leo XII in February 1829 to incorporate Madagascar in the Bourbon Prefecture Apostolic, but the pope died a few days later. His successor, Pius VIII, then did the incorporating on 3 May 1829. Pastre, whose broken health had made it necessary to find a successor, informed de Solages that the Holy See was planning to establish a vicar apostolic (usually a bishop) in Madagascar and intended to give this vicar apostolic charge of the Bourbon Prefecture Apostolic as well.

But meanwhile Madagascar was de Solages's responsibility. There were many priests in Bourbon, but none in Madagascar. He consequently had to provide missionaries for Madagascar and also for the South Sea Islands.[20]

Bourbon was to be the headquarters for his vast mission undertaking and there he would establish a kind of social pastoral institute to provide new missionaries with particularised training before sending them to Madagascar and to the south Pacific. 'According to arrangements already made with the Grand Almonry,' his report said, 'the institute to be established on the Isle of Bourbon is to render equal service for the Madagascar mission and for the Pacific Ocean mission, and the priests destined for both missions are to be taken from the community of the Reverend Coudrin, since the Holy Ghost Seminary cannot at present furnish the personnel needed for Madagascar.'

He thought that the French government should be asked to provide an annual subsidy of 12,000 francs for four or six missionaries to be employed exclusively in Madagascar. Since Île Sainte Marie was a French possession, the missionaries being sent there would automatically be paid a salary by the French government. Those being sent to the South Sea Islands, an area which had no connection with France, would be supported by the Grand Almonry or by the Association for the Propagation of the Faith.

De Solages said in his report that he had learned from a priest assigned to Bourbon for many years that there were old abandoned sheds in Bourbon that could easily be acquired. 'And since the Picpus Congregation is versed in the arts and crafts', he said, 'its members will be able to make them fit for lodging. Those who are to be assigned to the islands in the Pacific Ocean can do this work. . . .' The others were to go with him to Île Sainte Marie, where some would be left behind, and from there to Tananarive, the inland capital of Madagascar. Here he hoped to win the necessary protection for his missionaries from the powerful Queen Ranavalona. So as to have a greater guarantee of success with her, he petitioned the French government to send along presents for her and even to designate him a Special Ambassador for the occasion.

After providing for Madagascar he would return to Bourbon, his plan said, and there make immediate preparations for departing with those missionaries destined for the islands of the Pacific Ocean. 'One must not lose sight of the fact', he said, 'that the house to be established for missionaries at Bourbon must also provide formation for the most outstanding indigenes in the field of religion and also in those arts best suited for the advancement of civilisation in their respective countries. Nor shall I fail during my lengthy voyage to recruit a goodly number of these same indigenes to bring back with me.'

The project is vast, he admitted, 'and I do not know to what point God will give me the strength and the grace to execute it. But I believe it is my duty to submit this plan to the wisdom and insights of the Reverend Perreau, so that he might kindly indicate to me any changes that are to be made. And in case he approves of the plan completely, and if Divine Providence should dispose of my days before the plan is completely executed, then he could be my successor.'

In conclusion, de Solages said it was urgent to request Rome 'immediately' to grant the various faculties and spiritual powers necessary to carry out the project. This meant faculties for his missionaries as well as for himself.[21]

It was about the beginning of November when Father Perreau received a reply to the first letter that he had sent to Cardinal Cappellari in Rome, and its contents gave de Solages added reasons to rejoice. The cardinal said that the South Sea Islands project definitely merited consideration, and he even stated that he could wish for nothing better but to entrust it to Father de Solages as Perreau had requested. But at the same time he wanted to do nothing that might prove detrimental to the Picpus Fathers. Before making a final decision, therefore, he requested Perreau to check with Father Coudrin on how far the jurisdiction of his Sandwich Islands mission in the north Pacific extended. Overlapping of jurisdiction had frequently given rise to quarrels among prelates over the centuries and the cardinal wanted to avoid this very thing here.[22]

This very favourable reaction by Cardinal Cappellari committed Perreau now more than ever to work for the success of the de Solages mission in the South Seas which he himself had called to Rome's attention. De Solages all this time had been held in suspense by Coudrin, who during their visit a month before did not refuse to collaborate and yet did not formally agree either. De Solages took it for granted, however, that the Picpus Fathers would accept his invitation to collaborate and therefore had worked them into his plan.[23]

This new plan of de Solages, according to Perreau's undersecretary, won the admiration and hearty approbation of the Paris Council of the Association for the Propagation of the Faith, 'and particularly of the Reverend Perreau'. The undersecretary wrote that de Solages would render 'great services to religion because, as everyone knows, there is no place left but Oceania where religion has not yet penetrated, and there are more than a hundred islands here to conquer for Jesus Christ'.[24]

Since Perreau had been designated in the plan as the future successor of de Solages, it is not surprising that he decided to press for a definite commitment of personnel while seeing Coudrin in Rouen on 7 November about the clarification requested by Cardinal Cappellari. He explained how ready Cappellari was to make de Solages the Prefect Apostolic of the South Sea Islands and how the French government had also promised a ship and other assistance. But when he requested personnel for the new mission, Coudrin balked and said that his men would have to learn English, since this was the European language most used in the islands. He also pointed out that the relationship which his men must have with their religious order superiors could not be reconciled with the relationship that they would need to have with the Reverend de Solages, a secular priest, who would be the ecclesiastical superior. Perreau assured him, however, that these were no real obstacles and should not stand in the way of collaboration. Coudrin made no promise of personnel, but neither did he refuse. De Solages was again left in suspense.[25]

The visit by Perreau had proved somewhat embarrassing for Coudrin, because at Rouen he had no record of the jurisdiction granted by the Holy See to his missionaries in the Sandwich Islands. The next day, 8 November, he wrote to Father Raphaël Bonamie, prior of the house on rue de Picpus in Paris, and told him about the visit by Perreau. 'I see', he wrote, 'that the Reverend de Solages would like to have some of our members and ape the little bishop in their midst.'

He admitted to Father Raphaël that he had been 'too modest' in his replies to Father Perreau who, like himself, was one of the vicars general of Cardinal Prince de Croÿ of Rouen. He asked Raphaël to go and see Perreau with the pertinent excerpts from the decree that Father Hilarion Lucas, the secretary general, had on file. And if Hilarion could control his tongue, he said, the two men were to go together. They were to find out precisely what islands de Solages wanted to evangelise, and whether from them one could reach the Sandwich Islands.

As for the extent of jurisdiction, which was the original query of Cardinal Cappellari, it was clear from the documents that the jurisdiction of the Picpus Fathers covered only the Sandwich Islands in the north Pacific. There could consequently be no conflict of jurisdiction between this mission and one located completely in the south Pacific.

The two priests visited Perreau and reported back to Coudrin that there were islands below the equator which in fact did have contact with the Sandwich Islands. If some Picpus priests were to be sent there, de Solages could place one of them in charge as his vice-prefect. Coudrin agreed with this proposal of Raphaël and Hilarion, but insisted that their archipelago had to be 'independent' of de Solages.[26] In laying down this condition Coudrin was being consistent with the principle that he had expressed on 15 July 1825 when announcing to the Evangelisation Congregation that his community was prepared to undertake foreign missionary work. 'The only request we make,' he said, 'and one that we consider necessary, is that those who are sent should not depend upon anyone but the Evangelisation Congregation. And among those who are sent, there ought to be a superior, designated by the Superior General of our community and acceptable to the Sacred Congregation, who himself would see to it that the orders from the Sacred Congregation are carried out by the other members under his authority.'[27]

Raphaël and Hilarion correctly interpreted Father Coudrin's laconic reply as authorisation to seek an independent mission for the Picpus Fathers in some South Sea Islands which had contact with the Sandwich Islands. They learned that the two consuls from the United States and England based in the Sandwich Islands were also charged by their governments with the inspection of commerce in four South Seas archipelagoes below the Sandwich Islands, namely, the

Society Islands (with Tahiti), Marquesas Islands, Bad Sea Islands and Dangerous Islands. (The last two archipelagoes are the northwest and southeast island groups respectively in what is now called the Tuamotu Archipelago.) With this information in hand and with answers prepared beforehand for questions that might be asked, Hilarion and Raphaël on a day in mid-November went to pay a call on de Solages who was still waiting for a definite yes or no from Coudrin. Raphaël and Hilarion were now authorised to give him the answer.[28]

Hilarion minced no words in the condensed report of their visit that he sent to Coudrin. When de Solages asked for priests, they told him that the Picpus Fathers did not feel it was possible for them to give him any. 'This ecclesiastic has searched everywhere for priests who might accompany him,' Hilarion said, 'and we had reason to fear that this mixture of secular and independent priests with the members of our institute would be harmful for the common good. This was all the more true because just motives made one suspect that a number of priests not enjoying a very good reputation had succeeded in taking advantage of the good faith of the Reverend de Solages.'

They told him that the stretch of islands from the Friendly or Tonga Islands inclusive to New Zealand certainly would be a vast enough area to satisfy completely his own zeal and that of his collaborators. As for themselves, they would like to be entrusted by the pope with the four archipelagoes in the South Seas closest to the Sandwich Islands. And they would like him to agree to this division. These archipelagoes, they believed, could be created into an independent prefecture apostolic with one of their priests in charge as prefect apostolic.[29]

This Picpus proposal was disastrous for de Solages, because it would have split his plan for the evangelisation of Oceania right down the middle and would have removed from his competence Pitcairn Island, Marquesas Islands, and Tahiti in the Society Islands, three of the six areas in the South Seas where he had planned to set up missions. As for the island of Pitcairn, its tiny size and the small number of inhabitants were far surpassed by its religious importance. Since the inhabitants were bilingual and had been trained as Christians by John Adams, they were already 'half-formed' Catholics and 'lacked only Catholic teaching to become excellent catechists'. He believed that 'the small island of Pitcairn would furnish by itself the Christian teachers for all these archipelagoes'.[30]

As for the Picpus Fathers, 'they wanted to reserve for themselves alone', he said, 'the countries which were the more civilised, leaving the cannibals to us for our portion.' When de Solages said this he had perhaps forgotten that Dillon called the inhabitants of the Fiji Islands, which would have been in his portion, 'the most civilised people in the Pacific Ocean'.

He could not understand how the Picpus Fathers wanted more territory since 'they did not have enough priests for the Sandwich Islands of which they were in charge'. And so, being 'perfectly convinced that they were not able to send personnel' to the four archipelagoes which they wanted, he did not agree to the division that they requested. 'Why, not even the Jesuits would be big enough to take care of Oceania', he said, and therefore it was necessary 'to make an appeal to all religious congregations and pious ecclesiastics disposed to devote themselves to this kind of ministry'.[31]

But Father Coudrin used against de Solages the very same argumentation that de Solages used against him. He knew, he said, 'that the Reverend de Solages could never hope to have enough missionaries to spread them throughout all the islands', and so he had decided to ask for jurisdiction over four archipelagoes. He picked the ones closest to the Sandwich Islands 'so that the priests established in these two missions, animated by the same views, guided by the same spirit of obedience, and united by the same bonds, can be of assistance to one another'.[32]

But all the days for de Solages in this month of November were not cloudy. In his letter of 25 October to d'Haussez, he had tried to wipe out any suspicions that the minister might have regarding Dillon, insisting that he had been born in Martinique, that his Irish family was of French origin, and that he 'does not love England and would gladly attach himself to France'. Since there was 'no European' who had 'as many contacts as he with the diverse peoples of Oceania', his participation in the expedition was indispensable. And since de Solages realised that he could request only 'with difficulty' that an Irishman be placed in charge of a vessel of the French Navy, he suggested 'by way of compromise that he be made consul in the Fiji Islands'. In this way his valuable knowledge could be used and officers of the French Navy would not be offended.

It was happily the first compromise of de Solages, but unhappily also his last.

D'Haussez wrote to de Solages on 7 November that he was on his way at that moment to get the orders of King Charles for the expedition, and said that he had just informed de Polignac of the proposal that Dillon be named a consul.

De Solages then wrote to de Polignac on 15 November, once again praising Dillon highly. Six days later de Polignac gave his approval that Dillon become an honorary vice-consul of France, underlining the word 'Honorary', and King Charles X on 29 November officially named him 'Honorary Vice-Consul in the Islands Composing the Pacific Ocean Archipelago'. Dillon was assigned an income of 3,000 francs counting from the day of his nomination until the end of the expedition, or until such time as his services would no longer be required. De Polignac 'with pleasure' informed Dillon under date of 7 December of his appointment and said: 'His Majesty, while preparing to send to these islands missionaries charged with preaching Christianity, has wished to attempt at the same time the establishment of commercial and maritime contacts between these islands and France. You, sir, more than anyone else, have seemed suitable for accomplishing this mission with some chance of success, since your devotion has been tested already and you possess a knowledge of the customs and languages of those islanders. I have no doubt that your efforts will fully justify the honourable choice of which you today are the object.'

By this time Dillon was in London, so the document was sent to Baron Seguin, French consul general there, and he had it by 16 December. Besides learning of this appointment Dillon also got word that the corvette, *Dordogne*, had been assigned to the expedition and would be leaving Brest for Oceania on 1 February 1830. He immediately began preparations for the voyage.

De Solages had good reason to be happy; everything was working out just as he wished![33]

Without priests, however, he was helpless. He turned to Father Pouget at the large Jesuit residence of Grand-Montrouge at the gates of Paris and gave him a memorandum on his project for presentation to the provincial superior. Pouget replied on 18 November that the provincial alone was not able to take action in the matter; it would first have to be presented to the superior general. 'And if the Reverend Superior General should ask the Provincial's views', Pouget added, 'he would have to answer—although praising and admiring your zeal—that he could not collaborate without depriving his establishments in France of personnel, for they are all filled to capacity.'[34]

The prospect of getting Jesuits did not look good, so de Solages appealed to his good friend Goubert, the undersecretary of Perreau at the Paris Council of the Association for the Propagation of the Faith. Goubert then wrote to the Lyon Council on 26 November 1829, complaining that a letter by de Solages addressed to them asking for help especially in finding priests for his mission had gone unanswered. Goubert urged the Council of Lyon to support de Solages because 'this affair, which will bring so much honour to the Society, is very important and very urgent'.

Goubert wrote again on 14 December in the name of the Council of Paris and again asked them to inquire where the Reverend Count de Solages might find some priests 'because his project has now been authorised by royal ordinance and he will leave in January with 12 priests and 12 catechists for the islands of Pitcairn, Fiji, Tahiti, Marquesas and New Zealand'. After a month or two of getting affairs in order at Bourbon, he said, de Solages would leave for the above islands to place his missionaries, and would then return to Bourbon and evangelise Madagascar. 'The corvette is waiting for them at Le Havre and will leave in February. It will be commanded by M. Mathieu, brother of the canon of Paris, and Captain Dillon will take part in the expedition as guide with the title of Vice-Consul . . . Kindly communicate this recent news to the gentlemen there and tell them to look for personnel, because we still need some. The Reverend Perreau is of the opinion that a considerable subsidy should be allocated.'

Goubert wrote once again on 23 December and asked, 'Have you found any personnel for the Reverend de Solages? This is a very important affair. He would like you to make requests in Savoie, Piémont, etc. . . . .'[35]

The Council of Lyon actually had considered the letter of de Solages and had taken action, negative action, at its meeting of 10 December 1829. 'This zealous missionary', the minutes for the day read, 'would like to establish missions in all the islands of the South Seas, and even the entire earth would not appear to be a theatre too vast for his extensive zeal. For this end he solicits assistance from the government, and has no doubt but that our Association will furnish him with money and missionaries. After deliberating on the contents of this letter, the Council does not feel that it can fulfil this request, in view of the fact that if its entire funds were applied to this purpose, they would not suffice for a work so vast. Further, the Council is not able to supply any missionaries, and even less can it equip vessels at its own expense. At the most one could propose at the next allocation to grant some funds for the missionaries being sent to Madagascar, provided this project should offer desirable guarantees. It has been resolved to draw up a letter along these lines for the President of the Council of Paris.'[36]

Another who had misgivings about de Solages's extensive project was Father Jacques-Madeleine Bertout, the seventy-six-year-old head of the Holy Ghost Seminary in Paris who had been superior general of the Holy Ghost Fathers (C.S.Sp.) since 1805. As such Bertout was responsible to the Holy See and to the French government for adequate spiritual care being provided for the French colonies. Although he called the Oceania project 'great and praiseworthy', he believed that it was 'contrary to the spiritual good' of the colony of Bourbon which required 'an ecclesiastical superior in residence'. Bertout on 1 December 1829 sent these considerations in writing to d'Haussez, saying that he felt bound in conscience to do so. And he added: 'This affair was launched, conducted and terminated without my knowledge, and it is contrary to my expressed will which I made known to Monsieur de Solages.'[37]

De Solages was also strangely secretive with the Bishop of Pamiers for whom he was vicar general. Three days after Bertout's letter to d'Haussez, the bishop's secretary explained why a new vicar general was being appointed. De Solages, he said, had departed from Pamiers 'more than five months ago without saying a word to the bishop of his intention of transferring elsewhere. Neither did he send His Excellency any news. And so finally the bishop decided to replace him.'[38]

With no hope of getting priests through the Lyon Council of the Association for the Propagation of the Faith, de Solages decided to try the Jesuits again, and he wrote directly to Rome on 21 December 1829 to the Very Reverend Joannes Roothaan, S.J., who on 9 July that year had been elected the twenty-first superior general. Since a departure date of 1 February would give Roothaan less than a month to provide personnel, de Solages said his party would now be sailing at the beginning of March. He enclosed a summary of the Dillon memorandum 'in order to provide exact information on the project in question', and said he would place Jesuits over the other priests at each of the three or four main stations to be founded as a start in Oceania. 'Strictly speaking six priests of your Company would suffice for directing these foundations . . . but I particularly wish that you should appoint two others to help me found an Indian seminary at Bourbon.' De Solages asked for a speedy reply.

Roothaan received the letter on 2 January 1830 and answered it four days later, insisting that shortage of personnel for him would be no obstacle, since there were volunteers and he was 'convinced that Divine Providence will give back to us with interest those whom we give over to an enterprise so important for the glory of God and the salvation of so many abandoned souls'. Nothing interested him more, he said, than the foundation of a seminary at Bourbon, 'for the education of the natives of these islands and of Madagascar as well.' But two priests would hardly be enough. 'I tell you frankly that I would rather assign a larger number for directing such an establishment.' It could become a Jesuit centre, he said, 'and from there in time expeditions could set out for Madagascar and other islands.'

He felt, however, that the idea of placing Jesuits as superiors over other priests 'would cause a good number of difficulties'. And the fact that de Solages was sailing at the beginning of March left too little time 'for choosing the personnel, since some would have to come from a rather great distance'. More time was also needed to learn 'if and how the members of the Company [of Jesus] assigned to this mission could retain their status as religious and also remain dependent upon the superiors of the Company . . . And so I have to admit sadly the impossibility of complying with your wishes,' Roothaan said, 'at least on this occasion . . . But I would be very happy if later you were to honour me with news about your work. With a bit more time something worthy of your apostolic zeal could be arranged. . . .' The note was optimistic enough, but it did not provide the personnel that de Solages needed so desperately.

Roothaan, with one eye on the future, wrote about this matter six days later (12 January) to Father Druilhet, provincial superior of the Jesuits in France. Conducting a seminary in Bourbon, he said, 'would be most fitting for the Company' and 'would make possible sending missionaries from there to Madagascar, etc. . . . How happy I would be if only these projects were to materialise.'[39]

Fathers Coudrin and Hilarion were meanwhile engaged in feverish activity to obtain the desired four archipelagoes from Rome as a prefecture apostolic. Coudrin had Hilarion draft a letter for him which was mailed to Cardinal Cappellari under date of 6 December 1829. In it Coudrin admitted that he could immediately send only 'two or three priests' to the new mission. And as for the Picpus mission in the Sandwich Islands, no more men had been sent there since the first three priests and three Brothers left Bordeaux on 16 November 1826. But after a short time he hoped to send 'two or three other priests to facilitate the progress of this mission'.[40]

On 14 December both Raphaël and Hilarion had an audience with Prince de Polignac, Minister of Foreign Affairs, and laid before him their reasons for wanting the four archipelagoes. De Polignac requested a detailed memorandum on this which Hilarion submitted on 21 December. Coudrin on 2 January 1830, without yet having had a reply from Cardinal Cappellari, submitted an official request to de Polignac for free passage aboard a government vessel 'for two or three priests, three young theologians and three seminarians who, being furnished with powers from the Holy See and protected by His Most Christian Majesty, shall open a new mission in the Society Islands, Marquesas Islands, Dangerous Archipelago, and the Archipelago of the Bad Sea'.

De Polignac replied to Hilarion on 6 January 1830 and said that since the Reverend de Solages had already requested from Rome 'all of Oceania with the exception of the Sandwich Islands, it is naturally to the Holy See that the views of the House of Picpus in this regard will have to be submitted'. He gave assurance, however, 'that the government of His Majesty will grant equal protection in Oceania to all French houses'.[41]

In a supreme effort Coudrin on 11 January 1830, now having a promise of protection for his missionaries from de Polignac, made an official request to Pope Pius VIII for the archipelagoes. And on the same day he sent separate letters to Cardinals Cappellari, della Somaglia, Pacca and Caprano, asking each of them to lend their personal support to his petition. All four were active members in the Evangelisation Congregation, and the first three were the highest ranking members.[42]

Both Coudrin and Hilarion knew, and de Solages knew, that as long as the official decision had not been taken by the Sacred Congregation headed by Cardinal Cappellari, and as long as the pope had not approved this decision, there was still a possibility that the Prefecture Apostolic of the South Sea Islands, as envisioned by de Solages, might be split in two, as envisioned by Coudrin. And so de Solages, after getting the decisive no from Coudrin's two delegates in mid-November, and being convinced that such a split 'would cause grave obstacles for the success of the said mission', had hastened to set wheels in motion.[43]

He drew up a list of observations for Church authorities in Rome, pointing out in particular that there was no danger at all of the new mission in the South Sea Islands infringing upon the rights of the Picpus Fathers in the Sandwich Islands.

First of all, he said, a very great distance separated the two missions. Second, he had already broached the subject with the Picpus Congregation and neither Father Coudrin nor any of his priests had raised any objections. And when he had asked for priests, Coudrin said that he had only two available at the moment and these he had to send to the Sandwich Islands. Third, any eventual objection that might be raised by Father Coudrin would be based solely upon the knowledge that he had obtained from de Solages, because prior to their meeting Father Coudrin had been in complete ignorance of the project. Fourth, no one could imagine that the Picpus Fathers, being so few in number, 'would pretend to have the exclusive right of evangelisation in that part of the world where, because of the large number of islands, because of the enormous distances between them, and because of the extreme ignorance of the peoples that inhabit them, even thousands of priests would not be sufficient'. Fifth, the Picpus missions were all in the Northern Hemisphere and those of Father de Solages were all in the Southern Hemisphere, and no communication existed between the two hemispheres. Sixth, should the Picpus Fathers want to extend their mission westward, they could do so by going as far west as the Palau Islands in the western Caroline Islands. And, seventh, they could also go as far east as the coast of the North American continent, 'beginning at Nootka and going north, where there are people without number, and perfectly disposed, and where civilisation has already made no little progress'.[44]

The Palau Islands were near the Philippines. Nootka was halfway up the west coast of Vancouver Island in British Columbia, Canada, over a quarter of a world away.

Carefully de Solages added to these observations a copy of the letter that Dillon had sent him on 7 September 1829, a copy of the 16 October 1829 letter that he had received from de Polignac promising him a ship, a copy of his own letter of 25 October 1829 to the Minister of the Navy, and a list of ten faculties that he wanted, different from those that he had originally requested in the letter sent on 18 September 1829 by Perreau. He entrusted the packet to his friend, the Marquis de Pacca, who had made himself responsible for keeping Cardinal Pacca in Rome informed of all latest developments in this affair, and he urged the Marquis to use the greatest possible haste in transmitting the documents to Cardinal Pacca.[45]

In this way his papers quickly came into the hands of Bartolomeo Cardinal Pacca (1756–1844), one of the most influential cardinals in Rome, who that year had become dean of the college of cardinals. Pacca quickly handed over the documents to Father Castruccio Castracane, the new secretary of the Sacred Congregation for the Evangelisation of Nations, and asked him to call to Cardinal Prefect Cappellari's attention 'the very great interest' shown by the French Minister of Foreign Affairs in the project, also the fact that a ship was being provided by the Minister of the Navy, and also the haste urged by this minister. Pacca too was personally very much in favour of the project, he said, and he urged that Cardinal Cappellari be asked to take quick action.

On learning that Cardinal Pacca was so interested in the case, Cappellari said to him: Fine, we shall speed this up as you suggest, and put it on the agenda for our next meeting. And will you kindly be the *ponens*? Pacca agreed.

The *ponens* was that cardinal member of the Sacred Congregation who had the task of studying all the material on a particular project, doing further research on it, and then writing it up clearly and logically. He also had to show the pros and cons, and had to conclude his report with several specific points to be voted upon. The entire study, together with an appendix containing all or most of the letters and documents referred to, was then set up in type in the Sacred Congregation's own printing press so that each cardinal member and other experts could obtain an advance copy for personal study.

The de Solages project came up for discussion at the meeting of 22 December 1829, three days before Cardinal Pacca's seventy-third birthday.

It would have been difficult to find a better man than Pacca to be placed in charge of drawing up this project. He was an excellent writer, had a passion for history and literature, was a leader in educational reforms, and was expert in the principal languages of Europe. He had served as Nuncio Apostolic to Germany, Extraordinary Nuncio to King Louis XVI of France, and Nuncio Apostolic to Portugal. Pope Pius VII in 1801 had made him a cardinal and the same pope made him Pro-Secretary of State when the French entered Rome in 1808. Together with the pope he was arrested by the soldiers of Napoleon on 5 July 1809 at the Quirinal Apartments in Rome. Napoleon kept Pacca imprisoned in Fénestrelle, Fontainebleau and Uzès for nearly four years. When

8 Castruccio Cardinal Castracane (1779–1852), subsequently a cardinal member. *Source: OM vol. 2,* secretary of the Sacred Congregation for the *p. 560. (Chapter 2).* Evangelisation of Nations from 1828 to 1833 and

SAGRA CONGREGAZIONE
DE
PROPAGANDA FIDE

PONENTE

L'Emo , e Rmo Sig. Cardinale

BARTOLOMMEO PACCA

———

RISTRETTO CON SOMMARIO

Sul Progetto di una nuova Missione per la Polinesia Australe ,
ossia Isole del Mar Pacifico.

✤✤✤✤✤✤✤ (Decembre) ✤✤✤✤✤✤✤
ANNO MDCCCXXIX.
✤✤✤✤✤✤✤✤✤✤✤✤✤✤✤✤✤

9   Title page of the report attributed to Bartolomeo Cardinal Pacca discussed at the General Meeting of the Evangelisation Congregation on 22 December 1829 leading up to the foundation of the Prefecture Apostolic of the South Sea Islands. *Source: PF: Acta vol. 192 (1829) f. 462r. (Chapter 2).*

Eͫi, e Rͫi Signori

1 Con lettera del 28. Settembre decorso Mons. D. L. Perreau Vicario Generale dell' Eminentissimo Principe de Croy grande Elemosiniere di Francia espone all' Eͫo Prefetto, che il Sig. Ab. Solages Vicario Generale di Pamiers nominato da questa Sagra Congregazione alla Prefettura dell' Isola di Bourbon per la rinunzia emessa dal Sig. Ab. Pastre desidera ardentemente di mettere in esecuzione la brama accesasi nel suo cuore fin dagli anni giovanili, e sempre viva mantenutasi di portare la Fede di Gesù Cristo alle Isole del grande Oceano, ossia Mare del Sud; che all' esecuzione di cotal suo desiderio sembra avergli la Divina Provvidenza presentato nn mezzo opportunissimo nella persona del Capitano Irlandese D'Illon ottimo Cattolico, che per il corso di venti anni ha viaggiato all' Isole di detto Mare; ed ha stretto de' rapporti preziosi di amicizia, e di commercio cogli abitanti, e capi delle medesime.

2 All' esposizione di questo desiderio del Sig. Ab. de Solages unisce il Vicario Generale le notizie che lo riguardano sia della Famiglia, sia Personali, che di molto lo accreditano. Perciocchè scrive appartenere a famiglia di assai specchiata nobiltà, e lustro, esser egli facoltoso, nell' età di anni circa 42. di robusto temperamento, di un bello esteriore, possiedere inoltre la lingua Inglese conosciuta in alcuna dell' Isole del mare del Sud. Ma tra le qualità personali rimarca in particolare la santità della sua vita, e lo zelo di cui è divorato della gloria di Dio, e della salute delle anime, zelo, che lo ha di già condotto a trovare de' Missionarj Francesi, che vuole compagni del suo Apostolato nell' Isole del Mar Pacifico.

3 Conclude il Vicario Generale pregando l'Eͫo Prefetto a nome dell' Eͫo de Croy, che trovasi assente a volersi compiacere di ottenere al Solages da Sua Santità il titolo di Prefetto Apostolico accompagnato da tutti i poteri ordinarj, e straordinarj soliti accordarsi a tutti i Missionarj in *partibus Infidelium* per le Isole del grande Oceano cioè per le Isole intermedie all' Isola di Pasqua da un canto, e la nuova Zelanda dall'altro tra l'Equatore al Nord, e il Polo Antartico al Sud.

4 Oltre le facoltà di cui sogliono essere rivestiti i Prefetti di simili Missioni, altre più particolari ne chiede per il Sig. Solages delle quali se ne dà l'elenco in Sommario assicurando il Vicario Generale, che il sommo attaccamento dello stesso alla Santa Sede lo rende meritevole di ottenerle.

5 Questo progetto del Sig. Solages comunque Santissimo per lo scopo che prende di mira di dilatare il nome di Gesù Cristo a' po-

A

10 First page of Cardinal Pacca's report, as figure 9. Note that each paragraph of the report was numbered, as was customary, for easy reference. Such reports showed the entire evolution of a project, beginning with the first piece of correspondence on it to reach Rome. In the first line, however, '28 September' is a typographical error for '18 September'. *Source: PF: Acta vol. 192 (1829) f. 463r. (Chapter 2).*

Pope Pius VII made his triumphal return to Rome in 1814 after the fall of Napoleon, he wanted Pacca at his side. During the conclave attended by Coudrin early in 1829, Pacca had received many votes for the office of pope.

There were six cardinals present for the meeting and Pacca was given the floor. He at once explained how de Solages and Dillon had met and he called their project for a new mission in the south Pacific islands a fine and commendable one. As for the special faculties requested by de Solages, they seemed to be 'in proportion to the importance and difficulty of his project'.

The cardinal said that the geographical, jurisdictional and political aspects of the question had to be given special consideration and prudent reflection, and he divided his report accordingly.

1. Geographical aspect

What islands, precisely, are to be included in the new jurisdiction?

'According to the most exact research that has been done by using the new *Atlas* printed in Brussels and the most recent geographies,' he said, 'it is clear that the islands designated by the Reverend Solages for his apostolate are in that part of the world's sea area named Polynesia or, as some geographers prefer to call it, Oceanica.[46] Now Polynesia is divided into North and South, and so the mission of the Reverend Solages would include all the islands contained in the South, that is, those which form the following archipelagoes: Marquesas Islands, Dangerous Islands [now Tuamotu Islands], Society Islands, Roggewein Islands [now Manihiki Islands, Penrhyn Islands, or northern Cook Islands], Mangaia Islands [now southern Cook Islands], Navigators Islands [now Samoa Islands], Friendly Islands [now also Tonga Islands], Fiji Islands and Kermadec Islands.'

But why had de Solages included in his proposed mission Easter Island, he asked, which was of such little importance, and New Zealand, which certainly did not fit in with the other islands? Pacca answered his own question by saying that Easter Island was to be the mission's link with South America, and New Zealand was to be its link with Australia.

Cardinal Pacca's mentioning 'the new *Atlas* printed in Brussels' shows how careful the cardinals in those days were to have an accurate idea of the geographical areas with which they were dealing. The author of this particular *Atlas* was the famed Belgian cartographer Philippe Vandermaelen (1795–1869). It was titled, *Atlas universel de géographie physique, politique, statistique et minéralogique* (Universal Atlas of Physical, Political, Statistical and Mineralogical Geography). The work contained 373 maps in colour covering the entire world, all drawn to a scale of twenty-five miles to an inch, a much larger scale than that ordinarily used by cartographers today. The work was published in Brussels in 1827, just two years prior to the above meeting.[47] Vandermaelen's use of 'Oceania' as the title for one of the six huge tomes into which the *Atlas* was divided prompted the Evangelisation Congregation eventually to use this same generic term for Australia and all islands in the Pacific.

2. Jurisdictional aspect

Will the jurisdiction of the new mission collide with that of a pre-existing mission and so give rise to quarrels and dissensions between the prefects apostolic?

The precise geographical description already given, the cardinal said, made it clear that the jurisdiction of the new mission would not collide with that of any pre-existing mission. It was true that the Picpus Fathers were in the Sandwich Islands, he said. But since these islands were located in Northern Oceania, there was an immense distance separating them from the islands where Father de Solages proposed to found his mission. The Picpus congregation, he added, was also suffering from a very acute shortage of priests and so was powerless to evangelise the islands of Northern Oceania. 'This impotence excludes every presumption and even the distant possibility that the Picpus missionaries might decide to extend their apostolate to the islands of Southern Oceania', he said.

3. Political aspect

Does some European nation other than France exercise governing power over the area in question, or have commercial ties with it? And could such a country later complain to the Holy See that its interests had been prejudiced because the Holy See had authorised a foundation by French missionaries?

As for the political aspect, he said, 'the English pretend to dominate these islands. But it is necessary to consider the quality of this domination.' English-claimed islands are to be found interspersed on maps with Spanish-claimed islands. 'But in reality all the islands mentioned still retain their own form of government, which basically is a kind of feudal aristocracy. And in general they still preserve their own religious system, which in substance is a kind of polytheism.'

The cardinal admitted that of all European nations, England had the closest ties with these islands. 'But not believing that it was capable of subjecting them with arms', he said, 'England took recourse instead to means that were milder and more certain. She sought to create in those islands a desire for her arts, and she spread there her language and her social customs. But the means that she used most of all was religion. England has sent out many Methodist missionaries who have made conversions in various places, and in this way her culture has been introduced.'

He added that the peoples in the islands, being of a pleasant disposition and having an agricultural economy, had taken advantage of the good things proposed by the Methodists, who were the first preachers of the Gospel whom they had seen. 'For example, on the island of Tahiti the people have built churches. And here too the English have succeeded in founding a printing press with which the Bible Society has printed 3,000 copies of the Gospel of Saint Luke.'

At the end of the discussion that followed Cardinal Pacca's remarks, he presented several questions so that the Sacred Congregation could arrive at some practical conclusions. The questions that he asked were these. Is there any consideration which might prevent us from approving the project? The answer was no. Should we ask the pope to make Father de Solages the prefect apostolic of the new mission? The answer was yes. Should we grant him the faculties that he has requested? The answer was that he ought to receive the same faculties usually granted to other prefects apostolic. Is it proper for him to retain the Prefecture Apostolic of Bourbon together with this new Prefecture Apostolic of the South Sea Islands? The answer was, 'Yes, according to the good pleasure of the Sacred Congregation.'[48]

Father Castracane, the secretary, gave an account of the meeting to Pope Pius VIII after the Christmas holidays. His Holiness readily confirmed the decisions of the cardinals and thereby formally established the Prefecture Apostolic of the South Sea Islands. He ordered, however, that Father de Solages was to be provided with much broader faculties than usual because of the difficulty of his distant mission.

This important day in the history of the Catholic Church in the south Pacific was Sunday, 10 January 1830.[49] Coudrin had been too slow! His official request to Pius VIII for the eastern half of Oceania and his letters to Cappellari and three other influential cardinals begging them to support the project were not written until the following day, 11 January 1830.

Cardinal Prefect Cappellari on 16 January 1830 sent the long awaited news to Father de Solages. 'It is with great joy in my heart', he wrote, 'that I am able to send Your Excellency the enclosed decree appointing you Prefect Apostolic for the Islands of the Pacific Ocean, commonly called the South Sea Islands.' He also called attention to the very special faculties enclosed, stating that the pope had wanted them to be granted, 'so that you may take up with greater facility this work which is at once so holy and so difficult, and so that—God willing—you may also accomplish what you hope to achieve.'

All the faculties, the cardinal explained, could be delegated by him in whole or in part to any of his missionaries. But there was one very important exception, he said, and it concerned the writing of dimissorial letters. Pope Pius VIII had decided to give him personally the faculty of writing dimissorial letters in favour of those candidates whom he might find suitable for sending to nearby bishops for ordination. The bishops in turn were likewise authorised by this same faculty to ordain the candidates, even outside the times prescribed by church law, and also without observing the required time intervals between ordinations in the case of candidates receiving more than one of the seven minor and major orders.

'However, you are to make use of this faculty neither continually nor indiscriminately,' Cardinal Cappellari said, 'since it is a faculty proper to bishops and has never before been granted to any prefects in charge of missions. His Holiness, however, considering your mission's vast expanse and the great distance of the places, has not denied it to you. However, he did want to restrict this faculty by some limits and so allows you to make use of it only four times.'

De Solages was also informed by Cappellari that he could obtain from the nuncio apostolic in Paris the necessary letters patent for the missionaries whom

Copia 466

In Congregatione Generali de Propaganda Fide habita in Ædibus ejusdem Sacrae Congriς die 22 Decembris labentis Anni 1829, a me infraspto tria proposita fuerunt dubia circa novam Missionem in Insulis Magni Oceani sive Maris vulgo dicti *del Sud* constituendam, iisque dubiis Emi ac Rmi Patres responsa quae sequuntur dederunt.

1.um Dubium

Se vi sia alcun riflesso alla approvazione del progetto di Missione del Sig. Ab. De Solagy, e se dabba pregarsi il Santo Padre ad accordare al medesimo il titolo di Prefetto della Missione da stabilirsi

℞. Negative ad primam partem: affirmative ad secundam

2.um Dubium

Se dabba consigliarsi il Santo Padre a concedere al Sig. Ab. Solagy le facoltà da lui richieste, ed in quella estenzione, che le ha richieste

℞. Concedantur facultates quae aliis Praefectis concedi solent, et ad Dnum Secretarium cum SSmo

3.um Dubium

Se sia conveniente, che colla nuova Prefettura ritenga anche la Prefettura dell'Isola di Bourbon

℞. Affirmative; ad nutum Sacrae Congregationis

Datum ex Nostra Residentia apud Sam Mariam in Porticu Urbis hac die 24. Decembris 1829.

B. Cardinalis Pacca Conarς

11 The handwritten conclusions reached at the General Meeting of 22 December 1829, signed by Cardinal Pacca, indicating the intention of the Evangelisation Congregation to ask Pope Pius VIII to found the Prefecture Apostolic of the South Sea Islands. The three questions or 'Dubia' are in Italian, but the replies are in Latin. *Source: PF: Acta vol. 192 (1829) f. 466r. (Chapter 2).*

he wished to take along as well as other letters patent for the vice-prefects whom he might want to appoint in certain districts. He was advised to take counsel with the nuncio and to show wisdom and prudence in not admitting for missionary work any priests 'except those who are altogether acceptable on the basis of doctrine, piety, zeal for souls and prudence'. The names of those missionaries and vice-prefects to whom letters patent were eventually issued were to be forwarded to Rome.

'Insofar as you can and insofar as it seems opportune to you,' the cardinal said in conclusion, 'make use of the occasions that arise and send letters to the Sacred Congregation about yourself and about your missionaries. Also compose an accurate report on the beginnings of the mission and its progress. I do not have the least doubt but that you will do this with all zeal and diligence. In conclusion, I earnestly ask Our Lord that he graciously assist your efforts with his grace, and that he grant you and your companions every success.'[50]

The decree enclosed with the letter spoke of the multitude of islands contained in that 'very vast ocean area stretching from Easter Island westwards to New Zealand, and from the equator southwards to the Tropic of Capricorn, where they say the light of the true faith has not yet begun to shine'.[51]

In entrusting such an immense area to a single ecclesiastical superior the Evangelisation Congregation did not for one moment think that this one man with his handful of assistants could ever evangelise all of it. But at least he could make a start. And who could tell in advance where the best place or places to begin might be? After arriving on the spot the mission head might well find that circumstances of the moment would require decisions unforeseen in even the most carefully worked out plan. Later, after he had succeeded in solidly establishing the Catholic Church, a subdivision of the mission could be made, and then another, and another, and so on indefinitely. Since 1622 when the Sacred Congregation was founded, this had always been its practice in North America, South America, Africa, Asia and Europe. This same endless process was now being launched in the south Pacific, so long neglected, and precisely for this reason the action taken in Rome at this time was so very important.

The letter meant for de Solages, the decree, and the list of special faculties were all sent by Cardinal Cappellari to Father Perreau, the vicar general of Cardinal Prince de Croÿ, with the request that he pass them on to de Solages. In an accompanying letter for Perreau the cardinal praised him for his 'zeal and concern for souls'. He wanted the documents to pass through his hands, he said, so Perreau could see that action had been taken on the proposal originally made by himself. The cardinal stated that this initiative of his was 'not a little responsible' for the new mission coming into existence, and he thanked him for it.[52]

The cardinal then addressed one last letter to Archbishop Luigi Lambruschini (1776–1854), Archbishop of Genoa, who had been serving in Paris since 8 February 1827 as nuncio apostolic. He informed him that a new prefecture apostolic had been founded for the South Sea Islands, and that Father de Solages with whom he was acquainted had been placed in charge. 'He will visit Your Excellency to get the letters patent for the priests whom he will be taking with him', the cardinal said. 'Consequently I am sending you the enclosed fifteen letters patent, with spaces left blank for the names of priests, and I am adding ten other letters patent for vice-prefects. It may be that the Reverend de Solages will find it necessary to establish a vice-prefect in more than one of the islands of the various archipelagoes through which he will pass. In that case he could choose suitable candidates for this office from among his missionaries.'

As long as de Solages was in France, however, he was to present the names and credentials of missionaries won for the cause to the nuncio apostolic who in turn was expected to use vigilance and prudence in providing them with letters-patent. Those letters patent that might still be unused at the time of de Solages's departure were to be consigned by the nuncio 'as they are to the same Reverend de Solages, upon whose prudence the choice of personnel will afterwards depend, since some candidates may present themselves to him in the course of his very long voyage.'[53]

The letters to the nuncio, to Perreau, and to de Solages, as well as the decree itself, were all dated 16 January 1830. With the mailing of these documents the church authorities in Rome had done their part. They could hardly have moved more quickly and been more magnanimous.

As for Father de Solages, his race with the Picpus Fathers was over and he had won. What remained now was for him to obtain some financial help, assemble his missionaries, get them aboard the vessel placed at his disposal by the French government, and then sail to the South Sea Islands.

But whether he actually succeeded in getting there, or whether others did whom he in late January 1830 accused of having 'the audacity of wanting to set up a separate group in order to take possession of a part of this mission and so close the door to everyone else except those of their own congregation', that is matter for another chapter.[54]

3

De Solages arrives in Bourbon

7 JANUARY 1831

Father de Solages had been correct in surmising that Father Coudrin might take action to have the Picpus mission in the north Pacific Ocean extended to include some islands in the south Pacific Ocean. On 6 December 1829, just sixteen days before the cardinals of the Evangelisation Congregation were to decide whether de Solages should be given spiritual jurisdiction over all of the South Sea Islands, Coudrin addressed a petition to Cardinal Prefect Cappellari in Rome. 'I have had occasion to learn of a project proposed to the French government', he said, 'which could prove very advantageous for the propagation of the faith. It concerns the establishment of missions in the south Pacific Ocean from New Zealand to the American continent. On this important subject I have made some reflections and believe I should submit them to Your Eminence.'

He explained that in the south Pacific Ocean about a thousand leagues distant from his Sandwich Islands (now Hawaii) mission, there were four additional archipelagoes known as the Marquesas Archipelago, Society (or Tahiti) Archipelago, Bad Sea Archipelago and Dangerous Archipelago (two groups in the Tuamotu Archipelago).[1] 'Would the Holy See be disposed', Coudrin asked, 'to give the title of prefect apostolic over the four archipelagoes to a priest of our congregation whom I would have the honour to designate?' This prefect apostolic, for facilitating contact with the Sandwich Islands mission, could be given jurisdiction also over all islands not yet evangelised which lay between the Marquesas Islands and the Sandwich Islands, extending as far east as the coasts of the two American continents. (Practically speaking these were only the Line, or Equatorial, Islands.) If there were also other priests interested in working in the south Pacific Ocean, Coudrin said, they surely would find scope enough for their activity in New Zealand, the Friendly Islands, and the many other islands west of the four archipelagoes mentioned by him.

Although able to supply immediately only 'two or three priests' for the new mission, Coudrin pointed out that he could easily send more personnel if he were allowed 'to choose candidates from among those who are not yet priests and who sense a vocation for such a holy work'. At the moment he had forty members in vows who were making theological studies at the Picpus seminary, and of these many desired to consecrate themselves to the foreign missions. 'I could send a fixed number and have them continue their theological courses under priests whom we would send with them', he said. 'They could learn the language of the indigenes at the same time, and consequently would begin practising their ministry immediately after their priestly ordination.'

Should this proposal prove acceptable, 'it would then be necessary' that one of the new missionaries being sent to the Sandwich Islands or to the four archipelagoes be a bishop, so that he could ordain to the priesthood the young men on completing their theological studies. 'In order to guarantee unity in the administration of the two missions' and to provide better for their welfare, Coudrin asked that the bishop be jurisdictionally superior to both prefects apostolic.

The Sandwich Islands mission, however, had received no new personnel since the first three priests and three catechists were sent there. But after a short time Coudrin hoped to send 'two or three other priests to facilitate the progress of this mission'. He asked Cappellari to send him word on Pope Pius VIII's reaction to this proposal, 'so that further steps can be taken to realise it, if His Holiness approves of the project'.[2]

The project here suggested by Coudrin seemed modelled after and prompted by that of de Solages, who wanted to found a seminary near Oceania for the training of seminarians whom he would bring along from Europe as well as of the indigenes whom he would get from Oceania. But Coudrin, in speaking of bringing seminarians from France and training them in the Sandwich Islands or in Oceania, made no mention of indigenes.

Without waiting for a reply from Cappellari to this December letter, Coudrin sent five more letters on 11 January 1830 to Pope Pius VIII and to Cardinals Cappellari, Caprano, Pacca and della Somaglia. He asked the cardinals, all of whom were members of the Evangelisation Congregation, to support the petition that he was sending that very same day to the pope. His petition pointed out five reasons why it was fitting that the four archipelagoes should be entrusted to his missionary community:

1. There were 'frequent contacts' between these archipelagoes and the Sandwich Islands, where he already had some men, and 'the same language' was spoken in both areas.
2. 'Communication among the priests in charge of both missions would be easy.'
3. Confiding a part of the Oceania missions to a missionary community would 'ensure stability', because secular priests 'easily become discouraged or they die and find no successors, whereas a community is always assured of finding within its own ranks the personnel to replace those who no longer can dedicate themselves to missionary work or who might happen to die'.
4. Both areas contain 'the same enemies to be combated, that is, the Protestant ministers from America, who established themselves there more or less around the same time'.
5. And because of the geographical location of the two areas, 'the English consul of the Sandwich Islands exercises the same powers in the Society

Islands and in the Marquesas Islands, and he has a ship at his disposal for travelling to and from those islands'.

These five points bolstered up by five separate letters showed how strongly Coudrin opposed a mission monopoly in Oceania. By this action he virtually declared himself a foe of de Solages at the court of Rome.[3]

De Solages had yet another foe in Father Jacques Bertout (1753–1832), superior general of the Holy Ghost Fathers, who was officially responsible to the French government for supplying clergy to French colonies. He had told d'Haussez, Minister of the Navy, on 1 December 1829 that the Oceania plan of de Solages was 'contrary to the spiritual good' of Bourbon. Bertout also sent a special messenger to inform the Picpus Fathers on 19 January that he in no way supported the Oceania project of de Solages. Nor did he want the Picpus Fathers to think that he shared any of the resentment toward them which de Solages manifested so often.[4]

Bertout had tried to reason with de Solages, explaining that the two offices of prefect apostolic over Bourbon and Oceania were incompatible. But de Solages would not hear of it. Then keep Oceania and give up Bourbon, Bertout suggested. But de Solages would not hear of that either, even though the former prefect apostolic of Bourbon was once again able and willing to resume office. Father Jean-Louis Pastre (1779–1839), prefect apostolic since 1821, had returned to Lyon seeking assistance for his prefecture apostolic in 1828. But his health did not allow him to return, he resigned his office, and on 18 June 1829 was named titular canon of Saint-Jean. Now his health was fully restored. In return for making this proposal, however, Bertout incurred the wrath of de Solages.

In view of this impasse Bertout wrote to Cappellari on 22 January announcing that de Solages, whose 'proximate departure' for Bourbon he had already announced in July, was still in Paris. And since de Solages wanted 'to establish a mission in many small islands' of the Pacific, there was little hope that he would get to Bourbon soon. After explaining his reasons for giving de Solages an alternative, Bertout shifted his own responsibility to the cardinal's shoulders and said: 'I ask Your Eminence in your wisdom to decide *whether these two posts are compatible.*'[5]

This letter of Bertout set many wheels in motion in Rome. Cappellari agreed in his reply of 25 February 1830 that it was 'certainly desirable that a suitable superior be sent immediately to Bourbon Island, lest the affairs of Catholics there suffer even greater harm by a longer absence of the mission head'. Who should it be? Pastre would be a good choice as prefect apostolic, he said, in case de Solages decided to resign from his position in Bourbon. And if he should not want to resign, he ought at least make Pastre vice-prefect, who then could leave at once for Bourbon and take charge of that mission.

Cappellari could simply have appointed Pastre the new prefect apostolic of Bourbon, if he had wanted to. But since the official documents appointing de Solages had been issued only five months earlier, the cardinal felt it was 'not expedient' to change a new decree of the Sacred Congregation. 'I am writing to de Solages and shall invite him to take up this affair with you,' the cardinal told Bertout, 'and I trust that he will show himself docile to your counsels in a matter of such great importance.' And so the cardinal placed the responsibility right back on Bertout's shoulders without answering his question.[6]

On that same day, 25 February 1830, Cappellari also wrote to Coudrin, saying that his two letters on a new south Pacific mission had arrived almost simultaneously. The cardinal very gladly would have supported the Picpus proposal, he said, except for the fact that de Solages by this time had already requested faculties 'to evangelise in all the islands of Southern Oceania from Easter Island to the island of New Zealand inclusive'. And since the faculties had in fact been granted to him, it was not fitting 'to create another prefecture at the present time in the islands designated by you, especially since no one knows in what particular islands he will be able to set foot, and where he will find it easier to establish his mission'.

This did not mean, however, that Coudrin's proposal of immediately sending some Picpus members to Southern Oceania had to be 'discarded altogether'. De Solages had been authorised 'to constitute vice-prefects as occasions demand', the cardinal said, and he had also been authorised 'to transmit to them his faculties'. So all that Coudrin had to do was come to an agreement with de Solages, something that the cardinal believed 'will not be difficult'. Instead of disapproving of any of the decisions reached by the two men on the basis of the powers granted to de Solages, the Sacred Congregation would 'learn with joy' that members of the Picpus community 'had joined forces in such a great mission'.[7]

Cappellari addressed a third letter that same day to de Solages, informing him that after Cappellari had mailed to him the decree establishing the Prefecture Apostolic of the South Sea Islands, letters had arrived from Coudrin requesting jurisdiction over the Marquesas, Society, Bad Sea and Dangerous Islands, but the Sacred Congregation had not acceded to this request, wanting the unity of the mission to be preserved 'at least at present'. The cardinal added, however, that a welcome solution to the problem would be for de Solages to accept for his mission some Picpus Fathers and appoint one of them as vice-prefect over the four archipelagoes in question. The Sacred Congregation would be pleased to see this happen 'in a mission so ample, one which embraces nearly the entire ocean'. The cardinal said that he had instructed Coudrin to approach de Solages. 'I trust that you will show yourself ready to comply with his wishes,' the cardinal said, 'keeping in mind such things especially which better contribute to the greater glory of God and which help propagate the faith more extensively and more easily.'

In the second part of his letter the cardinal brought up Bourbon. 'While you are applying yourself with all zeal to the new mission of Oceania, Your Reverence must also see to it that Catholic affairs do not suffer in the Island of Bourbon, that prefecture which the Sacred Congregation at its good pleasure permitted you to retain.' Cappellari pointed out that Pastre, now restored to

health, could be of great service to the Bourbon mission, and that consequently
he had already written to Pastre about the matter and had asked him to contact
both de Solages and Bertout. 'Indeed, the spiritual needs of that mission would
seem to require that the abovementioned Father Pastre should go there immediately,' the cardinal said, 'either with the faculties of prefect apostolic—if it
should please you to abdicate that prefecture—or at least as vice-prefect.' The
cardinal also urged de Solages, who was a brand new missionary, to seek advice
from Bertout about better methods for governing his several mission areas and
about easier ways of propagating the Catholic faith more extensively.[8]

Cappellari as highest arbiter of mission affairs after the pope could hardly
have been more calm, fair and wise in handling this ticklish problem and trying
to reconcile de Solages, Bertout and Coudrin. But the proposal that he made to
Coudrin was the very same one made earlier by de Solages and turned down by
Coudrin. So now Coudrin neither contacted de Solages nor answered Cappellari's letter, deciding instead 'to wait for other circumstances to provide the
means to enter this new mission'.[9]

And the proposal made by Cappellari that Pastre be sent to Bourbon was the
very same one made earlier by Bertout and rejected by de Solages. And so de
Solages also ignored Cappellari's letter. It only served to make him grow more
furious with Bertout and more resentful toward Coudrin for having appealed
to Rome against him.[10]

De Solages had still a third foe, Captain Mathieu of the *Dordogne*, the
corvette that was to take him and his missionaries to Oceania. All was still well
on 14 December 1829 when the ship was lying at Le Havre, awaiting the
February departure. The French Navy had endorsed the candidate suggested by
de Solages, and de Solages had been asked by the Grand Almonry to suggest
Mathieu, whose brother was a priest. 'I did not know that the brother of this
officer had close contacts with these gentlemen, and particularly with Abbé
Pieau, Secretary General of the Grand Almonry', de Solages later wrote, 'and
that the true motive of the choice proposed to me was not to render service to
the mission, as I was made to believe, but to procure the advancement of
Monsieur Mathieu.'[11]

Perreau informed Pieau and Pieau on 24 December informed de Solages that
Dillon had accepted the office of honorary vice-consul and was coming at once
from London to Paris. Pieau's letter contained this unexpected request: 'I ask
you to remain neutral in the struggle that might arise between him and Captain
Mathieu and let Providence take care of it.' De Solages was told that any active
intervention on his part in favour of Dillon could result in a 'very disagreeable
resignation'. Then Mathieu 'came to visit me,' de Solages said, 'not to thank me
for the steps that I had taken in his behalf, but rather to make me understand
that he wished to have Captain Dillon discharged.' But de Solages would not
hear of Dillon's removal.[12]

De Solages considered Dillon indispensable for the success of his Oceania
venture, and so in late January he had Dillon—now in Paris—draw up a letter
for de Polignac, listing concrete proposals for the voyage. The letter was aimed

at reducing Mathieu's influence to a minimum. It began by stating that Dillon would persuade Oceanians to cede to the French 'a certain number of places from which commerce could spread out to South America, New South Wales, the Philippines, China, Japan, and Kamchatka'.[13]

Dillon then went into detail on the supplies needed, asked for a 400–500 ton ship with a crew of eighty, and said that the missionaries and their party might total sixty to seventy men. It would be better to travel via the Cape of Good Hope than via Cape Horn, he said, since the former route would save eight months' time. And a small schooner ought to be sent along with the expedition, so that after the larger vessel returned to France, the smaller one could be used for visiting the newly established mission posts, conducting further explorations in Fiji, and bringing to France some of the exceptionally talented youths. 'It would be well for the commandant to be guided in his operations by a council composed of himself, the prefect apostolic, and the vice-consul of France,' Dillon said, 'and important questions should be decided by majority vote.' And finally, in order to avoid bloodshed and to prevent misunderstandings between the crew and the islanders, it was desirable 'that the commandant's instructions contain an insertion to the effect that Captain Dillon as vice-consul of the king be made responsible for negotiations with the indigenes in all matters concerning politics and commerce'.

De Solages added a postscript to Dillon's letter, saying that he already had '30 excellent men belonging to the Saint Joseph Association'. These were young men from distinguished families, some of them learned and others doctors of medicine, who had offered to assist the missionaries as catechists. Some of them also had the intention 'of entering the ecclesiastical state'. The heads of various dioceses had offered him priests, he said, and these were 'excellent men who desire to consecrate themselves to the foreign missions for a number of years'. And he told de Polignac 'with all certainty' that he would be able to obtain all necessary personnel without having recourse to Coudrin's group.

As for the plan drawn up by Mathieu, de Solages complained that 'it contradicts ours in all points'. Mathieu wanted Dillon excluded from the expedition and would take him aboard only if forced to do so. And even if Dillon were aboard, Mathieu said that he would not accept any advice or information from him. According to de Solages, Mathieu 'had changed entirely the purpose of the expedition, wanting it to be nothing but a scientific voyage. And thus the unique purpose for which it was ordered becomes simply a secondary matter over which he himself pretends to be the arbiter. He has already declared that he will not visit the places where we intend to found our chief establishments. And he gives as his reason the difficulties which he would have in getting there, for he has no knowledge of them and does not want to utilise in any way the presence of Captain Dillon aboard his ship.' But without Dillon's knowledge, insisted de Solages, 'it is impossible to succeed in this enterprise.'

In the same postscript de Solages then asked de Polignac to have the royal ordinance on the voyage revoked in favour of a new plan of his which would cost the French government only one-third of what the voyage would cost under

Mathieu. 'If the government were to grant the missionaries one of its vessels and a crew of 30–40 men chosen from the merchant marine, together with supplies for two years,' he said, 'then they will take charge of conducting the enterprise, buying territories from the indigenes so that establishments can be founded there later, and forming right from the start small establishments to receive the French ships that come for whaling or any other type of speculation . . . This vessel would not sail at the end of June or July, as Captain Mathieu would have it, but six weeks from now, going first to Bourbon for a sojourn of a month at the most. And from there it would continue on its way . . . As for the scientific research to be done by the present expedition [of Mathieu], this too would be accomplished and all possible things will be brought back for the Museum of Natural History. These tasks would be entrusted to learned men and naturalists chosen from among the most eminent in the field. . . .'

De Solages had decided to found his 'principal establishment' in the Fiji Islands, he said. And since the government vessel would have to return to France, he intended to construct in the South Seas 'right on the spot a small ship destined to transport us from one coast to another as mission opportunities and needs arise'. He asked de Polignac kindly to provide the rigging for this ship, as well as the salaries for a crew of 40 plus officers, and also two years of supplies (or their equivalent) for all 100 persons who would make up the expedition. He had still another request. He would like de Polignac to inform d'Haussez of this proposal, 'but in such a way that his bureaus will not become aware of it until after the affair has been definitively settled . . . , because for me great inconveniences would result if Captain Mathieu and the officers chosen by him were to learn that I am contemplating another plan.'

De Polignac, however, was shrewd, and could easily read between the lines. It was clear from Dillon's part of the letter that he was not content with being merely honorary vice-consul; he and de Solages wanted to overrule and outvote Mathieu on every important issue. And from the de Solages part of the letter it was clear that this priest was naive, proud, a visionary, and unable to work with others. He was also unstable, asking now at the end of January that the ordinance granted at his request at the end of November by King Charles X should be revoked and that a new ordinance should be issued.

As for Dillon being indispensable and Mathieu being helpless, this was hardly true. De Solages himself had said in his postscript that Mathieu had enlisted for the expedition 'certain officers who had been attached to the expedition of Captain d'Urville'. These officers had been aboard the *Astrolabe* in 1826–9 when Dumont d'Urville explored and reconnoitred various parts of Oceania along the route envisioned by de Solages. And so they were truly experienced men. But de Solages found fault with them.

The remarks by de Solages received no official comment. Those of Dillon were examined on 6 February 1830, apparently by de Polignac himself, and various judgments were scrawled in the margin. 'Impossible' was the answer to Dillon's request for a small schooner. 'Refused' was written alongside the proposal that he be mediator in all political and commercial dealings with the indigenes. In another place the scrawl read that Captain Mathieu alone, 'exercising the full plenitude of authority with which he is invested', was to make all decisions regarding supplies, crew, route, and all else concerning the expedition, 'according to what prudence shall dictate to him'. And in order that Mathieu might have 'a positive safeguard' against being overruled by Dillon and de Solages in the proposed council of three, he was 'to preside over the council concerned, he alone being the one who ought to direct the expedition'. Dillon had also suggested that some indigenes be brought to Paris, so that they could see 'the grandeur and the power of the French nation'. On their return to Oceania they could then make known to all 'that France is one of the first nations of Europe'. This was Dillon's only proposal that was considered worthy of examination, perhaps because the British had already brought such indigenes to London.

On that same day, 6 February, de Polignac sent a note to d'Haussez, saying that the President of the Council of Ministers had decided to report to the Ministry of the Navy all the observations of Dillon and de Solages. De Polignac was both Minister of Foreign Affairs and President of the Council of Ministers.

Having received no answer to his above remarks of January, de Solages wrote again to de Polignac on 18 February. 'I shall knock on all other doors, if those of the ministers remain completely closed to me', he said. 'I shall address myself to the royal family and, if necessary, to the king himself.' Seeking an excuse for de Polignac's silence, and unaware of his own guilt, de Solages placed the full blame on Bertout and Coudrin. 'No one is ignorant', he said at the end of his letter, 'of the intrigues that have been used and are still being used by the members of two congregations, the one group trying to oust me from my mission in the Pacific, and the other from that of Bourbon. I hope Your Excellency will give no support to any of their views.'[14]

It may have been this threatening letter that prompted de Polignac the very next day to examine the earlier postscript of de Solages. He answered briefly on 26 February, suggesting that the priest request an audience with d'Haussez, Minister of the Navy. Meanwhile the Director of Ports, Baron Tupinier, had issued orders on 19 February for Mathieu, who was then off the coast of Bayonne, to proceed to Toulon for an expedition to Algiers. The orders read that the *Dordogne* was to return from Algiers to Toulon and then depart from there 'for its trip around the world'.[15] This may have been a reaction to the January postscript of de Solages rejecting Mathieu and asking that the ordinance on the voyage be revoked. But de Solages was quick to attach a sinister significance to it, saying that Mathieu had requested service in Algiers 'in order to disgust Captain Dillon and oblige him to withdraw'.[16]

While negotiating with government officials for a ship, de Solages was also busy recruiting priests, catechists and craftsmen. 'I spent 10,000 francs of my own money during the rigorous winter of 1830,' he later told Cardinal Cappellari, 'most of it being used for recruiting and caring for a large number of priests and catechists destined for Oceania.'[17] Included in this amount was 'the small advance of 6,000 francs' that he had received for Bourbon.[18]

The man most interested in winning financial assistance for de Solages was Goubert, the undersecretary at the Paris Council of the Association for the Propagation of the Faith. He informed the Lyon Council on 20 February 1830 that de Solages would establish in Bourbon 'a kind of seminary' in which he would prepare his priests for missionary work. Besides, Goubert said, the French Minister of Foreign Affairs had authorised him to go as ambassador with presents to the queen of Madagascar. 'On this occasion he will ask the queen for permission to leave two missionaries in the island . . . , and probably they will even succeed in converting her. After that he will send missionaries to the three places in Oceania which he has especially in mind, namely, Tahiti, New Zealand and Pitcairn. These countries are already a bit civilised or tending in that direction. He will also send those islands some lay catechists to teach handicrafts. And later, if he can manage, he will try to go there himself, but first on arrival [in Bourbon] he will go around giving the jubilee blessing to the colony.'

Goubert assured the Lyon Council that Perreau was well pleased with the project. And lest they be mistaken about de Solages, he added that this priest was 'full of wisdom and sober-minded', a very handsome man in the prime of life. 'In him there is a rare union of piety and zeal', he said, and the plans and projects that he has conceived are 'neither those of a mischief-maker nor of an adventurer'. In addition to this he praised de Solages for speaking English 'perfectly, something precious for these countries'. But the Lyon Council seemed not to be impressed.[19]

Two days later, on 22 February, Father Guillaume Joseph Chaminade, founder of the Marianists, wrote to a fellow priest. 'I did not feel that I should take an active part in the vast enterprise of this South Seas mission', he said. But he did encourage the priest to render some services to the project, if he could. However, he advised him not to become completely involved. Chaminade himself had kept an Alsatian volunteer at Bordeaux for de Solages for three months, training him for missionary work in the Pacific.[20]

A gust of correspondence with government officials took place in March 1830. Bertout wrote to d'Haussez on 1 March that de Solages would be ready to sail for Bourbon by Easter (11 April), but that he did not want to leave except in the company of the priests and others whom he had assembled for his mission in the Pacific islands. D'Haussez answered on 5 March that the corvette, *Dordogne*, had been at de Solages's disposal since autumn, but was setting sail at that very moment for Algiers; it would not be available again 'until after the expedition'. De Solages wrote to de Polignac, stating that he wanted to bring twenty-five priests to Bourbon for his future foundation there. 'In this establishment', he said, 'we propose to educate in the knowledge of the arts and languages of Europe the principal islanders of Oceania and of Madagascar. And we have hopes of inculcating in them also the habits of civilised life.'

Earlier d'Haussez had told de Solages that he must choose between Bourbon, where he had a right to a government salary because it was a French colony, and Oceania, where he would get no financial aid from the government. De Solages then asked that he be at least authorised, in the event that he chose Bourbon, to found there or in Madagascar his proposed missionary establishment for propagating the faith in Oceania. D'Haussez answered on 19 March that such authorisation could not be granted. De Solages submitted counter arguments on 21 March and asked that the matter be reconsidered. He also wrote to the Minister of Finance, explaining how funds promised by the government had not been forthcoming; the Finance Minister forwarded this letter on 22 March to d'Haussez. And finally Dillon, by now thoroughly irate, complained vehemently on 31 March to de Polignac, stating that he had come from London to Paris bringing books, baggage and instruments, with the understanding that he would depart aboard the *Dordogne* on 1 February. He threatened to expose the whole matter in the press, if the requirements of justice were not met.[21]

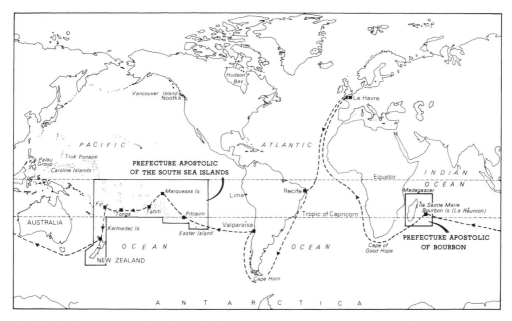

12 The Prefecture Apostolic of the South Sea Islands was founded on 10 January 1830. The plan of Prefect Apostolic de Solages was to leave Le Havre, place his missionaries on certain islands (indicated with a square), and take along from them the most talented young men to be trained by the Jesuits in his other Prefecture Apostolic of Bourbon. From there the ship placed at his service by the French Navy would return to Le Havre. (*Chapters 2, 3*).

D'Haussez waited until 20 April before answering de Solages's letter of 21 March. He could not authorise de Solages to found in Bourbon or Madagascar an establishment for training missionaries and indigenes, he said. 'Nor can I make any change in this regard. Further, your departure for Bourbon must not take place until you have renounced this project . . . I have the honour of requesting that you inform me of your definitive choice . . . I certainly leave you free to dedicate yourself to them,' he added, referring to the islands of Oceania, 'but once again I must declare to you that you shall first have to resign from your office as Prefect Apostolic of Bourbon.'[22]

Perplexed by the Bertout-de Solages-Coudrin feud, and wondering just how much authority had been granted to de Solages, the French government ordered Count Auguste de La Ferronnays, its ambassador in Rome, to request copies of official documents on the matter, which he did during a special audience on 28 April with Cardinal Prefect Cappellari and his secretary, Father Castruccio Castracane. 'In view of the most respectable urgency' manifested by the ambassador, Castracane on the following day sent him 'in duplicate all those things that were decreed by the Sacred Congregation concerning the new mission of the Pacific Islands'. He added that 'these duplicates show all that was done up to January 16 of this year'.[23]

After having asked d'Haussez on 21 March to reconsider the prohibition on founding a seminary, de Solages had written on 30 March to Roothaan, superior general of the Jesuits, making a much more enticing offer this time than in his previous letter of 21 December.[24] 'Let me explain', he said, 'how it would be possible to establish a seminary at Bourbon, if you judge it opportune to choose a certain number of Fathers of your Company and place them in charge of this establishment. All obstacles would be removed by the simple purchase of a piece of property. Then we shall have indigenes come from Madagascar and from Oceania; these you will educate as you see fit. I would also take advantage of every favourable opportunity of having entrusted to you the professorships at the college in such a way that you will also be in charge of the instructions that are given. And you would get not only the colonists from Bourbon [as students], but also those from l'Île de France [now Mauritius] and from other nearby establishments. You could also take charge of a part of the mission of Madagascar ... I would suggest that you begin by taking charge of the Archipelago of the Marquesas along with Easter Island, and that you then spread to the Dangerous Archipelago and the Archipelago of the Bad Sea (also called the Low Islands) ... The populated Navigators Islands [today Samoa] would also later be in need of your concern.'

De Solages here spitefully offered to the Jesuits the very part of Oceania that the Picpus Fathers were eager to get! And yet he was honest enough to admit to Roothaan that 'in the beginning everything seemed to be in my favour, but then everything turned against me'.[25]

Roothaan answered briefly—and coldly—on 22 April, noting that the present state of his order, his lack of personnel, the lack of necessary information on the suggested project, and the speed with which it was necessary to act, all made it impossible for him to collaborate in these 'pious designs'. But he did express his 'very sincere wishes' that the project would turn out happily.[26]

At this point the only ones who still had faith in de Solages were Goubert and Rome. And finally Goubert succeeded in having the Central Council of Lyon reconsider its earlier refusal of funds, since he could now show that the project had been officially sanctioned by Rome. However, the Lyon Central Council judged on 3 May 1830 that 'it would not be possible to fix an allocation at this time, since we do not as yet know precisely how the project will be realised and what needs he will have'. It decided to ask the Superior Council 'to estimate the subsidy to be granted for this purpose'.

The Superior Council discussed the repeated urgent requests from de Solages for funds on 11 May and noted that 'this enterprise has not begun to be carried out; it seems it will not be carried out soon; M. de Solages has given neither precise indications on how it could succeed nor positive information on the time of his departure and on the extent of his real needs; and nonetheless he has received very ample powers and very complimentary approbation after describing his apostolic projects to the Most Holy Father.' Keeping all of this in mind the Superior Council resolved 'to hold some funds in reserve for application to this mission upon the receipt of proof that the mission is carried out and that needs do exist'. This was item number seven in a long list of subsidies signed that day by Perreau.

Item number thirteen in the same list reported that Coudrin's mission in the Sandwich Islands (Hawaii) had not as yet made great progress and so did not need 'considerable funds'. Keeping in mind, nevertheless, 'that this mission has three priests and three Brothers to support', the Superior Council resolved 'to allocate two per cent [of available subsidies] for this project'.[27]

Goubert informed de Solages of the Superior Council's decision on the evening of 16 May 1830. 'Nothing has been allocated for the mission in the Pacific or even for Madagascar', de Solages wrote in anger to Perreau the next day. 'Never did I expect to receive treatment like this after all that I have done in behalf of the mission of Oceania. Please pardon the expression, but this is adding insult to injury.' He then explained how, 'trusting in your promises, I incurred expenses for more than 4,000 francs, and I request above all else that I be reimbursed for this amount. I myself have spent my last penny, since I was counting on the favours of the government and the support of the Grand Almonry.' He had been 'cruelly deceived', he said, and now could only plead 'in all seriousness' for the 4,000 francs. Through this letter he lost any sympathy that Perreau may have had for him or his cause.[28]

Nearly despairing about this time of getting a ship from the French Navy, de Solages made up his mind to go to Oceania by commercial vessel and wrote directly to Cardinal de Croÿ for funds. 'In that case I would take along four or five priests and as many catechists and artisans,' he said, 'and we would establish ourselves at once in the most suitable place.' But Pieau, attached to the office of de Croÿ, quickly informed de Solages of the consequences. He 'made known to me', de Solages later said, 'that if I did not await the return of Captain Mathieu, and if I decided to use any other way to get to my Oceania mission, I would be deprived of the funds promised me by the Association for the Propagation of the Faith.' The purpose of the threat according to de Solages was to keep Mathieu from losing 'this beautiful opportunity for making himself famous'.[29]

The barrage of correspondence by de Solages seemed never to end. He had written to de Polignac on 13 May, just three days before getting the above bad news from Goubert, thinking that once again he was in the good graces of the

Minister of Foreign Affairs. He spelled out the four promises made to him by the government, including the salary of 3,000 francs for Captain Dillon, 'so there will be no mistake on either side'. Apparently cowed into submission by circumstances, he likewise asked for government authorisation to send 'an ecclesiastic to Bourbon after the shortest possible delay, vested with my powers and charged with administration in my name'. He himself would go to Oceania. He also asked that the salary that he would have received in Bourbon as prefect apostolic 'should be counted from that day in the month of October last when I would have departed, if the government had not judged it opportune to keep me here to put into execution the [Oceania] project which I mentioned above. I have all the more reason to make this request', he explained, 'because I have been involved in very considerable expenses for this mission, not counting those which I shall have to incur in the future by taking care of so many persons over whom I shall be in charge.' He asked for a speedy reply so that he would know what steps to take.[30]

De Polignac handed over the letter to d'Haussez who replied on 25 May that the government could not reimburse him for the expenses made in behalf of his Oceania mission, since this was not French territory. And he added that orders had been issued 'this very day' to the commissary general at Bordeaux to take measures for the embarkation of de Solages. But three days later de Solages sent a further appeal for funds. D'Haussez answered categorically on 15 June that no funds would be granted. 'If for some reason you are hindered from departing immediately,' he said, 'I shall be obliged to propose to the king that he provide for your replacement.'[31]

De Solages did find a reason hindering his immediate departure! 'A grave indisposition' had struck him down, confining him to his room for the whole month of June and part of July.[32] It was during June that he sent a lengthy letter to King Charles X, pointing out the advantages for France of his project and asking that the king reconfirm the original plan and allow him to retain both missions. For if the Oceania foundations were to succeed and be of value to France, he said, they would have to be supported and sustained by Bourbon, the only French colony nearby. Otherwise 'the missionaries and their collaborators would be deprived of help from France for many years, would be constrained to get in contact with foreign establishments nearby, and perhaps would even have to ask them for protection'.

But all these inconveniences could be avoided if only 'the spiritual chief of these future colonies would have his residence at Bourbon, where it would be possible and even easy for him to establish a seminary of the Indies destined not only for the education of the principal islanders of Oceania, but also those of Madagascar. For it is by educating them in a French Colony that one can hasten the development of their intelligence and attach them irrevocably to France.' He concluded his lengthy letter with the wish that the king would 'revive an enterprise so honourable for France, so advantageous for commerce, and so useful for religion'.

But the only reaction from the government was still another letter from the

Ministry of the Navy dated 2 July informing de Solages that its previous letter of 15 June remained in force. And by this time Dillon, the man who was 'so essential for the success of this enterprise', had officially been relieved of his office as honorary vice-consul.[33]

At his wits' end de Solages sent a confidential letter to Father Warnet, one of the Holy Ghost Fathers in the house where he was residing in Paris, offering him the Vice-Prefecture of New Zealand, 'with the liberty of choosing' whatever island in Oceania best suited his health. Warnet in four large pages declined the offer, tried to show de Solages how harmful for Bourbon his Oceania project would be, and urged him to leave for Bourbon as soon as possible.[34]

Nuncio Lambruschini of Paris informed Cappellari in Rome on 7 June that he still had in his possession the many letters patent for Oceania which the cardinal had sent. He promised to make use of them, however, each time that a candidate might be presented to him by de Solages. 'But I am beginning to fear that the project will disappear into thin air', he said. Arrangements for the expedition had all been made, he explained, when the rigid position taken by de Solages regarding Dillon caused the French government to lose interest in the project. According to Lambruschini, the government's indisposition 'has been increased perhaps by the intrigues of the gentlemen of the Holy Ghost Seminary who look upon this undertaking with an evil eye'. Although the nuncio himself had taken a stand in favour of the priest, he could not provide the money that was needed for the project. And recently he had heard that the Grand Almonry also was opposed to de Solages. 'I do not know what will come of it all', he said. De Solages was 'a pious and excellent ecclesiastic', according to the nuncio, 'but one without keen intellectual powers'. However, he had not lost courage and was making new efforts to succeed. 'In my opinion,' the nuncio concluded, 'we ought to let him continue, and particularly so because he has found people to support him.' These details, he said, would help Cappellari know what steps to take.[35]

Father Hilarion, secretary general of the Picpus Fathers, did not see the de Solages project in such an optimistic light. In that same month of June he wrote: 'We learned with certitude that the plans of M. de Solages had completely failed and that he had been obliged to discharge the priests who had agreed to join him.'[36]

Cappellari wrote back to Lambruschini on 13 July 1830 that he had learned 'with displeasure that the execution of the projected mission in the South Sea Islands had been retarded and that there is reason to fear that it will come to naught'. He stated that the mission had been established on the basis of very favourable information and he agreed with the nuncio that 'it seems wise . . . to let the Reverend de Solages do what he wants in this matter'.

The cardinal then brought up the 'intrigues' mentioned by the nuncio and explained for him how de Solages, Pastre, Bertout and Coudrin all fitted into the picture chronologically. He also described the instructions that had been sent to each of these priests on 25 February. 'No reply has yet been received to any of these letters', he said. As for the Isle of Bourbon, 'the longer the head of that mission is absent, the worse its condition will become'. The urgency was all the greater, he explained, 'because the jurisdiction of the prefect apostolic of Bourbon temporarily has been extended to include Île Sainte Marie and also provisionally the large and important island of Madagascar.' Île Sainte Marie was adjacent to the east coast of Madagascar and, unlike Madagascar, was politically dependent upon France.

'I therefore have to beg Your Excellency', the cardinal continued, 'to take opportune steps in this matter both with the Reverend Bertout and with the Reverend de Solages, urging them to give a prompt reply to my letters, and to make above all a definite decision on what is immediately to be done for the Isle of Bourbon. If the South Sea Islands mission has become a lost cause, then let de Solages leave at once for Bourbon. Otherwise let him renounce the Prefecture of Bourbon so that the Reverend Pastre can be invested with it anew. Or else let the Reverend de Solages at least see to it that the Reverend Pastre or some other suitable candidate goes there with the title of vice-prefect.' It was the nuncio's responsibility to have these directives carried out, the cardinal said, 'even by letting it be known—if necessary—that you have been given this charge by the Sacred Congregation'.[37]

In Paris on 13 July, the same day that the above letter was written in Rome, J. E. Filleau de Saint-Hilaire, Director of the Colonies (1826–42) at the Ministry of the Navy, informed de Solages that no matter what letters the two of them might exchange, nothing would be able 'to discharge you of the responsibility which weighs on you in case you delay executing the orders given for your departure by the Minister'.[38]

Somehow de Solages had persuaded himself that the Superior Council wanted to give him 4,000 francs for opening a mission in Madagascar, and so he informed Goubert on 10 July that he was on the point of departure. The 4,000 francs should be sent to him 'now or never'. But King Charles X signed his famous ordinances fifteen days later on 25 July, making Paris rise in revolt. When the royal troops were defeated after three days of fighting (27–29 July), the king fled to Rambouillet, where he abdicated. He was succeeded by Louis-Philippe (1773–1850), who accepted the crown on 9 August and called himself king of the French (1830–48). But this revolt in no way was responsible for the failure of de Solages; he had failed long before the revolt took place.[39]

Not yet having obtained the money from Goubert, de Solages wrote on 4 August to Cardinal de Croÿ, the Grand Almoner, asking what steps he should take to get it. He had addressed his query to de Croÿ because Perreau had gone into hiding since the revolution. But as the Lyon Council wrote into its minutes on 6 September, the methods used earlier by de Solages in claiming these funds had made Perreau, secretary of the Superior Council, 'reconsider his too favourable dispositions' and so all help was refused. That same day, 6 September, or the day after, de Solages left Bordeaux for Pauillac at which port he was to board the *Elizabeth*. After waiting three weeks for a favourable wind, and without donations from any of his hoped-for benefactors, he finally set sail for Bourbon on 27 September 1830.[40]

Because Nuncio Lambruschini had failed to answer the July inquiry from Rome, Cappellari on 16 October wrote again and asked what had happened. Lambruschini answered on 1 November that, docile to directives issued by himself, de Solages had in fact left for Bourbon two months earlier. Before the month was over Cappellari wrote back that he was highly pleased with this news.[41]

The voyage from France to Bourbon took four months. There were only two priests and a layman with de Solages. One of the priests had been born in Bourbon and was simply returning home after completing his studies for the priesthood at Saint-Sulpice. The other was Father Jean-Pierre Dalmond from de Solages's home diocese of Albi; he had been to Guadeloupe and now wished to dedicate himself to Madagascar. De Solages was still Prefect Apostolic of the South Sea Islands, but he did not have in his company a single man for Oceania! When he reached Bourbon on 7 January 1831, it was the end of his dream and the beginning of harsh reality.[42]

4

The Vicariate Apostolic of Eastern Oceania

2 JUNE 1833

The 25 February 1830 letter of Cardinal Cappellari, head of the Evangelisation Congregation, had said that no division of de Solages's mission could be made 'at the present time', and so Father Coudrin and his priests were forced to wait before taking any further steps to obtain spiritual jurisdiction over the coveted archipelagoes of Eastern Oceania. But by June of that same year the Picpus community had learned 'with certitude' that the plans of de Solages 'had completely failed and that he had been obliged to discharge the priests who had agreed to join him'. Coudrin then wrote on 14 July to Hilarion, his secretary general in Paris, instructing him 'to keep pressing Rome' for the four archipelagoes.

But the Paris revolt against King Charles X erupted only two weeks later, and on 28 July the revolutionaries broke into the Picpus house and threatened to burn it down. That night they came back with flaming torches, but spared the house. Two days later they were back again. 'In the midst of these troubles it would have been rash to undertake new projects', Hilarion wrote. And so the matter for the time being was dropped.[1]

The aftermath of the July 1830 revolution lasted for many months and was particularly trying for the Church. This made it impossible for the Picpus community to take any new action to obtain jurisdiction over the Marquesas, Society, Bad Sea and Dangerous archipelagoes.[2]

In an earlier effort to win state support for this mission, Father Hilarion Lucas had written to de Polignac, then Minister of Foreign Affairs, arguing that 'a community of priests always provides stronger guarantees for the perpetuity of a mission. If a priest should be lacking, another can take his place. But isolated priests die off, or lose interest, and they do not readily find others to succeed them. It is therefore important for the government to entrust one part of the Southern Oceania missions to a community of priests who can guarantee their continuance.'[3]

His petition to the government was ill timed, as he learned later, because on the following day in Rome, 22 December 1829, the cardinals of the Evangelisation Congregation held the General Meeting at which they decided to entrust the whole of the south Pacific, stretching from Easter Island to New Zealand, to Father de Solages, making him Prefect Apostolic of the South Sea Islands.[4]

As late as February 1831 the Picpus house in Paris was devastated and the majority of priests were dispersed. Hilarion wrote that it was therefore out of the question 'to think any more about the Oceania mission'.[5]

At this time, however, de Solages in Bourbon was thinking very much about the Oceania mission, especially since five of the priests whom he had recruited in France for Oceania had come to join him. He had also received letters via London from Dillon who like himself was still most interested in the Oceania project. This prompted de Solages on 5 May 1831 to address a lengthy report to Cappellari with all this news. He also described in minute detail the numerous 'intrigues' that had been used against him in Paris to block his plans for Oceania.

Before his departure from Paris, he added, Nuncio Lambruschini had given him orders from Cappellari to go to the large island of Madagascar. This he would do, he promised, as soon as he had provided for certain urgent needs in Bourbon. And while in Madagascar he hoped to obtain the queen's permission to establish a number of foundations. He also mentioned how he had learned in Paris from Pastre that the Holy See intended to establish a vicar apostolic in Madagascar with Bourbon being included under the vicar apostolic's jurisdiction. It was precisely Bertout's fear of losing the island of Bourbon through this arrangement, he maintained, that had prompted Bertout and his seminary to oppose the plans of de Solages to establish in Bourbon a centre for preparing and training priests for service in Madagascar.[6]

Unknown to de Solages, Cappellari was now pope! His predecessor, Pius VIII, had died on 30 November 1830 after only twenty months in office, and in the long and difficult conclave which followed Cardinal Pacca once again received many votes. But when the final ballot was counted, thirty-two out of the forty-one votes were for Cardinal Cappellari who had headed the Evangelisation Congregation for four years and four months. Elected pope at the age of sixty-five on 2 February 1831, he took the name Gregory XVI and was to reign for the next fifteen years. On the second day after his election he named Carlo Maria Cardinal Pedicini (1769–1843) to head the Evangelisation Congregation. Pedicini was very well acquainted with the work of this congregation, having served as its substitute secretary and then as its secretary from 1814 to 1823. In 1823 he had become a cardinal and since that year had served as a member of the board of cardinals charged with all business of the Evangelisation Congregation.

Also unknown to de Solages, his Oceania project was being discussed in 1831 in places as far apart as New Zealand and Paris. In October that year Captain Cyrille-Pierre-Théodore Laplace (1793–1875) arrived at the Bay of Islands in New Zealand with his royal corvette, *Favorite*, mounting twenty-four cannon. In a conversation with Mrs Henry Williams at Paihia, where a foundation of the Church Missionary Society was located, he said that the revolution of July 1830 had caused the French government to abandon its plan of sending a Catholic bishop to New Zealand aboard his ship.[7] But the captain surely was mistaken, because no one but de Solages could come into question here. And he was not a bishop, there had never been any talk of making him one, no plans existed for him to sail aboard the *Favorite* which had left Toulon (France) by 13 January

1830, and the Oceania plan of de Solages had been abandoned by the French government long before the July Revolution broke out.[8]

In Paris on 8 November 1831 the Central Council of the Association for the Propagation of the Faith considered a new appeal for funds submitted by de Solages. Its decision was brief: 'Since nothing has been pledged to him, there is nothing to be done at the present time.' In this same year, however, the Paris and Lyon Central Councils gave a total of 5,940 francs to Coudrin's mission in the Sandwich Islands.[9]

The long letter of de Solages addressed to Cappellari was read by Pedicini, the new cardinal prefect of the Evangelisation Congregation. In this letter de Solages told at great length how he had been victimised in Paris by officials of both church and state. Trying to comfort and at the same time encourage the disconsolate priest, Pedicini sent him a carefully phrased reply on 14 February 1832. He wanted to remind the prefect apostolic, he said, 'that in this world nothing happens unless it is willed or permitted by God, and all things are governed by his wisdom. Consequently, whether it was inexperience or the perfidy of men which has been responsible for your not being able to realise the voyage which you had prepared, you nevertheless ought to acquiesce to the will of God. Perhaps he has postponed to a later date the bringing of those island peoples to the light of the gospel . . . There is something, however, which meanwhile can alleviate your great grief and pain. It is the goodness and kindness of God who will know how to keep our wishes and our plans, although as yet unfulfilled, from falling back into nothingness. Nor will God allow them to go unrewarded.'[10]

Before receiving these words of Pedicini along with the special faculties that he had requested for Madagascar, de Solages learned that Cappellari was now pope. Quickly he sent his congratulations from Saint-André in Bourbon on 12 March 1832. He explained to Gregory XVI that while 'waiting for Divine Providence' to help him find the means to realise his projected Oceania mission, he was busy restoring discipline among the priests of Bourbon. He also hoped to bring the faith to Madagascar and to found schools 'in the interior of that country for the instruction of the indigenes'. His numerous struggles with the undisciplined clergy of Bourbon, however, had worn him out so much that he had 'almost made the decision' to designate another priest as vice-prefect over the two islands of Bourbon and Madagascar. 'I myself would go to Oceania,' he said, 'since my wishes carry me there continually.'

In fact, the Oceania project that could not be realised from France might now be realised from Bourbon, he said. Some inhabitants from a district of Bourbon, where morals were very good, had conceived 'the idea of buying and equipping a ship at their own expense to transport themselves and their families to certain islands of Oceania about which they had heard very favourable reports. They also want some priests to accompany them . . . And although their departure date is still indefinite, I propose to go along on the first voyage and shall try to help them with the knowledge that I have of these lands. At the same time I shall at last be able to put my hand to the work that you so kindly entrusted to me.

I do hope that eventually this plan can be realised and shall do everything in my power to remove the obstacles and make it come true.'

He was confident that in Oceania itself he would find the catechists that he needed for launching the various missions to be established there. 'I shall find them in New Holland,' he said, 'where there are so very many Catholics who are Irish by birth or by origin.' (New Holland is today called Australia.) 'As for the Gambier Islands, the indigenes that one finds there can really and truly be called neophytes. The only thing that they lack in order to become excellent catechists is Catholic doctrine, since they already have been halfway trained by Protestant missionaries. As for the small island of Pitcairn, whose inhabitants are so religious, it by itself could furnish the Christian teachers needed for all of these archipelagoes. So you see, I am far from despairing over the fact that I can no longer draw support where I at first expected to find it. Instead I shall always keep pushing forward, trusting more than ever in the inexhaustible resources of Divine Providence.'

He added that he planned to visit Queen Ranavalona of Madagascar 'as soon as the bad season so fatal to foreigners is past'.[11] But was he not aware that a French commissioner had tried to reach this xenophobe queen at Tananarive as late as June 1830 but had not got there, because he was arrested en route? The commissioner's companion had managed to reach Tananarive, but spent fifteen unsuccessful days there trying to negotiate with the queen.[12] Did de Solages have reason to believe that he would be more successful than they?

In that same month, on 30 March, he wrote to King Louis-Philippe, also explaining his plans and requesting financial aid for the Oceania project. But he never received an answer.[13]

His letter addressed to Pope Gregory XVI could not possibly have reached Rome by the time Father Bertout, head of the Holy Ghost Seminary in Paris, on 15 May 1832 wrote to Pedicini and requested the removal of de Solages from Bourbon. Bertout stated frankly that he himself could 'neither approve nor condemn the conduct' of de Solages, not having received from him a single letter on this or any other subject since his departure from France. 'But it is a fact that there is trouble and discord among the clergy in Bourbon', he said. 'And I am certain that, if Your Eminence were to judge it appropriate to advise him to resign—for his position must now be annoying to him and a source of much pain—or even if you were to recall him, the government would look upon this gesture with pleasure.' Bertout also assured the cardinal that he had good reason to believe that Pastre, if asked, would consent to take up once again his former post as prefect apostolic in Bourbon.

Pedicini answered on 9 June with a question: Would it not be possible to remove de Solages from Bourbon by giving him another office elsewhere?

Bertout replied promptly on 24 June that he was practically certain the French government would not agree to send de Solages to any other colony. And since Pastre was now ready and waiting to depart for Bourbon, Bertout suggested that Pedicini at once ask de Solages to resign, or else have him go to Oceania, a place for which he 'always appeared to have a great attraction'.[14]

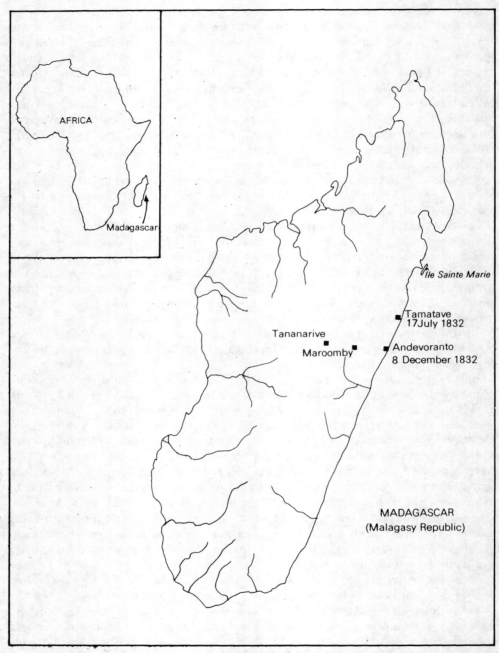

13   Prefect Apostolic de Solages landed at Tamatave, Madagascar, on 17 July 1832, was arrested at
Maroomby when trying to reach Tananarive and died
at Andevoranto on 8 December 1832. *(Chapter 4).*

While the fate of de Solages was being determined in Europe, he was taking it into his own hands in Bourbon. He had Sister Rosalie Javouhey (1790–1868), superior of the Sisters of Saint Joseph of Cluny at Saint-Denis in Bourbon, write a letter to Queen Ranavalona on 9 June, the same day that Pedicini wrote to Bertout. She explained that the Sisters of Saint Joseph conducted schools for 'little girls' and she asked the queen to accept the enclosed 'program of studies', since it listed the subjects that the nuns would be happy to teach in Madagascar. The nuns had also prepared some gifts for the queen, which de Solages was to give her when presenting the letter. These nuns were known for their progressive methods and as early as 1816 had been invited to Bourbon by its governor to open schools.[15]

Father Dalmond, the close and trusted friend who had sailed with de Solages from France to Bourbon, was temporarily placed in charge of the colony and was given the title of vice-prefect. Then on Friday, 13 July 1832, de Solages left Bourbon with two companions and arrived at Tamatave on the east coast of Madagascar on Tuesday morning, 17 July. He had been seasick all the way and had eaten almost nothing during the entire voyage. Tamatave, he had thought, was a large port town, but instead he found only a small village with native huts. By 8 P.M. he managed to find a hut for himself. 'It had no doors, nor was there anything for closing the windows', he said. 'I used a board for my bed and my trunks had to serve as table and chairs.' Casimir, his Negro aide from Bourbon, died from fever two weeks later. And Jean-Baptiste, his white catechist, rushed back to Bourbon when he became seriously ill.[16]

De Solages thought that it would be a simple matter for him to follow the coast southwards from Tamatave to Andevoranto and then go from there inland to the mountain fastness of Tananarive where Queen Ranavalona held her court. But he had failed to reckon with thirty-two-year-old Aristide Coroller, half French and half Madagascan, the ambitious and unscrupulous governor and commandant of Tamatave, an appointee of the queen, whose task it was to serve as buffer between her and arriving foreigners. Coroller informed de Solages that he could not leave for Tananarive until he had received an invitation from the queen. And so on 21 July, just four days after his arrival, he sent her a letter in which he identified himself as 'Count Henri de Solages, Spiritual Prefect of Bourbon and Former Grand Vicar of the Diocese of Pamiers in France'. He explained that he wished to deliver some gifts which he had brought her from Europe, and that he would also like to ask her permission for 'some virtuous persons to teach in your country, as they do in all others, for the benefit of your people'. With his own letter he enclosed that of Sister Rosalie Javouhey. He also explained how he had learned from the commandant of Tamatave that he must first have an invitation. 'I come to do good to your country', he assured her, 'and I am confident . . . that you will allow me to explain my plan and present these gifts . . . I shall wait for your reply.'[17]

A runner could reach Tananarive in four days. It was the fourth day, 25 July, when de Solages wrote to Dalmond that 'the Sisters' proposal is being discussed at this moment'. He was so confident that the queen would want the nuns, that he told Dalmond it was necessary for Sister Rosalie 'to have three of them ready to depart as soon as I have smoothed the path for them'.[18]

But by the end of that month there was still no reply from the queen. He sent her a second letter with the same request, using as an excuse for his apparently impatient action the fact that his health was 'deteriorating more and more'. Later, on 12 August, he admitted to Dalmond, 'Although I have no fever, I do have constant headaches'. One week later he wrote to him again, saying that he was not at all bitter about how slowly things were moving in Madagascar, nor did he look upon his trip to that country as a useless move. 'I feel certain it was the will of Providence for me to make this voyage, although I had little idea then how it would all turn out. I might even say that, since being here, I have tasted more of what it means to be truly content in God, than I did during all the time that I was in Bourbon.'[19]

Meanwhile a chain of events originating in the Sandwich Islands was beginning to involve ever more seriously de Solages and his Prefecture Apostolic of the South Sea Islands. On 12 June 1832, just three days after Sister Rosalie had written her letter to the queen and also three days after Pedicini replied to Bertout on the proposed removal of de Solages from Bourbon, a Picpus missionary from the Sandwich Islands arrived in Paris. He was Brother Leonard Portal and he had been sent by Prefect Apostolic Bachelot as a special messenger to Coudrin. The gist of his message was that at the time of his departure on 15 December 1831 orders had already been issued for the deportation of Alexis Bachelot and Patrice Short to California on the west coast of North America. These two were the only Picpus priests in the Sandwich Islands.[20]

At the time of their arrival in the Sandwich Islands in 1827 the Picpus missionaries were tolerated, but government authorities as early as 6 August 1829 announced that people were forbidden to take part in prayer services conducted by the French missionaries. Then on 2 April 1831, the day after Queen Tamanu promulgated new laws, both Bachelot and Short were told that they would soon be expelled. Although no immediate action was taken, matters continued to worsen until 11 December, when the two priests were ordered to board a brig lying in the harbour. To forestall this action they sent a strong letter of protest to the English consul. Then Brother Leonard on 15 December left for France to report the matter to Coudrin. And finally on Christmas Eve both Bachelot and Short were forced to embark on the *Waverley* and were deported by Captain William Sumner to Alta or Upper California which was then a province of Mexico. They received lodging from the Franciscans at San Gabriel Mission (founded 1771) and on a temporary basis took up priestly work in the area. The Frenchman Bachelot became the first resident pastor of Los Angeles, then a settlement cared for by the San Gabriel Mission, and the Irishman Short founded the first school near Monterey. Because Brother Melchior was not a priest, he managed to remain behind in the Sandwich Islands to protect the school and property of the Picpus missionaries at Oahu.[21]

Father Coudrin was in a predicament. Where could he send these missionaries and also other volunteers as long as the Sandwich Islands were closed to his community? The answer, of course, was simple: Eastern Oceania. And so once again he drew up arguments in favour of his religious community's being entrusted with the eastern half of de Solages's Oceania mission. But before presenting this request to Rome, he decided to wait for an opportune moment.

He did not have to wait long! Father Raphaël Bonamie, prior of the Picpus house in Paris, was named Bishop of Babylon, the Roman Curia's name for Baghdad, Iraq, and on 26 August 1832 was advised by the chargé d'affaires at the nunciature to go to Rome for his episcopal ordination. Bonamie was extremely well qualified to represent and defend Coudrin's position, since he had earlier discussed it with Perreau, with de Solages, and with de Polignac. And as bishop-elect he would have direct access not only to Pedicini, head of the Evangelisation Congregation, but even to Pope Gregory XVI himself. This time Coudrin's petition was bound to meet with success.[22]

Coudrin on 31 August composed separate letters on Oceania for Pope Gregory XVI, for Cardinal Prefect Pedicini, and for Cardinal Pacca. Cardinal-Archbishop de Croÿ of Rouen also obliged by writing under the same date to Pedicini, lending his support to the proposals of Coudrin. Bonamie took along these letters when he left Paris for Rome on 11 September. He visited Pedicini on 15 October, was given lodging in the Evangelisation Congregation's college, had an audience with the cardinal on 3 November and with the pope on 8 November. He was ordained a bishop on 18 November, had Mass at the tomb of Saint Peter the next day, and on 18 December left Rome for France.[23]

By a strange coincidence de Solages was en route from Tamatave to Tananarive at the very same time that Bonamie was en route from Paris to Rome. He had waited in Tamatave two full months for a reply from the queen, but it never came. His suspicions steadily grew that Coroller was keeping his letters from reaching her. And so one day in late September he stealthily left Tamatave, contrary to Coroller's orders, and headed for Tananarive. His plan was to camp a good distance from there, send the queen word of his arrival and of his mission, and then await her invitation. He followed the coastal road south for a hundred kilometres until he came to Andevoranto at the mouth of the Iharoka River. From there he travelled by boat to Maroomby, a village on the Lavenona River. But here he was captured and arrested by the large party of soldiers sent after him by Coroller.

While under arrest in Maroomby he wrote to Queen Ranavalona on 26 September 1832, describing his mission, explaining the reasons for his course of action, and suggesting that she might not have received his letters due to the treachery of Coroller. He called himself an envoy of the most high sovereign of Rome. 'The soldiers wanted to take me back to Tamatave by force,' he said, 'but I absolutely refused to go and said to them: Treat me in this way and you will pay for it by harm coming to your country.' They had deprived him of his servants, kept him under watch day and night, and would let him go nowhere but to Tamatave, 'where I do not want to return as yet ... I have come to negotiate with the queen of the Madagascans and with her government, not with an insignificant commander of some distant outpost.'

He was convinced that the king of France would be angry on learning of the harsh treatment meted out to him by Coroller, especially since 'the French government at present has good relations with your people'. What he desired most of all was for her to have him 'come to Tananarive without delay. There I shall explain my plan to you. I have brought along articles for you from France; part of them I have with me here and the other part is still in Tamatave.' He added that no foreigner in all her land wanted to do it more good than he, 'and there is no one who loves you like I do. . . .'[24]

On 7 October, just eleven days after the above letter of de Solages was written, Bertout in Paris informed the Minister of the Navy that he had petitioned Rome to order de Solages either to resign from Bourbon or to go to Oceania, since his 'zeal for ecclesiastical discipline and for the honour of religion' in Bourbon were 'perhaps not always regulated by prudence'.[25]

That same month of October the Paris Council of the Association for the Propagation of the Faith considered the appeal for funds sent by de Solages to Gregory XVI; Pedicini had sent a copy of it to this fund-raising group in Paris. Its decision can be read in the minutes of 22 October: 'Nothing will be done by the Council regarding this memorandum.' And yet that same year the Paris Council informed Coudrin that his Sandwich Islands Mission had been allotted 8,370 francs, even more than the year before. The council perhaps was unaware that Brother Melchior, a carpenter by trade, was the only Picpus missionary in the islands at the time.[26]

In Madagascar at Tananarive on 25 October three members of the London Missionary Society, which had been in Madagascar since 1818 and in Tananarive since 1820, signed a letter to Queen Ranavalona. They were David Griffiths, David Johns and Joseph John Freeman, and they said that they had heard of a 'white, a Frenchman, being held under arrest by soldiers at Maroomby'. They suggested that he not be allowed to stay there a long time 'for fear that he die of fever'. And they themselves were convinced that 'he does not have the prosperity of your country of Madagascar at heart, nor are his purposes in making the journey very upright'.

The queen answered them on 27 October. 'I have received your letter about the white in Maroomby . . . I agree and approve.' That very same day she wrote to de Solages, telling him that she had received his letter, had understood its contents, and now wanted him to return to Tamatave. 'My representative, the governor, is there. Relate to him the affair that you wish to discuss [with me] and then he can give me a report.' She wrote again two days later: 'If you are truly an envoy of the king of France, then where are your credentials?'

On 27 November she wrote: 'I have had word about you. You have no credentials on your person and you are not an envoy of the king of France. Now take heed and return to Tamatave, for my country is hot and fever abounds. And if you have something to say, then tell it to A. Coroller, or to Rainihova, or to Philibert. They will send your message on to me here; your words will not go astray.' Under the same date she wrote in a similar vein to the three Tamatave officials, and she ordered the chief of Vohiboahazo carefully to transfer the white at Maroomby to Tamatave.

The queen sent de Solages still another letter on 7 December, saying that she was sending him back to Tamatave because he had lied in saying at Tamatave that he was an envoy of the king of France and had credentials, whereas he denied this at Maroomby.[27]

The foes of de Solages seemed only to increase! Would he be able to succeed in spite of them? Would he ever see his Oceania dream come true? And while he was having so much misfortune in Madagascar, was the Picpus community perhaps enjoying better fortune in Rome? What was the reaction there to Coudrin's three letters of 31 August 1832 addressed to Gregory XVI, Pedicini and Pacca, all carried to Rome by Raphaël Bonamie when he went there to be ordained a bishop?

'About three years ago,' Coudrin said in the first letter, 'when Your Holiness was prefect of the Sacred Congregation for the Evangelisation of Nations, I explained that a new harvest could be obtained in the South Seas, especially in four archipelagoes . . . Your Holiness wrote us on 25 February 1830 that the Reverend de Solages had obtained the title of prefect apostolic over all the islands of the South Seas from Easter Island to New Zealand inclusive and from the equator to the tropic of Capricorn, and that consequently the same faculties could not be granted to others "at the present time". We waited until it was clear to us that all plans of the foresaid de Solages had vanished. . . .' It was the arrival of letters from Prefect Apostolic Bachelot announcing the expulsion of missionaries from the Sandwich Islands, he explained, which had prompted his taking up the matter again.

He also admitted that he had sent no new missionaries to the Sandwich Islands since the first group had been sent there six years ago. But now, when he finally did have another group ready to depart, it was impossible to send them because of the difficulties created for his men with the government by 'pseudo-reformers'. But if the pope had no objection, the missionaries who at the moment were hindered from going to the Sandwich Islands could go instead to the four archipelagoes south of the equator. Bachelot could remain in office as prefect apostolic over the Sandwich Islands and Father Chrysostome-Charles-Auguste Liausu could be named prefect apostolic over the four archipelagoes. Coudrin proposed thirty-four-year-old Father Étienne Rouchouze (1798–1843) for the office of bishop and vicar apostolic and asked that both prefects apostolic be placed under the bishop's jurisdiction. A note enclosed from Cardinal de Croÿ supported these three candidates for the offices indicated.[28]

De Croÿ had also sent a letter to Pedicini, explaining that Coudrin was his first vicar general and had been his companion during the 1829 conclave which elected Pius VIII. The French cardinal gave his warm support to Coudrin's proposals and highly praised his zeal and that of his priests.[29]

Pedicini found himself in a real dilemma! On the one hand he did not want to infringe upon the rights in the south Pacific granted to de Solages. And yet on the other hand he did not want to lose this fine opportunity of starting work

14 The Most Reverend Étienne Rouchouze (1798–1843), first Vicar Apostolic of Eastern Oceania. *Source: SSCC. (Chapter 4).*

there at once with the personnel that Coudrin was willing and ready to send. Hoping to resolve this dilemma he placed Coudrin's proposal on the agenda for 7 January 1833, one month from the day on which Queen Ranavalona had accused de Solages of being a liar.

Cardinal Pacca, now seventy-six, was entrusted with drawing up the report for the cardinals who would be attending the meeting. He titled it, 'A New Proposal for a Southern Polynesian Mission'. Coudrin had cultivated Pacca's friendship and had sent him a special letter requesting his support for the proposal. But this cardinal also owed some allegiance to de Solages, since it was Pacca who had pushed so hard to have de Solages named prefect apostolic of the South Sea islands. In fact, it was Pacca who had explained, promoted, and defended that project when it came up for discussion by the cardinals at their general meeting of 22 December 1829.[30]

Pacca's report for the 7 January 1833 meeting explained in detail what had happened to 'the brilliant project' of de Solages. According to Coudrin, Pacca said, there was not the least doubt that de Solages 'had renounced his project two years and five months ago; and now he lacks all the means necessary to carry it out'.

But Coudrin's 'principal reason' for once again requesting the four archipelagoes, Pacca said, was the Methodist persecution which had resulted in the expulsion of the Picpus missionaries from the Sandwich Islands. In fact, Bachelot, the prefect apostolic in charge of those islands, had no idea when he or his missionaries would be able to enter them again. Consequently, when asking Coudrin recently for another priest to be assigned to his mission, he had added the request that all his present and future missionaries be granted more extensive jurisdiction so that they might 'go and preach the gospel in those other islands of the Pacific Ocean, both north and south [of the equator], where no Catholic missionary has yet penetrated'.

Coudrin's letter to the pope had reported that he had five priests who could leave for the South Pacific at a moment's notice, Pacca said. He also had many seminarians taking theology who wanted to dedicate themselves to missionary work immediately after their ordination to the priesthood. In fact, according to Coudrin, it would be possible and on many counts advantageous for these seminarians to leave at once and complete their theological studies in their mission. This would make it possible for them at the same time to learn the local language, teach catechism, and baptise some of the more than ten thousand babies said to die in those islands each year. But from this consideration, the cardinal said, Coudrin 'deduces the need for a bishop who can ordain the seminarians to the priesthood when they finish their studies'.

Pacca also called attention to the warm letter of recommendation for this project addressed to Pedicini by de Croÿ, the Cardinal-Archbishop of Rouen.

Up to this point it appeared that Pacca was supporting only the position of Coudrin, but then he presented counter arguments. 'All of this presupposes that the project of de Solages must be considered a lost cause,' he said, 'or that he in fact has given up the idea and has actually lost every hope of seeing his plan realised.' If that were the case, the Prefecture Apostolic of the South Sea Islands could simply be taken away from him. 'But at this point it will be helpful to know what the Reverend de Solages thinks of this,' the cardinal said, 'or at least to know what he wrote about it to the cardinal prefect in a letter dated 5 May 1831.'

De Solages in this letter announced that five priests recruited earlier in France for Oceania had come to join him. Further, Captain Dillon had sent him a letter from London, saying that he was still very much planning on the expedition, that he would soon be contacting French government officials, and that he was quite optimistic about the outcome. This news had encouraged de Solages to such an extent that he in turn had written to the Minister of the Navy and of the Colonies, to the Minister of Foreign Affairs, and also to many priests in France. If the new French government should decide to support his project, de Solages had said, he would send the priests in France wishing to join him to see the nuncio apostolic in Paris, who then could decide which ones ought to receive letters patent for the South Sea Islands.

A negative factor, however, was that de Solages in his reformation work at Bourbon had been perhaps 'too heated and did not manifest a proper degree of prudence', since he had suspended a pastor, had interdicted a church, and had antagonised other priests and also large numbers of the faithful. Bourbon civil authorities were dissatisfied with his behaviour and reported it to the Minister of the Navy and of the Colonies in Paris. Pacca said that this information had been reported to Rome the previous May by Bertout, superior of the Holy Ghost Seminary.

At the end of his report Cardinal Pacca placed two questions before the cardinals for careful consideration: (1) How valid are the hopes of de Solages for realising his project? (2) In view of these hopes, would it be better to deny or to defer the concession requested by Coudrin?

The cardinals then discussed the pros and cons and decided that de Solages's Prefecture Apostolic of the South Sea Islands ought to be divided and that part of it should be given to Coudrin. But before making this decision they wanted both men to have the opportunity of indicating where the border line should be drawn. And because of previous experience in the difficulties of trying to get Coudrin and de Solages to come together, the cardinals thought it would be wise to ask the chargé d'affaires at the nunciature in Paris to serve as intermediary. As for the contents of the letters to be sent to each of these three men, the following detailed instructions were issued:

1. 'Give thanks and due praise to Father Coudrin for his pious and zealous plans to promote a work so advantageous for the spiritual salvation of so many people still immersed in the darkness of idolatry. Also make known to him the Evangelisation Congregation's desire and hope of quickly being able to put his plan into execution once it has acquired the necessary information.'

2. 'Write likewise to Father de Solages and ask for information on the actual

state of the mission over which he has charge. Inform him also that the Sacred Congregation, considering it extremely difficult and well-nigh impossible for him to extend his jurisdiction over such a vast territory containing countries so very distant from one another, has decided to divide his mission and to assign a portion of it to other worthy priests of his nation, who have offered themselves for this useful and holy enterprise. Forward the letter to him through the chargé d'affaires at the nunciature in Paris.'

3. 'Also make known the mind of the Sacred Congregation to the chargé d'affaires of the nunciature in Paris, enjoining him to confer with the Reverend Father Coudrin, or with a person delegated by him, and with some agent of the Reverend de Solages. After he has informed them of what the Sacred Congregation has decided, they can together draw up a geographical chart on which will be indicated how the proposed division of that immense territory into two different missions could be made. This proposal will then be presented to the Holy Father for his supreme approval.'[31]

Nuncio Lambruschini had lost favour with the new authorities after the fall of King Charles X and so had been recalled by Pope Gregory XVI, who created him a cardinal on 30 September 1831. At the time of Lambruschini's departure from Paris on 6 July that year, Father Antonio Garibaldi became chargé d'affaires at the nunciature and was called monsignor by some and even internuncio.

After Garibaldi received his letter from Pedicini and the one meant for de Solages, he spent several weeks searching in vain for the agent whom the cardinals presumed de Solages had appointed. Since Coudrin was also absent from Paris, Garibaldi finally wrote on 9 March 1833 to Hilarion, the secretary general and plenipotentiary of Coudrin, inviting him to come to the nunciature with proposals for a border line to be used for a new Picpus mission in the South Sea Islands.

Three days later Hilarion arrived at the nunciature with Father Philippe and announced that 'it would seem most easy to us' to designate the border line with the help of a map. He suggested that the Picpus community should receive all islands in the Pacific Ocean north and south of the equator from the Sandwich Islands to the tropic of Capricorn, and from Easter Island on the east to the Roggewein Archipelago inclusive on the west. As for de Solages and his priests, they would retain jurisdiction in the south Pacific Ocean from the equator to the tropic of Capricorn and from the Mangaia Archipelago on the east to New Zealand inclusive on the west.

The division appeared satisfactory to Garibaldi and so on the following day, 13 March, Hilarion wrote up in Latin a memorandum on his proposals for forwarding to Rome. On presenting this to Garibaldi on 14 March, he assured the chargé d'affaires that implicitly it had the full approval of Coudrin. Then Coudrin arrived in Paris and on 16 March also visited Garibaldi to give his explicit approval to Hilarion's proposals. Finally Garibaldi on 18 March sent Pedicini a detailed report on all that had happened and enclosed the memorandum prepared by Hilarion.

He added his own judgment on the matter. 'The project of the Reverend Hilarion seems very reasonable to me', he said, because 'it still leaves very vast regions to the Reverend de Solages and precisely those which are closer to his present residence'. And it also designates for the Picpus Fathers those islands which have contacts with the Sandwich Islands, 'where they already are'.

As for writing to de Solages, he said it would take almost a year to get a reply, and then the reply might necessitate still another letter before a decision could be reached. 'Further, there seems to be no doubt that it would be extremely difficult or even impossible for the Reverend de Solages to go to Oceania and successfully establish a mission there, especially in view of the circumstances in which he now finds himself and after all his previous plans have failed. Nor do I know if he really has the qualities so necessary to succeed in such an enterprise. At least he would seem not to have given any proof of this from the time of his arrival in Bourbon.' Garibaldi nevertheless said that he would keep the letter meant for de Solages, in the event that Pedicini might not find the Picpus proposal acceptable.[32]

Pedicini quickly placed the Hilarion-Garibaldi proposal on the agenda for 20 May 1833. The cardinals at the meeting were told that the map requested from Coudrin had arrived and that Hilarion had used the 159th meridian west of Paris as the dividing line, because it ran through the Sandwich Islands.[33] And although the viewpoint of de Solages was not known, the matter was nonetheless to be decided at this time, since writing to de Solages would take a year or more, and since, 'there is recent news that the Reverend de Solages has suffered a terrible sickness in Madagascar and has returned from there to Bourbon in a state of health to make one despair of his life'. After all, the Picpus proposal was a 'distinguished and reasonable' one and had been placed on the agenda 'so as not to cause greater delay in executing a plan so advantageous for the spiritual salvation of so many peoples still immersed in the darkness of idolatry'. But of course, the relator said, the decision rests 'with you cardinals'.

It was also pointed out that if the cardinals should decide in favour of the division, they would also have to indicate whether the southern archipelagoes were to receive a prefect apostolic of their own, whether a bishop was to be placed over the two prefects apostolic north and south of the equator, and whether the one to be named bishop should be Father Rouchouze.

The unidentified relator then reminded the cardinals that during their meeting of 7 January that year they had already heard (1) how highly Cardinal de Croÿ recommended the entire proposal, (2) how advantageous it would be to have a bishop in such a remote and vast area, (3) how this would make it possible for theologians to go there and learn the local language, catechise and baptise, while completing their studies, (4) how they would have a bishop to ordain them, and (5) how both prefectures north and south of the equator would constitute only one mission if a bishop were placed over them.

The cardinals gave their full approval to the entire proposal.

The secretary at the meeting was Father Angelo Mai, successor to Castracane, who five weeks earlier had been made a cardinal. Mai, who may have been the relator at the meeting, reported the substance of it to Pope Gregory XVI on Sunday, 2 June 1833. 'It was resolved to beg Your Holiness to sanction the division', he said. 'And because of the many advantages that can result from establishing in those places a vicar apostolic with episcopal character', the cardinals also request that you make Rouchouze a bishop with authority over the two prefects apostolic.

To all of this Gregory XVI agreed, thus formally (1) extending the jurisdiction of the Prefecture Apostolic of the Sandwich Islands to the equator, (2) creating the new Prefecture Apostolic of Southern Oceania and reducing the size of de Solages's mission, (3) creating the new Vicariate Apostolic of Eastern Oceania, (4) naming Rouchouze a bishop and placing him in charge of the vicariate apostolic, and (5) stating that the two prefectures apostolic were distinct from one another but integral parts of the new vicariate apostolic and subject to it.[34]

The public document containing these papal decisions, dated 8 June 1833, was drawn up by the Evangelisation Congregation and stated that the two prefects apostolic had been made dependent upon the episcopal vicar apostolic 'in order to ensure unity in the said mission'. Neither this document, however, nor others related to it, listed the border line as 159° west of Paris. Instead it specified the extent of the new mission geographically, precisely as it had been spelled out in Hilarion's proposal of 13 March. The mission was not entrusted to an individual, as in the case of de Solages, but to Coudrin's religious community known as the Congregation of the Sacred Hearts of Jesus and Mary.[35]

Two documents dated 12 and 14 June were addressed by Pope Gregory XVI to Bishop-Elect Rouchouze, informing him of his appointment as bishop and vicar apostolic, of his episcopal title 'Nilopolis' (today called a titular see), and of the limits of his vicariate apostolic. In the second document the pope urged the new bishop to teach by deeds as well as by words. He likewise stated that it was his pastoral concern and vigilance which now prompted him to send Rouchouze 'to regions which are very remote from this Apostolic See, so that the Christian religion and the Catholic faith may spread more and more as time goes on'.[36]

Although naming a bishop was the pope's prerogative, it was within the competency of the cardinal prefect of the Evangelisation Congregation to name prefects apostolic. And so Pedicini, following Coudrin's suggestion, reappointed Father Alexis Bachelot as prefect apostolic north of the equator, and chose Father Chrysostome Liausu as the new prefect apostolic south of the equator.[37]

These decisions meant that every single request made by Coudrin in his original petition of 6 December 1829 to Gregory XVI, who then was cardinal prefect of the Evangelisation Congregation, had been granted. In fact, Coudrin now received even more than he had requested at that time, because then he had

15   The original decree issued by the Evangelisation Congregation on 8 June 1833, signed by Cardinal Prefect Pedicini and Secretary Mai, announcing the foundation of the Vicariate Apostolic of Eastern Oceania by Pope Gregory XVI on 2 June 1833. *Source: SSCC: 1–1–4H1. (Chapter 4).*

asked only for the Line Islands north of the equator and for the Marquesas Islands, Society Islands (or Tahiti Archipelago), Bad Sea Islands and Dangerous Islands (two groups in the Tuamotu Archipelago), south of the equator. But now in addition to these he received the Gambier Islands, Tubuai (or Austral) Islands, the entire Tuamotu Archipelago, Easter Island, Pitcairn Island and the Roggewein Archipelago, as well as other scattered islands within the area.

The Evangelisation Congregation's document dated 8 June 1833, mentioned above, spoke first of the South Sea Islands mission of de Solages and stated that he had not yet been able to go there 'because of vicissitudes of the times'. And to all appearances—the document continued—it would be 'very difficult' for him, 'in view of the circumstances in which he now finds himself', to extend his jurisdiction 'to such vast regions so widely separated from one another'.[38] These words were surely meant to soften the blow for the fiery priest and to assist him in accepting Rome's unilateral decision which deprived him of a good portion of his Oceania mission. But such concern on the part of officials was unnecessary, because unknown to them de Solages had died from fever and starvation in solitary confinement in Madagascar on 8 December 1832, exactly six months to the day before these words were written!

Eleven days before the death of de Solages the chief of Vohiboahazo had been ordered by Queen Ranavalona to transfer him from Maroomby to Tamatave. But because of weakness, or intransigence, or a combination of these, de Solages never got farther than Andevoranto. Here he was placed in solitary confinement by order of Coroller, and Madagascans were forbidden to give him food or help under penalty of death. Mr Hély, a young European living nearby, paid a visit to the sick priest. De Solages begged him for some soup, which he could not eat after it was prepared. On the next day, 8 December, he died at 5 P.M. at the age of forty-six. A businessman from Tamatave happened to be in Andevoranto at the time and after seeing the corpse testified in writing to the place, day and hour of de Solages's death, saying that he had died 'after a week of fever'. Having no casket Hély and a friend buried the body deep in the sand between two sleeping mats. They marked the grave with a fence and a wooden cross.

Slightly more than twenty-four hours later, on the night of 9 December, Father Bertout, the superior general of the Holy Ghost Fathers, died in Paris at the age of seventy-nine. Was it a mere coincidence that he and de Solages, two missionaries who had manifested such little understanding for one another in life, should be called to render accounts to their Maker almost simultaneously in death?

Admiral Cuvillier, governor of Bourbon, informed Vice-Prefect Dalmond on the last day of February 1833 that word had just arrived from Coroller announcing the death of de Solages at Andevoranto on 8 December. Dalmond sent the news to Gregory XVI on 3 March, stating that 'the zeal, the devotion, and the resignation which he manifested make me consider his death to be that of a true martyr'. And in a letter to the Evangelisation Congregation dated 14 July, Dalmond said that 'the patience in adversities and the zeal for souls that

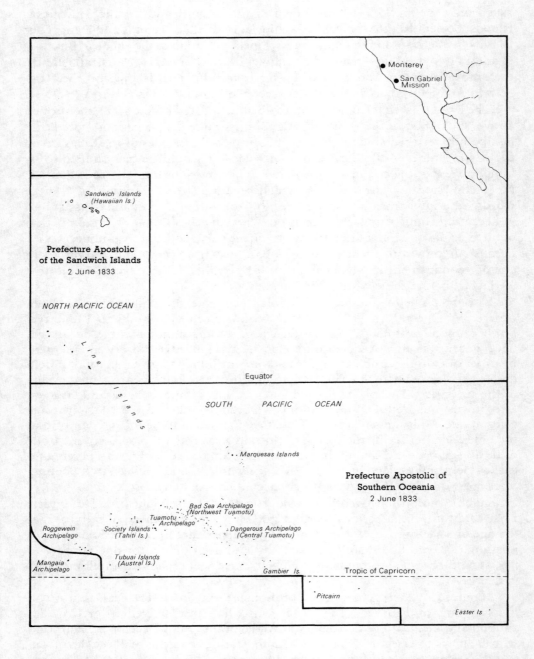

16 The Vicariate Apostolic of Eastern Oceania, founded on 2 June 1833, was composed of the Prefecture Apostolic of the Sandwich Islands and the Prefecture Apostolic of Southern Oceania, both of which were also founded on 2 June 1833. *(Chapter 4).*

he constantly manifested convince me that his death was a martyrdom of charity if not of religion'.[39]

L'ami de la religion, an ecclesiastical, political and literary journal, published the news that de Solages had died in Madagascar. Undoubtedly it was this notice that prompted Coudrin, then in Rouen, to write on 6 June 1833 to Father Hilarion Lucas in Paris, urging him 'to go and visit the internuncio. Offer him the homage of my respect and press him to tell you what he thinks, especially now after the death of M. de Solages. . . .'

The letter reached Hilarion the next day, 7 June, a Friday, and he visited Internuncio Garibaldi immediately. He presented him with a memorandum in which he said that the Picpus community had received no reply to its earlier memorandum which had requested a new mission in Oceania and which Garibaldi had forwarded to Rome in March. 'I presume the matter has been delayed', Hilarion said, 'because of the difficulty in reconciling the powers requested by us with those already granted to the Reverend de Solages. But this difficulty no longer exists, since the death of de Solages in the island of Madagascar removes all obstacles.' He asked Garibaldi to forward this news to Pedicini and also urged him to recommend once again for the cardinal's consideration the Picpus request.

Garibaldi that same day, 7 June, wrote to Pedicini, enclosing the original draft of Hilarion's memorandum and suggesting that meanwhile the cardinal must also have seen the notice in *L'ami de la religion*. He was able to confirm this news, he said, because the Reverend Amable Fourdinier (1788–1845), successor to the lately deceased Bertout at the Holy Ghost Seminary, had recently received word from Bourbon that de Solages had died.[40]

Pedicini had Garibaldi's letter within two weeks and he answered it in haste on 22 June. Even before your letter arrived, he said, 'everything regarding the Oceania mission had already been settled in accordance with the wishes expressed by the Reverend Coudrin'. Rouchouze had been chosen bishop and vicar apostolic, he announced, and all the official papers would be sent 'without delay'. On receiving this letter the chargé d'affaires informed Hilarion on 4 July that Rome had granted every Picpus request. Then Pedicini on 27 July sent three separate letters to Garibaldi, to de Croÿ, and to Coudrin, explaining the action taken by the Evangelisation Congregation. 'I am happy to notify you', he said in the letter addressed to the indomitable Coudrin, 'that we have conformed our decisions to the ideas and wishes of Your Reverence. . . .'[41]

De Solages was dead, but not his dream. Others would make it come true: the Picpus Fathers in Eastern Oceania, the Marists in Western Oceania and the Jesuits in Madagascar. On 23 December 1840, just eight years after the death of de Solages, Father Roothaan, the superior general of the Jesuits, assigned three of his priests to take up work in Madagascar. And the Sisters of Saint Joseph of Cluny, the congregation to which Sister Rosalie belonged, were sent there in 1844. When the country became a vicariate apostolic in 1848, it was entrusted to the Jesuits who have worked there ever since, early establishing the kind of seminary envisioned by de Solages.[42]

As so often happens in life, a man's dreams are realised by those who come after him. This was the case with Father Henri de Solages and Captain Peter Dillon. They were the dreamers! They did not establish the Catholic Church in the South Sea Islands or in Madagascar; some might even say they made no contribution. But really they did, because it was the plan of these two men, so colossal in conception, which fired the interest of the Evangelisation Congregation in this part of the world, and made Coudrin feel that his Sandwich Islands mission was much too small. For these reasons, and particularly because Dillon and de Solages helped unleash the immense spiritual force of the Picpus Congregation in the south Pacific, no church history on this part of the world dare pass over them in silence.

Dillon's work, however, was not yet done. For many a year he would still concern himself with Catholic missionaries in Oceania, especially the Marists, performing for them numerous and valuable services in view of his experience and his contacts. As for de Solages, abandoned in life but never completely forgotten in death, his mortal remains lay buried for ninety-nine years in the sands at Andevoranto. Then on 4 January 1932 they were solemnly exhumed and transferred to Saint Joseph's Cathedral in Tamatave where they have been venerated ever since.[43]

5

The Picpus missionaries reach the Gambier Islands

7 AUGUST 1834

Father Hilarion Lucas, secretary general of Father Coudrin, who was superior general of the Picpus Fathers, received the official papers concerning the Vicariate Apostolic of Eastern Oceania on 21 September 1833 from Monsignor Garibaldi, the chargé d'affaires at the nunciature in Paris. Bishop-Elect Rouchouze, the vicar apostolic, then went with Coudrin to visit the Archbishop of Paris and Garibaldi on 8 October. One week later the Paris Council of the Association for the Propagation of the Faith set aside 5,000 francs for the new mission. Since it had been suggested that Rouchouze receive his episcopal ordination in Rome, Coudrin on 24 October wrote letters for Rouchouze to take along to Cardinal Prefect Pedicini, head of the Evangelisation Congregation, to Cardinal Pacca, Coudrin's 'protector' in Rome, and to Cardinal Lambruschini, the former nuncio in Paris who had been called to Rome in July 1831 and was made a cardinal two months later by Pope Gregory XVI.

Coudrin in these letters told the cardinals that it would be more advantageous for him to send his missionaries to Eastern Oceania in two groups, so as 'to draw less attention from the enemies of the faith'. *L'ami de la religion* had unfortunately publicised the new mission on 19 October 1833, as had other newspapers. This caused 'as much affliction as surprise for us', Coudrin wrote, since he now feared that Protestants would be aware of what was happening and would 'create obstacles' to keep his missionaries from entering the islands of Oceania. But 'we are not too disturbed', he assured the cardinals, 'since we feel that the Lord himself will deign to guide the missionaries and open the way for them to propagate the Gospel'.[1]

Rouchouze left Paris for Rome on 28 October with Father Hilarion and with Father Frédéric Pagès, one of the missionaries assigned to Eastern Oceania. They made some stops en route and reached Rome on 19 November. It was Hilarion's third trip to Rome and his task was to gather all possible information on the new mission.

Once in Rome the bishop-elect lost no time in making contacts. During his first two days he saw Pedicini, and Father Angelo Mai, who had become secretary of the Evangelisation Congregation on 15 April, and Castracane, who had been secretary until 15 April, the day on which he was made a cardinal. By the end of November he had also visited Cardinals Lambruschini, de Gregorio, Fesch, Zurla, Macchi, Weld, Rivarola and Fransoni. And on 28 November, at the insistence of Pedicini, he saw the ambassador of France, M. de Latour

Marbourg. Rouchouze visited six more cardinals by 28 December: Gernetti, Pacca, Sala, Caprano (who had been secretary of the Evangelisation Congregation from 1823 to 1828), Justiniani and Barberini. This meant that he had visited sixteen cardinals in forty days.[2]

Cardinal Prefect Pedicini himself ordained Rouchouze a bishop on 22 December 1833 in the church built by the French at the top of the Spanish Steps called 'Trinity on the Mountain'. That date—it was the fourth Sunday of Advent—marked exactly four years since the Evangelisation Congregation's meeting at which it was decided to found the Prefecture Apostolic of the South Sea Islands. Rouchouze had Mass on the tomb of Saint Peter on 23 December and on Christmas Day assisted Pope Gregory XVI during his Solemn Mass in Saint Peter's Basilica. Then on the missionary feast of Epiphany, 6 January 1834, the pope—who himself had earlier been the cardinal prefect of the Evangelisation Congregation—received in audience Bishop Rouchouze and Fathers Hilarion and Frédéric. He granted them a second audience on 21 January, the day before their return to Paris. While in Rome, Rouchouze and his two companions had been lodged at the expense of the Evangelisation Congregation.[3]

Meanwhile the first group of missionaries had been trying to leave France for Eastern Oceania. The group was composed of Prefect Apostolic Chrysostome Liausu (who also was delegated as religious superior by Coudrin), Fathers François-d'Assise Caret and Honoré Laval, and Brother-Catechist Colomban Murphy. (Because of their religious educational mission Brothers were called 'catechists'.) They had gathered at the seminary in Bordeaux and their sailing vessel, *Sylphide*, engaged to bring them to Valparaíso for 1,300 francs each, was anchored at Pauillac in the Gironde. The missionaries were not there when a favourable wind blew one day in December pushing 130 other fast sailing vessels out to sea. A storm arose, however, and 6 of these vessels were lost.

On the day after Christmas the missionaries transferred to Pauillac and took rooms near the place where the *Sylphide* was anchored. On 6 January 1834 their ship fired a cannon to announce imminent departure and the missionaries went aboard. It was the same day on which Rouchouze, their bishop, was having his audience with Pope Gregory XVI in Rome. But the wind changed and kept them from leaving. They went ashore again and embarked a second time on 22 January, the very day that their bishop left Rome. Finally on 1 February 1834, after they had waited for two months, a favourable wind pushed the *Sylphide* out to sea. When they arrived at the port of Valparaíso, it was 13 May 1834; their voyage had lasted three and a half months.[4]

When the missionaries went ashore the next day, they met an elderly Franciscan priest who received them with the greatest cordiality and invited them to lodge in his nearby retreat house. The man in question was sixty-five-year-old Fray Andrés Caro (1769–1844), and Liausu later told Coudrin that 'everyone in town considers him a saint'. He had been born in Granada, Spain, and as a twenty-six-year-old priest arrived in 1795 in Upper Peru (now Bolivia), where he taught and did other missionary work for thirty-three years. Then in

1828 because of age and political developments he went to Valparaíso, intending to return to Spain and retire. He took passage aboard the *Comète*, the same ship which had taken Prefect Apostolic Bachelot to the Sandwich Islands in 1827. But the ship began to leak so badly at Cape Horn that the captain was barely able to make it back to Valparaíso. Fray Andrés then began building a retreat house and when the *Comète* was dismantled, he used parts of it for constructing his buildings. He had some thirty small rooms available for those wishing to make retreats and he himself conducted them every month. In spite of being very infirm, due to his rugged missionary life, he retired each night at ten and got up at three.[5]

Liausu wrote at length to Coudrin on 19 July, telling him that for two months they had searched in vain to find an inexpensive way of getting to Eastern Oceania. They had also made many a novena imploring God's assistance and had contacted all sorts of people, in particular the captains of ships plying those waters. 'All of them tell us that we shall not find a ship willing to transport us as far as Tahiti for less than 200 piastres or 1,000 francs per person', he explained. 'They say that there we would find ships headed for the other archipelagoes, that all of the archipelagoes are under the influence of the Protestants who certainly would not permit us to disembark, and that in the small number of islands where there are no Protestants the inhabitants are cannibals.' This information was reliable, he argued, because it was the same as that received from a Spanish sea captain, a good Christian, and from the Dutch consul, Juan Francisco Doursther, a Catholic. The consul had said that 'he was on the point of being devoured by the natives of Marquesas Islands, who had already eaten two of his party, when he had the good fortune to escape'.

Captain Arnaud Mauruc, a Frenchman, had told Liausu that the Marquesas Islands were ruled by American Protestant ministers and that with his own ship he had brought Protestant missionaries there. 'Some of these [ministers] had formerly been on the Sandwich Islands,' Liausu told Coudrin, 'and had collaborated in sending away our Fathers.'

In one of their talks Captain Mauruc had called to Liausu's attention the Gambier Islands, said to be five in number, with Mangareva as their capital. The population was estimated at eight hundred to a thousand. 'The inhabitants, though cannibals and idolaters, are quite friendly', Liausu told Coudrin. 'They steal to excess and you have to let yourself be robbed by them. You even have to laugh it off, or else you will become victimised by their capriciousness. Now these are the islands to which Captain Mauruc advises us to go.'

The captain had also spoken to them about Rapa or Opara Island, where he had gone fishing for fine pearls. 'But the population there is no larger than three or four hundred souls.' As for Easter Island, with which he was also acquainted, 'the inhabitants are very great thieves'. And besides, since this island has nothing of commercial value, 'there would be no vessels going there'.

These considerations made Liausu choose the Gambier Islands as the first Picpus mission field in Eastern Oceania. 'But the difficulty was to find a vessel to take us there', he said. 'Only every five or seven years do ships go there for pearl fishing, since no other object of commerce is to be found there, and even this does not always cover the costs involved. Captain Mauruc told me that he did not believe anyone would bring us there for less than 100 piastres or 500 francs per person, supposing of course that we would be using a vessel which normally takes this route.'

On 9 July, the feast of Our Lady of Peace to whom the Picpus Fathers have a very great devotion, Liausu sang a Solemn Mass. That same day he paid Captain Mauruc another visit, going aboard his ship with Brother Colomban Murphy. 'He showed me a map of Oceania that he himself had made,' Liausu wrote, 'and on it he had indicated an infinite number of islands which I did not know.'

Liausu and Colomban left Captain Mauruc and went to visit Captain Sweetland from Boston whose ship, the *Peruvian*, was to sail for Tahiti. This captain by way of concession had offered to bring the missionaries there for 150 piastres (750 francs) per person. 'But we feared this island,' Liausu said, 'since according to the law of the land we could not disembark there without paying 30 piastres (150 francs) per person. So we did not accept the offer.'

Sweetland many years earlier had been baptised in Boston by Father Jean-Louis Lefebvre de Cheverus (1768–1836), a French missionary who reached Boston in 1796, served as its first bishop from 1810 to 1823, and since 1826 had been the Archbishop of Bordeaux in France. On learning this Liausu spoke to Sweetland about the archbishop, 'and of the great goodness that he had manifested towards us'. The captain said he was most eager to see the archbishop again and wished that he might be able to perform some service for him. Finding the captain in such a generous mood Liausu replied, 'I should very much like to have you take us aboard. But we cannot possibly give you the price you quoted.' The captain then asked what the missionaries would be able to pay. Brother Colomban spoke up and said 460 francs, but the captain immediately replied that this was not enough. Liausu persisted, however, and finally the captain agreed to Colomban's price. 'After all, you seem to be good fellows', he said. Sweetland was 'to bring us to the Gambier Islands and put two of us ashore there, or even all four of us, if we so wished'.

The other missionaries, on learning of the arrangements made by Liausu and Colomban, said that it was Our Lady of Peace who had taken care of everything. That same day they decided that Fathers Caret and Laval should take up work on the Gambier Islands and that Colomban and Liausu should go to Tahiti. It was 9 July 1834.

Fray Andrés, in whose retreat house they were lodged, quickly learned of their plans. On the following day he approached Liausu and said that he did not consider it at all prudent for the entire group to depart. He suggested that Caret be left behind in Valparaíso. 'I do believe that God has prepared a haven here for you and that he inspired me to take you in. You know what they are telling you about your islands . . . You will not be able to gain entrance to them unless you give presents.' This would prove a serious drain on the limited resources of the missionaries. 'What would happen to you, if you should find yourselves obliged to rent one or two rooms here and should have to pay for your meals? Six piastres a day would not be enough! And to this you would have to add your other living expenses and laundering costs as well. What will you do if all four of you go to these islands and are not able to get in? . . . And what will Bishop Rouchouze do on his arrival? Where will he go to join you? What information will he get? Would it not be better to endanger only a part rather than the whole group?'

Fray Andrés then suggested that after Rouchouze's arrival Liausu could decide together with him and with Bachelot (who was still prefect apostolic north of the equator even though he was now aiding the Franciscans in California) what ought to be done about Valparaíso. They really ought to take over his retreat house for the good of their mission, Fray Andrés said. 'It would serve as a land base for future personnel arriving from Europe, who otherwise would be in danger of spending here the little money that they have for continuing their journey. Take care not to go against the will of your superior, who would act differently than you think, if he were to know the difficulties in which you find yourselves.'

These remarks so impressed Liausu and his companions that they agreed one of them ought to stay behind in Valparaíso. Liausu, like Fray Andrés, wanted Caret to stay behind, but the rest in the group thought that it should be Liausu. 'I was not able to share their views,' he told Coudrin, 'because it seemed to me that I ought to be the first to make the assault.' Caret agreed to stay behind, if necessary, but said that he would not be happy to do so.

Fray Andrés then asked if he could speak with Caret privately. 'I do not know what they discussed', Liausu told Coudrin. 'But after their meeting Fray Andrés called for me. With tears in his eyes he embraced me and said, "Let Father François-d'Assise [Caret] go and you stay here. I believe that you will not be able to prevent his departure, nor should you, because it is the will of God." And so I stayed.'

Liausu said that the good of the mission 'seemed to require this'. And he was convinced that his companions were going where obedience wanted them to be. 'But for me, what account must I render to God, if my conduct does not please him?' He confided in Coudrin and wondered whether 'in this circumstance I have acted in conformity with your will? And if I have not, then I have failed in my duty! . . . If only I could have consulted you! My good Father, do not forget in your prayers him who by his conduct has possibly proven unworthy to be your son.'

On the eve of their departure from Valparaíso the missionaries renewed their religious vows. 'They told me that they intended to dedicate their first church to Our Lady of Peace', Liausu said. 'This gave me all the more pleasure, because I had made this resolution myself in Paris at Our Lady's feet.'

On 16 July 1834, feast of Our Lady of Mount Carmel, the missionaries went aboard the *Peruvian*. They took along enough grain and other food supplies to last nine or ten months. Various sea captains had said that the islanders, fearing mistreatment, would 'hide in the earth all their food, and for this reason it would be well to bring along provisions for themselves and for attracting the people'.

'We accompanied them to the ship,' Liausu wrote, 'and Fray Andrés in spite of his age wanted to go aboard to make sure that everything was in order. Again and again he asked the captain to look after them. The spectacle tore my heart to shreds, seeing them continue their journey while I myself remained in Valparaíso.' Many leading people from the town accompanied the missionaries as well and that evening Fray Andrés said special prayers with his congregation for them.

But the ship was not able to leave port until the following day. 'I climbed a hill from which I was able to see it', Liausu said, and his missionaries on seeing him 'waved their handkerchiefs'. As soon as Fray Andrés saw the ship leave, he had the church bells rung at his monastery and at other monasteries in order to recommend the missionaries once again to the prayers of the faithful.[6] People began referring to these missionaries as 'los Padres Francéses', that is, 'the French Fathers', a name that is still used for the Picpus Fathers in Chile today.

On 15 July, the day before the three Picpus missionaries boarded their ship, Fray Andrés wrote to Father Coudrin: 'I do not know how your sons came to my house. Surely, it was Divine Providence that brought them here, so I could take care of them. These services I performed because of their kindness, their humility and their other virtues which I noticed when we met the first time. It makes me happy to provide them with lodging. And I am doing my best to give them as much help as religious poverty allows, since I do not want them to have to spend a single cent . . . They have won the hearts of all by their piety. And they are models for everyone, but especially for me and for all the religious and secular priests of this town. I feel that I must tell you, my Reverend Father, that I pray to God continually, asking him to send to the people of Chile priests who are zealous for the glory of God, the salvation of souls, and piety. We need such priests in this port of Valparaíso where the people are inclined to be good, but where they are so abandoned. May God hear my prayers! And may I one day see some of your zealous priests consecrate themselves to these souls. I could then die in peace.'

Fray Andrés said that he would always be happy to see other Picpus missionaries pass through Valparaíso and promised to be as good to them as he had been to this first group. 'I am attached to missionaries, I love them with all my heart, and I shall do all in my power to help them. In return I ask only one thing, a remembrance in your Masses that I may die in the kiss of peace and in the heart of Our Lord Jesus Christ.'[7]

Meanwhile Bishop Rouchouze one month earlier on 17 June had left Paris for London to be co-consecrator of Australia's first bishop, the English Benedictine, Bishop-Elect John Bede Polding (1794–1877), and at the same time to obtain more precise information on Oceania.[8] As early as 3 July 1832 the cardinals of the Evangelisation Congregation had chosen Polding of Downside Monastery to be bishop and head of the Vicariate Apostolic of Madras in India.

But he had refused this office, the cardinals were told, 'wanting rather to go as a simple missionary to New Holland' (now Australia).

At the Evangelisation Congregation's meeting of 12 May 1834 his name came up again. The cardinals said that experience had proved that communication between New Holland and the island of Mauritius was unsatisfactory. Consequently the bishop located on Mauritius, who up until this time had been entrusted with the spiritual care of New Holland, found that he could not properly fulfil his task. (Mauritius in the Indian Ocean was some 11,100 kilometres from modern Sydney, where most of New Holland's Catholics were to be found.) The cardinals at this meeting therefore decided to create a new vicar apostolic with the rank of bishop and place him in charge of 'the affairs of Catholics dwelling in great numbers in the foresaid region of New Holland and in nearby Diemen Island' (now Tasmania).[9] They agreed to ask Pope Gregory XVI 'graciously to name as vicar apostolic of the foresaid New Holland and adjacent Diemen Island, the Very Reverend John Polding, monk of the Benedictine family in England, who had already been chosen for the office of bishop. . . .' On that same day Father Mai, secretary of the Evangelisation Congregation, presented the nomination to Pope Gregory XVI who gave his approval and ordered apostolic letters to that effect to be issued.[10] By this act the pope established the Vicariate Apostolic of New Holland and Van Diemen's Land and gave Australia its first bishop who would take up residence in modern Sydney.

The episcopal ordination of thirty-nine-year-old Polding was set for 29 June 1834, the feast of Saints Peter and Paul. Bishop James Bramston, Vicar Apostolic of London District, performed the episcopal ordination which took place in his own private chapel in London.[11] Three weeks after the ceremony Rouchouze wrote: 'I had the consolation of being assistant bishop for the consecration of Msgr. Polding, [Titular] Bishop of Hierocaesarea and Vicar Apostolic of New Holland. Both of us are destined to evangelise Oceania and so necessarily we shall be in close contact with one another.'[12]

Rouchouze was back in Paris on 9 July and on 20 July he wrote three important letters to Secretary Mai, Prefect Pedicini and Pope Gregory XVI. The first two letters apologised for his letter to the pope. In them he explained that the chargé d'affaires in Paris had strongly advised him 'to solicit from the Holy Father an extension of powers' in view of the important observations that had been made to him 'at both Paris and London on the present state of religion in the islands of Oceania'.

His letter to the pope said that in Paris and again in London he had contacted many seamen who in the past few years had visited the islands now entrusted to his spiritual care. They had been 'unanimous in maintaining that very many of those islands, and in particular the Society Islands, are completely dependent upon and dominated by the ministers of the pseudo-reformers. . . .' Hence there was serious reason to doubt 'whether it will be at all possible to gain admission to the islands mentioned'.

But these same seamen had told him that 'the pseudo-reformers have not yet invaded the islands of New Zealand, of Friends, called also Tonga, and other islands nearby'. For this reason 'both the Vicar Apostolic of London and the Vicar Apostolic of New Holland', as well as many other individuals, had urged him to have recourse to the pope 'in order to obtain more extensive jurisdiction, namely, over New Zealand, the islands called Chatham, the islands called Kermadec, the Islands of Friends or Tonga, the Islands of Navigators known also as Samoa, and the islands of the Mangaia Archipelago also called Cook's'. All of these islands, he said, would fall within the territory of the Prefect Apostolic of Southern Oceania and make his jurisdiction extend 'from Easter Island to New Zealand inclusive, whereas the jurisdiction of the Prefect Apostolic of Northern Oceania would remain within the limits already assigned to him'.

Others had given Rouchouze additional reasons for approaching the pope 'to obtain this new concession'. First of all, communication would be greatly facilitated 'because of the very frequent contacts between Europe and New Holland', and New Zealand was not far from New Holland. Secondly, modern geographers of both France and England now included 'under Eastern Oceania all the above-mentioned islands, because their inhabitants all use practically the same languages'.

Rouchouze admitted of great hesitation in approaching the pope on this matter, however, since he feared that such extensive jurisdiction would prove too heavy a burden. But when explaining the entire matter to 'the Most Excellent [Antonio] Garibaldi, chargé d'affaires of the Holy Apostolic See in France', he had been strongly urged to submit the entire matter to the pope's judgment. What 'especially motivated' Garibaldi in suggesting this procedure, he explained, was the fact that this added territory would guarantee for Rouchouze and his missionaries 'at least a sure way of gaining access to the missions'.

After presenting all these reasons the bishop made his 'most humble request' that the pope should enlarge the mission of the Picpus Fathers in such a way that it might contain all the islands mentioned. And in conclusion he referred to 'the various apostolic decrees of 8 June 1833, 14 June 1833, 6 July 1833, 21 July 1833, 10 January 1834 and 16 June 1834', and asked that the faculties and privileges which they contained for him, his missionaries, their neophytes and other members of the faithful in Eastern Oceania should be extended as well to those living and working in the islands to the west.

Rouchouze, however, already had jurisdiction over half the Pacific Ocean. He now wanted jurisdiction over three-fourths. But this letter meant for the pope apparently never got beyond Pedicini's desk, because the cardinal quickly wrote back on 9 August. 'The domain of the Vicar Apostolic of Eastern Oceania is extensive enough and there is no need for any addition', he said. 'We therefore advise Your Grace to abide by the boundaries as already indicated, especially since a clause appended thereto allows you to exercise your apostolic ministry provisorily even in islands located outside your domain, in the event that you or your priests should arrive there, and provided also that these islands are under no one's jurisdiction and are in need of Catholic priests.'

This blunt and businesslike reply from Pedicini put an end to Rouchouze's aspirations and on 28 October 1834 with six fellow missionaries he sailed from Le Havre aboard the *Delphine* for Valparaíso.[13]

Meanwhile both Caret (who had been named vice-prefect by Liausu) and Laval had arrived in Eastern Oceania. They passed the San Felix Islands on 21 July and at about 10.30 A.M. on 7 August 1834 they saw the Gambier Islands in the distance. 'We at once recited the Salve Regina', Caret wrote Coudrin on the following day, 'placing these poor people under the protection of Our Lady of Peace to whom we have dedicated this mission. We also invoked the three Archangels, Saints Michael, Gabriel and Raphael, whom we have chosen as our protectors.' They dropped anchor near the islands at about 7 P.M. that evening and the next day Caret wrote that, when setting foot on land at Akamaru Island, their first words were, 'Peace to this island and to all who dwell on it'. With them were two natives, he added, 'one from New Holland and the other from the Society Islands, who will be very helpful to us, I hope'. A Frenchman named Chédin fishing in the islands for mother-of-pearl gave them their first shelter. And on 15 August, Feast of the Assumption of the Blessed Virgin Mary, the two priests celebrated their first Masses on land at Aukéna Island.[14]

On 14 October 1834, two weeks before Rouchouze set sail from Le Havre, the Reverend David Darling (1790–1867) of the London Missionary Society (L.M.S.) addressed a letter 'To the two French missionaries who are in the Gambier Islands'. He wrote the letter from Vaitahu on Tahuata Island in the Marquesas Islands, where he had arrived on 6 October. His letter read: 'My dear Gentlemen: The missionaries of Tahiti having learned that you have disembarked at the Gambier Islands, have judged it apropos to charge me to address you with these few lines. We would like you to withdraw to some other group of islands, since we have taken possession of the Gambier Islands before you, and since we have stationed schoolmasters in some of the islands. There are enough other archipelagoes in this vast sea which have not yet been visited and which are open to you. In virtue of our previous possession it would seem to us that we ought to occupy the Gambier Islands, and that it should be up to you to leave them and go to some other islands. In the name of the missionaries of Tahiti, I am your very affectionate, D. Darling.'

The London Missionary Society had its headquarters in Tahiti. In spite of the contents of the above letter the Tahiti missionaries closed their schools in the Gambier Islands and left in February 1835, the very month that Rouchouze and his companions reached Valparaíso.[15] Were they rearranging their forces in accord with new strategy?

Fray Andrés on 23 February wrote to the Bishop of Santiago that the Vicar Apostolic of Eastern Oceania had arrived and had won his heart. 'He has informed me that the superior general of his order told him to accede to my requests in behalf of my retreat house.' Consequently Fray Andrés had asked for still another priest and also a lay Brother, both of whom he received from Rouchouze 'in view of the recommendation from his general'.[16] The priest assigned to him was Father Frédéric Pagès. Giving his reasons for this action to Coudrin on 2 April 1835, Rouchouze said, 'Their staying in Valparaíso is

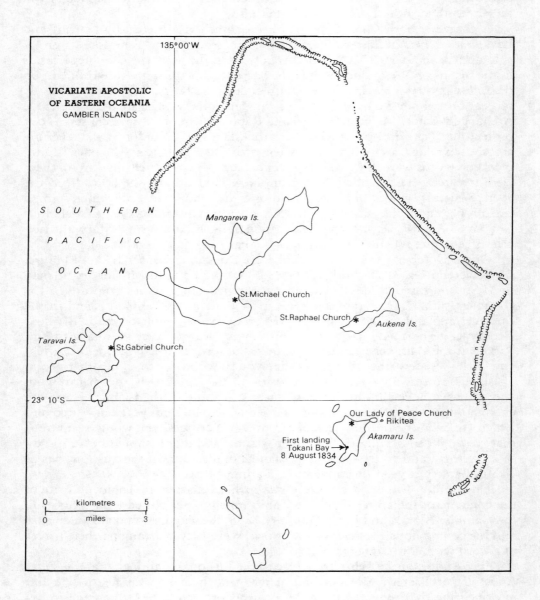

**VICARIATE APOSTOLIC
OF EASTERN OCEANIA**
GAMBIER ISLANDS

135°00'W

S O U T H E R N

P A C I F I C

O C E A N

Mangareva Is.

✳ St.Michael Church

St.Raphael Church ✳   *Aukena Is.*

Taravai Is.   ✳ St.Gabriel Church

23° 10'S

Our Lady of Peace Church
✳   ○ Rikitea
Akamaru Is.

First landing
Tokani Bay →
8 August 1834

0 _____ kilometres _____ 5
0 _____ miles _____ 3

17   The Picpus Fathers landed on Akamaru Island
in the Gambier Islands, their first mission in the south
Pacific, on 8 August 1834. *Source: Honoré Laval,*
Mémoires pour servir à l'histoire de Mangareva,
p. 673 and map 2. (Chapter 5).

18 Giacomo Filippo Cardinal Fransoni (1775–   Evangelisation of Nations from 1834 to 1856.
1856), prefect of the Sacred Congregation for the   *Source: OM vol. 1, opp. p. 913. (Chapter 5).*

essential for the welfare of the mission . . . It certainly will be necessary for us to see that we get established in this town . . . If we had not met Father Andrés Caro, the lack of supplies would have made it impossible for our missions to succeed. It was necessary not so long ago to ship supplies to our friends in the Gambier Islands, items most necessary for them to keep alive.'[17]

Bishop Rouchouze finally arrived in the Gambier Islands on 9 May 1835 with two priests, who were also doctors of medicine, two lay Brothers, and a layman who had resigned as director of the University School of Mende in order to dedicate himself to educating the people of Oceania. He was the first Catholic lay missionary to come to Oceania and his name was Viscount Urbain de Florit de La Tour de Clamouze. Before the month was over, Rouchouze wrote to Coudrin that Caret and Laval had accomplished wonders. 'These people, whom the sailors called so ferocious, so inhospitable, so untractable, have become friendly and humane at the voice of our missionaries.'[18]

The Gambier Islands had an area of about thirty-one square kilometres and Mangareva, the largest of them, was only about nine kilometres long. Only four of the islands were inhabited and these were grouped in a semicircle, none being more than about five kilometres away from its neighbour. Rouchouze divided his personnel among three of them: Mangareva, Akamaru and Taravai. In this way his men had mission fields of their own and still were close enough to help and encourage one another. Although the area was very confined, it was an excellent training ground for inexperienced missionaries. And that is what Rouchouze had.[19]

In the next month in Rome on 20 June 1835 the cardinal prefect of the Evangelisation Congregation wrote to Coudrin. Pedicini no longer held this office, but had been replaced by Giacomo Filippo Cardinal Fransoni (1775–1856), who told Coudrin that it would be most expedient for him to found as soon as possible an establishment of his own in Valparaíso. This was to be a mainland base for the island missions.[20]

In saying this Fransoni was merely supporting what Caret had written to Coudrin on 8 August 1834, the day after he and Laval had reached the Gambier Islands. 'From Valparaíso it will be extremely easy to provide for the needs of all the missions of Oceania as well as for those of Chile.' A foundation in Valparaíso, he had said, could serve 'as a communications centre with France and will prove just as useful for us as the Goa foundation was for the Jesuits and for their missions in India and Japan at the time of Saint Francis Xavier'.[21]

A start had been made in the Vicariate Apostolic of Eastern Oceania and the next step was for the mission to take roots and grow.

6

The Vicariate Apostolic of Western Oceania

10 JANUARY 1836

The premature death of Father Henri de Solages in Madagascar on 8 December 1832 left vacant the two offices of Prefect Apostolic of Bourbon and Prefect Apostolic of the South Sea Islands. Without losing any time Cardinal Prefect Pedicini of the Evangelisation Congregation on 27 July 1833 wrote to Father Fourdinier, successor of Bertout as superior general of the Holy Ghost Fathers in Paris, saying that 'the Reverend Pastre can now go as soon as possible to the Island of Bourbon to take up once again his office as Prefect Apostolic, since there is no more doubt regarding the death of de Solages . . .And because you said that he would go the more gladly if the Reverend Minot were to accompany him as collaborator, we are writing to Minot and asking him to comply with the wishes of Pastre. . . .'

Rome had great confidence in Father Jean-Louis Pastre of Lyon, whom Bertout as early as 15 January 1823 had described for Pro-Prefect Consalvi of the Evangelisation Congregation as a priest in Bourbon 'who is truly an apostolic man and has worked wonders in that colony'. Pastre had arrived there on 18 May 1817, became curé of Saint-Paul, and was named prefect apostolic in 1821. But ill health had forced him to resign in 1829 while he was in France collecting funds and seeking personnel for his mission. It was then that de Solages had been named his successor. Pastre's health, however, had long since been restored. Minot, a priest from Nantes in France, had served with Pastre in Bourbon from 1822 to 1826 and currently was serving as chaplain for the Visitation nuns at Nantes. On 20 July, a full week before writing to Fourdinier, Pedicini had already written to Minot, saying that 'action must be taken for electing a new prefect' for the colony of Bourbon since de Solages had died in Madagascar. And because Pastre had indicated that he would not object to taking up office again 'if he could have you as his companion on the journey and as his helper in his apostolic labours . . . , I therefore ask that you show yourself docile to the wishes of the Reverend Pastre. . . .' Minot had been his close associate in Bourbon earlier and Pedicini asked Minot to contact Fourdinier who was responsible for missionary personnel in the colony.[1]

On the day that Pedicini wrote to Fourdinier about Minot, he sent all of the papers and documents regarding the newly created Vicariate Apostolic of Eastern Oceania to Antonio Garibaldi at the nunciature in Paris, stating that in the enclosed decree on the new vicariate apostolic, 'the Reverend de Solages is mentioned as still among the living, since only afterwards did news arrive of his death'. As for the remaining western half of his prefecture apostolic, Pedicini said, 'we shall provide for that part in due time. . . .'[2] He wanted to wait and see what would happen to the Picpus Fathers after their arrival in Eastern Oceania and what success they would have.[3]

One year later, on 20 July 1834, Bishop Rouchouze wrote from Paris requesting that the remaining western half of de Solages's prefecture apostolic be added to his own Vicariate Apostolic of Eastern Oceania.[4] But Pedicini on 9 August answered that the bishop's 'domain' was 'extensive enough, and there is no need for any addition'.[5]

Fransoni succeeded Pedicini as cardinal prefect of the Evangelisation Congregation on 21 November 1834. In the months that followed, news began to reach him that the Picpus Fathers in spite of difficulties and in spite of their fears had succeeded in establishing themselves within the limits of their own territory in Eastern Oceania. He therefore began looking for someone else to take over responsibility for the western half of the Prefecture Apostolic of the South Sea Islands. Fransoni knew this prefecture apostolic very well, having been present at the meeting of 22 December 1829 when it was thoroughly discussed and the resolution was taken to have it established.

Minot had not been able to free himself from his responsibilities and consequently neither he nor Pastre had gone to Bourbon. Pastre, an experienced missionary, was known in Rome as 'a hard worker' and was highly esteemed. Believing that he was still interested in devoting himself to missionary work, Fransoni wrote to him on 4 July 1835, asking if he would like to become head of the mission of Western Oceania left vacant by the death of de Solages.

The cardinal prefect explained that two years earlier the Picpus Fathers had been entrusted with a vicariate apostolic 'in that part of Oceania which includes all the islands of the Pacific Ocean, both north and south, from Easter Island to the islands of the archipelago called Roggewein inclusive, and from the Sandwich Islands to the Tropic of Capricorn'. The Sacred Congregation was now thinking of constituting 'another mission in the remaining part of Southern Oceania which stretches from the above-mentioned Roggewein Archipelago exclusive, to the island of New Zealand in the west, and from the equator to the Tropic of Capricorn in the south, including especially the archipelagoes called Navigators, Friends and Fiji, and in addition to these also the Kermadec Islands and the above-mentioned New Zealand. We shall soon be taking up the business of choosing a head for this mission', Fransoni said. 'In fact, we have actually been thinking of Your Reverence, since I know that you have not yet given up the idea of devoting yourself to missionary work among the heathen.' But before making a decision in 'this very grave matter', Fransoni wished to be informed by Pastre whether or not he would accept the office if it were offered to him.

In 1829 when Pastre was making his plans for returning to Bourbon, he had written to the Evangelisation Congregation that he could easily obtain excellent priests, especially from his own Archdiocese of Lyon, for taking up work on the nearby island of Madagascar. 'Can we reasonably hope that the same will now be true for this mission [of Western Oceania]?' Fransoni asked. He assured

Pastre that the Sacred Congregation itself would provide part of the funds required, but at the same time he inquired whether Pastre knew of some other way 'of paying for the expenses of this mission, which will be considerable'.[6]

Pastre thanked Fransoni by return mail on 17 July for 'the great honour of offering me this mission'. The fact that he was Honorary Canon of the Lyon Archdiocese was no obstacle at all to his 'affronting the perils of navigation involved', nor did he fear possibly becoming stranded on some South Sea island and getting lost among its people. But of what use would a priest like himself be, he asked, deprived of the knowledge and qualities so necessary and so befitting for a vicar apostolic? 'And especially how can I at the age of *fifty-five* learn new languages, circumnavigate Cape Horn and Tierra del Fuego, or resolve to cross overland through the immense forests of South America? . . .Such a vast mission as this would require no one less than another Saint Francis Xavier . . . I regret that I am not able with good sense, and without temerity, to subscribe to the honourable proposal of Your Eminence and to dedicate the rest of my days to such a beautiful task as this.'

He asserted that, if he had been able to accept the mission, he would have managed to obtain passage to the Cape of Good Hope and from there even to New Holland (now Australia) 'at the expense of the French government'. And as for priests, he would have obtained them from bishops who were heads of dioceses, especially from the Archbishop of Lyon, by simply stirring up in the bishops interest in Western Oceania. 'But at my age. . . .'[7]

Pastre showed Fransoni's letter and his reply to it to Archbishop Jean-Paul-Gaston de Pins (1766–1850), the apostolic administrator of the Lyon Archdiocese. The archbishop in a letter of the same date as Pastre's explained to Fransoni that he had been asked to forward the reply to Rome with some remarks of his own. 'I gladly would have done all in my power to assist the apostolate of Father Pastre', de Pins wrote, 'if he had been able to accept the mission of Oceania. But unfortunately his very feeble health, his present age, and his ever increasing infirmities, which prevent him from applying himself to a given task for more than half an hour at a stretch—not to mention the languages that he would have to study and the voyage that he would have to under-take—are some of the obstacles that he cannot overcome. All of this afflicts his zealous spirit, and I hasten to vouch to Your Eminence for all of the above. . . .'[8]

Was Pastre bluffing when he said that he would have been able to get personnel and funds, if he could have accepted the mission? Cardinal Fransoni decided to find out. He wrote right back on 15 August, stating that although he 'vehemently desired' to have Pastre head the mission, he could well appreciate his reasons for turning it down. But since Pastre could not go personally to the assistance of the peoples of Oceania, Fransoni suggested that he 'at least indicate for the Sacred Congregation' what it must do in order to acquire for this mission the personnel, financial aid and transportation which he had mentioned in his letter. 'Explain this whole matter to me more clearly', the cardinal said.[9]

Pastre was no bluff. In fact, as if by intuition he had anticipated Fransoni's question of 15 August regarding personnel and had posted a letter to him dated 7 August with the answer. His letter and the cardinal's crossed in the mail.

Pastre's letter said that on the very day on which he had written his first letter to the cardinal, he had spoken briefly and confidentially 'with a priest of the society called Marists'. He explained that this society so far had been approved only by the bishops of Lyon and Belley, but was to receive papal approbation very soon. The priest with whom he had spoken—Pastre did not mention the name—was 'esteemed by the clergy of Lyon', and the two of them had discussed 'the Vicariate Apostolic of the Friendly Islands, Fiji Islands, etc., etc., and also New Zealand', which the Sacred Congregation was planning to found in Western Oceania.[10] This priest then consulted with his companions for very many days, Pastre added, 'and has finally received a letter on this subject written by his superior. He showed me the letter and I considered it opportune to forward it to Your Eminence. I should be very happy indeed if this proves to be of some use to the Sacred Congregation, since I do not want to manifest less concern over the success of this mission than is proper.'[11]

What had happened was this. Pastre had approached Father Jean Cholleton (1788–1852), a vicar general of Archbishop de Pins, and told him how vexed he was at not being able to accept the invitation from Rome to head a new mission planned for Western Oceania. 'I would at least like to have someone whom I could present to His Eminence', he said, and he asked Cholleton whether he knew a priest 'who would satisfy the cardinal's wishes'. 'I do know a zealous priest who wants to dedicate himself to the missions,' Cholleton replied, 'and I believe that he would suit you well. His name is Father Pompallier and he is chaplain of La Favorite [a boarding school in Lyon], which belongs to a young society.'[12] The 'young society' was the society of Marists. Cholleton had been a seminary professor teaching moral theology in 1816 when the Marists were being founded and had offered his room as their first meeting place. From that time on he kept abreast of Marist affairs and eventually joined the Marists himself in 1840.

The priest mentioned by Cholleton was thirty-three-year-old Father Jean-Baptiste-François Pompallier (1801–71), one of the approximately twenty Marist priests residing either in the Diocese of Belley or the neighbouring Archdiocese of Lyon. Pastre interviewed him without delay.[13]

The 'superior' who had written the letter to Pompallier, which Pastre in turn forwarded to Rome, was forty-five-year-old Father Jean-Claude Colin (1790–1875), founder of the society of Marists, or Society of Mary as the group of priests came to be called. The members in 1830 had elected him as their provisional central superior. His own residence in the town of Belley served as headquarters for the loosely knit society. And it was from here that Colin had written on 3 August 1835 to Pompallier.

'It would give me great pleasure to see you set out for this foreign mission', Colin said. 'Nor would I refuse to accept what the Lord himself is offering us. That same Providence will also find companions for you, so be filled with courage. By devoting yourself to the salvation of those poor heathen you would

19 The Very Reverend Jean-Claude Colin (1790–1875), founder of the Society of Mary, better known as the Marists. *Source: OM vol. 3, p. 393. (Chapters 6, 15).*

be serving the Society of Mary usefully. Apparently God is asking this development of our society, since our agent in Rome recently requested some personnel from me for the foreign missions.'

Colin went on to explain how he had reacted to Rome's earlier request for missionaries. He had sent word back to Father Paul Trinchant, who was handling their affairs in Rome, explaining that he and his priests were 'still entirely under the hand' of their respective bishops. 'Considering the position in which we find ourselves,' he had said, 'we think it would be prudent not to rush headlong into any affair connected with these foreign missions. It would be best for us first to become an organised group, and therefore we shall await the Brief which we requested at the Roman Curia.'

Colin here was referring to the formal request that he had made for papal approbation for his society. One result of such approbation would be greater autonomy. Bishop Alexandre-Raymond Devie, sixty-eight-year-old head of the Belley Diocese in which Colin lived, was insisting for example that members of the Society of Mary who came from his diocese should also make his diocese their lifelong field of labour.

Being shrewd and seeing in Pastre's proposal a further motive for Rome to grant the desired papal approbation, Colin told Pompallier that he ought to show himself interested and ought to accept the role being offered him, because otherwise 'we would be hurting ourselves at the Roman Curia'. If Pastre were to tell the cardinal prefect of the Evangelisation Congregation that members of the Society of Mary were available for Western Oceania, Colin reasoned, 'this offer of ourselves could not but be well received, and it would also prove of advantage to our society'.

Colin's strategy was simple. If Fransoni had the well-founded hope of getting Marist priests for Western Oceania and if he saw that Colin was holding out for papal approbation of his society prior to assigning priests to that mission, the cardinal most likely would use his influence with other cardinals of the Roman Curia and even with the pope himself to obtain for the Society of Mary the desired papal approval.

Colin even asked Pompallier to tell Pastre what he ought to say in his reply to Fransoni. There ought to be mention of the two branches of the society, both priests and Brothers, since 'both could devote themselves to this mission'. And in case Pastre actually were to write to the cardinal in this vein, and were to suggest the availability of the Marists for staffing the mission, 'and if he offers you as a member of the society to be sent there', Colin added, 'I would ask you to write me at once. I myself would then write to our agent in Rome to have him treat of this whole matter with the Prefect of the Evangelisation Congregation and with the other cardinals who are informed of our affairs.'

Colin heaped praise on Pompallier's head. 'I hope that the good God will indeed strengthen you in this vocation,' he said, 'because at the present moment I can think of no one else but you who can fill the position that is offered to you. And so do not neglect this matter, but be full of courage and full of confidence in God.' The letter was signed: 'Your very humble servant, Colin.'[14]

Pastre's letter with Colin's letter enclosed was mailed from Lyon on 7 August and must have reached Rome about 21 August. But for some unexplainable reason Fransoni did not reply. Was he put on his guard by Colin's letter—never meant for Rome—which so frankly spelled out Marist strategy for dealing with the Roman Curia? It seems so, because he quickly looked elsewhere for personnel.

He wrote on 12 September 1835 to Father Marin Ducrey, founder and superior of a college at old Mélan near Taninges in Savoy, a duchy of the kingdom of Sardinia. Ducrey had opened the college in an old Carthusian abbey which he had bought in 1804. Although the college was not specifically for training missionaries, it fostered missionary vocations and those students who became priests and went to the foreign missions were reimbursed by Ducrey in full for the board and tuition that they had paid him. In fact, Ducrey in 1832 had taken official steps to convert his college into a missionary seminary for the whole world, offering it to the Evangelisation Congregation. That year Father Castracane, secretary of this same congregation since 1828, visited Mélan to inspect the buildings.

Back in Rome he reported on the project favourably to the cardinals and began making arrangements to send Italian members of a religious order there to staff the seminary. Since Castracane was well acquainted with the delicate Marist negotiations, and also a member of the Evangelisation Congregation, he may have suggested to Fransoni that he offer the mission to Ducrey.

'Since I am now thinking of founding another very interesting mission in Southern Oceania,' Fransoni told Ducrey, 'I wish to inform you about it. If you should have some suitable and zealous priests to propose for it from among those educated for the missions in your seminary, kindly send me the pertinent information.'[15]

But Fransoni's invitation fell on deaf ears. He no doubt was unaware that the Mélan seminary had been handed over by Ducrey to the Jesuits two years earlier on 24 August 1833. Castracane also pointed out later that the king of Sardinia had blocked the project of the seminary's being taken over by the Evangelisation Congregation by saying no to the Italian religious order personnel being sent there as faculty members. The king wanted no foreigners in his kingdom.[16]

Shortly after writing to Ducrey, Fransoni received a third letter from Pastre, this one written on 2 September 1835. It was a reply to Fransoni's of 15 August. Five missionaries would suffice for the first group, Pastre said, because 'in the beginning there will be very serious difficulties with the language. And may God grant that the English Methodists stir up no persecution against them!' He was confident that it would be easy for him 'to obtain this small number of missionaries without even leaving the limits' of the Lyon Archdiocese. 'I wish to tell Your Eminence *confidentially*', he said, that Archbishop de Pins of Lyon 'has already furnished personnel for many missions . . . and would accept with pleasure a recommendation from the Sacred Congregation for some particular mission. A goodly number of generous souls in this city would also collaborate in the project by providing financial aid.'

As for the route which the missionaries ought to follow, he listed three possibilities. The shortest and least dangerous route, but one that might not be feasible, would be to cross the Atlantic Ocean, go overland through Mexico and New Spain (now Central America), and then sail across the Pacific Ocean. Another route would be via Cape Horn at the southernmost tip of South America, but this route was very much feared and was little known by French sailors. A third route, he said, was via the Cape of Good Hope at the southernmost tip of Africa. Although quite roundabout this route was the most common and perhaps also the most expeditious of all. It was this last route, he said, to which he had referred in his first letter to the cardinal.

He went on to explain that the government 'of our Very Christian King' had never refused when asked to give Catholic missionaries free passage aboard the ships that it employed to transport government personnel and supplies to French possessions. This was true for the islands off the east coast of Africa, for the Indies and elsewhere. Pastre said that he was speaking from experience here, since he himself had been stationed at Bourbon.

'But how will missionaries reach the Pacific islands from the African islands, or from the Indies, or from the Cape of Good Hope?' he asked. 'We must not flatter ourselves, Your Eminence, by thinking that free passage will be provided for this stretch, because it means going around New Holland to arrive at Botany Bay [adjoining modern Sydney], and from there to Norfolk, an English island with settlements not very far from the Friendly Islands or from New Zealand. This stretch cannot be covered except by English ships which are very little inclined to oblige Roman Catholic missionaries. However, one would be treated tolerably well if he were furnished with letters of recommendation from the English Ambassador addressed to the English governments in the countries where English settlements have been multiplying.'

In conclusion he assured the cardinal that he would continue to 'desire ardently that the vast and praiseworthy project of the Sacred Congregation might obtain happy and lasting success', so that it can contribute to 'the glory of God, the conversion of those distant peoples, and the consolation of the Church of Rome'.[17]

What caught Fransoni's attention most of all in Pastre's latest letter was the assurance that sufficient personnel for the new mission could be obtained from the Archdiocese of Lyon. He now wanted confirmation of this from the archbishop himself and so without even waiting for a reply to his letter sent only ten days earlier to Ducrey, he mustered all the diplomacy at his command and wrote to Archbishop de Pins of Lyon on 22 September 1835.

'The Reverend Pastre because of age and ill health', he said, 'cannot accept the government of the mission to be established in the western portion of the Pacific Ocean, which was offered to him by this Sacred Congregation. He has indicated to us that from your diocese alone, according to Your Excellency's own testimony, it should not be difficult to acquire with your consent—or rather with your help—as many diligent workers as are necessary for this task.' Since a decision was soon to be made about the mission in the western Pacific, Fransoni said, the Sacred Congregation would be 'most grateful to you for the concern that you manifest for the propagation of religion among the heathen'.[18]

The letter from Fransoni unfortunately went unnoticed among numerous papers that came to de Pins's office and, although it must have arrived about 4 October, it was not opened until around 10 November. The contents were made known to Pompallier in Lyon who at once wrote to Colin in Belley. Finally on 20 November the archbishop sent Fransoni the assurance that he would use all his zeal 'to procure excellent workers for the missions of Oceania in the West Pacific Ocean'. He stated that 'the Society of Priests of Mary, who are doing successful work in the dioceses of Lyon and Belley, and who at this moment are seeking approbation from the Holy See, could furnish at once five or six good men as a start. They would also take upon themselves the responsibility of supplying the number of missionaries that might be needed in the future.' He added that the Association for the Propagation of the Faith in Lyon was also prepared to contribute its share of aid by adding this mission to the others that regularly received its funds.[19]

The letter from Archbishop de Pins was so favourable, indicating a source of present and future personnel, that it prompted Cardinal Fransoni without more ado to place the formal foundation of this new mission on the agenda for the next general meeting of the Evangelisation Congregation to be held on 23 December 1835. The one chosen to deliver the report 'On the Establishment of a Vicariate Apostolic in Western Oceania' at this meeting was Napoleon Bonaparte's uncle, seventy-two-year-old Joseph Cardinal Fesch (1763–1839), who had become Archbishop of Lyon in 1802 and France's ambassador to the Holy See in 1803. After Napoleon's defeat at Waterloo in 1815, Fesch was exiled by Louis XVIII and from that time on resided in Rome, governing the Archdiocese of Lyon from there. Fesch was soon asked to resign his archbishopric, not being there to govern it, but he refused. Pope Pius VII in 1817 then entrusted its government to an apostolic administrator, leaving Fesch as the nominal head. Early during his exile Fesch had become a member of several Sacred Congregations in Rome, including the Evangelisation Congregation. Fransoni invited him to be the relator for this report apparently because it directly concerned priests from his Archdiocese of Lyon. Fesch accepted the invitation and was indicated as *ponens* (in English, relator) in the printed copies of the Latin report which were distributed to the cardinal members for study in advance of the meeting. But at the last moment something unforeseen must have happened because Fesch did not attend the meeting and Cardinal Castracane, who had been secretary of the Evangelisation Congregation in 1829 when the Prefecture Apostolic of the South Sea Islands was established, presented the report instead.[20]

The lengthy study contained twenty-one points. Its purpose was to help the cardinal members determine whether 'that most extensive and very important portion [of the Pacific Ocean] containing principally the archipelagoes of the

Navigators, Friendly Islands, Fiji, and also the Kermadec Islands and New Zealand, should become a new mission'.[21] The report was also meant to help them decide what form the mission ought to take 'and to whom it might be entrusted'. After some introductory remarks on the 'grandiose project' of Father de Solages, it was pointed out that the Picpus missionaries in the south Pacific 'already have had some success, although the results produced by them have been quite meagre due to adverse circumstances'.

Then followed a detailed report on the difficulties and success of the Picpus missionaries. Prefect Apostolic Liausu had expressed great concern over the possibility of the Methodists' erecting barriers against his missionaries in all of the archipelagoes within his territory. He therefore wished to have his mission territory south of the equator enlarged toward the west. 'The Protestants cannot be everywhere at the same time', he wrote. 'And there are islands, like those of Fiji, to which we have been invited and where much good can be done. The islands where we are able to remain could serve as supply bases and likewise as a refuge for those missionaries whom the Methodists succeed in driving out. From these islands the gospel could then gradually reach out, first to those people who are nearby and later to those who are more distant. . . .'

There were also reports telling how these same missionaries were making headway in the Gambier Islands and how well they had been received there. They had also succeeded in putting the language of those islands into writing and had started schools on each of the islands. Further good news came from Bishop Rouchouze. He had left Valparaíso on 17 April 1835 with his companions and was headed for Tahiti via the Gambier Islands, where he planned a stopover of eight days. The captain of his ship had a house on Tahiti and had offered it to Rouchouze, promising to mediate and make it possible for him to reside there peacefully in spite of the opposition that could be expected from the Methodists. Rouchouze was very optimistic and hoped also to found a mission in the Marquesas Islands, since the people there had expelled the Bible Readers that had come from Tahiti.

All of these letters brought the Sacred Congregation up to date as of April 1835, Castracane said, and showed that the Picpus missionaries actually were making headway in the area entrusted to them. And in case of expulsion Rouchouze had been given extensive faculties for himself, for the two prefects apostolic under him, and for all his missionaries. These faculties could be used in any land or island whatsoever, wherever violence or need might drive them, and for as long a time as they might need to stay in these places. The only condition was that no other missionary be already stationed there, and that the lands or islands in question be not under the jurisdiction of some other prelate.

This argumentation was calculated to show that it was unnecessary to extend the jurisdiction of the Picpus missionaries into Western Oceania.

The report then went on to explain how Father Pastre had been contacted in July of 1835 and it also told of Pastre's suggestion regarding free passage for at least part of the way to Western Oceania. But this particular problem was not considered very important, because the Picpus Fathers were already in Eastern

Oceania and this was proof enough that it was possible to get there. The missionaries going to Western Oceania could follow the same route. 'The question to be decided now is whether some similar provision—and what kind?—ought to be made to procure the salvation of those many peoples deprived of the true light of the faith, who inhabit the islands to the west, both north and south of the equator.' To be excluded, of course, were those areas in which other Catholic ecclesiastical authorities had already been established.[22]

It is interesting to note here that Castracane speaks of 'the islands to the west, both north and south of the equator'. Until this point there was talk only of the western half of what had been the Prefecture Apostolic of the South Sea Islands, with the equator as its northern boundary. How can one explain this unexpected reference to the islands north of the equator, known today as Micronesia?

A letter of 30 January 1832 written in Rome by Petrus Maria Heredia del Rio to 'the Secretary of Propaganda Fide Congregation', who then was Castracane, the same man now reading this report, seems to provide a clue. Heredia del Rio begins his letter in this way: 'In accord with your desire to get some news on matters concerning the mission once decreed by His Holiness Clement XI for the New Philippine Islands, that is, the Carolines, I read through the letters of Jesuit missionaries in the library of the Roman College. The same letters can perhaps also be found in your library. There is a report and also a map of the foresaid islands prepared by the Servant of God, Father Giovanni Antonio Cantova, S.J., sent to the confessor of King Philip V of Spain on 20 March 1722. . . .' The letter goes on to speak of the Marianas and states that they depended upon the Old Philippines 'in spiritual matters and temporalities'. Accompanying the letter were extensive reports on both the Carolines and the Marianas.[23]

When Castracane was originally seeking this information, Coudrin was trying hard to have his mission of the Sandwich Islands extended into part of the territory of de Solages south of the equator. Because of the bitter opposition of de Solages to Coudrin's proposal, Castracane may have played with the idea of extending the Picpus mission westward to the Carolines and the Marianas, which would have made one mission of the islands along the north Pacific trade route. But as matters developed Coudrin eventually did receive certain islands south of the equator and so the Carolines and the Marianas were left unattended. Therefore it was only natural that Castracane, now delivering this report on the proposed creation of a new vicariate for Western Oceania, should once again think of these same islands north of the equator. Adding to the new mission the islands north of the equator would also balance it with the Vicariate Apostolic of Eastern Oceania which also had jurisdiction over islands both north and south of the equator. So instead of dividing all islands of the Pacific into two mission areas stretching from east to west and separated by the equator, the proposal now being made was to divide the Pacific islands into two vast mission areas stretching north to south.

But who would supply the staff for Western Oceania? The Picpus Fathers were eager to branch out into that area, Castracane said, 'and it seems that one could count on their good will, activity and zeal'. But he called attention to an earlier remark of de Solages to the effect that Coudrin's congregation was so small that it would not be able to staff both the Sandwich Islands and the islands of the south Pacific. Four archipelagoes in the south Pacific had nevertheless been assigned to the Picpus Fathers on 2 June 1833, he said, and this new mission required 'not a few members to staff it'.

A further reason against assigning Western Oceania to the Picpus Fathers, Castracane said, was a new project in Chile that would require more Picpus personnel. The President of Chile, his ministers, and the Bishop of Santiago had all urgently requested the Picpus Fathers to establish themselves in Valparaíso. They could continue the work of the aged Fray Andrés Caro, O.F.M., he said, giving spiritual exercises or retreats to the Catholic population there. Or they could devote themselves to the conversion of the Araucanian Indians in central Chile and to other tribes which had no missionaries to care for them since the Spaniards had been expelled.

Fray Andrés had offered to the Picpus Fathers his own completely furnished retreat house, which had extensive living quarters for priests, a very large section for retreatants, and a church capable of holding 600 people. 'By now the contract for handing over this house is probably completed', Castracane said. As for the mission to the Indians, the government had offered to the Picpus Fathers the Colegio de los Angeles on the frontier of the Indian missions, a school formerly staffed by Spanish Franciscans. It also promised to pay the French priests the same salary given formerly by Spain to the Spanish priests.

'Beyond a doubt', Castracane said, 'it would be important and advantageous *for all the missions of Oceania* if the Picpus Congregation were to establish itself at Valparaíso. This would facilitate communications between these islands and France and at the same time would speed up communications and make them safer.' One of the Picpus priests based there could be given the title of Procurator General for the Missions of Eastern Oceania. He would be kept informed by the bishop of the current needs in each mission as regards personnel, funds and supplies. The missionaries coming from Europe would assemble there in order to receive their assignments to the various archipelagoes, and alms collected in Valparaíso would help provide them with some necessary funds.

Valparaíso would become 'for the missions of Eastern Oceania what Macao is for the missions of China and neighbouring countries', Castracane said, 'and there is no doubt at all about these advantages. But in order to realise them at least two members will have to remain permanently in this city.' This section of the report concluded with the statement that in view of their many existing obligations the Picpus Fathers would hardly be able to supply the necessary personnel for the contemplated new mission of Western Oceania.

By this time Castracane had read through nineteen of the twenty-one points in the printed report, which covered nine solid pages, and he had not yet mentioned the Marists. But on the second to last page, in point number twenty, it was explained how Pastre and the Marists fitted into the picture. Castracane also mentioned that Pastre had spoken confidentially with 'a highly esteemed priest of the clergy of Lyon who was also a member of a society called Marists, or rather Society of Mary, established until now in the two dioceses of Lyon and Belley, and not yet approved by the Holy See. The institute, which differs little in its activities and in its rule of life from the Jesuits, has been granted to date only a Laudatory Brief.'

The report went on to explain that the name of the priest contacted by Pastre was not known, but that Father Colin of Belley, the superior, had praised this priest for his 'readiness to dedicate himself to the conversion of the heathen in Oceania, and does not judge this work foreign to his institute'. Colin, however, before accepting this mission wanted to have his group better organised and had decided to wait for the brief containing papal approbation. 'He is eager to know whether the Sacred Congregation would accept the members of his society for the proposed mission', the report said, 'so that he can immediately make contact, in case the reply is affirmative, with his representative [in Rome] . . . , instructing him to treat of the matter with the cardinals who are informed of these affairs.'

The final point in the report stated that when the apostolic administrator of the Archdiocese of Lyon was invited by the Sacred Congregation to procure excellent priests for the mission of Western Oceania, he had praised the priests of the Society of Mary, had said that it could provide five or six members to start the mission, and had announced that the society would also oblige itself to supply as many priests as would be needed to maintain the mission in the future. The archbishop-administrator had also said that the Association for the Propagation of the Faith in Lyon had agreed to do its share in helping the mission financially.

Castracane then asked the other seven cardinals at the meeting to decide what action should be taken on these two questions:

1. Should a new Vicariate Apostolic of Western Oceania be established?
2. If so, to whom should the new mission be entrusted?

The cardinals answered the first question in the affirmative.[24]

As for the second question, it was clear from the report that the Picpus Fathers had responsibilities enough in the Sandwich Islands, in the archipelagoes south of the equator in Eastern Oceania, and in Valparaíso. It was therefore proposed that the new mission should be entrusted to the Marists, if there were no objections.

Of the fifteen cardinals residing in Rome who were members of the Evangelisation Congregation, only eight were present at this meeting. Six of these eight were also members of the Sacred Congregation for Bishops and Religious, the congregation immediately concerned with the final approbation by the Holy See of religious congregations like the Marists. Of these six cardinals, one was seventy-three-year-old Giuseppe Antonio Sala (1762–1839), head of the Congregation for Bishops and Religious since November 1834. He spoke up at the meeting and said that he would immediately contact Colin to assure him that there were good hopes of his receiving the kind of papal approbation that he desired for his society. Sala said that he would also urge Colin to accept the mission of Western Oceania.[25]

Although Cardinal Sala had no objection, Cardinal Castracane did object, and strongly so. Since September 1833 he had been a member of the congregation now headed by Sala, and was assigned to study the rule of the Society of Mary submitted by Colin in December of that year. He had made a very negative report on the rule at the meeting of the Sacred Congregation for Bishops and Religious held on 31 January 1834.

According to Colin's rule the Society of Mary was to be composed of four distinct groups: (1) Society of Priests, (2) Society of Lay Brothers, (3) Community of Religious Sisters, and (4) Confraternity of Laymen Living in the World. Each of the first three groups was to have its own rules, its own houses, and its own superior. But the superior of the Brothers—a priest with the title of provincial—and the superior of the Sisters were both to be 'dependent upon the superior general of the priests'. The fourth group would admit 'persons of both sexes in every part of the world, who will be recognised as Third Order members of the religious congregations mentioned; they will be permitted to participate in the spiritual benefits of these religious congregations in dependence upon the superior general who is over all of them'.

As for the structure of the Society of Mary, Castracane had asked at that meeting how it could be expedient 'for three institutes having diverse activities to be subject to one superior general'. The superior general of every religious order knows well enough, he said, 'that he can hardly manage to conduct all the affairs of his own order, if he wants to attend to them conscientiously. How then would he be able to manage the affairs of three orders?' As for the 'confraternity to consist of men and women of every walk of life and of every country, likewise to be presided over by the superior general', this proposal was 'extravagant and out of order', since confraternities according to Church practice were not worldwide, but were dependent upon local bishops.

Further, what difference was there between the three religious congregations proposed by Colin and others already existing? Approval by the Holy See had been made a necessary condition for the formal recognition of new religious congregations, he said, 'in order to avoid the confusion that could be created by multiplying them'. One could hurt the other. As for the Marist Brothers, he said, their aim is to instruct the poor, but in nearly all dioceses of France the Brothers of the Christian Schools (F.S.C.) are already doing this excellently. 'What advantage would there be for the Church if the scope is the same and there is no other difference but the name?' Rivalries could arise 'which might paralyse or at least diminish the good being done at present by the Brothers of the Christian Schools'. The same could be said about the Sisters, because 'such foundations for the education of youth are so numerous in France that it is now difficult to number them'.

Castracane did make one concession, however. 'If the only issue in question were the setting up of mission congregations, particularly for foreign countries, multiplying their number could perhaps be approved without fear of any difficulty.' He concluded his report by saying that to him the plan of Colin seemed 'inadmissible', 'extravagant', 'monstrous', 'inopportune', 'and without precedent in the history of religious institutes'. Castracane had told the cardinals at the January 1834 meeting that he had discussed the matter with Colin (who was in Rome at this time awaiting the outcome), 'and he too is persuaded that the plan is monstrous. He therefore intends to simplify it . . . , limiting his plan to the establishment of only a congregation of priests'.

The Sacred Congregation for Bishops and Religious had then voted unanimously not to give approval to the Society of Mary as presented in Colin's rule, a decision confirmed on 20 June 1834 by the pope. Colin knew from his earlier talks with Castracane that this would happen. Writing from Rome to a friend on 30 January 1834, the day before the important meeting was held, Colin had said: 'If we had proposed only the priest group and had presented a complete set of rules, we would be on the right road toward obtaining approbation.' Colin had been told by Castracane that he could not hope 'at this time to receive from the Holy See any act of approbation'. The entire body of rules had to be revised first and presented anew for examination and study by the Holy See before a decision could be reached.

After half a year or more of waiting, and receiving no official word on the action taken by the Sacred Congregation for Bishops and Religious, Colin through his representative in Rome submitted still another request for approbation, omitting this time the part about Third Orders, but for the rest suggesting the very same structure. Cardinal Castracane in March 1835 was called upon to give his comment on this document and was puzzled that Colin should press once again for the very same thing which he had been told by Castracane himself could not be granted, and which Colin had agreed to change. And yet the cardinal wanted to issue no official word of disapproval, since the three branches of priests, Brothers and Sisters were doing such good work. The best thing to do, he concluded, was 'to leave the decision in this matter to the most prudent of counsellors, namely to time, which will discover whether or not it is fitting for three institutes to be united under a single superior'.

This was the background against which Castracane saw Colin's most recent request for papal approbation, now up for discussion at the 23 December 1835 meeting of the Evangelisation Congregation, and so intimately bound up with his acceptance of the proposed mission.

Castracane spelled out clearly for the other seven cardinals his serious objections. His position was the same as it had always been: papal approbation could be granted for the society of priests without difficulty, but not for all three or four groups together. And if Colin persisted in his view that papal approbation must cover the various groups, the pope should not be asked to grant the desired approbation.[26]

But then the question was asked: Will Father Colin accept the mission of Western Oceania if he does not receive papal approbation in the form that he has insisted upon so forcefully, resolutely, and repeatedly?

The cardinal members of the Evangelisation Congregation were anxious to have personnel for Western Oceania immediately, and they knew of no other available source. They consequently decided to apply pressure on Colin through separate channels in order to have him change his mind. Not only would Cardinal Sala write to him directly, but both Archbishop de Pins and Father Pastre would also be asked to approach him personally. These three men were to do all they could to persuade Colin to accept the mission, something to which he was not averse, according to the testimony received from both de Pins and Pastre. At the same time they were to tell him that if he did accept the mission, he could 'hope to obtain approbation more easily for his institute insofar as the official recognition of the congregation of priests is concerned'. The pope, however, would have to give his support to the scheme if the cardinals were sincerely to hold out to Colin the hope of papal approbation.

Father Angelo Mai, secretary of the Evangelisation Congregation, read a summary of this meeting during an audience with Pope Gregory XVI on Sunday, 10 January 1836, calling attention to the plan devised by the cardinals. When telling the pope the names of some of the islands contained in the new vicariate, he explicitly mentioned 'New Zealand, the Friendly Islands, the Navigators, the Solomons, the Hebrides, and the islands of Ralik and Ratak' in the Marshall Islands. He added that the mission extended even farther to the west and to the north 'until one reaches the few Dutch, Portuguese and Spanish missionaries, who would seem to be in the Marianas, the Carolines and the Moluccas'.

After hearing the report and learning of the decisions of the cardinals, Pope Gregory XVI created the Vicariate Apostolic of Western Oceania and entrusted it to the Marists. At the same time he authorised Cardinal Sala and the Evangelisation Congregation to proceed with their strategy as planned. He also said that after Colin had accepted the mission, the matter should be taken up of finding a suitable candidate for the dignity of bishop and vicar apostolic.[27]

Gregory XVI by creating this new vicariate apostolic showed once again that he was deeply and personally interested in Oceania. As Mauro Cardinal Cappellari, prefect of the Evangelisation Congregation from 1826 to 1831, he had been largely responsible for the creation of the Prefecture Apostolic of the South Sea Islands on 10 January 1830. And as Pope Gregory XVI, he had already created the Vicariate Apostolic of Eastern Oceania on 2 June 1833. Not without reason does his tomb in Saint Peter's Basilica portray him sending missionaries to Oceania.

Within the brief span of six years *to the day*, the dream mission of de Solages had evolved into two vicariates apostolic.

7

The Marists accept responsibility for Western Oceania

10 FEBRUARY 1836

Cardinal Fransoni informed Father Pastre under date of 23 January 1836 that the Vicariate Apostolic of Western Oceania had now been established and had been entrusted with the pope's approval 'to the priests of the Society of Marists'. Fransoni also praised Pastre for his zealous initiative and said that he must now help bring this project to a successful conclusion. Enclosed were detailed instructions on the method of procedure for Pastre to follow, but the cardinal advised him to take action only 'after having taken counsel with the Most Reverend Archbishop Administrator of the Church of Lyon, to whom we are also writing'.[1]   On the same day Fransoni wrote to Archbishop de Pins and told him much the same thing. He said that the archbishop's letter of 20 November 1835 had been read during the meeting of cardinals, and he reminded him of his promise to lend his help so that the entire affair 'can more easily turn out successfully'. The cardinals had given 'all due praise to the outstanding zeal' which de Pins had manifested for the propagation of religion. They now wished him to see to it that Colin would not refuse this mission, since by accepting it he could more easily obtain the desired approbation for his congregation of priests.[2]

Both Pastre and de Pins's vicar general Cholleton informed Colin and his priests of the letters received from Cardinal Fransoni. The tiny community was elated with the news that the Evangelisation Congregation wanted it to take over 'the western part of the islands in the Pacific Ocean'. Colin at once wrote to Fransoni from Belley on 10 February 1836, saying that 'the superior and the priests of the Society of Mary, full of confidence in the help of the Lord, joyfully seize this favourable occasion of fulfilling one of the purposes which they propose for themselves. They accept with gratitude the offer of the Sacred Congregation.' Colin gave assurance that the cardinal would learn very soon through Archbishop de Pins the number and names of the priests preparing to take up work in this new mission.

But shrewd Colin wanted papal approbation in fact, not only in promise. 'Our joy in the Lord would be complete', he added, if before the departure of the missionaries 'a Brief from the Holy See were to encourage our enterprise and to permit at least the priests of the society to tighten even more securely the bonds which have united us in a common purpose'. Colin added that Fransoni would acquire a new claim on the eternal gratitude of the Marists and at the same time would hasten the departure of the first missionaries, if he would 'kindly obtain

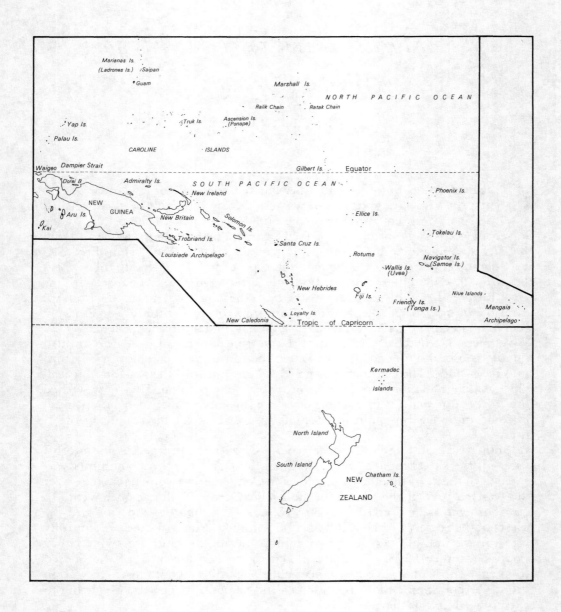

20 All this territory was included within the boundaries of the Vicariate Apostolic of Western Oceania founded on 10 January 1836. (*Chapters 6, 7, 8, 10*).

this special favour for us, about which I shall take the liberty of writing anew to His Eminence, Cardinal Castracane'. Colin's strategy was working out perfectly![3]

Pastre also wrote to Fransoni on 10 February, saying that he had received the cardinal's letter 'with the greatest exultation', and had 'at once made it known to the superior of the Marists in the presence of a representative of the Administrator Apostolic of the Diocese of Lyon'. Colin had not only accepted the mission, he said, but also the limited type of approbation for his community, and as quickly as possible would make known to Archbishop de Pins the names of five priests and two Brothers whom he intended to send to Western Oceania. Then a few days later de Pins would advise Fransoni which one of these priests he considered the best candidate to govern the new mission. 'The one in question up to now', Pastre said, 'appears to be the one with whom I first spoke confidentially (namely the Reverend Pompallier), who is a man of God possessing knowledge, prudence and zeal for souls.' He added that Colin was most anxious for Rome quickly to approve his congregation of priests, so that a superior general could be elected before the departure of the missionaries, since they of necessity would have special contacts with their superior general. Pastre assured Fransoni that the Reverend Cholleton, Vicar General of Lyon, had made 'wise provisions' for the expenses of the mission, and added that he himself was obtaining data for the missionaries about their voyage around Cape Horn. He was also hoping, he said, that he would be able to accompany to Rome the one chosen to head the new mission.[4]

Colin also sent a letter to Cardinal Castracane on 10 February, telling him much the same as he had told Fransoni, but adding that 'something essential' was still lacking for his joy to be complete. This was the authorisation for the members to bind themselves more closely together by taking simple vows before the departure date. And he added by way of compromise: 'We request this Brief on behalf of the priests of the society alone, and Your Eminence can make those additions or deletions that you see fit in the rule submitted to you.' The brief had been 'so long desired', Colin said, and was now urgently needed so that the present provisional superior (namely, Colin himself) could be replaced before the departure by a newly elected 'superior general who would be recognised by the two bishops of Lyon and Belley'. But such an election could not take place 'without previous word from the Holy See'.[5]

After these letters were posted to Rome, another letter arrived from Rome for Archbishop de Pins. It was from Cardinal Sala, prefect of the Sacred Congregation for Bishops and Religious. Father Mai, secretary of the Evangelisation Congregation, had informed Sala on 15 January of the pope's decision and had suggested that he should now 'please write to the superior, Reverend Colin, according to the agreement reached at the meeting', and urge him to accept the mission of Western Oceania for the members of his society.[6] Long-standing practice in the Sacred Congregation for Bishops and Religious, however, prompted Sala to send his letter to de Pins rather than to Colin. But before forwarding the letter through Mai, he sent a copy of it for correction on

24 January to Cardinal Castracane. 'I find myself somewhat embarrassed at not having at hand the papers regarding the confirmation of this new institute,' Sala said, 'and I would not want to advance some promises which may not be realised.'

Castracane replied without delay and sent Sala a revised draft for a very inexact section of his letter. Castracane's text was quite strong, stating in part that if Colin's earlier efforts in Rome to get papal approbation 'had proved fruitless, the reason was that the structure of the proposed society had appeared very abnormal and strange, since it would be split up into three or even four groups of persons'. Approbation would be granted, however, if the society were composed only of priests. Sala accepted the corrections, but toned down the words 'very abnormal and strange', saying instead that the structure of the society as envisioned by Colin had appeared to be 'not at all opportune'.[7]

Sala was convinced that it would have been sufficient if the Evangelisation Congregation in its letter to de Pins had advised him of the above, and on 27 January he told Mai so. But since the Evangelisation Congregation wished that he write himself, he considered it 'his duty to do so'.[8]

Sala's letter to de Pins, dated 28 January, explained the above difficulty and then added: 'But if the society were to be presented to the Apostolic See for approval as composed only of priests who would duly collaborate in conducting sacred missions, spiritual exercises, preaching, and other offices of the divine ministry in a disciplined manner set down by rules, I do not doubt but that the decision of the Sacred Congregation would be favourable to the requests of these same priests.' Sala also asked de Pins to inflame the Marists with zeal for Western Oceania and urged him to strive to reconcile Colin to the facts of the case, 'since thereby the eternal salvation of so many peoples' will be realised so much sooner.[9]

De Pins quickly called this letter to the attention of Pompallier, residing in Lyon, who judged it to be most reassuring and most encouraging. 'This cardinal has no doubt at all about our obtaining from His Holiness the Brief so greatly desired, but it will be only for the priests', Pompallier wrote to a fellow Marist. 'Besides this he gives assurance that the Holy Father resolutely exhorts us to go ahead with the plan to take up the Oceania mission. How happy I am before God that from the beginning I accepted the burdens of this mission and that I have urged the entire society to devote itself to this very task. I have always foreseen that this mission of necessity would hasten and perhaps bring about that approbation which is the object of our common desires!'[10]

Sala's letter to de Pins, however, as he himself had anticipated, proved unnecessary to achieve the goal desired by the Evangelisation Congregation. Colin's letters of 10 February to Fransoni and Castracane and Pastre's letter to Fransoni of the same date had already given Rome the green light, and so members of the Sacred Congregation for Bishops and Religious hastily met in the Vatican apartments on 11 March 1836. Castracane reported to them orally on the rapid sequence of events and the cardinals immediately decided to grant Colin's request for papal approval. That same day the congregation's secretary informed Pope Gregory XVI of the decision taken by the cardinals. The pope at once confirmed their decision and ordered a brief drawn up to this effect.[11]

Castracane 'with very great pleasure' hastened to inform Colin on 12 March that the cardinals of the Sacred Congregation for Bishops and Religious had discussed his latest petition regarding the Society of Mary on the previous day and had decided to request the pope for the desired approbation. He would also be asked 'to provide the priest members with the faculty of taking simple vows and to authorise the head of the society to dispense from those same vows when this is necessary, with the reservation however that the rules of this same society must still be examined by the Sacred Congregation'.

His letter had a further point to make: 'I would like you to understand, however, that the Sacred Congregation was prompted to grant approbation to your institute by the thought that particularly in this way it could make you more eager to take upon yourselves the responsibility for a very difficult mission. And once you have begun the work, may you never cease to apply yourselves with ever greater diligence to your glorious task of planting the Catholic faith in . . . Oceania, an activity which will flourish with the help of God.'[12]

Colin received this letter at Belley on 23 March and the next day sent a copy of it to Cholleton, the one who months earlier had put Pastre on the track of the Marists, saying that 'this letter has filled all of us with joy and has aroused in our hearts the most sweet sentiments of gratitude and thanksgiving toward Our Lord'.[13]

Then on 29 April 1836, by a brief called *Omnium gentium*, Pope Gregory XVI formally and publicly announced that he was giving approbation to the Society of Mary. 'The salvation of all peoples', he said in part, '. . . compels us constantly to be vigilant and leave nothing untried through which the name of the Lord may be praised from the rising of the sun until its setting, and by means of which the most holy Catholic faith—without which it is impossible to please God—may thrive and shine forth all over the earth.'[14]

It was now the task of the Society of Mary to make the Catholic faith 'thrive and shine forth' all over Western Oceania.

8

Pompallier is named Vicar Apostolic of Western Oceania

17 APRIL 1836

Pope Gregory XVI, when creating the Vicariate Apostolic of Western Oceania and entrusting it to the Marists on 10 January 1836, had given instructions that the business of finding a suitable candidate for the dignity of bishop and vicar apostolic should be taken up as soon as Father Colin and the Marists had accepted the mission. The Evangelisation Congregation had to seek for no candidate, however, because one was presented spontaneously and without delay. His name was Father Pompallier.

When Pastre on 10 February 1836 had informed Fransoni that Colin had accepted full responsibility for Western Oceania, he had remarked that Archbishop de Pins of Lyon would be informing Fransoni after some days which priest, from among those chosen by Colin, he judged best for governing the new mission. 'The one in question up to now', Pastre had said, 'appears to be the one with whom I first spoke confidentially (namely the Reverend Pompallier), who is a man of God possessing knowledge, prudence and zeal for souls.'[1]

De Pins finally replied to Fransoni's letter of 23 January on 4 March. He announced formally that Colin had accepted Western Oceania, that the Marists would be sending five priests and two Brothers there, and that they had assumed responsibility for sending additional personnel as needed. In charge of the first group, he said, would be Pompallier, 'born in Lyon on 11 December 1801, a priest of rare merit and piety, whom I especially recommend to the goodness of Your Eminence as a person of distinction in all respects'. He added that if Fransoni so desired, 'this excellent priest will come to Rome to obtain instructions from Your Eminence, or he will wait here for any orders that you may want to send'.

On 28 March de Pins wrote again to Fransoni saying that 'if His Holiness were to judge it opportune to give some special powers to the superior of the Oceania mission', for this honour the cardinal should kindly recommend to the pope 'particularly the Reverend Pompallier, a priest of Lyon of the greatest merit'.[2]

Colin, too, was in favour of Pompallier, having encouraged him as early as 3 August 1835 to accept responsibility for heading the mission, because 'at the present moment I can think of no one else but you who can fill the position that is offered to you'.[3]

On the basis of the two recommendations received from de Pins and Pastre and the earlier one from Colin,[4] Fransoni had his secretary, Father Mai, take up this matter with Pope Gregory XVI at the very next audience devoted to business of the Evangelisation Congregation. Mai's audience was on Sunday, 17 April 1836, and the first item that he read to the pope from his long list of business was as follows: 'In the general congregation of 23 December 1835 the resolution was taken, later approved by Your Holiness, that Western Oceania should become a vicariate apostolic and be entrusted to the care of the Society of Marists of Lyon. The priest Jean-Baptiste Pompallier of Lyon, a member of that same society, is now being proposed for [the office of] vicar apostolic by the Archbishop-Administrator of that archdiocese, who recommends him, saying that he is a priest of merit and rare piety. The Reverend Pastre also states that this ecclesiastic *is a man of God as regards knowledge, prudence and zeal for souls*, and that therefore he enjoys *the greatest esteem among the clergy of Lyon*. On the basis of this data Your Holiness is requested kindly to designate Pompallier as Vicar Apostolic of the Western Part of Oceania with the title of an episcopal church *in partibus infidelium*.' The pope immediately gave his consent, thereby making Pompallier the first Vicar Apostolic of Western Oceania and raising him to the rank of bishop-elect.[5] He was thirty-four years old and had been a priest for six years and ten months.

It was customary for each mission bishop to be given the name of an extinct Christian community without his having jurisdiction over it or the responsibility of caring for it. Pompallier consequently was designated Bishop of Maronea on 9 May 1836,[6] just as Rouchouze, the Vicar Apostolic of Eastern Oceania, had been designated Bishop of Nilopolis. Since 10 June 1882 bishops with titles like this have been officially designated as 'titular bishops', a word still in use today, but in Pompallier's time they were classified as 'bishops *in partibus infidelium*' (that is, 'in heathen areas'). Contemporaries often used 'Bishop of Maronea' when speaking of Pompallier and 'Bishop of Nilopolis' when speaking of Rouchouze.

On 21 April, four days after the papal audience, sixty-year-old Fransoni wrote to seventy-year-old de Pins that his candidate had been accepted by Pope Gregory XVI. 'It seems preferable that he should come to Rome in order to receive here his episcopal ordination as well as necessary instructions', Fransoni said. 'I therefore ask you to see to it that he begins his journey as soon as possible, lest the spiritual welfare of so many peoples be delayed longer than is becoming.' Fransoni also told de Pins, who had requested 'special powers' for Pompallier, that 'the vicar apostolic will be provided with the most ample faculties in view of the enormous task which he is undertaking. Many of these faculties he will be able to delegate to the missionaries under him.'

De Pins had also brought up the matter of funds in his letter of 28 March, stating that a rough estimate placed the minimum costs for the mission at 40,000 francs. 'Would the Evangelisation Congregation be able to furnish part of this? If so, how much could be expected?' He pointed out that the Association for the Propagation of the Faith in Lyon had already promised 15,000 francs, and 'perhaps this amount may still be somewhat increased'. Fransoni replied to this by asking how much the Association for the Propagation of the Faith intended

21 The Most Reverend Jean-Baptiste-François Western Oceania. *Source: OM vol. 1, opp. p. 913.*
Pompallier (1801–71), the first Vicar Apostolic of *(Chapters 8, 15).*

to give over and above the 15,000 francs. He also wanted to know whether Pastre had been able to obtain any funds from generous people in the archdiocese, as he had earlier anticipated. But he assured de Pins that 'the Sacred Congregation after learning this will not hesitate to provide all that is needed to make up the required 40,000 francs'.[7]

The Association for the Propagation of the Faith subsequently did raise its contribution to 25,000 francs. The Evangelisation Congregation then promised 20,000 francs, making a total of 45,000 francs donated to the Marist mission.[8]

Fransoni's letter of 21 April to de Pins had said that Bishop-Elect Pompallier should be in Rome as soon as possible. He arrived there on 21 May, the day before Pentecost. Two days later, a Monday, he had a twenty-minute audience with Pope Gregory XVI. 'What goodness, what simplicity, what fatherliness there is in this august person and successor of Saint Peter', he wrote to Colin. 'And he squeezed my hands with such affection that I was embarrassed.' Pompallier said he was not worthy of his new office and asked the pope to relieve him of it, but the pope would hear nothing of the sort. In Colin's name Pompallier expressed the gratitude of the entire Society of Mary for the favour of papal approbation and for entrusting to the members the difficult mission of Western Oceania. During his first ten days in Rome he also personally thanked Cardinals Fransoni, Sala and Castracane for all that they had done in acquiring papal approbation and in having entrusted to the young society the Vicariate Apostolic of Western Oceania. In his free time he visited many of the shrines of Rome and prayed at the tombs of the apostles.[9]

Briefly Pompallier described his episcopal ordination for Colin: 'After I made a retreat of eight days, His Eminence, Cardinal Fransoni, brought me in his carriage to the Church of the Immaculate Conception. Here His Eminence himself ordained me on 30 June, feast of the Commemoration of Saint Paul. He was assisted by an archbishop and a bishop from the Holy City.' It was a very special grace, Pompallier said, that his episcopal ordination 'took place before an altar dedicated to Mary'.[10] The church, known to Romans as Santa Maria della Concezione (Saint Mary of the Conception), was built for the Capuchins near Piazza Barberini in 1624. It is very well known to pilgrims and tourists today because of its crypt with skeletal remains of some four thousand monks on view.

The first two weeks of July were spent visiting the 'whole College of Cardinals' and other prelates, and on 9 July Pompallier had his third audience with Pope Gregory XVI. 'He pleasantly surprised me by giving me the faculty of granting his apostolic benediction in my new and difficult ministry', he told Colin. 'His Holiness is well disposed to our society, its branches and all its activities . . . The cardinals have all given me testimony of their good will and of their great interest in the mission entrusted to our society. What an opportune moment for us to receive favours here!' All of this enthusiasm for the Society of Mary, he said, was generated by the hope in Rome that the mission of Western Oceania would be successful. 'And if there is evident so much benevolence on the part of the princes of the Church because of this hope, how much more will there be because of the success itself, *provided God gives it.*[11]

On Sunday, 10 July, the day after Pompallier had his audience with Gregory XVI, Secretary Mai had another papal audience. 'Your Holiness is requested to grant to the Most Reverend Pompallier, Bishop of Maronea and Vicar Apostolic of Western Oceania, the same faculties granted by Your Holiness to the Most Reverend Rouchouze, Bishop of Nilopolis and Vicar Apostolic of Eastern Oceania.' The pope without hesitation granted the request.[12]

Eleven years later in 'An Historical and Statistical Report on the Vicariate Apostolic of Western Oceania' prepared for Cardinal Fransoni, Pompallier would say that 'Pope Gregory XVI, after my episcopal ordination in Rome on the feast of Saint Paul, 30 June 1836, and in spite of my reservations, judged it proper' to increase the area of jurisdiction and add the islands of Oceania north of the equator.[13]

But Pompallier in writing this surely must have been confused. Or maybe he simply was not aware that the islands of Northern Oceania had already been included as part of his vicariate apostolic when it was created on 10 January 1836. Secretary Mai, telling the pope on that day the names of some of the islands contained in the new vicariate, had explicitly mentioned 'the islands of Ralik and Ratak' in the Marshall Islands. He had also said that the mission extended even farther to the west and to the north 'until one reaches the few Dutch, Portuguese and Spanish missionaries, who would seem to be in the Marianas, the Carolines and the Moluccas'.[14] Mai was simply spelling out more clearly the extent of the vicariate as already indicated at the general meeting of the Evangelisation Congregation held on 23 December 1835. Of course, Pompallier would not have seen the minutes of this meeting nor the text that was read to the pope.

But another document of the Evangelisation Congregation, the decree of 7 May 1836 announcing that the pope had chosen Pompallier to be bishop and Vicar Apostolic of Western Oceania, also said much the same.[15] It stated that his mission contained within its limits 'all islands in the western part of the Pacific Ocean, both to the north and to the south, including the archipelago called Mangaia, and starting from a straight line running through the same Mangaia Island from north to south, except for those places in which Catholic Church authority has already been legitimately established'. These words of 7 May were repeated verbatim in the brief *Pastorale officium* of 13 May by which the pope officially informed Pompallier of his new office and the limits of his spiritual jurisdiction.[16]

This meant that the Vicariate Apostolic of Western Oceania from the very beginning covered an area approximately 8,000 kilometres long from east to west and just as long from north to south. This was one-fifth the circumference of the earth in each direction, but the shape of the territory was more like a triangle than a square. Thus a vast array of islands which no man to this day has numbered fell within the spiritual jurisdiction of Pompallier. Their names could easily fill a paragraph!

They were the southern Cook Islands, Tonga or Friendly Islands, Samoa Islands, Tokelau Islands, Phoenix Islands, Kermadec Islands, Fiji Islands, Wallis Islands, Ellice Islands, Kingsmill Islands, Gilbert Islands, Marshall Islands, Loyalty Islands, New Zealand, New Caledonia, New Hebrides, Santa Cruz Islands, Louisiade Archipelago, Trobriand Islands, Solomon Islands, Bismarck Archipelago (New Britain, New Ireland, Admiralty Islands), New Guinea (the largest island), and also parts of the Moluccas or Spice Islands between New Guinea and Celebes, the Marianas or Ladrones Islands with Guam and Saipan, and the Caroline Islands which contained the Palau Islands, Yap Islands, Truk Islands, Mortlock Islands and Ponape.

Pompallier must have shuddered at the vastness of his vicariate and in his audience did ask the pope to exclude at least Micronesia, the part above the equator. But Gregory XVI as a former cardinal prefect of the Evangelisation Congregation knew better than Pompallier the difficulties connected with founding a first base of operations and wanted the new bishop to have as vast an area as possible in which to begin. In time parts of the territory could be cut off and entrusted to other bishops.

While in Rome, Pompallier met Father (now Saint) Vincenzo Pallotti (1795–1850) who one year earlier (4 April 1835) had founded there the Society of the Catholic Apostolate (S.A.C.) known also as the Pallottines. As Pallotti himself explained, his Catholic Apostolate 'was founded to deepen, defend and spread piety and the Catholic faith'. Missionaries and mission bishops, therefore, were fitted preeminently by vocation for membership in this organisation, and Pallotti accepted as members all who wanted to join. Rome was already at that time the crossroads of the mission world and he made innumerable contacts. By 1838 the Catholic Apostolate had members scattered throughout twenty-eight countries and Pallotti in turn empowered them to admit as members all the faithful in their territory. This international organisation of bishops, priests, religious and laity was thus very much like a confraternity. Pompallier on learning of it also joined, moved no doubt by Pallotti's aim of helping the worldwide mission effort of the Catholic Church both spiritually and materially. Pompallier hoped that some day he might even draw personnel from the organisation, because the Marists to whom his mission was entrusted numbered all told only twenty priests.[17]

'The pope was eager that I should get to my mission quickly', Pompallier said, 'and so I left Rome at the end of July . . .'[18] Once back in France he divided his time between Lyon, Belley and Paris, making numerous contacts and preparations for his mission. 'I stayed awhile with the members of the Society of Mary and visited their principal houses, where they had me officiate pontifically', he told Fransoni. 'I also had many talks with them, and particularly with the superior of the society, arranging matters for the mission of Western Oceania.'[19] It was around this time that *L'ami de la religion*, the principal religious newspaper of France, announced the departure of Pompallier in its issue of 20 August 1836. 'It is reported that the prelate will first visit the Friendly [or Tonga] Islands and the Society [or Tahiti] Islands, and then go to New Guinea.'[20]

Pompallier before leaving Rome submitted one or two delicate questions to Fransoni on 14 July and said he wished to have the replies in writing. Since these could not be drawn up before his departure, he left instructions with Secretary Mai that they should be sent to him in care of the secretary of the Association for the Propagation of the Faith in Lyon instead of to some Marist address. One of the questions seemed to flow from his conversation with Pallotti.

Although the mission of Western Oceania was entrusted to the care of the Society of Mary, he wanted to know whether he would be authorised to seek help from priests who were not Marists, and whether he could have them fill certain offices in the mission. He also wanted to know whether he could name one or two priests of the Society of Mary living in France as his delegates, so that they could grant ordinary faculties in his name to missionaries departing for Western Oceania. In this way the priests coming to his mission could have the use of faculties as soon as their ship brought them within the limits of his mission. If on the other hand they were obliged to get their faculties from him personally, they might well be inside the boundaries of his extensive mission for a long time, and still be deprived of faculties simply because of the difficulty in locating him or catching up with him. Fransoni answered on 18 August that he would send his replies soon, but they were slow in coming.[21]

From Paris on 10 September 1836 Pompallier sent Fransoni a report on his activities of the previous six weeks. 'I had an audience with the queen', he said among other things, 'and she showed me great benevolence and promised me a gift for my mission.'

In a postscript he said that on 14 September he would be leaving Paris for Lyon and then join the other Marists for the election of a superior general and for the retreat which was to precede the taking of vows. He then brought up a subject which he had already discussed in Rome with Fransoni and with Cardinal Prefect Sala of the Sacred Congregation for Bishops and Religious. It had to do with the problem of whether or not he should take vows along with the other Marists. 'As for myself', he said, 'I intend to make [instead] a solemn declaration regarding my relationship to the society. It will put my status on a par with that of a bishop who before his episcopal ordination was bound by vows of religion. For according to the views of Your Eminence and those of Cardinal Sala, I as a bishop ought no longer make vows to a mere priest, since this would be unbecoming, especially so after I have made a promise under oath to give immediate obedience to our Holy Father, the pope.'

Did Cardinals Fransoni and Sala actually say that he as a bishop ought no longer 'make vows to a mere priest'? Hardly, because vows are made to God, never to a priest, even though they may be made in the presence of a priest. Pompallier here must have been referring to certain obligations that he would incur by taking vows of obedience and poverty in the Society of Mary. Having taken an oath of obedience to the pope, it was not proper that he should now bind himself by vows to rules and constitutions which would command obedience to a lower ecclesiastical authority.

Twelve years later, however, on 29 May 1848, Luigi Cardinal Lambruschini would tell the cardinal members of the Evangelisation Congregation at a General Meeting that Pompallier had been allowed by Rome to make vows at this time, but never did so, and never afterwards considered himself to be a member of the Society of Mary.[22]

At the invitation of their provisional central superior, Colin, the twenty Marists from the two dioceses of Lyon and Belley along with Pompallier gathered on 20 September 1836 at the minor seminary in Belley where Colin was rector. They were to elect a superior general and to make the first profession of vows in the history of the Society of Mary. These bonds were to hold them closer together in their service of God, his Church and his people. For twenty years the group had waited for this day which was now made possible because of the papal approbation announced in *Omnium gentium*, Pope Gregory XVI's brief of 29 April 1836. Colin presided at the meetings and suggested that several days be devoted to recollection 'for asking God's help in electing a superior general, for acquiring a more profound knowledge of the rules, and for preparing oneself better for taking vows'. The retreat conferences were given by Pompallier and Colin explained the society's rule of life.

The voting for the superior general took place on 24 September, a Saturday, feast of Our Lady of Mercy, after nearly three hours of prayer. Pompallier cast the first ballot followed by all twenty remaining Marists. When the votes were counted, it was learned that Colin had been elected unanimously. He and the other nineteen priests then took 'the three simple and perpetual vows of chastity, obedience and poverty . . .', promising to observe them 'according to the rules and constitutions of the said Society of Mary and according to the tenor of the Brief of the Sovereign Pontiff Gregory XVI dated 29 April. . . .'

This ceremony was followed by Pompallier making his solemn declaration of spiritual attachment to the Society of Mary. After a solemn introduction he said, 'I, Jean-Baptiste-François, Bishop of Maronea, declare that I wish to hold fast with heart and soul to the Society of Mary, to which I have had the good fortune to belong up to this time. I declare that I wish to continue in its spirit and contribute toward making others abide by its spirit and its constitutions insofar as this shall be possible for me. And finally I declare that it will always be a joy and a consolation for me to listen very respectfully to the views of the superior general of the said society, as well as to accept delegated authority and other responsibilities not in conflict with the immediate obedience that I have promised to our Holy Father the pope. . . .' In conclusion he again mentioned the Society of Mary and said, 'I wish to be a member until my last breath'.[23]

Controversy and confusion would later arise over the stand taken by Pompallier on this day. Some would continue to consider him a Marist, not knowing what had happened, and others would maintain strongly that he had never been a Marist. Certainly he was a Marist just as much as Colin and the others were until he made up his mind not to take vows. When Cholleton directed Pastre to Pompallier, he—because he was a Marist—sought Colin's approval before accepting the offer. And his being a Marist was also the reason why Rome chose Pompallier to head the vicariate apostolic previously entrusted to the Marists. But after 24 September 1836, Pompallier in spite of his solemn declaration was no longer technically or juridically a Marist, because membership according to the rules and constitutions of the society could be acquired only by taking vows. Consequently the term 'Marist' is used improperly of Pompallier after this date, even though he continued to consider himself a Marist. In effect, a member of the secular clergy was now in charge of a mission entrusted to the Marists. Complications could be expected to arise, if Pompallier and the Marists were not extremely careful.[24]

It was 1 October 1836 when Fransoni sent Pompallier a reply to the special questions submitted in Rome on 14 July. 'Although the mission of Western Oceania has been entrusted explicitly by the Sacred Congregation to the care of priests of the Society of the Blessed Virgin Mary', he said, Pompallier was free to recruit non-Marists for the mission and could also confer offices upon them. 'But prefects and pro-vicars of the mission must be chosen from among the members of the Society of Mary', Fransoni said. As for the question of naming one or two priests of the Society of Mary living in France as his delegates, so that they in turn could confer faculties which future missionaries might use immediately upon entering the limits of his vicariate apostolic, there was 'certainly no obstacle in the way'. Pompallier had also requested a personal indult for a 'privileged altar'. Since this was not included in the powers already granted to him, Fransoni said, 'We shall request this indult from His Holiness, Gregory XVI, and send it on to you as soon as possible'.

Fransoni also sent Pompallier a large amount of money. 'Via the enclosed cheques', he said, 'we transfer to you the remaining funds which we promised as payment for your voyage. From the cheques you will see that we are now sending you 14,565 French francs. These are to be added to the 1,000 scudi which you have already received and which according to current exchange rates amount to 5,435 French francs. The enclosures therefore represent the balance of the 20,000 French francs that were promised you. The fact that we have not given you this amount sooner', the cardinal explained, 'must be attributed—as you may know—both to the present financial straits in which we find ourselves and to the enormous expenses which we had to incur recently when sending mission personnel to China and India.' Fransoni closed his letter with a prayer that God might grant Pompallier and his companions a successful voyage. 'We also ask from our heart that he may preserve Your Excellency for a very long time and keep you safe from harm.'[25]

Pompallier had so many urgent matters to attend to in Paris and Le Havre, the port from which he and his missionaries were to sail, that he was able to remain in Lyon and Belley 'only from 17 September to 10 October', as he told Fransoni. Before leaving France he made use of the special faculties that Fransoni had sent him under date of 1 October and drew up a document designating Colin his pro-vicar or vicar general for Western Oceania. He also asked Colin to be his correspondent and chargé d'affaires in France. 'I accepted these offices with all the more pleasure', Colin told Fransoni, 'since through them I can find opportunities for participating personally in the labours of the missionaries. This also makes it possible for me to foster and preserve contacts between our missionaries and the other members of the society remaining in France.'[26]

Colin asked Pompallier in turn to be the religious order superior over the missionaries being sent with him. The group was so small that he did not consider it advisable to have the religious order superior distinct from the ecclesiastical or mission superior. 'I accepted the office', Pompallier told Fransoni, 'but let me know if I should give it up . . . , so that I then can be occupied exclusively with the mission.'[27]

Unknown to Pompallier and Colin, the mutual pact which they now entered was to cause endless strife between them. It would even threaten one day to bring to an end the very work that now before God they had resolved to begin. The mission in Western Oceania in time would suffer great harm. In fact, it would almost certainly have been destroyed except for the wisdom, the patience and the ultimate severity of the Evangelisation Congregation in Rome. What had been calculated by these two men to help avoid an explosive situation was in reality destined to bring it about!

9

Pompallier sets sail from Le Havre

24 DECEMBER 1836

ishop Pompallier booked passage for himself and his missionaries aboard the *Delphine*, the same three-mast vessel on which Bishop Rouchouze and his missionaries had left Le Havre for the Vicariate Apostolic of Eastern Oceania on 28 October 1834. The ship was now scheduled to sail on 25 or 26 October 1836. It was Pompallier's plan to leave Lyon with his missionaries 'about 10 October', spend some time in Paris, and then go to Le Havre for embarking.[1] Before leaving Lyon they were all invited to Pastre's table. He was a most cordial host and showed himself overjoyed at having been responsible for calling the Society of Mary's attention to Western Oceania and Rome's attention to the Society of Mary. Two and a half years later he died in Lyon at the age of sixty. His death showed his wisdom in declining to accept responsibility for Western Oceania when it was offered to him by Rome.[2]

To gain God's special blessing and that of the Virgin Mary on his mission, Pompallier had a novena of Masses celebrated at the shrine of Our Lady of Fourvière in Lyon from 7 to 15 October. On the closing day, a Saturday, the missionaries dedicated themselves and Western Oceania to Our Lady of Fourvière. In the absence of Pompallier, called to Paris on urgent business, Father Pierre Chanel hung a heart-shaped locket around the neck of the Infant held by the Black Virgin. Inside was the text of the dedication signed by all the missionaries. It was in this same chapel that the Society of Mary had been founded on 23 July 1816.[3]

Chanel left Lyon on the following day for Paris, where Pompallier had obtained lodging for his missionaries at the Paris Foreign Mission Seminary. This veteran missionary organisation was able to assist the new missionaries with its 175 years of experience. Pompallier also visited the residence of the Picpus Fathers in Paris a number of times and on 25 October celebrated Mass there at the altar of Our Lady of Peace, placing the voyage under her protection. The Marists then left Paris for Le Havre with four Picpus missionaries who also had booked passage aboard the *Delphine* as far as Valparaíso.[4]

In the middle of October, Pompallier had been received in audience by King Louis-Philippe, by his queen, Marie-Amélie, and by his sister, Madame Adélaïde d'Orléans, princess of Orléans. 'The royal family and the French government not only expressed their benevolence and concern for the new mission of the Holy See in words', Pompallier wrote Fransoni, 'but also gave concrete proofs of it. I was received in a special audience and was treated most graciously.' The royal family also sent him gifts, he said. 'The king sent 1,000 francs; the queen, 500 francs; and Madame Adélaïde, a supply of white calico to clothe our future neophytes in Oceania.'

He also told Fransoni that Comte Louis-Mathieu Molé (1781–1855), Minister of Foreign Affairs, had provided him with excellent letters of introduction to the French consuls on the west coast of South America. And Claude-Charles-Marie Du Campe de Rosamel (1774–1848), Minister of the Navy, had given him a letter of introduction to the commander in charge of French naval forces based in the South Seas. 'And M. [J. E. Filleau] de Saint-Hilaire, Director of the Colonies, sent me one addressed to the Frenchman in New Zealand who is like a king.'[5]

De Rosamel's letter was addressed 'To the Commanders of the French Squadrons Based in the Southern Ocean at Valparaíso' and read in part: 'I request that you receive this prelate with the honours and the attention due to his office and to his person. And most particularly do I desire that you take every opportunity of rendering him that assistance which he may need and which you are able to provide. Similar instructions are to be issued by you for commanders of ships under your orders.' The letter was dated 24 September 1836.[6]

'The Frenchman in New Zealand who is like a king' was Baron Charles de Thierry, born in London in 1794 of emigrant parents; at times he claimed French nationality and at other times English nationality. He became deeply interested in New Zealand when he met a Maori chief named Hongi from the Bay of Islands area in New Zealand. Hongi, in England to help Professor Lee of Cambridge in compiling the first Maori dictionary, painted fantastic pictures for de Thierry about the extensive lands in New Zealand that could be purchased cheaply. Being eager to get funds for purchasing firearms, Hongi without being the real owner himself sold 40,000 acres (16,000 hectares) of land to de Thierry. The new landowner proceeded to call himself 'The Sovereign Chief of New Zealand' and in 1823 began writing long letters to British authorities, trying to interest them in the country. When unsuccessful, he approached the French government in April 1825 and presented plans for settling his territory. He directed requests to the Ministers of the Navy and of the Colonies for their support in the form of a warship and some transport ships, and he also wanted the title of French governor. But in March 1826 the French government declined to offer assistance.

De Thierry, who continued to live in England, kept writing long letters about New Zealand to the British authorities. In 1834 he informed both the British and French governments that he intended to set himself up as an independent sovereign in New Zealand.[7] It was this correspondence which may have prompted de Saint-Hilaire, Director of the Colonies, to draw up his letter of introduction for Pompallier. The interest shown on the part of the French government for de Thierry, and Pompallier's hope of receiving assistance and protection from him, may well be the reason that made Pompallier decide—even before leaving France—to go to New Zealand with his missionaries and take up work first in that part of his immense vicariate.

Leaving with Pompallier for Western Oceania were four Marist priests and three Brothers. The priests, besides Chanel, were Fathers Pierre Bataillon, Claude Bret and Catherin Servant. The Brothers, Joseph-Xavier Luzy, Marie-Nizier Delorme and Michel Colombon, were all skilled in numerous trades. Colin referred to them as 'Brother-Catechists'. They belonged to the Institute of the Little Brothers of Mary, today known as the Marist Brothers. This community had been founded on 2 January 1817 by Father Marcellin-Joseph-Benoît Champagnat, a Marist priest.[8]

Day after day passed but the missionaries at Le Havre waited in vain for a favourable wind, and so Captain Rouget finally postponed departure until 10 or 12 November. Pompallier used this opportunity to rush back to Paris to care for some last-minute business and from there he wrote to Fransoni on 7 November about all that had happened since his previous letter. He also asked Fransoni to give his enclosed letter to the pope, since it requested from His Holiness once more 'his apostolic blessing so that our voyage across the seas may be happy and so that our labours in the mission may be crowned with success'.[9]

The letter to Pope Gregory XVI, dated 8 November, said, 'I shall never forget your paternal kindness, our conversations, your precious gifts, and the even more precious apostolic blessing that you so frequently granted me.' He told the pope how the ministers of the French government and even the king himself along with other members of the royal family had given him gifts, commendatory letters and helps of every kind. 'Through your blessing may the Good Shepherd make the coming voyage a prosperous one for me and my companions. We are about to sail over the most vast seas in order to seek sheep wandering without a shepherd and we hope to lead so very many of them into the flock of the Church . . . May the sheep hear the word of God! And may they be docile and persevering unto the end!'[10]

But by 12 November there was still no wind strong enough to drive the ship out to sea and departure was again postponed. On 20 November, when Pompallier and his missionaries were still waiting in Le Havre, Secretary Mai of the Evangelisation Congregation went to see Pope Gregory XVI. 'The Most Reverend Pompallier, Vicar Apostolic of Western Oceania,' he said, 'requests the faculty for himself and for his missionaries of being dispensed from using wine in the two ablutions at Mass in view of the exorbitant price of wine and the difficulty in obtaining it in that very remote vicariate.' The pope granted the faculty.[11]

Finally on 23 December, after two months of waiting, Pompallier received word from Captain Rouget that he and his missionaries should be ready to sail the next day at 10 A.M. Father Bret wrote in his diary on 24 December 1836: 'There is a northeast wind. We have been waiting for this for two months . . . At 9 A.M. we went aboard and at 11 A.M. the *Delphine* left port.' There were fourteen passengers: Pompallier and his seven missionaries, four Picpus missionaries, and two other men. As the sails unfurled and caught the wind, the missionaries chanted the Ave Maris Stella, an antiphon in honour of the Virgin Mary.[12]

The harbour report on the *Delphine* read simply: 'Destination: The South Seas.' It was Christmas Eve!

Like most sea voyages in those days, this one was not to be without drama and tragedy. The diary entries of Fathers Bret and Bataillon help one visualise what it was like:

26 December:	The wind is strong and the waves are high.
31 December:	New Year's Eve, very rough, with strong winds.
1 January:	High waves. One sail is ripped off by the wind.
2 January:	The captain has been uneasy all night . . . He finds out during the day that something is wrong with the rudder and he heads for the Canary Islands . . . There is alarm and fear because the defect is serious . . . We are 80 leagues from land . . . It is calm, or there are contrary winds.
4 January:	Rain, rain, rain, and contrary winds.
5 January:	We are 64 leagues from Tenerife where we have to put into port. An English steamer is spotted and the distress flag is hoisted. But the steamer does not respond to the signal.
7 January:	We are still five leagues from Santa Cruz.
8 January:	We arrived [in Santa Cruz] this morning and are lying one-fourth of a league from port. For eight days we had bad weather or contrary winds . . . and we made hardly 100 leagues . . . We could have lost our rudder at any moment and so would have been exposed to every danger.[13]

Santa Cruz was a port on the northeast coast of Tenerife in the Canary Islands approximately 300 kilometres off the coast of Africa. A new copper rudder had to be made. Had the *Delphine*'s rudder dropped off at sea, it would have spun around helplessly like a top in the ocean. The rudder was dismounted on 11 January 1837. But when the company engaged to repair it had not yet begun the work by 4 February, the job was turned over to another company.

Pompallier on 22 February wrote to Fransoni from Santa Cruz that 'it will suffice here to tell you only that we nearly lost the rudder of our ship when we were on the high seas . . . Our passage aboard the *Delphine* has been paid from Le Havre to Valparaíso . . . and our cash on hand is 22,000 francs. People with experience tell us that this will hardly be enough for us to get to Western Oceania', because the voyage from Chile to the islands of Oceania 'is as costly as that from Europe to the coast of South America'. Furthermore, he added, funds were needed to establish a central station in his vicariate, something 'indispensable for the welfare of the mission'. It would keep him 'in contact with Europe and at the same time with the missionaries who will be working in the midst of the savage peoples whom we are to evangelise'.[14]

Nearly all the missionaries fell ill while waiting for the rudder to be repaired. It was finally attached to the ship again on 24 February. 'And the three anchors were raised at 9 A.M.', Bataillon wrote in his diary on 28 February. 'We sailed away after having been here for 52 days.' From then on his diary repeatedly mentioned Father Bret: 1 March: 'Father Bret has had a severe headache for several days and now feels worse.' 3 March: 'Father Bret definitely has a high fever.' 16 March: 'Father Bret is still very sick'. 19 March: 'Palm Sunday. The viaticum is carried to Father Bret after Mass.' 20 March: 'Father Bret suddenly worsens . . . His blood is renewed with leeches and mustard, but to no avail . . . He loses consciousness and falls into an agony. His Excellency gives him Extreme Unction and about 7.30 P.M. we have a new protector in heaven.'

All the missionaries were present when Bret died. 'His body was laid out in a small funeral chapel on the deck of the ship', Chanel said, and throughout the night the missionaries held a wake taking turns two at a time. The next day Pompallier offered Mass for the repose of his soul and said some moving words. Bret's body was then lowered into the sea and throughout the day the ship's flag was at half mast. Chanel, who had looked after Bret in his last illness, said that he 'had repeated often that it meant little to him whether his body were to be devoured by fish or worms, provided only that his soul would be with God'.[15]

Before leaving Le Havre, Bret had written words full of hope: 'We leave with a contented mind,' he said, 'calmly placing the success of our voyage in the hands of the Blessed Virgin. How many there must be who envy our good fortune, who merit more than I to be chosen for this mission.' But Father Bret, twenty-eight years of age, never reached the southern hemisphere. He died north of the equator in the middle of the Atlantic Ocean at 0°40′ north latitude and 24°30′ west longitude, halfway between Africa and South America. It was here that he was buried at sea.[16]

One week later in Paris, on 27 March 1837, Father Coudrin, the sixty-nine-year-old founder and superior general of the Picpus Fathers, also died. His last words were 'Valparaíso . . . Gambier'.[17]

The non-stop voyage of the Marist and Picpus missionaries to Valparaíso continued. The last time they sighted land was on 11 March when they saw Santo Antão, one of the Cape Verde Islands. Between 3 and 6 June they rounded Cape Horn and finally on 28 June 1837, after having sighted land the previous day, they reached Valparaíso. Reporting on the voyage in a letter to his mother, Chanel said that the weather en route had been 'good and bad. There was rain, thunder, lightning, hail, ice and snow. It was hot and cold.' And 'sometimes we had the good fortune of being able to celebrate the Holy Sacrifice of the Mass'. Bataillon's diary for that final day read: 'We dropped anchor one hour after midday in the roads before Valparaíso. There is news of war between Chile and Peru. . . .'

Four full months had passed since the missionaries had left Santa Cruz; and six months and four days since they had left Le Havre. They had crossed the Atlantic Ocean, had sailed over 16,000 kilometres, had seen one of their members die, and still had to cross the Pacific Ocean before reaching their final destination.

Before leaving Europe, Pompallier had informed Fransoni that his future address would be 'The Retreat House of the French Fathers, Valparaíso, Chile'. The French Fathers, of course, were the Picpus Fathers, and those based at

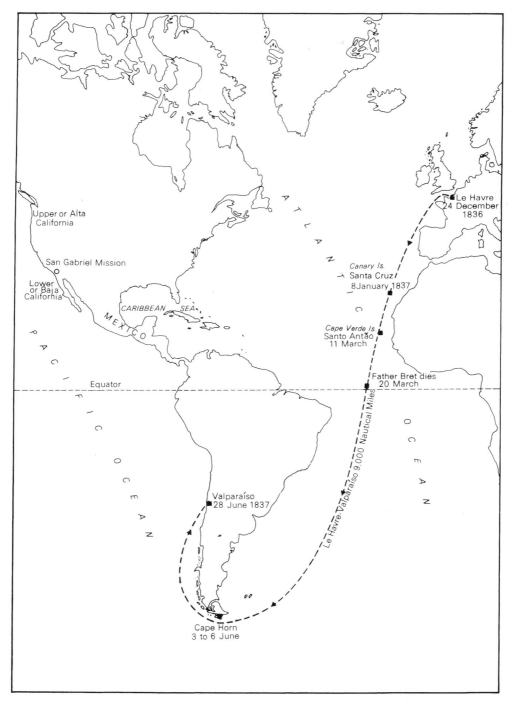

Upper or Alta
California

San Gabriel Mission

Lower
or Baja
California

MEXICO

CARIBBEAN   SEA

ATLAN

Le Havre
24 December
1836

Canary Is.
Santa Cruz
8 January 1837

Cape Verde Is.
Santo Antão
11 March

Father Bret dies
20 March

Equator

PACIFIC OCEAN

OCEAN

Le Havre-Valparaíso 9,000 Nautical Miles

Valparaíso
28 June 1837

Cape Horn
3 to 6 June

22   Bishop Pompallier and his missionaries sailed from Le Havre on 24 December 1836 for Western Oceania and reached Valparaíso on 28 June 1837. En route Father Bret had died and was buried at sea. *(Chapters 9, 35).*

Valparaíso came aboard and took the newly arrived missionaries to their chapel where the Te Deum and the Salve Regina were sung in thanksgiving to God and the Virgin Mary. The retreat house of the French Fathers was the one founded by Fray Andrés Caro, the Spanish Franciscan, whom the new missionaries met and who would continue to be active there until his death on 18 June 1844 at the age of seventy-five. His retreat house according to his own wish was now the property of the Picpus Fathers and Pompallier and his missionaries were given lodging there.

Pompallier's first plan, as announced in *L'ami de la religion* on 20 August 1836, was to visit the Tahiti and Tonga islands and then go to New Guinea.[18] But even before leaving France he had abandoned this plan in favour of starting in New Zealand. In Valparaíso, however, he found no ship that would take him there. This made him also abandon his second plan and he worked out the details of a new one, this time making Ponape in Micronesia his final destination. He succeeded in engaging Captain Stocks of the *Europa* to take him and his missionaries as far as the Sandwich Islands for 150 piastres per person. Pompallier signed the contract with Stocks on 18 July 1837.[19]

In a letter to Fransoni on 23 July, Pompallier explained what had happened. 'Up until now I had thought that New Zealand would be the first place where we would begin our labours, but in the waters of this town I do not find a ship that can take us there. Of course, I could wait here until an opportunity presents itself for us to get to that large island. But I would then have to stay here perhaps for several months and so consume a notable amount of our funds, which now are just sufficient or hardly sufficient for us to reach our mission. At this moment there is an American ship leaving for New Zealand, but the captain is Protestant and refuses to take Catholic missionaries aboard.

'Since there are no other possibilities for reaching the shores of my mission, I have been forced to take passage aboard another ship headed for the coasts of Micronesia. This is proof that God wishes us to begin our labours in the archipelagoes in the northern part of Western Oceania. I have already signed the contract with the captain of the ship *Europa*. He will bring us to the Gambier Islands, where I shall have the pleasure and advantage of visiting Bishop Rouchouze, whose Christian community provides many consolations. Then we shall put into port for a few days at Tahiti, where the Methodists do all they can to hinder the entry of Catholics . . . And from there we shall leave for Micronesia, stopping off at the Sandwich Islands.

'The island where I plan to begin missionary work is known here as Ascension Island, but geographers do not give it this name. I believe it is what they call Ponape . . . . , taken from the language of the natives. We are told that it has a population of some 10,000 souls and that the people are well disposed for the faith. I am taking all my companions there. Once this island is conquered for Jesus Christ, it will open the door for us to the entire far-flung archipelago of the Carolines. When I assign to other posts the new missionaries who are sent to me, I can then give them as guides one of the older missionaries. This way there will be uniformity of methods and the same progress will be made everywhere.

And since Ascension Island is just about in the centre of my mission,[20] I would find it easier to train my missionaries because so many archipelagoes surround us. From this island we can then reach out to New Guinea and the archipelagoes to the south as far as New Zealand.

'Missionaries coming in the future from Europe to join us at Ascension Island would do well not to go around Cape Horn. In other words they should not take the route which we took, being under the impression that here in Valparaíso we would find a good opportunity of getting passage to New Zealand. Instead the most direct route for them to follow would be the Caribbean Sea, Mexico and the Sandwich Archipelago; from there they should go to Ascension Island where we shall be.[21] If they take this route, their voyage will be about 4,000 leagues shorter than ours. Nevertheless I am very happy that this time we did come this way, because it gave us the opportunity of obtaining a vast amount of knowledge about the missionaries and the missions of Eastern Oceania. I shall also be able to learn many things from Bishop Rouchouze, the vicar apostolic.

'I did hear, of course, that one can go from Valparaíso to the Mangaia Islands, the Navigators, the Fiji Islands or the Friendly Islands. But the Methodists are there already and I am eager to begin my mission in a virgin island untouched by their errors and devoid of their threats and their hatred against Catholics. After we have obtained a foothold in our islands, we shall then more easily escape being persecuted by them and shall win over people in spite of all the efforts that they might make against us. Ascension Island, where we are going, is intact, not having any of them. Instead we shall have to combat idolatry, superstition and polygamy.'[22]

The situation in which Pompallier now found himself, of being forced to launch his missionary work in Micronesia, showed the wisdom of Pope Gregory XVI's refusal to disjoin that area from the Vicariate Apostolic of Western Oceania.

Why this sudden preoccupation and concern on the part of Pompallier with Protestant missions and missionaries, an aspect not at all in evidence in his correspondence prior to his arrival in Valparaíso? The explanation is that Protestant missionary activity constituted a major portion of that 'vast amount of knowledge about the missionaries and the missions of Eastern Oceania' which Pompallier had received from the Picpus Fathers and Brothers in Valparaíso. In fact on 13 June, just fifteen days before Pompallier and his party reached Valparaíso, Brother Colomban Murphy, the Irish Picpus missionary (who is not to be confused with Brother Michel Colombon, a Marist missionary), had just arrived in Valparaíso. He had been sent on a special mission by Bishop Rouchouze, who wanted firsthand information on Tahiti, the Sandwich Islands, and Prefect Apostolic Bachelot at San Gabriel Mission in Alta or Upper California. Murphy had sailed to Tahiti, Honolulu and Upper California. He told Pompallier that the Protestant missionaries were making preparations to prevent Catholic missionaries from landing in Tahiti. As for the Sandwich Islands, they were still closed to Bachelot, even though he was ready to return there at a moment's notice.[23]

Pompallier also learned more in detail about the difficulties that the Picpus missionaries were having with the London Missionary Society which had its headquarters in Tahiti. One of the ministers there named Darling had written as early as 14 October 1834 'To the two French missionaries who are in the Gambier Islands', inviting them to go elsewhere.[24] But the Picpus missionaries had remained and two of them, Fathers Caret and Laval, later even tried to open a mission in Tahiti. They disembarked at Tautira on 16 November 1836 and from there went on foot to Papeete at the other end of Tahiti to present themselves to Queen Pomare. They offered her a shawl and four ounces of gold which she graciously accepted as an arrival gift. But the benevolent indifference of the queen was quickly countered by the Reverend George Pritchard of the London Missionary Society. Eager to preserve his society's influential position and believing that French Catholic missionaries 'had no business in the country', he succeeded in having the two priests expelled. They were seized in their own house by Tahitian policemen on 16 December, exactly one month after their arrival, and were removed by force, put aboard a ship, and sent back to the Gambier Islands.[25]

Pompallier and the Marists heard about these difficulties from Father Désiré-Louis Maigret, the pro-vicar of Bishop Rouchouze. Maigret and Caret had both been sent by Rouchouze to Valparaíso to complain to the representatives of the French government there of the ill treatment that Frenchmen had received in Tahiti. They had arrived at Valparaíso on 22 March 1837 and had held frequent conferences with the French naval commanders and the staff of the French consulate. Two weeks after their arrival they had received a letter from Father Bachelot at San Gabriel Mission, saying that he intended to make a new effort to enter the Sandwich Islands. Caret had then sailed from Valparaíso for France aboard the man-of-war *Flore* on 6 May in order to plead the cause of the mission in Europe. Maigret had decided to wait in Valparaíso for Pompallier before returning to the Gambier Islands.[26]

Pompallier's letter of 23 July to Fransoni carried some further data to complete the cardinal's picture of how he was organising his mission. Chanel had been made pro-vicar of the mission. The mailing address for the mission would for the time being remain the same, the retreat house of the French Fathers, but Pompallier had decided against setting up a permanent supply centre at Valparaíso because 'this town is too far away from the place where we are going. It would be better to establish one on the west coast of Mexico or California.' He also had a question: 'Can I canonically assign patrons to the mission as a whole . . . and also to the prefectures apostolic that I might establish there in the future? . . . I would like the mission as a whole to be named after the Immaculate Conception . . . , a name that I have already used for it on many occasions without knowing whether or not the Holy See is agreeable.'[27]

In a letter to Colin on 28 July, Pompallier asked that he do his best 'to send four priests and three Brothers. Two priests and a Brother could be assigned to found a supply centre in California or Mexico.'[28]

'Nearly all our belongings are already aboard the *Europa*', Bataillon wrote on 30 July to a fellow Marist in France. He said that the bishop had received 'very detailed information' on Ascension Island 'from two travellers who have lived there for a long time'. The language there 'is completely different from that used in Eastern Oceania . . . , but one of the passengers travelling aboard our ship has lived on Ascension Island and will be able to give us an introduction to the language of this place. People say it is related to the language of Papua.'[29]

Chanel, who was always generous with details, had much to say about Ascension Island in a letter written the day before the *Europa* sailed. 'It is at 6°57′ north latitude and 155° east longitude and almost touches the Caroline Archipelago. Its inhabitants have neither idols nor sacrifices; they adore a Great Being without knowing who he is. Their chief priest is respected like a god and their government is monarchical. They have simultaneous polygamy and the king has as many as thirteen wives. There are some others who have five wives. The people are gentle and hospitable by nature. They are morally dissolute, although the sexes do preserve some modesty. Their clothing is a band worn around the loins which drops down to their legs. They have great respect for whites, whose knowledge they esteem highly. Their food consists of fish, turtles, breadfruit, bananas, coconuts, etc. And for drink they have good-tasting water. Someone presented the bishop with a piece of cloth that was made there and we all marvelled at its workmanship. Their tattoos are superbly designed, etc., etc. We shall tell you the rest of the news when we get there.'[30]

Pompallier's plan of reaching out from Ponape north of the equator to New Guinea, New Zealand, and other archipelagoes south of the equator sounded simple enough on paper. But vast distances, slow-moving sailing vessels, meagre funds, petty jealousies, limited personnel, and even death itself had already obstructed and would continue to obstruct the task ahead. The pace could hardly be expected to quicken once the missionaries found themselves in a tropical climate, wrestling with strange tongues and confronted with puzzling cultures. 'But the salvation of these peoples is so dear to us', Pompallier had told Fransoni from Valparaíso, 'that with help from on High we are ready to give up our blood and our life voluntarily for them.'[31]

The Vicar Apostolic of Eastern Oceania is given authority over New Zealand and the Archipelagoes of Tonga, Samoa and Fiji

14 JANUARY 1838

Bishop Pompallier's decision to go to Micronesia and make Ponape his headquarters was to have a swift reaction in France. The reaction came from Father Caret, Vice-Prefect Apostolic of Southern Oceania,[1] one of the two Picpus Fathers expelled from Tahiti. He had left Valparaíso seven weeks before Pompallier's arrival and had reached Paris on 7 September 1837, where he had been authorised by Bishop Rouchouze to plead the cause of Eastern Oceania with officials of church and state. He also had a list of difficult marriage cases and hoped to obtain solutions for them from Rome through correspondence.[2]

Coudrin had died in Paris on 27 March that year and Bonamie was elected to succeed him as superior general on 4 May 1837. Since Bonamie had been named Archbishop of Smyrna (nowadays Izmir), Turkey, early in 1835, he now resigned this see and late in 1837 was named Titular Archbishop of Chalcedon. On arriving in Paris on 1 October 1837 to take office as superior general, Bonamie found Caret waiting for him.

Writing from Paris to Pope Gregory XVI on 12 October, Caret said that the Vicar Apostolic of Eastern Oceania had sent him to France to report to the Picpus superior general 'on the state of the mission and on how necessary it is to obtain additional personnel'. He also explained why the missionaries at first had thought there was 'no true marriage in the islands of Oceania, since frequently and without serious reason a man leaves his wife—and a wife, her husband—and enters another marriage'. But the missionaries were beginning to doubt their initial stand on this matter, and in view of local customs were now confronted with difficult marriage cases. He submitted three typical ones and earnestly asked the pope for concrete solutions. He also asked that the special faculties received by the Jesuits from Pope Pius V for the Indies under date of 15 August 1572 be extended to Eastern Oceania. In a word, what the mission needed were special privileges 'better adapted . . . for spreading the faith more and more in Oceania'.[3]

Caret's letter, sent in care of Cardinal Prefect Fransoni of the Evangelisation Congregation, was forwarded on 11 November 1837 by Secretary Mai to Father Cornelius Van Everbroeck, a Jesuit consultor of that congregation in residence at his order's Roman College. Mai told Van Everbroeck that Caret had submitted 'various questions contained in the sheet attached and is anxiously awaiting replies to them, since he must return as soon as possible to his mission'.

Mai however, was 'eager to hear the views of some qualified consultor on the questions submitted', and therefore he asked the Jesuit 'kindly to indicate briefly' for him how he should judge the matter. Van Everbroeck on 21 November sent back a lengthy and detailed commentary of over a dozen pages 'on questions proposed and faculties requested' by Caret.[4]

But Caret did not wait for a reply from Mai, because on 13 November a letter arrived in Paris for the late Coudrin from Father Pagès, a Picpus priest in Valparaíso. It had been written on 18 July 1837, the very day on which Pompallier by contract had engaged Captain Stocks to take him and his missionaries aboard the *Europa* as far as the Sandwich Islands. 'Bishop Pompallier has already completed negotiations for his departure', Pagès reported. 'He will go to see Bishop Rouchouze, will then sail via Tahiti-Sandwich, and will establish himself on Ascension Island at 7° north latitude. . . .'[5]

This news about Ascension Island, startling as it was for Caret, seemed like an answer to a prayer. As vice-prefect apostolic of the southern half of the Vicariate Apostolic of Eastern Oceania, he was particularly responsible along with Bishop Rouchouze for mission strategy there, since Liausu, the prefect apostolic, was based at Valparaíso. Pompallier's going via Tahiti and the Sandwich Islands to Ascension Island meant that he was skirting and apparently avoiding heavily populated areas within his territory like New Zealand and the archipelagoes of Tonga, Samoa and Fiji, all of which were not too far distant from the Vicariate Apostolic of Eastern Oceania. A new type of strategy began to take shape in his mind and he discussed it at length with his new superior general, Archbishop Bonamie, and with Secretary General Hilarion.

His thinking, which he eventually spelled out to a large extent in a letter addressed to Pope Gregory XVI, went like this. By making Ponape his base Pompallier would be occupied for many years with the numerous islands of Micronesia and nearby Melanesia, and Protestant missionaries could meanwhile enter and gain a strong foothold in New Zealand, Tonga, Samoa and Fiji. Now the Picpus missionaries of Eastern Oceania, blocked as they were by Protestant missionaries from entering heavily populated areas within their own territory like Tahiti and the Sandwich Islands, could easily and immediately move into New Zealand, Tonga, Samoa and Fiji ahead of the Protestants, a decided advantage for missionary work. To make this possible nothing more was needed than for Rome to enlarge the Vicariate Apostolic of Eastern Oceania by separating these four areas from the jurisdiction of Pompallier and placing them under the jurisdiction of Rouchouze.[6]

Caret was of such a fiery and forceful temperament that he soon convinced Bonamie and Hilarion that directing such a request to Rome was absolutely necessary at the moment. But neither of these two officials cared to put such a petition in writing, since earlier similar requests by Rouchouze and Liausu had been ignored or refused. Prefect Apostolic Liausu had petitioned Rome from Valparaíso to extend Picpus missions westward to include 'islands, like those of Fiji, to which we have been invited and where much good can be done', but he was unsuccessful. And Rouchouze writing to the pope from Paris in 1834 had asked in vain that the Picpus missions be extended westward to include New Zealand, Chatham Islands, Kermadec Islands, Tonga Islands, Samoa Islands and Cook Islands.[7]

Bonamie and Hilarion could hardly present this petition in writing since it would prove embarrassing for them and for Rome if it had to be turned down. And even if it were granted, it could prove embarrassing because it could be considered an encroachment on the territory of Pompallier and the Marists. The plan ultimately agreed upon was for Caret to go to Rome under some pretext and there personally present his case to Pope Gregory XVI, to Cardinal Fransoni and to Secretary Mai. Caret, convinced that he would succeed where others had failed, believed that the officials in Rome—if only the matter were explained to them properly—could not but see the wisdom and urgency of the proposal. He left Paris for Rome on 4 December 1837.

Caret was armed with a letter of 3 December from Secretary General Hilarion to Secretary Mai stating that he was coming to Rome 'with the authorisation of his superior general'. His purpose was to give a report to the pope on Eastern Oceania and 'to ask for the solution of a number of difficulties'. He would also explain to Father Mai 'the enormous expenses necessary for the important mission of Eastern Oceania'. Hilarion pointed out that the voyage that Caret 'is obliged to make to Rome, and which all of us have judged indispensable if he is to be able well to explain the state of affairs and obtain a rather precise reply from the Holy Apostolic See, will cause even further expense'.

Four more priests had left for Valparaíso the previous week, Hilarion said, 'and we hope that Father Caret can take along with him an even larger number of priests and also catechists'. It was simply impossible, however, for the Picpus missionaries to perform the task expected of them with the limited financial aid that they had received from the Association for the Propagation of the Faith. But if the Evangelisation Congregation were to contribute 2,000 or 3,000 Roman scudi, he explained, this 'would facilitate the sending of two or three additional missionaries and consequently would contribute toward increasing the Kingdom of God. . . .'[8]

Superior General Bonamie also gave Caret a letter for Mai, dated 4 December, in which he explained that Caret had been sent to France by Rouchouze, 'to obtain there the solution of many difficulties regarding the marriages of savages'. Rouchouze also wanted him 'to arouse the interest of the French government in these missions'. The questions on marriage had been sent in care of Cardinal Fransoni, but there had been no reply. 'And since it is urgent that this missionary leave promptly for Oceania,' Bonamie said, 'we have considered it necessary to send him to Rome in order to solicit there the requested solutions and thus avoid very long delays. . . .'[9]

Caret arrived in Rome on the morning of 15 December 1837. Strangely enough on 16 December Cardinal Fransoni wrote to Lyon to Father Colin, superior general of the Marists, saying that his new missionaries should go to Western Oceania 'as quickly as possible'. He pointed out, however, that their speed 'would be slowed down, and the costs would be increased', if the missionaries 'assigned to Oceania were to come to Rome and spend time here'. He maintained that 'whatever is needed—like getting faculties and the necessary instructions—can be taken care of through the mail'. And he begged Colin 'not to give up this practice'. (A letter at this time covered the distance between Lyon and Rome in two weeks.) Was this advice for Colin perhaps prompted by Caret's unannounced arrival in Rome?[10]

Caret on 17 December had a private audience with Pope Gregory XVI. An undated memorandum addressed to the pope and submitted at this time, or perhaps later, stated that Caret considered it his duty to inform the pope 'on the status of various islands of Oceania which he himself has examined with his own eyes, or about which he has received information from the mouth of those who repeatedly have visited them'. He hoped that His Holiness, 'after becoming better acquainted with the inhabitants of Oceania, might provide even more suitable means for procuring their salvation'.

The three-page memorandum was devoted chiefly to a comparative study of the population of Eastern and Western Oceania. 'Many of the islands of Eastern Oceania, which are described in such great numbers on geographical charts, have absolutely no human inhabitants', Caret said. He could testify to this 'with his own eyes'. There were other inhabited islands but the people on them were few in number. 'One can therefore say that the total number of inhabitants on the various islands in the southern part [of Eastern Oceania] does not exceed 40,000. But statistics issued by the Protestants for the Sandwich Islands indicate that these islands have approximately 128,000 people.' He attributed this large population to the fact that the Sandwich Islands had 'fertile land, which produces various fruits'. The same was true for the better populated Gambier, Tahiti and Marquesas islands south of the equator. 'On the remaining islands the people eat nothing but fish and a certain kind of fruit which Europeans call the coconut. But this is found in abundance only on the island called Anaa or Chain.'

In Western Oceania 'three archipelagoes with very numerous inhabitants' were quite near to Bishop Rouchouze's vicariate, he said, 'namely, the *Tonga* or *Friendly* Archipelago, the *Navigators* [now Samoa] Archipelago, and the *Fiji* or *Viti* Archipelago'. Fiji, the one farthest away, he placed at 'approximately 175° longitude'. He added that 'the Protestants have already visited these archipelagoes, it is true, but they have not yet made much progress in disseminating heresy'.

Under a separate heading he also mentioned New Zealand and said that it alone had 'many more inhabitants than the entire vicariate of Bishop Rouchouze'. And since 'the Methodists' had already been active there for many years, it was to be feared 'that Catholics will find it most difficult to enter there once the power of heresy becomes firmly entrenched'.

Caret then said that Pompallier would be 'unequal to the task of collecting so great a harvest', since his missionaries were 'so few in number' and since his vicariate apostolic included 'so many other peoples in addition to the three designated archipelagoes and New Zealand'.[11] It must have been at this point during his audience that Caret said Pompallier would be launching his missionary work from Ponape—something not included in his memorandum—and that consequently the three archipelagoes and New Zealand could be entrusted to the Picpus missionaries.

Fransoni had Mai formally bring up this matter during his regular audience with Pope Gregory XVI on 14 January 1838, and the secretary went into great detail. He first gave the pope a quick survey of Picpus requests for broader jurisdiction in Southern Oceania and mentioned that the pope as early as 21 July 1833 had given Rouchouze Extraordinary Faculty no. 31. This authorised the bishop and through him his missionaries to make use of all faculties granted for his own territory also 'in any lands or islands whatsoever to which he might be compelled to flee by force or necessity, or be transported, as long as they had to stay there, provided only that no [other] missionary is there and the said lands or islands are not within the limits of someone's jurisdiction'.

On receiving these faculties Rouchouze had submitted a query, asking how the words 'lands or islands that are not within the limits of someone's jurisdiction' were to be understood. For example, when the Vicariate Apostolic of Eastern Oceania had been created, the islands of Southwest Oceania had been left under the jurisdiction of de Solages. 'But now that he is dead', Rouchouze had asked, 'are they still to be considered as being under someone's jurisdiction?' Mai reminded the pope how on this occasion he had authorised the cardinal prefect of the Evangelisation Congregation to draw up a reply. Rouchouze was accordingly advised on 10 January 1834 that he could exercise jurisdiction in the islands of Southwest Oceania, 'provided only that no missionary or priest has been placed there by another Ordinary'. (This meant in effect that Rouchouze's jurisdiction reached as far west as New Zealand inclusive and his territory south of the equator consequently was as vast as the earlier Prefecture Apostolic of the South Sea Islands.)

Mai then became very precise. 'The Vicariate of Eastern Oceania ends at 165° longitude', he said. 'Now very close on the other side of this longitude are three large and thickly populated archipelagoes: 1. Tonga or Friendly, 2. Navigators [now Samoa], and 3. Fiji. In addition there is New Zealand, which is very vast. At the same time one must keep in mind that Bishop Pompallier, the Vicar Apostolic of Western Oceania, has headed northward with a few companions toward Ascension Island. But in this area the islands to be visited are very numerous, and it seems also very large, and consequently he will be able to take up work in the three archipelagoes mentioned above and in New Zealand only with difficulty or at a later date. But in the meantime the souls of the heathen are perishing and the islands are being occupied daily by the Methodists, Bible Society, etc. The question has therefore been directed to Your Holiness, whether the missionaries of Eastern Oceania, who are near the places mentioned, could be authorised to assist these [places] without delay. The understanding is that as yet there are no missionaries of the western vicariate there. The stipulation would also be made that when these do arrive, the other missionaries would either hand over the area to them or would place themselves under the jurisdiction of the Local Ordinary.'

It is interesting to observe that this particular paragraph of Mai's notes is not in his own handwriting, and one cannot but wonder if the text was composed by Caret and then translated and edited for Mai. What lends weight to this assumption is the fact that the boundary in this report has been pushed from the Roggewein Archipelago (northern Cook Islands), which marked the end of the Eastern Oceania Vicariate, and the Mangaia Archipelago (southern Cook Islands), which marked the beginning of the Western Oceania Vicariate, to a point half a dozen degrees of longitude farther west. This naturally made it look as though the Samoa and Tonga islands were right on the other side of the border of the Eastern Oceania Vicariate, which technically had never been said to be 165° longitude.[12]

Pope Gregory XVI authorised the extension of Rouchouze's jurisdiction precisely as outlined by Mai. However, knowing how sensitive bishops were about their jurisdiction and how necessary it was to avoid complications in this area, he insisted that Pompallier be advised of the entire matter.[13]

The granting of this request seemingly placed the two vicars apostolic of Eastern and Western Oceania in competition with one another, since Rouchouze received temporary jurisdiction over those areas which he or his missionaries might reach before the arrival of Pompallier and his missionaries. But the concession primarily had to be looked upon in a soul-saving way, since it was a rather ingenious method of assuring the earliest possible arrival of missionaries in the three archipelagoes and in New Zealand. It was a case of mission strategy based on known or supposed factors. The feelings of Pompallier and of the Marists might be hurt, but this could not happen if they truly wished to promote the common good. And it was the common good about which the pope had to be concerned.

Cardinal Fransoni lost little time and broached the delicate matter in a letter to Pompallier on 25 January. 'The Sacred Congregation, of course, knows the vastness of the territories contained within Your Grace's vicariate apostolic', he said. 'And therefore it well understands that of necessity you will be able to take up your pastoral role in so very many of its areas only after a rather long period of time and with exceptional difficulty. Therefore it has been decided that in the meantime some other arrangement ought to be provided for these areas in order to safeguard our religion and foster its growth. This arrangement, however, in no way will lessen your jurisdiction and authority.'

Fransoni then said, 'I am referring to the very large tracts of islands called Tonga or Friendly, Navigators, and Fiji, and I am also referring to the very vast region of New Zealand. All of these places, of course, are contained within the jurisdiction of your vicariate apostolic.' But since the bishop had gone to Ascension Island with some of his missionaries in the interests of religion, and since he would be 'so intensely occupied looking after ecclesiastical matters throughout the surrounding islands', it was clear that much time would pass and many difficulties would have to be overcome before he could 'solicitously provide for the places' which Fransoni had mentioned. In the meanwhile 'the Methodists, Bible Society' and also others 'shall certainly be trying to spread their errors in these places. . . .'

Only after this long introduction did Fransoni tell Pompallier what the Evangelisation Congregation had actually done 'with the approval of His Holiness, Pope Gregory XVI'. It was the pope who had granted Rouchouze 'necessary and adequate faculties so that personally or through priests sent by him he can exercise jurisdiction without delay in those islands and in New Zealand, just as he can in areas contained within the limits of his own vicariate. . . .' Fransoni also mentioned in detail the various conditions under which these faculties had been granted.[14]

On the same day Fransoni sent Rouchouze a decree which described the new jurisdiction that would be his 'on an interim basis'. He also assured the bishop that Caret had been given solutions to his difficult marriage cases and that he had received as well a special 'Instruction' on the matter approved by the pope. This 'Instruction' dealt with 'heathens living in polygamy who become Catholics'. A copy had also been enclosed with the letter sent to Pompallier so that a uniform practice could be followed in Oceania.[15]

On 21 December 1837, just four days after Caret's audience with the pope, he had addressed a lengthy petition for funds to Fransoni. He said that Rouchouze had spent 'the last of his money' to send him to implore help from Rome, and he hoped that he had not made 'this voyage of almost 6,000 leagues in vain'. He believed that 'the missionaries of Oceania truthfully have greater need of funds than those living on continents, because the former are obliged to use ships or at least large boats . . . We would need a schooner strong enough to withstand the sea and transport us from one island to another for a distance of a thousand leagues or so.' Such a ship, he thought, could not be obtained for less than 20,000 or 30,000 piastres.

Caret reminded the cardinal that 'our antagonists, the Protestants, have ships . . . and their own ships bring them wherever they want to go and whenever they want to go there!' According to him the Protestants had at their disposal 'huge sums of money which they use to win over all the chiefs'. Now if the Evangelisation Congregation were to make a donation , he said, then Catholic missionaries could 'counterbalance to some extent the ministers of heresy, especially by furnishing clothes for our people so they can cover themselves and tools so they can work the land and cut down trees'. If we cannot give such gifts to the people, 'it is to be feared that we shall not only be unable to found new missions, but we shall also lose those which seem to promise so much consolation for the Church'. He was well aware that Jesus Christ 'has no need of human means, and I do have full confidence in him and in his august Mother. But Your Eminence knows much better than I that these human means do help.'

He stressed how difficult it would be for Catholic missionaries to counteract 'the Protestants who are always calumniating the Holy Roman Church and who make themselves heard by their money'. If the Catholic missionaries were to insist 'that the Church of Rome is not as bad as the Protestants maintain, but on the contrary that it is good, that it loves them, that it is their mother, and that the pope is their father, how shall we prove this to these savages, who are so simple, if we have nothing to give them from our Holy Father, the Pope? But if the Evangelisation Congregation should give us some money, we shall say to them: "Look how good our Holy Father, the Pope, is, and how much he loves you! He is the good father who sends you these clothes for covering yourselves and these tools for improving your status by working." Only then, Your Eminence, will the savages listen to us and be deaf to the calumnies of the Protestants.'

He concluded where he should have begun, he said, and asked how the missionaries could build even reasonably decent churches without money. 'If Your Eminence could see where we celebrate Holy Mass, you would weep. And if Your Eminence could witness the kind of life' led by Bishop Rouchouze, 'you would take all possible measures to give not only what I ask, but a hundred times more'. In order to spare His Eminence the pain of having to refuse, however, Caret said he would ask 'for no more than 3,000 Roman scudi'. In the name of 'poor Oceania which holds its arms outstretched to the Holy Father', he earnestly begged for 'at least' this amount.[16]

Caret was most successful and obtained the desired amount of money.

Fransoni on 25 January 1838 wrote to Archbishop Bonamie, the Picpus superior general, that Caret himself 'will tell you with what benevolence he was received by us and by His Holiness. . . .' Fransoni then went into some detail about where and how the money was to be used. 'Since the Sacred Congregation is eager to make sound provisions for the growth of our Catholic religion in the very vast Vicariate Apostolic of Eastern Oceania, it has decided that action must be taken to achieve this in every way possible. And although its treasury is hard pressed and has very serious daily obligations, it has nevertheless decided that 3,000 Roman silver scudi should be allocated for this project so beneficial to religion.' The letters of credit for receiving that amount were also enclosed and Bonamie was instructed to make sure 'that this sum of money in its entirety is given to the Reverend François [-d'Assise] Caret, who on returning to Eastern Oceania will hand it over to the vicar apostolic. And he in turn, according to the will of the Sacred Congregation, will use it for the good of religion within the territory of Eastern Oceania. . . .'[17]

In his letter of the same date to Rouchouze, Fransoni also indicated the specific sum, mentioned that the bishop would receive it from Caret, and pointed out that the grant had been made because the Sacred Congregation wanted to provide in a substantial way 'for the increase of religion in the very vast district of your vicariate apostolic'.[18]

From these two letters to Bonamie and Rouchouze it was clear that the Evangelisation Congregation was most eager for the Picpus Fathers to make serious efforts toward establishing the Church in Eastern Oceania—the only place where the donation could be used—before considering anything like a transfer en masse to Southwest Oceania. Having more than two hundred years of experience in conducting missionary work, the Sacred Congregation was well aware that it would not be long before additional vicariates apostolic would be established in Oceania. And it was important that someone be concerned about Eastern Oceania, no matter what the possibilities were elsewhere.

Caret thanked Cardinal Fransoni for the donation on 24 March 1838 and soon after sailed from France for Valparaíso with four priests and three Brothers.[19] Would some of these go to New Zealand and the archipelagoes of Tonga, Samoa and Fiji? At this point no one could tell.

Caret's request that Rome extend his bishop's jurisdiction to New Zealand and other archipelagoes of Western Oceania was better founded and more opportune than he himself realised. On 18 December 1837, the day after his audience with Pope Gregory XVI, *An Ordinance Rejecting the Catholic Religion* was issued by Kamehameha III, sovereign of the Sandwich Islands, at Lahaina, Maui. This *Ordinance* in part read:

' . . . I, with my chiefs, forbid, by this document that any one should teach the peculiarities of the Pope's religion, nor shall it be allowed to any who teaches those doctrines or those peculiarities to reside in this kingdom; nor shall the ceremonies be exhibited in our kingdom, nor shall any one teaching its peculiarities or its faith be permitted to land on these shores; for it is not proper that two religions be found in this small kingdom. Therefore we utterly refuse to allow any one to teach those peculiarites in any manner whatsoever. We moreover prohibit all vessels whatsoever from bringing any teacher of that religion into this kingdom. . . .

'If the master of a vessel shall refuse to obey this law and shall set on shore the teacher prohibited by this act, in contempt of the government, then the vessel shall be forfeited to the chiefs of these islands and become theirs, and the cargo on board the vessel shall likewise become theirs, and the master of the vessel shall pay the sum of ten thousand dollars, but it may be optional with the chiefs to remit any part of the sum.

'Moreover if a stranger shall present himself as a mechanic, a merchant or of any other business, and it shall be granted him to reside here, and afterwards he shall be found teaching the doctrine of the Pope or any thing else whereby this kingdom shall be disturbed, this law shall be in force against him and he may be retained a prisoner or banished, after he shall have paid a fine at the discretion of the chiefs.

'That this law may be extensively known, it shall be printed and published, and on the arrival of a vessel, it shall be the duty of the Pilot to carry with him this law and give it to the master of the vessel that he may not be ignorant of the law. . . .

'If any one, either foreigner or native, shall be found assisting another in teaching the doctrine of the Pope's religion, he shall pay to the government a fine of one hundred dollars for every such offence.'[20]

Kamehameha III, who signed the *Ordinance* and had succeeded to the throne in 1825 after the death of Kamehameha II in England, would reign until 1854.

I I

Pompallier leaves Valparaíso for Ponape in Micronesia

10 AUGUST 1837

Bishop Pompallier and his three priests and three Brothers left Valparaiso aboard the *Europa* on 10 August 1837 with Ponape in Micronesia as their ultimate goal. With them were Father Maigret and Brother Murphy, the two Picpus missionaries who wished to give Bishop Rouchouze in the Gambier Islands a personal report on the assignments that he had entrusted to them. Also on board was Picpus Father Potentien Guilmard, on his way to Mangareva. It took thirty-four days to reach the Gambier Islands due to eight days of calm and three days of contrary winds.

'Aboard ship we applied ourselves diligently to the study of English', Pompallier wrote Colin. 'This language is indispensable for missionaries in Oceania both for travel and for various apostolic activities.' He said that almost the only ones to sail these seas were Englishmen and Americans 'and they can be found on all the islands. There are also many natives who understand English.' Although the French missionaries found English to be 'quite difficult because of the pronunciation', they did have 'some success' in learning it. Their teacher was Brother Murphy whose mother tongue was English. Pompallier excused the three Brothers from studying English because 'they will not have as great a need for it as the rest of us'.[1]

Gambier Islands

The *Europa* reached Mangareva, largest of the Gambier Islands, on Wednesday, 13 September 1837. It was about 8 P.M. when the ship dropped anchor. At once Maigret and Murphy accompanied Pompallier, Chanel and Brother Michel Colombon by rowboat to the small island of Aukéna where Rouchouze had his residence. 'It took three hours of rowing and we arrived by bright moonlight at 11.30 P.M.', Pompallier said. Nearly all inhabitants of the island were waiting with Rouchouze to greet the newcomers. On the following morning, feast of the Exaltation of the Holy Cross, Pompallier celebrated a solemn Mass in his brother bishop's 'cathedral', which was 'made of reeds and covered with thatch'.

After Mass and a 'frugal breakfast', Rouchouze and Pompallier in pontifical robes left for Mangareva 'where the king of the entire Gambier Archipelago lives'. His name was Maputeoa and he had been baptised just the year before on 25 August at Taku in a class of 160. Maputeoa had taken 'Gregory' as his baptismal name in honour of Pope Gregory XVI who had sent the Picpus missionaries to Eastern Oceania. On 15 August, one month prior to Pompallier's arrival the king had solemnly placed his islands under the protection of the Blessed Virgin Mary.

After the two bishops had paid their respects to the king, Rouchouze conducted Pompallier to a slight elevation for the *Tapena* ceremony which was to be held in his honour. At the order of the king issued through a member of his court, one person after another presented gifts, piling them at the feet of Pompallier. There were coconuts, bananas, sugar cane, breadfruit, fish, poultry, etc. 'Everyone took part in this offering of presents', Chanel later reported. This ceremony was followed by a war dance depicting the fighting tactics earlier used by the Mangarevans.[2]

Pompallier and his missionaries spent that second night at Mangareva, had Mass there the next morning, and then went back to Aukéna for dinner and for further discussions with Rouchouze at his residence. 'I was able to speak with His Grace on many things of importance concerning the missions of Oceania', Pompallier told Colin. 'And we delegated our faculties to one another, something which could prove useful during times of persecution or in other difficult circumstances.'[3] This mutual delegation of faculties meant that each bishop was empowered by the other to authorise his own missionaries to work in the vicariate apostolic of the other. The situation being such as it was in Tahiti and in the Sandwich Islands, where English and American Protestants had influenced local leaders to oppose French Catholics, Rouchouze was beginning to fear that he would be able to place men nowhere but in the Gambier Islands.[4]

When Pompallier and his missionaries boarded the *Europa* again on the afternoon of 15 September, Rouchouze joined them for further discussions until the captain hoisted the anchor. About 10.30 P.M. the ship set sail for what Pompallier called 'the intolerant island of Tahiti, where I expected nothing good'.[5]

One of the early decisions that Rouchouze had made on hearing that Pompallier was headed for Ponape via the Sandwich Islands was to have Maigret and Murphy accompany him part of the way. Their instructions were to attempt to take up residence in the Sandwich Islands in case Bachelot's new attempt to do so should fail.[6] Unknown to Pompallier and his missionaries, they now had aboard a newly ordained priest. In a secret ordination ceremony early that same morning, 15 September 1837, Brother Colomban Murphy had become Father Colomban Murphy. Bishop Rouchouze had ordained him on Taravai Island in the presence of no other witness but his pro-vicar, Father Maigret. If Murphy's ordination should become known, Rouchouze thought, it would jeopardise his chances of getting into the Sandwich Islands, and so it had to be kept secret from everyone.[7]

Bishop Rouchouze on 14 November, when the next ship passed through the Gambier Islands, sent some details about Pompallier's visit to Father Coudrin in Paris.[8] He had not yet learned that Coudrin had been dead for nearly eight months and that Archbishop Bonamie on 4 May had been elected to succeed him as superior general.

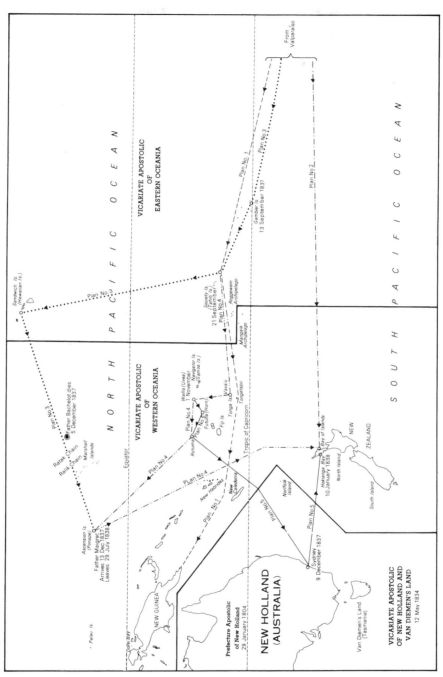

23 Bishop Pompallier's plans for reaching Western Oceania from Valparaíso had to be changed repeatedly. Initially he had New Guinea as his goal (plan one), but New Guinea was subsequently dropped in favour of New Zealand (plan two). Difficulties then caused him to choose Ponape as his residence and he arranged to sail there via Tahiti and the Sandwich Islands (plan three). After reaching Tahiti, however, he found it possible to go to Ponape by a more direct route, but he now planned only to visit it and then make his residence in New Zealand (plan four). After reaching Wallis he decided to forego a visit to Ponape for the time being and instead to go to New Zealand via Futuna, Rotuma and Sydney (plan five). He reached New Zealand on 10 January 1838. (Chapters 11, 12, 13).

Tahiti

The voyage from the Gambier Islands to Tahiti lasted five and a half days. 'It was about midday on 21 September [1837] when we arrived', Chanel wrote. 'Canoes surrounded our ship and we received visitors of every sort. Among the many who embarked was Mr Moerenhout, the American consul, who came to offer all the services in his power to the bishop and to Father Maigret.'[9]

Jacques Antoine Moerenhout (1796–1879), born in Belgium while it was annexed to France, had been named United States consul in 1835. At a reunion of Tahiti chiefs at Moorea in the presence of Queen Pomare IV on 27 January 1836 he was authorised to perform his new functions at Papeete. In November of that same year, when Fathers Caret and Laval had attempted to found a Catholic mission in Tahiti, Moerenhout gave them lodging and protected them, but was not able to prevent their expulsion one month later. He nevertheless took energetic action with the Tahitian government on behalf of the two priests. As a result the Tahitian government sent a protest to the United States government and Moerenhout on 18 July 1837 was relieved of his office.[10] This action took place two months prior to the arrival of Pompallier, but apparently the news of Moerenhout's dismissal had not yet covered the distance from Washington to Tahiti.

The *Europa* was still anchored at Tahiti when the French government on 29 September 1837 sent a dispatch from Paris to its chargé d'affaires at the Holy See. 'In your meetings with His Eminence, Cardinal Lambruschini,' it read, 'you will be able to inform him of an item of special interest to the Holy See. Namely, the king's government has learned that two French missionaries of the Gambier Islands were violently expelled from Tahiti as a result of intrigues by English missionaries . . . It has therefore charged the commander at the French base in the South Seas to send ships to the Society Islands to ask redress from the government of these islands and to demand that French missionaries shall not be exposed to similar treatment there in the future.'

Lambruschini as nuncio apostolic in Paris had earlier dealt with de Solages and was well informed of the entire mission effort in the South Seas. He had been a member of the Evangelisation Congregation since becoming a cardinal and was now also secretary of state for Pope Gregory XVI. On receiving this message he forwarded a copy of it to Cardinal Fransoni of the Evangelisation Congregation, saying that from it Fransoni could see that 'the government itself will be providing protection for French missionaries in Tahiti'.[11]

'The first favour' that Moerenhout performed for Bishop Pompallier and Pro-Vicar Maigret, Chanel said, was 'to obtain permission from the queen for them and all their missionaries to set foot on the island'. Dressed in his episcopal robes and accompanied by his missionaries, Pompallier was preceded and followed by a large and curious crowd as he walked toward the residence of Moerenhout. It looked as if the consul's home was being 'besieged by the crowd'. And in spite of the bias that had been spread, Chanel said 'the people did not at all seem frightened by our presence. On the contrary, a large number even loudly maintained that they wanted us to remain there among them.' Pompallier also paid a courtesy visit to the queen.[12]

Writing to Colin from Tahiti on Monday, 2 October, Pompallier could not say enough about the goodness of Moerenhout. He was full of kindness toward the bishop and his missionaries and had made himself their protector. 'Nearly each day we go walking and people greet us', Pompallier said. 'Yesterday I celebrated Mass in the home of the American consul, but of course the authorities of the country were not aware of this.'

Pompallier also told Colin that on 1 October he had baptised a boy 'about six years of age who was born in New Zealand. The father is employed on our ship, is a Catholic, and has promised to raise him according to the Church's teaching. Up until this time people in Tahiti have been caring for him, but now he is going out to sea with his father. I baptised him solemnly aboard ship in my cabin before the makeshift altar where I say Mass. I also gave him confirmation and all priests and catechists were present. This tiny Christian has thus become for the Church the first of its New Zealand children. Doesn't it seem as though he is anticipating the good news that we so happily are bringing to these distant peoples?'

(Father Maigret on 23 September had already solemnly baptised Marie-Célestine Brémond, about two years old, most probably the first person to receive solemn Roman Catholic Baptism in Tahiti. Her mother was Tahitian; her father was French.)

But the biggest news Pompallier had for Colin was his new plan for reaching Ponape. 'Here in Tahiti I am chartering a schooner which belongs to Mr Moerenhout himself . . . At the price of 400 piastres a month I can have the ship for an unlimited amount of time and am free to have it stop at whatever islands I point out as we pass through the Friendly [or Tonga] Islands, Navigators [or Samoa] Islands, Fiji Islands and Ponape Archipelago. Our captain, who is an excellent sailor and had already made many voyages to the archipelagoes of Oceania, has even resided on the island of Ponape or Ascension. He is known there and is well liked. I shall most probably go on to Sydney and try to enter New Zealand from there with a priest and one or two of our Brothers. In this case, as you can see, I shall be making two groups out of my small and dear company. Nevertheless I have no intention of leaving for New Zealand until after I have visited Ponape and have checked on the dispositions of the islanders, about whom I have received such very satisfactory reports.'

Moerenhout's schooner, called the *Raiatea*, was named after the most populated island among the Îles sous le Vent, a group in the Society Islands. The word meant 'clear (atea) sky (rai)'.

Seeing the vast possibilities and recognising the inadequacy of his staff, Pompallier asked Colin to send him more personnel as soon as possible. He also wished him to pass on all the latest news to the Association for the Propagation of the Faith in Lyon and to try to obtain more funds from that organisation. 'My cash box will be empty at any moment', he said, and he needed abundant funds in order to be able 'to cross the seas of Oceania in all directions'. Without such funds his missionary activity would be greatly hampered. 'Heresy will make headway in those archipelagoes, where we do not go, and numerous souls will be lost . . . Oh God! Who will give us wings to transport ourselves with speed and so make it possible to multiply our presence in all places!'[13]

Pompallier now had a fourth plan! He would open one mission in Ponape and another in New Zealand. But with two missions so far apart and a cash box that was nearly empty, how would it be possible for him to sail back and forth between his two missions in order to supervise the work of his men? Circumstances had forced Rouchouze to keep his men close together; Pompallier seemed intent on spreading his far apart.

Fransoni was informed by Pompallier of the reasons which prompted him to transfer to the *Raiatea*, whose captain and crew were ready to sail immediately. 'By chartering this schooner I could avoid losing the month that it would take to travel from Tahiti to the Sandwich Islands. But far more important than this consideration, was the fact that with the schooner I would be able to pass right through the islands within my jurisdiction on my way from Tahiti to Ponape. And I could have the captain stop at any islands of my choice.'

Pompallier admitted to Fransoni that he thereby would lose the money already paid in Valparaíso for the balance of the *Europa* voyage from Tahiti to the Sandwich Islands. But the voyage from Tahiti to Ponape aboard the *Raiatea*, he said, 'was not to be any more expensive' than the additional voyage that he would still have to make from the Sandwich Islands to Ponape.[14]

Maigret and Murphy, however, continued their voyage aboard the *Europa*. While in Tahiti they had learned that Bachelot had indeed gone to Honolulu, but officials there would not allow him to remain permanently in the country. Since Maigret had never been expelled, and since Murphy was not known to be a priest, both felt that they might well succeed where Bachelot had failed. The *Europa* set sail from Tahiti on 6 October for Honolulu.[15]

Two days earlier, on 4 October 1837 about 10 A.M., the *Raiatea* left Tahiti. 'I had the intention of going to Ponape,' Pompallier said, 'stopping en route at Vava'u, Wallis and Rotuma, and then finishing the voyage in New Zealand.'[16] In separating from Murphy at this time he had lost his English teacher and his interpreter. 'I could understand English a little when it was written', he said, 'but not at all when it was spoken.' And since the captain of the *Raiatea* was an Englishman, Pompallier used his dictionary whenever talking to him. The captain, in order to be understood by the bishop, had to put in writing whatever he wanted to say.[17]

Vava'u

The first inhabited island within the limits of his vicariate apostolic visited by Pompallier was Vava'u in the Tonga Archipelago. 'On our arrival there God spared us from a shipwreck which seemed inevitable', he said. 'The wind had died down and the current was pulling us toward the rocks. Rain, lightning and thunder added to the horror of our predicament. And the foam created by the sea crashing against the rocks had already encircled our ship. We were on the point of being dashed to pieces! But at that very moment, when all of us were resigned to die, a stiff breeze came from the direction of the rocks themselves, something that the captain had never expected. Immediately it pushed us out to sea and away from all danger.'[18]

The captain waited until daybreak to bring the ship into port. Pompallier then had his missionaries recite the Veni Creator, Ave Maris Stella and Miserere for God's blessing on the people of Vava'u. He prescribed the same prayers for nine consecutive days and said that this should be done each time the *Raiatea* dropped anchor at an island. He himself said a prayer of exorcism.

The natives tried to speak English with Pompallier. Fortunately he found an interpreter, a French sailor named Charles Simonet, who had been living on the island for nearly twelve years. He had served under Captain d'Urville of the *Astrolabe* and was able to supply Pompallier with useful data on Vava'u and neighbouring islands. He was also well informed on the activities of the Wesleyan Missionary Society (Methodist).[19] This Protestant group had opened a mission in Tonga in 1822, discontinued it one year later, and then sent John Thomas and John Hutchinson to reopen it in June 1826.[20] Thomas was active in the Vava'u group when Pompallier arrived.

Thomas Boog, an American Protestant and trader who knew the Vava'u language, gave further assistance. Boog and Simonet together arranged an interview for the bishop with the king and also served as interpreters. When Pompallier asked if he could leave two of his missionaries there to study and to teach, the king gave his consent on condition that John Thomas, the chief Methodist missionary, then absent, had no objection. The king also accepted Pompallier's invitation to dine aboard the *Raiatea*.

One day with Simonet as guide the missionaries climbed a hill and buried at the top of it some religious articles. They also chanted the Ave Maris Stella, thus taking spiritual possession of this first island in their vicariate in the name of Mary. But after the return of Thomas, the king informed Pompallier that none of his companions would be allowed to remain at Vava'u. Not being able to speak his language, the bishop decided not to object and left on good terms with the king, promising to visit him again after having learned the Tonga language.[21]

It was during this week at Vava'u that Pompallier began to have misgivings regarding his plan of assigning Chanel to head one group of missionaries in Ponape while he himself headed another in New Zealand. He had noticed that in the Friendly or Tonga Islands the Wesleyan Missionary Society was using 'occupancy' as a title to spiritual ownership, just as the London Missionary Society had done at Tahiti and elsewhere. 'Occupancy' is the actual taking possession of a thing, which belongs to no one, with the intention of making it one's own. Simonet and Boog confirmed the fears of Pompallier about the activity of the Methodists.

Actually, as early as 1821 the Anglican minister Samuel Marsden of New Holland, wanting to intensify missionary work in Oceania, had made a concrete suggestion along these lines to the various Protestant missionary groups. 'It appears to me', he said, 'that it would be a wise and prudent measure for each

Society to select their separate fields for their missionaries to labour in . . . New Zealand for the Church M[issionary] S[ociety], the Friendly Islands for the Wesleyan Society & the Society Islands for the London M[issionary] S[ociety].'[22] Pompallier had no alternative but to follow suit. 'I judged that they were on the point of taking over Wallis and the surrounding islands', he wrote Fransoni about the Methodists in Vava'u, 'and therefore I hastened to get there before them.'[23]

Two other reasons influenced him in the choice of Wallis. There was the assurance that its population was over 2,000.[24] And Boog, the American trader, knew the language of Wallis and had agreed to act as interpreter there. In exchange for this service he was to get free passage as far as Futuna, where he hoped to start a trade store.[25]

Wallis (Uvea)

On All Saints Day, 1 November 1837, three days after leaving Vava'u, the *Raiatea* arrived at the island of Wallis, often called Uvea. As the ship came into port two chiefs came out in a canoe to meet it. One was Pelo, an acquaintance of the captain, and the other was Tahangara, who lived on a nearby island. Both had acquired a smattering of English from American and English sailors who periodically lived in their midst. Pelo later accompanied the captain, Pompallier, Bataillon and Boog to the house of King Lavelua for a presentation of gifts. For two hours they walked through village after village filled with friendly people before reaching Lavelua's house. Pompallier had instructed the captain to identify his party as travellers interested in learning the Wallis language. And he was to add that they would leave the island at once if the king did not wish to have them remain.

From a French sailor and other Europeans living on the island, Pompallier had learned that a foreigner could live quite well if he enjoyed the favour of the king and had a supply of trade goods. The people there had fruit, vegetables, fish, birds, pigs and fowl in abundance. During a second visit to the king Pompallier's party included Father Bataillon and Brother Joseph-Xavier Luzy, a carpenter. Lavelua agreed to Pompallier's request and allowed these two missionaries to take up residence in his village. Bataillon, who was twenty-seven years old at this time, was placed in charge. The king promised to provide them with food and lodging.

Pompallier dedicated this first mission in his vicariate to Saint John the Baptist. He gave Bataillon a few hundred francs for buying provisions from passing ships and a large quantity of trade goods that were supposed to last for nine months. When the baggage of the two missionaries was transferred to Lavelua's house, the locks were broken open en route and some articles were stolen, but Lavelua ordered that the stolen goods had to be returned. The bishop gave him assurance that within six months he or some of his priests would again be paying a visit to Wallis.[26]

'We were on the point of leaving for Rotuma', Pompallier said, 'when a dozen people sent word asking if I would take them along to the island of Futuna, their native land.' They had come to Wallis to visit relatives and friends. 'After reaching an agreement with my captain, I gladly took them aboard. I had wanted to visit Futuna on the way', Pompallier said, 'and this circumstance made me decide definitely to do so.'[27]

Futuna did not appear in the original plans drawn up by Pompallier in Tahiti. 'But God with time makes his will more clearly manifest and obliges us to make decisions other than those which we first conceived', he said. 'And as I approached these islands, that is what happened to me!'[28]

Futuna (Horn)

The *Raiatea* reached Futuna or Horn Island southwest of Wallis on 8 November after a voyage of less than a day.[29] One of the men who came aboard was Keletaona, whose father once was one of the two kings who ruled the island. He spoke some English, having worked on an Australian whaler for five years, during which time he was nicknamed Sam. Because of his travels he at once recognised Pompallier and his companions as missionaries. 'Stay on this island and instruct us', he said.

Keletaona took Pompallier, Chanel and the others to pay their respects to Niuliki, the more powerful of the current two kings. 'After spending four days at this island and seeing all the favourable conditions which it offered for the holy ministry', Pompallier later told Fransoni, 'I offered the king my pro-vicar, Father Chanel, and also a catechist to assist him. Both of them were accepted.' Chanel was thirty-four years of age, eldest of the priests assigned to Pompallier. The catechist was Brother Marie-Nizier Delorme. Pompallier estimated the island's population to be about a thousand and said 'they seemed to be even better disposed than the people of Wallis'. He dedicated this mission to Saint Francis of Assisi.

Pompallier was not able to pay his respects to the second king, because a sudden change in wind made it necessary for the *Raiatea* to set sail immediately. He left presents with Chanel, however, for delivery to this king.[30] When reporting to Fransoni where he had made his first two foundations, Pompallier said that they were 'only 40 leagues' distant from one another and so 'the two priests can visit each other from time to time'.[31]

Rotuma

While in Futuna, Pompallier had met '14 shipwrecked English Protestants', the captain, officers and sailors of the whaler *Ariete*, which had made one of its last stops at Fiji. 'On learning that I was going to visit the island of Rotuma, and then go on to Sydney in order to proceed from there to New Zealand . . . , they approached me through their captain and asked to be taken aboard my schooner. Some wanted to go to Rotuma and others to Sydney. I was not able to say no to their requests . . . , and so all of them full of gratitude came aboard.' It was 'about 15 November' when Pompallier reached Rotuma, an island some 640 kilometres north of Suva, Fiji, but not a part of the Fiji Islands. He stayed there 'only a day', landing according to local tradition at Oinafa on the northeast corner of the island. He said that two of the principal chiefs on the island offered him hospitality. 'But I could only promise them that after a while I would send them some of my companions,' Pompallier said, 'because I had only one priest and one catechist left, and it was necessary for me to take them along to New Zealand. This place is an island—or rather two islands—that are heavily populated. And from Tahiti onwards I have been receiving the most favourable information about them.'[32]

Pompallier was becoming more and more preoccupied with New Zealand. 'I decided to go there myself and start the mission,' he explained to Fransoni in a long report, 'because I feared that I would run the risk of not getting into New Zealand, if I did not take action at once.' He knew that various Protestant groups had already opened missions there. And so, like Rotuma, Ponape was also not to receive any personnel at this time. 'The Lord showed me by circumstances', he told Fransoni, 'that it was necessary to let Ponape wait until the arrival of a new group of missionaries, whom I expect to receive from the Society of Mary.'

Six of the shipwrecked sailors disembarked at Rotuma, where they hoped to be picked up by a hospitable whaler. The other eight, including the captain and the officer, stayed aboard for the voyage to Sydney. In explaining to Fransoni why he decided to visit Sydney, when his real destination was New Zealand, Pompallier pointed out several reasons. At Sydney he could become personally acquainted with Bishop Polding, the Vicar Apostolic of New Holland. Also, he hoped to find a safe place to store temporarily his vast amount of mission supplies. But his chief reason for going to Sydney, he said, was to obtain from the English authorities there the assurance of their protection, something which would 'assist me in surmounting the difficulties that awaited me in New Zealand'.[33]

Pompallier's fourth plan, designed to bring him to Ponape and then to New Zealand, was now dropped in favour of a fifth plan which would by-pass Ponape and bring him from Rotuma to New Zealand via Sydney. In retrospect it is interesting to note that Father de Solages on 25 October 1829 had envisioned practically the same route that was ultimately followed by Pompallier after unforeseeable factors had made him alter or reject his four previous plans. When indicating the route to be followed by the ship promised to him by the Ministry of the Navy and of the Colonies, de Solages was very precise about the places where he wished his missionaries to begin work. 'From the Society Islands', he said, 'we shall head for the Friendly Islands, visiting Vava'u, Tongatapu, etc. . . . And from the Friendly Islands, otherwise known as Tonga, we shall sail for the Fiji Islands . . . And then the ship shall pursue its course toward New Zealand. . . .'[34]

The *Raiatea* on leaving Rotuma took a course between the Fiji Islands and New Caledonia and was still en route to Sydney when Colin on 1 December sent Fransoni the sad news that Father Bret had died at sea. 'We can reasonably presume', he added, that the missionaries have now reached their destinations. He told the cardinal that he intended to send three or four more priests and two Brothers to Western Oceania in 1838.[35]

Ponape

As Bishop Pompallier was fast approaching Sydney, he could not have known that Father Maigret was just as quickly approaching Ponape! He and Murphy had reached Honolulu by 2 November, the day after Pompallier had reached Wallis. The two Picpus missionaries upon arrival had to sign a statement for the Queen Regent Kaahumanu II in which they said, 'The undersigned passengers on board the *Europa* promise not to interfere with the laws and regulations of the Sandwich Islands during their sojourn, and promise to leave the islands at the first favourable opportunity.'

The queen regent replied on the same day: ' . . .You have not stated definitely to me in writing what countrymen you are, what your employments are, and how long you wish to stay.' She also wanted to know 'to what country you wish to go by the first favourable opportunity . . . And if you or either of you are priests of the religion of the pope, or of any other office, make it known to me, do not hide it from me, for this is the only reason why I hesitate to allow you to land. I do not desire propagators of that religion to dwell here. That is tabu.' Murphy made no reply, fearing that his words might reveal his ordination and spoil his chances of landing. When the British consul subsequently declared that Murphy was not a priest, he was allowed to land. Maigret on 3 November said merely that he was a Frenchman seeking 'passage to the Marquesas or the Dangerous Archipelago Islands. . . .'

But the queen regent after questioning Dudoit, the French consul, found out that Maigret was a priest and accused him of deceit. Then Dudoit on 6 November presented her with a lengthy memorandum in French on Maigret's case and that of Father Bachelot, who had come from California. He was still there but had been ordered to leave. Dudoit requested that both of them be allowed to remain on the basis of a recent agreement made with France. And he asked that she make her reply in writing so that he could present his request and her reply to his government.

She answered on 8 November; it was the same day that Pompallier had arrived at Futuna. 'We protect all strangers', she said. 'But on account of former difficulties and dissensions, our minds are made up not to consent that Roman Catholic priests come here from any country . . . Moreover, I want to make known to you that the Romish priest Maigret concealed from me his country and his being a priest, as though he wished to land privately and dwell here, so we could not remove him. And when he could no longer conceal this, he stated that he was a Frenchman wishing to go to the Marquesas. We know, however, that vessels do not sail directly from these islands to the Marquesas. And if they do, they usually touch at the Societies, whence he has come. I cannot therefore by any means confide in his word . . . If you have the power to do so, I beg you to put Bachelot on board the ship *Europa*, about to sail for China, so that he may leave the country in accordance with the word of the commodore. If the governments of France and England and America desire the peace and quiet of my country and my king, they will allow us to enforce our laws prohibiting priests of the Roman Catholic religion. This is my reply to your letter. Moreover, let Monsieur Maigret go away in the ship in which he came. And you will please make known my letter to the Government of France with kindness.'

Maigret maintained that the Sandwich Islands authorities had been deceived about his position by others, since he himself had 'made no secret of it to anybody'. And when asked 'to what nation I belonged and if I was a priest, I answered at once, and did not hide anything.' But the authorities 'pretended to believe that I had connived with those that had deceived it, and this was one of the reasons why I was forbidden to go ashore. I protested . . . It was all in vain.'

Bachelot, also banned from the Sandwich Islands, had been waiting in Honolulu all this time for a vessel to take him to the Gambier Islands, but none appeared. And by no means did he or Maigret want to go to China aboard the *Europa*. Fortunately the two men found a happy solution: they decided to accept an offer made by Dudoit and purchased his schooner, the *Honolulu*, then lying in the harbour. It was their only means of leaving the Sandwich Islands and getting to the Gambier Islands. But before the ship was to become their property, it had to visit some islands south of the equator and then sail for Valparaíso, a voyage for which it was already chartered.

Instead of staying aboard ship for the long voyage south of the equator, the two priests agreed by contract that the *Honolulu* should drop them off at Ponape, where they could use their time well by helping Bishop Pompallier found his mission. On the *Honolulu*'s return in July or August, it would pick them up and take them via the Gambier Islands to Valparaiso. A contract was signed, the missionaries paid the first 1,000 dollars (with 2,000 dollars more to be paid in Valparaíso), and they rechristened their ship *Notre Dame de Paix* (Our Lady of Peace).[36] Oddly enough this same schooner had once belonged to the American Board of Commissioners for Foreign Missions under the name *Missionary Packet* and had carried missionaries to the Sandwich and Marquesas islands.[37]

In Rome on 18 November 1837, the day after Maigret transferred from the *Europa* to *Notre Dame de Paix*, Cardinal Fransoni addressed a letter to Bachelot at San Gabriel Mission in Alta California, thinking he was still there. He was answering Bachelot's letter of 22 November 1836, which had arrived 'late, indeed, but finally'. The cardinal was 'deeply moved' by Bachelot's great zeal in propagating the faith and by the constancy of his neophytes. And he thanked God 'for inspiring and setting up such outstanding examples of virtue in these terrible times when our Catholic religion is suffering so much'.

Bachelot had enclosed a catechism of Christian doctrine composed by himself in 'the Sandwich language'. Fransoni explained how he had turned it over to a theological commission for examination and had personally sent some brief amendments to the Picpus house in Paris.

The rest of the letter concerned the return of Bachelot and his companions to the Sandwich Islands. In an effort to hasten their return, the cardinal had seen to it 'that the king of France should also be approached'. The king was first reminded 'how Catholic priests were brought back to the Island of Tahiti under the patronage of a French vessel', and was then asked 'to help you and your companions get back to your Sandwich Mission in the very same way, if at all possible. There is now nothing else for you to do', Fransoni concluded, 'but to keep up your courage and your zeal until you have reached the goal merited by your efforts.'[38]

A French warship did in fact come to Honolulu while Bachelot was there, but it was unsuccessful in obtaining permission for him to remain.[39]

On 23 November, when Pompallier had completed one-third of his voyage from Rotuma to Sydney, the *Notre Dame de Paix* with Bachelot and Maigret aboard left Honolulu for Ponape. But Bachelot had been suffering from a long illness and the schooner was at sea hardly twenty-four hours when he fell sick again. Soon his mind became very confused and he imagined that he saw and heard the strangest things. He wished to be moved constantly from place to place and talked incessantly. Before falling into this state of delirium he offered up his life to God and expressed the wish to see Bishop Rouchouze. He received the Last Sacraments from Father Maigret and at 2 A.M. on 5 December he died. At that moment the *Notre Dame de Paix* was northeast of the Ratak Chain in the Marshall Islands at 13°14′ north latitude and 176°33′ east longitude.[40]

Maigret later sent details of Bachelot's death to Superior General Bonamie. 'I feared greatly that they would throw him into the sea, but I obtained permission to have his body preserved. It was wrapped and sealed as well as possible and was placed on the bridge at the foot of the mast. Then eight days later, that is, on 13 December, we arrived at Ascension . . . On the following day I buried the first apostle of Oceania on a small island called Naha in the Ascension group. Two Sandwich islanders, not baptised, and also two Tahitians carried the body; the natives of the local village had dug the grave. When alone, I threw myself down and prayed for him. . . .'[41]

Maigret kept a diary as well and wrote into it on 13 December: 'Ascension Island came into view this morning and we arrived there about four o'clock in the afternoon. The Bishop of Maronea is not here.'[42]

Meanwhile Pompallier, the Bishop of Maronea and Vicar Apostolic of Western Oceania, had completed another portion of his seemingly endless voyage. On 9 December 1837, nearly a year after leaving Le Havre, he sailed into Sydney harbour. A subtropical storm was raging. But nevertheless it was an exciting and very happy night for all on board.[43]

12

Pompallier arrives in Sydney and meets Polding

9 DECEMBER 1837

The continent reached by Bishop Pompallier on 9 December 1837 was called New Holland by some and Australia by others. The name Australia came from the Latin expression *Terra Australis* (i.e. South Land) which ancient geographers and voyagers used for an imagined continent in the southern hemisphere. They reasoned that it must exist in order to counterbalance Asia, just as Africa and South America counterbalanced Europe and North America. The Dutch East India Company's vessel *Duyfken* sailing southward along the eastern shore of the Gulf of Carpentaria in 1606 made the first recorded contact with the Australian continent. Other ships of the Dutch East India Company by 1644 had fairly well established two-thirds of the Australian coast, beginning from Cape York in the north and going counterclockwise to Ceduna in South Australia. Dutch navigators, who called the whole of their discoveries 'New Holland', had also sighted Van Diemen's Land (now Tasmania) in 1636 and named it after the Governor-General of the Dutch East India Company. They also discovered and named New Zealand in 1642.

The first known shipwreck on the Australian coast was the English East India Company's galleon *Tryal* which foundered in 1622 on the reefs between the Monte Bello Islands and the northwest coast of Western Australia. It had aboard the first Englishmen known to have set foot on Australian territory.[1]

Cristoforo Borri

Pope Gregory XV on 6 January 1622 founded the Sacred Congregation for the Evangelisation of Nations. Its task was to supervise and direct the propagation of the Roman Catholic faith not only in European countries, where Protestantism had taken hold, but also in newly discovered lands. Letters in its archives dated 24 April and 31 December 1630 from Father Cristoforo Borri, a Jesuit from Milan who had served in Siam, tell of great missionary opportunities in a land which he called 'New India', discovered in the southern hemisphere by the Dutch.

Addressing his letters to Pope Urban VIII, who generally attended Evangelisation Congregation meetings and shared his letters with the cardinal members, Borri described this 'New Land of Australian [that is, Southern] India' (Terra Nuova dell'India Australe). He explained first of all how he had been called to take part in a meeting of the King's Council in Lisbon two years earlier. By order of His Catholic Majesty the council discussed 'a certain Dutch vessel which was sailing the seas in the vicinity of the Cape of Good Hope when it was driven off course by a storm and eventually reached a New Land . . . , designated generally on world maps as "An Unknown Land". They themselves [the sailors] reported to us on this land which they saw, stating that it was very large, very vast and very full of people. . . .' Experts and learned men attending the meeting readily agreed when it was said that the climate of this new land 'was the same as that of Europe, since God had created it like a second Europe in the southern hemisphere, equal in size and goodness and also equal in the quantity and quality of its peoples'. The King's Council therefore decided that 'it would be fitting for His Majesty to send ships to explore it'.

Borri told the pope that later he learned in Madrid that no action had been taken. He therefore had personally approached a captain with galleons in Lisbon, suggesting that he undertake the journey himself and he agreed. 'But when he made his proposal to the Royal Ministers and to the Council of Portugal, he was told that the king had more lands than he could manage and he did not want to look for any new ones. Hence all came to naught. . . .' But Borri, interested in having some missionaries accompany such a vessel of discovery, continued making efforts to find one.[2]

Jean Paulmier de Courtonne

One generation later 'the unknown Australian land' was brought to Rome's attention again, this time at a General Meeting of the Evangelisation Congregation held on 25 February 1666 in the presence of Pope Alexander VII (1655–67) in his Quirinal Apartments with fourteen cardinals present. Giambattista Cardinal Pallotta (1594–1667), Bishop of Frascati, addressed the pope as follows:

'By means of a printed memorandum Your Holiness is asked by the Reverend Jean Paulmier, a French priest, to grant him the apostolic blessing and faculties to go as missionary to the unknown Australian Land, from where he says he has his origin. He asks that he be enabled to transfer these faculties to other priests of Paris who have volunteered to go with him, in order to bring there the light of our Holy Faith and to plant there a mission for the salvation of so many millions of souls. These people would [then] be able to come to the knowledge of the truth, [but] now live without anyone to announce the gospel, since no one has ever arrived there.'

Cardinal Pallotta pointed out that according to Paulmier support for the missionaries would be provided for 'sufficiently by France without any cost to the [Sacred] Congregation and by alms of various pious people, who already have collected a goodly sum of money for this purpose as an endowment for the said mission. . . .' If His Holiness should deign to grant the request, Pallotta added, letters patent could be sent to the Most Reverend Nuncio of France with orders for him not to hand them over to anyone, if he were not convinced of the authenticity of the proposal.

The rescript for this sixth item on the day's agenda indicated that 'the Most Holy [Father] consented, but with the proviso that the mission and the missionaries must depend completely upon the Sacred Congregation in matters concerning missions'. The nuncio in Paris was also to be requested to send further information on the proposal.

The printed memorandum referred to by Pallotta was certainly the widely distributed *Mémoires tovchant l'établissement d'vne mission chrestienne dans le troisième monde autrement appelé la Terre Australe, méridionale, antarctique et inconnue.* It was written by the Reverend Jean Paulmier de Courtonne (1636–?), printed in Paris, dated 1663, and contained a dedication to Pope Alexander VII, a 10-page letter addressed to him, and 215 pages of text. Paulmier was one of the canons in the cathedral of Lisieux. Some 130 years earlier, he said, a Norman vessel en route to the East Indies was blown off course, landed on the shores of Terra Australis, and brought back to France from there a certain Essomerie. This man became a Christian, married, raised a family, and was one of Paulmier's ancestors; this fact explained the author's special interest in that part of the world. There was 'no land so miserable or so destitute of help as Terra Australis', Paulmier said, and only France could convert it.

His text, in effect a book, was divided into chapters with some sixty pages devoted to geographical questions. Chapter seven was devoted to personnel and stated that no less than sixty or eighty persons were needed to found the proposed mission in Terra Australis. The main category of professional people in addition to priests were farmers for cultivating the soil, he said, so that the mission would not prove a burden to the indigenous population. Also needed were artisans such as carpenters, joiners, dyers and blacksmiths, as well as musicians who played various instruments, and 'a small number of persons knowledgeable in medicine, pharmacy and surgery'. Some sailors would also be needed, he said, in order to man the small vessel that would be left behind with the settlers once the main vessel bringing them to Terra Australis had returned to France.

Chapter eight was devoted to self-support and to aid from abroad. The settlers would take along a goodly supply of items for barter, like trinkets, bowls, knives and mirrors. They could fall back on a fund to be set up for them in France and periodically a ship from France would bring them supplies. But for subsistence they would rely on the fertility of the land, which Paulmier called an assured source of income. He devoted four pages to the coconut palm. Having nothing else but this tree, he maintained, was 'like having a whole farm in which the owner perpetually finds something to pick'. In spite of all these guarantees, however, he said that the settlers would have to rely 'above all on Providence'.

Chapter nine, dedicated to indigenous clergy, stressed the importance of founding seminaries 'and filling them with youth from these new countries'. If there were seminarians, Paulmier said, they would facilitate acquiring knowledge of these new lands and they would also 'provide admittance to various places'. Also 'indispensable' was developing the Catholic hierarchy and having 'pastors, bishops and curés'.

The nuncio in Paris, who meanwhile had received the orders sent to him after the General Meeting of 25 February, duly made his investigations and reported back to the Evangelisation Congregation. His report came up for discussion at the General Meeting held on 20 September 1666 attended by fifteen cardinals; this time the pope was not present. The relator informed the cardinals that the nuncio had interviewed Paulmier and also 'questioned him about his project of founding a mission in unknown Terra Australis'. Paulmier 'wishes to take advantage of the fleet which by coincidence the king has resolved to send to Madagascar [nowadays Malagasy Republic],' the relator said, 'since he believes that the passage to America [read: Terra Australis] is safe from that island'. Paulmier, in fact, wanted to use Madagascar as a supply depot for his mission. Because of these circumstances, the nuncio said in his report, Paulmier believed 'it will be easy for him to launch the said mission, the more so because in France a new company has been formed of persons who wish to undertake sailing to this Terra Australis, both for the sake of trade and for providing him and his companions with an opportunity to sow the gospel there.'

In fact, the nuncio had reported, Louis XIV, king of France (1643–1715), had given his approval to this new company which, together with the East Indies Company, 'had established a fund to support the missionaries to be sent out under the direction of the Sacred Congregation'. Paulmier, the relator said, 'plans to go there with seven or eight companions, substituting others in case of death'. Priests attached to the seminary of Saint-Sulpice Church in Paris, according to the nuncio, had volunteered to send personnel there from time to time and had also agreed to serve as agents in Paris with the king and with the Evangelisation Congregation in all matters touching the new mission. The nuncio further had given assurance, according to the relator, that Paulmier 'in everything wishes to depend completely' upon the Evangelisation Congregation.

The relator then indicated some specific requests submitted by Paulmier, one of which was that the usual faculties for missionaries should be granted to him and to his priest companions and that one of them should be named superior. Paulmier had also suggested that Rome name 'a vicar apostolic to reside in Madagascar and superintend the good government of the said mission'. In fact, the cardinals were told, Paulmier had met a princess (d'Aiguillon?) 'who wishes to make a grant-in-aid for the support' of the vicar apostolic.

The relator reminded the cardinals that some years earlier it had been suggested that a member of the Capuchins (in full: Order of Friars Minor Capuchin, abbreviated: O.F.M. Cap.) be made bishop in Madagascar. But the project was subsequently dropped because the majority of missionaries working there belonged to the Congregation of the Mission (C.M.) and it seemed best that one of them ought to become the bishop instead. Moreover, the Capuchin candidate soon died. But it might be well to take up this proposal once again, the relator said, 'in order to have a person in authority to govern the missions of these Frenchmen. Otherwise as these missions multiply the Holy See would run the risk, if it had no ministers there dependent upon itself . . . , of seeing the closer French bishops, those namely in the ports of France, interfering and wanting to govern by themselves both these missions and the new Christians.'

He pointed out 'the experience of Canada where similar disorders were remedied by means of a vicar apostolic.'

The nuncio's description of Paulmier was also presented to the cardinals. He was a priest 'about thirty years of age, in good health, and of such character and intelligence' that the nuncio could not help but wonder whether a man of his calibre really wanted to engage in an undertaking of this sort. In fact, Paulmier was also 'the incumbent of the king of Denmark, looking after his affairs in Paris'. These reasons had prompted the nuncio to question Paulmier 'a number of times on this matter'. But each time the priest had answered that his mind was made up. And since he had promised always to be dependent upon the orders of the Evangelisation Congregation, the nuncio was convinced that 'a great service would be done to God by granting him faculties as a missionary'. As for companions, the nuncio reported that Paulmier 'has not yet obtained any, since he was not certain that he would obtain faculties. But once he has them, companions will be found.' The nuncio promised to examine the qualifications of these new men and report to Rome on them.

After further discussion the cardinals at the General Meeting made these resolutions: 'Let the new mission in unknown Terra Australis be erected in dependence upon the nuncio in France and let Jean Paulmier be named its superior with authority to transfer faculties to the companions of his mission, those [namely] who have been approved and appointed by the Sacred Congregation.' The Holy Office was to be approached for these faculties. 'As for a vicar apostolic in the island of Madagascar,' the resolution read, 'let the promised grant-in-aid be made first, and then let the request be presented again.'

The only item not touched upon in these resolutions was a minor one, namely Paulmier's request for 'a Brief containing both a blessing for this new mission, for those who promote it, and for those who in the future shall assist it, as well as an invitation to the faithful to contribute to this pious enterprise'. It was not Rome's custom to issue such formal exhortations for projects, or special blessings upon them, before they had proved their worth. And so this brief was not granted. The above decisions fully authorised Paulmier to go ahead with his plan for a French mission in Terra Australis. Rome had done its part.

Paulmier lost little time. On 7 January 1667 he sent word to King Louis XIV that those interested in the Terra Australis project had 'happily found His Holiness well-intentioned' and that the pope had even gone so far as to consent 'to the creation of a French bishop to work more efficaciously to found this new church, provided however that in France a fitting and sound income should be assigned to him . . . .' On the same day Paulmier wrote to the king's chief minister, Jean-Baptiste Colbert (1619–83), a man who vigorously supported the East Indies Company and who is best remembered for founding the French Navy. Paulmier told Colbert that he wanted 'no other protector' in the king's court but him for this proposed Christian mission and French settlement 'in the Australian Lands', and assured him at the same time that this Australian project would bring glory to his ministry.

Paulmier was no mean writer and drew up an outstanding set of articles for his proposed 'Australian Lands Company', which in French he called 'Compagnie des Terres australes'. In describing these Australian Lands he said that they stretched over the torrid, temperate and frigid zones 'opposite to ours'. The Antarctic, as was evident from the title of his *Mémoires*, was also included. More than 4,000 leagues of coast had already been visited, he said. In the initial pages of his *Mémoires* or memorandum dated 1663 he published a world map showing the location of these various lands. Except for a few alterations the map was identical with that contained in *Trésor des cartes géographiques des principaux estats de l'univers*, an atlas published in Paris in 1653. Explaining why he called this part of the world 'the third world', he said that it was the practice of 'modern geographers'. They called the Australian Lands 'the third world, or unknown world, giving the title of first or old world to the continent in which Europe, Asia and Africa are located, and that of second or new world to that large island which constitutes both the Mexican and the Peruvian America'.

A protest against Paulmier's project was sent to Rome by Father René Alméras, superior general of the Congregation of the Mission (C.M.), founded in Paris in 1625 by Saint Vincent de Paul (1576–1660). (Lazarists and Vincentians are other names for the same congregation.) Since Madagascar was distant 'not less than 3,000 miles from Terra Australis', Alméras said, it was 'incompatible to have the two [areas] under one vicar apostolic. . . .' He therefore appealed to the Roman authorities to make one of his priests the vicar apostolic in Madagascar instead of Paulmier or one of his men, since the Congregation of the Mission had been working in Madagascar for twenty years already.

Paulmier quickly and wisely resolved this difficulty. He paid Alméras a visit, said that he agreed completely with the superior general's logic, and without delay wrote to the nuncio in Paris, upon whom he was now officially dependent because of Rome's decision. Madagascar and the Australian Lands ought not to be under one and the same vicar apostolic, he told the nuncio, since Madagascar was within the territory entrusted to the French East Indies Company, whereas the third or unknown world was within territory entrusted to the French Australian Lands Company. This latter company, having 'the propagation of the faith as its principal goal and purpose, intends to designate as one of the chief members of its administration, even in temporal matters, the vicar apostolic who is to be appointed'. Consequently it was impossible for the vicar apostolic to reside in Madagascar; he would have to reside in the Australian Lands themselves.

Paulmier had meanwhile decided to recruit the priests for his mission, no longer from the seminary attached to the Saint-Sulpice Church of Paris, but rather from the new Paris Foreign Mission Seminary. It had been founded in 1660, the year in which Vincent de Paul had died, and was formally approved by Rome in 1664. Now in 1667 Paulmier tried to persuade its founders, whom he knew well, to send their personnel with him to Terra Australis instead of to East Asia. But he did not succeed.

Unfortunately, as often is the case with men of great vision, Jean Paulmier de Courtonne—unlike a Christopher Columbus and unlike a Michelangelo—did not have the pluck and perseverance so vital for the realisation of his great plan. Records suddenly go silent about him and about his enterprise, conceived with such fine detail, saying only that he died in Cologne.[3]

Victorio Riccio

An Italian contemporary of Paulmier in the Philippines also wanted to bring the gospel to Terra Australis. He was Father Victorio Riccio of the Order of Preachers (O.P.), a religious community better known as Dominicans. Born on 18 January 1621 at Santa Maria a Cintoia near Florence, he began his studies at Saint Dominic Monastery in Fiesole and completed them at the Dominican college in Rome alongside the Pantheon. His superiors named him professor of philosophy and assigned him to the Fiesole monastery. But Father Juan Bautista de Morales, O.P. (1597–1664), back from the Far East to report to Rome on the Chinese rites being used by the Jesuits and to recruit forty Dominicans, recognised Riccio's extraordinary talents, enlisted him immediately for the Philippines, and took him from Rome to Madrid in June 1644.

When Innocent X (1644–55) became pope that same year on 15 September, de Morales sent Riccio back to Rome as his delegate with orders to win pontifical university status for the Dominicans' Colegio de Santo Tomás in Manila. Armed with letters from King Philip IV (1605–65) addressed to the pope and to Spain's ambassador to the Holy See, Riccio saw the pope twice and succeeded in spite of opposition from many cardinals. The papal bull was dated 20 November 1645, was ratified by the king's council on 31 July 1646, and was welcomed with festivities in Manila in 1648, being brought there by Riccio who had sailed from Spain via Acapulco, Mexico. (The Pontifical University of Santo Tomás exists to the present day.)

Riccio was assigned to work among the Chinese of Luzon. According to his own estimate dated 22 June 1651, the Chinese on this largest of the Philippine Islands numbered 10,000 although there had been as many as 25,000 earlier. The majority lived at Manila, but their dwellings and places of business since 1581 were outside the city's walls and within range of artillery fire. Because of political reasons the Spaniards had expelled them from the walled city and had given them a marshy area to the east of the city and on the south bank of the Pasig River, which the Chinese quickly transformed into a veritable Chinatown. At once it became Manila's centre of commerce called Parian and its shops were kept supplied by junks and sampans from Amoy and other ports along China's southeastern coast. Silk, porcelain, chinaware, glass, textiles of cotton and linen, fresh fruits, domesticated birds and animals, trinkets and finely carved furniture could all be had for a price. Many of these items eventually followed the 'Manila galleon' trade route to Acapulco and from there reached Europe.

The Dominican monastery to which Riccio was assigned was also located outside the walled city and alongside the Parian. He was to work among the Chinese, study their language, and in time learned it remarkably well. Superiors in 1655 sent him to Amoy in the Formosa Strait to care for the Chinese there

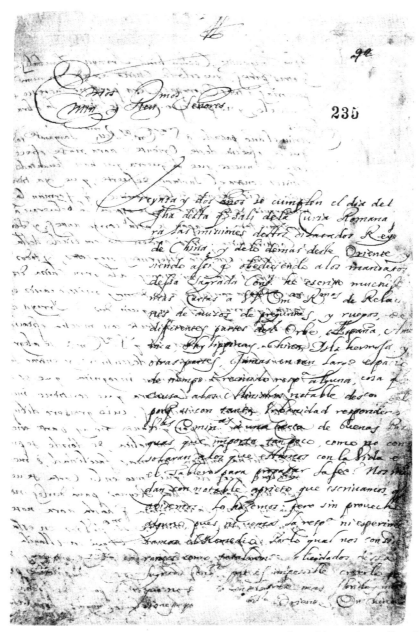

24 Father Victorio Riccio, a Dominican priest, wrote from Manila on 4 June 1676 to the cardinal members of the Evangelisation Congregation, suggesting that the newly discovered 'Australian Land' be created a prefecture apostolic. He envisioned it as embracing in a single continent modern Papua New Guinea, Australia and Antarctica, and he volunteered to serve as its first prefect apostolic with the assistance of a group of Franciscan missionaries from Manila. This is page one of his four-page Spanish letter. *Source: PF: SOCG vol. 493 (1681) f. 235r. (Chapter 12).*

25   For the benefit of the cardinal members of the Evangelisation Congregation, Father Riccio's Spanish letter of 4 June 1676 was translated into Italian. This first page speaks of Japan, Tonkin, Cochin China, Formosa and other lands in the Far East, and especially of China's war against the Tartars. *Source: PF: SOCG vol. 493 (1681) f. 237r. (Chapter 12).*

26 This second page of the Italian translation of Father Riccio's letter, as figure 25, first tells of the discovery of the Australian Land and then how the prefecture apostolic should be organised. *Source: PF: SOCG vol. 493 (1681) f. 237v. (Chapter 12).*

27   On this third and final page of the letter, as figure 25, Father Riccio asks the cardinals to intercede with the king of Spain on behalf of the proposed mission.

Source: PF: SOCG vol. 493 (1681) f. 243r. (Chapter 12).

who had become Catholics in Luzon. Koxinga (1623–62), the pirate lord of Amoy who succeeded in expelling the Dutch from Formosa, used Riccio as his ambassador to Governor General Don Sabiniano Manrique de Lara of Manila, even threatening the priest with death if his mission proved unsuccessful. Koxinga's less warlike son and successor, Kinsie, also used Riccio who negotiated for Kinsie in 1663 a commercial treaty between Formosa and the Philippines.

In 1675 fellow priests elected Riccio to the office of prior of Saint Dominic Monastery alongside the Parian outside the walled city of Manila. From here Prior Riccio wrote on 4 June 1676, the feast of Corpus Christi, to 'The Most Eminent and Reverend Lords' of the Evangelisation Congregation in Rome, saying that thirty-two years had passed since his original departure from Rome for the distant and vast kingdoms of China and the Far East. 'And although in obedience to the orders of this Sacred Congregation I have written very many letters to Your Most Reverend Eminences containing reports, news, questions and requests, still I have never received a single reply in this very long period of time . . . Since Your Eminences answer with such great pleasure a letter wishing you happy holidays, something of such little consequence, why do you not console those (like us) who expose their very lives to a thousand dangers in order to propagate the faith? . . . We get to think that the Sacred Congregation has completely forgotten about us, something [quite] incredible, since no missions in the world are more flourishing than these in the Orient. . . .'

There was nothing new to add to his lengthy report of the previous year, Riccio said, except to mention that the Chinese were waging war 'with such great valour' against Tartary that they had succeeded in regaining 'six kingdoms out of the fifteen which form the great monarchy of China'. And there was hope that they might regain the others as well.

As for himself, he was currently busy making plans to launch 'a rare mission, one that will give Your Eminences very great satisfaction'. He wished 'to explore and to enter Terra Australis, called the Unknown, the fifth part of the world, a land containing innumerable kingdoms and nations'. For the cardinals he enclosed 'a rough map' so that they could see 'where the Australian Land is and how vast it is'. And since the kind of expedition which he envisioned could be launched from no other Catholic land in the world 'with greater facility or with less difficulty than from here, as is evident from my map, I therefore wish to go to these kingdoms in order to bring them the knowledge of God'.

Men born on the coasts of Terra Australis had been brought to Manila in Dutch vessels, Riccio explained. They had been 'made slaves by the Dutch who discovered parts of the said land' and 'they are adust in colour—some are black—and they are courageous and strong'. On his map he pointed out that at a place called Cape Concordia 'there are men of remarkable stature'. He had spoken with the Dutch explorers and they had told him that one could walk through the interior of this new country 'for more than two years without ever seeing the sea'. It was 'deplorable', he added, 'that in such a vast and immense part of the world no one has yet heard the most holy name of God mentioned'.

He had further been told that red and white races, 'like the rest of us', populated this new land. He accepted this as 'credible', because being in the southern hemisphere they were at the same latitudes 'in relation to the Antarctic Pole as we are to the Arctic Pole'.

Only two things were needed to make his project a reality: (1) the authority of the Sacred Congregation and (2) a request addressed by it to the Catholic king (of Spain) inviting him to instruct the governors in the Philippines to assist Riccio and place no obstacles in his path. 'Should it please Your Eminences', he added, 'I offer myself to be head of this mission. And if I should die in it, I shall die performing an action of the greatest service to God.' He suggested strongly that Terra Australis ought to be made a prefecture apostolic, but in such a way that 'in case of death or grave infirmity, someone else could be substituted'. He also urged the cardinals to spell out his faculties clearly and explicitly, something that they had neglected when he was given the Prefecture Apostolic of the Island of Formosa.

Riccio explained that he was not at present in the mission field 'because they have me in Manila now, this metropolis of the Philippines, where I am serving as prior of the Saint Dominic Monastery'. But once all preparations for the expedition to Terra Australis would be completed 'and by the time your reply comes back, my [term of] office will have expired, making me free. And although I am 58 [55?] years of age, I trust that God will none the less give me strength and life to carry out this project, since the only difficulty consists in opening the door. Once it has been opened, there will then be others who can enter it.' In fact, he added, Franciscan priests had promised to accompany him provided that he received the necessary authorisation from Rome. 'But everything rests in Your Eminences' hands and in the hands of His Catholic Majesty.'

Riccio pointed out that King Charles II of Spain would be highly pleased at seeing a new world explored in the very beginning of his reign. (Charles II had succeeded Philip IV in 1665 and now was fourteen years old.) A letter from their Eminences to the king would make him highly esteem the project, 'something which would not be the case if a poor religious like myself were to write to him'.

The map enclosed by Riccio measured thirty by forty centimetres and was drawn in colour. On it he indicated how he would start from Manila, sail through the Philippines to Gilolo (nowadays Halmahera), and from there go via Papua and New Guinea to 'the Australian Land once Unknown and now Partly Known'. (On his map New Guinea, Australia and Antarctica were all drawn as parts of the same continent, since it was not known in 1676 that these land masses were separated from one another by bodies of water.) In closing his letter Riccio described himself as 'The Prior of Saint Dominic of Manila of the Order of Preachers, Prefect Apostolic of the Island of Formosa, and Missionary for the same see to the Great Empire of China'.

In those days Spaniards sailing from Manila to Spain travelled via Acapulco; their vessels often made numerous stops en route for the sake of trade, getting fresh water and food, making repairs due to storms encountered at sea, or simply because there was no wind. Apparently Riccio's letter addressed to the cardinals

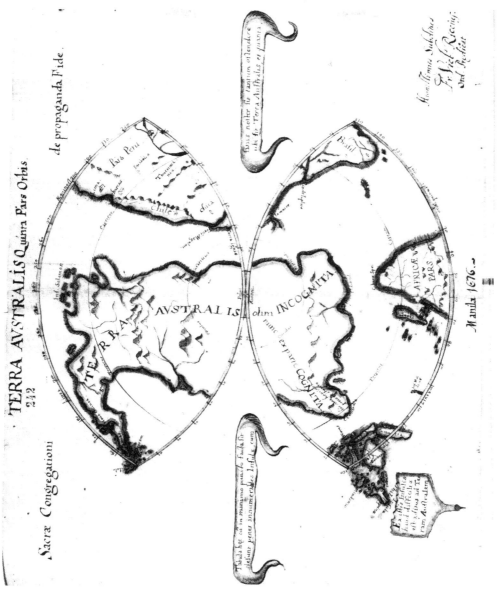

28 Ninety-four years before Captain Cook explored Australia's east coast Father Victorio Riccio of Manila sent this large coloured map of 'The Australian Land: The Fifth Part of the World', dated 1676 and measuring thirty by forty centimetres, to the Evangelisation Congregation in Rome. The Latin text in the lower lefthand corner says: 'From these islands it is not difficult to enter the Australian Land.' Specifically mentioned are the Philippine Islands, Mindanao and Gilolo, and also Sumatra, Java, Borneo, Celebes, Flores, Timor and Ceram. Beginning with Gilolo at the upper left and going around 'Terra Australis' clockwise the names given are these: Papua, New Guinea, Solomon Islands, Cape Landt, Cape Concordia, Pygmies and Ceram. A note near Cape Concordia reads: 'Here there are men of remarkable stature.' The Latin text across the middle of the map says: 'This chart has been made on a very small scale and as a result innumerable islands are altogether lacking, since our only purpose was to show where the Australian Land is and how vast it is.' The three latitudes shown are the equator, the Tropic of Capricorn and the Antarctic Circle. The chart is signed: 'Your most humble subject, Father Victorius Riccius [Latin for Victorio Riccio] of the Order of Preachers.' *Source: PF: SOCG vol. 493 (1681) f. 242r. (Chapter 12).*

in Rome had the misfortune of being on vessels which experienced an unhappy combination of all of these delays because the letter was en route for five full years! Cardinal Prefect Paluzio Altieri of the Evangelisation Congregation had the original Spanish letter translated into Italian.

Riccio would have been pleased to know that his proposal was considered so important that it was placed first on the agenda for the General Meeting of 15 July 1681. Archbishop Edoardo Cibo, secretary of the Sacred Congregation, summarised Riccio's letter for the nine cardinals present. He told them that Terra Australis was so vast 'that one can walk through it for more than two years without ever seeing the sea', that it was considered to be 'the fifth part of the world' and that it contained 'innumerable kingdoms and nations'. He repeated all the essential points in Riccio's letter, saying that this veteran missionary had volunteered to head the mission and that he wished the cardinals 'to take steps with His Catholic Majesty to have the governors of the Philippines assist him and show him favour. He asks further that a prefecture [apostolic] be established, but in such a manner that in case of death or grave infirmity he could substitute someone else. He also asks that his faculties be well expressed. And he hopes to be able with ease to render the mission in that part [of the world] very fruitful.'

The cardinals supported Riccio's proposal completely. They created the Prefecture Apostolic of Terra Australis (including modern Papua New Guinea, West Irian, Australia and Antarctica), made Riccio its prefect apostolic, and ruled that all opportune faculties should be given to him.

Riccio's letter of 4 June 1676 had taken five full years to reach the cardinals in Rome. If their reply and the accompanying documents also took five years to reach Manila, they would have arrived in 1686! But Riccio died on 17 February 1685 at Saint Dominic Monastery bordering on the Parian outside the walled city. Dare one speculate on his state of mind in the final years of his life? Did he die thinking that Rome's cardinals had ignored still another of his many letters? Or did the news of his appointment as Prefect Apostolic of Terra Australis perhaps arrive on time, brighten his last days, and assure him that his idea of bringing the gospel to Terra Australis was in no way considered by Rome an impossible dream?[4]

James Cook

The first European known to have set foot on the east coast of this new continent was James Cook, England's greatest naval explorer. As captain of the *Endeavour*, a 370-ton sailing vessel, he landed on the beach at Kurnell, about ten kilometres south of Sydney, on 29 April 1770. The bay where he anchored had so many plants new to science that it was called Botany Bay. He wrote into his log on 23 August: 'I took possession of the whole of the eastern coast by the name of New Wales.' Later he changed the name to New South Wales and called himself 'the real discoverer of Australia'.[5] During a second voyage to the South Seas he discovered Norfolk Island (about halfway between Sydney and Fiji) on 10 October 1773.

29 These minutes of the General Meeting of the Evangelisation Congregation held on 15 July 1681 show that the first item on the agenda was Father Riccio's proposal. The upper half of the page lists all the cardinals present. *Source: PF: Acta vol. 51 (1681) f. 205r. (Chapter 12).*

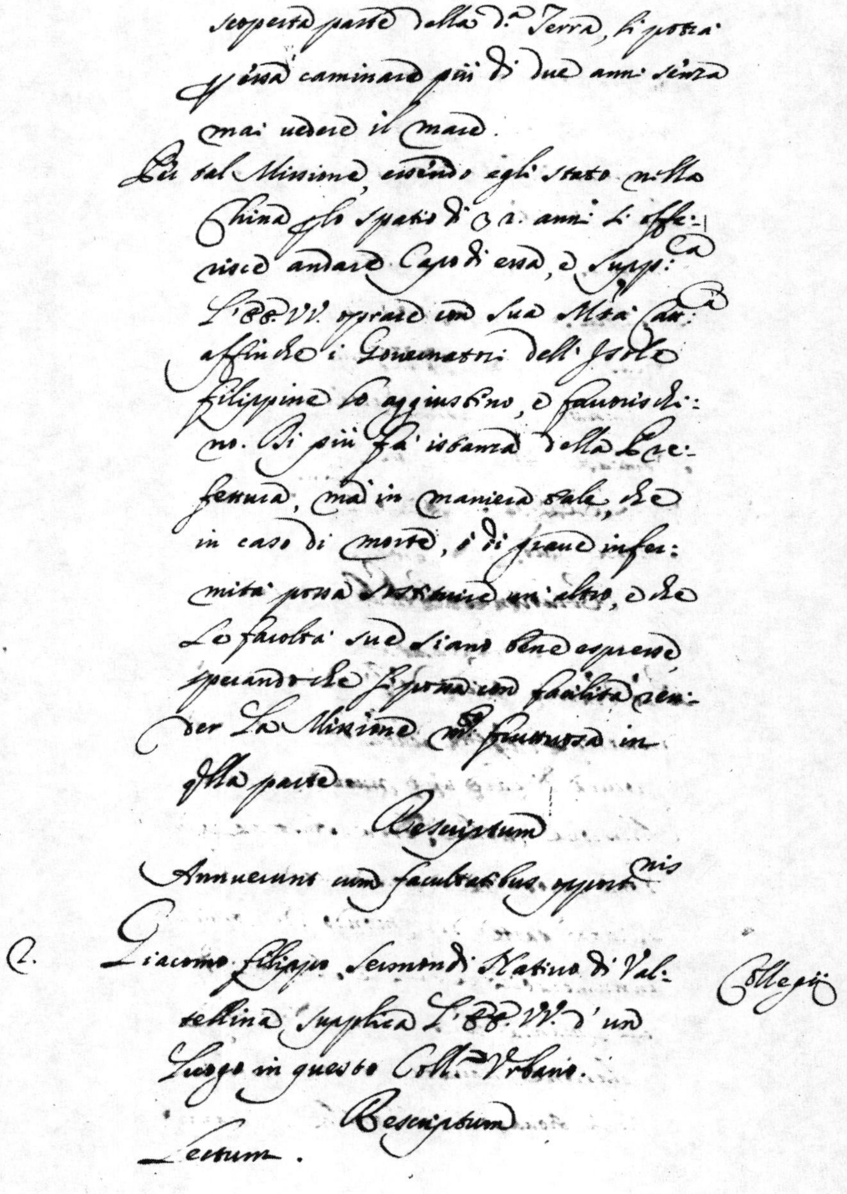
scoperta parte della d.a Terra, si potrà
per essa caminare più di due anni senza
mai vedere il mare.
Per tal Ministero, essendo egli stato nella
China per lo spatio di 32 anni si offe-
risce andare Capo di essa, e supp.ca
l'EE. VV. operare con Sua Maestà Catt.ca
affinchè i Governatori dell'Isole
Filippine lo aggiustino, e favorischi-
no. Di più fa istanza della Eccel-
lenza, ma in maniera tale, che
in caso di morte, ò di grave infer-
mità possa [illegible] un'altro, e che
le facoltà sue siano bene espresse
sperando che si porrà con facilità render lo Ministero [illegible] fruttuoso in
quella parte.
Rescriptum
Annuerunt cum facultatibus opportunis
C. Giacomo Filippo Seramondi Nativo di Val-
tellina supplica l'EE. VV. d'un
luogo in questo Coll.o Urbano.
Collegii
Rescriptum
Lectum.

30 The reaction of the cardinals on 15 July 1681 was 'Annuerunt cum facultatibus opportunis', that is, 'They accepted the proposal and granted the needed faculties'. *Source: PF: Acta vol. 51 (1681) f. 205v. (Chapter 12).*

England chose these two areas, New South Wales and Norfolk Island, to serve as penal colonies after New England in North America became independent in 1776. Its Colony of Port Jackson was officially established at Sydney Cove in New South Wales on 7 February 1788. And the second British settlement in the south Pacific was founded on 6 March of that year at Sydney Bay on the south side of Norfolk Island.[6]

Nicolò Paccanari

Ten years later, on 7 November 1798, the Evangelisation Congregation entrusted New Holland 'to the care and zeal of the priests of the Society of the Faith of Jesus'. This society, also known as Paccanarists, was a union of priests founded at Caravita Oratory in Rome on 15 August 1797 by Nicolò Paccanari. Born at Valsugana near Trent in 1773, the year in which Pope Clement XIV suppressed the Society of Jesus (or Jesuits), he dreamed of reviving the order. After serving as soldier and sergeant at Castel Sant'Angelo in Rome, his original profession, he wrote his society's rule in Loreto, adopted Jesuit garb, introduced a fourth vow like the Jesuits, and with papal permission accepted former Jesuits and other priests into his society. Early in 1798 he opened a house in Spoleto (Italy) with twelve companions. Quickly his society grew in numbers and began to spread.

In February of 1798 the French had occupied Rome, causing the head of the Evangelisation Congregation, Hyacinthe-Sigismond Cardinal Gerdil, to flee to Piemonte. He was so occupied with other things that Pope Pius VI on 18 March 1798 made Archbishop Cesare Brancadore, secretary of the Evangelisation Congregation, its pro-prefect. This official had fled to Firmi in Piceno and it was here that he signed the document on 7 November 1798 entrusting New Holland and other areas to the Society of the Faith of Jesus.

Stefano Cardinal Borgia residing in Padua had also been appointed pro-prefect of the Evangelisation Congregation by Pope Pius VI on the same day as Brancadore, 18 March 1798. At odds with Brancadore because of overlapping authority, Borgia explained the problem to Pius VI who then divided the mission world between the two pro-prefects. But Borgia wanted to have everything in his own hands and was so successful a diplomat that by 7 February 1799 he was able to inform Cardinal Prefect Gerdil that 'the Holy Father has expressed the wish that I take upon myself the task of serving all the missions. On 5 January just past he informed me of this and declared Padua to be the temporary location for the Sacred Congregation for the Evangelisation of Nations, appointing me its Pro-Prefect, giving me all its faculties, and ordering the Most Reverend Secretary (Brancadore) to come to Padua.' This confusion and in-fighting in the Evangelisation Congregation as well as the vastness of the areas entrusted to the priests of the Society of the Faith of Jesus—the Cape of Good Hope and adjacent territories, Ethiopia, Madagascar, l'Île de France (now Mauritius), Bourbon, Seychelles, New Holland and the parts adjacent to it, Ieso Islands and Japan—alone would make it easy to understand why nothing concrete was done for New Holland at this time.

But what actually happened to Paccanari? His society on 18 April 1799 absorbed an almost identical group called the Society of the Sacred Heart of Jesus and quickly had sixty-nine members. It spread from Italy to Austria, Germany, Hungary, Switzerland, France, Netherlands and England, growing in numbers all the time. The Jesuits in White Russia had never been suppressed because Catherine II (1729–96), empress of Russia, had not promulgated Pope Clement XIV's brief. Paccanari declared on 11 August 1799 that he would accept these Jesuits into his society, but would not hear of his society being incorporated by them. When Pope Pius VII authorised the activity of the Jesuits in White Russia in 1801, and in the Kingdom of the Two Sicilies in 1804, even allowing them to accept recruits from elsewhere, many of Paccanari's members joined them. Then in 1808 Paccanari after a papal investigation received a ten-year prison sentence in Castel Sant'Angelo. Freed by the French in 1809, he was back in prison for another offence in 1810. His name then disappears from historical records. When Pope Pius VII revoked the brief of suppression and completely restored the Society of Jesus around the world on 7 August 1814, the Society of the Faith of Jesus for all practical purposes ceased to exist.[7]

James Dixon

In 1798 when Pro-Prefects Borgia and Brancadore were vying for jurisdiction over mission lands, an Irish rebellion broke out and as a result the English deported large numbers of Irish prisoners to New Holland. Among them were three Catholic priests: Fathers James Dixon (1758–1840), James Harold (1745–1830) and Peter O'Neil (1757–1846). Dixon and Harold arrived at Port Jackson in January 1800 on the *Friendship* and the *Minerva* respectively and O'Neil in early 1801 on the *Anne*. All three were convict ships, euphemistically called transportation vessels. Dixon was conditionally emancipated by Governor Philip Gidley King's proclamation of 19 April 1803 which read:' . . .I have judged it expedient and admissible, in consequence of a [29 August 1802] communication from His Majesty's Principal Secretary of State for the Colonies and War Department, to grant unto the Reverend Mr. Dixon a conditional emancipation, to enable him to exercise his clerical functions as a Roman Catholic priest, which he has qualified himself for by the regular and exemplary conduct he has manifested since his residence in the colony, and his having taken the oath of allegiance, abjuration, and declaration prescribed by law. . . .'

Things began to look bright for the Catholic Church in this penal colony because the government even granted Dixon a salary. Eager to have the same faculties which were enjoyed by other missionaries around the world, he applied for them to the Evangelisation Congregation through Father James MacCormick, Guardian at Saint Isidore College in Rome, a foundation of the Irish Franciscans. MacCormick often channelled Irish requests to the Holy See.

The request described Dixon as a secular priest who for many years had done parish work in Ireland in the diocese of Ferns. It said that he 'devoutly explains how he was deported by order of his government to New Holland in the Pacific Ocean and there met various Roman Catholic colonists from the three kingdoms of Great Britain and from other European nations'. Not being able to reach 'any of the vicars apostolic in the East Indies because of immense distances and lack of communication by sea', he had presumed the necessary jurisdiction. For two years he had been administering the sacraments and was still doing so, 'intending to have recourse to the Holy See when there should be an opportunity'. He now asked the cardinals 'to grant him all the necessary faculties which customarily are granted to missionaries' who are based in areas where the Church is not established.

Archbishop Domenico Coppola, secretary of the Evangelisation Congregation at this time, presented this petition to Pius VII on 29 January 1804, and the pope granted 'all faculties which seem expedient'. Although Dixon had asked only for the faculties 'customarily granted to missionaries', the Evangelisation Congregation and the pope went much further, creating on this day the Prefecture Apostolic of New Holland and naming Dixon the first prefect apostolic.[8]

Borgia meanwhile had been advanced to the rank of cardinal prefect and on 25 February he wrote to Dixon, addressing him as 'the Most Reverend James Dixon, Prefect of the Missions of New Holland'. The Sacred Congregation 'had already been concerned for some time about the faithful who are living in New Holland', he said, 'and repeatedly was terribly disturbed because such great difficulties of time and place made it impossible to send personnel into this very vast section of the vineyard of the Lord.' But while the Sacred Congregation was filled with these thoughts, he said, 'we learned with very great pleasure that Your Reverence, about whose piety and doctrine outstanding testimony has been relayed to us, has fortuitously arrived there. And the Catholics living there, lacking all spiritual assistance for such a long time, not only received you most joyfully as if you were sent by God, but almost even forced you to administer the sacraments to them. But since you knew that legitimately you had no faculties, you hesitated for a long time. Then overcome finally by the requests of the faithful, and thinking that their need was so great that you could presume the faculties, you did not hesitate to administer the sacraments to them.'

The cardinal said that he would not go into the theoretical question as to whether faculties could be presumed in this case, or whether presumed faculties 'would make not only licit, but also valid, such acts which require express jurisdiction'. Pius VII, however, was 'desirous of using as efficacious a remedy as possible for this evil', and therefore he 'used the fullness of power that has been granted to him by Christ our Lord and graciously rectified all of the acts performed by you, which are capable of being rectified'. As for the future, 'this Sacred Congregation, filled with confidence in your piety and zeal, elects Your Reverence at its good pleasure and makes you Prefect Apostolic over all the missions which are contained within the boundaries of New Holland. It has also seen to it that our Most Holy Father would provide you with suitable faculties, as you can see from the enclosed document.'

What Dixon had to be concerned about 'most of all', Borgia said, was bringing into the country 'suitable priests from Europe or elsewhere, who under your rule shall assist the faithful and shall also strive to propagate our Catholic religion far and wide'. So that Dixon could carry out this task, the cardinal promised to place 'this Sacred Congregation at your complete disposal'. To be of real service to him, however, it was necessary for the Evangelisation Congregation to receive 'an accurate and full report on the state of Catholic affairs in New Holland'. Dixon was to draw up such a report 'according to the questionnaire contained in the enclosed booklet'. He was also instructed to indicate to Borgia 'without delay whatever can contribute toward the permanence and spread of the orthodox faith in that province'.[9]

But that very year (1804) several hundred Irishmen decided to take vengeance on their English jailers at Castle Hill just outside of Sydney, and they rebelled. The rebellion was quickly suppressed, but Dixon was held personally responsible, his permission to celebrate Mass publicly was withdrawn and his government salary was discontinued. He remained in Sydney a few more years, ministering privately to Catholics, and then left New Holland after obtaining permission from the government to return to Ireland. Father Harold, who meanwhile had served in Norfolk Island and Van Diemen's Land, then took Dixon's place in Sydney until he too left New Holland in 1810 via Rio de Janeiro and the United States for Ireland. Father O'Neil of Ballymacoda parish in County Cork, who had received 275 lashes before being transported in 1800 to Sydney and Norfolk Island, had been freed from Norfolk Island's penal colony as early as 15 January 1803 by government order and was returned to Ireland that same year.[10]

Dixon, born at Castlebridge in Wexford County, had been deported to New Holland with a certain Michael Hayes of Wexford Town, who had a younger brother Richard (1787–1824), a Franciscan priest, attached to his order's monastery at Cork. Michael wrote frequently to Richard about the abandoned Irish Catholics in Sydney Cove, urging him to come and be their parish priest. But Richard had become deeply involved in the fight against the veto which Pope Pius VII was being pressured to grant to the British government so that it would have a say in the nomination of bishops for Ireland. Because of his knowledge of Italian and Roman life (Richard had studied for the priesthood at Saint Isidore College in Rome from 1802 to 1810 and now was twenty-eight years old), a lay organisation called the Catholic Association of Ireland chose him as a one-man delegation to Rome to lodge its protests against the veto. He arrived there on 25 October 1815 and on 9 November, 22 December and again on 16 January 1816 had papal audiences arranged by Cardinal Prefect Lorenzo Litta of the Evangelisation Congregation.[11]

While in Rome on this mission Father Hayes discussed the matter of New Holland with Cardinal Litta and on 28 August 1816 submitted a memorandum. Its contents were based on personal interviews and on 'many letters received from my brother (Michael Hayes) who in every letter has bewailed the deplorable state of those Catholics, who are abandoned and without a priest, and he has urged me to go there. Although this is something that I have wanted to do, circumstances have not permitted me to attempt it.'

Io Sotto certifico, che nella colonia di Sydney Cove, dove
si trovano molte migliaja di Cattolici Irlandesi,
nè in nissuna altra parte della Nuova Ollanda,
non si trova presentemente alcun Missionario o
Sacerdote Cattolico.

Nell'anno 1804, D. Giacomo Dixon, Sacerdote
nativo della Contèa di Wexford, Diocesi di Ferns, in
Irlanda, (deportato nella Nuova Ollanda insieme con
molti altri Cattolici Secolari dell'itessa Contèa,
tra' quali il fratello carnale maggiore dello Sotto,
il Sig.e Michele Hayes) fù nominato Prefetto Aplico
in quella Regione dalla Sa Conge di Propa Fede
sull'istanza fatta in di lui nome dal P. Guard.o di
S. Isidoro.

Certifico, che il sud.o D. Giacomo Dixon, che è da
me personalmente ed intimamente conosciuto, risiede
ora nella casa del di lui fratello, il Sig.e Nicola
Dixon, a due miglia dalla Città di Wexford in Irlanda
(città nativa del Deponente); dove io l'ho veduto e
trattato continuamente e familiarmente dall'anno
1811 fino all'anno 1815; che il d.to D. Giacomo Dixon
è da molto tempo incommodato colla podagra e non
è nell'intenzione di mai tornare nella Nuova

31 First page of a three-page memorandum dated 28 August 1816 submitted by twenty-nine-year-old Father Richard Hayes, a Franciscan from Ireland, to Cardinal Prefect Litta, testifying that Sydney Cove had thousands of Irish Catholics without a single priest to care for them. Source: PF: SC Oceania vol. 1 (1816–41) f. 7r. (Chapter 12).

Hayes testified that 'in the Colony of Sydney Cove, where there are many thousands of Irish Catholics, and in all other parts of New Holland as well there is at the present time not a single Catholic missionary or priest'. After explaining how Dixon had got to New Holland along with Michael Hayes and how Dixon had been made prefect apostolic in 1804, he said, 'I certify that the above-mentioned Father James Dixon, who is personally and intimately known to me, now resides in the house of his brother . . . , two miles distant from Wexford Town in Ireland . . . , where I have dealt with him continually from 1811 to 1815 . . . He is suffering from the gout and intends never to return to New Holland which he left in 1809. . . .' Hayes also testified that Father Harold of the Diocese of Dublin 'had stayed for some years in that region with Dixon, but left in 1810 for Rio de Janeiro in Brazil, went from there to North America, and finally returned to Ireland three years ago.'[12]

Jeremiah Francis Flynn

By this memorandum Hayes intended to prove to Cardinal Litta that there was no obstacle to appointing another prefect apostolic, or at least that it was most urgent to send a priest to Sydney Cove (now Sydney). As Providence would have it, there was in Rome just at this time a priest who was eager for some such mission and who no doubt was in close contact with Hayes, since the two were Irish. He was a Cistercian named Jeremiah Francis Flynn—called O'Flynn in the records of the Evangelisation Congregation—who in March 1813 had gone to the West Indies with the Abbot of La Trappe, France, who intended to found a Trappist mission there. Flynn was left behind at Saint Croix, largest of the Virgin Islands, where he stayed until April 1816. The Abbot of La Trappe, however, left immediately for North America and later for some reason suspended Flynn from performing priestly functions and declared him an apostate. When Flynn learned this, he went to Rome to defend himself, not knowing where to find his abbot. Thanks to the testimony of others, he was absolved from all these censures by Pope Pius VII on 28 July 1816.

Then on 1 September that same year, just four days after Hayes had presented his memorandum to the Evangelisation Congregation, Secretary Pedicini informed Pius VII that Flynn had spontaneously volunteered to go as a missionary to New Holland 'where many thousands of Irish Catholics are without help'. And since New Holland had no Cistercians, he told the pope, Flynn also wished to be relieved of all responsibilities to his order. At this audience Pius VII granted 'all faculties whatsoever that are necessary and opportune', and in virtue of these Flynn ceased to be a Cistercian and was named 'Prefect of the Missions in New Holland', thus receiving the prefecture apostolic left vacant by Dixon. In signing official documents he used: Jeremiah F. Flynn, Prefect Apostolic of New Holland.[13]

Before publishing the faculties granted by Pius VII on 1 September, Secretary Pedicini contacted Stefano Pietro Damiani of the Sacred Apostolic Penitentiary at the Vatican and requested a judgment on Flynn. Damiani wrote back on 9 September, saying, 'I have examined at length the qualifications of the Irish priest, Jeremiah O'Flynn, as you requested, and concerning his morals, etc., he seems satisfactory as a missionary . . . for the Colony of Botany Bay. . . .'[14] Pedicini saw the pope again on 15 September and obtained further faculties for Flynn including the authorisation to administer the sacrament of confirmation.[15]

Flynn in turn requested from the Evangelisation Congregation sacred vessels, letters of recommendation and funds. Cardinal Litta then wrote a letter of introduction for him on 21 September to the Most Reverend Archbishops of Ireland and to their suffragan bishops. He said that the Evangelisation Congregation had learned 'with the greatest of sorrow that Catholics living in exile in New Holland had been deprived of all spiritual help, lacked ministers of the Church and found themselves in great spiritual trouble'. He then said that Flynn, 'an Irish priest whose piety and zeal have been abundantly documented', had offered himself spontaneously to care for those Catholics and the Sacred Congregation had decided 'to place him in charge of this distant and abandoned mission and to provide him as well with suitable faculties through the authority of our Most Holy Father'.

But Flynn was still in need of money, he said, 'both to make the journey and to buy church goods'. And since the Sacred Congregation 'was able to give only a little help, because its funds were so low', it earnestly requested them to help the priest in every way possible in view of the charity which they ought to have for their countrymen living in such misery in New Holland. Further, they should try to arouse the piety of their faithful as well, 'especially those who by ties of blood are joined to those in exile', so that all Flynn's needs would be met. Litta himself was convinced, he said, that the archbishops, bishops and other Catholics of Ireland would readily supply all that was needed.[16]

Had Flynn been wise, he would have requested Bishop William Poynter (1762–1827), Vicar Apostolic of London District, to announce his newly acquired official status to British authorities and to petition from them some consideration on his behalf. Poynter could have done this easily, since the government considered him an unofficial representative of Roman Catholic interests in the realm. Nor was Poynter a stranger to Flynn; he had ordained Flynn to the priesthood on 29 March 1813 prior to his leaving for the West Indies mission.

But Flynn was no diplomat. He himself wrote to Lord Bathurst, the Colonial Secretary, composing his letter in such a way and with such poor orthography that it at once aroused 'a suspicion of his fitness'. After repeated inquiries Flynn eventually received word from Mr Henry Goulburn, secretary of Lord Bathurst, 'to the effect that it was not the intention of the Government to send any Roman Catholic clergyman to New South Wales, and that, under no circumstances, would Lord Bathurst accede to his request to be permitted to proceed thither without previous conference being had with the Right Reverend Dr. Poynter'. Flynn then visited Under Secretary Goulburn, showed him his official papers from Rome, and suggested that Goulburn invite Poynter to see Bathurst. Goulburn agreed.

When Poynter and Bathurst met on 27 February 1817, Poynter was told that

Flynn's letter to Bathurst was written in a style that showed him to be a person of no education. Poynter, describing his meeting with Bathurst, said: '. . . He asked me, whether I considered Mr. Flynn as a person of education; he should not think so from his letter. I said that I did not know much of Mr. Flynn, but that certainly I had heard the same observation from others who had received letters from him.'

Three days later Under Secretary Goulburn wrote to Flynn: 'I am directed by Lord Bathurst . . . to acquaint you that, after a full consideration of all the circumstances, his Lordship does not consider it advisable to authorize your proceeding to New South Wales.' Not being a man to accept no for an answer, Flynn proceeded anyhow as a private citizen, something which was not forbidden by law. He reached Hobart Town in Van Diemen's Land in October 1817, was well received by Lieutenant Governor Sorell and even dined with him, and also celebrated the first publicly recorded Mass there.[17]

It was 14 November 1817 when Flynn landed at Sydney Cove and on the following day he visited Governor Lachlan Macquarie, who gave the priest a cold reception. Subsequently Macquarie's secretary wrote to Flynn that the governor commanded him 'not to use any of the ceremonies of the Roman Church, in any public manner, in any part of this colony'. Flynn was also ordered 'to depart from this colony' by the ship that had brought him. Poynter when informed of these details by Michael Hayes of Sydney, brother of Father Richard Hayes, forwarded them to Bathurst. Under Secretary Goulburn then wrote to Poynter 'by direction of Earl Bathurst' on 24 July 1818 'that as Mr. Flynn went out there without any permission, or recommendation from His Majesty's Government here, the Governor of New South Wales acted perfectly right in directing him to leave the colony forthwith. . . .'

Flynn had proved popular among the Roman Catholics of Sydney, however, and they helped him go into hiding. But finally he was caught, was put aboard ship, and was sent back to London on 20 May 1818, arriving there in November, never to return to New Holland.

Since Archbishop John Thomas Troy (1739–1823) of Dublin had been misinformed on this entire affair by Flynn, Poynter sent Troy details on 19 August 1818. Lord Bathurst, Poynter said, 'did express his readiness to grant his protection and favour to any Catholic clergyman of respectable character who should be recommended to him as a fit person to go out to the colony of New South Wales . . . Lord Bathurst sent for me at Mr. Flynn's request, but I certainly did not know enough in Mr. Flynn's favour to remove the impression made on Lord Bathurst's mind, or to make myself responsible for him. The character of Mr. Flynn, which I had received [sic!] from his late superior, was sufficient to deter me from committing myself with Lord Bathurst by a positive recommendation of Mr. Flynn . . . On Your Grace's recommendation of a respectable clergyman . . . , I should be happy to be instrumental in obtaining the protection and favour of our Minister, without whose protection a Catholic clergyman is exposed to be much molested in some places. But I should be at a loss to know from whom the clergyman sent could receive his spiritual faculties, as, at the appointment of Mr. Flynn, whatever jurisdiction I held with regard to that colony expired. I should rejoice much to see a good Catholic mission established in New South Wales.'[18]

Father Giovanni Grassi, S.J. (1775–1849), the Jesuit rector of the Reale Collegio del Carmine in Turin, Italy, informed Secretary Pedicini on 22 April 1822 that Flynn had been sent back by the Governor of New Holland on the pretext that he had no passport. However, there was a French priest attached to a college in Maryland in the United States of America, Grassi said, who had volunteered to serve among those who had been deported to New South Wales. He had a private library of 4,000 volumes that he wanted to take along. Pedicini wrote to the Archbishop of Baltimore for more information. The priest was Father Simon-Guillaume-Gabriel Bruté de Rémur (1779–1839), who in 1815 had become president of Saint Mary's College in Baltimore and since 1818 had been on the faculty of Mount Saint Mary's College in Emmitsburg, Maryland. He did not go to New Holland, however. In 1834 he became the first Bishop of Vincennes, Indiana.[19]

When expressing his grief about Flynn's unexpected return from New Holland in a letter to Bishop Poynter of London on 13 February 1819, Francesco Luigi Cardinal Fontana (1750–1822), the new prefect of the Evangelisation Congregation, had begged the vicar apostolic 'with all earnestness' to seek out diligently 'other missionaries who may devote themselves to that mission, no less neglected than it is extensive, and to obtain the Government sanction for their proceeding thither'. About this time, in fact, the Evangelisation Congregation had requested Pope Pius VII to entrust the care of the Catholics of New Holland to Bishop Poynter, and this the pope did. However, at an audience with the pope on 4 April 1819, Pedicini mentioned that letters had recently arrived from Bishop Edward Slater still in England stating that the British government would help him send priests to New Holland. Slater, an English Benedictine, had recently been appointed Vicar Apostolic of the Cape of Good Hope, Madagascar and Mauritius, and was therefore 'in a better position to care for New Holland than the Vicar Apostolic of London'. Giving jurisdiction over New Holland to Bishop Slater would cause no problem, Pedicini said, because the pope's earlier decision had not yet been transmitted to Poynter. And so Pius VII decided at this audience that jurisdiction over New Holland should be given to Slater, who at this time was cultivating good relations with the British government and making preparations for his departure. After receiving the appropriate faculties Slater wrote from London on 24 September assuring Cardinal Prefect Fontana that he had 'already sent two missionaries to New Holland'.[20]

Sydney Cove or Port Jackson was a British colony and so it was only natural that the British government should want to have an English bishop as the local ecclesiastical authority. Yet it was just as natural that the two priests to be sent by Slater to New Holland should be Irish, because nearly all Catholics there were Irish. The ones delegated by him were Father Philip Conolly, senior chaplain, born in the Diocese of Kildare and Leighlin, and Father John Joseph Therry, born in the city of Cork. They sailed aboard the convict ship *Janus* and arrived at the Colony of Port Jackson (Sydney) on 3 May 1820. The two priests quarrelled, however, and Conolly left for Van Diemen's Land, arriving at Hobart on 14 April 1821. Soon Therry was also at odds with the government, which in 1825 dismissed him as official Catholic chaplain and discontinued his salary.

There were about 6,000 Catholics in the Colony of Port Jackson when Conolly and Therry arrived and by 1828 the census listed 11,236 Catholics in a total population of 36,598.

William Bernard Ullathorne

Slater, too, was having difficulties. Reports sent to Rome asking that he be suspended from office resulted in a meeting of the Evangelisation Congregation on 22 December 1829 at which it was decided to request the pope to send a bishop to Mauritius to investigate. Slater's investigator and successor was another English Benedictine, Bishop William Morris. He sent a twenty-six-year-old English Benedictine, Father William Bernard Ullathorne (1806–89), to New Holland to settle disagreements there among the Irish priests and to establish good relations with local government officials. To make this possible Morris had named Ullathorne his vicar general with residence in Sydney. And the British government had named him His Majesty's Catholic chaplain in New South Wales, providing him as well with specific funds.[21]

Ullathorne while en route to New Holland stopped off at Van Diemen's Land on 30 January 1833 for a twelve-day visit with Father Conolly. And in February he arrived unexpected at Port Jackson where by now there were three Irish priests: Therry in Sydney Cove; Christopher Dowling, a Dominican, who had gone to Newcastle after a row with Therry; and John McEncroe, who somehow managed to put up with Therry. Daniel Power, another Irish priest, had died in 1830.

McEncroe (1795–1868) from 1822 to 1829 had served under Bishop John England in the Diocese of Charleston, South Carolina, United States of America. In 1832 he arrived in Sydney aboard the same vessel with John Hubert Plunkett, Solicitor General of New South Wales, as one of the Roman Catholic chaplains of the colony with a salary of £150 per annum. As early as 2 November 1832 he wrote from Sydney to Archbishop Daniel Murray of Dublin, saying: 'The Holy See should provide this place with a Bishop. It is the most neglected portion of the Catholic world. The Vicar-Apostolic at the Mauritius can do but little for this place; by proper care it can become an interesting portion of the fold of Christ . . . I have an arduous mission in Sydney with a Catholic population of five thousand souls, and am called at an average of once or twice a week to attend sick calls at the distance of from 20 to 40 miles.' He said that all told 'there are 16,000 or 18,000 Catholics in this colony, not one half of whom hardly ever see a priest'.[22]

John Bede Polding

Young and active Ullathorne quickly made his influence felt in official circles.

Insisting that three priests in New South Wales and one in Van Diemen's Land were far too few for Roman Catholic needs, he soon persuaded Sir Richard Bourke, new liberal-minded Irish governor in the colony, to petition His Majesty's Government to send four more priests without delay. Ullathorne told Bourke that none of these ought to be sent without the approval of the Vicar Apostolic of London. His Majesty's Government consequently approached Bishop James Bramston, successor to the late Bishop Poynter, with its urgent request. Bramston in turn sent a detailed report on this to Rome with still another urgent request, namely, that Rome assign a bishop to New Holland and Van Diemen's Land. His letter, dated 26 April 1834, was addressed to Cardinal Pedicini who three years earlier had become prefect of the Evangelisation Congregation.

'There are more than 20,000 Catholics' in New Holland and Van Diemen's Land, Bramston said, 'of whom the greater part are convicts banished from England for their crimes. . . .' He mentioned the concern shown for these Catholics by Governor Bourke and Vicar General Ullathorne and indicated their eagerness to receive four more priests without delay. 'It has also been distinctly intimated to me', he said, 'that the clergy to be forwarded should be English, and the Colonial Secretary has for this purpose asked me to select four ecclesiastics, natives of England. Having none among my own subjects whom I could send, I consulted on the matter with the Very Reverend President of the Anglo-Benedictines, John Birdsall, and I am persuaded that it will be easy to find four subjects of this religious Order, deserving of every commendation and willing to engage in this mission.'

Bramston went on to explain that the Vicar Apostolic of Mauritius currently had jurisdiction over New Holland, a circumstance which made communications between the vicar apostolic and his priests in New Holland difficult and even impossible. Therefore 'the president of the Anglo-Benedictines and the other Superiors of the Order in England have come to the conclusion, in which I wholly concur, that it would be impossible to make due provision for the spiritual wants of the faithful in these parts, unless a resident Vicar-Apostolic, invested with the Episcopal dignity, be appointed for that Church.' Bramston had discussed this issue with the Colonial Secretary, he said, 'and I am convinced that, so far as he is concerned there will be no difficulty in the matter'.

'The better to insure success', Bramston suggested that Rome appoint Father John Bede Polding, an English Benedictine monk, the vicar apostolic. 'Your Eminence will probably be surprised at this recommendation,' he quickly added, 'holding in mind how the same religious acted when he was appointed to the Diocese of Madras [India]. But my recommendation is based upon the attestation of the President and other Superiors of the Benedictines on his fame for learning, zeal, and piety among his religious brethren, and on my own knowledge of him.' Polding would also be 'most acceptable to the Government'. In fact, Polding was 'admirably suited' for the office, Bramston said, and had refused the Madras Vicariate precisely because of his great desire to go to New Holland. The Benedictines who showed a readiness to go to New Holland also

32 Minutes of the report given to the cardinal members of the Evangelisation Congregation on 12 May 1834 proposing Father Polding, a Benedictine from England, to head the Vicariate Apostolic of New Holland and Van Diemen's Land. *Source: PF: SC Oceania vol. 1 (1816–41) f. 196r. (Chapter 12).*

di destinarlo a tale incarico.
Di questo Religioso ne sono già stati
fatti all'EE. SS. RR. gli elogii al-
lorché fu eletto Vicario aplico di
Madras, per cui non vi è luogo a
temere, che non sia per riuscire un
buon Pastore.
In mani di Mgr Vicario Aplico di
Londra sono i Brevi ancora per
poterlo consagrare Vescovo di Hier-
ocena per cui con la massima
sollecitudine potrà portarsi al suo
destino, non mancando altro che
fornirlo delle facoltà opportune; e
del Breve di Vicario aplico della
Nuova Missione.
Il Presidente poi dei Benedettini
ha assicurato il Vicario aplico di
Londra che i Religiosi del suo ordine
lascieranno la patria per portarsi
alla Nuova Olanda.
Spetta ora all'EE. VV. ame il
decidere, se credono di approvare
quanto il Vicario aplico di Londra
ha esposto, ed in pari tempo se si
debba supplicare il Santo Padre
per l'opportuna sanzione di tutto,
non che a concedere al Nuovo Vica-
vio aplico le opportune facoltà
per governare con frutto i Cattolici
dimoranti nella Nuova Olanda; e
nell'Isola Van-Diemen

33 Page two of the report, as figure 32. *Source: PF:
SC Oceania vol. 1 (1816–41) f. 196v. (Chapter 12).*

wanted to have Polding as their ecclesiastical superior. Bramston therefore asked that Rome 'with as little delay as possible' make Polding vicar apostolic with jurisdiction over New Holland and Van Diemen's Land.

Pedicini considered Bramston's letter so urgent and so important that he at once passed on its details to the cardinals present for the General Meeting of 12 May 1834, just sixteen days after the letter had been written! The cardinals were told that a particular advantage in choosing Polding for this new office was the fact that 'he will be able to leave for his destination with the utmost haste', since most of the preliminaries in his case had already been attended to. Character references, for example, had been heard by the cardinals when Polding was considered for the office of Vicar Apostolic of Madras at their meeting of 3 July 1832, 'and so there is no need to fear that he will not succeed in being a good pastor'. At that time, also, he had been designated (Titular) Bishop of Hiero-caesarea, a decision that had never been revoked, and the corresponding briefs were still in the hands of the Vicar Apostolic of London. 'All that needs to be done is to provide him with suitable faculties and with a Brief designating him as vicar apostolic of the new mission.' And besides, the report said, Bramston had been assured by the president of the Benedictines 'that four other members of his order will also leave their homeland and go to New Holland'.

Like all reports presented to the cardinals for deliberation, this one ended by giving the gist of the entire proposal. 'It is up to Your Most Reverend Eminences', Secretary Mai said, 'to decide now whether you wish to give your approval to what the Vicar Apostolic of London has suggested. Also, should the Holy Father be asked to give appropriate sanctions for all of this and to provide the new vicar apostolic with corresponding faculties so that he may effectually govern the Catholics living in New Holland and Van Diemen Island?'[23]

The cardinals accepted all points in Bramston's proposal and that same day, 12 May 1834, Pope Gregory XVI, after hearing a report from Secretary Mai, gave his 'gracious approval'. He thus created the Vicariate Apostolic of New Holland and Van Diemen's Land and made Polding its vicar apostolic with the rank of bishop. When the Evangelisation Congregation published this decision in a decree dated 20 May, it said that the new vicariate apostolic had been created because experience had proven that it was extremely difficult to have any kind of suitable communication between New Holland and the island of Mauritius. And it was the bishop and vicar apostolic residing in Mauritius who up until then had been charged with 'the spiritual care . . . of the large number of Catholics living in . . . New Holland and in nearby Van Diemen Island'. The only apparent way to remedy the matter, the decree said, was to give that distant part of the world its own vicar apostolic with the rank of bishop. Then he could 'reside in that most extensive region and look after its ecclesiastical affairs'. The decree also announced, of course, that Polding had been chosen for this new office.[24]

Who was John Bede Polding? He was born in Liverpool on 18 October 1794, joined the Benedictines at Downside, Stratton on the Fosse, Bath, and right after his ordination to the priesthood was assigned to the faculty of Saint Gregory College at Bath. In February 1819 he became novice master at Downside and

34 The Most Reverend John Bede Polding (1794–1877), the first Vicar Apostolic of New Holland and Van Diemen's Land and also the first Bishop and Archbishop of Sydney. *Source: Catholic Weekly (Sydney). (Chapter 12).*

from August 1826 onward was also subprior. Both terms of office ended on 24 June 1834 and on 29 June the thirty-nine-year-old monk was ordained a bishop by Bramston in his private chapel in Golden Square in Soho, London, about two blocks from Piccadilly Circus.[25] Bramston's assistants were his own coadjutor bishop, Thomas Griffiths, and Bishop Étienne Rouchouze, the newly appointed Vicar Apostolic of Eastern Oceania.

Polding formally accepted his new office in a letter to Rome on 14 June and he wrote again to Cardinal Pedicini from Bath on 24 July, saying that he had many letters in his possession attesting to the numerous evils existing in his new vicariate. For example, 'Catholics lack nearly every type of education, and so non-Catholic ministers have taken advantage of this to bring harm to the Catholic religion . . . And, as you know well enough from experience, many of the priests who go to foreign lands are generally such whose morals are not acceptable at home.' He said that 'nothing, therefore, will benefit the propagation of the Catholic religion so much as founding in that vicariate a seminary in which the most upright youths can be trained in virtue and zeal for religion under the very eyes and practically by the hand of the one in charge'. Through soliciting funds and assistance of all kinds from Catholics in England, Polding 'had already in some way laid the foundation for this work', he said, and likewise had been assured by his fellow Benedictines assembled in Chapter 'that they will not desert me when it comes to concrete action and subsidies'.

Van Diemen's Land, he told the Italian cardinal, was 'hardly smaller in size than the Island of Sicily and has only one priest serving 4,000 dispersed Catholics; nor do these [Catholics] have any kind of education for their youth, nor even a chapel'.[26] As for New Holland, it had 'more than 25,000 Catholics in an area 200 miles long and 7 miles wide', not to mention those in other scattered areas. And in addition, 'about one thousand Catholics a year migrate to these lands'. Polding said that the only way to provide efficacious help for all these Catholics was to erect a seminary. True, there were four priests on the Australian mainland, and they 'certainly are men inflamed with zeal for God's glory and the salvation of souls', but they simply could not cope with the task.

What was the purpose of this report? Polding said that through it he hoped to receive 'from the Apostolic See every kind of grace, favour and help' for his proposed seminary. He said it was a matter of such great importance because it concerned 'God's glory and the salvation of nearly 30,000 souls'. (The official census of 1836 gave the precise number of Catholics as 21,898.)[27]

Polding left Brunswick Dock, Liverpool, for Sydney aboard the *Oriental* on 27 March 1835, five months after Rouchouze had left Le Havre for Eastern Oceania, and he arrived at Hobart Town in Van Diemen's Land on 7 August. After spending a month there and leaving behind one of his three priests as a companion for Father Conolly, he set sail for Sydney where he arrived on 13 September. Polding went ashore the next day and on the following Sunday, 20 September 1835, was solemnly installed in Saint Mary's Church as Vicar Apostolic of New Holland and Van Diemen's Land. His first two letters to the Prior of Downside describing his arrival and initial activities were lost en route but his third letter of 13 November 1835 reported that at present he was busy 'building a church at Parramatta (the second largest town in this colony) which will be about 70 feet long and 40 feet wide . . . The cost is estimated at 600 pounds sterling (about 3,000 scudi), of which half will be paid by the government and the other half by the inhabitants of the colony.' In the coming week he planned to visit the Illawarra District, 'about 40 miles from Sydney, in order to choose a site for the monastery'. Land was sold there 'ordinarily at five shillings an acre'. But the price was expected to rise considerably 'as soon as the new road now being made is completed'. He said that he was fortunate having in Sydney 'an excellent and generous governor, a man with vision and with an affectionate heart'. The governor was Sir Richard Bourke.

This particular letter from Polding reached Downside on 1 April 1836 and excerpts from it were forwarded to Cardinal Fransoni on 20 May by Father William Bernard Allen Collier, the procurator general of the English Benedictines in Rome residing at San Calisto Hospice at Piazza Santa Maria in Trastevere.[28]

Ullathorne, a former student of Polding at Downside, at once became his vicar general and confidant. On 10 May 1836, when Polding had been in New Holland no more than eight months, he had Ullathorne leave Sydney for Europe to accomplish various missions. He was to try to recruit for New Holland priests and candidates for the priesthood. In Rome he was to obtain formal authorisation for the erection of a seminary. In England he was to take action to improve the lot of convicts in New Holland, Norfolk Island and Van Diemen's Land. And in Ireland he was to win a community of Sisters to work for the moral betterment of female convicts and a community of teaching Brothers to take up work in Sydney schools.

Attempts had already been made to obtain teaching Brothers, but all had failed. McEncroe in his letter of 2 November 1832 from Sydney to Archbishop Murray of Dublin, in which he had asked that a bishop be assigned to New Holland, had said: 'We want very much five or six competent schoolmasters; each would get about £50 a year. I have the appointment. What a blessing, if I could procure two or three of Mr. Rice's brothers. Please speak to him. I will pay their passage money on their arrival in Sydney. We would soon have subjects for their Order, and thus be able in time to supply all the Catholic schools with proper teachers.'

Rice was none other than Brother Edmund Ignatius Rice (1762–1844), the widowed businessman of Waterford, Ireland, who had founded the Congregation of the Brothers of the Christian Schools of Ireland or the Christian Brothers of Ireland, nowadays called simply the Christian Brothers (C.F.C.). On 20 January 1822 at the age of fifty-nine he had been elected the community's first superior general. Archbishop Murray called Rice to his office and showed him McEncroe's letter. But nothing came of it.

Several months after his arrival in Sydney in February 1833 Ullathorne as vicar general of Bishop Morris made a similar request. He asked Polding, who at this time was still novice master and subprior at Downside, to write in his name to Rice. Polding obliged and Rice then had a letter sent on 21 November 1833 to all his teaching Brothers in vows to learn their views. This letter spoke of New Holland's 'total want of well-regulated schools for the religious and moral education of the rising generation', and said that Polding in Ullathorne's name had 'pressed in a most suppliant manner for four or six of our brothers to assist in this great and meritorious work'. Free passage would be provided by the government, which allowed £300 annually for Catholic education, and 'there are three boys' schools already established. . . .' But in this case as well Rice's response was negative. So now Ullathorne intended to try personal contact.

In England he would give graphic testimony to Sir William Molesworth's Committee on Transportation on the horrors of the system, for he had witnessed them for three full years in New Holland, Norfolk Island and Van Diemen's Land. 'The number of criminals annually transported is about 6,000', he wrote in 1837 in a London publication. 'In 1835, the last year of which I have a full account, there were transported to New South Wales, 3,006 males and 179 females; to Van Diemen's Land, 2,054 males and 922 females, making a total of 6,161 criminals. The entire number in actual bondage is, in New South Wales, nearly 30,000, whilst, in Van Diemen's Land, there are nearly 20,000, to which must be added 3,000 for the penal settlements of Norfolk Island, Moreton Bay, and Port Arthur . . . Of all these, one third are Irish Catholics. . . .'

All of the convicts, he said, 'arrive in numbers of from two to three hundred in a ship, under the authority and superintendence of a surgeon of the Royal Navy'. They are 'thrown together for four months [the length of their voyage], with no occupation . . . They are closed down at night under hatches, each rolled in his blanket, three or more placed together in one wooden crib . . . In 1835, the number of men in chain gangs was, in New South Wales, 1,191; in road gangs, 982. In Van Diemen's Land, the number in chain gangs was 805; in road gangs, 2,919 . . . In 1835, there were 116 capital convictions in the criminal court of Sydney, all for crimes of violence; whilst the convictions for petty offences, for the same year, throughout this one colony, amounted to nearly 22,000. The Reverend Mr. McEncroe has himself attended 74 executions in the course of four years . . . The number of criminals at the [Norfolk Island] settlement in 1835 was 1,200 of whom 450 were Catholic . . . They are worked in heavy irons, and fed on salt meat and maize bread. . . .'[29]

On 12 July 1836, only two months after Ullathorne had left Sydney en route to Europe, the Nuncio Apostolic of Vienna picked up his pen to inform Cardinal Fransoni of an interesting conversation regarding Norfolk Island. 'When I was speaking with the esteemed Countess Hügel several days ago she told me about her son, who for several years has been travelling all over Asia and Oceania. From time to time he sends home reports on his voyages and she narrated to me the contents of one of them. In it he speaks of persons from Great Britain who in exchange for the death penalty are deported to Norfolk Island. And he depicts them as very miserable, especially as far as religion is concerned.'

The nuncio told Fransoni that since the information would be of special interest to the Evangelisation Congregation, he had asked the Countess whether he might borrow the passage concerned. 'She complied with my request,' he said, 'giving me the report referred to above, and I have faithfully translated it from the original German into Latin.' Fransoni would see from the report, he said, that two-thirds of those deported to Norfolk Island were Catholics and that there were 600 Catholics all told 'on that island where there is not a single priest'.[30]

Norfolk Island, first settled in 1788 from Sydney Cove, had been abandoned in 1814 when the convicts were all transferred to Van Diemen's Land, then in need of development. But in 1824 the British government decided to reopen it as a penal colony 'for the worst type of criminals'. Governor Brisbane in 1825 stated that 'the felon who is sent there is forever excluded from all hope of return'. For the next thirty years the worst criminals from New South Wales, Van Diemen's Land and eventually straight from England were sent there and suffered the severest inhumanity of the convict system.[31]

The nuncio's letter to Fransoni closed with the good news that a benefactor had provided 'the sum of 10,000 fine Austrian florins, equivalent to 5,000 Bavarian florins', so that the Evangelisation Congregation 'could have at least one Jesuit missionary take up work' on Norfolk Island. And the money could be had immediately by Rome, as soon as word arrived that a Jesuit had been found for this mission. The donor, not mentioned by name in the letter, was a certain Canon Schmidt.

A quick exchange of correspondence followed. Fransoni contacted the superior general of the Jesuits, who pleaded inability to accept Norfolk Island as a mission. On being advised of this the nuncio wrote back to Fransoni on 19 August, saying that the benefactor was disappointed. However, knowing that the Jesuits usually sent two missionaries to a post, and thinking that the amount consequently was insufficient, the donor had increased the fund by 5,000 fine Austrian florins, making a grand total of 15,000 fine Austrian florins. 'And in case the Father General should persist in his refusal,' the nuncio added, 'the pious benefactor, although sorry at not being able to obtain Jesuits as missionaries for the indicated island and colony, will be well pleased with whatever arrangement the Sacred Congregation might make in order to provide the faithful there with necessary spiritual assistance and two zealous priests.' The money meanwhile would be invested, the nuncio said, so that it could draw interest. But this offer as well was turned down by the Jesuit superior general and nothing was done for Norfolk Island at the moment.[32]

Ullathorne visited Rome in 1837 and on 13 May wrote to Fransoni from San Calisto Hospice in Trastevere. He pointed out that New Holland—which he also called Australia—was made up of six colonies located at great distances from one another. Four of them had been founded recently on the southern coast: King George's Sound, Spencer's Gulf, Gulf St. Vincent and Port Philip. Swan River on the west coast he listed in the fifth place and said that he had visited it a few times. But most of his energies, he said, had been dedicated to the colony of New South Wales, 'which was chosen by the British Government as a substitute penal colony for North America which had separated from England'. The first Europeans to arrive in 1788 'totalled 1,030 souls of whom over 700 were convicts'. The population was less than 8,000 by 1800, Ullathorne said, but by 1837 it had grown to 100,000.

The many whaling vessels in the Pacific Ocean, he said, sailed frequently into the harbours of Sydney and Hobart Town, coming from New Zealand where they stopped to take on fresh supplies. As for the Aboriginal population of New Holland, it was considered 'to be the last portion of mankind and also the least intelligent by all authors who have written on the subject. The same is said about the Papuans of New Guinea and the inhabitants of the Indian Archipelago [now Indonesia].'

His report, however, ended on a very optimistic note. 'In concluding this document of mine on the colonies,' he said, 'I must state that their rapid growth in recent years in population, commerce, and general importance is altogether without parallel. This is a country whose progress and whose prospects are already exciting much interest, since it employs a vast number of ships for commerce, not only with England, but also with the East Indies, America and islands scattered across the ocean. It seems evident that this country by reason of its resources and its central position is destined to exert after a short time a very great influence on the Southern Hemisphere. Consequently getting religion well established in these colonies will affect not only Australia, but even half the world.'[33]

The Evangelisation Congregation placed New Holland and Van Diemen's Land on its agenda for the General Meeting of 3 July 1837, since it now had much information on both places from Polding and Ullathorne. (Just five days before this date Pompallier and his missionaries had arrived in Valparaíso.) The report which was read at the meeting of cardinals briefly indicated the activities of individual priests in New Holland and Van Diemen's Land prior to the arrival of Bishop Polding. It stated among other things that 'the number of those condemned to slavery is 30,000 in New Holland and 17,000 on Van Diemen Island. And about 3,000 have been condemned for new crimes to the more severe penal colonies of Norfolk and Port Arthur.'[34] Others had already finished their prison terms and had been emancipated from slavery. According to the report, morality in those places was 'as corrupt as one could possibly imagine'.

Cardinal Castracane, a former secretary of the Evangelisation Congregation, had prepared the report and said that Polding unfortunately had no more than seven priests and so was able to care for only the southern part of New Holland, 'now to be called New [South] Wales'. He had not been able to send any spiritual aid at all to those in the north and to the west. In Van Diemen Island he had only one priest, the cardinal said, and none at all in Norfolk Island, 'distant about a thousand miles from the capital of New [South] Wales'.

The Anglicans in 1836 had appointed a Bishop of Australia with residence in Sydney, he reported, and the Methodists had also taken up missionary work there. These groups 'let no means go untried, but until now they have been little successful in making converts among Catholics and the indigenous population'.

Polding, however, needed teachers for his schools so that Catholic children would not be forced to go to Protestant schools. Castracane also pointed out that Polding's priests were receiving from the government not only a salary but other financial assistance as well. His report ended with some practical questions.

'In view of the copious subsidies and funds that the mission has received from the British Government,' Castracane said, 'and in view of the government's assurance that it will remain favourably disposed in the future, should the Sacred Congregation for the present provide the mission only with personnel?' The cardinals answered that the Sacred Congregation should provide not only more missionaries, 'but also so much financial aid as possible, in order to help the vicar apostolic erect institutes of Christian learning for youths of both sexes, and especially a seminary'.

Another question was whether the Sacred Congregation, in order better to achieve this purpose 'and to facilitate for Father Ullathorne his negotiations with the English Government' concerning the improvement of moral conditions for condemned Catholics, should furnish him with letters of recommendation 'to the Archbishop of Dublin and to the Vicar Apostolic of London, so that through their contacts and influence his efforts might be more effective'. The cardinals replied that such letters were indeed to be given to Ullathorne. But in addition to these he was to receive other letters as well addressed not only to the Archbishop of Dublin, but also to all other archbishops of Ireland, 'exhorting them to assist Father Ullathorne both in finding missionaries and in obtaining Sisters of some pious institute and Brothers of Christian Doctrine'. The archbishops of Ireland were to send the Sisters and Brothers 'to New Holland for the education of youth'. The name used here, Brothers of Christian Doctrine, was a misnomer for the Brothers of the Christian Schools of Ireland founded by Brother Edmund Ignatius Rice and nowadays known simply as Christian Brothers (C.F.C.).

After the questions formulated by Castracane were all answered, the cardinals discussed the matter even further and 'pointed out that there exist in New Holland six colonies properly so called which from the time of their foundation have been deprived of all the helps that come from religion'. In order that 'they might not remain in this calamitous state any longer', the cardinals deemed it 'most advisable to procure missionaries from the Institute of Charity', whose founder was Father Antonio Rosmini Serbati (1797–1855). They decided to write and ask him 'kindly to indicate whether among the priests of his society there might be found some so disposed as to take upon themselves gladly the role of foreign missionaries and go to New Holland'. Rosmini was one of Italy's leading educators and was well known in Rome. He had founded his religious community at Santo Monte Calvario near Domodossola on 20 February 1828 and in 1833 had founded a community of nuns known as Sisters of Providence.[35]

While in Rome, Ullathorne had heard of the Vienna fund which was available on condition that two priests be sent to Norfolk Island. From England on 15 December 1837 he wrote to Collier, the Benedictine procurator general in Rome, that 'the Reverend [John] Brady, named expressly for Norfolk Island, has already left England accompanied by another priest and they are en route for New Holland. Five other priests are ready to leave immediately and I give my word of honour that one of these will accompany the Reverend Brady to Norfolk Island. Thus I hope that I shall be able to obtain the Vienna fund.' Father Brady, who later became the first Bishop of Perth, had served for twelve years in the Bourbon-Mauritius mission, had met Ullathorne in Rome in 1837, and had volunteered for the Australian mission. He sailed aboard the *Upton Castle*, arriving in Australia on 24 February 1838.

Collier hastily got this information from Ullathorne into Fransoni's hands, telling him at the same time that 'the British Government grants to Catholic clergy at the service of religion in New Holland a sum equal to that which they themselves manage to acquire elsewhere' for religious purposes. Therefore, he said, 'Father Ullathorne would immediately obtain a right to such an advantage, if this said fund should be entrusted to him . . . Further, it will be difficult to transmit this money to New Holland if it is not entrusted to Father Ullathorne before his departure, which is to take place very soon'.

Collier also told Fransoni that Polding 'for a long time has been desirous of seeing a Benedictine monastery established' in New Holland. Since Benedictines make a vow to occupy themselves with missionary work, 'they would be adapted to spread religion in those vast areas'. Ullathorne while in Rome, he said, had requested faculties from Fransoni for Polding to establish such a monastery in Australia and Secretary Mai later had given assurance that the desired faculties had been granted and the rescript sent to the Vicar Apostolic of London for Ullathorne. But this rescript had never arrived and now Ullathorne through Collier requested a new one.

Ullathorne had also informed Collier that the British government 'has decided to colonise New Zealand and to send a Protestant bishop there'. Ullathorne's own letter read: 'Now we shall see those two islands [of New Zealand] covered rapidly by Englishmen. I foresee bloody revolutions and a war of extermination against the indigenes. An exclusively Protestant society has been founded in London and has published a manifesto of its aims, namely, to form a new colony in the southern part of Australia, but in such a manner that neither idolator nor Catholic will ever be able to possess land in that colony.'[36]

Rome had acted on the Vienna fund more quickly than Ullathorne! Five months before he even wrote his 15 December 1837 letter saying that he was now able to fulfil the Norfolk Island conditions, the Evangelisation Congregation had taken action to have the fund allocated instead to Polding for his seminary. It had written to the nuncio in Vienna immediately after its meeting of 3 July 1837, asking whether the donor might agree to have his grant, earmarked for sending two priests to Norfolk Island, allocated instead to Bishop Polding for his proposed seminary in Sydney. The nuncio informed Fransoni on 23 July that the donor had 'promptly and very willingly' agreed to have the money allocated 'for the erection of a seminary at Sydney in New Wales, granting for that purpose the sum which he had wanted to devote to the maintenance of two religious missionaries in Norfolk'. The Evangelisation

Congregation would have to see to it that the Vicar Apostolic of New Holland actually used the funds 'for students of that seminary instead of for spiritual needs of the Catholics of Norfolk'.[37]

Because of the urgency now indicated by Collier, Fransoni quickly issued instructions for the nuncio in Vienna to transfer a large portion of the fund immediately to Ullathorne. Nuncio Ludovico Altieri replied that the fund, which originally totalled 15,000 fine Austrian florins, now because of interest amounted to 16,492.14 fine Austrian florins. He made the transfer as requested.[38]

Six days before Ullathorne penned his above letter of 15 December 1837 to Collier in Rome, Bishop Pompallier had arrived in Sydney aboard the *Raiatea*. Showing true Benedictine hospitality Polding took the bishop and the priest and Brother with him into his own home for the duration of their stay. Just as Pompallier had sought to learn all that he could from Bishop Rouchouze about the foundation, growth and difficulties of the Vicariate Apostolic of Eastern Oceania, he now tried to learn all that he could about the Vicariate Apostolic of New Holland and Van Diemen's Land from Polding who would be his nearest fellow bishop.

Pompallier was well received by Polding and was also well received by government officials in Sydney. He had to pay neither customs nor storage fees of any kind on the supplies that he had brought into the country. These he entrusted to Polding until such time as he would know where he wanted to make his New Zealand headquarters.[39]

Polding suggested that Father McEncroe, in addition to his regular duties, serve as Pompallier's contact in Sydney for making purchases and for forwarding his mail to Europe. Polding also had McEncroe write a letter of introduction for Pompallier on 21 December to 'the Roman Catholics of New Zealand and of the South Sea Islands', and added a postscript of his own: 'We invite all to receive in the name of Christ Jesus, the Bishop whom He Himself by His Vicegerent has appointed over them.'[40]

Polding wrote a separate letter of introduction on 27 December to Mr Thomas Poynton, saying among other things that he had made over to Pompallier 'the ten acres of land for a church and burying ground' that New Zealand Catholics had earlier made over to him. Poynton, an Irish Catholic, had come to Sydney Cove in 1822 and in 1828 became the first Catholic settler in New Zealand, opening a store and sawmill at Hokianga. His wife Mary, daughter of Thomas Kennedy of Wexford County, was born in Sydney in 1811 and was baptised by Father Jeremiah F. Flynn in 1817. She sailed from Hokianga to Sydney Cove to have their first daughter baptised by Father Therry and two years later returned to have him baptise their first son.

On receiving word in 1835 that Polding had arrived in Sydney, Poynton in the name of all New Zealand Catholics went to see the new bishop and requested a priest. He received instead a letter dated 29 October 1835 in which Polding said he had 'great pleasure in sending Some Books of Instruction and Devotion to the faithful in New Zealand'. He exhorted them 'most earnestly in our Lord to continue in the faith', and urged them to 'join in spirit in the Prayers of your Brethren who enjoy the consolations of Religion of which at present you are deprived. . . .' About twelve months later Poynton was back in Sydney looking for a priest, but again in vain. On a third visit, however, he was assured by Polding that missionaries were on the way. Since Pompallier had made up his mind long before reaching Sydney Cove that New Zealand would be the headquarters for his Vicariate Apostolic of Western Oceania, Polding naturally recommended that his first contact there should be Poynton.[41]

Pompallier on 22 December wrote from Sydney to the Commander of the French Station at Valparaíso. He mentioned the various circumstances which had made him decide not to go to Ponape after all 'in spite of the project that I had conceived at Valparaíso and about which I wrote to the Minister of the Navy in France . . . God at times shows his will more clearly and obliges one to make decisions different from those which are at first conceived. This is what happened to me. . . .' He added that the governor in Sydney had written a letter of introduction for him to the British consul at the Bay of Islands in the northeast part of New Zealand. Pompallier was to deliver this letter personally.[42]

On the following day Pompallier wrote to Colin, head of the Marists, saying that the purchasing office for his mission should not be established in California or in Mexico, as he himself had earlier suggested, but at Sydney. As for Ponape, it would have to wait until he received more personnel from France.[43]

Pompallier and Polding celebrated this Christmas of 1837 together. Later, when describing his visit in a letter to Fransoni, Pompallier said that he and Polding had become friends. And telling Colin about his host, he wrote: 'In the short time that we were there, he had two portraits made, his and mine . . . He kept mine . . . and I took his to New Zealand.'

Finally Pompallier and his two missionaries boarded the *Raiatea* for the last time and sailed from Sydney on 30 December 1837 for New Zealand. It was the second consecutive year in which these three men would spend New Year's Eve aboard ship on the open sea while en route to their mission.[44]

And Ullathorne? Had his many letters of recommendation from the Evangelisation Congregation proved helpful in achieving his goals? When he sailed aboard the *Francis Spaight* from Gravesend on the River Thames on 18 August 1838, he had eleven others in his party. There were three priests and three candidates for the priesthood. And there were four Sisters of Charity from Dublin and a postulant provided by their superior general, Mother Mary Aikenhead, with the blessing of the Archbishop of Dublin. These were the first Sisters of any religious congregation to go to New Holland. But Ullathorne had no teaching Brothers in his party. 'Our brothers did not then sail for Sydney,' one of Rice's members said in his memoirs, 'as our Superiors did not think well of it, neither had they brothers to spare.' As for Rice himself, he submitted his resignation as superior general at the age of seventy-six. By coincidence this happened less than a month before the *Francis Spaight* sailed.

While in England, Ullathorne had testified before government bodies on the transportation system, had published tracts on it, and had described its evils in a course of lectures in the churches of Lancashire. When he reached Sydney with his party on 31 December 1838, he soon learned that some officials in the colony and many influential persons had taken offence at his statements made in Europe against the transportation system. Difficulties began to spring up for Vicar General Ullathorne on every side and by some he was nicknamed 'Agitator General'. He had been absent from Sydney for two years and seven months. Before another two years and seven months would pass, he would be back in England, never to return to New Holland.[45]

13

Pompallier makes New Zealand his headquarters

10 JANUARY 1838

Bishop Pompallier left Sydney aboard the *Raiatea* for New Zealand on 30 December 1837. Describing his arrival, he said: 'On Wednesday, the 10th of January, 1838, we arrived at the entrance of the Hokianga River, which is on the north-west coast of the North Island of New Zealand, after a pleasant passage of twelve days. We proceeded about eighteen leagues up this big river into the interior of the country on the schooner. A European pilot stationed at the mouth of the river took us up safe and well.' Thomas Poynton, the Irish timber merchant about whom Pompallier had learned from Bishop Polding, met the party and took them to Totara Point. Here Poynton and his wife Mary had their house and they spontaneously loaned it to the bishop and his two companions, Father Catherin Servant and Brother Michel Colombon. One of the four small rooms was soon converted into a chapel and here on Saturday, 13 January 1838, Pompallier celebrated the first recorded Mass in New Zealand. Pompallier later designated 10 January 1838, his date of arrival, as the foundation date for 'the Roman Catholic Mission of New Zealand'.[1]

Bishop Polding's letter had asked Poynton to use all his influence in obtaining for Pompallier 'a favourable reception with the chiefs', and urged him to 'present this good man as equal in spiritual power with myself'. Polding also wanted Poynton to share with the new bishop the immense knowledge about New Zealand that he had acquired through experience.[2]

Thirty-six-year-old Pompallier found a second friend in forty-three-year-old Baron Charles de Thierry, with whom he finally caught up in New Zealand. Unwittingly Pompallier in meandering across the Pacific had been following close behind de Thierry. On arriving in Tahiti on 21 September 1837, the bishop learned that the baron had been there for twenty-one months and had left the island on 3 May of that year. And when Pompallier arrived in Sydney on 9 December 1837, he learned that de Thierry had also been there. The baron had arrived on 30 July aboard the American Brig *Draco*, had issued a proclamation on 20 September regarding his New Zealand intentions, and had recruited approximately a hundred interested settlers. Then six weeks prior to Pompallier's arrival in Sydney, de Thierry had departed for New Zealand aboard the *Nimrod* with his would-be colonists, arriving there on 4 November. (This was two months and six days before Pompallier arrived at Hokianga Bay.) To the baron's great surprise, however, and to the utter disenchantment of his party,

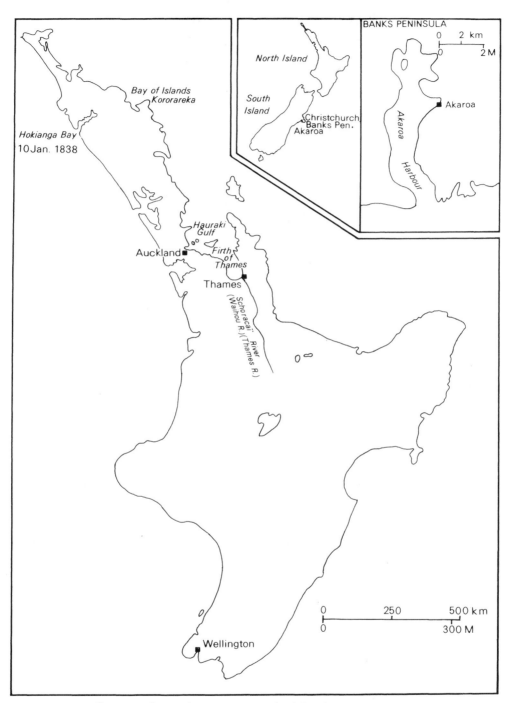

BANKS PENINSULA

0 — 2 km
0 — 2 M

North Island

South Island

Christchurch
Banks Pen.
Akaroa

Akaroa

Akaroa Harbour

Bay of Islands
Kororareka

Hokianga Bay
10 Jan. 1838

Hauraki Gulf

Auckland

Firth of Thames

Thames

Schoracaï River
(Waihou R.) (Thames R.)

0 — 250 — 500 km
0 — 300 M

Wellington

35 Bishop Pompallier arrived at Hokianga Bay, New Zealand, on 10 January 1838, took up residence in the immediate vicinity, but soon afterwards moved to Kororareka in the Bay of Islands. The de Solages-Dillon plan of 1829 had envisioned a New Zealand foundation on the Schoracaï River, better known today as the Waihou River or Thames River. The insets show the location of Banks Peninsula and the French settlement of Akaroa. *(Chapters 2, 13, 14)*.

his New Zealand 'kingdom' had meanwhile dwindled from 40,000 acres (16,000 hectares) to something like 300 acres (120 hectares)!

In addition to receiving a letter of introduction to de Thierry from de Saint-Hilaire, Director of the Colonies in Paris, Pompallier had received a letter of introduction from Polding. Impressed at being addressed by two such high dignitaries of state and church, and sincerely eager to be helpful, de Thierry made good use of the little influence that he had. He printed and distributed copies of Pompallier's letter from de Rosamel, Minister of the Navy, addressed to the commander of the French naval forces based in the South Seas. This letter, which ordered the commander to give Pompallier special protection, was also published in the newspapers of New South Wales. Besides this, de Thierry wrote a circular letter of his own. By 20 March 1838 Pompallier had met de Thierry and he wrote to de Saint-Hilaire that the baron's property was quite a distance away. Soon after arriving Pompallier had sent a messenger to de Thierry with the letters of recommendation addressed to him. 'But in this country I am told that one does not put much faith in what he does', Pompallier told de Saint-Hilaire.[3]

Unexpectedly Pompallier found yet a third friend who had all sorts of contacts with Maoris and European settlers and whose practical knowledge of New Zealand and even of Western Oceania was exceptionally vast. He was Captain Peter Dillon, the same man who had worked so closely in 1829–30 with Father de Solages, Prefect Apostolic of the South Sea Islands. Dillon had arrived at the Bay of Islands on New Zealand's northeast coast in February 1838 and had learned that Pompallier had settled just one month before at Hokianga. Subsequently both men met at the Bay of Islands and had long talks together. Dillon was soon to leave for Europe, but promised to return in charge of a ship, if one was donated in Europe, in order to bring Pompallier and his missionaries to the various islands of Western Oceania. His only complaint later about the bishop was that he could not speak English.

Comte Molé, French Minister of Foreign Affairs, apparently was aware of Dillon's movements, because he had written about him on 30 January 1837 to a certain Prince d'Eckmühl, then contemplating a journey from France to Australia. 'At Sydney you will find Captain Dillon, an officer of the English navy', the minister said. '. . . I would be interested in knowing whether it might be expedient and possible to give him the title of consular agent at Sydney.' But d'Eckmühl never reached Sydney and Dillon never received this post. The Irish sea captain nevertheless proved of great help to Pompallier and from London for years to come would continue to assist the mission.[4]

It soon became clear to Pompallier that the real centre of shipping and activity in New Zealand was at the Bay of Islands, which was a two days' trip overland from Hokianga. Pompallier was back at the Bay of Islands for five days in May 1838 to receive from Captain Cécille of the French corvette *Héroïne* part of the supplies which he had left in storage at Sydney. The two men had a conference on 10 May, discussed among other things the assistance received by Pompallier from de Thierry, and visited Maori tribes in the vicinity of the Bay of Islands. Before leaving that area Pompallier promised the Maoris that he would found a mission station among them as soon as more priests should arrive from France.[5]

Four days later, on 14 May, Pompallier wrote to Colin: 'It shall be necessary, my Reverend Father, for you to send me as soon as possible at least 14 priests and 7 Brothers. That is, 10 priests and 6 Brothers for New Zealand, 2 priests for the islands of Wallis and Futuna, and 2 priests and 1 Brother for the Ponape Islands. . . .' From these words it is clear that Pompallier wanted to live up to the Marist ideal of having a minimum of two priests and one Brother on each mission station. Wallis and Futuna each already had one priest and one Brother. Aware that Colin would have difficulty in supplying all the priests needed, Pompallier asked him to request the Evangelisation Congregation in Rome to provide the balance. Funds were also needed because the money brought along from France had all been used up in establishing the three missions of Wallis, Futuna and Hokianga. In fact the bishop said that he was already 1,200 francs in debt.

Much of his letter was devoted to decisions undoubtedly reached because of his conversations with Dillon. He pointed out that it would be faster and more economical for mission personnel in the future to travel to New Zealand by taking the route around the Cape of Good Hope and New Holland. It was true that New Zealand could not at all be considered the geographical centre of his vicariate, he said. But the prevailing winds there and the large number of ships which regularly visited New Zealand were 'more important considerations' than mere geography.

As indicated in his letter Pompallier did want to bring reinforcements to Wallis and Futuna and he also hoped to begin a new mission at Ponape or Rotuma. He admitted that the missionaries at Wallis and Futuna were 'a bit abandoned' and stated that as yet he had received no news about them. He had been assured earlier by captains that many ships dropped anchor at those two islands, but the truth was that ships stopped there very rarely. And the ships that did go from the Bay of Islands were owned by the Protestant mission and did not care to take Pompallier aboard.

It was only natural then that Pompallier, apparently following Dillon's advice, should try to acquire a schooner of 100–120 tons. 'A small ship of this size would cost about 20,000 francs', he said, and it would be 'good for the longest voyages'. This would mean that money otherwise spent for passage on ships could be saved, and it would be a simple matter to contact even the farthest mission stations. But how could he get enough money to purchase a schooner? Pompallier had an idea. He told Colin that he was expecting funds from the Evangelisation Congregation in Rome and from the Association for the Propagation of the Faith in Lyon for building a purchasing office outside the limits of his own vicariate. But this was an expensive operation. He had now decided to set up that office at the Bay of Islands, 'a very safe place for this and one which offers frequent contacts with Europe via Sydney, Tahiti and Valparaíso'. The money originally earmarked for the extra-territorial purchasing office, therefore, could now be used to purchase the schooner!

Pompallier had one last request for Colin to fulfil. What he needed most of all in New Zealand after personnel and funds was 'a printing press and a skilled operator for it'. With a printing press he could counteract 'the heretical missionaries' who were constantly circulating books, brochures and fliers, 'whereas we have nothing but our voices and our pens'.[6]

But how could Colin in 1838 possibly provide Pompallier with fourteen priests? The first group to take vows as Marists on 24 September 1836 had numbered only twenty priests and four of these had left Le Havre with Pompallier! Apparently convinced that Colin alone could not fulfil his needs, Pompallier addressed himself to Cardinal Prefect Fransoni on 21 May 1838, one week after writing to Colin. He explained all that had happened since he had left Valparaíso and he gave a picture of the current religious situation in New Zealand.

The country, he said, was 'covered with ministers of several kinds of sects. . . .' He had had to endure 'the menace of persecution during the first two months at Hokianga' and was meant to be the victim in 'a violent attempt which had death as its goal . . . But now the Catholic ministry can be practised freely in New Zealand.' In fact, he already had been able to baptise a tribal chief whom he named Gregorio in honour of Pope Gregory XVI. This was 'the first chief and even the first native whom I baptised'. He had also baptised 'the princess daughter of another great chief' and had named her Marie Anne. 'Conditions for the establishment of the Kingdom of God in the entire southern portion' of Western Oceania 'are now more favourable than ever before', he said, since 'news of the arrival of a legitimate minister is being spread among the archipelagoes. . . .'

In order to reap this potential harvest, however, he needed more priests than Colin could supply, and so he suggested to Fransoni three other possibilities. First of all, the Evangelisation Congregation had its own seminary in Rome called the Urban College and he would be happy to receive any good priests who had attended courses there. Secondly, he could send candidates directly from New Zealand whom the Evangelisation Congregation and the Marists might be kind enough to train. This would be a good way, he said, for both organisations 'to cooperate in getting religion established in this country . . . But it would be impossible for me to cover the cost of their voyages and their education.' Thirdly, Pompallier suggested that he also might obtain some priests from the Society of the Catholic Apostolate founded at Rome in 1835 by Father Vincenzo Pallotti. Pompallier had met Pallotti while in Rome in 1836 and this priest had shown 'lively interest in my mission and had promised to help me through the society that he directs. He even wanted to receive me into it as a member.' Enclosed for Pallotti was an unsealed letter which Pompallier wanted Fransoni to read and then forward, 'if Your Eminence should judge it apropos'.

Fransoni did forward Bishop Pompallier's letter dated 22 May 1838. In it the bishop reminded Pallotti of his promise to give every kind of assistance. 'How I need collaborators', Pompallier said. 'Reverend Director, if among your colleagues you should be able to find some priests with a divine vocation for taking up work in my mission, kindly speak with His Eminence, Cardinal Fransoni, about them, or with the Very Reverend Secretary of the same Sacred Congregation', so that they 'can be sent to me at once'. The Marists, he believed, 'will perhaps find it difficult to supply a sufficient number of workers for so vast a mission'.

Pompallier also reminded Pallotti of the letter that he had written from Paris in November 1836 before leaving for Oceania. In it he had mentioned 'many things useful for the missions'. It would be of great help, for example, 'if some members of the Catholic Apostolate, whether priests or laity—and especially those skilled in some profession—were to prepare themselves' under Pallotti's guidance for Pompallier's mission. His 1836 letter had also asked for tools, clothing made of cotton or wool, and other items, all of which 'can be of great service in relieving the needs of the inhabitants and in winning for ourselves their affection and confidence, so that the faith and the kingdom of God may become rooted more easily'.

On 28 July 1838, however, two months and a week after Pompallier had posted his New Zealand letter, Pallotti began having problems which threatened the very existence of his organisation founded on 4 April 1835. The problems were caused by the Association for the Propagation of the Faith in Lyon, which was lobbying in Rome to obtain a monopoly over the collecting of funds for distribution to the foreign missions. It already had this kind of monopoly in France and now wanted it in Rome and Italy. The association charged that Pallotti's group simply collected funds for the missions and therefore was duplicating what the Association for the Propagation of the Faith had been authorised by Rome to do. The lobbying of the French group was so successful that Pope Gregory XVI on 28 July 1838 ordered that a decree be drawn up suppressing Pallotti's group. Archbishop Ignazio Cadolini, secretary to the Evangelisation Congregation, personally on 30 July gave Pallotti notice of the pope's decision.

In desperation Pallotti appealed for the survival of his organisation to the pope, visiting him from mid-August onwards, indicating that his group had many other goals and activities besides fund collecting, and that consequently it was specifically different from the association in Lyon and so had a right to exist. Pallotti succeeded in having Pope Gregory XVI rule on 1 October 1838 that the proclamation of the decree of suppression should be postponed. Pallotti's case then came up at a General Meeting of the Evangelisation Congregation on 11 December 1838. And although the pope's decree of suppression was in fact never promulgated, the action taken by him and by the Evangelisation Congregation understandably caused Pallotti to reduce greatly his activity on behalf of the foreign missions. Therefore he was unable to supply Pompallier with the assistance requested in 1838.[7]

Letters between New Zealand and Europe took five or six months to reach their destinations. Colin on 10 November 1838 wrote to Fransoni, saying that 'very recently' he had received Pompallier's letter of 14 May requesting personnel, funds and also 20,000 francs for the purchase of a schooner. To show

Fransoni that he personally was doing everything possible to provide personnel, Colin pointed out that in September he had sent three priests and three Brother-Catechists and he hoped it would be possible in 1839 'to send eight or ten priests'. For Fransoni's information he enclosed a copy of Pompallier's letter which had asked that he request from Fransoni the balance, if he himself could not supply 'at least 14 priests'.[8]

About two weeks later, just as Colin's letter of 10 November was reaching Fransoni, a letter from Fransoni also written on 10 November reached Colin. It said that Pompallier in a letter dated 21 May had informed the cardinal how urgently he needed more men and that he had requested them from Colin. Fransoni said he wished to give his support to that request.[9]

Also on 10 November, when Fransoni and Colin were writing letters to one another, Pompallier was once again at the Bay of Islands where a small hill at Kororareka (nowadays Russell) was deeded over to him on that day. Not long after this he transferred his headquarters from Hokianga to Kororareka, where local Catholics had asked him to open a chapel.[10]

The second group of Marist missionaries to leave for Western Oceania, the group mentioned in Colin's letter to Fransoni, had left Bordeaux on 2 September 1838. By this date the new instructions contained in Pompallier's letter of 14 May had not arrived and so this group like the first one sailed across the Atlantic and around Cape Horn to Valparaíso. Nor did they know that this same letter mentioned his plan of purchasing a schooner.

While the Marists were crossing the Atlantic, Father Maigret, vicar general of Bishop Rouchouze of Eastern Oceania, was crossing the Pacific. He had left Ponape aboard *Notre Dame de Paix* on 29 July 1838 and on 22 December reached Valparaíso, where he was to make the final payment on his ship purchased in the Sandwich Islands in November of the previous year. At Valparaíso he met the Marists looking for a ship to take them to New Zealand.[11]

Father Claude-André Baty, leader of the Marist group, soon saw the advisability of purchasing *Notre Dame de Paix* in partnership for Bishop Pompallier. Maigret had difficulty providing alone the necessary capital and so he too welcomed the proposal. According to the agreement reached by Baty and Maigret, each bishop by turn could use the ship for six months, since each had 'a right to half of the services of the schooner . . . for the price of 2,000 piastres'. Baty considered the transaction most advantageous, since the ship was completely furnished and well supplied with provisions. The price also included the voyage to New Zealand for the six Marists. But neither Baty nor Maigret knew the views of their bishops and so they agreed that the ship could be sold if either of the two bishops did not agree to the purchase or to the sharing arrangement.[12]

There were also other items, of course, like salary for the crew, keeping the ship in repair, and numerous other expenses, and these were estimated at 1,900 piastres a year. But in spite of this Father Liausu, the Prefect Apostolic of Eastern Oceania based in Valparaíso, considered the outlay necessary, since 'a schooner is indispensable for us. Without it our missionaries will forever be prisoners in the Gambier Islands.'[13]

36 This final page of a three-page letter to Cardinal Prefect Fransoni dated 10 November 1838 at Bay of Islands, New Zealand, shows the handwriting and signature of 'Jean-Baptiste-Francois [Pompallier, Titular] Bishop of Maronea and Vicar Apostolic of Western Oceania'. *Source: PF: SC Oceania vol. 1 (1816–41) f. 510r. (Chapter 13).*

214 FOUNDING OF THE ROMAN CATHOLIC CHURCH IN OCEANIA

Maigret left Valparaíso on Sunday, 27 January 1839 about 6.30 P.M., with the six Marists aboard and travelled with them as far as the Gambier Islands, where they arrived on 15 March. It was here, at Mangareva, that the transaction between Maigret and Baty was signed and sealed. On 2 April the Marists left, but the ship was to return to the Gambier Islands immediately after taking them to New Zealand. Bishop Rouchouze, in the Marquesas Islands at the time, was later convinced that Pompallier would not hesitate 'to accept the conditions, but what is lacking is the money for it'.

Earlier Rouchouze had expressed some reservations about purchasing a ship. When writing on 19 August 1838 to Archbishop Bonamie, superior general of the Picpus Fathers in Paris, he said that owning a ship would bring with it 'a number of disagreeable aspects', since the missionaries thereby would 'create the impression that they are engaged in commerce'. He also wondered who would look after the numerous details, like provisions, maintenance and finding a captain.[14]

The Marists arrived at Tahiti in April 1839 and received from Moerenhout, now serving as French consul, a letter from Pompallier written the previous September, in which he expressed concern about the abandoned missionaries at Wallis and Futuna. *Notre Dame de Paix* then sailed for Wallis, arriving there in May. Since the ship was also going to Futuna, Bataillon went aboard and remained with Father Chanel in Futuna for six weeks. Their islands were about 190 kilometres apart and the two had seen one another only once before when Chanel in March 1838 had gone to Wallis for about two months to join Bataillon for language studies.[15]

It was 14 June 1839 when *Notre Dame de Paix* finally arrived at the Bay of Islands in New Zealand. The poorly built ship had almost capsized en route. Pompallier nevertheless agreed to the purchase and sharing arrangement, but instead of sending the ship back immediately to Rouchouze, he used it for some New Zealand voyages. But two or three months later the ship nearly capsized again and so he eventually sold it for 600 pounds, sending half of the amount to Rouchouze. This unilateral action displeased Rouchouze, who needed a small ship in order to visit the nearby Tuamotu Islands.[16]

With the arrival of six new missionaries (three priests and three Brothers) aboard *Notre Dame de Paix* in June 1839, Pompallier was now able to begin consolidating his position in New Zealand and he started with Kororareka at the Bay of Islands. In July he purchased a piece of property there near the beach and set up his residence and a storehouse. As Pompallier explained to Colin on 14 August 1839, the Bay of Islands was much safer for ships than Hokianga Bay and also far better for international communications 'since American, French and English ships' came to the Bay of Islands frequently. The first mission station at Hokianga had been dedicated to Saint Joseph; this one was dedicated to Saints Peter and Paul. At this time about seventy whites were living at Kororareka and in the vicinity were four Maori tribes with a total population of approximately four hundred.[17]

Pompallier now had four priests in New Zealand, one on Wallis and one on

Futuna. This number seemed pitifully small to him and he told Colin so in no uncertain terms in his 14 August letter. '[There are] twelve or fifteen million souls in the thousands of islands contained in my mission', he said. And although he found 'many tribes of islanders' well disposed towards the Catholic faith, it tore his heart asunder because he was not able to grant their requests. 'In France, my Catholic fatherland, there are over 30,000 [priests]', and yet 'in my entire mission I have no more than six . . . Oh God! What a disproportion!' With so few priests he could not even begin to think 'about instructing these people thoroughly', and much less 'about each one of them learning only the act of faith in God or, what in theology we call, the truths necessary as a means to salvation. And yet I am supposed to establish schools, some colleges, and even some seminaries.' He appealed in desperation to the church at large to send him priests.[18]

This outburst may have been due in part to Pompallier's being under great psychological pressure since the arrival of Fransoni's altogether unexpected letter of 25 January 1838, which must have reached him half a year or so before the arrival of Baty and the other two priests. The letter had announced that jurisdiction over New Zealand, Tonga, Samoa and Fiji, by order of Pope Gregory XVI, had been given temporarily and conditionally to Bishop Rouchouze of Eastern Oceania.[19] This was very exasperating for Pompallier, who had hardly set foot within his vicariate apostolic when nearly half of it was given conditionally to someone else. He must have wondered what had happened behind the scenes to cause Rome to take such a step. To all appearances, if one could judge from the letter, the only cause for the decision was his lack of priests. And he knew no one else to blame for this but Colin. Thinking that Pompallier would be making his headquarters at Ponape in Micronesia, as reported by Father Caret, Pope Gregory XVI had authorised this arrangement on 14 January 1838,[20] just four days *after* Pompallier had founded the New Zealand mission. This meant, in effect, that Rouchouze never had any authority over New Zealand, not even on paper, since Pompallier's presence there—in virtue of the conditions laid down—negated the jurisdiction which was being granted to Rouchouze. But this was not true for Tonga, Samoa and Fiji, since Pompallier had no personnel there. Consequently Rouchouze was perfectly free to send his men to those three archipelagoes.

Had Pompallier only known fully what was happening in Eastern Oceania, however, his concern over Fransoni's puzzling letter would have been greatly diminished. The concession won in Rome by Caret, for example, was not at all well received by his fellow Picpus missionaries. Writing from Valparaíso to Fransoni as early as 31 October 1838, Caret announced that Pompallier had not gone to Ascension (or Ponape) Island after all, as he had originally intended, but to New Zealand instead! 'And the condition laid down that we must depart, if Pompallier or his priests should arrive, or that we must work under his jurisdiction, has cooled the zeal of our men a bit'. Caret also told Fransoni that the Picpus missionaries in Valparaíso were saying, 'If we can be sent away from an island after we have worked hard there and have done some good, it would be better not to go to the islands within the jurisdiction of Pompallier. We shall limit ourselves instead to those which are entrusted to our own vicar apostolic.'[21]

What contributed most of all to this cooling of interest on the part of the Picpus missionaries was the fact that conditions in Eastern Oceania had changed so very much since Caret had made his original request. This request had been granted on the supposition that Picpus missionaries were being blocked from entering the islands within their own territory. But this was no longer the case. As Caret's own letter reported, for example, a French frigate had taken two Picpus priests and a catechist to the Marquesas Islands where they were well received. They had arrived at the island called Santa Cristina or Tahuata on 4 August 1838.[22]

This was only part of an extensive program of energetic action launched by France in Eastern Oceania. On 29 August, just three weeks after the arrival of the first Picpus missionaries in the Marquesas Islands, the warship *Venus* arrived at Papeete in Tahiti and Commandant Dupetit-Thouars demanded and received a written apology from local authorities for the earlier expulsion of Fathers Caret and Laval. And on 4 September an agreement was signed by the local authorities there which guaranteed for all Frenchmen complete freedom of movement in all islands of the Tahiti Archipelago.

Similar action was taken one year later at Honolulu where Captain Cyrille-Pierre-Théodore Laplace arrived with his frigate *Artemise* mounting forty cannon on 10 July 1839 and demanded reparation for the expulsion of Father Bachelot and for other infractions of an earlier signed agreement. He too insisted that all be granted freedom to practise the Catholic religion and that permission be given to build churches. A clause added on 13 July made specific provisions for French Catholic missionaries. In Tahiti that month Laplace exacted complete religious freedom for Catholic missionaries similar to that enjoyed by Protestant missionaries from England. Eager to maintain cordial relations with France at this time, the English government permitted this concession, thus theoretically opening also this territory for Catholic missionary work. Except for some additional difficulties which were still to crop up in Tahiti, the many archipelagoes in the Vicariate Apostolic of Eastern Oceania now provided sufficient scope for the zeal of the Picpus Fathers and they quickly lost all interest in Western Oceania.[23]

Colin informed Fransoni on 26 April 1839 that recently he had received a letter from Pompallier dated 16 September 1838. 'He is truly in distress,' Colin said, 'not yet having received any letters from Europe since his departure from France. Besides this, he has no money and has only one priest to gather so abundant a harvest.' But what disturbed Colin most of all was the fact that Pompallier had not yet received any word about the two missionaries whom he had left at Wallis and Futuna. Colin's letter also contained some good news. 'I have just received word today', he said, 'that the missionaries whom we sent last September have arrived at Valparaíso.' He was referring to the group under Father Baty. Soon another group of three priests and some Brother-Catechists would be sent, he said, but they would sail 'no longer via Valparaíso, but via

Sydney . . . The entire voyage to New Zealand should take no longer than five months.'[24]

Pompallier had suggested this change in route to Colin in his letter of 14 May 1838. 'Now that experience has made me better acquainted with these seas,' he said, 'I am even more convinced that the fastest and most economical voyages from Europe for us are those which take the route around the Cape of Good Hope and New Holland and then go to the Bay of Islands in New Zealand.'[25]

Colin's decision to send his missionaries via the Cape of Good Hope, however, was not based only on these words of Pompallier. Captain Peter Dillon was now back from New Zealand and had written to Colin from London on 18 February, two months before Colin wrote to Fransoni. Dillon had suggested very strongly that in the future Colin should no longer send his missionaries via Valparaíso, since there 'they have to wait too long' to get a ship for New Zealand. Instead they should come to London and from there sail to New Zealand via New Holland. 'The passage as far as New Holland would cost 70 pounds sterling or 1,750 francs per person', he said. And at Sydney Bishop Polding 'would look after them until a ship sails for New Zealand'. He said that ships left Sydney for the Bay of Islands and for Hokianga 'once, twice and occasionally three times a month'. The additional cost per person for the segment of the voyage from Sydney to New Zealand 'would be 10 pounds sterling or 250 francs'. Colin could hardly have wished for more details and he would soon learn that in Dillon he had a tireless travel agent.

Dillon's letter also introduced Mr Daniel Cooper Esq., a shipowner whose wife was a Roman Catholic. Father Ullathorne, assistant to Bishop Polding of Sydney, and eight priests had sailed to Sydney on one of his ships and Dillon had learned from the Catholic bishop of London that they were treated very well throughout the voyage. Cooper had another ship sailing for Sydney at the end of May, Dillon said, and would be very happy to take aboard French missionaries as passengers. 'They could come from France to London via Calais and would . . . arrive at their destination [in the South Seas] after four or five months, whereas sending them via Valparaíso as formerly would ordinarily take a year for the voyage.' Dillon asked Colin to reply quickly if he was interested and he also enclosed Cooper's address: Jerusalem Coffee House, Cornhill, London.[26]

Colin was indeed interested and sent four priests and a Brother-Catechist to London. Their ship sailed in June 1839 and they arrived in Sydney on 23 October. On 8 December they arrived in New Zealand.[27] On the previous day Pompallier had sent Colin, his purchasing agent in France, an order to buy a brig. Colin consulted Monsieur Le Normand at Le Havre, as instructed by Pompallier. But when he learned that the cost would be 60,000–70,000 francs, he postponed making the purchase.[28]

Since the French government by this time had a foothold in Eastern Oceania, it took action throughout the latter part of 1839 to gain a foothold in Western Oceania as well. It had taken a long time for France to react to the enticements offered years before by Father de Solages, Captain Dillon and Baron de Thierry. Dillon in 1835 surveyed the New Zealand coast 'for a location for a French colony', and in 1837 he was seriously considered by France for the position of consul in Sydney. The French consulate in Manila was raised to the status of consulate general on 8 July 1839. And on 8 August that year a French consulate was established in Sydney, but not with Dillon in charge.[29]

The French government considered close collaboration with the Marists a help toward achieving its aims in Western Oceania. And the Marists believed that protection from the French government was necessary for success. And so Colin was happy to report to Pompallier on 9 November 1839 that two of his priests, Fathers Dubreul and Poupinel, had been very well received by several ministers and that Nicolas-Jean-de-Dieu Soult (1769–1851), who had become Minister of Foreign Affairs that year and was also President of the Council of Ministers, had been particularly kind. Through his two priests Colin had requested protection for his missionaries. But what he had asked for above all was that a French consul be assigned to New Zealand. Soult in turn had asked Colin to submit a report on the Western Oceania mission.

Colin passed on this information to Pompallier and said that the letter containing it would be delivered by Captain Charles-François Lavaud (1798–1878) of the *Aube*, who had received important instructions concerning the islands of Oceania. Lavaud, like the captains of all other French vessels in Oceania, he said, had received formal orders to protect Catholic missionaries. The French ministers wanted to make settlements in Oceania to repress somewhat the English advances, and therefore they wanted to protect Catholic missionaries.[30]

Soon Colin found himself in correspondence with Emmanuel-Gabriel-Jacques Eveillard (1803–?), a man in Paris who was eager to become French consul in New Zealand. Eveillard wrote Colin on 15 November 1839 that 'the government for quite some time has been trying to set up a plan for the deportation of criminals. It has long been undecisive in choosing a place, but now seems to have decided upon New Guinea. The spot which it is considering for a possible settlement is to the north at Dorei Harbour in a vast bay. . . .'

Eveillard wanted to know whether this spot was contained within the boundaries of the Marist mission. He also asked whether Colin might be willing to collaborate with the French government in the realisation of this project and he even suggested that Colin submit to the authorities 'a detailed plan for such an establishment'. Rather than see it become the project of philanthropists, Eveillard hoped that the Marists would be placed in charge. In fact, Colin would do well, he said, to offer his missionaries to the French ministry spontaneously for this penal colony, expressing at the same time the readiness 'to go and prepare the way for this establishment by trying to convert the Papuans'. And if Colin's zeal should prompt him to labour for the salvation of the Papuans in New Guinea, Eveillard said, it should also make him do something for the condemned Frenchmen to be sent there, since 'our condemned are just as valuable as the Papuans'.[31]

But meanwhile Colin had more urgent business to attend to, since he had to draw up his report on missionary work in Western Oceania for Soult, the

Minister of Foreign Affairs. He submitted the report on 22 November 1839 and it contained many details, like the size of the mission, the launching of missionary work there, the obstacles encountered by his missionaries, and the kind of people whom they had found. The population of New Zealand, he said, was estimated at 150,000–200,000. He thanked Soult for the assurance given to his two priests that the government intended to continue its practice of providing protection for missionaries through its ships visiting those shores. He also expressed the hope that French consuls would be placed in various parts of Oceania, above all in New Zealand. 'And we are sincerely grateful', he said, 'for Your Excellency's kindness in granting our missionaries passage aboard French ships and in allowing our correspondence to be transmitted either by state ships or through the French ambassador in London.' He and his missionaries also hoped that they could be 'useful to France in these distant countries'. And since Soult had expressed to Dubreul and Poupinel his great eagerness to see all possible reports arriving from Western Oceania, Colin promised that he would 'hasten to make them known to Your Excellency' as soon as they arrive.[32]

Colin's secretary Poupinel informed Eveillard on 23 November that the mission report had been sent to Soult on the previous day and that it requested above all a consul for New Zealand. At the same time he begged Eveillard not to mention the matter in the press. He also pointed out that there would be no difficulty at all for the Marists in making a foundation in New Guinea, if the government should request this, provided only that the Holy See and Bishop Pompallier gave their consent.[33] Colin then on 4 December wrote to Internuncio Garibaldi and to Curé Olivier of Saint-Roch, ecclesiastics in Paris in close contact with royalty, and requested each of them to propose Eveillard to the French royal family as a candidate for consul in New Zealand.[34]

Soult received another letter from Colin dated 30 November 1839 saying that 'at this moment' news had arrived from the second group of missionaries who had left France the previous year for Western Oceania via Valparaíso. They had written from Tahiti on 15 April 1839 that some nine or ten French whalers had visited the island that very month. Colin added more news and said that Soult's 'powerful protection' would 'contribute much to the success of the missionaries'. Discreetly trying to learn the position of the Minister of Foreign Affairs on New Guinea, he also affirmed that 'far greater progress will be made in New Zealand' than in New Guinea, whose tribes he judged to be very backward. 'But since they are men, our missionaries would be happy to go there as well, if Divine Providence should seem to call us to evangelise that island.'[35]

The French government was meanwhile becoming ever more deeply involved in Western Oceania. It signed a contract on 11 December 1839 with the Société Nanto-Bordelaise, a company formed on 8 November 1839. King Louis-Philippe in virtue of this contract approved government transport for eighty colonists who were to found a French settlement at Akaroa in Banks Peninsula halfway down the east coast of New Zealand's South Island. In exchange for this transportation and further material assistance, the company obliged itself to cede to the state one-fourth of its lands acquired in Banks Peninsula. France's intention at this time was to install in its lands a naval base and a penal colony.

A commissioner of the king invested with special powers was to reside in this New Zealand settlement and it was this office which Eveillard formally but unsuccessfully requested from the Minister of Foreign Affairs. His program, spelled out for the minister, was to include having the pope name only French bishops for New Zealand; having French Catholic priests far outnumber English Catholic priests; having Trappists, for example, introduce agriculture to tribes in the interior and civilise them; and having the bishops found schools in which teaching of the French language would predominate. This method, he said, would counterbalance the English population, resist it and perhaps some day subject it.[36]

When Soult on 16 December 1839 thanked Colin for his mission report on Western Oceania, he said that he had read the details 'with lively interest'. His real purpose in writing, however, was to inform Colin that France now had an opportunity to penetrate Western Oceania. 'An expedition is about to depart for southern New Zealand', he said. The corvette *Aube* commanded by Captain Lavaud was already at Brest preparing for the voyage and would set sail very soon. 'I have the honour of proposing to you, Monsieur, that you send along two of your missionaries. They should depart for Brest immediately and there they will be taken aboard the vessel which I have just mentioned. And if you wish, you may also send with them two laymen as assistants; they will be received on equal terms.'[37]

Colin thanked Soult on 24 December for the offer and stated that he would definitely take advantage of it. Full of optimism he quoted from Pompallier's letter of 17 March 1839 in which the bishop said that everything was moving along well and that he needed 'only men and money'. Soult had asked Colin to use his influence in having Pompallier get in touch with the French commissioner to be based at Banks Peninsula and Colin assured him that Pompallier certainly would do so. He was careful to mention, however, that his missionaries in Oceania had to be very circumspect. 'Your Excellency understands that our primary purpose is the salvation of infidels', he said. And since 'the Methodists are very ardent adversaries', his missionaries needed 'to take care not to expose themselves to their calumnies. . . .'[38]

Wanting to keep Pompallier posted about latest developments in France, Colin wrote him on 29 December that the French government had decided to name a consul for New Zealand and that it was also planning to found a penal colony in New Guinea.[39] Meanwhile in New Zealand on 8 December 1839, Pompallier had received four more priests and a Brother-Catechist from France. A brig happened to be leaving the Bay of Islands on 17 December for Fiji and Tonga, so Pompallier sent one of these priests and the Brother-Catechist to Wallis and Futuna to assist Bataillon and Chanel.[40]

Dillon in London, like Eveillard in Paris, wanted Colin to help him become French consul in New Zealand. Dillon informed Colin on 25 January 1840 that he was planning to leave for New Zealand on one of Cooper's vessels the following April. He therefore urged Colin to approach the royal family and request that it name him French consul for the Pacific islands. But this time the position should be salaried, he said, and not merely honorary as it had been ten years before. 'This coming October it will be 31 years since my first visit to New Zealand', he said. 'I am the oldest acquaintance that New Zealanders have.'

He was still in London when he wrote to Colin on 24 April, saying, 'It is absolutely necessary for France to send a Consul to New Zealand to protect its interests, the whalers, etc., etc.' In the previous year he had addressed a letter to Princess Adélaïde d'Orléans, sister of the king, giving his qualifications and expressing his readiness to serve as consul for France. He had now received a reply from her secretary, dated 25 February 1840, stating that she had received his letter and had 'placed it under the eyes of the king'. Dillon enclosed the original for Colin to see. But since Colin on 4 December 1839 had already asked Internuncio Garibaldi and the Curé of Saint-Roch to suggest Eveillard for this office, he could now hardly suggest Dillon. And so Colin avoided the issue.

Dillon did not sail for New Zealand in April as planned. From London he wrote to Colin on 25 November 1840, saying how sorry he was that the latest group of missionaries to pass through London had placed their money in the bank of Mr Wright and had lost it all. Had he been consulted, he would have told them that Wright's bank had become altogether unreliable. Still, he would do all that he could to see if at least part of the money could be recouped. He apologised for writing this particular letter in English, but explained that his daughter, who usually translated his letters into French, was not at home. 'I shall conclude by once more assuring you that I will assist the mission as far as lies in my power.'[41]

The *Aube* under command of Captain Lavaud arrived at the Bay of Islands on 10 July 1840 with the two priests and two Brother-Catechists aboard sent by Colin. Pompallier had a conference with Lavaud on the following day and told him that some 25,000 Maoris were on the way to becoming Catholics. Pleased on one hand by Pompallier's progress, Lavaud was disturbed on the other hand by the news that the British had concluded the Waitangi Treaty with the Maoris on 6 February that year, thereby placing New Zealand under the British Crown. Had the French waited too long to found their colony in South Island?

Lavaud sent a report on 19 July to the Minister of the Navy in Paris, stating that Great Britain had already taken possession of New Zealand and that Lieutenant-Governor Hobson at Bay of Islands had an administrative staff, a small garrison and the services of three warships. He then sailed to Banks Peninsula in South Island where he patrolled the area and made possible the founding of the planned French colony. The first sixty-three settlers arrived at Akaroa, a bay and a harbour, aboard the *Comte de Paris* on 19 August 1840. At the rear of the bay there was an English colony alongside the French one. Both colonies were protected by vessels from their own countries.[42]

This show of strength on the part of France, her definite commitment to New Zealand by founding a colony there, and also the many assurances of protection that Colin and Pompallier had received from various French officials made the bishop extremely optimistic about the future. Since selling the *Notre Dame de Paix*, he had been chartering ships to make his missionary journeys. After returning from such a New Zealand voyage in May 1840, he reported to Colin that during this voyage he had won over to the Catholic faith some forty tribes or approximately 15,000 people.[43]

His missionary force was also growing. On the islands of Wallis and Futuna he now had three priests and three Brother-Catechists and in New Zealand after the arrival of the *Aube* he had nine priests and five Brother-Catechists. Eager to begin placing his men on islands other than New Zealand, and having the opportunity to purchase a ship, Pompallier in July 1840 bought the *Atlas*, a 135-ton topsail schooner, which he rechristened *Sancta Maria*. Perhaps he had forgotten that seven months earlier he had sent orders to Colin to purchase a vessel for him in France, orders which were only reaching Colin about this time. Pompallier then sent him word on 10 September that he himself had purchased a vessel, the *Sancta Maria*, for 25,000 francs. It had cost him another 14,000 francs, he said, to get it in running condition, since a number of items necessary for remaining at sea for several months were lacking. Pompallier planned to use it to visit some New Zealand ports and other islands of his vicariate.[44]

The slow but steady progress of Bishop Pompallier and his missionaries was not going unnoticed. The Wesleyan missionary James Watkin at Waikouaiti, New Zealand, wrote into his journal on 21 November 1840 that 'the Popish missionaries . . . are doing all they can to ingratiate themselves with the natives' by means of presents. He said they were 'very anxious to obtain influence among the natives, and giving largely is the most effective way'.[45]

In Rome on 21 November, the same day that Watkin made his journal entry, Cardinal Fransoni wrote about New Zealand to Bishop Thomas Griffiths, Vicar Apostolic of London District. The latest news to arrive from that mission, he said, had made his office both happy and sad. The good news was that 'the missionaries through their labours are preparing a most abundant harvest' and the peoples of New Zealand 'show themselves very predisposed to receive the seed of faith'. The bad news was the creation of serious obstacles by Protestant missionaries and the fact that 'a new English colony is being established in that region'. The Western Oceania missionaries, he said, wanted Griffiths to appeal to Her Majesty, Queen Victoria, and beg for equal liberty for Catholic and Protestant missionaries. And since missionaries leaving for Western Oceania in the future might have to travel via London, they said that they would greatly appreciate receiving assistance from Griffiths. Fransoni said that 'the Sacred Congregation urgently recommends both requests [of the missionaries] to Your Grace and is confident that you will comply with their wishes'.[46]

At this moment in its history the Vicariate Apostolic of Western Oceania was making advances on all fronts. It was clear that Fransoni in Rome would immediately do whatever he could to foster its growth. The government of England could now be expected to take action on the mission's behalf. And there were guarantees enough that the government of France was interested in its success. Pompallier with more personnel and funds at his disposal was becoming optimistic and had great plans for the future; with such a large ship he could easily distribute his personnel. Colin back in France was tireless in writing letters and reports to win whatever interest and support he could. His community was expanding rapidly and it seemed there would be a steady stream of missionaries available. God too seemed to be blessing the venture. With all this divine and human help the mission should have succeeded brilliantly. And it would have, except for one obstacle. That obstacle was Pompallier's inability to get along with the Marists and their inability to get along with him.

14

The Vicariate Apostolic of Central Oceania

8 AUGUST 1842

Father Catherin Servant, who had accompanied Bishop Pompallier to New Zealand in January 1838, was in this mission for two years and three months when he filled seven pages with criticism of his bishop and mailed them to Father Colin, his superior general. It was necessary for Colin to have this information, he said, 'and I entrust the following details to your prudence after having taken counsel with our dear Fathers Baty, [Maxime] Petit and Epalle'. These three priests were the ones longest in New Zealand after Servant; they had arrived on 14 June 1839, ten months before he wrote this letter on 26 April 1840.

In each of nine categories of complaint Servant listed numerous examples to show the harm that Pompallier was doing. When describing how the bishop treated his personnel, Servant mentioned what had happened as early as 1837 at Vava'u in the Tonga Islands; the bishop and his first missionaries were aboard ship and still en route to their missions. 'Believing that he noticed a spirit of estrangement among us in his regard', Servant said, 'he fulminated against us, going so far as to treat us as if he wanted to set us aside, as if he wanted to separate us from himself, even threatening to excommunicate us. His tone was so vehement that it could easily reach the ears of our crew, but they fortunately did not understand French.'

Servant warned Colin that he should not take literally the marvellous conversions that had been reported from New Zealand. 'These natives are far removed from the initial dispositions required for true conversion . . . Except for those few in each of our places, who really give reason for hope, the rest are so avaricious that it is frightening.' And in regard to the administration of temporal goods, although Pompallier had 'no understanding' for this at all, 'he still wishes to do everything by himself', even though he appointed a priest for this work. 'It is painful for us to hear strangers say that the bishop allows himself to be duped and that he has no understanding for business matters.'

'The wise distribution of gifts to natives', Servant said, 'is indispensable when a mission is being founded in the midst of savages, because it is through gifts that one wins their friendship and their confidence. But it does not seem right for the bishop alone to be the one who should distribute these gifts', since this reflects badly on his missionaries. Nor did Pompallier keep his word. One day he would promise clothing to the natives and the next day he would not give it to them, thus hurting the mission cause and destroying the confidence that the people had in their missionaries.

Servant had not been allowed to send news about his own mission back to France without having it read first by the bishop. Even his letters addressed to Colin were all censored. But this situation improved somewhat after the arrival of the second group of missionaries. 'Father Baty and I,' Servant told Colin, 'knowing the mind of the other Fathers, insisted vigorously on the freedom to send you sealed letters and to receive sealed letters from you.'

The chief criticism that Servant had against Pompallier, however, was his almost utter neglect of the innumerable islands and archipelagoes in the tropics that along with New Zealand made up the Vicariate Apostolic of Western Oceania. The bishop had kept so much of his personnel and funds in New Zealand, that little was left over for the other islands. 'The mission is already in its third year,' he said, 'and the bishop is occupied completely with New Zealand.' Only twice did the Wallis and Futuna missionaries receive any assistance, and that was when the second group of missionaries aboard the *Notre Dame de Paix* had stopped there and again when Pompallier sent Father Joseph Chevron (1808–84) to assist them. He himself had never returned. Nor could Servant see how funds and personnel in the near future could be distributed proportionately, because even in New Zealand most of the funds were being used at the Bay of Islands.

'It therefore appears expedient and desirable', he said, 'that a new vicariate apostolic should be created for the islands in the tropics.' New Zealand with its adjacent islands was the only part of the Vicariate Apostolic of Western Oceania which was not in the tropics, since it was below the Tropic of Capricorn. Servant's proposal seemed drastic and was aimed at restricting Pompallier juridically to the New Zealand area to which circumstances of the moment had bound him.

Servant then proceeded to list arguments in order to convince Colin that missionary work in the tropics would be much more successful than in New Zealand and that it could be conducted on a much more solid basis. In New Zealand large numbers of Europeans were streaming into the country and were bewildering the natives by their immorality. This invasion en masse was not taking place in the smaller islands. Nor were the inhabitants of the smaller islands so covetous for temporal goods as in New Zealand, where the newly arrived whites had made this spirit grow through commerce. They were also more hospitable. And it would be a much simpler matter to reach the island peoples, since they would be practically under the eye of the missionary. In New Zealand, however, 'they can be visited very rarely and . . . they do not come to the mission very often.' It would be necessary, of course, for the new vicar apostolic to have a small ship for his own use, so that he could move about from island to island.

Some of Servant's eloquence may have been caused by the fact that he was eager to free himself from close contact with Pompallier and even from his jurisdiction. In fact, he had already submitted a petition to the bishop, requesting that he be transferred to the tropics. In concluding his letter he asked Colin kindly to support this petition 'by a letter from yourself, if you judge it proper'.[1]

Colin wrote back and urged Servant and the others to be patient with their bishop. He also wrote to Pompallier, counselling him to use prudence, moderation and suavity toward his priests.[2]

Captain Peter Dillon wrote to Colin from London on 9 February 1841, urging him to take up work in the tropics and specifically in the Friendly (or Tonga) Islands. Enclosed with his letter was a printed copy of a letter which he had sent to the Admiralty in London 'on the subject of the murders committed by the English missionaries at the Friendly Islands'. He informed Colin that the natives 'have banished their cruel oppressors, the [English] missionaries, from Tongatapu', and that they were asking for French missionaries and for the French king to protect them. He had already informed Princess Adélaïde that he would be able to obtain for her brother, King Louis-Philippe, sovereignty over all the Friendly Islands. And he advised Colin to 'act expeditiously by taking advantage of the chance thrown into our hands by God in the expulsion of the Wesleyans from Tonga and the wish of the natives to have protection [provided by] the French government and . . . French missionaries'.

Dillon was always eager to save as much money as possible for Colin and suggested that he ought to buy a vessel, if he intended to send out more missionaries, since 'the passage money of the last missionaries and their goods would have paid for a brig or schooner of 150 or 200 tons. That vessel could be placed under the orders of Bishop Pompallier at New Zealand and could take him about from one island to another where he has missionaries.' And if it were to engage in trade, he said, it would 'defray the expense of your mission in the South Seas'. He explained that Colin could purchase 'a brig or schooner of the above tonnage for about 800 or 1,000 pounds sterling'.[3]

Since the Tonga Islands were also in the tropics and close to Wallis and Futuna, and since Dillon suggested the purchase of a ship for inter-island service, he unwittingly confirmed the proposal of Servant, even though he did not suggest the founding of a separate vicariate apostolic. Colin, however, began to see the many benefits that would flow from an independent vicariate. The missionaries at Wallis and Futuna, for example, would no longer be isolated. A higher concentration of missionaries in the tropics would mean that his priests could find their way into many new areas before the Protestants, whose presence would automatically make missionary work more difficult. And no longer would all his members in Oceania be subject to the temperamental character of Pompallier and to the strain of trying to have harmonious relations with him.[4]

These thoughts prompted Colin to write to the Association for the Propagation of the Faith in Lyon on 2 March 1841, announcing his plans for a new vicariate apostolic. If God in his Providence were to supply him with sufficient personnel, he said, 'we would contemplate petitioning the Holy See for the erection of a new vicariate apostolic consisting of the Navigators Islands [or Samoa], the Friendly Islands [or Tonga] and Fiji'. These archipelagoes, about which he had received 'some good reports' formed a semicircle around Wallis and Futuna.

But the main purpose of his letter, and the item which he called to the attention of the officials first, was the need for funds in New Zealand. Bishop Pompallier had none and 33,000 francs had been lost when the Wright Bank collapsed in London. To show that in Oceania the money was being put to good use, he pointed out that the Vicariate Apostolic of Western Oceania in August 1840 had eight residential mission stations: Wallis, Futuna, Banks Peninsula in New Zealand's South Island, and in New Zealand's North Island Kororareka (where the vicar apostolic resided), Hokianga, Wangaroa, Tauranga and Kaipara.[5]

Having received no reaction from Colin to his earlier letter, Dillon wrote again on 16 April, stressing that in Oceania he had 'more influence than any other man who has visited these regions' and that he therefore could obtain Tongatapu for France through his friends living there. And if France should not be interested, he said, 'I would then address myself to the Austrian Empire or to Russia . . . in order to obtain help from one of these large nations for my poor friends in Oceania. . . .'[6] Dillon as well as Colin knew that French Marists would have no difficulty in gaining access to Tongatapu, the principal island of the Tonga Archipelago, if the French had sovereignty over it. Dillon consequently half-expected Colin to serve as his liaison in urging the French government to take action on his proposal.

Colin did reply on 16 May, saying that he had transmitted all data on the Tonga Islands to Soult, the Minister of Foreign Affairs, who had shown himself deeply interested. And he added that ever since the arrival of Dillon's earlier letter with the printed copy of his letter sent to the Admiralty in London, 'I have made the resolution to send a certain number of missionaries to the archipelagoes in question, and I hope that they will be able to depart this year. One of our missionaries has already baptised a chief from Tongatapu, who was at Wallis. . . .'[7]

Four days later, on 20 May 1841, Colin sent Cardinal Fransoni, head of the Evangelisation Congregation in Rome, the latest information about his missionaries on Wallis and Futuna. It was a good opportunity, he told the cardinal, for submitting at the same time his ideas on those two islands and on the thickly populated archipelagoes surrounding them. He stated his cause in one sentence: Because of the distances between those islands and New Zealand, the difficulties experienced by Bishop Pompallier in visiting them, the isolation of the three priests and three Brother-Catechists stationed there, and the religious movement bound to follow if a bishop were to be sent to the well-disposed peoples of Wallis, Futuna, Fiji, Tonga, Samoa, etc., 'we think it would be singularly advantageous for religion to have a bishop based there with the title of Vicar Apostolic of Central Oceania'. And should the cardinal be agreeable to the project, Colin promised to prepare 'a sufficient number of priests and catechists to accompany the new bishop or, if one should be chosen from among the priests already on the spot, to go and join him there'. He stated further that these new missionaries could be ready to leave Europe before the end of the year.

To be sure that his letter would reach Fransoni without delay, he had it personally delivered by two of his priests.[8] They quickly got word back to Colin that Fransoni liked the proposal, but first wanted to write to Pompallier for his views on it. Colin then hastily sent off a letter on 6 June 1841 to Pompallier, informing him of his letter to Rome and requesting that he conform with the views of Fransoni on the proposed Vicariate Apostolic of Central Oceania. He also asked Pompallier to leave Fransoni completely free to form a second vicariate apostolic in the direction of New Britain.[9]

Fransoni's letter to Pompallier, dated 12 June, stated that Colin 'has recently suggested to us the erection of another new vicariate, to be called Central, in the islands of Wallis and Futuna and other islands in their vicinity, in order to lessen your very heavy burden, to reduce your labour and to promote Catholicism more and more in your territory'. The cardinal explained that 'these islands would be separated from the Western Mission entrusted to you', and the government of the new vicariate apostolic would be entrusted to the Marists. Pompallier did not need to fear that the new vicariate would withdraw personnel from New Zealand, because it would be staffed by new personnel coming from Europe. 'But before making any decision in this matter, even though the project appears to be extremely advantageous for the propagation of the faith, we think Your Grace should express your views on the subject. And if you agree to the future execution of this proposal, as we believe you will, we would ask you to indicate for us from among your missionaries whom you judge to be most suitable for ruling the new vicariate'. Fransoni also asked Pompallier to indicate precisely what regions and islands ought to be included in the new Central Vicariate. 'We expect that you will be able to give us a very prompt reply on these matters', the cardinal added.[10]

That same day Fransoni wrote to Colin, stating that his 20 May proposal 'of erecting a new Central Vicariate Apostolic in the islands of Wallis, Futuna and vicinity to lessen Bishop Pompallier's heavy burden and to facilitate the conversion of so many souls', seemed to him 'most opportune'. But since the affair 'directly concerns the excellent prelate just mentioned, I should be pleased to have his consent', Fransoni said. 'Therefore kindly do me the favour of sending him the enclosed letter which asks his opinion on the matter.' The cardinal had no doubt 'that he will agree with pleasure to the proposed division', and he gave assurance to Colin that he could make all the necessary arrangements for establishing the new mission 'as soon as Bishop Pompallier's reply arrives'. He urged Colin himself to describe the proposal for Pompallier in a separate letter, to ask the bishop to suggest candidates to head it, and to request him to indicate precisely 'which places he would see fit to have subject to that Central Vicariate'. After obtaining this data, the cardinal would be able to make his report for a General Meeting and for the Holy Father.[11]

On 10 June, just two days before Fransoni wrote to both Pompallier and Colin, Dillon had written to Colin again from London, saying that there was no time to lose in sending missionaries to Oceania, and that his friend Cooper, the shipowner, had another vessel leaving London in September for Sydney and New Zealand. 'I fear that the Wesleyans will be making peace with the inhabitants of Tongatapu Island and will take root there once again', he said. And as he was writing the thought also came to him that Colin ought to transfer all his men from New Zealand, now an English colony, to Tonga and Fiji, where there would be more benefit for France. Nor did he let Colin forget that in Tongatapu he had 'the greatest influence'. He had met Bishop Polding who had come to London from Sydney aboard a French whaler which had sailed the Pacific route and had stopped off at New Zealand. 'He told me that Bishop Pompallier and his missionaries have converted 35,000 inhabitants of New Zealand and that the French are much loved there.'[12]

On 15 June, just five days after Dillon wrote his letter, eleven more Marists arrived at the Bay of Islands with the printing press earlier requested by Pompallier. The newly arrived missionaries were given a quick course in the Maori language and Maori customs at Kororareka while Pompallier prepared the *Sancta Maria* for another voyage. With missionaries aboard, and also some Maori chiefs who had come looking for priests, the bishop set sail from the Bay of Islands on 23 July 1841 intending to visit the coasts of New Zealand and also Wallis, Futuna and the Tonga Islands. At this time he was completely unaware of the correspondence going on between Servant, Dillon, Colin and Fransoni.

After visiting 'nearly all the bays on the east coast of New Zealand', Pompallier sailed to Akaroa at Banks Peninsula in South Island, where he had two priests and a Brother-Catechist assigned to the developing French colony. It was here that he drew up a statistical report for Rome. He listed a total of fourteen mission stations within his territory as of 14 September 1841. Of these, one was on Wallis, another on Futuna and the rest were in New Zealand.[13]

While at Akaroa, Pompallier received letters from France. 'But instead of announcing that funds would be arriving for me, as I had been hoping and as I had been led to expect by my missionaries at the Bay of Islands, the letters informed me that doubts had arisen about my administrative ability.' This news made him change his plans drastically.

In order to obtain the funds that he needed so urgently and at the same time to relieve himself of his biggest expense, he planned to sell the *Sancta Maria* in Valparaíso. But first he wanted to send it back to the Bay of Islands, load it with supplies that recently had come from France, and ship these to Wallis and Futuna. 'As for myself, I prepared to make a journey to France and to Rome in order to benefit all of my missions, to seek personnel and assistance, and to give a clear picture of the entire situation in these missions and in my vicariate apostolic.'[14]

It was Colin's letter which had so disturbed Pompallier, undoubtedly the one that Colin had written after reading Servant's long list of grievances. Pompallier later wrote to Rome that 'false reports' were being sent to Europe by his young priests in which he was accused of poor administration. He believed that these reports 'have paralysed my community's confidence in me'.[15]

Pompallier then wrote from Akaroa to Captain Lavaud of the *Aube* on 18 October 1841. 'Circumstances which concern in an important manner the general good of my mission labours in Oceania oblige me to make a prompt voyage to France and to Rome; but I am meeting with the greatest hindrances to carrying this out. . . .' Pompallier therefore begged Lavaud to allow him to make this voyage aboard the *Aube* 'which you are about to take back to France'. And if the government should not be willing to bear the costs (he wanted to take along a few companions), he said that he himself would reimburse the Ministry of the Navy 'when I am in France'. In a postscript he also requested letters patent from Lavaud which would guarantee 'protection for the mission schooner that I am going to leave behind'.[16]

Lavaud kindly provided free passage for Pompallier, as well as for one of his priests and two Maori youths whom he hoped to have trained for the priesthood at the Urban College in Rome. The bishop had already moved into his private cabin when the *Héroïne* under Captain Lévêque dropped anchor at Akaroa on 4 November 1841. That same day Lévêque gave the bishop a letter from Father Bataillon of Wallis with news that Father Chanel had been killed on Futuna six months earlier and that the Futuna mission had been closed. Fearing a chain reaction Bataillon added that the Wallis mission might also have to close down and that consequently all future missions in the tropics were in danger. 'Their success would be compromised for a long time', Pompallier said, 'if I would not hasten there as soon as possible'. This news made him cancel his voyage to France.[17]

The tragic news had also been sent to Colin in France by Father Chevron, who had worked with Chanel on Futuna until shortly before his death. In a very detailed report dated 28 May 1841, Chevron explained that Chanel had won to the Catholic faith the son of the king of Futuna, who became exasperated over this. The son went into hiding and his father found him in a village on 27 April 1841, but the son would not recant. Then on the following morning at about seven o'clock a native arrived at the residence of Chanel and asked him to dress a wound. Chanel was preparing the dressing when 'the native struck him with a tomahawk on the forehead'.

Unknown to Chanel, his house was completely encircled by armed natives. 'One of these advanced and struck him repeatedly with a club. The victim fell to his knees, prayed and wiped away the blood which flowed from his forehead. A third assassin pushed a bayonet into him at the shoulder which came out below his arm. Without saying a word the priest himself drew the blade out of the wound.' And while the others were busy looting, the murderer who had struck the first blow picked up a carpenter's tool and with it struck Chanel again, 'taking off the upper part of his head'. Chevron added that Brother Marie-Nizier Delorme and also an Englishman living with Chanel had left the house earlier that day to visit a sick person of the Vaincus tribe, and so escaped. 'These people generously protected them until a ship arrived which then brought them to Wallis, where they have been with us for the past ten days.'[18]

On 6 November, two days after receiving news of Chanel's death from

Bataillon, Pompallier wrote to Lavaud that he was now 'obliged to go myself, or to send at least one of my pro-vicars to the islands of Wallis and Futuna in order to visit the two missions that I established there four years ago'. He complained that ships of the French Navy had not visited either of those two missions for two years and that Bataillon at Wallis had been threatened several times with exile and even with death. 'Once even he was left for dead after being struck blows by a club. . . .' His schooner had to visit 'these two unfortunate missions, to deliver my colleagues from these people if they are determined to make themselves unworthy of them'. He also wished to collect, if possible, the remains of Chanel, 'the first martyr of my mission'.

In this letter he told Lavaud that 'the people of Wallis in the past have seized three-masted schooners and massacred the crews. If then these islanders are still in bad dispositions with regard to my missionaries, or if they [meanwhile] have killed them as those of Futuna killed the Reverend Chanel, it is probable that my schooner, on appearing there, will be in great danger of being taken and all hands on board being plundered and massacred.' He judged it wise and prudent, therefore, to request a French Navy escort for the voyage to Wallis, where he had two priests and three Brother-Catechists. Lavaud agreed and ordered the corvette *Allier* under Captain Eugène Dubouzet to accompany the *Sancta Maria* which left Akaroa at the end of November with Pompallier and Father Viard aboard.[19]

That same month of November had been a very disconcerting one for Colin back in France for an altogether different reason. About 8 November, when ten more Marists set sail from London for New Zealand,[20] he received a rather upsetting letter from Pompallier dated 18 May. If this letter had arrived a few days earlier, he said, he would not have sent these missionaries without first taking counsel with Cardinal Fransoni.

He described the bishop's letter as being filled with 'many bitter reproaches', criticising Colin particularly for 'delays in sending men and money'. Pompallier also 'makes it a crime for us to have authorised our members to write to us, as is our practice, and to do so without submitting their letters for his inspection. And he told us in formal terms that, in virtue of the letters from the Holy See which named him Vicar Apostolic of Western Oceania, he recognises no other superior over his clergy than himself alone. Consequently, he forbade us as well as everyone else to give any advice to the priests and Brothers of the society who, he said, are in fact exclusively under his hand.' The bishop also said that without his consent no Marist for any reason whatsoever could leave the mission and return to Europe, unless he wanted to incur the gravest censures. And he threatened to send back to Europe every priest and Brother who wanted to remain attached to the Society of Mary and to its superior.

The Marist priest who mailed Pompallier's letter to Colin enclosed a note of his own dated 21 May. 'I am taking advantage of this occasion to send you this note secretly', he said. 'His Grace read to me the letter which he addressed to you. With abundant tears I told him what pain his letter caused me . . . And I said that if I had known what was to happen, I never would have come to this mission. He replied that if I wanted to be dependent upon the society and upon its superior general, I could return to France. He also told me that he was going to make the same proposal to everyone. I begged him not to do anything of the sort, saying that each of us was too attached to the society and to the superiors . . . I am confident that he will stop there for the moment.'[21]

At this time both the limits of authority of Bishop Pompallier, whose staff was made up completely of Marists, and the limits of authority of Superior General Colin, whose religious community of Marists was entrusted with the same territory over which Pompallier had jurisdiction, were not clear. This easily led to misunderstandings between the two men.

Once again Colin sought a territory outside the jurisdiction of Pompallier, or rather sought to have one created quickly, because he wanted to send Pompallier no more personnel. And since Rome had decided to wait for a reply from the bishop before establishing the Vicariate Apostolic of Central Oceania, Colin made a compromise proposal on 28 December 1841, one that could be realised at once. 'With the permission of Your Eminence', he said, 'we shall send personnel to New Caledonia, from where they can gradually penetrate the other islands. Or we can send them to the Wallis Islands and from there they can easily pass over to the Tonga and Fiji archipelagoes, which are not far away. It would be sufficient for the priest who is to be placed in charge of this new colony of apostles to be given the title of prefect apostolic.'

Wanting to prove to Fransoni that he had fulfilled his duty toward New Zealand, Colin said that the group of missionaries sent in the previous month raised to forty-two the total number of missionaries sent by the Society of Mary to Western Oceania. In this number there were twenty priests, three students of theology (one had meanwhile been ordained a priest by Pompallier), and nineteen Brother-Catechists. He said that Pompallier had assigned all of his personnel to New Zealand except three priests and three Brothers, who were stationed on Wallis and Futuna.[22]

Colin's presentation here was not very objective, since Pompallier had not assigned six missionaries out of forty-two to Wallis and Futuna, but six out of twenty-one. Colin could not have known at this time the assignments of the remaining missionaries. His mentioning New Caledonia referred, of course, to his earlier proposal made to Pompallier on 6 June 1841, asking not only that the bishop favour the founding of a Vicariate Apostolic of Central Oceania, but also that he leave Fransoni completely free 'to erect another [vicariate apostolic] toward the islands of New Britain. . . .' If the prefect apostolic and his companions were to be sent to New Caledonia, they would then form a nucleus for this projected third vicariate apostolic in Marist territory reaching from New Caledonia to New Britain. 'Your Eminence', Colin concluded, 'will find us completely docile in following the line of conduct which you decide to trace out for us.'[23]

Fransoni apparently considered the foothold by three priests and three Brother-Catechists in Central Oceania sufficient, because on 29 January 1842 he 'seconded with great pleasure' Colin's proposal to send his next group of missionaries in the spring or late summer to 'New Caledonia, New Britain and the numerous islands lying to the north-west[24] of New Zealand, regions until now uncared-for'. Thus they would arrive there 'before the sowers of cockle'. The necessary letters patent for the one to be named prefect apostolic were enclosed, Fransoni said, and the choice was left up to Colin. All that he had to do was to insert the candidate's name in the space provided. 'And as soon as the requested information arrives from Bishop Pompallier, his vast vicariate will be divided in two and the Central Vicariate will be established.' Fransoni magnanimously added that he was ready to do whatever else Pompallier and Colin might care to suggest 'for the good and the advancement of those missions, which are so close to my heart'.[25]

When Colin wrote his letter to Fransoni about the new Prefecture Apostolic of New Caledonia-New Britain, the corvette *Allier* under Captain Eugène Dubouzet was escorting the *Sancta Maria* on its way to Wallis. En route the two ships had stopped at Vava'u in the Tonga Islands where Pompallier celebrated Christmas Mass aboard the *Allier*. Captain Dubouzet called a meeting there of the local chiefs and rebuked them for having refused to allow Pompallier to remain at Vava'u when he stopped there four years earlier. At Dubouzet's insistence the chiefs promised that never again would any French subject suffer such intolerance.

From Vava'u the two ships sailed to Wallis, where they arrived on 30 December 1841. Bataillon and his companions had worked unhindered and had made so much progress in giving instruction that countless people were ready to receive the sacraments. Bishop Pompallier decided to remain behind in Wallis to baptise and confirm, while Father Viard and Brother Marie-Nizier Delorme aboard the *Sancta Maria* sailed to Futuna escorted by the *Allier*. The bishop had asked Dubouzet to collect Chanel's remains there and had begged him to shed no blood in vengeance.[26]

All this time Colin in France was looking forward to the day when Rome would remove Wallis and Futuna and the surrounding archipelagoes from Pompallier's jurisdiction, not suspecting that the bishop was then living in Wallis and studying its language. In fact, Pompallier was still on Wallis when Colin finally decided to notify Fransoni on 18 March 1842 of the shocking letter that he had received from Pompallier. 'Only after long reflection do we dare bring Your Eminence up-to-date on the little human difficulties which seem to exist between our members and the Vicar Apostolic of New Zealand. . . .'

It was strange that Colin should use this title for Pompallier in a letter to Rome, since the bishop's official title was Vicar Apostolic of Western Oceania. Had Colin in his own mind already begun to restrict Pompallier to New Zealand, as he hoped Rome would do officially by removing all islands in the tropics from his jurisdiction?

By way of introduction Colin told Fransoni that members of his society for three years had been complaining in their letters about Pompallier's severity toward them, of his threats to place them under interdict for simple oversights, and of his insistence on inspecting and censoring their letters, even those directed to the superior general. He then explained how he had exhorted his members to be patient, since he was well acquainted with the sensitive character of Pompallier and knew how difficult it was to get along with him. Colin said that he had also written to Pompallier, counselling him to use prudence, moderation and suavity toward his priests. He admitted that the bishop 'really had every desirable authority over them', because he was not only their ecclesiastical superior, but also their religious superior, having been named so by Colin.

Then Colin in some detail informed Fransoni of the various reproaches that Pompallier had made in his letter of 18 May 1841, pointing out that he never would have sent the last group of missionaries, if that letter had arrived some days earlier. He not only mentioned Pompallier's threat to send back to France all Marists who felt an attachment to their society and to their top superior in France, but also quoted at length from the letter of 21 May 1841 written by one of his priests who had begged Pompallier in tears not to publish this decision.

Pompallier's letter of 18 May also indicated that he had been obliged to make a loan at a high rate of interest, Colin said, and was in immediate danger of losing his property, unless he soon received money from Europe. Then less than three months later the bishop withdrew 35,000 francs from Colin's account to cover a loan, perhaps the one in question; he had already withdrawn 18,000 francs before that. 'We earnestly wish that this practice of drawing on our account without forewarning us should discontinue', Colin said, since in this way Pompallier could 'compromise us or compromise the mission'. Colin asked Fransoni for advice on what steps he should take to remedy these matters and added that he would be contacting the cardinal soon on 'the mission to New Caledonia'.[27]

Fransoni reacted immediately and wrote on 12 April to both Colin and Pompallier. He told Colin that he was very sorry to learn about the disagreements existing between the Marist missionaries and Pompallier. The evils had to be remedied, he said, and he hoped to achieve this by a letter addressed to the bishop, which he enclosed for Colin to read and forward.[28]

The letter for Pompallier said that Fransoni 'with great sorrow' had learned that there did not exist between him and his missionaries 'that concord of minds which is to be desired and which is necessary for the welfare of your mission'. The missionaries were right, he said, in complaining that their bishop was not treating them properly, since he was using threats and censures to keep them from fulfilling duties toward their superior general which flowed from their vows. On the other hand, everyone praised Pompallier's zeal and realised the difficulties and the dangers in which he found himself. 'However, the right thing to do would be . . . to determine in a more mature manner, and after taking counsel, what is more important to do and then complete it, instead of rather often discontinuing what has been undertaken and making expenses beyond measure.'

He would quickly notice, the cardinal warned, 'that little by little your mission is being brought to the brink of destruction, since the personnel of the society entrusted with the mission will be removed. . . .' To obviate this he advised Pompallier to foster unity in the Society of Mary, because this would also promote the good of the mission. The cardinal also made it clear that the members ought to be allowed to communicate regularly with their superior general. 'Nor does your dignity suffer, if at times you seek counsel from those sharing your labours and your ministry, and if you act toward them as an equal and as a colleague, rather than as a superior, so that all things may be accomplished in the Lord and in charity.'

Fransoni described Colin as ceaselessly giving Pompallier testimony of his 'devotion, love and confidence'. And Pompallier's unique task for God in Western Oceania was, in fact, a task which he had in common 'with the superior of the Marists'. He therefore exhorted Pompallier, in conclusion, to fulfil his pastoral duties, 'not in fighting and jealousy, but in the bond of peace, working together harmoniously with him and with your helpers'.[29]

The cardinal's letter of 12 April for Pompallier did not impress Colin very much. 'I understood at once that it would produce no more than an ephemeral effect', he later told Fransoni, 'even though it was filled with wise advice.' He was certain 'that Bishop Pompallier would reply in the same way that he replies to me, stating that he should not want to be in the shoes of those who submit false reports [about him]'.

Instead of quieting Colin, the cardinal's letter seemed only to make him more disturbed and he began to consider 'a journey to Rome as absolutely necessary for the interests of the mission of New Zealand'. (Only six months earlier Pompallier, too, had considered a journey to Rome absolutely necessary for the good of his mission, but the news of Chanel's death had changed his plans.) Colin decided to take along all the correspondence which he had received from Pompallier and from the members of his society, as well as copies of the letters that he himself had written. As he later told Fransoni, it was his intention 'to place under the eyes of Your Eminence all of our correspondence, so that you could have a just knowledge of the condition of the mission and take the necessary steps for maintaining peace and preventing abuses'. But he postponed the trip to Rome until near the end of May.[30]

By the time Colin left for Rome, he had a detailed plan ready which divided all of Western Oceania into five geographical districts which step by step could become independent vicariates apostolic. The document drawn up by Colin and his priests was titled: 'An Overall View of the Islands of Western Oceania to Help Determine the Borders to Be Laid Down between the New Missions That Could Be Founded There'. The five proposed divisions of Western Oceania were called 'approximate and natural' and all longitudes were based on the prime meridian of Paris. The divisions were as follows:

1. The Vicariate Apostolic of New Zealand with its surrounding islands, reaching from 160° east longitude to 175° west longitude and from the Tropic of Capricorn (23°30′ south latitude) to the Antarctic.

2. The Vicariate Apostolic of Tonga, Samoa, Fiji, etc., including Wallis and Futuna, reaching from 170° east longitude to 170° west longitude and from the equator to the Tropic of Capricorn.

A.M.D.G.   *et A.M.D.G.H.*

Renseignements sur l'océanie occidentale par les pères Maristes. Lyon. 26 mai 1842.

Coup d'œil général
Sur les îles de l'Océanie occidentale
pour servir à fixer des limites entre les missions nouvelles qu'on
pourrait y établir.

L'océanie occidentale formant actuellement le vicariat apostolique de Monseigneur de Maronée, érigé en l'année 1836, s'étend depuis le 165° de longitude occidentale du méridien de paris, jusques vers les archipels de la Malaisie, par des limites qui restent encore à déterminer. Dans un autre sens, si l'on s'en tient aux bornes généralement adoptées pour l'Océanie, elle occuperait un espace d'environ 2,000 lieues, depuis le 40° de latitude septentrionale, jusqu'au 55° de latitude méridionale.

Deux points seulement de cette immense étendue ont été visités et sont devenus la demeure de missionnaires catholiques. Ce sont la Nouvelle-Zélande, résidence actuelle de Monseigneur de Maronée, et les îles Wallis et Futuna, résidences des pères Chevron Bataillon et Chanel. Les principaux archipels de cette vaste contrée sont: 1° la Nouvelle-Zélande, 2° les groupes tonga, samoa et viti, 3° la Nouvelle-Calédonie, les Nouvelles-hébrides et les îles Salomon. 4° la Nouvelle-Guinée, la nouvelle-Bretagne la nouvelle-irlande, les îles de l'amirauté, de Seguiou &c... 5° enfin les îles Carolines dont il faut excepter les îles Mariannes possédées depuis longtems par les espagnols, et soumises à la juridiction ecclésiastique des philippines.

Les limites respectives de pays encore si peu connus ne pouvant pas être données exactement, voici peut être la manière d'établir entre elles une division approximative et naturelle.

1°

Vicariat apostolique de la Nouvelle-Zélande et îles circonvoisines, depuis le 160° de longitude orientale, jusqu'au 175.° de longitude occidentale (méridien de paris), et dans un autre sens, depuis le tropique du Capricorne, 23° 30′ de lat. mérid, jusqu'aux terres polaires

Le P. Chanel a été martyrisé le 28 Avril 1841.

Lyon 26 Mai 1842. Coup d'œil sur les missions de l'océanie occidentale

37   The Marists in May 1842 drew up 'An Overall View of the Islands of Western Oceania to Help Determine the Borders to Be Laid Down between the New Missions That Could Be Founded There'. Although not officially submitted to Rome, it greatly influenced the subsequent proposals made by the Marists for carving new vicariates apostolic from the original Vicariate Apostolic of Western Oceania. *Source: SM: 410/SCPF. (Chapter 14).*

4°

Vicariat apostolique de la nouvelle-Guinée et îles circonvoisines depuis le 127° jusqu'au 152° de longitude orientale (méridien de paris) et dans un autre sens depuis la ligne équinoriale 0° jusqu'au 12° de latitude méridionale.

1° la nouvelle-Guinée est une terre considérable longue de c 400 lieues du sud-est au nord-ouest, sur une largeur ordinaire de 130 lieues. elle est échancrée dans sa partie septent.le de manière à former une presqu'île qu'on nomme la terre des papouas. rien n'est comparable à tout ce que l'on dit de la fertilité et de l'admirable végétation de cette Contrée. sa population est inconnue. les habitans sont une

assez belle race d'hommes à la peau noire aux cheveux laineux et frisés. ceux de l'intérieur sont réputés sauvages et féroces, mais ceux qui habitent aux environs du hâvre dori, par le 131° 30' de longitude orientale à 1° de l'équateur ont eu de fréquentes relations avec les navires européens, et il serait facile de faire parmi eux un établissement de missionnaires attendu qu'ils paraissent assez doux et déjà bien disposés pour recevoir la foi.

2° la nouvelle-Bretagne et la nouvelle-irlande à l'Est de la nouvelle-guinée; deux îles magnifiques ayant chacune une longueur de 60 à 80 lieues sur une largeur de 10 à 15, et une population de 100 mille âmes. ces insulaires ont paru assez pacifiques envers les étrangers qui les ont visités. en remontant le long de l'équateur on trouve encore le groupe de l'amirauté assez considérable, composé d'une trentaine d'îles; les îles jobie, véguiou dont la population est estimée à 100 mille âmes. en descendant le long de la côte occid.le de la nouvelle-guinée on rencontre plusieurs îles dont les plus remar quables sont les îles Arrou très-nombreuses et bien peuplées; &c...

nota. Nous n'avons rien dit de la religion de ces peuples, qui varie selon les distances, mais en général ils croient à l'existence des mauvais génies dont la nature et l'occupation est de faire du mal aux hommes. aussi ils tâchent de les apaiser par des offrandes de différentes choses, quelquefois même par des sacrifices humains. beaucoup de ces peuples sont anthropophages.

38   As figure 37, p. 4. This page contains information on the Vicariate Apostolic of New Guinea as
proposed by the Marists. *Source: SM: 410/SCPF.*
(*Chapter 14*).

3. The Vicariate Apostolic of New Caledonia, New Hebrides and the Solomon Islands, reaching from 152° to 170° east longitude and from the equator to the Tropic of Capricorn.

4. The Vicariate Apostolic of New Guinea and the surrounding islands, including New Britain, New Ireland, the Admiralty Islands, Waigeo, etc., reaching from 127.° to 152° east longitude and from the equator to 12° south latitude.

5. A very extensive fifth division of Oceania could also be formed into a vicariate apostolic, reaching from 128° to 171°40′ east longitude and from the equator northward to the last latitude accepted as the boundary for Oceania. This vicariate apostolic would include the Carolines but exclude the Marianas, which were under the jurisdiction of a bishop in the Philippines.

The 'Overall View' indicated not only the above boundaries of the proposed vicariates apostolic, but also contained a small map of each together with a description of the geography, population, culture, produce and commercial contacts. As is clear from the divisions that it contained, the territory reaching from New Caledonia to New Britain inclusive, originally proposed by Colin as a possible vicariate apostolic, was now presented as parts of two distinct vicariates apostolic. The news of Chanel's death in no way affected this report, since it was composed before that news arrived.

After learning from Father Chevron in Wallis that Chanel had been killed, Colin wrote to Fransoni on 26 May 1842. This letter accompanied the 'Overall View' and both documents were designed to help Colin win his case at Rome for the immediate foundation of the Vicariate Apostolic of Central Oceania, with others to follow in the near future. Having a bishop in each of those areas, Colin said, would 'inspire the natives with respect' and would also 'attract new personnel'. This was something that 'the presence of a simple priest' could not do, since a bishop 'alone is capable of founding a church and of assuring its prosperity'. Furthermore, Pompallier was 'more than absorbed by the urgent needs of the people around him and new colleagues in the episcopate would be of the greatest benefit for him in advancing the cause of truth against the intrigues of error'. In fact, Colin added, Chanel's being massacred 'must in part be attributed' to Pompallier's finding it impossible to visit the islands of Wallis and Futuna as promised. (He lifted this argument almost verbatim from Father Chevron's letter.)[31]

Instead of mailing the 'Overall View' and his letter to Rome, Colin added them to the pile of correspondence that he wanted to present personally to Cardinal Fransoni, head of the Evangelisation Congregation. But just as he was about to leave Lyon for Rome, he received a letter from Oceania which seemed to indicate that affairs in New Zealand were improving. Partly because of this letter he decided not to show Fransoni the disturbing correspondence from Pompallier and the complaints from his priests. A second reason for withholding these letters was the coolness that he sensed after arriving in the offices of the Evangelisation Congregation in Rome. He interpreted this coolness to mean that his letter of 18 March 1842, which pointed out his difficulties and those of his missionaries with Pompallier, was looked upon 'as an attempt to encroach upon the rights of the vicar apostolic'. Certain remarks helped confirm this idea.[32] He therefore restricted his business with the Evangelisation Congregation to urging the immediate establishment of the Vicariate Apostolic of Central Oceania and to making the proximate preparations for launching missionary work among the Kaffirs of South Africa. This new mission had been offered to his community some months earlier by Rome.

In a formal petition written from Rome on 21 June 1842 and addressed to Fransoni, Colin pointed out that it was difficult to make progress in a mission area after the arrival of Protestant missionaries. He therefore wished to send his missionaries at once 'to the thickly populated archipelagoes of Tonga, Fiji and Samoa, all of which are near the Wallis Islands'. He said that this reason and 'the necessity of bringing prompt assistance to our members, who have been completely isolated for five years in the Wallis Islands more than 600 leagues from New Zealand', had made him decide the previous year to request that the three archipelagoes mentioned should become a new vicariate to be called the Vicariate Apostolic of Central Oceania. He now dared to repeat that request, he said, and his reasons for it were the same as he had submitted the year before.

For the office of vicar apostolic he presented the usual list of three candidates, giving his preference in this order: Bataillon of Wallis, Baty of New Zealand, and Chevron of Futuna-Wallis. In the event that difficulties might stand in the way and make it impossible to create this new vicariate apostolic at once, he requested authorisation to send some priests immediately to join the missionaries at work in the Wallis Islands 'without having recourse for this to Bishop Pompallier'.[33]

Colin was still in Rome when he received word from his headquarters in Lyon that a letter had arrived from Bataillon in Wallis dated 31 May 1841 on Chanel's death. Colin then informed Fransoni on 2 August that 'the details on the martyrdom of Father Chanel' that he had submitted earlier were confirmed by Bataillon. In his letter Bataillon also reported that the Wallis Islands had been converted to the Catholic faith, that five churches had already been built and that he needed priests urgently. Colin passed on all this information to Fransoni.[34]

Six days later, 8 August 1842, the cardinals of the Evangelisation Congregation assembled to decide whether a new Vicariate Apostolic of Central Oceania should be established. The name of Cardinal Mai, a former secretary of the Evangelisation Congregation, was printed on the first page of the report, indicating that he was responsible for it. But he happened to be absent that day and in his place Cardinal Prefect Fransoni presented the report. It filled six large printed pages and the information was divided into eight points:

1. The introduction said that the assembled cardinals were well acquainted with the rapid progress being made by the Catholic faith within the two vicariates apostolic of Eastern Oceania and Western Oceania. At a later date steps would have to be taken to create new divisions in the Vicariate Apostolic of Eastern Oceania, 'which now also seems to need them'.

2. A glance at a map would show how 'immeasurably vast' Western Oceania

was, since it included all islands north and south of the equator and reached westward from Mangaia Island (in the southern Cook Islands). In these islands, according to a report from Bishop Pompallier, there were 'some 15 to 20 million inhabitants'.

3. Hardly five years have passed since the arrival of Bishop Pompallier and the Marists and yet the mission has already produced 'abundant results and promises even more'. Although Vicar Apostolic Pompallier has over forty missionaries already, he keeps asking for more. But since he has so much work to do in New Zealand, he has kept nearly all of them there. By the end of this year he should have close to sixty priests and Brothers. 'And since these latter serve as catechists, they are hardly less efficient than the former in propagating the faith.'

4. Here were listed all the reasons presented by Father Colin in favour of a new vicariate apostolic since his first letter of 20 May 1841. The task in Western Oceania was simply too great for a single vicar apostolic because of the extensive territory and the great difficulties in communications between the islands. Having a bishop of their own would remedy the isolation of the missionaries on Wallis and Futuna and at the same time would have a very beneficial influence on the people there and in the archipelagoes of Fiji, Tonga and Samoa. And if the number of missionaries should continue to grow and if the results should keep up as in the past, even additional vicariates apostolic could be formed later.

5. Although Colin's proposal 'had to be looked upon as most opportune', it had been deemed proper to obtain first the views of Vicar Apostolic Pompallier on boundaries and candidates. Colin had written again on 28 December, stating that more missionaries had been sent and that a new group was soon to leave, and he asked that one of these be made prefect apostolic even prior to the creation of the vicariate apostolic. Much detail was given here on the personnel that Colin had already supplied and would continue to supply for Western Oceania. Colin was quoted as saying that Pompallier was so occupied with the affairs of New Zealand, 'where alone two vicariates apostolic would be necessary, one for the north and the other for the south of this extensive island', that he had no time to think of the other parts of his vicariate. 'However it would be extremely important that the Catholic faith be brought as soon as possible to these numerous populations before the error of the Methodists has taken deep root in their hearts.'

6. Over a year has passed since the letter of 12 June 1841 was sent to Pompallier, but no answer has arrived. Colin, in Rome on some other business, believes that the letter must have been lost en route and now he is urging more than ever that a decision on the new vicariate be made. The threat of Protestant missionaries moving in is greater than ever before, and so 'a longer delay could become very dangerous for the interests of the mission'. Colin also maintains that Pompallier could not at all object to the foundation of a new vicariate apostolic, because 'he never ceases to complain—and with reason—about the very enormous burden on his shoulders and he asks for some relief'.

7. The boundaries suggested by Colin for the new mission are these. On the north the equator and on the south the Tropic of Capricorn (23°27′ south latitude). On the east the meridian passing through Mangaia Island, that is, the line which divides the Vicariate Apostolic of Western Oceania from that of Eastern Oceania. And on the west the meridian passing through the most eastern point of San Cristóbal Island in the Solomon Islands, without however including that island. The new Vicariate Apostolic of Central Oceania would therefore include the Wallis Islands, which are almost completely converted, Futuna Island, where Chanel shed his blood, and the archipelagoes of Tonga, Samoa, Fiji, New Caledonia and New Hebrides, as well as a large number of smaller islands within the area.

8. Presented as first choice for the office of Vicar Apostolic of Central Oceania was Father Pierre Bataillon. He was recommended 'because of his personal qualities' and also because he had been active in the Wallis Islands for several years already and had obtained there 'the most brilliant success in his preaching and in his apostolic work'.

The cardinals were then asked whether the pope should be requested to separate the above-mentioned places from the Vicariate Apostolic of Western Oceania and form them into a new Vicariate Apostolic of Central Oceania, and also whether this new territory should remain entrusted to the Marists. The cardinals answered in the affirmative in both instances. And when asked who ought to be named vicar apostolic, they chose Bataillon, saying that the pope should be requested to raise him to the rank of bishop.

Cardinal Fransoni then presented one further proposal, which was not on the printed report and which he said Colin had suggested. He asked the assembled cardinals whether Bataillon should be given a coadjutor bishop, that is, an assistant bishop with the right of succession. The coadjutor could be chosen from among the next group of missionaries preparing to leave for the Vicariate Apostolic of Central Oceania and Colin had already presented three candidates in the following order of preference: Fathers Douarre, Procedaire and Dupont. The two reasons given by Colin for requesting a coadjutor were these: (1) The coadjutor could be ordained a bishop in France and on arriving in Wallis could at once ordain Bataillon a bishop, thus making it unnecessary for Bataillon to lose time by going elsewhere for his episcopal ordination, and (2) in the event of Bataillon's death the mission would not be deprived of a shepherd, since the coadjutor could immediately take charge. The cardinals of the Evangelisation Congregation considered the reasons valid and named Father Guillaume Douarre as the one to be presented to the pope for this office.

That same day, 8 August 1842, Archbishop Ignazio Cadolini, secretary of the Evangelisation Congregation, reported on the meeting to Pope Gregory XVI, who sanctioned all the decisions reached. He thus formally established the Vicariate Apostolic of Central Oceania with the boundaries indicated, made Bataillon the vicar apostolic with the rank of bishop, and gave him Douarre as a coadjutor bishop.[35]

Two of the decisions reached by the cardinals give rise to much speculation.

39   The Most Reverend Pierre Bataillon (1810–77),
the first Vicar Apostolic of Central Oceania. *Source:*
OM vol. 4, p. 257. (Chapter 14).

Why were New Caledonia and New Hebrides included in the Vicariate Apostolic of Central Oceania and why at the last minute was Bataillon given a coadjutor bishop? The fact that this latter proposal was not in the printed report proves that it was made much later than the one to extend the boundaries of the Central Vicariate. And although New Caledonia and New Hebrides were mentioned in point number seven of the report, they had never been mentioned as a possible component of the Central Vicariate previous to Colin's coming to Rome.

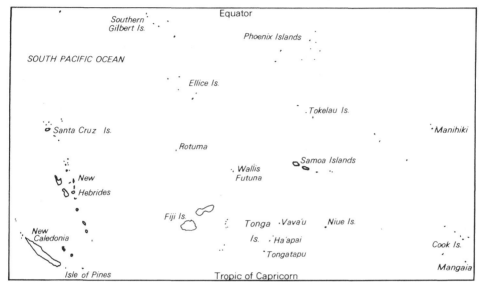

40 The Vicariate Apostolic of Central Oceania, created on 8 August 1842, was the first new ecclesiastical territory to be carved from the Vicariate Apostolic of Western Oceania. The territory remained entrusted to the Marists. *(Chapter 14)*.

Both Colin and Fransoni had wanted to send a prefect apostolic to New Caledonia so that he and his missionaries might serve as a nucleus for a later vicariate apostolic. Perhaps they considered it more practicable to separate that territory at this time from Pompallier's jurisdiction, so that the missionaries for it would depend upon the Vicar Apostolic of Central Oceania, since more understanding could be expected from Bataillon than from Pompallier. If this was the thinking of the two men, it is understandable how the next step could follow, namely, sending a coadjutor bishop to Bataillon in Wallis instead of a prefect apostolic to New Caledonia. If Bataillon were still alive, the coadjutor could then try to establish himself in New Caledonia-New Hebrides. Once he were established there, his territory could be extended to include the Solomon Islands and then become an independent vicariate apostolic containing the very archipelagoes indicated by Colin for one of the proposed vicariates apostolic in his 'Overall View'.

Colin had succeeded admirably and returned to France with a happy heart, having received much more in Rome than he had ever thought of requesting from

Lyon. Cardinal Fransoni and the Evangelisation Congregation could hardly have been more magnanimous.

Pompallier, too, was returning home about this time with a happy heart, for he had done much to promote missionary work in the tropical islands. At Wallis in five weeks he had learned the language well enough to assist his priests in caring for their people. 'At the end of four and a half months', he said, 'I was able to baptise and confirm the whole population, including the King and all his family.' He estimated the population at 2,700.

It had been arranged that Bishop Pompallier should remain in Wallis and that the *Sancta Maria* should go to Futuna to take aboard Father Chanel's remains and deliver them to New Zealand before returning to Wallis to pick up the bishop and then bring him to Futuna. Consequently the *Sancta Maria* escorted by the corvette *Allier* under Captain Dubouzet had sailed from Wallis to Futuna, arriving there on 18 January 1842. Sam Keletaona, whom Pompallier had met at Futuna in 1837 while en route from France to New Zealand, had fled to Wallis after an August 1839 war between Futuna's two kings and had begun taking instructions in the Roman Catholic religion at Wallis. On leaving for Futuna, Captain Dubouzet had invited him to come aboard the *Allier* in order to serve as his interpreter in Futuna. Dubouzet encouraged the young chief to help in restoring peace to the island and hoped that he would also foster Christianity. Keletaona accepted the invitation, promised to do his best, and stayed behind on Futuna when the *Sancta Maria* with its precious cargo and the *Allier* left for New Zealand on 20 January 1842.

Several months later when Pompallier reached Futuna on 29 May, he was astonished to see how much Keletaona and his companions had accomplished in this short interval in giving religious instructions. The bishop found an occasion to address the island's leaders, telling them that Futuna was much too small to have two kings, a system of government which could only lead to repeated civil wars. He suggested that from among their chiefs they choose a single one to be their king. They did this and unanimously chose Keletaona. (He ruled Futuna until he was deposed in 1851.) Pompallier, whose stay in Futuna lasted less than two weeks, then baptised and confirmed 120 of its inhabitants, including the new king, his queen, and their daughter. Keletaona at this time received a third name, Petelo, for Pierre, his baptismal name. On 9 June when Pompallier sailed for Fiji, he left behind Brother Marie-Nizier Delorme, who originally had been assigned to Futuna with Chanel, and also two priests, one of whom was Father Catherin Servant who had asked to be transferred from New Zealand to the tropical islands.

In Fiji the bishop stopped at the small islands of Oneata and Lakemba, 'to inform these peoples that Mother Church thinks of them and is concerned about their salvation'. And from Fiji he had sailed to Tongatapu. He estimated its population at 10,000 or 12,000 and was able to boast that he had won the favour of all but 1,000. 'The great chiefs of Bea have received one of my priests whom I offered them with a catechist', he said. 'The principal chief of Bea has already turned to the Faith with several others of his celebrated fort, where I said the first Mass on 2nd July.'

After visiting Vava'u and returning to Wallis for another week, Pompallier returned to New Zealand to take care of the business that had accumulated there. The *Sancta Maria* sailed into the Bay of Islands on 26 August 1842 and anchored before his residence at Kororareka.[36] He had been absent for one year, one month and three days. Among the letters in his possession waiting to be answered was Cardinal Fransoni's of 12 June 1841 requesting his views on the foundation of the Vicariate Apostolic of Central Oceania.[37] The *Sancta Maria* had delivered it to Pompallier in Wallis in May 1842, but he had had neither time nor occasion to answer it.[38]

15

Tension mounts between the Marists and Pompallier

20 OCTOBER 1842

Bishop Rouchouze, whose missionary work in Eastern Oceania was expanding, had sailed from Honolulu on 3 January 1841 to discuss in France and Rome his need for more personnel and funds. He left Paris on 27 December 1841 for Rome to report on the development of his Vicariate Apostolic of Eastern Oceania and while there he submitted questions to the Evangelisation Congregation about religious order members (the Picpus Fathers) assigned to his vicariate apostolic. His questions were aimed at clarifying in some concrete cases the authority of the *ecclesiastical* superior who represents a mission (bishop, prelate, vicar apostolic, pro-vicar, prefect apostolic, pro-prefect) and the authority of the *religious* superior who represents a religious order (superior general, provincial superior, vice provincial).

His first question was whether 'a religious superior at will can change or recall a missionary, employing him outside the mission or in some other post of the mission, without consulting the ecclesiastical superior and without obtaining his consent. Above all can he keep a pro-prefect outside the mission?' Cardinal Fransoni handed over the question to the Evangelisation Congregation's archivist for research. The archivist replied on 15 April 1842 that religious superiors on many occasions and by various decrees had been forbidden to remove members of their religious communities from missions, unless they previously had obtained the Evangelisation Congregation's consent. One of the first decrees in the matter was dated 2 February 1631 and had been confirmed on 13 March 1668. He added that in 1646 the Society of Jesus (Jesuits) was dispensed under certain conditions from observing the decree and also that the superior of the Paris Foreign Mission Seminary, in fact, 'recalls his missionaries at will'.[1]

Cardinal Fransoni on 21 April 1842 answered Rouchouze's question by repeating verbatim the text of the 1631 decree, but without mentioning a word about the Jesuits or the Paris Foreign Mission Seminary. According to this decree all missionaries who were members of religious communities were 'subject in all things and for all things to their [religious] superiors, except in the case of their removal from the mission'. Religious superiors could not remove missionaries 'for any pretext, reason or complaint whatsoever' without first consulting the Evangelisation Congregation. And even if a prefect apostolic at the same time happened to be a provincial superior, he would not be allowed to remove missionaries from his territory 'unless in the case of public scandal, and then the Sacred Congregation must be informed as soon as possible about the scandal and about the removal of the missionaries'. In all other cases when prefects apostolic might judge that a missionary ought to be removed, 'they must first inform the same Sacred Congregation of their reason for wanting to remove him and they must await a reply before removing the said missionary, or barring him from the mission or denying him the use of faculties'.

A second question of Rouchouze was: 'Can the provincial or vice provincial serve simultaneously as the pro-vicar, prefect or pro-prefect?' Fransoni's reply to this was very brief: 'We think that this question must be answered not only affirmatively, but that it is even expedient to join together offices of this kind whenever possible, since this will foster unity.'

Rouchouze had also brought up the question of the Picpus missionaries writing to their superior general, so Fransoni also clarified this issue. According to the decrees of the Sacred Congregation the missionaries, and primarily the ecclesiastical superior, 'are bound to correspond directly and immediately with the Sacred Congregation on all things strictly pertaining to the mission. This is the case because many things either may not be made known to others or at least should not be made known.'

But this does not mean, he said, that these same individuals are prohibited from corresponding with their superior general, or from informing him of the progress of the mission, its needs and other business, except for the more confidential matters already mentioned. 'They inform him either by a letter addressed to him personally, or by transmitting through him to the Sacred Congregation the letters not included among those mentioned above, so that he may read them. As for matters pertaining to religious discipline, as well as other things mentioned in the above decrees, the Sacred Congregation not only considers it fitting, but it altogether approves their making these things known to the superior general of the society and their seeking counsel from him. In a word, it earnestly exhorts both the missionaries and the vicar apostolic always to preserve and to foster unity and concord with the above-mentioned [religious] superior, so that all things may be carried out in charity and in the bond of peace. . . .'[2]

Just nine days before Fransoni wrote this letter, he had also informed Pompallier (on 12 April 1842) that the Marists had a right to correspond with their superior general.[3] Apparently he was trying to establish a uniform practice for the missions of Oceania. But more important than this, he was interested in the entire missionary team's working harmoniously together, since only then could it be assured of God's blessing. Striving to achieve this harmony among missionaries had been a constant concern of the Evangelisation Congregation ever since its foundation in 1622. As late as 19 December 1839 a meeting of cardinals had discussed some questions on the relationship of missionaries to vicars apostolic and to diocesan bishops. The result was the publication of a new instruction to which Pope Gregory XVI gave his approval on 28 December 1839. It was based upon a similar instruction issued in 1783.[4]

Fransoni had sent Colin for forwarding (and reading) the 12 April 1842 letter for Pompallier. Colin, with his secretary Poupinel, in the next month, on 28 May, left Lyon for Rome with 'the sole purpose' (as he said later) of resolving problems with Pompallier that had come to light in New Zealand correspondence. Colin wanted Rome to issue some guarantees for himself and for his missionaries serving in Western Oceania and on 21 June 1842 he gave a formal request to Fransoni. He asked him 'to authorise us in the interests of the mission:

'1. To establish in New Zealand a provincial to represent the superior general of the society, who without prejudicing the rights of jurisdiction of the vicar apostolic, would in accord with the latter watch over each missionary.

'2. To withdraw a missionary and replace him by another, where there is need for this, having previously given notice to Your Eminence. Obviously we shall use this faculty only in serious cases.

'3. To require that missionaries ordinarily be not isolated, as they have been for entire years in the past. Charity and prudence would seem to require that in the rigorous existence which they must endure, they ought to be given the consolation of being in a group of at least two or three.

'4. To recall one of the missionaries about every four or five years in order to have him inform Your Eminence and the superior of the Society [of Mary] on all points that might concern the good of the mission and of the individual missionaries.'[5]

Cardinal Fransoni was most cooperative and nine days later, on 30 June 1842, issued a decree signed by himself, which he gave to Colin. Its purpose, clearly spelled out in the decree itself, was 'to foster unity of spirit' among the priests of the Society of Mary, 'who are labouring in areas in Western Oceania, and also to promote the observance of the religious life as much as possible. . . .' It was likewise aimed at eliminating 'contentions, abuses and other inconveniences, so they may carry out their evangelical task with greater fervour and may work in harmony. . . .' The decree was divided into the four points which Colin had judged indispensable for the good of the mission. However, they had been qualified in such a way as not to jeopardise the rights of either the vicar apostolic or the Evangelisation Congregation. The points would prove 'beneficial for the prosperity and growth of the same mission', the decree said, and they were to remain in effect until 'changed times and circumstances' or something 'more expedient and useful for the mission' might prompt the Evangelisation Congregation to revise or revoke them.

In the first point Colin was authorised to name a provincial superior in Oceania who in turn would be able to subdelegate vice provincials as circumstances might require. The provincial and his vice provincial 'together with the vicars apostolic, while leaving intact all the rights of these vicars apostolic and their authority, are to devote particular care to watching over the internal religious discipline of the members and their manner of life'.

In the second point the superior general 'for grave reasons' was allowed to recall one or other of his missionaries, provided he had first informed the Evangelisation Congregation and had received its reply, and provided also that the vicar apostolic had been informed. But he was obliged 'to substitute other suitable priests without delay' for those recalled, 'lest the faithful be deprived of spiritual helps and lest the work of propagating the faith suffer harm'.

The third point stated that every missionary 'should live with at least one other member and even, if possible, with two', taking care of a particular region together, since in this way they could find strength and companionship in one another. No missionary was ever to live alone, 'except in case of necessity and for a limited time'.

In the fourth and final point the superior general was authorised 'to recall one of his missionaries every four or five years, after informing the vicar apostolic, and have him give the Sacred Congregation a more detailed and complete report on the state of the mission and missionaries, their activities, needs, growth of the faith and other matters'. But this report did not exclude 'the report which the vicar apostolic himself is bound to transmit to the Sacred Congregation at fixed times'.[6]

This decree, which Colin received in handwritten form while still in Rome, protected and strengthened his position in many areas.

Bishop Pompallier had returned to the Bay of Islands on 26 August 1842, but inexplicably he waited almost two months before answering Cardinal Fransoni's letter of 12 June 1841. This letter had requested Pompallier's views on the foundation of the Vicariate Apostolic of Central Oceania and Fransoni had said that he expected 'a very prompt reply'. Finally answering on 19 October 1842, Pompallier said that he had been busy with missionary work in the tropics when the cardinal's letter arrived. Before replying to it, though, he mentioned that grave misunderstandings had arisen between him and the Marist head-quarters in France, since 'a number of priests are writing things about my administration to their superior general which are evidently false'. This in turn had affected the Association for the Propagation of the Faith in Lyon, he said, because no funds had arrived from that organisation. Consequently he had been obliged to make a loan, 'since without it the mission would have collapsed. Thanks to the services of the Protestants in this country, I have been able to keep the mission going.'

In regard to the proposal of founding a vicariate apostolic in Central Oceania immediately, he listed numerous reservations:

1. The territory should not contain 'too many different languages'.

2. He had no guarantee that any of his New Zealand mission stations would survive and even those in the tropics had also 'just been born'. In addition to this consideration there was the danger that the English, who 'one year ago took possession of all the islands of New Zealand', might not allow him, a French subject, to remain there.

3. In the event that circumstances should force him to leave New Zealand, where would he go? He knew English and the New Zealand language well, he said, and also the two languages of Wallis-Futuna and of Tongatapu well enough for exercising the ministry there. But if these tropical islands were to become parts of a new vicariate apostolic, he said, he would have to seek territory elsewhere. This would mean that 'all my linguistic knowledge, acquired in the

missions which I have founded until now, will have been in vain, and I am close to 40 years of age'.

4. 'In one or two years' an English vicar apostolic ought to be assigned to New Zealand, since understandably the French government 'would not be pleased' to have a French bishop in English territory. 'And if I remain here, its protection will become non-existent for me and for my missions, whereas I owe to that protection—after God—the freedom to carry out my ministry and the safety of my personnel.'

5. He had moreover won the hearts and the confidence 'of the peoples of Wallis, Futuna and Tongatapu', and so Rome could eventually give him that area and the surrounding archipelagoes as a vicariate apostolic.

6. Nor could he understand how Colin, the superior general of the Marists, 'can propose to you the foundation of another vicariate apostolic to be administered by the same society, since it cannot furnish enough personnel even for New Zealand'. He himself had earlier advised Fransoni, he said, that three or four new vicariates apostolic were needed within the limits of his jurisdiction, and not just one, 'in order to free it from the heresy with which it is ravaged on almost every side'.

If in spite of all these considerations 'the Holy Father in your person' should decide to establish a new vicariate apostolic in the tropical islands, then it ought to contain 'those islands which have much contact with one another because of language', namely, Tongatapu, Vava'u, Ha'apai, Wallis, Samoa and Futuna. But he asked that these islands be left within his jurisdiction 'for two years in order to see what will happen to New Zealand under English authority'. Fiji, on the other hand, could immediately become a vicariate apostolic, he said, 'because the paramount chief there, whom I have seen, asked me for priests. And the population is very numerous there and has only about one language.' He counselled Fransoni to begin with Fiji.

In the event that Fiji or the other group of islands were to become a vicariate apostolic, his candidate for vicar apostolic would be Father Viard, 'whom I left at Wallis to direct mission work in all the islands of the tropics'. Pompallier praised his talent for languages and said that he was loved by the natives. He called Viard a learned, prudent and holy man with all the virtues proper to a cleric. He also knew how to make missions in his charge 'succeed wonderfully'.

Pompallier's letter concluded on a happy note. 'God has blessed our seven months of work in the islands of Wallis, Futuna and Tongatapu prodigiously', he said. 'All of Wallis is baptised and confirmed (2,800 souls) with the exception of four or five persons. Futuna has 120 baptisms and confirmations . . . And I have two priests and a catechist at Wallis, the same at Futuna and the same at Tongatapu.' Also Ascension Island (or Ponape) in the Archipelago of the Carolines 'has urgently requested to have a mission founded there'.

In a lengthy postscript, which consisted chiefly of another attack on the Marists, Pompallier said that during his absence his pro-vicar, Father Epalle, 'without any authorisation on my part had wanted to found a new station with two priests and a Brother on Ascension Island in the Carolines', and had even thought of using for this purpose personnel that Pompallier had assigned to New Zealand. 'This same pro-vicar', he said in the body of his letter, 'has left for France without my authorisation as the result of a small sort of plot among my priests.' Leader of the 'plot' was Father Garin, whom Pompallier himself had named provincial superior. (Colin much earlier had designated Pompallier as top religious superior of the Marists in Western Oceania, thus enabling him to make such an appointment.) This provincial superior 'took over the reins of the vicariate apostolic and imperceptibly pushed aside the vicar apostolic', managing all affairs in New Zealand, Pompallier charged, while Colin acted the part of vicar apostolic in France. 'Even my pro-vicars collaborated with the provincial in this matter and were guilty of serious imprudence, not even following the instructions that I sent them by letter. . . .'

It was in his own residence, he said, that the priests had gathered to decide that Epalle should go to France and to Rome 'to report on my mission to the superior general, to the Association for the Propagation of the Faith and to Your Eminence'. He explained that Epalle on leaving New Zealand had delegated Father Jean-Baptiste Petit-Jean as pro-vicar. But Petit-Jean soon after left for Sydney and subdelegated Father Garin, the provincial superior, as pro-vicar. 'I cannot but be discontented before the Lord about all these things that have taken place', he said.

Pompallier told Fransoni that in spite of all this he had written to Epalle a number of times since his departure, 'so that he will not be discouraged from collaborating on behalf of this mission. But I no longer believe that he is fit to bear important responsibilities. I would be happy, though, if he were to remain at Lyon as correspondent for this mission in the purchasing office there.' Before concluding his lengthy postscript on the Marist intrigues, he pointed out that his funds were so low that he had been obliged to sell his mission schooner 'to the great detriment of the salvation of souls'.[7]

The reason why Pro-Vicar Petit-Jean had left New Zealand for Sydney in July 1842 was to get financial aid for the foundering New Zealand mission. He returned late that year with donated sheep, pigs, cows, fowl, pigeons and bees. Epalle had left the Bay of Islands, New Zealand, for France on 22 May 1842.[8]

Pompallier's letter of 19 October 1842 to Fransoni concluded with these words: 'There is more to tell you later. . . .' On 30 October he wrote twenty-four more pages, listing his difficulties in three categories and expanding on them. Some had arisen because of England's taking possession of New Zealand. Others stemmed from 'the heretics'. And still others were caused by 'my own congregation, which does not understand the affairs of this mission. . . .' He repeated his perplexity over Epalle's departure and accused him, Petit-Jean and Provincial Superior Garin of changing in his absence nearly everything in New Zealand and in his residence. The Marist Society through its superior general 'seems to inculcate in all of its members . . . the obligation of reporting to the superior general himself all the faults that one finds in my administration of this vicariate apostolic'. There is a tribunal at Lyon, he said, referring to the Marist headquarters in France, 'where I am accused and condemned without being heard. . . .'[9]

Unfortunately Pompallier and Colin consumed much valuable time in uncharitable criticism of each other. By a queer coincidence Pompallier in October 1842 severely criticised Colin in two letters, as shown above, and Colin in the same month severely criticised Pompallier in two letters. The difference was that Pompallier's letters were addressed to Cardinal Fransoni and Colin's were addressed to Pompallier.

Colin's two letters were dated 20 October 1842. From their date and content they appeared to be an unconscious retaliation for Pompallier's letter of criticism written the day before half a world away. They were, in fact, a retaliation, but in answer to Pompallier's earlier letter of 15 November 1841, written from Akaroa. Colin had received it in early September 1842, just two days after returning from his long stay in Rome.[10]

'God is the spirit of peace and charity, not of contention', Colin's rebuttal began. Pompallier would find it impossible to carry on 'war' with him, 'because I shall not quarrel with you over your rights, and you will always find me ready to abandon even those rights of mine which are the most reasonable. . . .' He requested the bishop, however, 'and probably for the last time, for permission to make the following observations to you for no other reason but your own benefit and that of the mission'. The 'observations' that he listed were nine in number.

'I should have to do nothing else but follow the line of conduct which you have adopted', Colin said, 'if I wanted to destroy in a very short time' the most solidly founded project. He then questioned Pompallier's prudence in assigning a single priest with a Brother-Catechist to isolated posts like Wallis, Futuna and various New Zealand missions. Although the Brother-Catechist would have a confessor at hand when needed, this was not the case for isolated priests. With time they 'might no longer take account of their conscience when finding it necessary to mount the altar and exercise their priestly functions, doing so at times with a doubtful conscience because they do not have at their side a priest to whom they can make their confession'. Colin had described Pompallier's practice to 'experienced and prudent vicars apostolic', and their reaction, he told Pompallier, was 'to sigh and shrug their shoulders'.

Colin was ignorant of 'what real purpose you have in mind and upon which church law you base your right to inspect and censor the letters of your priests to their colleagues, to their friends and to their superior. I add, *to their superior*, because you do not permit them to correspond with him except for spiritual guidance alone. . . .'

Then there was also Pompallier's contention, as mentioned in his letter of 18 May 1841, that no Marist priest without his consent could leave the mission and return to Europe for any reason whatsoever without incurring the most serious censures. 'Is this true?' Colin asked. He had consulted leading theologians in France and Italy 'who think differently and are inclined to believe that in the present case your censures would be abusive'.

Certainly anyone in Pompallier's position could put to good use several million francs in realising a number of excellent projects, Colin said. 'But since they are not available to you and since it is not in our power to acquire them for you, prudence rigorously demands of you, Your Excellency, that you undertake nothing but those good measures which God asks of you, that you never go beyond the means which Providence places in your hands and that you do not get involved imprudently in a labyrinth of debts, which compromise your honour and the mission itself and which reduce your co-workers to go begging even at the doors of the Protestants. Do not say that the bank failure in London has reduced you to this state of distress; this bank failure has been of far less harm to you than you pretend, as I prove to you on the enclosed sheet.'

He added that his contributions made to Pompallier's mission had been made by him as superior of the Society of Mary 'and not as your treasurer or your pro-vicar'. Pompallier was free to submit requests, he said, but it was up to him and to his council to decide whether it was possible to fulfil these requests. 'To expect that we shall give you all that you request and in the manner in which you request it, is to suppose that we have the gift of miracles. . . .'

Colin said that he would not contest Pompallier's right to refuse the services of the Marists and his personal services as chargé d'affaires for Pompallier in Europe. 'You made use of that right and by your letter of 18 May 1841 you have indicated a complete rupture with us in the most formal terms possible, even to the point of threatening to send back from the mission every priest or every Brother who might remain loyal to the superior and to the society'. This 'brusque declaration' had surprised Colin, especially when later he saw 'come raining down on us from you a heap of bank notes, letters, requests for personnel and for money, etc., etc.'

'The sole purpose' of his journey to Rome in mid-1842, Colin added, was to resolve the problems which had come to light in previous letters. 'For a moment I thought that my hopes had been fulfilled, but your letter of 15 November 1841 has destroyed my hopes.' It was filled with invectives and epithets and it told Colin that he knew nothing about administration, that he was at fault for Pompallier's not having received any money in 1841 from the Association for the Propagation of the Faith in Lyon, and that the greatest enemies of the Western Oceania mission were not outsiders and heretics, 'but rather the superior and the members' of the Marist Society.

Since the two Pompallier letters of 18 May 1841 and 15 November 1841 had confirmed one another, Colin drew what he considered unavoidable conclusions and formally declared 'that you are no longer our representative among our members as religious and consequently you cannot command them in virtue of the obedience vowed into our hands; that every bank note or other contract of whatever nature coming to us from you or concerning you, will be rejected; and that every contact between you and us will be broken off, whether it concerns personnel, money, or any other matter . . . These measures contain nothing that can surprise you. They are your work. You have provoked them and you would be unjust to complain about them.'

In signing his four-page letter Colin called himself, as usual, 'Your most humble and most obedient servant'.[11]

It is interesting to note that incorporated in this letter were elements from three of the four points of the 30 June 1842 decree that Colin had received in Rome a few months earlier: the isolation of priests; recall of priests; and the appointment of a provincial superior. But Colin made no reference to that decree, nor did he mention any of the many qualifications in it which safeguarded Pompallier's rights. And the way he presented the whole affair was so tactless that it could serve no other purpose but to widen even more the breach between him and Pompallier.

The second letter of Colin to Pompallier, also written on 20 October 1842, went into very great detail about the financial situation of Pompallier's vicariate apostolic. By listing income and expenses it intended to prove that all funds due to the bishop had been credited to his vicariate apostolic and it showed further that he had greatly overdrawn his account.

Colin finally told Pompallier that God in his Providence 'has used Your Grace to make us understand that it is not fitting for our society to provide the foreign missions with vicars apostolic having the rank of bishop. Nor is it fitting for our society by letters and negotiations to have direct contact with the said vicars apostolic, who through the episcopacy naturally have also been withdrawn from the ranks of our society. Consequently my contacts in behalf of your mission from now on will be made only through the provincial. And if in New Zealand our priests cannot depend upon a provincial without injuring the rights of jurisdiction of the vicar apostolic, whereas in France they depend upon their superior general without causing the least conflict with bishops, then we shall discontinue sending you new personnel. . . .'[12]

Just before mailing these two letters to Pompallier, Colin received from Rome printed copies of the 1842 decree, now in revised form, dated 16 September 1842, and approved by Pope Gregory XVI the day before. As revised it 'does not remove all the difficulties for us', he said. In fact, it now had a new point—his other points had not been excluded—which he knew would aggravate his position with Pompallier.

The new point, put in the first place, read: 'Vicars apostolic and prefects or other heads of missions must send a report to the Evangelisation Congregation at least once a year on the areas entrusted to them and also letters dealing with more serious mission affairs. They must send these things unsealed to the superiors general, so that they can read them, make copies, and then transmit them to the Evangelisation Congregation. The Evangelisation Congregation will follow the same procedure in reverse, unless it judges some other way more expedient.'

Colin knew that Father Roothaan, superior general of the Jesuits, had intervened in altering his decree and he resented this. Roothaan, who was interested in getting a stronger hand over the mission bishops of his own order, had been approached by Secretary Archbishop Cadolini of the Evangelisation Congregation in connection with the decree prepared for Colin on 30 June 1842.

Cadolini, who highly esteemed the Jesuits, showed Roothaan a copy and asked for his opinion. Roothaan liked it, seeing the possibilities that it would offer him if it were extended to include Jesuit vicariates apostolic as well and not only those of the Marists, as was the case in the original decree. However, he did not find it explicit enough, counselled strengthening it, and even suggested that it be published and be made applicable to vicariates apostolic generally. When he said 'strengthening it', he meant in favour of superiors general. And he insisted on the importance and necessity of the new first point as a mark of confidence on the part of the Holy See in superiors general who were providing the missions with personnel. This was the best possible way, he argued, of keeping them abreast of their mission territories.

Such a new draft was issued by Cardinal Fransoni on 31 August 1842, applicable generally to vicariates apostolic and all other missions; it had in the first place Roothaan's point on reports and letters going through the hands of superiors general, and Roothaan was able to make use of it for his purpose. A handwritten copy was hastily forwarded by Fransoni and Cadolini to Colin—he had left Rome on 28 August—and they thought that he would be as pleased with it as Roothaan was. It had the opposite effect on Colin.

Meanwhile back in Rome it appeared advisable to the authorities to make the decree even stronger by printing it and by having it sanctioned explicitly by the pope. The pope's approval was only implicit in a decree signed on Fransoni's authority alone. But the Evangelisation Congregation now had second thoughts about giving all superiors general such power over the bishops in mission territories entrusted to them. Since Roothaan's purpose had been achieved by the 31 August decree, the new version of 16 September was restricted to the Oceania missions of the Marists and Picpus Fathers and to the Ava-Pegú (now Burma) Mission of the Oblates of the Virgin Mary of Turin. A decree could hardly be made applicable to Western Oceania and not to Eastern Oceania, and the Turin group as well had wanted guarantees in dealing with vicars apostolic. Copies of this new forceful decree were sent to Colin for forwarding to Bishops Pompallier, Bataillon and Douarre.

Colin would for many years bear a grudge against Roothaan for his intervention. As late as 30 January 1848 he said at a meeting of his council: 'The Jesuits intervened in the 1842 decree and they had things introduced which suited them. Of course, the Jesuits have this fault: they refer everything to themselves and they embarrassed me by what they had introduced in the decree. Consequently the fourth time I went to Rome, I did not contact them. . . .' Pompallier eventually learned that Roothaan had had a role in the issuance of the 1842 decree and he concluded falsely—knowing only of the *third* version restricted to Oceania and Ava-Pegú—that it was the Jesuits, approached by Colin, who had been responsible for the decree. He then called Father Colin 'an ignoramus' and charged that he had to have the Jesuits take care of his affairs. It was this attitude of Pompallier which made Colin break off contact with the Jesuits in Rome, lest he confirm Pompallier in his opinion.

Having this forceful decree of 16 September 1842 from Rome in his hands with instructions from Fransoni to forward a copy to Pompallier, Colin began to reconsider the tone and content of his two strong letters. In fact, the decree now made many parts of his letter superfluous.

Before taking any further action, therefore, he wrote to Cardinal Fransoni on 27 October 1842. He explained that after returning from Rome to France in early September, he had received a packet of letters from Bishop Pompallier. One of them was dated 15 November 1841, was filled with much abuse, and had exhausted his patience. 'In agreement with my eldest colleague I then took the only stand left for me and I wrote Bishop Pompallier the two enclosed letters, which I dare to submit to Your Eminence before mailing.'

As for the decree presented to him while in Rome, it 'seemed at first sight to present very serious difficulties of a practical nature. But I refrained from making any observations at that time, since I regarded the decree as a private reply meant for me personally. . . .' He requested that its promulgation be postponed, that he be allowed to present observations on it, and that pending Rome's decision he be excused from dispatching the copies meant for Pompallier and Bataillon. (As for Douarre, who was still in Europe, he could always be given his copy personally, if Rome were to insist that the decree should stand.)

Colin's letter ended with the happy news that Douarre, Bataillon's coadjutor, had been ordained a bishop 'some days ago and is making preparations for his departure. Five priests and four Brothers will accompany him. . . .' The episcopal ordination had taken place at Lyon on 18 October.

In the course of his letter Colin had recalled how coolly he had been received at the Evangelisation Congregation during his visit there and how this had given him the impression that he was suspected of encroaching on the rights of Vicar Apostolic Pompallier. He explained that this had also caused him to bring back to France the correspondence from, to, and concerning Pompallier which originally he had intended to show to the cardinal.[13]

Fransoni replied on 10 December 1842. He expressed surprise and great displeasure over the letters that he had received and said that he could not understand 'what reasonable grounds' Colin might have for being 'little satisfied' over the business which had been transacted at the Evangelisation Congregation, since everything possible had been done to give him a hearty welcome and to fulfil all his wishes in the best possible way. And as for other requests 'which could not be taken care of at the moment', the Evangelisation Congregation had promised that these, too, would all be granted. Again, the outcome of its meeting on whether or not the Vicariate Apostolic of Central Oceania should be founded was further proof by the Evangelisation Congregation of 'the unlimited confidence which it places in you'. Also the special decree of 1842, which was 'issued in your favour to bind the missions more tightly together with your society, and which by order of His Holiness and with his approval was even amplified . . . , confirms how anxious the Sacred Congregation is to support the zeal and wishes of Your Reverence'. The purpose of the decree, he said, was 'to remove the misunderstandings that have arisen with Bishop Pompallier and at the same time to prevent any disagreement with the other prelates entrusted with, or to be entrusted with, the care of those regions which receive missionaries from your society'.

However, it was not possible for him to grant 'the unusual and altogether extraordinary powers', which Colin now requested, 'without violating the sanctions of the Holy See in this matter and breaking down the structure of pastoral rule'. And even if permissible, it would have been imprudent to grant such exceptional powers, he said, since there was no guarantee that Colin's successors would follow his example and make 'only good and moderate use of them'.

The cardinal then told of his 'displeasure at reading through the pages' meant for Pompallier. 'In fact, they are a declaration of estrangement, cutting off contact with him, and abandonment of the mission.' And even though Colin's complaints might well be justified, Fransoni wanted him to 'keep in mind that the Sacred Congregation in an attempt to bring to an end precisely this disagreeable affair' had sent a written admonition to the bishop. And even though the tenor of his 15 November 1841 letter was like that of his previous letter of 18 May, 'it nevertheless seems most just to me that you ought to wait for the effect that the exhortations of the Sacred Congregation will produce in him. Because when he wrote the letters referred to by Your Reverence, which reached you in the beginning of September, he could not yet have known of these exhortations, since the Sacred Congregation's letter was dated in Rome on 12 April of this year.'

And even if the Sacred Congregation's 'first loving admonitions were to prove useless', the cardinal added, 'it still does not seem appropriate to me to have recourse at once to extreme remedies, which will bring very great harm to religion, before experimenting with other remedies, which the Sacred Congregation will be able to try in the case in question. The decree that was sent to you recently will also without doubt be a help in attaining the desired goal, since it has the approbation of the Holy Father, a fact that His Holiness expressly wished should be made known to the prelates of Oceania. You must therefore absolutely refrain from sending Bishop Pompallier your threatening letters, and without any further delay you will transmit to him and to the other prelates the decree in question.'

Cardinal Fransoni's letter did not end here. He said that the Society of Mary had won great merit because of its contributions to Western Oceania, but the merit of Pompallier was no less, since he 'can justly be called the founder of that important and flourishing flock of Christ'. And so it was only fitting that Colin should use more regard towards him than toward any other prelate and ought 'to exhaust all ways of reconciliation'. He urged Colin meanwhile 'to continue corresponding with Bishop Pompallier with the same spirit of mildness, sweetness and peace with which you told me in an earlier letter that you had always answered his disagreeable letters'.

Nor did the cardinal understand why Colin considered the episcopacy incompatible with membership in the Society of Mary. By way of example Fransoni pointed out that very many members of the Paris Foreign Mission

Seminary had become vicars apostolic with the rank of bishop and 'the most perfect concord and harmony had always reigned and still reigns between these same prelates and the [seminary] directors and there is not the slightest friction'.

In conclusion Fransoni asked Colin 'to seek out with all diligence the cause of these differences which have arisen', and give more thought to them, since the quarrels would disappear immediately 'with the removal from the mission or from the society of the one sowing discord'.[14]

Colin wrote to Fransoni on 23 December 1842 that he had received his letter of 10 December 'with the most profound respect and the most complete submission'. He asked the cardinal 'to accept my very humble apologies and likewise the very sincere assurance that I wish to follow no other line of conduct but that which Your Eminence will kindly trace for me'. By his two strong letters to Pompallier he had hoped 'to open his eyes to the consequences of his way of acting', so that he might reform 'or at least decide to make a voyage to Europe, where the paternal advice of Your Eminence by tracing the line of action to be followed would easily be able to remedy everything'. He assured Fransoni that he had suppressed the two letters and he promised to send the decree of 16 September 1842 to the two vicars apostolic of Western Oceania and of Central Oceania as soon as possible.

But Colin did not accept Fransoni's stand on Marists becoming bishops. 'The members of the Paris Foreign Mission Seminary do not at all bind themselves by vows', he said. 'Our position under this aspect is different from theirs, since the missionaries of our society depart with the idea that everywhere they remain under the attentive surveillance of their superior. They make known to him in confidence their internal and external difficulties and await help from him for whatever needs they have.' The director of the Paris Foreign Mission Seminary, on the other hand, was more an administrator than a religious superior, he said. Besides, the priests of his society in France had decided earlier that year not to accept any dignities either in the church or outside of it 'unless ordered to do so by His Holiness'. The example of Bishop Pompallier, he said, was greatly responsible for their making this decision.

Nor did Colin believe that any Marist in Oceania or in France was fomenting the discord between him and Pompallier. He had 'prudently' left all members in France in ignorance about what was happening in New Zealand. Only after his return from Rome did he give out any information, but then 'only to a small number of my most prudent counsellors. They therefore could not have excited me against Bishop Pompallier.' And in New Zealand not only one, but all the members were clamouring and complaining. 'Many asked me if they might transfer to another mission and some wanted to return to Europe. I sincerely regret that I did not leave their letters at the Sacred Congregation.'

Colin added that in November just past he had been obliged to pay out unexpectedly 30,000 francs to cover a bank draft drawn against him on behalf of the New Zealand mission, and this happened immediately after he had taken steps to have other funds transmitted by his bank in London. Epalle, pro-vicar in New Zealand and now in France, but not yet in Lyon, had sent Colin word on the bank draft adding—Colin told Fransoni—this comment: 'What can we do? Must we scandalously allow the mission to collapse? If you happen to have new missionaries on the point of leaving for New Zealand, stop them very quickly. It is money and more money that we need. It is necessary to put the past in order.' Colin underlined all of Epalle's remarks. And to show how unrealistic in view of them Pompallier was in making requests for personnel, Colin pointed out that six months earlier he had asked for 130 more men, both priests and Brothers.

Epalle was expected to arrive shortly in Lyon and Colin told Fransoni that he would try to 'have him go as soon as possible to Rome'. Colin was convinced that in this way the cardinal would obtain as objective a picture as possible of conditions in Western Oceania and then could determine his policy accordingly.[15]

Because Colin wanted to keep Fransoni 'perfectly informed of all our steps so that you can guide us and remedy the imprudence which may escape us', he enclosed a report that he had received three days earlier. It was from Father Jean Forest who had been sent by Colin to Western Oceania as visitator, that is, a kind of inspector sent by a society to take a close look at the religious life of its members and to see how they are observing the rule.

Together with this report Colin enclosed a letter dated 20 October 1841 written by himself 'to the Priests and Brothers of the Society of Mary Working for the Glory of God in New Zealand and in the Tropical Islands'. This letter introduced thirty-six-year-old Forest, one of the oldest members of the society, as 'a second self'. It gave Forest no authority and stated that his sole function was to bring Colin up to date with the life and activities of Marist missionaries. 'His age, his experience, his tried virtue, his perfect knowledge of the spirit and orientation of the Society of Mary, give us promise that most happy results will come from his visits and from his charity in your midst.' Forest had left London on 8 November 1841 with nine other missionaries and arrived in New Zealand on 6 April 1842 while Pompallier was still at Wallis Island.

Colin's letter of introduction listed seven areas into which Forest was to inquire. Above all, he was expected always to seek out the views of Pompallier and of the Marist superior and then reach an understanding with them on all issues regarding the welfare of the Marists. It was also his task to visit all priests and Brothers of the society as soon as possible, or reach them through correspondence, in order to learn if they were at peace, what privations they endured and to what dangers they were exposed, how these could be prevented, and what the best means might be 'for establishing and strengthening the Catholic faith in these islands and above all in New Zealand. . . .'

Forest was also supposed to consult with Pompallier and the Marist superior about 'the possibility and necessity of having a house at the Bay of Islands'. Colin thought that it might serve as the residence for the provincial superior, with whom he would correspond, and for the 'Father Procurator, who will be responsible for looking after the needs of members of the society. . . .' His letter also pointed out that annual allocations from the Association for the Propagation of the Faith in Lyon were 'evidently insufficient'. And so he wanted Forest to inquire what resources the mission had for the support of the missionaries. Also, 'what items can the missionaries buy for themselves locally at the same price, in order to cut down for us the very high cost of shipping these supplies from Europe?'

Colin's letter concluded with the assurance that he would make 'as detailed a report as possible' to Cardinal Fransoni in Rome on the basis of Forest's answers. He would also report in detail, he said, on any other information that Forest might submit as a result of discussions with Pompallier and the Marists serving under him.[16]

Father Forest's report forwarded to Fransoni was dated 2 June 1842, before Bishop Pompallier had returned from the tropical islands. None of the things that Forest had to say about the bishop were complimentary. For example, the report stated that Pompallier believed there was no other way to win over the Maoris in New Zealand than by giving them gifts. He made his visits with pomp and circumstance aboard a ship which cost him 100 francs per day and had a crew of eight or nine, taking along most of the goods that he had received from France and distributing them during his travels. In this way Pompallier received the reputation for being 'a rich and opulent man', so much so that many came to believe that he was related to King Louis-Philippe.

On learning that the bishop was expected to pass by, Forest said, people would come running from all directions because they wanted to receive something. 'The bishop, thinking that everyone was joining ranks on his side, refused nothing, provided only that they said to him: *Je suis Episcopo*, that is, I am a follower of the bishop.' And when he no longer had any gifts left, 'he took out loans at the interest rate of 12 to 15 per cent for three months', so that he could buy more gifts. And when these too ran out, he would promise everyone that in time he would have gifts for them and that they would also get priests. 'This way of acting easily won a great multitude to his side, and it was a simple matter to estimate the conversions at 33,000.'

Forest added that Pompallier had spent much time in Akaroa and after that had gone to the tropical islands. 'I believe that he does not dare to return from there for fear that his ship will be confiscated and that he himself will be arrested for lack of payments. This would cause great harm for the New Zealand mission.' Meanwhile the prospective New Zealand converts 'have been as prompt in returning to their former state as they were in leaving it', because the priests and gifts promised by Pompallier did not arrive.

'All that I am telling you here', Forest said, 'I have heard from the mouths of all the members whom I have been able to interview. All of them, except Father Epalle, have this idea of the mission. Father Epalle is a bit more optimistic. It seems to me that he is a bit too favourable, because the facts which we have before our eyes speak loudly and clearly enough . . . What Father Epalle tells you will be true, but I fear that much of what he tells you will not be the whole truth . . . I heard that he would not tell you everything, in order not to afflict you. . . .'

Forest's report then made some very concrete proposals. 'If Bishop Pompallier were to receive some priests from England or elsewhere, he could be master over them, as he desires, and he might get along with them better, or *perhaps worse*. The priests of our society could then take up work in the tropical islands, if they had one or two good bishops over them, who are very good Marists holding fast with all their heart to the society. Being completely united in heart and mind, they incontestably could do much more good there than in New Zealand. And the natives there are not spoiled as yet, as they are here.' Expenses also would be less in the tropical islands and dangers would not be so great. 'New Guinea, they say, offers a vast field to the zeal of a group of missionaries.' And since it had such a 'large number of inhabitants', he said, it would be possible to pick out the best place to start.

When suggesting the qualities necessary for the 'one or two good bishops', Forest said it would be desirable to have someone old enough, 'who could assert himself a bit, and would not fear to speak up to His Grace, always preserving at the same time the most profound respect'. The general feeling among the missionaries was 'that Father Epalle has succeeded as well as he could in his position. But he is not able to stand up to the bishop, who looks upon him as a child.' Epalle was very much loved, however, by the English. Forest added that he had found the Marists very well united in spite of all their difficulties, something that had surprised him. He called this a very great grace from God for the society, but wanted Colin to remember that all were 'in great hopes of seeing a change made soon'.[17]

When Bishop Pompallier eventually returned to New Zealand and saw the letter of introduction written by Colin, he became embittered because it appeared to him that Colin had overstepped his powers. The bishop objected, for example, to the words, 'the general good of the mission', as Forest explained to Colin under date of 5 November 1842. 'He told me', Forest said, 'that everything concerning the general and particular good of the mission was his affair and that he had to render an account of this to the Holy See and to no one else.'

Another section had made Pompallier 'even more angry', because Colin had asked Forest to inquire about the best method, 'above all in New Zealand', for establishing and strengthening the Catholic faith. According to Pompallier, Colin was to concern himself about nothing in New Zealand 'other than the observance of the rule by the members and their interior life'. And as for building a Marist house at the Bay of Islands, Pompallier saw no purpose in this, Forest reported, but he was willing to request the necessary authorisation from Rome.

Pompallier was also displeased with the question, 'What are the presumed resources which the land offers for the maintenance and subsistence of the missionaries, at least for the future?' His reply again was, 'All this regards me and the Holy See'. Forest said that every time anyone mentioned anything about administration, no matter how slight, Pompallier would always give the same answer. This topic had become 'something so sacred that no one dares to say a word to him about it'.

But Pompallier's chief complaint, Forest said, and the one that they heard every day, was that the Marist headquarters in Lyon was retaining his funds, thus causing the entire mission to collapse. Forest therefore counselled Colin to cease handling all monies meant for Pompallier, including the forwarding of it, and have someone outside of the society take care of this. 'You would free yourself from a great burden', Forest said, 'and would eliminate many of the complaints made against you. . . .'[18]

Eager to obtain funds at this time so that he could develop missionary work in New Zealand, Pompallier on 6 November 1842 (the day after Forest wrote to Colin) sent an appeal to the Association for the Propagation of the Faith in Lyon. Because he was pressed for time, he asked that this same letter be forwarded by the association to Cardinal Fransoni. In it he spelled out his plans for development. 'In New Zealand I wish to open three new stations each year for the next four years, that is, ten or twelve new stations . . . , and so I shall need [an additional] six priests and at least three Brothers each year. . . .' The maintenance cost for a single mission station when run economically, he said, was 5,000 francs a year. And since he had ten mission stations in New Zealand already and intended to found three new ones each year, he listed his needs as 50,000 francs for the year beginning with November 1842; 65,000 francs for the next year; 80,000 francs for the year after that; and 95,000 francs for the year beginning with November 1845. He explained that this money was to be over and above the costs of sending missionaries and mission supplies from France to New Zealand and he also specified that the money should be sent directly to him.

He also hoped to found new mission stations for the tropical islands and said that the funds meant for them 'naturally should not prejudice the funds meant for New Zealand'. For example, he needed two more priests and two more Brothers for Tongatapu and also another priest and another Brother for Wallis. Then he also intended to found two or three mission stations in the Samoa Islands and hoped to gain access to Vava'u and Ha'apai in the Tonga Islands. But since it would take time to consolidate missionary work in the tropics and to establish a uniform mission method there, it would be 'necessary to wait about two years' before these islands could become an independent vicariate apostolic. This would also give him time to see what would be happening to him and to the French clergy in New Zealand, now completely under English authority. 'But I do regard expulsion as quite improbable', he said.

Pompallier added the news that the *Sancta Maria* was being sold; he hoped that the sale price would make it possible for him to buy another schooner of 60 tons. But the important thing, he pointed out, was for the Lyon fund-collecting organisation not to believe readily any bad reports that might be circulating about his mission and its administration. As for new ecclesiastical territories, he said that 'at this moment two interesting vicariates apostolic could be founded within the area of my present jurisdiction'. The first could be established in the Fiji Archipelago, 'where there is practically only one language'. Some Europeans had already settled there and the total population numbered five million. A second possible vicariate apostolic could be established 'at Ascension, that is, Ponape . . . for the entire archipelago of the Carolines'.[19]

Later that month he wrote to his mother that three young women at Wallis, daughters of the greatest chiefs of the island, had earnestly requested permission 'to consecrate themselves to God in a special manner by the vow of chastity'. They arrived at this idea by themselves 'and by the sole inspiration of grace', he said, knowing that this was an evangelical counsel and that fulfilling it freely was pleasing to the Lord. In building up the church in Western Oceania, he said, 'I must water with my sweat each stone of the edifice that I erect and . . . I should like to cement [it] with my blood'. But his mother never received this letter; she had died during the previous May while her son was in the tropical islands.[20]

It was not until 2 January 1843 that Pro-Vicar Epalle finally reached Lyon. Colin had promised Fransoni that Epalle would leave for Rome immediately upon arrival, but Epalle had to wait for mail from Pompallier containing official papers meant for Rome. In giving this information to Fransoni on 14 January 1843, Colin explained that Epalle had taken out a loan at Valparaíso in the amount 'of 30,000 francs to be reimbursed by me', precisely to avoid the scandal which would follow if the New Zealand mission were to collapse financially.[21]

In France Epalle busied himself soliciting funds to cover the balance of the huge New Zealand mission debt and Colin gave him all possible assistance. They succeeded in collecting 100,000 francs and Colin informed Fransoni on 22 February 1843 that Epalle at that moment was leaving for London, where he hoped to find a safe way of transmitting these funds to New Zealand. 'We are instructing Father Petit-Jean to use 80,000 of these francs exclusively to wipe out the debt', Colin said. 'The balance can be used for their most pressing needs.' Petit-Jean, as pro-vicar named by Epalle, would be in charge of the mission in the absence of Pompallier, Epalle thought. 'We are addressing ourselves to Father Petit-Jean', Colin said, 'because we doubt that Bishop Pompallier is in New Zealand and also because we do not have complete confidence in him.'

Colin in the same letter informed Fransoni that a complication had arisen regarding the Vicariate Apostolic of Central Oceania. According to Epalle's considered opinion, Bataillon had been sent from Wallis to Ascension Island in the Caroline Archipelago (Micronesia) to open a Catholic mission there in answer to a request brought to New Zealand by James Hall, a Protestant Scotsman. If Epalle was correct, Colin said, this would place Coadjutor Bishop Douarre in an embarrassing situation, since he was going to Wallis precisely to ordain Bataillon a bishop. At the same time Central Oceania would be without its vicar apostolic for a protracted period, since it would take very long to get word to Bataillon about his new appointment and have him return. In order to provide for such an eventuality Colin suggested to Fransoni that the powers attached to the office of Vicar Apostolic of Central Oceania be given to Douarre pending Bataillon's return. In this way the new vicariate apostolic could begin functioning without further delay. Douarre at least would have to be able to place personnel, Colin indicated, since eleven other Marists were leaving with him for this new mission aboard a French Navy vessel scheduled to sail in mid-March.[22]

Showing the flexibility of Rome and its readiness to promote missionary work in Oceania in any way possible, Fransoni answered Colin on 18 March 1843 that Pope Gregory XVI 'grants to Bishop Douarre use of the faculties given to the Vicar Apostolic of Central Oceania. . . .' He was disturbed, however, over the latest news about Pompallier's vicariate apostolic and called it 'very unpleasant'. But he assured Colin that after Epalle's arrival in Rome 'the Sacred Congregation will not fail to take the matter into serious consideration and provide for it an adequate and efficacious remedy'. The cardinal also found it 'surprising that Bishop Pompallier has not yet replied to the letter of admonition sent to him such a long time ago and has not altered his conduct in any way.'[23]

Having returned to France from England, Epalle himself wrote to Fransoni from Lyon on 3 May and asked how much longer he should stay there waiting for letters to arrive from Pompallier. He explained that he had received word from the bishop dated 3 September 1842 instructing him to remain in France until special letters arrived. These were to be sent three weeks later on the next ship. Other letters mailed after that date had arrived, making Epalle believe that the special letters had been lost as often happened with mail coming from New Zealand. Meanwhile Colin had received new requests from missionaries in New Zealand asking for permission to return to France. But just recently, Epalle said, the Anglican Church had sent a bishop of its own to New Zealand accompanied by many ministers,[24] and it would be 'extremely regrettable' if precisely at this time 'the Catholic ranks were to thin out'. So it was urgent and necessary, he felt, 'for me to go back and join my discouraged colleagues as soon as possible and bring them the solutions which Your Eminence will devise for the evils causing their discouragement'.

He added that the many details already sent to Fransoni about 'the sad state of affairs' in Pompallier's territory were 'unfortunately only too true'. And since the cardinal was already so well informed, his own purpose in coming to Rome was not so much to expose the condition of the mission, 'but rather to receive from Your Eminence the orders which will remove the obstacles blocking the progress of this nascent church. . . .' In view of all these considerations he therefore wondered whether he should keep waiting for the letters, 'or should I come to Rome before receiving them, because of the necessity to leave again as soon as possible for New Zealand?'[25] Fransoni did not answer.

The mail from Pompallier finally did arrive and with it was a letter of 28 November 1842 by which the bishop named Epalle his new chargé d'affaires in France, authorising him to give faculties to all missionaries departing for the Vicariate Apostolic of Western Oceania. This appointment for Epalle meant implicitly that Colin had been discharged from the office which he had held ever since Pompallier had gone to Western Oceania.

It was Colin who sent all this information to Fransoni on 18 June 1843. He was now relieved of all responsibilities, 'and I bless Providence for it'. But he pointed out that Epalle was only thirty-four years old 'and would not at all like to see his missionary career among the infidels come to an end. However, he will readily follow whatever line of conduct Your Eminence may wish to indicate for him.' Colin begged Fransoni to receive Epalle kindly, since he now definitely would be leaving for Rome. And he praised Epalle for his ability and 'the delicacy of his manners', adding that 'he has constantly won the esteem and confidence of Bishop Pompallier, who made him his pro-vicar and mission procurator at the Bay of Islands'. According to Colin, the purpose of Epalle's journey to Rome was 'to reveal to Your Eminence the actual state of the mission in New Zealand'.

There was another serious matter on Colin's mind. Early in the previous year the Evangelisation Congregation had requested his community to take up missionary work among the Kaffirs in South Africa and some of his priests had already volunteered to go. Preliminary negotiations between the Evangelisation Congregation and Colin were also far advanced. 'But for lack of financial means', Colin now told Fransoni, 'it is impossible for us to take over this mission among the Kaffirs. We beg Your Eminence to discharge us of this important mission and give it to an older organisation.' What had happened to his funds? 'The altogether extraordinary expenses which we had to make so recently on behalf of the missions of Western Oceania and Central Oceania', he explained, 'have exhausted our resources.'

Enclosed for Fransoni's information were also some excerpts from Father Forest's letter, subsequent to his report, indicating the points to which Pompallier had so strongly objected in Colin's letter of introduction. 'We are still novices in these deliberations', Colin admitted.'But we cannot imagine that a mission should be entrusted by the Holy See to a society and that this same society cannot inquire about the general welfare of that mission without wounding the rights of the vicar apostolic, and that it cannot acquire for itself within that mission a residence at its own expense without obtaining new authorisation from the Holy See.' And as for Pompallier's choice of Father Viard, then serving as pro-vicar in the Wallis Islands, for the office of vicar apostolic, Colin said that he had an excellent character and was pious, but 'his talents are very ordinary and, above all, he has no aptitude for administration. . . .'

In conclusion, Colin 'dared' to request Fransoni to concentrate his attention on New Zealand. 'Beyond a doubt Bishop Pompallier has some good qualities', he said. 'He has zeal, but his zeal is not always guided by knowledge and prudence. He is lacking in vision, tact, justice and constancy in his ideas. He is not an administrator. And very often his good heart, or rather his lack of caution, has caused him to make serious mistakes in financial matters. Besides, he is so sensitive that no one can tell him anything. No doubt Your Eminence's wisdom will find an efficacious and moderate solution to restore the broken courage of the missionaries and to prevent the ruin of such a fascinating mission.'[26]

There was nothing more that Colin could do. Epalle would now go to Rome in his dual role as representative of Colin and as representative of Pompallier. The future of the Catholic Church in Western Oceania would depend on what Epalle would say and on what he would do and on what Cardinal Fransoni and his Evangelisation Congregation with the authority of Pope Gregory XVI would decide. This was responsibility enough for two men, one a priest thirty-four years of age and the other a cardinal thirty-three years his senior. As for Colin and Pompallier, they would never cease to quarrel and would carry their mutually inflicted wounds to the grave.

16

A French Carthusian in Rome proposes a
Northern Oceania Vicariate

6 APRIL 1843

Early in 1842 a Carthusian monk wrote to the Evangelisation Congregation and manifested a deep desire to see the Catholic faith propagated in the Palau (also Pelew) Islands, an island group in the western Caroline Islands of Micronesia. He was Father Paul-Laurent-Marcel Supriès (1800–88) born in the Diocese of Fréjus in France. He had joined the Paris Foreign Mission Seminary in 1829, left that same year for India and from there in 1834 went to the Isle of Bourbon, Nicobar Islands and Siam (now Thailand). In France in 1838 to restore his health, he was deeply moved at seeing the contemplative life of the Order of Carthusians (O. Cart.) and at once asked for admission. After a year's probation he was accepted into the order on 29 June 1839 and was given the new name of Thadée. Early in 1842 when he wrote to the Evangelisation Congregation about the Palau Islands, he was assistant superior of the Carthusian monastery attached to the Basilica of Saint Mary of the Angels in Rome.

Cardinal Fransoni wrote back on 14 April 1842 and praised him for his zeal in wanting to see the gospel propagated 'among the most distant and abandoned peoples'. But the Palau Islands belonged to the Vicariate Apostolic of Western Oceania, he explained, and there was 'reason to hope' that Bishop Pompallier 'has already sent some of his co-workers there'. Convinced that Supriès would be pleased to know the latest developments in that part of the world, Fransoni told him 'that at present Oceania is divided into three vicariates apostolic . . . staffed by a large number of missionary priests and catechists, who for a number of years have been busy cultivating that vast portion of the Lord's vineyard with much success'. The vicars apostolic in charge were all bishops, he said.[1]

The three vicariates apostolic referred to by Fransoni were Eastern Oceania, New Holland and Van Diemen's Land, and Western Oceania, founded in that order. The Vicariate Apostolic of Central Oceania was in the planning stage at this time and was founded four months later. It is difficult to see how Fransoni could say there was 'reason to hope' that Pompallier had sent personnel to the Palau Islands, since the chief reason for founding the Central Oceania Vicariate was precisely Pompallier's failure to send personnel to the tropical islands in his territory.

Supriès again wrote to Fransoni about the Palau Islands one year later, on 6 April 1843, and this time greatly elaborated on his project, apparently forgetting what Fransoni had said about the Palau Islands being within Pompallier's territory. He had noticed that the Holy See had sent Picpus Fathers and

Marists 'to the vast expanses of Oceania', and so there seemed to be hope 'that the day of salvation has finally arrived for these unfortunate peoples'. They would at last be freed 'from their very gross superstitions and from their most barbarous customs'.

He was afflicted, however, 'at seeing the emissaries of diverse Protestant sects competing zealously with Catholic missionaries and arriving before them in many places, spreading among these poor islanders their deadly doctrines, which later are so difficult to eradicate'. Numerous Catholic missionaries, therefore, would have to hasten to Oceania, because 'the danger draws nearer from day to day as the commerce of the English, Dutch and Americans becomes ever more active on these shores'. There was now an added peril, he said, 'in view of what very recently has happened in China'. He was referring to the English-Chinese treaty of August 1842 by which China had ceded Hong Kong to Great Britain and had opened its five principal ports of Canton, Amoy, Foochow, Ningpo and Shanghai to international commerce. These ports now were also open to Protestant missionary activity. The islands of Oceania closest to the Chinese Empire, therefore, were 'the ones most exposed to surprises from the enemies of our faith'. He meant, of course, the islands of Northern Oceania, since it was precisely here that Catholic missionaries had not as yet penetrated. And this was 'the principal reason which makes me humbly ask your permission to go out from my seclusion to take up again a missionary career and consecrate the remainder of my strength to a work so beautiful in the eyes of faith'. In other words he was asking to be dispensed from his vows as a Carthusian monk.

Erroneously thinking that the equator was the northern boundary for both the Central and the Western vicariates of Oceania, he believed that 'the immense expanse of lands' between the equator and Japan had no bishop over it. 'Therefore', he said, 'I request that a new mission to be called the Mission of Northern Oceania should be erected there with these boundaries: the equator at the south, 30° latitude at the north, 200° longitude at the east, and 150° longitude at the west. This area includes the Palau Islands, the Carolines, the Mulgraves, the archipelagoes of Magellan, Anson, etc., etc.' The missionaries would go first to the Palau Islands, he said, 'because I know from the report of a voyager who stayed there for a very long time that the inhabitants are peaceful and hospitable.' Apparently Supriès did not know how to read maps, or he used a very poor one. His '200° longitude at the east' would have been equivalent to 160° west longitude; and since he was using the prime meridian of Paris, his boundaries would have included many of the Hawaiian Islands in Picpus territory and would have excluded the Palau Islands.

Understandably he also needed financial support for his project and hoped to obtain this from the Association for the Propagation of the Faith in Lyon. And in France, he said, he would be able to recruit 'a goodly number of co-workers, something which I believe will not be very difficult, since I already have in mind two or three good prospects'. He went so far as to promise that he would found a new Congregation of Missionary Priests at Our Lady of Victory Church in Paris. It would be modelled after the Paris Foreign Mission Seminary and would be joined to the Confraternity of the Immaculate Heart of Mary for the Conversion of Sinners. In conclusion he assured Cardinal Fransoni that his project had no other aim but to promote the greater glory of God and the salvation of souls. 'I have confidence', he added, 'that the same motive will make you accept it favourably.'[2]

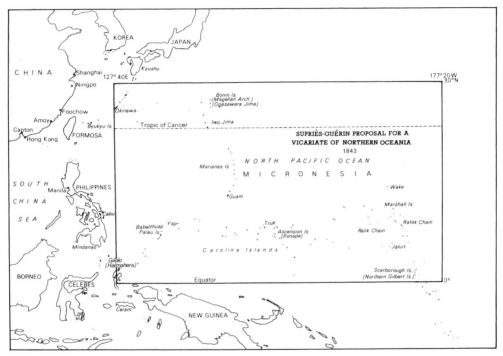

41 The English-Chinese treaty of August 1842 by which China ceded Hong Kong to Great Britain and opened its five principal ports of Canton, Amoy, Foochow, Ningpo and Shanghai to international commerce, prompted the Supriès-Guérin proposal of 1843 for a Vicariate Apostolic of Northern Oceania. *(Chapter 16).*

The Supriès proposal placed Fransoni in somewhat of a dilemma. He could have separated Northern Oceania from Bishop Pompallier's jurisdiction and placed Supriès in charge. But when he received this proposal, he was expecting Pro-Vicar Epalle to arrive in Rome any day for special consultations meant to settle once and for all the explosive situation which had arisen between Pompallier and the Marists. The cardinal therefore had to hold in reserve the remaining sections of Pompallier's extensive Vicariate Apostolic of Western Oceania for possible placement there of the bishop or of the Marists, in the event that it proved absolutely impossible for them to work together.

Cardinal Fransoni nevertheless answered Supriès on 27 April 1843, saying that his project of founding 'a new Vicariate Apostolic of Northern Oceania' seemed 'most advantageous for the progress of the Catholic religion in those regions and archipelagoes'. And he praised him for his readiness 'to look after it and facilitate the foundation of the above-mentioned vicariate'. But he made it clear that much reflection was necessary, 'since it would not be fitting to decree its foundation without having reached an understanding with the present vicars apostolic among whom the missions in question are now divided'. He urged Supriès meanwhile 'to recommend this important affair to the Lord', while the Evangelisation Congregation studied the matter. And if the project were to seem feasible in all of its parts, it could be carried out after some time.[3]

Fransoni's reply surprisingly enough spoke of founding 'a new Vicariate Apostolic of Northern Oceania' and therefore went much further than the letter of Supriès which had suggested nothing more than a 'mission' of Northern Oceania. The cardinal's words meant that Northern Oceania would be headed by a vicar apostolic, and it had become customary for nearly all vicars apostolic to be named bishops. Supriès in his excitement now began to envision himself as a bishop and would not let the matter rest. He quickly found a sympathetic supporter in a friend of his based in Rome, who fourteen years earlier had worked with him in the Pondicherry mission in southeastern India. He was Abbé J. F. M. Guérin, curate and treasurer for the Church of Saint Louis of France in Rome. Because of his position Guérin was well known at the Holy See and was skilled in promoting the interests of French Catholics.

Guérin lost no time and paid a visit to Father Giovanni Brunelli, who had been named secretary of the Evangelisation Congregation on 27 January 1843. Brunelli was greatly pleased with the project as outlined by Guérin and asked him to put his ideas in writing for Cardinal Prefect Fransoni. This Guérin did on 24 May 1843. His sixteen-page report, written in French, was titled, 'Memorandum on the Northern Oceania Vicariate'. Its twofold aim was to have the vicariate established 'as soon as possible' and to have Father Thadée Supriès placed in charge.

A glance at a map of Oceania, Guérin said in his report, reveals approximately five hundred islands between the equator and 30° north latitude and between 125° and 180° longitude east of the meridian of Paris. (His longitudes, different from those of Supriès, were correct.) These islands, he said, were inhabited by a large number of infidels and they included these groups: Palau, Marianas, Bonin (now also Ogasawara), Liou-Tchou, Caroline, Ralik, Marshall, Mulgraves and Gilbert. Mistakenly believing that the Vicariate Apostolic of Eastern Oceania had 180° longitude as its western boundary and that the vicariates of Western Oceania and Central Oceania both had the equator as their northern boundary, he deduced incorrectly that 'no vicariate apostolic has these islands within its boundaries'.

According to Guérin the language used in the islands of Northern Oceania was Malay. He therefore suggested that its missionaries should go first to Manila, since there they could learn this language, which was composed of 'Chinese, Japanese, Burmese, Indian and some Arabic'. It was a language 'quite different from the languages spoken in the three vicariates apostolic located on the other side of the equator'. And since the island of Luzon in the Philippines, where Manila was located, contained slaves taken from all the islands of Northern Oceania, some of these, once converted, could be taken along by the missionaries as catechists and would be 'a great help for bringing the light of the gospel to their own country'. Supriès, moreover, had spent a year and a half in the Nicobar Islands in the Andaman Sea in the Bay of Bengal, Guérin added, and so 'he already knows a bit of the Malay language and tells me that learning to speak it is not too difficult'.

Then Guérin indicated where missionary work in the Northern Vicariate should start and in which direction it could expand. The vicar apostolic ought to begin his activity in the Palau group, 'which consists of 26 very fertile and well-populated islands of which Babelthuap is the principal one'. Not very far from these islands were the island groups known as Martyre, Goulou, Gouap, Elivi and Phillip, 'totalling more than 50 islands'. After launching work in these areas, the vicar apostolic could expand his mission northward, bringing Christianity to Guam, which 'is more than 50 leagues in circumference and is the principal island of the Marianas'. Next he 'ought to visit Bonin Island, which gives its name to an island group. And from there he could go to plant the cross on Liou-Tchou Island, which dominates a hundred islands at the southern tip of Japan.'

To refute any possible objection that some of these islands might be cared for by bishops residing in the Philippines, Guérin quoted statistics from the 1840 directory of the Manila Archdiocese. Although the archdiocese had approximately a thousand priests, half of whom were Filipinos and the rest from Spain, they devoted all their care 'to about three million Manilans living in 182 perfectly organised parishes' and were not at all engaged 'in converting the infidels' outside the Philippines.

Guérin pointed out that it was possible to expand also in an easterly direction, going from Palau or Guam to Hogolen, then to Ponape and then to Ualam (also Oulea), all of which were in the Caroline Islands. From there the vicar apostolic could proceed to the groups known as Ralik, Ratak, Mulgraves, Marshall and Gilbert. The sequence 'depends upon the success obtained' and also 'upon the island chosen as the headquarters for the vicariate'.

The lengthy memorandum also contained some ethnological and religious information. The peoples of these islands were described as 'generally peaceful, benevolent, generous, hospitable, but terrible in their vengeance and most voluptuous'. For example, 'the inhabitants of the Bonin Islands, known also as the Magellan Archipelago, are peaceful, gay, simple, hospitable and generous. . . .' The English, Dutch and Americans often bartered with them because their location was so very advantageous as a merchant or military base for vessels travelling the north Pacific route from Hawaii to China. Their location would prove particularly advantageous 'for voyages around the world if the Isthmus of Panama is ever opened'.[4]

In the Carolines, Guérin said, the gospel would certainly make great progress, 'if one could win over the paramount king of all these islands, who resides at Hogolen, the centre of some 20 islands. . . .' Although low, the islands were well populated, very fertile and healthy. 'The inhabitants on the principal island number more than 6,000.' Another very important island was Ualam, 'where perpetual peace reigns'. Since the inhabitants of other islands were often at war with one another, this island could always serve as a refuge. And from it one could advance to the Marshall Islands and Gilbert Islands. But all of this would depend on further information to be gathered at Manila or Palau. Moreover he was happy to point out that in the islands of Northern Oceania the people 'do not at all eat one another out of habit, or because they relish it, like the Papuans do. . . .'

Guérin then proceeded to indicate the qualities necessary for a vicar apostolic 'in these infidel and barbarous lands'. The candidate had to be 'a man completely dedicated, endowed with a firm character and with perseverance, and one who is ready—if necessary—to die by poison, by a club in the hand of a savage, or by serving as a human sacrifice for the horrible banquets of the cannibals'. But where could one find 'this apostle, this future martyr, who would want to go and plant the cross on an island which could become a gallows'? A voice in answer to this appeal 'has made itself heard in the silence of Chartreuse', he said, and belonged to the Very Reverend Father Thadée Supriès, 'whom one of the directors of the Paris Foreign Mission Seminary in 1834 had included among the *Most Distinguished Missionaries* of the Pondicherry Mission in the East Indies'. Fourteen years earlier Guérin himself 'had the honour' of knowing Supriès in that mission and he listed some six well-known ecclesiastics who had highly praised Supriès for his 'abundance of zeal, piety, energy, constancy and firmness'.

As for staff, Guérin suggested that the Vicariate Apostolic of Northern Oceania 'could become a vast and glorious field of activity for the old and ever new zeal' of the Jesuits. In fact, 'in their capable hands Palau and the surrounding islands' could become another Paraguay where the Jesuits had introduced 'a magnificent system of Christian living which has astonished the universe'. He was referring to the so-called reductions, where Jesuit missionaries had gathered together Indians from scattered areas to form highly developed and self-sustaining communities. Guérin was convinced that there were many Jesuits 'ready to march everywhere, even into the midst of cannibals, to combat paganism, idolatry, or, in a word, Satan in his empire, in order to win souls for Jesus Christ at the price of their own blood'. Supriès esteemed the Jesuits highly 'and he would take along as many of these religious as the Most Reverend Father General would like to give him'. Having such collaborators would make him very happy and would give him more hope of success.

It appears that Guérin also had reason to suspect that the Evangelisation Congregation would call the candidacy of Supriès into question on grounds of instability. To provide himself with a rebuttal for this objection, Guérin in advance had approached Supriès and had asked him to state in writing 'in all frankness and sincerity how he justified the apparent inconstancy that he had shown in leaving the Pondicherry missions for those of Siam'. Fearing that

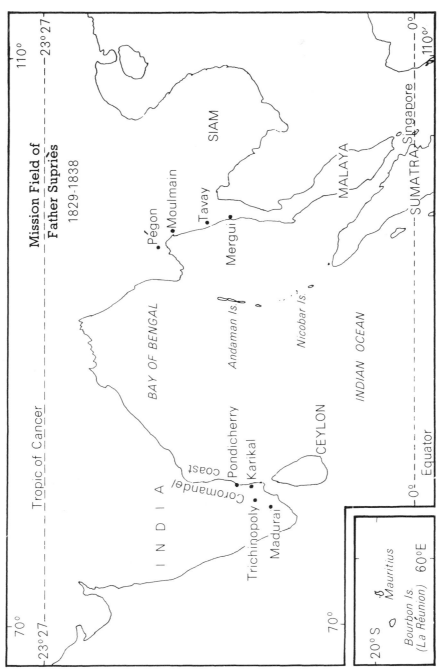

Mission Field of Father Supriès
1829-1838

42 Father Supriès, a Carthusian monk based in Rome who proposed a vicariate apostolic for Northern Oceania in 1843, previously was a member of the Paris Foreign Mission Seminary and served in many missions in the East Indies from 1829 to 1838. *(Chapter 16).*

excerpts would detract from the value of the replies, Guérin attached the complete statement by Supriès to his memorandum and gave both documents to Fransoni.[5]

The Supriès statement had been written on 20 May, four days before Guérin wrote his memorandum. Addressing himself to Guérin, Supriès said that 'in our last meeting you accused me of inconstancy'. All that he needed to clear himself of this charge, he said, was 'a short word of explanation'. That 'word' stretched over four full pages! From the time he was sixteen or seventeen he had wanted to become a missionary. He joined the Paris Foreign Mission Seminary and on 1 March 1829 left France as a priest for the East Indies. In August of that year he reached the Coromandel Coast of southeastern India and served as a missionary in Pondicherry, a French settlement.

But soon he began to lose his peace of mind. 'Continually I was experiencing internal grief and remorse of conscience at seeing myself obliged to tolerate certain remnants of superstition, certain practices which seemed to me clearly condemned.' He believed that these had been outlawed by 'the decrees and ordinances of the Holy Apostolic See covering the Malabar Rites'. He admitted that he may have deceived himself, or perhaps he was too scrupulous, 'but I do not believe this was the case', he said. Even after submitting his doubts to his superiors, the replies that he received 'were never capable of bringing me peace'. He therefore asked to be transferred from Pondicherry.

His bishop then sent him in early 1833 to Madurai, a city in southern Madras state in India. The Christians in this Portuguese mission had risen in revolt because of the scandalous conduct of their priests. Supriès entered the fray, 'fighting at the risk of my life and my liberty against the schismatics to defend the rights and prerogatives of the head of the Church'. He was then denounced 'as a vagabond and a disturber of the public peace', was kept prisoner for twenty days, and was finally expelled into French territory at Trichinopoly (also Tiruchirappalli). Finally he arrived at Karikal in July 1833 and worked there until September 1834.

Because the Malabar Rites still gave him no peace of mind and because his health had deteriorated as a result of persecutions endured at Madurai, he then asked permission from the Bishop of Pondicherry to transfer to Siam, which also was a mission of the Paris Foreign Mission Seminary. At first the bishop refused, 'but he did let me go for some time to Bourbon in order to restore my health there'. Supriès arrived at the French colony of Bourbon (now Réunion) in early November 1834, took charge of Saint Rose parish and gave instruction to slaves, 'above all to Kaffirs, the most abandoned of all'.

He finally received authorisation from the directors of the Paris Foreign Mission Seminary in May 1835 to transfer to their mission in Siam and left without delay, arriving in Singapore around the end of September that year. His new bishop sent him and another missionary 'to the Nicobar Islands inhabited by peoples who were entirely savage. We stayed there one and a half years, that is, all of 1836 and half of 1837.' Although the mission gave good prospects of success, his colleague fell dangerously ill. 'And to complicate matters the

Mohammedans from Achin on the Island of Sumatra had arrived at this island and persuaded these poor inhabitants that our purpose among them was to harm them and to prepare the way for Europeans, who would soon arrive to make all of them slaves. From this moment they treated us like enemies and on several occasions tried to kill us.' Supriès then boarded a Chinese ship with his dying colleague and went to the coast of Pégon, visiting places like Tavay, Mergui, Moulmain and others. Here he found large numbers of pariahs from Madras employed as domestic servants for agents of the English East India Company, who had been deprived of religious helps for many years. So he also did some missionary work among them.

Having lost contact with his bishop in Siam and being 'extremely afflicted by all sorts of evils and almost discouraged by all this misfortune', Supriès left the East Indies in 1838 for France to regain his health and arrived there on 13 May of that year. 'In order to obtain perfect peace of conscience, I also intended to go to Rome and cast myself at the feet of the Holy Father to be absolved from the censures which I always feared that I had incurred.' En route to Rome he stopped at La Grande Chartreuse in the French Alps where Saint Bruno had founded the Carthusians in 1084. 'The peace and tranquillity enjoyed by those living in this beautiful solitude made the most profound impression upon me. I then compared this quiet and peaceful life with the life full of agitation and anxiety which I had led up to that time, and I sensed an immense need for repose, solitude, prayer and union with God.' He was permitted to remain at La Grande Chartreuse and on 29 June 1839 he became a Carthusian monk. His autobiographical account to Guérin ended with the words, 'You know the rest'.[6]

It is difficult to imagine what Fransoni and Brunelli thought after reading this autobiographical account. Was this the man whom they wanted to have as bishop over the Vicariate Apostolic of Northern Oceania? And what about Guérin's proposal that Supriès have Jesuits under him? Surely, if the Jesuits were interested in the mission and were able to supply the staff, they would want to have one of their own men named vicar apostolic and not a Carthusian.

Six anxious weeks of waiting passed for Supriès, but the Evangelisation Congregation remained strangely silent. He then paid Fransoni a visit about 4 July to see how matters stood. To his great disappointment he learned that there was no longer talk of a vicar apostolic with the rank of bishop being placed in charge, but instead a priest with the title of prefect apostolic. Supriès objected to this, saying that as a mere priest he would never be influential enough to obtain the necessary personnel. But Fransoni remained firm in his stand. He added that the Evangelisation Congregation was investigating the matter, since it intended soon to reorganise the mission territories in Western Oceania.[7]

Fransoni, in fact, took the Supriès-Guérin proposal much more seriously than the two men imagined and on 12 July 1843, shortly after the visit from Supriès, sent Guérin's detailed memorandum of 24 May to Archbishop Joseph Segni of Manila in order to obtain his views on it. He told the archbishop that the boundaries of the Vicariate Apostolic of Western Oceania 'still extend much too far', even though it had been reduced in size in the previous year by cutting off territory for the Vicariate Apostolic of Central Oceania. And since Bishop Pompallier simply could not 'promote the eternal salvation of so many widely scattered tribes or islands entrusted to him, this Sacred Congregation intends to cut off still other areas from the Western Vicariate just mentioned in order to erect another vicariate shortly and several more in the course of time'. An increase in the number of 'prelate bishops and preachers of the word of God', he said, 'should prove beneficial to the Catholic faith and to the conversion of these same tribes.'

Fransoni then explained that while thinking along these lines he had received a concrete proposal for a Vicariate Apostolic of Northern Oceania, which he enclosed. 'Although in many points it would not be easy to carry out because of apparent difficulties . . . , we nevertheless thought it most opportune to submit the project to Your Excellency in order to learn your views in this matter.' In particular Fransoni wanted him to indicate which places mentioned in Guérin's memorandum could be incorporated in the new vicariate, 'so that neither your jurisdiction nor perhaps that of another bishop might suffer, since some of the places might already be entrusted to you or to some other bishop'. And in addition to the Jesuits mentioned by Guérin, he wanted to know whether Archbishop Segni knew of any other tried and tested missionaries to whom the government and care of the proposed Northern Vicariate could be entrusted.[8]

Meanwhile Father Epalle had reached Rome and, as Providence would have it, took up residence at the Church of Saint Louis of France, where Guérin was curate and treasurer. The two men immediately began discussing the proposed Vicariate Apostolic of Northern Oceania. Epalle strongly suggested that Ponape, and not the Palau Islands, should be the headquarters. Guérin passed on this information to Brunelli, who in turn asked him to put these ideas in writing. Instead of doing so himself, Guérin contacted Epalle who on 14 July 1843 wrote for him 'A Note on the Island of Ponape and the Hopes Which It Offers to Catholicism'.

Epalle's 'Note' stated that 'Ponape or Ascension Island, located at the centre of the Archipelago of the Carolines . . . , has a population of about 8,000 souls'. It was one of the most important islands in the Carolines, he said, and also one of the most important in what he called 'the projected Vicariate of Micronesia or Northwestern Oceania'. It seemed as though Christianity had earlier penetrated this island, he said, because the officers of a passing American warship discovered an iron cross on a spot believed to contain the ruins of a village.

The balance of Epalle's 'Note' stressed the importance of starting missionary work at Ponape at once because of the eagerness of European settlers there to have Catholic priests. He explained that many Europeans had been attracted 'by the beauty and fertility' of Ponape and 'by the peacefulness and friendliness of its inhabitants', and therefore had taken up residence there. For a number of years, however, they had done everything possible to keep out both Catholic and Protestant missionaries. But one of the settlers, a Scots Presbyterian, James Hall, 'prayed to the Lord to obtain for the inhabitants of Ascension (Ponape) the benefits of Christianity'. Eventually he won over some of the most influential settlers, including a Frenchman. 'Without further delay eight of them got together, all Protestants except for the Frenchman, and unanimously decided that one of them should go immediately in search of Catholic missionaries. The lot fell upon the Scots Presbyterian.' After providing for the care of his wife and children, he boarded a passing whaler and six months later arrived at the Bay of Islands.

Here he was warmly received by Bishop Pompallier, who for a long time had been thinking of founding a mission in this island,[9] and so he promised to give him two priests for Ponape. But since the bishop first had to make a voyage of six weeks or less along the coast of New Zealand with the *Sancta Maria*, he invited the Scotsman to remain at his residence in Kororareka until his return. To all appearances Pompallier wanted to take the Scotsman and the two missionaries to Ponape aboard the *Sancta Maria*. But it was during this time that Pompallier was forced to change his plans due to Father Chanel's death, and he was therefore unable to pick up the Scotsman and the two priests.

The Scotsman meanwhile led a most edifying life in the bishop's residence, Epalle said, and in the course of his nine months there 'to his great surprise he became a Catholic'. When the *Sancta Maria* returned from the tropical islands without Pompallier, but with the remains of Father Chanel, Pro-Vicar Epalle thought 'that the moment had come to fulfil the bishop's promise'. He therefore sent two priests with Hall aboard the *Sancta Maria* back to Wallis so that the priests could receive their formal appointment to Ponape directly from Bishop Pompallier. 'But His Grace on passing Futuna gave in to the requests of the inhabitants of this island and the two priests destined for Ascension (Ponape) were assigned to them.'

According to Epalle, 'there was never the slightest suspicion that this man might have been motivated for reasons of personal gain; on the contrary he was considered to be one of the most beautiful souls that one could find'. And if since that time his dispositions had not changed, today 'it would be a very simple matter, humanly speaking, for missionaries to get into Ponape'. But the fact that the Scotsman had made such great sacrifices to achieve his goal, and had been unsuccessful, 'exposes him to very severe temptations'. Therefore Epalle suggested in conclusion that it would be 'expedient to take advantage quickly of the influence and good dispositions of this convert'.[10]

On the following day, 15 July, Guérin presented Epalle's 'Note' to Secretary Brunelli. 'I have the honour of sending you the promised report on the Island of Ponape, which is located in the projected Vicariate of Northern Oceania', he said. According to this new information 'Ponape could be visited before Palau and could be chosen as the centre of the new vicariate, since it already is the geographical centre. Also, it would be altogether useless to go to Manila to learn the language and to look for interpreters. This eliminates great expense and saves a considerable amount of time.'

Wanting to provide the Evangelisation Congregation with as many incentives as possible for founding the projected vicariate without delay, Guérin added that it would be risky to ignore or even to postpone fulfilling the

Scotsman's request for personnel. Any delay would make him and those who had sent him 'turn to Protestant ministers, who travel these seas, and they without delay will take advantage of such a beautiful opportunity for spreading their errors. This will make our entrance to these islands at a later date very difficult, at least, if not altogether impossible.' A delay here could cause a repetition of what earlier had happened in the Sandwich Islands (now Hawaii), he warned. 'I have learned many other interesting things about this island and about the proposed vicariate,' he added, 'and so I earnestly request Your Excellency kindly to contact for more ample information the Reverend Father Epalle, the Marist who communicated these things to me.'[11]

The Evangelisation Congregation followed Guérin's final recommendation and discussed the entire matter with Epalle.[12]

Apparently Guérin and Supriès kept one another well informed of the individual steps they took in connection with the proposed Vicariate Apostolic of Northern Oceania, because on 18 July, just three days after Guérin submitted Epalle's report to Secretary Brunelli, Supriès once again wrote to Cardinal Fransoni. 'I have the consolation of announcing to you that Divine Providence has given me personnel for the mission of Northern Oceania in an altogether unexpected way', he began. A few days earlier one of the directors of the major seminary of Fréjus, his home diocese, had paid him a visit and said that he had three mission-minded candidates who would be happy to go to Northern Oceania. Now these three candidates with the two others mentioned in his letter of 6 April, he said, made five. In addition there was a young Carthusian lay Brother born in Savoy 'who for more than a year' had asked for a mission assignment. This meant that the new mission already was assured of six priests (including Supriès) and a catechist, he said, 'and many missions have begun with less'. And once the mission were actually founded, 'there would be many others whom the voice of God will call to come and share our labours'.

Supriès had a confession to make in this letter. 'During the visit which I had the honour of paying Your Eminence some two weeks ago', he said, 'I allowed myself in the complete simplicity of my soul to make some remarks to you, all in a spirit of candour, testifying to some repugnance on my part at being named a prefect apostolic.' (Supriès until that moment had imagined that he would be named vicar apostolic with the rank of bishop.) He now explained that the only reason for the repugnance which he had felt 'was the fear that I had of not having enough influence to obtain co-workers for myself. But today, since this obstacle has been removed in a way which seems altogether extraordinary, I no longer have any objections to make.' He placed himself completely in the hands of the Evangelisation Congregation, so that it could dispose of him 'as it sees fit for the greater glory of God and the welfare of the Church'.[13]

Fransoni answered the 18 July letter of Supriès on 20 July, saying that he was 'greatly pleased with the zeal and new concern' shown by the Carthusian. He added, however, that 'the undersigned Cardinal Prefect ... believes it opportune to remind you of what he already made known to you orally, namely, that the Sacred Congregation is now obtaining for itself all the information

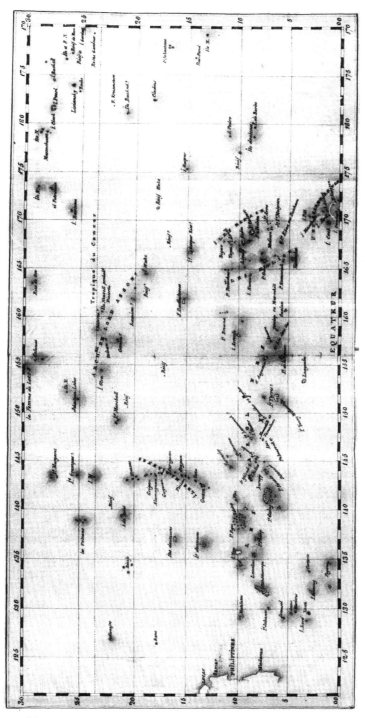

43 When requested by Archbishop Segni of Manila for his views on a proposed Northern Oceania Vicariate, Father Balvino Consuegra, a former Franciscan provincial superior, submitted this map along with his comments on 9 April 1844 from Bocavi in the Philippines. *Source: PF: SC Oceania vol. 2 (1842–5, Part II) f. 679r. (Chapter 16).*

needed for this purpose and for reorganising the entire Western Mission. Consequently, if in the course of time provisions are made in line with your petitions, the writer will let Your Paternity know in Grenoble, where you say you must go shortly. . . .'[14]

About the time that Supriès was pressing so insistently to be made head of the new mission of Northern Oceania, Epalle was in the offices of Secretary Brunelli suggesting that 'it might be better' if Bishop Pompallier with a new group of Marists were 'to go to the Carolines where he originally intended to start'. Another possibility would be to assign some other archipelago to Pompallier and give the Carolines 'to another community'. After their conference Brunelli asked Epalle to submit in writing all of the ideas that they had discussed and he did this on 24 July 1843.[15]

In December of that year Archbishop Segni of Manila received Cardinal Fransoni's letter of 12 July. He answered at once and promised that the desired information would follow as soon as possible. But on New Year's Day he left Manila for a pastoral visit to the two provinces of Batangas and Bataan in southern Luzon and did not return to Manila until 20 March. It was after his return, apparently, that he commissioned Father Balvino Consuegra, a former provincial superior of the Franciscan order, to make a study of the Guérin memorandum. This priest was 'very expert in geography' and was asked to indicate what the archbishop should advise Rome in the matter.[16]

Father Consuegra's reply to Archbishop Segni, dated at Bocavi on 9 April 1844, was written in Spanish. Ever since his arrival in the Philippines in 1815, he said, he had thought about the possibility of uniting the islands of Northern Oceania 'under the dominion of a great and wise nation through whose protection the Malayans could acquire unity, civilisation and virtues. . . .' The letter now received from his archbishop, he said, with the enclosed letter from Cardinal Fransoni and the memorandum of Abbé Guérin, made him understand 'that the great, wise and judicious nation whose protection was destined for the Malayans was the Catholic Apostolic Roman Church, from which alone they will obtain the great benefits which they need so much and which I have desired for them so often'.

The Franciscan then clearly set forth his ideas on the matter. He suggested that the headquarters of the new vicariate apostolic should be at Hogolen, the principal island group in the Carolines. Once missionary work was launched there, 'the light of the gospel should go to the Palau group which is to the west'. He pointed out that the Jesuits in the beginning of the eighteenth century had done much work there and had lost many lives, 'but without any considerable success'. Going eastward from the Carolines, 'the light of the gospel should be brought to the groups called Marshall and Mulgraves and also to other islands dependent upon them, reaching as far as the Scarborough group [now the northern Gilbert Islands], situated between the equator and 5° north latitude and at 170° longitude. We have no special information about all these islands east of the Carolines, except what modern geographers say about them, particularly Adrien Balbi who says that among the multitude of peoples who populate them, there are blacks, there are those the colour of copper, and there are peoples so poor that they could be the poorest of Oceania.'

The work by Balbi (1782–1848) referred to here by Father Consuegra was a geographical compendium of 1,392 pages called *Abrégé de géographie* first published in 1833 in Paris. On pages 1260–84 it had sections on Micronesia, Melanesia, Polynesia, New Zealand and Australia. Frenchmen called this popular book 'the Bible of geographers' and within five years two French editions and an Italian translation were sold out. These were followed by a third French edition in 1837, published also in Italian in 1840. Both the first French edition and this second Italian edition are in the Evangelisation Congregation's library. Balbi, who was Italian by birth, spent most of his life in France and published his works there, calling himself 'Adrien' in his French works and 'Adriano' in their Italian translations, often made by himself.

Consuegra excluded the Marianas Islands from the proposed vicariate. Not only were they very distant from the Carolines, but their seas 'are very stormy, especially at the time of hurricanes and typhoons in the months of August to December'. Jesuits at various times had left the Marianas to go in search of the Palau Islands, but did not succeed in reaching them. 'And others left from the Philippines in search of the Carolines and only seldom reached them.'

Another reason for excluding the Marianas was 'the certainty that the Spaniards have in those islands a governor dependent upon Manila'. Consuegra was also certain that 'the Bishop of Cebu is in charge of ecclesiastical government in the Marianas Islands'. Except for this he agreed completely with Guérin that the Vicariate of Northern Oceania should be erected and should include the islands listed in the memorandum. For the sake of greater clarity Consuegra enclosed for Archbishop Segni 'a small map which includes that vicariate and indicates the parts belonging to the Bishop of Cebu which must be excluded'. He also enclosed Guérin's memorandum and Fransoni's letter, saying that he hoped God would greatly enlighten the cardinal 'so that he sends to these islands many Jesuits and a number of vicars apostolic like Father Thadée [Supriès]. . . .'[17]

It was 17 April 1844 by the time Archbishop Segni finally answered Cardinal Fransoni's letter of 12 July 1843. He explained how he had commissioned Father Consuegra to look into the matter and said that a reply from him had arrived just a few days before. 'And because in my judgment it is so very well written, I am sending it to Your Eminence with the hope that it may be of some use in increasing the number of Christians in these parts of Oceania.' He also enclosed Consuegra's geographical chart because it showed 'very clearly—so it seems to me—what boundaries in his judgment ought to be given to the proposed vicariate'. Segni called Fransoni's attention to the fact that on the chart the Marianas Islands and Mindanao were marked in red and would have to be excluded from the vicariate 'because they are subject to Spain and are governed in spiritual matters by the Bishop of Cebu. . . .' As for priests who might staff the Northern Vicariate, Segni knew of no one, because the priests assigned to

44 First page of the 17 April 1844 letter of Archbishop Joseph Segni of Manila answering Cardinal Prefect Fransoni's inquiries of 12 July 1843 regarding possible boundaries for a new Northern Oceania Vicariate proposed by Father Thadée Supriès, a Carthusian monk in Rome. *Source: PF: SC Oceania vol. 2 (1842–5, Part II) f. 680r. (Chapter 16).*

the Philippines were 'unequal to the task of ruling so great a multitude of Christians. . . .'[18]

It had taken five months for Cardinal Fransoni's letter to reach Archbishop Segni and so probably it also took five months for Segni's reply to reach Rome. This meant it would have arrived about 16 September 1844. But exactly *one full year* before that date, on 16 September 1843, Fransoni had written to Father Colin in Lyon, assuring him that the Vicariate Apostolic of Northern Oceania—wanted so much by Supriès—would be entrusted to the Marists according to Epalle's plan as soon as the matter could be brought up at a general meeting of the Evangelisation Congregation.[19] How this came about is a story in itself.

17

The Vicariates Apostolic of
Melanesia and Micronesia

16 JULY 1844

By taking up residence in Rome at the Church of Saint Louis of France, where Abbé Guérin was curate and treasurer, Pro-Vicar Epalle immediately became aware of the far advanced Supriès-Guérin plans for founding a vicariate apostolic in Northern Oceania, known also as Micronesia. In fact, on 13 July 1843, the day after Cardinal Fransoni sent Guérin's detailed memorandum of the previous 24 May to Archbishop Segni of Manila, announcing that the above vicariate would soon be established, Epalle had a meeting with Secretary Brunelli and with Oceania expert, Reverend (?) Clemente Maria Buratti, in the offices of the Evangelisation Congregation. Here he explained how a mission in the Caroline Islands of Micronesia might help solve the Pompallier-Marist conflict.

The meeting did not begin with this proposal, but rather with an examination of Pompallier's recent administration and his conduct toward Colin and the Marists. Epalle sensed immediately that Brunelli and Buratti were rather annoyed with Colin, seeing in his every letter a constant clamouring to have Pompallier recalled to Europe. But Brunelli had decided against this, since Pompallier was just as prolific in defending himself. The most recent case in point was a letter from Pompallier dated 6 November 1842, forwarded to Cardinal Prefect Fransoni by the Association for the Propagation of the Faith in Lyon on 17 June 1843, and Colin's rebuttal to it, also forwarded to Fransoni by the same association four days later.[1]

Brunelli and Buratti suggested the following solution. They would send Pompallier a coadjutor bishop, whether he wanted one or not, and the coadjutor would be in charge of administration on all levels and in such a way that Pompallier would be able to take no action without first consulting him. After this measure went into effect, if Colin should still have reason for complaint, Pompallier would be summoned to Rome. Meanwhile, Colin should continue recruiting vocations for New Zealand.

Not convinced that this was a satisfactory solution guaranteeing collaboration between Pompallier and the Marists as well as success for the New Zealand mission, Epalle ventured to make two proposals of his own. The first, which he considered 'the more efficacious remedy', called for transferring Pompallier from New Zealand to another part of his own vicariate. Epalle did not believe that Pompallier because of his French nationality would be forced to leave New Zealand, but he did feel it would be wise for him to leave spontaneously. The fact that New Zealand since 1840 had been an English colony, with a foreign population almost exclusively British, seemed to suggest this. He was convinced that the colonists 'will soon outnumber the native population, which is not over 100,000', and the best interests of the Church in New Zealand would seem to require that Rome 'place British Clergy in charge'. Priests from England would speak English well and would also better understand the customs of the colonists.

But if Pompallier were to leave New Zealand, he would have to go somewhere else. 'While he was on Wallis', Epalle said, 'he . . . asked me whether I thought it might be better for him to remain there and to request that Rome send an English bishop to New Zealand.' Epalle was not at all in favour of Pompallier's remaining in the Wallis area, however. He thought that the bishop should rather go to the Caroline Islands, since he much earlier had intended to make his first foundation there. 'In this new place, having new clergy, he could make a new start, and this would be less difficult for him than having to change his ways. . . .' Aware of the Supriès-Guérin proposal for Micronesia, Epalle said that if the Evangelisation Congregation 'were to judge it preferable to give the Carolines to another community', something which he himself highly recommended, another archipelago could be separated from the Vicariate Apostolic of Western Oceania and be entrusted to Pompallier.

Epalle added that if Pompallier were to be removed from New Zealand in this way, 'the Society of Mary could let its missionaries stay in New Zealand and could send even a larger number of them to evangelise the infidels, if the Evangelisation Congregation and the new [English] bishop were to desire it'. He envisioned the English clergy as taking care of the colonists and the Marists as taking care of the Maoris. He was not certain, however, whether Colin would be willing to send Marists to staff a new mission headed by Pompallier. 'I know that he would not at all oppose the orders of Rome, but . . . he fears disputes and is anxious to separate himself from collaboration where peace does not reign.'

Brunelli's reaction to this first proposal of Epalle was 'Impossible for the moment'.

His second proposal concerned the distribution of funds. He suggested that separate bookkeeping be introduced for the bishop and for the Marists and that Rome should also give its funds separately to the bishop and to the Marists. In practice this would mean that Colin would receive from the Association for the Propagation of the Faith the money necessary to send his missionaries overseas and to support them. As for Pompallier's funds, he would obtain them directly from the Evangelisation Congregation, just like other vicars apostolic. Or he could be given the option to name someone, not a Marist, to take care of this for him and to act according to his orders. 'This system would have the double advantage of assuring for the missionaries what they need, and of putting an end to the serious accusations being made by Bishop Pompallier. . . .' But Epalle feared that if this system were put into effect, it might make Pompallier even more furious.

On returning to his residence Epalle at once wrote Colin a report on this meeting, saying that he had been asked to submit his two proposals in writing. He had also been instructed to write first of all to Colin and ask him to present quickly a candidate for the office of coadjutor for Bishop Pompallier. And if he should find for this office an Englishman in whom he had confidence, so much the better. Without going into any detail whatsoever about the geographical area concerned, Epalle told Colin that Brunelli also wanted him to submit names for 'a vicar apostolic and a coadjutor for a third vicariate in Oceania'. And Epalle advised Colin, 'Answer each letter promptly, because the Most Reverend Brunelli wastes no time.'[2]

The fact that Epalle added no further explanation about this 'third vicariate in Oceania' is evidence that he and Colin had reached an understanding on it in France.[3] Colin referred to it vaguely when he wrote to Fransoni on 18 June 1843, announcing that Epalle would soon be coming to Rome. The thirty-four-year-old Epalle did not wish to remain in France as chargé d'affaires for Pompallier, Colin had said, but wanted instead to present plans in Rome 'for a new project'.[4] The 'new project' was to found a vicariate apostolic in Melanesia, something to which Brunelli had agreed without hesitation.

This proposal was not completely new to Brunelli, since it was partly contained in Father Visitor Forest's letter of 2 June 1842, which had reached the Evangelisation Congregation early in 1843. Forest in this letter had spoken highly of Epalle when suggesting that the remaining tropical islands within Pompallier's territory should be divided among 'one or two good bishops who are very good Marists'. At that time a secretary at the Evangelisation Congregation had summarised Forest's letter as follows: 'Let Bishop Pompallier remain in New Zealand, now almost completely an English colony; send him some English priests; and give the rest of Oceania and New Guinea to the Marists.'[5]

On 14 July, the day after the meeting with Brunelli and Buratti, Epalle at Guérin's request wrote 'A Note on the Island of Ponape and the Hopes Which It Offers to Catholicism'. Guérin presented this to the Evangelisation Congregation on the following day and suggested that Brunelli 'kindly . . . contact for more ample information the Reverend Father Epalle, the Marist who communicated these things to me'. Guérin's letter and Epalle's report were read and summarised as follows: ' . . . The Island of Ponape belonging to the Vicariate of Northern Oceania—Favourable dispositions of its inhabitants for embracing Catholicism—Urgency of sending some missionaries there—Imminent danger that Protestants may enter there.' And this was followed by a further note in another hand: 'Discuss this entire matter with Father Epalle.'[6]

Then Supriès on 18 July informed Fransoni that he could assure him of six priests (including himself) and a catechist for the contemplated mission of Northern Oceania. But Fransoni answered two days later that the Evangelisation Congregation was busy 'obtaining for itself all the information needed . . . for reorganising the entire Western Mission', and would let him know in due time, if his services were needed.[7]

It was not until 24 July that Epalle put down in writing his two proposals as requested by Brunelli at the 13 July meeting. He did not want to influence the Evangelisation Congregation one way or the other in its decisions regarding Pompallier, he said. 'But the knowledge which I have about Bishop Pompallier does not allow me to have any brilliant hopes, no matter what guidelines might be traced out for us. . . .' As he saw it, the question was not which solution was good, but which would be the lesser evil. He also assured Brunelli that Colin was not clamouring for Pompallier's recall to Europe, but merely considered it 'his duty to acquaint Rome with the evil as he himself knew it'.[8]

Epalle during the following week had a scribe write out neatly and legibly his proposal on a third vicariate to be entrusted to the Marists. He addressed it to Cardinal Prefect Fransoni and dated it 1 August 1843. In the first part of the proposal he spoke only about Melanesia and suggested that New Guinea, New Britain, New Ireland, the Admiralty Islands, the Solomon Islands and all surrounding islands should become a new vicariate apostolic. It is interesting to note that this territory, except for the Solomon Islands, coincided exactly with the territory labelled 'Vicariate Apostolic of New Guinea' in the 1842 Marist proposal called 'An Overall View of the Islands of Western Oceania to Help Determine the Borders to Be Laid Down, between the New Missions That Could Be Founded There', which originally Colin had intended to submit in its entirety to Cardinal Fransoni.

From a large number of men who had visited these islands, Epalle explained, he had learned how thickly populated they were. Among his informers was a French naval officer, Commander Joseph du Bouzet (he had sailed with Dumont d'Urville in 1837–40), who 'has often recommended to me that I take up with Your Eminence the cause of these poor peoples, especially of those in the Solomon Archipelago'. The population per unit area in the islands of Melanesia was no greater than in other mission territories of Oceania, but 'because these lands are so much more extensive, their population will be so much greater'. Epalle told Fransoni that he considered the reports by navigators to be exaggerated, like the one which said that the island of Waigeo 'has a population of 100,000'.

This is precisely the population given for Waigeo by Conrad Malte-Brun (1775–1826) in his *Précis de la géographie universelle*, a widely distributed geographical work of the last century which went into numerous editions. It was highly authoritative since each new edition contained the latest information gleaned from the journals and reports of navigators. Malte-Brun, in fact, founded with others in Paris in 1822 the Société de géographie, the first modern geographical society. He was also its first secretary. Epalle eventually acquired his book to take along to Oceania, perhaps the fifth edition which was published in Paris in 1843, the very year when Epalle was writing his letter to Cardinal Prefect Fransoni.[9]

Epalle added that 'the islands in question have not yet been invaded by heresy'. And without telling Fransoni where he obtained the information, he said that 'today we know that Europeans have been able to live for a long time

45 Father Jean-Baptiste Epalle as pro-vicar apostolic of Western Oceania submitted a report from Rome on 1 August 1843 to Cardinal Prefect Fransoni suggesting that both Melanesia and Micronesia be made independent vicariates apostolic. This is the first page of his eight-page report. *Source: PF: SOCG vol. 965 (1844) f. 453r. (Chapter 17).*

46 The last page of Father Epalle's report, as figure 45, containing the date, his signature, and eight short lines in Italian by the secretary of the Evangelisation Congregation condensing the eight-page French report. *Source: PF: SOCG vol. 965 (1844) f. 456v. (Chapter 17).*

290 FOUNDING OF THE ROMAN CATHOLIC CHURCH IN OCEANIA

without great peril in New Guinea, where the natives were dreaded so much. We also know that the inhabitants of New Ireland are very sociable and that the Louisiade and the Solomon archipelagoes give no great reasons for fear.' Protestantism meanwhile had been 'allured by the bait of the considerable progress' which could be made there, 'and it was consequently preparing to make new sacrifices to become heroic' by sending preachers 'toward these beautiful and vast lands'.

Catholic missionaries in Oceania had always arrived on the scene after the Protestant missionaries, he said, and so it was desirable 'for the Catholic religion to be first' in penetrating Melanesia. 'The Oceanian is disposed to Catholicism and nothing else is needed to win him but steadfastness and fearlessness in the face of privations, especially hunger.' He pointed out, however, that 'according to the mentality of these people it is essential, in order to have influence over them, to be the first to arrive'.

The northern and southern boundaries that he indicated for the new Melanesia Mission were taken directly from those indicated in Colin's 'Overall View' for the proposed Vicariate Apostolic of New Guinea, namely, 12° south latitude on the south and the equator on the north. He suggested 125° longitude east of Paris as the western boundary and 160° longitude east of Paris as the eastern boundary. Thus the eastern boundary of the new mission coincided with the western boundary of the already established Central Vicariate. These limits made the entire territory 700 leagues long and 240 leagues wide and within it, he said, 'there are at least 200 islands, of which the more considerable are: New Guinea, which is one of the largest islands on the globe, Tobie, Willem Schouten, Waigeo, Les Deux Vessets, Timorlaut, Four Aroe Islands, Admiralties, New Hanover, New Ireland, New Britain, Louisiade, Bougainville, Choiseul, [Santa] Isabel, Guadalcanal, [San] Cristóbal, etc. . . . .'

Another factor very much in favour of starting missionary work without delay in Melanesia, Epalle pointed out, was the fact that 'many governments covet these islands'. Holland 'has declared part of New Guinea to be a Dutch possession, but until now to no avail'. England on the other hand 'claims exclusive rights over it, but fears that European powers will not respect its claims, and so it is hastening to occupy these vast and fertile lands in order to vindicate its claims'. Epalle believed that once these governments were to take possession of these islands, 'it will not be easy for Catholic missionaries to penetrate there. . . .' He added that 'France has designs on the Solomon Archipelago—I know that positively—but it wishes to begin with New Caledonia, which is part of the Central Vicariate Apostolic.' Instead of being a help to Catholic missionaries, however, this would prove a hindrance, since the bulk of French immigrants were known for their bad example and scandal. Religion had no other choice, therefore, 'but to go there first in order to win over these peoples' and provide them with 'an education that is thoroughly Christian'.

'I think that the Society of Mary could furnish the missionaries necessary for this enterprise', Epalle said, if Fransoni were to judge it 'fitting to establish a vicariate apostolic in the territory called Melanesia. It would be impossible for me, however, to designate anyone [for the office of vicar apostolic or coadjutor] without previously consulting the Reverend Father Colin. In view of instructions that I have received on this matter from His Excellency, Monsignor Brunelli, I have already written to Father Colin on this subject.'

Brunelli or Buratti had meanwhile discussed with Epalle the matter contained in his 'Note' written for Guérin and the proposal of Supriès and Guérin as well. And so, after clearly marking off the Melanesia section of his letter to Fransoni, Epalle said: 'I must also speak to Your Eminence about another part of Oceania, where it would be even more pressing to establish a vicariate apostolic. I mean Micronesia, that is, Northwestern Oceania. It seems to me that those who go there will certainly be successful, since the principal archipelagoes are not only disposed to receive the gospel, but are even crying out for missionaries.'

The boundaries listed by Epalle for this new Vicariate Apostolic of Micronesia were not those contained in the 'Overall View' of Colin, but—with one exception—those given by Guérin in his memorandum of 24 May 1843, namely, the equator on the south, 125° longitude east of Paris on the west, 180° longitude east of Paris on the east, and—the exception—13° north latitude on the north. This placed the northern boundary directly under Guam and far below the Marianas Islands, thus avoiding any possible conflict of jurisdiction with some bishop in the Philippines. Apparently Epalle was adhering closely to the maps provided in Vandermaelen's *Atlas universel*, available for consultation in the offices of the Evangelisation Congregation, which indicated all islands of Melanesia and Micronesia in great detail as far as 12° north and south of the equator. He pointed out, however, that although the Gilbert Islands were mostly north of the equator, some of them did reach below the equator and formed part of the Central Vicariate Apostolic. He therefore suggested that the complete Gilbert Archipelago ought to belong to the new Vicariate Apostolic of Micronesia.

'Ascension or Ponape would seem to me the point where one should go to start the mission without delay', he said. 'It was here that Father Bachelot, the first Prefect Apostolic of Eastern Oceania, was buried; he . . . died as a result of bad treatment received while being persecuted in the Sandwich Islands. Because of its geographical position, its size and its population, this island deserves to become a central station.' Epalle then repeated almost verbatim the account that he had given two weeks earlier in his 'Note' to Guérin about the Protestant Scotsman, James Hall, who had come from Ponape to New Zealand seeking Catholic missionaries.

Epalle went on to explain how deeply moved Colin had been on learning that Protestants had tried in vain to get Catholic missionaries from Bishop Pompallier for the inhabitants of Ponape. 'If the difficulty of finding missionaries for this vicariate should prove to be an obstacle to its formation—and its establishment seems to me an urgent matter—the Reverend Father Colin . . . might agree to the following solution, if Your Eminence were to request it: A single vicariate could be erected for the moment, but it would contain the two parts of Oceania about which I have spoken. Missionaries would then be sent there in sufficient numbers to make two foundations, one at Ascension and the other at New Ireland, two points which are not too far distant from one another. It would take about two years to get a mission centre established in each of these two islands.' With missionaries being right on the spot, they could advise Fransoni when the proper moment had arrived for creating the new vicariate and sending a new bishop and new missionaries to take charge of it.[10]

When Epalle submitted his 1 August 1843 report to Fransoni, he was still full of optimism, because he had not yet received Colin's answer to his letter of 13 July, which had reached Lyon on 23 July. Colin's reply, written two days later, reached Epalle on 7 August, just as he had taken paper in hand to write another letter to Colin. What Epalle read was this:

It is good that Pompallier is remaining at his post.

'. . .You are offered a new mission and are asked to provide a vicar apostolic, a coadjutor for him, and a third bishop as coadjutor for the Most Reverend Pompallier. A great task! For the moment it is impossible for us to give a precise reply without being rash. We need time to recommend this important matter to God and to examine our resources. Therefore ask for a delay and on your return we shall together examine the question and search out the means to make all of this contribute to the greater glory of God. Do not forget about our scanty financial resources and the immense expenses of such an enterprise in lands so distant and so poor, where the possibility of correspondence is so rare.'

'. . .Dividing goods between Vicar Apostolic [Pompallier] and his co-workers, as I see it, offers grave inconveniences . . . The moment has not come to insist on this article.'

. . .And in view of Bishop Pompallier's attitude, 'the idea of giving him a coadjutor as a counsellor in administrative matters frightens me. I fear there will be a collision of powers, confusion, disunion among the clergy, scandal, etc. . . . It would seem better to keep the status quo for a while . . . We want only what the Sacred Congregation wants.'

'. . .I am surprised to learn that my letters make the Evangelisation Congregation think that I want to have Bishop Pompallier recalled. . . .'[11]

Disappointed over Colin's reply and wondering what steps should be taken next, Epalle spent the evening walking alone on the banks of the Tiber River. His thoughts depressed him even more and he succeeded in returning to his residence at Saint Louis of France Church only with difficulty.

Epalle answered Colin the next day, 8 August, that negotiations at the Evangelisation Congregation had come to a standstill. It had decided to suspend all action until it learned Pompallier's reactions to the measures that it had taken to date and to others that it soon would be taking. The Sacred Congregation had recently told Pompallier 'that he would be receiving a coadjutor', Epalle said, 'and after he arrives, the bishop will be able to come to Rome. But when does it intend to send him the coadjutor? I have no idea.' Colin had sent Epalle new complaints against Pompallier which he had received from New Zealand, and which he wanted Epalle to present to the Evangelisation Congregation. But it 'is tired of this affair and does not read the documentation presented to it', Epalle replied. He personally, however, had no reasons for complaint, because he had always been well received and had always been given a hearing. But he did want to know from Colin how much longer he should stay in Rome.[12]   Two days later, on 10 August, Epalle informed Fransoni that Pompallier had named Forest the fourth provincial superior over the Marists, once again making the nomination independently of all consultation with Superior General Colin. This led to a further meeting with Evangelisation Congregation officials, especially after Epalle submitted Colin's letter of 25 July and also the letters from New Zealand accompanying it, including two pages of regulations that Pompallier had given newly appointed Provincial Superior Forest on 19 March 1843.[13]

It was 22 August when Epalle reported to Colin his most recent meeting with the Evangelisation Congregation. 'In its embarrassment', he said, 'I believe that it will do whatever you want. And if what you want is the status quo, I believe that this can easily be obtained in spite of the letters that have already been sent to Bishop Pompallier, saying that a coadjutor was being sent to him.' Epalle, however, felt that the status quo represented no progress at all and was of benefit to no one. He asked Colin therefore to give some thought to his own ideas on the matter, which were the following.

'The measures taken by the Evangelisation Congregation without asking us for advice were to give Bishop Pompallier a coadjutor, saying to him in effect: "Come to Rome; the good of your mission requires it. Then when you return to your vicariate, if this first coadjutor should not suit you at all, you shall receive another according to your choice." Now the Evangelisation Congregation in addition to this tells us that once Bishop Pompallier is in Rome, it will be possible gently to persuade him not to return to his mission, or to go elsewhere, if the affair should not turn out satisfactory for everyone concerned. Or, if circumstances should call for it, other steps could still be taken.'

Epalle pressed Colin to nominate a coadjutor for Pompallier at once, saying that the Evangelisation Congregation wanted him to choose a candidate who enjoyed both his confidence and that of Pompallier, 'but in the first place yours'. Epalle himself had been asked by officials specifically about the qualifications of Father Forest for this office, but he asked Colin to consider Fathers Petit-Jean and Baty as well. 'But might it not be best of all to send someone who is ignorant of all that has transpired there?' The Evangelisation Congregation wanted to have the candidate's name in time for its next meeting on 10 September, he said. 'According to all appearances a new vicariate will also be decreed at this meeting, but the nomination of the vicar apostolic will be postponed until word is received from you, since your reply is not expected until after my return to Lyon.' Epalle was racing with time, since it was already 22 August and the reply had to be back in Rome before 10 September. 'I have just time enough to get to the post office before it closes', he said.[14]

Mail service was good, and Colin answered on 1 September. He was well pleased with the Sacred Congregation's 'wise suggestion' about a coadjutor, he said, but he needed a bit more time to gather information and could suggest no one for the moment, although he was inclined in favour of Baty. 'But we can decide that when you get to Lyon', Colin said. But before his letter reached Rome, Epalle had already left for Lyon and the Evangelisation Congregation had postponed naming a coadjutor for Pompallier and establishing the new vicariate apostolic.[15]

Epalle while in Rome had succeeded in obtaining a concession from the Evangelisation Congregation, persuading it to allow the Marists to suspend sending personnel to Pompallier until the differences with him should be resolved. This meant that all of the missionary personnel who normally would have gone to New Zealand could now be sent to Melanesia and Micronesia. But Colin would not hear of the Marists taking over any responsibility whatsoever for Micronesia, and he was even hesitant about assuming responsibility for Melanesia. Epalle evidently had detected this earlier, and also from Colin's letter of 25 July, because he was convinced that his society 'did not at all want to take over charge of these missions'. He then tried 'to have them given to the Jesuits', but was not successful. After leaving Rome and discussing the matter more in detail with Colin, and finding him still hesitant, Epalle began visiting the various dioceses of France 'intending to make known the missions of Oceania and their needs'. Meanwhile the Evangelisation Congregation, as Epalle told a friend, 'did not cease to press the Reverend Father General to accept the new missions'.[16]

Fransoni was not slow in applying the promised pressure. He wrote to Colin on 16 September 1843, saying that 'as soon as possible' the matter of giving a coadjutor to Pompallier would be placed on the agenda. But at the same general meeting, he promised, 'we shall deal with the proposed foundation of the two new vicariates apostolic of Northern Australasia and Southern Micronesia, according to the plan suggested by Pro-Vicar Father Epalle'. The cardinal explained that these two vicariates 'at the moment will form only one mission entrusted to the esteemed Society of Marists, until the Sacred Congregation shall be able to relieve it of the responsibility for one of these [vicariates] by sending other missionaries there, since it would be too difficult to manage', as Epalle had remarked, if the Marists were 'to keep charge of both missions for a long time'.

The cardinal said that there could be no doubt about 'the usefulness and necessity' of erecting these two new vicariates. And he requested Colin 'meanwhile to arrange what is needed for sending a group of missionaries to the new vicariate' and to submit the names of those whom he judged the most suitable candidates to head the mission. From these the Evangelisation Congregation would choose 'the vicar apostolic and his coadjutor, as was done for Central Oceania'.[17]

Colin took his time and answered Fransoni on 28 October, sending a list of candidates only for the office of coadjutor for Pompallier. Three years earlier, he told the cardinal, he had 'dared to suggest to Bishop Pompallier the idea of asking for a coadjutor for New Zealand'. And since the country was so vast, 'the interests of religion and the salvation of souls seemed to require that there be one bishop in the northern part and another in the southern part. Such an arrangement would provide a new impetus for the spread of the gospel, it would prevent the missionaries from becoming isolated from their bishop, and it would avoid endless travel which is always very costly.' Colin therefore called Fransoni's decision to give Pompallier a coadjutor 'a measure full of wisdom', and as candidates for the office he suggested three of his priests already in New Zealand: Father Baty, age thirty-three, Father Petit-Jean, age thirty-three, and Father Forest, age thirty-nine. Colin told Fransoni that Epalle had the same qualities as Baty, and was perhaps even a better choice, since he had 'a stronger character, greater vision and more talent for administration'. But Colin did not dare to suggest Epalle, since Pompallier might be very suspicious of him 'because of the circumstances connected with his voyage to Europe and to Rome'.

In the same letter Colin promised 'soon to submit our reply on the new vicariate apostolic to be established in that part of Oceania which includes the archipelagoes of the Carolines, New Guinea, New Britain, etc.' His delay was 'commanded by prudence', he said. But this could not at all harm the mission, because he would be able to accept it only in view of the funds that might be granted to him by the Association for the Propagation of the Faith in Lyon. And its next allocation of funds would not take place until 1844.[18]

Just as Fransoni was about to bring up the matter of a coadjutor for Pompallier at a general meeting, he received an important letter from Pompallier dated 19 October 1842 in reply to his of 12 June 1841. In it Pompallier explained that he had received Fransoni's letter while he was on Wallis in May 1842 and he had had no proper ship connections by which to answer it earlier. Like so many of Pompallier's letters, this one too was very long and highly critical of the Marists. In five different places, for example, the bishop reprimanded his own pro-vicar, Father Epalle, for having wanted to place missionaries at Ponape, for having gone to Europe 'without my authorisation as the result of a small sort of plot among my priests', and for having sub-delegated another pro-vicar to govern the mission in his absence.

But what interested Fransoni most of all was what Pompallier had to say about the inadvisability of setting up Central Oceania as an independent vicariate apostolic, something which in fact had been done at Colin's insistence and without the bishop's knowledge on 8 August 1842. Pompallier gave six reasons why it was *not* opportune to found a vicariate apostolic in Central Oceania! If the Evangelisation Congregation nevertheless should decide to do so, he said, then the new vicariate ought to contain no other islands but Wallis, Futuna, and the Samoa and Tonga archipelagoes, since their inhabitants spoke related languages. He would prefer, however, that these islands should remain under his own jurisdiction for two more years, since after that time he would know whether English authorities in New Zealand intended to expel him. He suggested further that the first vicariate apostolic to be created should be the Fiji Islands, because a paramount chief there had asked him for priests and because its large population spoke practically one language.

Pompallier also offered Fransoni a candidate for the office of bishop and vicar apostolic over the Fiji Islands. He was Pro-Vicar Viard, also a Marist, whom Pompallier earlier had placed in charge of all tropical islands within his vicariate.

Or, if the Evangelisation Congregation wanted to wait two more years, Viard could then be made bishop and vicar apostolic over the Tonga and Samoa islands, including Wallis and Futuna. Pompallier added in a postscript that still another vicariate apostolic could be founded in the Caroline Archipelago by opening a mission on Ascension Island.[19]

Before answering this letter the cardinal wrote to Colin on 12 December 1843, explaining how the matter of Pompallier's coadjutor was about to be brought up in a general meeting, when 'some recent mail from the prelate persuaded the Sacred Congregation to further postpone this election . . ., otherwise he will have another reason to complain that he is not being treated properly'.[20] Fransoni, in fact, had asked Pompallier as early as 4 October 1842 to let him know 'who from among your priests in your judgment would be a worthy and suitable candidate' for the office of coadjutor, and he may have expected a reply to arrive soon.[21]

The cardinal also informed Colin that Pompallier was 'very much opposed' to the idea of separating from his vicariate apostolic 'the islands of Wallis, Fiji, etc., which at present are entrusted to Bishop Bataillon, and for his stand he gives various reasons, which are not to be despised'. But Pompallier had also suggested founding a new vicariate, Fransoni said, that 'might be composed of the Caroline Islands, Ascension, and other islands about which we have an understanding with Your Reverence, all of which are to be set up as a third vicariate apostolic . . . And in case the Carolines Vicariate should be erected, he proposes some candidates for the office of vicar apostolic, agreeing more or less to those proposed by Your Reverence in your letter of 28 October as candidates for his coadjutor. . . .'[22]

It is difficult to see how Fransoni was being honest when he told Colin that Pompallier 'more or less' had suggested for the office of vicar apostolic in the proposed Carolines Vicariate the same candidates whom Colin had suggested for Pompallier's coadjutor. For coadjutor, Colin had suggested three candidates: Baty, Petit-Jean, and Forest. And for vicar apostolic, Pompallier had suggested only one, Viard, and he had not suggested him for the Carolines.

Colin was absent from Lyon for two months and so could not answer Fransoni's letter of 12 December 1843 until 8 February 1844. He was pleased with the news that the election of Pompallier's coadjutor was being postponed, 'because under the present circumstances it would have caused some difficulty. . . .' But he was also puzzled by the cardinal's letter, because he could not tell from it 'whether the foundation of the third vicariate in Oceania was also being postponed'. Clarification on this issue was urgent, he said, 'since the moment is arriving for presentation of the 1844 budget on behalf of the foreign missions to the two councils of the Association for the Propagation of the Faith. . . .'[23]

Before answering Colin's letter Fransoni received still another letter from Pompallier, dated 9 February 1843, in which he said: 'It seems opportune to me to found the following new vicariates apostolic in Western Oceania as soon as possible: Fiji, the Navigators [now Samoa], and the Archipelago of the Carolines in which Ponape or Ascension, one of the principal islands, has been asking for Catholic missionaries for more than four years.' The English Catholics of New Zealand, he added, 'often let me know that they would prefer to have English priests and above all an English bishop.'[24]

Fransoni answered Colin's letter on 12 March 1844. 'Although the creation of the third vicariate apostolic already planned for Western Oceania has been postponed,' he said, 'it nevertheless will be realised as soon as possible.' In fact, now there was further reason to go ahead with the project because Pompallier, although not in favour of the Vicariate Apostolic of Central Oceania, had suggested 'as most opportune' the foundation of a third vicariate apostolic 'composed of the Carolines, Ascension, etc.' The cardinal urged Colin to make all necessary preparations for launching the new vicariate and to obtain special subsidies from the Association for the Propagation of the Faith in France. And once the missionaries had been appointed, Colin was to send Fransoni the names of those whom he judged 'more suitable for governing the new mission and being chosen vicar apostolic'. And if Colin felt that there was need for a coadjutor bishop, as was the case in Central Oceania, he was asked to submit names of candidates for this office as well. But the missionaries were to be sent off at once, even before the actual foundation of the vicariate apostolic and the naming of the vicar apostolic. Meanwhile, Fransoni said, he would inform Pompallier that the new group of missionaries being sent to Western Oceania 'should be directed to the above-indicated regions in order to prepare for the foundation of the agreed-upon vicariate'.[25]

Four days later, on 16 March, Fransoni true to his word wrote to Pompallier, answering his two letters of 19 October 1842 and 9 February 1843. He expressed his regrets that it had been impossible to postpone the foundation of the Central Oceania Vicariate, because Pompallier's reasons in favour of postponement, although sufficient, had arrived too late, after the vicariate had been founded. And so nothing could be done about reserving the Tonga, Wallis and Futuna islands for Pompallier. But there was a new place of refuge to which he could go in case of need. Fransoni explained that 'the formation of another Vicariate of Northern Australasia [or Melanesia] and Southern Micronesia, which you seem to approve', could serve as a substitute place of refuge for the Tonga, Wallis and Futuna islands. 'Then whenever the time arrives in the territory of New Zealand for an English prelate to be placed in charge of the mission, Your Grace could take over the government of the very extensive vicariate to the north mentioned above.[26] We therefore insisted with the superior of your society that he should supply you as quickly as possible with more personnel. Then, once these have been sent on ahead to begin work in the above-mentioned regions, the final steps can be taken to establish the separate vicariate mentioned above.'[27]

Fransoni's letter spurred Colin to action, causing him to write to the Lyon Central Council of the Association for the Propagation of the Faith on 23 March 1844 and two days later to the Paris Central Council. Both received identical letters. 'For about a year[28] the Holy See has been pressing us to bring the faith to that part of Oceania commonly called Melanesia and Micronesia, which it is thinking of forming into a new vicariate apostolic. For a long time we hesitated to accept this third vicariate . . . But finally a letter dated 12 March from His Eminence, Cardinal Fransoni, Prefect of the Evangelisation Congregation, brought our hesitation to an end by definitively charging us with this new mission, which in fact is nothing else but a section of the mission of Western Oceania.' Colin explained that 'this third vicariate' would contain both Melanesia—and then he listed all the islands mentioned by Epalle in his 1 August 1843 proposal—and Micronesia, 'which consists of the Carolines subdivided into a large number of archipelagoes like the Marshalls, Gilberts, etc., etc. . . . .'

Colin said that 'Rome desires one vicar apostolic with a coadjutor bishop for this vast mission.[29] The coadjutor according to the desires of the Holy See is supposed to bring the faith to Micronesia north of the equator, and first of all probably to Ascension Island, whereas the vicar apostolic shall remain in Melanesia and preach the gospel there.'

The purpose of these two letters was to justify the enclosed budget being presented to this fund-collecting organisation. Since 'really two new missions' were being founded simultaneously, Colin said, it was necessary for the Marists to send in addition to the two bishops 'at least eight priests and six catechists', or a total staff of sixteen. And they had to have enough supplies for eighteen or twenty-four months, since they would be isolated for that length of time.

Under seven headings he itemised the costs, totalling 175,400 francs. This included transportation to the mission (52,800 francs), transportation within the mission (8,000 francs), personal effects (33,600 francs), supplies for eighteen or twenty-four months (34,000 francs), building a central station in Melanesia and another in Micronesia (20,000 francs), and 7 per cent interest to be paid on 100,000 francs at Sydney (7,000 francs). The remaining 20,000 francs were budgeted for tools and other equipment needed to teach skills and agriculture; it was 'of the greatest importance' to bring such things to the inhabitants of these islands, since these were 'a means to win them over and would prove useful to them'.[30]

Then on 16 April, Colin wrote to Fransoni, 'Not without trembling have we decided to accept a third vicariate apostolic in Oceania'. He thus formally accepted the new mission, or at least the Melanesian part of it, since he made no mention at all of Micronesia in his letter. It was a great responsibility that he was assuming, he said, since such distant missions were filled with dangers and difficulties of every kind. 'It is necessary to supply them from Europe with even the smallest items and the opportunities for communication are so rare and costly.' He had approached the Association for the Propagation of the Faith, he said, 'to obtain some special help in the course of this year so that we can send off a certain number of missionaries appointed to the new vicariate, which shall be founded in that part of Oceania called Melanesia'.

Colin's choice for vicar apostolic was Father Epalle, age thirty-five, and for coadjutor, Father Antoine Dubreul, age thirty-four. He said that he would soon be sending them to Rome, where he wished them to remain for several months, so that they might obtain advice and information from Fransoni about the new mission territory and might absorb 'the true apostolic spirit at its source'. Before presenting them definitively, however, he wanted them to be 'fully known' to the Evangelisation Congregation. 'May Your Eminence receive them kindly, encourage them and help them with your usual goodness.'

In order to facilitate communication with the missionaries of all three vicariates in Western Oceania, Colin now wanted to establish a procure or supply centre at Sydney, Australia, with some of his priests in charge. The success of missionary work in these three vicariates, he told Fransoni, could be assured if there were such a supply centre in Sydney. He asked Fransoni to intercede on his behalf with Archbishop Polding of Sydney.[31]

Without waiting for a reply, Colin wrote to Fransoni again on 8 May. 'Recently we announced to Your Eminence that soon Fathers Epalle and Dubreul would be arriving in Rome', he said. 'They shall have the honour of presenting you with this letter. . . .' It contained three names for the office of vicar apostolic 'of the new vicariate to be established in that part of Oceania called Melanesia'. The order of preference was: Father Jean-Baptiste Epalle, age thirty-five; Father Jean-Baptiste Gouchon, age thirty-nine; and Father Claude Raccurt, age thirty-five. There were also three names for the office of coadjutor bishop in this order: Father Antoine Dubreul, age thirty-four; Father Jean-Pierre Frémont, age thirty-three; and Father Jean-Louis Rocher, age thirty-four.

Fransoni had earlier asked Colin whether he wanted to send a coadjutor, but in this letter Colin now asked the same of Fransoni: 'Your Eminence, do you intend to give a coadjutor to the vicar apostolic of this new mission at this time? Would it not be rather inconvenient to have two bishops arriving at the same time with a small number of missionaries in the midst of a savage and infidel population. . . ?' He felt that the number of young bishops in his society was growing much too quickly. 'We would earnestly beg Your Eminence by no means to allow the coadjutor to be ordained a bishop in Rome or in Europe', Colin said. 'Instead, please keep the bulls secret until he arrives in Sydney, where he then could receive his episcopal ordination.'[32]

Colin was suddenly pressuring Fransoni to have the new vicariate founded quickly; just three weeks earlier he had written that he would formally submit the names of the candidates only after Epalle and Dubreul had become 'fully known' at the Evangelisation Congregation. He was also showing a lack of interest in Micronesia.

Fransoni had reacted favourably to the supply centre idea and almost at once, on 6 May, had written to Archbishop Polding of Sydney, saying that such a centre would make it easier for the Marists 'to expedite the affairs' connected with their missions in Oceania. He praised Polding's missionary zeal and said that it alone was guarantee enough 'that you will receive these excellent priests with every benevolence' and be of help to them.[33] That same day Fransoni wrote to Colin, enclosing the letter for Polding, assuring him that Polding would give his full cooperation to the Marists in opening a supply centre at Sydney for 'the important missions' of Oceania.[34]

When Colin on 3 June 1844 thanked Fransoni for his letter to Polding, he used the opportunity to present new reasons against the immediate appointment of a coadjutor bishop. He had earlier submitted three candidates for this office, he said, so that the Sacred Congregation would have the list at hand in case it wanted to name a coadjutor. 'But the more I study the matter, the more it seems to me that naming a coadjutor is premature.' Colin believed that unnecessary trouble would be caused, if 'two young bishops depart simultaneously with a small number of priests, not knowing in which island they will settle or in what manner they will be received'. He suggested that the naming of a coadjutor be postponed for one or two years, because 'by that time the vicar apostolic will have fixed his residence definitely in those regions. . . .'[35]

Epalle and Dubreul arrived in Rome on 14 May 1844 and took up residence at Via Bocca di Leone, 55, near the Piazza di Spagna offices of the Evangelisation Congregation. On 17 May they visited Cardinal Fransoni and had a short conversation about the new vicariate. He was friendly, but gave them only vague replies. Epalle told Colin about this visit on 23 May and said that he was keeping himself busy studying canon law. Dubreul spent his time seeing the city and sleeping. And Father C. M. Léopold Verguet, their twenty-seven-year-old companion, spent most of each day 'perfecting himself in painting at one of the better schools in Rome'.[36]

Sending Colin more information on 13 June, Epalle said that they had spoken with Fransoni, Brunelli and Buratti, and had been told that the formation of the new vicariate was on the agenda for July. They had also learned that no coadjutor would be appointed 'according to the wishes of the Very Reverend Father Colin', and Epalle told Colin that he was in full agreement.[37]

In the following week Epalle received a letter from Monsieur Michel-Victor Marziou, a young businessman and fervent Catholic of Le Havre in France. This gentleman, aware of the transportation difficulties which missionaries in Oceania and elsewhere were having, envisioned a religious and commercial shipping company. It was to provide trans-oceanic and inter-island service for missionaries and was to support itself by commerce. Epalle, having served as pro-vicar in New Zealand, knew concretely how great a service this would be for the missions. And so he became deeply interested when Marziou said that his organisation was readying a ship of 300–400 tons for Oceania and that it had already engaged one of the best sailors in Le Havre as captain.

Epalle quickly passed on this information on 22 June to Secretary Brunelli of the Evangelisation Congregation, telling him that the ship would sail 'about the end of September, the favourable season for sailing vessels'. Moreover, Marziou had offered passage 'to all of our missionaries who will be ready to leave'. Epalle prodded the officials with this news (although he denied it later when writing to Colin). 'If the Sacred Congregation for the Evangelisation of Nations is still planning to send some missionaries to Melanesia', he said, 'it perhaps would be necessary to take advantage of this providential opportunity of bringing the missionaries to their destination. Ships leaving Europe go little farther than New Zealand or New Holland. And from those points small ships from time to time leave for the islands of the Central Vicariate, but hardly ever for the islands of Melanesia. Therefore, if we do not take advantage of this opportunity, we shall have to charter a ship for ourselves at Sydney to complete the voyage, something which would be so very costly that we could hardly afford it.' Epalle added that, in order to take advantage of this offer, he 'would have to be in Lyon by the beginning of the month of August at the latest'.[38]

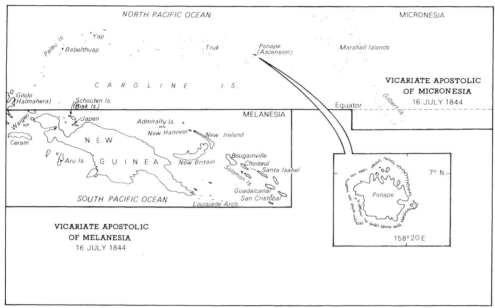

47 The Vicariates Apostolic of Melanesia and Micronesia, founded on 16 July 1844, were originally proposed by Father Epalle of New Zealand on 1 August 1843 while he was in Rome. *(Chapter 17).*

When Epalle wrote to Colin again on 28 June, he told him about passing on the Marziou data to Brunelli, but 'I do not believe that I have failed in my principle of reserve. . . .' The immediate result of his action was that Brunelli considered it necessary to speed up the whole procedure in order not to lose the opportunity which the new shipping company had offered. 'And Monsieur Buratti on his own initiative, without my saying a single word and without his mentioning anything about it to anyone, drew up the report in order to hasten the erection of the vicariate in question.' Epalle had been told that 'in 11 more days all will be completed'.[39]

'The meeting has been postponed to the 15th of this month', Epalle told Colin on Saturday, 13 July. 'And so I cannot tell you anything new today . . . , except that we are certain they will bring up the matter this coming Monday and intend to finish it quickly . . . At the offices of the Evangelisation Congregation we were assured that we would be able to leave [Rome] at the end of July, something which I do not believe.'[40]

It was Monday, 15 July 1844, when the cardinal members of the Evangelisation Congregation gathered to discuss 'The Foundation of a New Vicariate Apostolic in the Western Mission of Oceania'. The project was given added prestige because Cardinal Prefect Fransoni himself was the one who presented and explained it. The purpose of the project, he said, was 'to promote spiritual advantages for the important and very vast missions of Oceania'.

Fransoni's presentation, prepared by Buratti and set up in type, was divided into six sections:

1. Superior General Colin had commissioned Father Epalle, the pro-vicar of Bishop Pompallier, to visit Rome, he said, 'not only to settle some differences that have arisen between his society and the praiseworthy bishop, but also to take up the matter indicated above of founding a new third vicariate'. Number 1 of the *Appendix*, Fransoni pointed out, contained Epalle's detailed report of 1 August 1843 in which he 'explained very accurately the project in question'. (Each presentation prepared for the cardinals contained an *Appendix*, when necessary, in which the more important incoming correspondence connected with a project was printed in full and numbered for easy reference.)

2. After listing Epalle's reasons in favour of the new vicariate and stating that Pompallier would still have sufficient territory left to govern, since New Zealand itself in the course of time would need another bishop to ensure proper vigilance, he explained that 'the new vicariate will be made up of two parts: Melanesia and Micronesia'. Both territories were to remain united for the present, he said, but later could be divided quickly, if exact boundaries for them were determined now. Fransoni then described the two areas geographically, just as Epalle had done in his report of 1 August 1843, suggesting also that those islands of the Gilbert Archipelago which were south of the equator should be removed from the Central Oceania Vicariate and be added to Micronesia, since most of the archipelago was north of the equator. Fransoni then said that Epalle had given assurance that the Marists were prepared to take over both territories—here Fransoni called them 'vicariates'—and would send many missionaries there 'with the clear understanding that, when the moment should come to subdivide it, one of the two [vicariates] would be left in the hands of that society or group of missionaries. . . .'

3. There had been reasons enough to bring the matter to the attention of the cardinals earlier, Fransoni said, 'but it nevertheless seemed very prudent to defer the proposal' in order to learn Pompallier's views about it, 'since it is from his jurisdiction that the territories in question will have to be separated'. Nor had any reaction been received from Pompallier to the creation of the Central Oceania Vicariate. But letters from Pompallier had meanwhile arrived, he said, 'and so it will be up to Your Eminences to decide whether there now are no more obstacles'.

4. Although not a direct reply to the Sacred Congregation's query on the Melanesia-Micronesia proposal, a letter from Pompallier dated 9 February 1843 had mentioned 'the Archipelago of the Carolines' as a possible new vicariate. This meant that he 'agrees almost entirely with the proposal of his pro-vicar. . . .'

Pompallier, however, would have liked 'to keep within his jurisdiction the Wallis Islands and others, which he and his missionaries catechised and which now form the Central Mission, so that he might be able to transfer his residence there in case he should be expelled from New Zealand'. But giving those islands back to Pompallier was out of the question, because they were now part of the Central Oceania Vicariate. This need of Pompallier for a place of refuge, however, was an added reason in favour of founding without delay 'the third vicariate now proposed'. The Marists, namely, would move into both Melanesia and Micronesia and would develop them simultaneously. This would make it possible, should the need arise, 'to separate one from the other in order to form a fourth distinct mission', in order to provide a place 'for Bishop Pompallier to take up residence, as mentioned above'.

There was no immediate need, however, 'to provide New Zealand with an English prelate', Fransoni said, nor was there any necessity to relocate Pompallier and his missionaries at the moment. In fact, even after separating Melanesia and Micronesia, 'many other islands' outside of New Zealand would remain within Pompallier's jurisdiction and 'would still form a very vast vicariate'. One had every reason to hope, Fransoni said, that 'the truly apostolic zeal' of Pompallier would make mission work flourish in these islands. 'Therefore, if it should become necessary to relocate the staff now in New Zealand, there will be no lack of suitable places within his own Western Vicariate in which he can settle and have a very large territory to look after.'[41]

5. Meanwhile Colin, informed by Fransoni of these plans, was 'hastily making preparations to send many missionaries there' and on 8 May 1844 had submitted a list of candidates 'from whom Your Eminences might choose the new vicar apostolic, if you should be in favour of founding this vicariate'. Fransoni mentioned Epalle's name and gave his qualifications, passing over the other two candidates in silence.

6. Fransoni said that Colin had also been invited to present candidates for the office of coadjutor, if he considered it expedient for the mission to have one, and at first he did submit a list of candidates for this office. But serious reservations about sending two bishops at the same time prompted him in a further letter of 3 June to beg 'that the choice of a coadjutor be postponed to a later date, when the new mission is sufficiently established'.

In conclusion Fransoni presented two questions for the vote:

(1) 'Should we approve, and decide to erect as planned, the new vicariate of Melanesia and Micronesia, keeping [the two territories] united for the present, to be formed later into two distinct vicariates?'[42] (2) Should His Holiness be asked to appoint a vicar apostolic with episcopal rank and, if so, who should it be from among the proposed candidates?[43]

The first question repeated exactly the proposal made by Epalle in his report of 1 August 1843, calling for *one* vicariate apostolic containing both Melanesia and Micronesia. Fransoni's report, however, had been somewhat vague on this point. Although often mentioning the proposal as stated by Epalle, Fransoni in one place had referred to Melanesia and Micronesia as *two* vicariates apostolic. The cardinals discussed this particular issue before voting and then decided in favour of founding two vicariates apostolic, one to be called Melanesia and the other Micronesia, which for the present were to remain united under one vicar apostolic with episcopal rank. They chose Epalle to head the new mission.[44]

Decisions of the Evangelisation Congregation were usually brought to the pope for ratification on the following Sunday, and this meeting had been held on Monday. But because it was 'absolutely necessary' for Epalle 'to be in Lyon by the beginning of the month of August', if he was to take advantage of the ship leaving for Melanesia in September, Secretary Brunelli saw Pope Gregory XVI the very next day.

He informed the pope that the cardinals of the Evangelisation Congregation intended to separate some additional territory from the Vicariate Apostolic of Western Oceania. They had decided 'that two other distinct vicariates should be erected, one of which would include Melanesia and the other Micronesia, but in such a way that for the present both missions are to be governed by one and the same vicar apostolic. . . .' Brunelli added that 'the responsibility for this double vicariate, united for the present', would be entrusted to the Marists, who also would provide a vicar apostolic to be given the rank of bishop. The candidate presented was Epalle, a priest 'very highly renowned for his piety, prudence, doctrine, mission experience and zeal for religion. . . .'

Pope Gregory XVI 'benignly approved' the project 'in all its parts and ratified it, ordering that an apostolic letter in the form of a brief be issued both for the creation of the double vicariate and for the election of the vicar apostolic'.

Through this action Pope Gregory XVI on 16 July 1844 founded the Vicariate Apostolic of Melanesia and the Vicariate Apostolic of Micronesia and entrusted them to the Marists under the leadership of Bishop-Elect Epalle.[45]

The decrees and other documents subsequently prepared for public consumption did not indicate the real and immediate causes for this unique arrangement. They merely stated the general principle that 'fostering and promoting the Catholic cause as much as possible requires the foundation of new and separate missions by dividing certain missions and reducing their excessive territory, insofar as this is possible, and by increasing the number of missionaries and bishops'.[46]

Pope Gregory's apostolic letter in the form of a brief telling of the two new vicariates and of Epalle's appointment was dated Friday, 19 July.[47] On the next day Epalle took his oath of fidelity to the pope and made the required profession of faith.[48] And on Sunday, 21 July, Cardinal Prefect Fransoni ordained him Titular Bishop of Sion in the chapel of the Evangelisation Congregation's office building at Piazza di Spagna.[49] The two prelates assisting Fransoni were Archbishop Bonamie, superior general of the Picpus Fathers, then in Rome on business in connection with his order's missions in Eastern Oceania, and Bishop Donald MacDonald of Charlottetown, Canada.[50]

On the day that Cardinal Prefect Fransoni ordained Epalle a bishop,

Secretary Brunelli visited Pope Gregory XVI to obtain for Epalle the spiritual faculties usually granted 'to the vicars apostolic of those far-distant regions', and also a few more faculties that Epalle had specifically requested. The new bishop was allowed 'to promote [candidates] to sacred orders without having dimissorial letters and to dispense from impediments arising from illegitimacy'. He also received 'the indult of a daily privileged altar in perpetuity' and was authorised 'to grant a similar privilege three times a week to the priests of his vicariate'.[51]

Epalle's two companions in Rome, Fathers Dubreul and Verguet, had assisted at his episcopal ordination on Sunday. And on Monday, 22 July, they were received with him in private audience by seventy-eight-year-old Pope Gregory XVI, who showed himself most gracious and friendly toward the young missionaries. 'The French and Irish cross the seas with the same facility as if America and Oceania were on the other side of the Tiber', he quipped, 'but we Italians believe that we are being sent into exile, if we go only as far as Civitavecchia!' He complimented Epalle especially on the sacredness and vastness of the work which he was about to undertake on behalf of religion.[52]

Epalle was still in Rome on 25 July when Fransoni wrote to Pompallier, informing him of the latest turn of events. 'I hope that you long ago have received my letter of 16 March', he said, 'from which you learned among other things that the Sacred Congregation has given its complete approval to your idea proposing that a new vicariate be founded in Northern Australasia (that is, in Melanesia and Southern Micronesia).' Fransoni in that March letter had told Pompallier that the new Marist missionaries arriving in his territory were to make preparations in Northern Australasia *so that at some future date* it could become a vicariate apostolic, in case Pompallier needed a place of refuge.

But since a group of missionaries was ready to leave, he now wrote, and since it was necessary to take advantage of the good dispositions of the people there prior to the arrival of 'the heretics', the cardinals of the Evangelisation Congregation had decided to take action immediately. He explained, however, that Melanesia and Micronesia 'must be considered as two distinct vicariates', which 'shall remain joined together under the authority of one and the same vicar apostolic . . . The reason for this provision was your premonition that you and your personnel at some time might have to leave New Zealand and that you would have to be replaced there by a British bishop. One or other of the vicariates mentioned would then be given to you to govern.'

But there were other possibilities, Fransoni pointed out. Pompallier might never have to leave New Zealand! Or, if he did have to leave, there might be other islands within his jurisdiction where missionary work was flourishing so well that he could settle there! 'In this case another prelate will be chosen for Micronesia or for Melanesia. And if that happens, we would really have reason to rejoice because it would mean that the Western Mission, once so very extensive, would have developed into four or even five (if New Zealand should have to be divided) vicariates, which are not at all small and are most promising. And as time goes on they may have to be divided again. Also the number of bishops placed in charge would be increased to four or five, something that has been found to be most advantageous for the spread of the faith.'

Fransoni assured Pompallier that similar provisions would also be made for the Vicariate Apostolic of Eastern Oceania and for other vicariates. 'For it is clear that individual bishops can more easily and more intensively concern themselves over the needs of the flock entrusted to them, if the size of their territory is restricted.' In his final sentence Fransoni told Pompallier that from the enclosed decree, which established the new mission, he could see that 'the government of the new double vicariate, at present undivided', had been entrusted to Father Epalle, whom His Holiness had raised to the dignity of bishop.[53]

On the same day, 25 July, Fransoni also wrote to Colin, urging him to make haste with the necessary preparations for 'this new and most important mission'. And he told Colin that in his letter to Pompallier he had tried 'to avoid everything which might cause unpleasant surprise'.[54]

Shortly after Epalle received from Fransoni the letters for Colin and Pompallier, he left Rome and arrived in Lyon on 8 August. One of the letters that he delivered to Colin asked him to provide the staff for a college in the Archdiocese of Smyrna (nowadays Izmir), Turkey, entrusted to Archbishop Antonio Mussabini. Colin on 9 August, however, sent his regrets to Fransoni, saying that 'the three vicariates, which the Holy See has desired to entrust to us, claim all the energies of our society at this time. We believe it prudent to concentrate our feeble forces for the moment on Oceania. We even see the vague future possibility of being able to erect a college at Sydney, something which could not fail but have the best results for the missions in these lands.' He urged Fransoni to accept 'our humble excuses' and requested him to forward his regrets to the Archbishop of Smyrna. At the same time he thanked Fransoni for the goodness showered upon Epalle and his companions in Rome and said that the preparations for their departure to Melanesia were already under way. 'The priests destined for this mission will be divided into two groups and we are confident that the first group can leave during the month of September. The others will follow quickly.'[55]

It is interesting to note that in all of Colin's correspondence with Fransoni he consistently speaks only of Melanesia. Epalle gave an explanation of this later in a letter to a colleague in New Zealand, saying that 'the society did not accept anything but Melanesia'.

Epalle from Lyon on 27 August 1844 wrote to Marziou, the businessman in Le Havre. 'Several months have already passed since you kindly informed me that you proposed to prepare a ship for Oceania', he said. 'I would like to let you know immediately that I am altogether ready to book passage together with my colleagues . . . But before making the arrangements definitive, I should have to submit to the Sacred Congregation the plan which you hope to realise with such great zeal.'

He told Marziou that 'in Rome they attach great importance to the realisation of your plans and they will give powerful support to your praise-worthy efforts'. Epalle was well pleased with Marziou's price and other requirements and said that his party would number '15 to 20 . . . Kindly make your arrangements in such a way that I can sail from France toward the end of this coming October. . . .'[56]

Father Dubreul soon departed with two other Marists to found a supply centre in Sydney. But Epalle and his missionaries were still in Lyon on 30 November 1844, when he wrote to Fransoni that '13 of us are going to the mission, both priests and catechists'. Fransoni had donated some funds, and Epalle now thanked him for them. But the Marziou plan had failed, since there was no telling when that company's first ship would sail from Le Havre for Oceania, and so Epalle frankly told the cardinal that the donated funds were far too little for his needs. 'The cost of arriving at our destination will be immense', he said, 'because to all appearances we shall be obliged to charter a ship at Sydney to bring us to Melanesia, whose islands are still so seldom visited.'[57]

When in Paris doing research to learn where it would be best for him to start, Epalle was surprised to see how interested the business world was in Melanesia. He told Colin on 15 December 1844 about a company which called itself Société cosmopolite and drew settlers from France, England, Holland and Germany. 'It is being organised at this moment', he said, 'and its first ship is scheduled to leave from Holland with 50 families headed for New Guinea.' Epalle had received these details from the principal French agent of the company, who had sought him out after seeing news in the press that he soon would be leaving for Melanesia. 'If I am not mistaken, this company is far from being religious,' Epalle said, 'even though it puts no obstacles in the way of the propagation of the gospel.'

He told Colin that daily he was discovering 'that many heads are occupied with the Melanesian archipelagoes, and above all with New Guinea. This makes me reflect a great deal on which area I ought to occupy on my arrival.' He wanted to bring glory to Catholicism and to the Marist Society and so he was thinking of occupying as quickly as possible the principal archipelagoes of Melanesia and sending as soon as possible 'three or four priests and as many Brothers to the Solomon Islands', the same number to 'New Ireland and New Britain, each of which can become a diocese', and also the same number 'to each of the four or five principal points in New Guinea'. Then, after these bases were firmly established, each one would become 'a vicariate as soon as possible'.[58]

Word somehow reached Captain Peter Dillon in London that Epalle was preparing to leave for Western Oceania with a large number of missionaries, and so he wrote to Colin on 21 December: 'I have not heard from you for a long time. . . .' He had a Roman Catholic friend named Captain Jackson, he said, 'who had visited the New Hebrides, Santa Cruz, New Guinea and all the other islands', and could speak native languages fluently. Jackson had bought a 200-ton ship and was sailing to Sydney soon. Dillon said that Jackson's fees certainly would be cheaper than those of anyone else and that he would bring the bishop and his missionaries directly to the islands where they wanted to go. There would be no other passengers aboard, only missionaries.

Six days later, on 27 December, Dillon again wrote to Colin, saying that he himself intended to make the voyage with Captain Jackson to Sydney and Tahiti. 'I own some houses and some land in Sydney, which I want to sell, and I have several hundred head of cattle in Tahiti, which I plan to slaughter and sell. . . .' He would be most happy to share his knowledge of Western Oceania with the new missionaries, he said, since he was 'the only person now alive who has visited these islands in the Western Pacific, namely, the [New] Hebrides Islands, New Caledonia, Santa Cruz, New Ireland, New Britain and the eastern part of New Guinea'.

But four days later, on 31 December, Dillon wrote again, saying that Jackson had changed his mind about taking passengers to Sydney. The ever-resourceful Dillon, however, had another plan. He suggested that Colin's missionaries take the 430-ton sailing vessel *Ganges* to Sydney. He had gone aboard, found it satisfactory, and enclosed a sketch showing the location of all cabins.[59]

Meanwhile Epalle had been in Paris for a month making final preparations for his departure. Illness had incapacitated him for nearly a week. 'I have taken advantage of this time to acquire more extensive information about the islands of Melanesia', he wrote Fransoni on 2 January 1845, 'and I am all the more convinced of the urgency for Catholicism to make haste, if it wishes to have the glory of arriving first in these lands so little known up to this era.' He told the cardinal that various business ventures were concentrating on Melanesia and he referred especially to Société cosmopolite, about which he had already written to Colin. 'It is made up of born Protestants and of businessmen who have preserved nothing of Catholicism but the name', he said. 'This causes me the greatest alarm.'

Wanting to acquaint Fransoni with his mission strategy, he said that three distinct areas in Melanesia 'will certainly arouse the cupidity' of businessmen: New Guinea, New Ireland-New Britain, and the Solomon Archipelago. Formerly 'their fear of the ferocity of the inhabitants' had kept them away, but now they had begun to understand this ferocity better. But once the Europeans should begin to penetrate these islands, Epalle said, the conversion of the inhabitants would become more difficult, 'since then we shall have to combat not only paganism, but also heresy and disbelief'.

Repeating with some modifications the project which he had spelled out for Colin eighteen days earlier, Epalle told Fransoni that it was 'of the utmost importance to found as quickly as possible a base of operations in the Solomons, a second one in New Ireland-New Britain, and four others in New Guinea'. He assured the cardinal that Colin was occupied 'more than ever with the means of implanting Catholicism firmly and without delay' in Oceania, and that from Colin he expected to receive the priests necessary to realise his project. His proposal to Fransoni was that these six bases of operations ought to be made independent vicariates apostolic soon after their foundation. 'I believe that this would be the way to implant the faith there more solidly, to ward off heresy from those places more surely, to avoid isolation for the missionaries, and to multiply those institutions which give a firm foundation to the church and assure its perpetuity.'

Epalle insisted, however, that 'it is altogether impossible for one bishop to look after the needs of such extensive lands, since New Guinea alone has an area one-third larger than that of France'. He therefore begged the cardinal 'not to wait for replies from me [to your letters] before you alleviate my episcopal responsibilities . . . , since such delays could create obstacles to the progress of the gospel in these areas'. Epalle wanted Fransoni to feel perfectly free in giving him a coadjutor or in dividing his territory.[60]

On the same day, 2 January 1845, Epalle sent a lengthy report on Melanesia and Micronesia to the Central Council of the Association for the Propagation of the Faith in Lyon. He had said nothing at all about Micronesia in his letter to Fransoni and in this letter spoke only briefly about it. 'Micronesia was not accepted by the Society of Mary except in the last instance, when the Holy See promised to discharge us of this responsibility as soon as possible.' The responsibility assumed by the Marists consisted in 'sending at least two priests to Ascension in the Caroline Archipelago to supply a particular need which is too complicated to explain here . . . And for this reason a temporary union of the two vicariates was agreed upon. . . .'

The young bishop spoke in great detail about Melanesia. He said that its land masses were separated, 'so to speak, only by channels or straits'. And from San Cristóbal to the southeast, as far as Gilolo, the point farthest to the northwest, a distance of 875 leagues, 'the largest body of water separating one area from another is not more than 26 or 27 leagues long'. He said that 'New Guinea alone, whose position makes it the centre of the mission, has a surface area of 40,000 square leagues . . . And you know, gentlemen, that it will not fail to contain numerous natives, since the coasts that have been only half explored contain 700,000 people according to the estimates of voyagers.' He added that the Solomon Islands had an area of more than 2,200 square leagues, that New Britain had 3,200 square leagues, and that Waigeo had 'at least 100,000 inhabitants'.

Although Catholicism would be first to arrive in these new territories, he said, businessmen and Protestant missionaries were sure to follow. His plan for establishing bases in Melanesia was spelled out here much more precisely than in his letters to Colin and Fransoni. He said that there would be one each in New Britain, New Ireland, and the Solomon Islands, and four in New Guinea. Each of these seven bases was to receive four priests and four Brothers, making a total of twenty-eight priests and twenty-eight Brothers. These seven focal points, he explained, would give him control over the islands concerned and from them he could acquire influence over all other islands in Melanesia. He assured the Lyon fund-collecting organisation that he had submitted this plan to Father Colin who 'approves of it and has kindly promised to send me the necessary personnel, since at this time the good God is providing numerous vocations for the apostolate. . . .' He also reminded them that nearly one-fourth of his personnel requirements were already taken care of since seven priests and six Brothers 'will be departing with me'.

He explained that he was assigning 'a rather large number of Brothers' to each central station, because 'being the first ones to arrive there, we shall obtain land at little cost and shall begin to cultivate it at once. In this way I hope that soon I shall no longer be a [financial] burden to you', because 'a place firmly founded suffices to assure the conquest of an island and also the future material welfare of a mission. . . .'[61]

Epalle had not forgotten Marziou and sent him new encouragement from London on 14 January 1845. 'Tell me a bit about the progress and the difficulties connected with your work, which interests me to such a great degree. Every piece of information that I receive about Oceania convinces me more and more that the richest country in that part of the world is New Guinea and that commerce will discover resources there. Do not fail to send me some news about Monsieur Marceau.' Marceau had agreed to take command of the ship.

Writing to Colin from London on 18 January 1845 Epalle said that the Bishop of London was most friendly to him. 'I go to say Mass in his private chapel each day and [he is so hospitable that] I have not yet been able to pass up taking breakfast with him.'[62]

As if by afterthought Colin on 20 January hastily informed Epalle that he had been chosen to serve as religious superior over his missionaries and that Father Frémont had been named his admonitor.[63]

It was 2 February 1845 when Epalle and his thirteen young missionaries finally set sail from London aboard the *Bussorah Merchant* for Sydney.[64] Their ultimate destination was Melanesia, where the young and zealous bishop would immediately be greeted by Death!

18

The Vicariate Apostolic of the Sandwich Islands

18 JULY 1844

The French government took energetic action with the Sandwich Islands (now Hawaii) government after Fathers Bachelot and Maigret were expelled in November 1837. As a result Bishop Rouchouze was able personally in May 1840 to bring three new missionaries to the Sandwich Islands, the northernmost part of his Vicariate Apostolic of Eastern Oceania. Three more missionaries joined them before the end of that year and from then on Catholic missionary work could be carried on with little interference.[1]

With new opportunities springing up everywhere it was clear that Bishop Rouchouze needed more missionary personnel. He also needed a ship of his own to transport his missionaries to their island outposts and to keep in contact with them. In order to achieve both objectives, he decided that it would be far more effective for him to appear on the scene personally than merely to correspond with Europe. So he sailed from Honolulu on 3 January 1841 via Valparaíso to France, bringing with him two Mangareva youths from the Gambier Islands and two young Hawaiians.

Bishop Rouchouze was most successful in getting a ship and personnel. With funds received in France he had a brig built at Saint-Malo in northwestern France. It weighed 128 tons and was registered as a French vessel on 15 November 1842. It was christened *Marie-Joseph* in honour of the late Superior General Marie-Joseph-Pierre Coudrin, who had always signed himself simply Marie-Joseph in letters to his priests, and was considered by them to be the founder of the Eastern Oceania missions.

Rouchouze had confidence in a certain Eugene O'Sullivan of Boston, who had captained the ship on which he had sailed from Hawaii to Valparaíso on his way to France. He wrote to Captain O'Sullivan, invited him to bring the *Marie-Joseph* from Saint-Malo to Valparaíso and Hawaii, and O'Sullivan agreed. When the captain left the east coast of the United States for France, his twenty-year-old bride left for Hawaii to await her husband there.

Bishop Rouchouze was also most fortunate in the number of missionaries he enlisted. From his own Picpus community he received six priests, one subdeacon, and seven lay Brothers. From the Sisterhood branch of the Picpus community, also founded by Coudrin and bearing the same name as his community of men, Rouchouze received eight teaching Sisters and two non-teachers, whom he destined for Valparaíso and Honolulu. Captain O'Sullivan arrived from Boston, gathered together a crew of thirteen, and set sail with

Bishop Rouchouze and his twenty-four missionaries from Saint-Malo on Thursday, 15 December 1842. Also on board was one of the Mangareva youths; the other had died from the climate. One of the Hawaiians had also died, and the other wanted to remain in France. Superior General Bonamie, who saw his missionaries off, described the venture in detail in a circular letter which he immediately sent to the men and women members of his communities. It was the greatest Roman Catholic missionary enterprise ever undertaken on behalf of Oceania.[2]

As Bishop Rouchouze left France behind and headed toward the high seas in his own ship and with a host of missionaries at his disposal, he had good reason to hope that missionary work and schooling could now advance at a rapid pace in his Vicariate of Eastern Oceania.

Five months, ten months, fifteen months passed. But no word on the safe arrival of Bishop Rouchouze and his twenty-four missionaries in Valparaíso or Honolulu reached the Paris headquarters of the Picpus Fathers! Superior General Archbishop Bonamie began to fear that all the missionaries had been lost at sea, perhaps shipwrecked while rounding perilous Cape Horn. And with each new day his fears increased. His letters to Cardinal Prefect Fransoni of the Evangelisation Congregation in Rome carried the terse refrain: Still no word about Bishop Rouchouze and his companions!

It was only natural that Bonamie should be concerned about providing a new ecclesiastical superior to head the important Vicariate Apostolic of Eastern Oceania if Rouchouze actually had perished. When Rome did not react to the fears that he had expressed, he visited Archbishop Raffaele Fornari, nuncio apostolic in Paris, and discussed the matter with him on 17 April 1844. According to Fornari, Bonamie said that Bishop Rouchouze must have been lost at sea, 'since for 18 months no news has arrived about him, nor about the ship on which he was sailing. . . .' Bonamie therefore believed that the Evangelisation Congregation could safely take up the business of naming a new vicar apostolic to succeed Rouchouze, 'or at least a coadjutor with right of succession, who would be authorised to declare himself to be the vicar apostolic at the time when confirmation should reach the vicariate that Bishop Rouchouze in fact has perished'.

Bonamie asked Fornari if he would kindly get in touch with Rome on the matter and he did so the very next day, 18 April. 'Archbishop Bonamie has no doubt at all about their having perished', Fornari said in his letter to Cardinal Fransoni. He strongly supported Bonamie's request that a successor or at least a coadjutor bishop should be appointed for the missing Bishop Rouchouze. 'Both the need for having present a bishop in those archipelagoes, which are so far away from other archipelagoes and from every continent, and the fact that those places have been deprived [of a bishop] for such a long time, made me readily consent to the archbishop's request', he said.

But there was another proposal made by Bonamie to which Nuncio Fornari did not give any support. In fact, he strongly opposed it and told Fransoni why. Bonamie was of the opinion that he ought to inform the Minister of the Colonies of France that the pope most likely would soon name a successor for Bishop Rouchouze. The Picpus superior general had stated that the French government now looked upon the Marquesas Islands, part of the Vicariate Apostolic of Eastern Oceania, as a colony, 'and because of this it provides funds for divine worship and for the needs—at least in part—of the clergy'. Bonamie's thinking was that the French government in view of this financial assistance might expect to have a say in the nomination of the new vicar apostolic. He also thought that the government, if not advised beforehand, might take action to impede the bishop 'in the exercise of his jurisdiction'.

Fornari, however, forbade Bonamie to approach the Minister of the Colonies without first obtaining the view of Cardinal Fransoni. 'I for my part', Fornari told Fransoni, 'shall never allow the government to usurp the right of nominating vicars apostolic. I have already informed both the king and his ministers that the Holy Father cannot in any case allow . . . a king, whosoever he may be, to nominate a vicar apostolic. This would be a monstrosity! Just as the King of France would not allow the pope to name a civil or military governor in a [French] colony, so too the pope cannot allow one of his vicars apostolic to be named by the king.' If the king were to have a part in the nomination of any one of them, 'this would create a very great obstacle to the exercise of spiritual jurisdiction, because the king might claim that his consent would be needed in order to revoke the faculties' originally granted by Rome.

This argumentation, Fornari said, had proven satisfactory to the king and his ministers, and so interference from them 'need no longer be feared'. But he felt that the government, in view of the fact that it would be providing support for the bishop, 'would want to know ahead of time at least the name of the candidate'. He was convinced, however, 'that it would exact nothing else but that he be a *persona grata*'. Fornari gave Fransoni his own views, he said, 'so that you, who have greater knowledge of the matter, can take that stand which you consider more suitable for the case in question'.[3]

Not yet in possession of Fornari's letter of 18 April 1844, and consequently unaware of the nature of his discussion with Bonamie on the previous day, Cardinal Prefect Fransoni reacted as if by mental telepathy on 25 April in a letter to Bonamie. 'The fact that there is still no news of Bishop [Rouchouze] of Nilopolis and his companions makes it practically certain now that the ship transporting this expedition, as you feared, has become lost at sea. This urges me to recommend all the more that you zealously take action to repair the deplorable loss suffered by that important and vast mission and provide it with new personnel. Further, it would seem opportune not to postpone any longer the choice of another bishop, who with the title at least of coadjutor to Bishop Rouchouze (as long as there is still some hope of his being alive) would assume pastoral care of the vicariate after being endowed with the requisite faculties.' Fransoni also asked Bonamie to submit several candidates from among his missionaries already on the spot and to indicate at the same time who among them was the most worthy of the episcopacy. 'Without delay' the cardinal could then bring up the matter at the next General Meeting of the Evangelisation Congregation.[4]

When Cardinal Fransoni's letter arrived in Paris, Bonamie was visiting various Picpus foundations in France, and so the letter was forwarded to him. He replied on 16 May that the majority of his General Council had voted for the following candidates: (1) Father Simplicien Duboize, born on 31 January 1800; (2) Father (Désiré-) Louis Maigret, born on 14 September 1804; and (3) Father François-Toussaint Caret, born on 14 July 1802. He said that Duboize was in the Marquesas Islands, Maigret in the Sandwich Islands, and Caret in Tahiti. 'It seems to me that the most capable of these three priests would be Father Duboize.' And he added that there still was no news about Bishop Rouchouze.[5]

Bonamie on his return to Paris hurried to the offices of Nuncio Fornari, curious to learn whether he had received a reply from Rome. Fornari did have a letter from Fransoni, dated 11 May, in which the cardinal expressed his complete readiness to supply Eastern Oceania with a coadjutor drawn from the candidates to be presented by Superior General Bonamie. At the same time he praised Fornari for dissuading Bonamie from speaking about this matter to the Minister of Colonies. By doing so Bonamie 'would have created obstacles instead of removing them', Fransoni said.[6]

But Bonamie was also curious about Rome's reaction to another request. He had asked that the Sandwich Islands be set up as an independent vicariate apostolic. During his earlier visit with Fornari on 17 April he had discussed this matter and had asked him to sound out Rome on the proposal. Fornari had done this in his letter written the next day. In that letter he informed Cardinal Fransoni that Bishop Rouchouze before leaving Paris had told Superior General Bonamie that 'he believed his vicariate apostolic ought to be divided because of the immense distances between the various places . . . From the Sandwich Islands to the Marquesas Islands alone there was a distance of 1,500 leagues.' According to Rouchouze this distance made it 'expedient to create a separate vicariate apostolic for the Sandwich Islands', especially since these islands already had 'more then 12,000 Catholics and also some schools'.[7]

The Rouchouze-Bonamie-Fornari proposal that the Sandwich Islands should become a separate vicariate apostolic was a complete surprise to Fransoni, but he did not present a single objection. In fact, he welcomed it, saying that Bonamie should be told to submit a list of names longer than originally requested, so that from it 'a vicar apostolic can be elected for the Sandwich Islands and, if need be, also a coadjutor for him, in order to avoid every danger of such remote regions being completely deprived of having a shepherd'. He also instructed Fornari to urge Superior General Bonamie 'to make good insofar as possible' the loss of priests by sending other priests to take their place.[8]

Fornari had pointed out in his letter of 18 April to Fransoni a special reason which seemed to him to indicate the urgency and advisability of separating the Sandwich Islands from the Vicariate Apostolic of Eastern Oceania. He had said that the Marquesas Islands, part of the Eastern Oceania Vicariate, were now considered by the French government as a colony. But the Sandwich Islands, also part of the Eastern Oceania Vicariate, had nothing at all to do with France. The bishop in charge was of course French, and his activity in the Sandwich Islands might well manifest influences 'coming more or less directly from France'. This could in turn antagonise the other powers and lead them 'to obstruct the exercise of his jurisdiction and also ask for his expulsion'. This danger would be obviated by making the Sandwich Islands a separate jurisdictional area.[9]

For Fransoni, however, the argument of distance and of 'more than 12,000 Catholics' was sufficient for making the Sandwich Islands an independent vicariate apostolic. Although he had not anticipated such a proposal, he readily agreed, when writing to Fornari on 11 May 1844, that it 'too can become part of the same position paper which will treat of the choice of a coadjutor for the Eastern Vicariate'. Bonamie, therefore, was asked to send Rome 'with haste' his list of candidates. And Fransoni gave assurance that 'in any event the coadjutor of Bishop Rouchouze will be in charge of the Eastern Mission, with the exception of the vicariate to be erected in Sandwich'. He added that 'the Marquesas Islands will also be excluded, since they will constitute a mission to be cared for by the Holy Ghost Seminary, there being no other arrangement possible'. The cardinal was here referring to the practice adopted by the Evangelisation Congregation of entrusting missionary work in all French colonies to the priests of this Paris seminary. By this time the Marquesas Islands for all practical purposes were a French colony.[10]

Bonamie, however, was not at all pleased at hearing this news and gave Fornari arguments in favour of letting the Marquesas Islands remain part of the Picpus Vicariate of Eastern Oceania. Fornari's new letter of 18 June 1844, reporting to Fransoni on this second meeting with Bonamie, said that the Picpus superior general 'believes it would be best to leave all the rest of the Oceania mission like it is now, separating from it only the Sandwich Islands (which are so very distant). He does not think it advisable to separate the Marquesas Islands from the rest of the mission.'

Fornari, thinking that Fransoni might go ahead with his plan in spite of Bonamie's request, added a word of caution, advising the cardinal 'not to decide quickly about giving the new mission to the Holy Ghost Seminary'. Using information that was strictly confidential, he said 'it appears that this seminary is on the verge of collapse for lack of personnel and students and because of the [type of] education which it provides. The Reverend Abbé Fourdinier foresees that his seminary can no longer continue and has come here just now to tell me that he is busy with a plan of reorganisation. He will try to win over a certain number of priests—men respected for their piety, zeal and knowledge—and have them join his community. In this way he hopes to give his community and his seminary new life and new splendour. As soon as he completes his plan and informs me, I shall dutifully submit it to Your Most Reverend Eminence so that you may pass on it whatever judgment you in your wisdom should consider more correct. I shall then wait for corresponding instructions from you . . . I do not know, however, whether he will succeed in having this institution regain the reputation which it unfortunately has lost. . . .'[11]

Cardinal Fransoni had told Nuncio Fornari that 'the project mentioned by you of erecting a new vicariate in the Sandwich Islands . . . can become part of the same position paper which will treat of the choice of a coadjutor for the Eastern Vicariate'. Knowing that Fransoni wasted no time, Fornari assured him in his 18 June letter that Bonamie would hasten to send the additional names of candidates needed for the Sandwich Islands. 'Perhaps by the time I finish writing this, he will already have carried out this new order of Your Most Reverend Eminence.' Fransoni waited, but no letter came from Bonamie, and so he held the General Meeting on 15 July 1844.[12]

The position paper had a very general heading, 'Some Measures to Be Taken for the Vicariates Apostolic of Western and Eastern Oceania', and was presented by Cardinal Prefect Fransoni himself. Its two parts, he said, were 'aimed at promoting the spiritual advantage of the important and vast missions of Oceania'. Part one was devoted to the Marist proposals on Melanesia and Micronesia and was discussed first, as already described in the previous chapter of this book. Part two was titled: 'On the Choice of a Coadjutor for the Reverend Bishop [Rouchouze] of Nilopolis, Vicar Apostolic of Eastern Oceania, and on the Erection of a New Vicariate Apostolic in the Sandwich Islands'. The report said that the proposals for Eastern Oceania were 'no less important and necessary' than those for Western Oceania.

The cardinals were told how Bishop Rouchouze had come to Paris and Rome for 'serious matters concerning his mission', had purchased a ship, and had then set sail again for Eastern Oceania with many priests, lay Brothers and nuns. The lay Brothers would be 'so helpful because they evangelise those infidel populations' and the nuns would 'instruct girls and give them a Catholic education'. But it was now feared that the bishop and his missionaries had all been shipwrecked, Fransoni said, because almost two years had passed since their departure and still 'no news has been received from any port about the ship in question stopping there'. It was therefore advisable to appoint a coadjutor for the missing Bishop Rouchouze and 'the most meritorious and capable' candidate for this office was Father Duboize.

After explaining to the cardinals how Superior General Bonamie had wanted to advise the French Minister of Colonies of the imminent appointment of a coadjutor, and how Nuncio Fornari had 'wisely opposed' such action and thus guaranteed that there would be 'no ugly dispute with the [French] Court', the cardinal gave the background on the Sandwich Islands proposal. Bonamie had discussed with Fornari 'the erection of a separate vicariate apostolic in the Sandwich Islands in view of the immense distances between the places, the large Catholic population of those same islands, and other similar wise reflections'. Fornari at Rome's request had then invited Bonamie to submit a list of candidates for the office of Vicar Apostolic of the Sandwich Islands 'in the event that Your Eminences should approve of the project'. Although Bonamie's list of candidates 'at the moment' had not yet arrived, the cardinals nevertheless could decide to erect the new vicariate apostolic, if they wished to do so. He promised that 'as soon as a reply comes from Archbishop Bonamie, a verbal report will be made on it at the next meeting'.

Two separate articles were then voted upon. (1) Should His Holiness be asked to name for Bishop Rouchouze, Vicar Apostolic of Eastern Oceania, a coadjutor 'with the right of future succession and with the faculty of taking upon himself immediately the government of the vicariate, if it unfortunately proves true' that Rouchouze has died, 'which is feared to be the case'? The vote was affirmative and the cardinals chose Duboize as their candidate. (2) 'Should a new and distinct Vicariate Apostolic of the Sandwich Islands be erected by separating these from the other islands contained in the Eastern Mission, with the choice of a vicar apostolic being left dependent upon the report expected soon from Archbishop [Bonamie] of Chalcedon?' The vote on this point, too, was affirmative. As for the choice of candidate, the cardinals delegated their authority to Cardinal Fransoni, saying that he in consultation with the pope should determine which candidate on the list ought to be made vicar apostolic.[13]

On 16 July, the day after the decisions were made and before they could be presented to Pope Gregory XVI for ratification, Bonamie arrived in person at the offices of the Evangelisation Congregation. He urgently requested Fransoni to present to the pope for the office of coadjutor in place of Duboize a different candidate, namely Father Joseph Baudichon, born on 18 September 1812. 'He has been in the Marquesas Islands since the beginning of this mission', Bonamie said. 'Moreover, he is loved and esteemed by both the indigenes and the French living in the islands. And the King of France has sent him the Cross of Honour in recompense for services rendered to the French Expedition at the time when this archipelago was taken in possession.' As for Duboize, also an excellent candidate, Bonamie asked that he be placed in charge of the Sandwich Islands Vicariate. He insisted that 'this substitution and change has been suggested for the greater good of the two respective missions. . . .'[14]

Three days after the cardinals had reached their decisions, Secretary Brunelli in an audience with Pope Gregory XVI explained why Superior General Bonamie now wanted some of those decisions changed. The pope had no objections and named Baudichon the coadjutor of Bishop Rouchouze, just as Bonamie had requested. He also established the Vicariate Apostolic of the Sandwich Islands (now Honolulu Diocese) and named Duboize its first bishop and vicar apostolic. The date was 18 July 1844. The two papal briefs promulgating these decisions were dated 13 August 1844. Baudichon was in the Marquesas Islands when he received news on 29 March 1845 of his appointment. The closest bishop was in Santiago, so he had to go there for his episcopal ordination. He had to wait until 31 May before a ship left the Marquesas Islands, bringing him to Tahiti, and from there on 2 July to Valparaíso, Chile, where he arrived on 14 August 1845. The two papal briefs for him and Duboize, necessary for the episcopal ordination to be licit, came via France with missionaries en route 150 days and finally arrived on 10 December. On Sunday, 21 December 1845, Baudichon was ordained a bishop in the Santiago cathedral and the next day sailed with newly

48   The *Marie-Joseph*, named in honour of the Very Reverend Marie-Joseph Coudrin, was lost at sea early in 1843 with Bishop Rouchouze aboard and six priests, one subdeacon, seven lay Brothers and nine Sisters. *Source: SSCC. Painting by Richard Reimans (1931). (Chapter 18).*

arrived missionaries for the Marquesas Islands, arriving there on 23 January 1846.[15]

Duboize, however, refused the office of Vicar Apostolic of the Sandwich Islands and was merely a spectator in the Santiago cathedral on 21 December 1845. Rome asked Bonamie on 7 March 1846 to write to Duboize and have him return the papal briefs if he had not yet been ordained a bishop. Duboize then wrote to the pope. He said that 'some truly grave circumstances' made it impossible for him 'to accept the episcopal dignity and the pastoral rule of this mission', and he begged the pope to choose someone else in his place. But Pope Gregory XVI, who had made Duboize both vicar apostolic and bishop, died on 1 June 1846. He was succeeded later that month by Pope Pius IX, who on 30 August 1846 accepted Duboize's resignation. That same day at the request of the Evangelisation Congregation the pope named in his place 'the Reverend [Désiré-] Louis Maigret, a priest highly to be commended for his piety, prudence, doctrine and zeal for religion, who for a long time has excellently fulfilled the duties of prefect apostolic in the same mission'. Cardinal Fransoni on 30 September sent Superior General Bonamie the news about the appointment of Maigret, who like Duboize before him was made Titular Bishop of Arad and Vicar Apostolic of the Sandwich Islands.[16]

But what had happened to Bishop Rouchouze and his missionaries, to Captain O'Sullivan and his crew? The *Marie-Joseph* had nearly crossed the Atlantic Ocean when twenty-four-year-old Sister Calliste Le Gris died at sea on Friday, 20 January 1843. Since the missionaries were reluctant to give up her body to the waves, and since the *Marie-Joseph* was only three days off the coast of Brazil, Captain O'Sullivan made an unscheduled stop to bury her on 23 January at São Miguel (on the mainland) near Florianópolis, capital of the state of Santa Catarina.[17] But before the *Marie-Joseph* was ready to sail again, Evaristo, the Mangareva youth, took sick and needed hospital care. He entered Caridade hospital at Florianópolis on 16 February and died there five days later. Some time afterwards the *Marie-Joseph* left 'for Chile', as the records at Florianópolis say.

In the following month a Frenchman on the high seas in the vicinity of the Falkland Islands saw a sailing vessel, readily identifiable as a French ship, fighting a storm and heading toward Cape Horn. He noted in his diary or log that it was 13 March 1843 and that the position of his ship at the time was 51° latitude and 62° longitude. Much later, on learning of the *Marie-Joseph*'s disappearance, he informed the Picpus Fathers of what he had seen. Perhaps it was the ship of Bishop Rouchouze, he said.[18] Yes, perhaps. No other word was ever heard.

19

Tonga is returned to Pompallier

12 JANUARY 1845

Father Guillaume Douarre, a Marist priest, was named coadjutor for Bishop-Elect Bataillon, Vicar Apostolic of Central Oceania, and was ordained a bishop in Lyon, France, on 18 October 1842.[1] He had been given this office so that he in turn could ordain Bataillon a bishop on the island of Wallis (or Uvea). This he did on 3 December 1843 'in the principal church called Saint Joseph . . . in the presence of the king, various local leaders', French naval officers and sailors, and a large crowd of neophytes.[2]

Bataillon thanked Cardinal Prefect Fransoni of the Evangelisation Congregation on 8 December for making him a bishop. 'In the new Vicariate Apostolic of Central Oceania', he said, 'there are until now no more than three islands which have been able to receive the benefits of the faith. On the island of Uvea or Wallis all 3,600 souls with only a few exceptions have been converted and baptised . . . Futuna Island with about 700 souls . . . has also been entirely converted, but all have not yet been baptised . . . And on the island of Tongatapu there are about 12,000 souls. . . .' All other archipelagoes in his vicariate, he said, had not yet been evangelised.[3]

One of the first decisions for Bataillon to make was where to send his coadjutor, since he did not need a second bishop on the tiny island of Wallis. At this time the Marists knew that France had 'designs on the Solomon Archipelago', and that it wished to prepare for the seizure of those islands by first taking possession of New Caledonia.[4] Bataillon was also aware that New Caledonia was 'very little explored'. Douarre was eager to go there, however, thinking that the French would begin colonising it without delay. And so Bataillon placed New Caledonia and nearby New Hebrides, both parts of his vicariate apostolic, under the young bishop's care.[5]

Julien Laferrièrre, captain of the French corvette *Bucéphale*, was present with his officers at the episcopal ordination of Bataillon. Some days later he brought Bishop Douarre and his missionaries via Futuna (9 December) to New Caledonia, which they sighted on 19 December. The following day the ship anchored at Port Balade and on 21 December, feast of Saint Thomas the Apostle, Douarre went ashore for the first time. Chief Païama of Mahamata village nearby had come aboard ship on 20 December. Douarre decided to build his first mission station alongside his village, because the chief was friendly and because his village was close to the port. Mass was said aboard ship on Sunday, 24

December, and on Christmas Day the bishop celebrated Mass at Mahamata, the first Mass on land in New Caledonia.

A residence for the missionaries was completed on 15 January 1844 and their goods were put ashore on Sunday, 21 January. The following day Laferrièrre sailed away, leaving the missionaries behind as the only Europeans on the island. He had succeeded on New Year's Day in having Chief Païama and also Chief Pakili-Pouma of the Pouma tribe sign a statement that they 'recognised from this date forward the full and entire sovereignty' of France. And on his departure he promised them that a French warship would visit the island five months later. He also gave the missionaries enough flour for five months.[6]

Laferrièrre's mailbag contained a letter written by Douarre on 16 January to the cardinal prefect of the Evangelisation Congregation. The bishop explained that he had been placed in charge of New Caledonia and New Hebrides by Bishop Bataillon, Vicar Apostolic of the Central Vicariate. 'We are in urgent need of reinforcements at the moment,' he said, 'and I really fear that it will take a good while for this help to arrive, as long as the division [of the Central Vicariate], which the Superior General of the Society of Mary gave me reason to hope for, does not take place.' An incident had already come up, he added, which indicated the kind of treatment that he could expect from Bataillon. Namely, he had left France with four priests and four Brothers, all from the Diocese of Clermont, and their bishop was happy that they would all be working together in New Caledonia. But Bishop Bataillon 'in spite of this sent me [to New Caledonia] with one priest and two Brothers'. Douarre felt himself obliged to mention this, he said, so that the cardinal might help him obtain additional funds and additional personnel. Only then could he manage 'to occupy these archipelagoes before the Protestants themselves return here'. Protestant ministers had been in both New Caledonia and New Hebrides, but had left, he said, and now he and his men were the only missionaries in both islands.[7]

After leaving New Caledonia the *Bucéphale* sailed to New Zealand, arriving at the Bay of Islands on 7 February 1844. Having been present at the episcopal ordination in Wallis and also at the landing of the first missionaries in New Caledonia, Captain Laferrièrre was able to give Bishop Pompallier a first-hand report of all that had happened. In return for this information and for other services rendered to the Catholic missions of Western Oceania, Pompallier celebrated a special Mass for the captain and his crew on Sunday, 11 February, in the new church at Kororareka still under construction. He also presented the captain with a statistical report on the twelve Catholic mission stations of New Zealand in the order of their foundation. The total number of indigenes baptised by this time in all mission stations was 2,166 and the total number of European Catholics cared for by the missionaries in these same stations was 1,385. This made a grand total of 3,551 Catholics being served in New Zealand.[8]

With the arrival of Bishop Douarre on the Western Oceania scene Bishop Pompallier now had someone new to suspect. Four years later, on 9 March 1848, he would write to Cardinal Fransoni that Douarre was 'a young bishop . . . who came to Oceania as an active agent of the Reverend Colin; he does nothing in his office as coadjutor for Bishop Bataillon except out of obedience to the Superior General.' Nor was Pompallier pleased with Rome's creation of the new Central Vicariate, because this had removed 'from my jurisdiction all the principal archipelagoes in the Torrid Zone. How much this went against my plans! For at this time the political circumstances in New Zealand seemed to be forcing me to establish my centre of administration at Wallis, whose entire population, including the king and his family, I had baptised and confirmed eight months earlier.'[9]

And on 3 March 1845 he had told Fransoni that he was 'on the point of going to fix my residence at Tongatapu or Wallis, when I learned of the erection of the Central Oceania Vicariate. This kept me from executing my project. . . .' He considered these islands in the Friendly Archipelago as an ideal refuge for himself 'in the event of political differences arising between these peoples, especially between the French and English, and between these latter and the New Zealanders'. His plan was to continue 'governing the New Zealand mission through one or two pro-vicars' until such time as it might become clear that an English Catholic bishop should be placed in charge.[10]

Although the Evangelisation Congregation was not aware of these wishes and plans of Pompallier when it fixed the boundaries for the new Central Oceania Vicariate on 8 August 1842, it was aware of them on 15 July 1844, when it established the Vicariates Apostolic of Melanesia and Micronesia. On this latter occasion Cardinal Fransoni as relator of the report had said that it would be impossible to give back to Pompallier 'the Wallis Islands and others', since they were part of the already established Vicariate Apostolic of Central Oceania. But he did use Pompallier's supposed need for a place of refuge as an added reason for establishing the Melanesia-Micronesia Mission, saying that then, should an emergency arise for Pompallier, one area could be separated from the other to provide a place for Bishop Pompallier to take up residence.[11]

On 28 August 1844, however, just forty-four days after Fransoni gave the above solution, two letters arrived from Bishop Pompallier dated 26 November 1843 and 16 February 1844, which altered the entire picture.[12] They contained his reaction to the official news from Fransoni that the Central Oceania Vicariate had been established and also indicated the name of the candidate whom he wanted to have as coadjutor.

The 26 November letter at first seemed positive enough, since it began by conveying Pompallier's 'ardent wishes for the success of the new vicariate apostolic'. After expressing regret that his earlier objections had not arrived in time to be taken into consideration, he said: 'But may the designs of the Lord be adored! The thing is done; may he bless it!' He did ask Fransoni, however, please to listen to his thoughts on the matter.

Then at great length he once again tried to show why the Friendly (or Tonga) Archipelago should never have been removed from his jurisdiction and why now it ought to be returned. 'I am indeed of the opinion that great good is accomplished by multiplying vicariates apostolic in Western Oceania', he began. But it would be morally impossible for the new Vicar Apostolic of Central

Oceania to succeed, he said, 'because the archipelagoes assigned to the Central Vicariate according to my knowledge have more than four different languages'. He explained that the Navigator (or Samoa) Archipelago and the Fiji Archipelago were both 'very populous and completely ravaged by heresy, and they [alone] have two totally different languages'. It was his opinion that 'the Navigator Archipelago needs a bishop of its own and the Fiji Archipelago also needs one . . . Another bishop is needed for the [New] Hebrides Archipelago and still another for New Caledonia.' (Pompallier, of course, had no way of knowing that Bishop Douarre would be setting foot on New Caledonia less than a month after he had written these lines.)

Since these four archipelagoes were all within the newly founded Central Vicariate, Pompallier was implying that Rome could have assigned Bataillon—or could *now* assign him—to any one of them and he would still have plenty of work to do. He also implied that neither Bataillon nor any other bishop would find nationality a problem when moving into these archipelagoes, because they were still independent from 'France, England and North America', all rival powers seeking to acquire new possessions and colonies in the Pacific. He then went on to explain in great detail why 'it would have been expedient and perhaps would still be expedient to have the Friendly or Tonga Archipelago attached to the Vicariate Apostolic of Western Oceania'. His principal reason was the danger of his being expelled from New Zealand by English authorities because of his French nationality and the need he had of another place where he then could take up missionary work. He also reminded Fransoni that officially he had the title 'Vicar Apostolic of Western Oceania', but in fact he was nothing more than Vicar Apostolic of New Zealand.[13]

Fransoni was not at all convinced that Pompallier was in any immediate danger of expulsion. But evidently he sensed that the bishop was quite discouraged and he decided that granting this rather reasonable request might raise Pompallier's spirits. As for Bishop Bataillon, he had four other archipelagoes within his vicariate which needed evangelising, as Pompallier had explained, and so he would have sufficient apostolic work to keep himself occupied. Perhaps for this reason Fransoni did not write to Bataillon to ask whether he objected to having the Friendly Archipelago removed from his Central Vicariate and returned to Pompallier's Western Vicariate. Nor did he ask Superior General Colin for a judgment on Father Viard, the Marist priest chosen by Pompallier as his sole candidate for the office of coadjutor, although there was ample time to do so. There was little reason, however, for Fransoni to write to Colin, because from long experience he knew in advance that Colin would surely disagree with any proposal made by Pompallier.

Four months after the arrival of Pompallier's two requests, they were brought up at a General Meeting on 23 December 1844. Cardinal Prefect Fransoni himself was relator and explained to the cardinals that the Vicar Apostolic of Western Oceania had asked 'that he be granted a coadjutor and that a certain change be made in regard to the boundaries of his own vicariate and that of the Centre'. Since the boundaries of the Central Oceania Vicariate had been discussed at the General Meeting of 8 August 1842, he asked the cardinals to take up these minutes again, as well as those of 15 July 1844 on Melanesia and Micronesia. The minutes of both meetings would prove a help, he said, in 'getting clarification on the present issue'.

In the minutes of 8 August 1842, he said, they would find the reasons prompting the foundation of the Central Oceania Vicariate. But at that time Pompallier's views on the matter, although requested long before, had not yet arrived. And in the minutes of 15 July 1844 on Melanesia and Micronesia, he said, they would find extracts from a Pompallier letter dated February 1843 (not 1842 as the printed text incorrectly states here) indicating 'the reasons why he did not believe it expedient' to found the Central Oceania Vicariate. Fransoni also pointed out that 'the principal cause' of Pompallier's dissent was 'his fear of finding himself one day obliged to abandon New Zealand with his personnel, after it completely becomes an English colony'. In this predicament 'he would have liked to retain under his jurisdiction some islands now contained in the Central Mission, islands already evangelised by himself and whose language he knows'. Then, if need be, 'he could transfer [to those islands], and while living in peace there he could care for the rest of his vicariate'.

Referring to the Melanesia-Micronesia deliberations Fransoni said that the cardinals had believed that by erecting 'the two new Vicariates of Melanesia and Micronesia, governed for the present by only one vicar apostolic . . . , but meant to be separated later, the feared emergency would be solved'. For if Pompallier actually were expelled from New Zealand, he 'could be transferred to govern one of these vicariates which, to his advantage, had already been founded and was being cared for by priests of his own Society'. The Marists were also in charge of the Central Oceania Vicariate, he said, and its vicar apostolic certainly would not deny 'hospitality to his Marist colleagues' in case they were expelled from New Zealand.

'Added to this is the fact that there is no reason to believe that the danger of expulsion for the French prelate from the British colony is imminent,' Fransoni said, 'nor that he will soon have to be replaced in that very vast island' by an English bishop assisted by English clergy. After listing several more possibilities where Pompallier could find a new field of activity, Fransoni pointed out that there was always the expedient of returning to him some island territory not far distant from New Zealand. Because of these numerous possibilities word had been sent to the bishop after the Melanesia-Micronesia meeting that his 'reasons for opposing the creation of the Central Oceania Vicariate, already established, were not found to be plausible'.

Up to this point it appeared that Fransoni believed there was no need to make any change in the boundaries established two years earlier for the Central Oceania Vicariate. But he then told the cardinals that Pompallier, after receiving the official news of the erection of the Central Oceania Vicariate, had written 'another long report on the matter on 26 November 1843, in which he developed more profusely the very same motives for his contrary position. He had also manifested the most earnest desire that the separation already agreed upon ought to be modified by returning at least the Friendly or Tonga Archipelago to the Western Vicariate.' Even though these views had already been considered at the General Meeting of 15 July 1844, Fransoni said, 'perhaps nonetheless this new presentation by the well-deserving prelate might merit some regard, or at least be of help in giving him a more tranquillising and reassuring reply. And so it seems opportune to bring this affair once again to the attention of Your Eminences and to invoke your prudent judgment.'

A verbatim copy of Pompallier's reasons for wanting the Friendly Archipelago was given to the cardinals. In his first argument he said that he knew 'the language of this archipelago, having practised the holy ministry in this place. Further, the language of New Zealand and that of the Friends are so closely related, that it is easy for a missionary who knows the New Zealand language to learn to speak that of the Friends after a month and a half or two.'

Pompallier's second argument was that ever since New Zealand had become an English possession, he and his French clergy had been in an awkward position and their ability to exert influence was paralysed. He himself felt very much 'like a French bishop who is sent to Ireland or England. The only ones who love me cordially and have complete confidence in me are the New Zealanders. All the others, the Europeans, esteem and respect me, but they would show more love for a Catholic bishop who is English. This, of course, is only natural and even reasonable. But if a war should break out between England and France, there would be reason to believe that I and all my French missionaries would be expelled from New Zealand, since the authorities governing it are both English and heretical. Then where in Western Oceania would I find refuge and be able to take up work? It would have to be a French area, or at least an independent area, like the Archipelago of Friends, whose language I know and whose language my missionary priests from New Zealand could also learn quickly.' He stressed that France and England were always on the verge of war.

His third argument was rather confused and dealt with a host of items, some repetitious. He was 'over 40 years of age' and therefore would find it 'difficult to learn new languages with the perfection required for matters of faith'. It would also be 'morally impossible' for him to master languages in new vicariates to be established by the Evangelisation Congregation. He needed the Friendly Archipelago in order to continue enjoying the protection of the French government. By being restricted to an English colony, he said, 'my mission no longer provides France with a reason for concern . . . But if the Holy See were to attach the Archipelago of the Friends, an independent country, to the French Vicariate Apostolic of New Zealand, France would still have some reason to be interested in me and would give me its attention, its protection, etc. . . . .' And to this protection 'I owe the security of my personnel, our victory over the . . . intolerance of heresy and our deliverance from death. . . .'

Fransoni then mentioned another concern of Pompallier. He was anxious to have an English bishop named at once to succeed him, Fransoni said, and he also wanted to have his French missionaries replaced by English missionaries without delay. But Fransoni's own judgment in the matter was that 'it seems premature to take any action along this line other than keeping a watchful eye on the progress of events. At the same time we shall make arrangements in advance for a prompt substitution, in case that should be needed.'[14]

The cardinals then discussed the question of a coadjutor. Much earlier when Pompallier had expressed the desire to visit Europe in order to take care of urgent business, he had been asked to suggest a candidate for the office of coadjutor. 'In view of all the circumstances,' Fransoni wrote to him on 4 October 1842, 'we once again would like to persuade you not to desert your mission until you have a coadjutor bishop to whom you can entrust the government of the vicariate . . . Let us know who from among your priests in your judgment would be a worthy and suitable candidate.'[15]

Pompallier devoted two paragraphs to this subject in his 26 November 1843 letter. This was the same letter in which he made his lengthy plea for having the Friendly Archipelago returned to his vicariate and he proposed his candidate in such a way that Rome, in providing him with a coadjutor, would have an added reason for returning the Friendly Archipelago. Eager to remain in New Zealand himself as long as possible, he began his argumentation by stating that he did not at all consider it 'expedient at present' to choose a coadjutor for New Zealand from among his missionaries, since they 'are all French subjects', and the candidate of necessity would have to be an Englishman. 'Now I have here only one missionary who is English. He is the Reverend Father O'Reily of Ireland and at the moment he is working in Port Nicholson . . . But he is new and I have never seen him.' Pompallier therefore did not 'dare' to suggest him. 'Instead I leave it up to Your Eminence and to His Holiness to make a wise choice of some English subject to be coadjutor bishop for New Zealand.'

But then in the next paragraph Pompallier stated that he did have a candidate after all. This candidate, however, being French, would have to be assigned to some area outside of the English colony of New Zealand. And so Pompallier said: 'If it should please both the Sacred Congregation for the Evangelisation of Nations and His Holiness to allow the Friendly [or Tonga] Archipelago to remain attached to the vicariate apostolic with which my unworthy person is charged, I would venture to propose for the office of coadjutor bishop in this same archipelago one of my pro-vicars, the Reverend Father Viard. I therefore request your authorisation to ordain him for this purpose. . . .'[16]

Nearly three months after making this proposal Pompallier received another letter from Fransoni, dated 22 July 1843, advising him that the Marists had charged him with giving out enormous sums for the upkeep of his sailing vessel, *Sancta Maria*.[17] On 16 February 1844, the day after receiving this letter, Pompallier wrote to Fransoni in self-defence and again brought up the subject of a coadjutor. He insisted that competent authorities had certified that his ship expenses had been 45.15 francs per day, or 1,377.07 francs per month, or 16,479.75 francs per year. 'Here, then, you see the error of those young and inexperienced missionaries to whom the Reverend Colin, Superior General of the Society of Mary, seems to give more faith than to myself', he said. 'Those missionaries have maintained that the cost of the ship was approximately 100 francs per day or 36,000 francs per year.'

He then brought up the matter of his coadjutor. 'I do feel the need more and more of having a coadjutor bishop', he said, 'and I would like to have the Reverend Father Viard, a man of apostolic virtue and talent.' Thinking that Fransoni might have some other candidate in mind, Pompallier begged him 'not to choose for me any missionary included in the number of those who maintained that the cost of the *Sancta Maria* was 100 francs per day!' In any event, he said, the Holy See would have to decide 'whether this new bishop should be an English or French subject. As for myself, I am in doubt.' As an afterthought, however, he assured Fransoni that the English Catholics would be well pleased with Father Viard. And in a postscript he promised to do everything possible 'to avoid making the voyage to Europe. Nor do I think that circumstances will oblige me to make it. I myself can see that the absence of the bishop from this mission could be a cause of ruin for the flock.'[18]

Cardinal Fransoni told the cardinals attending the General Meeting that the first of Pompallier's letters had requested a coadjutor conditionally. That is, he wanted a coadjutor 'if the Friendly Archipelago were to be returned to his Western Vicariate'. But in his second letter he 'urgently requests' that Your Eminences give him a coadjutor, stating that he 'now feels a more pressing need for one'.[19]

In his first letter, Fransoni added, Pompallier had wondered 'whether it might be more fitting to choose an English subject for the office of coadjutor. But in spite of this he was in favour of the excellent French missionary, Father Philippe-Jacques [read Philippe-Joseph] Viard [1809–72], his pro-vicar of the same Society of Marists, for whom he has the highest praise.' And in the second letter, Fransoni continued, Pompallier had laid down no conditions, but had simply asked the Sacred Congregation 'to grant him the praiseworthy priest Viard. And he gives assurance that of all his collaborators, he is the most worthy by virtue, talent and apostolic zeal. In addition to this he knows the languages of those places, enjoys the love and esteem of those in authority and also of the English people, and therefore his nomination generally would be well received.'

Fransoni summed up the matter like this: 'In view of the fact that these places are so far away, and in order to provide for every eventuality, it would be fitting for Your Eminences to consent to the request of Bishop Pompallier. You may also wish to give him the faculty of electing and ordaining some other worthy and experienced missionary, if the priest Viard chosen [for this office] should be dead on arrival of the papal briefs, or if the bishop for some other just cause should no longer believe that the choice [of Viard] is satisfactory.'

The cardinals were then asked to vote on three separate questions:

'1. Would it be fitting to separate the Friendly Archipelago from the Central [Vicariate] and return it to the Western Vicariate of Oceania, rescinding in this way—at least provisionally—a part of the papal brief on boundaries that has already been mailed?

'2. And if the answer is negative: What reply should be given to the proposal of Bishop Pompallier and should some action be taken now—what kind?—to give him some reassurance for the emergency that he fears will take place?

'3. Should Bishop [Pompallier] be given a coadjutor with the rank of bishop in the person of the missionary and pro-vicar Philippe-Jacques Viard and should His Holiness be approached on this?'

Before the vote was taken, there was some discussion on the wording of the first proposal. As the text stood, it called for the return of the Friendly Archipelago to Pompallier's Vicariate Apostolic of Western Oceania by dismembering it from Bataillon's Vicariate Apostolic of Central Oceania. This implied a revision of boundaries and at the same time a rescinding of the papal brief of demarcation already dispatched. But since Pompallier needed only a provisional solution, it was suggested that he should be granted merely the administration of the Friendly Archipelago instead, since then the boundaries of the Vicariate Apostolic of Central Oceania could be left intact. And if it should later prove unnecessary for Pompallier to leave New Zealand, the administration of the Friendly Islands could be restored to Bataillon without changing the boundaries again.

This revision was acceptable to the cardinals, who then proceeded to vote. Their replies were brief and to the point:

'1. Yes, at least until some other arrangements are made.

'2. Provided for under number one.

'3. Yes, and request that His Holiness designate as coadjutor for the Very Reverend Vicar Apostolic of Western Oceania the Reverend Philippe-Jacques Viard with right of succession, with episcopal rank and with a title *in partibus*.'[20]

On 12 January 1845, three weeks after the cardinals had reached these decisions, Secretary Brunelli of the Evangelisation Congregation presented them to Pope Gregory XVI. 'After giving mature consideration to all the issues, he ratified the decisions of the Most Eminent Cardinals . . . , gave his complete approval, and ordered that an apostolic letter in the form of a brief should be issued.'[21] Viard at this time was thirty-five years old.

It was not until 22 February 1845, however, that Cardinal Fransoni wrote to Pompallier and enclosed two papal briefs. One of these returned to him the administration of the Friendly Archipelago and the other authorised him to ordain one of his missionaries as his coadjutor. On the same day by separate letters Fransoni informed Bishop Bataillon and Superior General Colin of the decisions that had been reached.[22] This was two months after the General Meeting of 23 December 1844 and six months after the arrival of the two Pompallier letters which gave rise to these decisions. Why the long delay? Did Cardinal Fransoni believe that before the completion of negotiations a new letter from Pompallier might arrive, stating that he did not need the Friendly Islands after all? One can only guess. What was clear, however, was the fact that the

Evangelisation Congregation did not at all consider the danger of expulsion for Pompallier so imminent as he had made it appear.

20

Bishop Epalle is killed in the Solomon Islands

19 DECEMBER 1845

Bishop Epalle, Vicar Apostolic of Melanesia and Micronesia, set sail from London aboard the *Bussorah Merchant* on 2 February 1845 with a missionary staff of seven priests and six Brothers. Two of the priests and one or two of the Brothers were meant to be the pioneers at Ascension (or Ponape) Island in Micronesia and the rest were to help the young bishop launch missionary work in Melanesia.[1] The *Bussorah Merchant* brought them only as far as Sydney, however, with a stopover en route at Cape Town on the southern tip of Africa, where they arrived on 1 May. This stopover was fortunate for Epalle. It gave him an opportunity to have a complete rest, since he was recovering from a serious illness which had almost cost his life. After three days the ship weighed anchor and sailed for Sydney.[2]

'The first land that we saw in Oceania was King Island', said Father Léopold Verguet, chronicler of the voyage. This island lies between the Australian mainland and Tasmania at the western end of Bass Strait, which the *Bussorah Merchant* entered at noon on 17 June 1845. And it was '21 June, Saturday, shortly after midnight, that is, the first hour of the day in the week consecrated to the Blessed Virgin Mary, when we approached the lighthouse at Sydney', Verguet reported. 'The captain joyfully shot off a cannon to announce our arrival and to let it be known that he wanted a pilot. Then he lighted a torch. . . .' It glowed for ten minutes, helping the pilot locate the ship. When the *Bussorah Merchant* dropped anchor at Sydney at 8 A.M., two Marists immediately came aboard to welcome the newcomers. They were Fathers Dubreul and Rocher, who had been sent on ahead to open a supply centre in Sydney for the fast growing Marist missions of Western Oceania.[3]

Epalle waited until 12 July before writing to Superior General Colin. 'We experienced no real danger during our long voyage and also no tempest properly so called.' But his missionaries needed some rest, he said, before going out to sea again and taking up their strenuous missionary work. 'All are suggesting that New Guinea be the field of battle, but I cannot tell you yet where we shall go.'[4]

When he wrote again on 17 August, more than a month had passed and he admitted that he was making Colin wait a long time 'to learn in which island of Melanesia we think we shall start. If I did not prefer my own opinion to that of all those around me, including Archbishop Polding,[5] we would start in New Guinea. Although I do not dare to contradict this general opinion, I could perhaps modify it, because I see great advantages in taking up work at a place where it is possible to become complete master. Now in the Archipelago of New Guinea there is an island called Waigeo, separated from the [New Guinea] mainland only by Dampier Strait. This island is important and they say that it has a population of 100,000.[6] It has two magnificent harbours and is located on the route used by ships going from Sydney to China. Very likely we shall try to start on this island, which I consider to be a small part of New Guinea.'

In order to get there, however, 'we shall have to pass through the whole of Melanesia and it is impossible for me to know today all that Providence may have in store for us during this voyage. It could be that something providential will be waiting for us at the door by which we are to enter [Melanesia], that is, in the Solomon Islands . . . My health has improved far beyond what I had dared to hope and I feel within myself a new force and a new vigour which I thought had been lost forever. . . .' He added that New Caledonia was along his route and so he would interrupt his voyage to visit Bishop Douarre.[7]

Epalle had left the Bay of Islands in New Zealand on 22 May 1842 in order to obtain personnel and funds in France for the New Zealand mission. Now he was back in Sydney with a staff of seven priests and six Brothers for Melanesia and Micronesia, but without a single priest or Brother for New Zealand. He felt that he should send an explanation to some Marist in New Zealand and on 18 August 1845, the day after writing to Superior General Colin, he wrote to Father Maxime Petit with whom he had come from France to New Zealand in 1839. Epalle explained how he had succeeded in persuading the Association for the Propagation of the Faith in Lyon to allocate the necessary funds for him to bring twenty-six Marists to New Zealand. But letters from Bishop Pompallier later caused the association to cancel the funds, and as a result the appointments of the twenty-six missionaries for New Zealand were also cancelled. Matters had become so bad between Pompallier and the Marists, he explained, that the Marist Society 'was allowed to suspend sending missionaries [to Bishop Pompallier]. This will remain in force until new arrangements are made.'

Then Epalle explained that much of his time in Rome had been taken up with negotiations leading to the foundation of the Vicariates Apostolic of Melanesia and Micronesia, temporarily united. But the Marist Generalate 'did not accept anything but Melanesia', he said. 'Micronesia is to be separated from it as soon as possible. It was united to Melanesia because of Ascension Island and I must send two priests there to good James Hall.' Hall was the Protestant gentleman who had come to New Zealand just prior to Epalle's departure, seeking priests for Ascension Island, known nowadays as Ponape.

The young bishop also confided to Petit that he hoped soon to receive a coadjutor. 'And before long I expect to see my Vicariate of Melanesia divided among several vicars apostolic. . . .'[8] Here he was referring to his concrete plans made in France for the rapid development of the Church in the Melanesian part of his mission. He had spelled out his plans in detail on 2 January 1845 in separate letters from Paris to Cardinal Prefect Fransoni in Rome and to the Association for the Propagation of the Faith in Lyon. In these letters he had suggested that Melanesia should be divided quickly into seven vicariates: four in New Guinea and one each in New Britain, New Ireland and the Solomon Islands. He had urged Fransoni simply to cut off from his Vicariate Apostolic of Melanesia whatever territories he wished and to establish them as new vicariates without consulting him on the matter. And also, if Fransoni thought that Epalle ought to have a coadjutor in that part of his vicariate which eventually would remain under his jurisdiction, the cardinal should simply go ahead and send him one.[9]

Superior General Colin had also been informed of this ambitious program by Epalle and had supported it wholeheartedly. In fact, he had written to Epalle in London and had suggested that an excellent candidate for heading a second vicariate apostolic in Melanesia might well be Father Jean-Georges Collomb.[10] Epalle heartily seconded this choice and told Colin so from London on 18 January 1845. 'You caused me great joy by announcing to me your project concerning the Reverend Collomb', he said. But he did ask Colin to keep a special consideration in mind.

If prior to Collomb's departure from France it would already be known where in Melanesia Epalle had settled with his missionaries, Colin could simply ask Rome to designate some other part of Melanesia as a separate vicariate apostolic for Collomb. But 'if at the moment of the Reverend Collomb's departure you do not yet know at what place we shall have made our foundation, it would be perhaps more apropos', Epalle counselled, 'to send him as coadjutor.' What Epalle feared was that Rome might designate unintentionally for Collomb that very part of Melanesia in which he, Epalle, had already settled. Such a procedure, he told Colin, could expose him and his men 'to the danger of having to give up a post, where we have already begun to speak the language'. But if Collomb were to arrive in Melanesia as coadjutor, he would be under Epalle, who could then send him to some new section of Melanesia. That new section could subsequently be erected by Rome into a separate vicariate apostolic for Collomb.[11]

Colin, however, did not immediately propose Collomb to Rome for the office of vicar apostolic or coadjutor. His reason for this may have been Collomb's age: he was twenty-eight years old and the canonically required age for a bishop was thirty.

For four full months Bishop Epalle and his thirteen missionaries remained in Sydney recuperating from their first voyage and preparing for the next. They also used the time to make many friends, although Verguet certainly was exaggerating when he said that 'the entire city [he placed the population at 40,000] spoke of nothing else but the 14 missionaries on their way to attempt to bring the faith to the cannibals'. Many thought that they 'would probably become victims of the ferocity' of the peoples whom they intended to evangelise. 'And Bishop Epalle was looked upon as a holy martyr who would not be seen again . . . All asked for his blessing. And in the churches the people said prayers and received Communion so that the grace of God might descend upon the missionaries.'[12]

Wanting to give Colin some idea of what was delaying him and his men in

Sydney, Epalle wrote on 27 August 1845 that their goods had to be unpacked for drying, since they had become damaged en route. And on 6 September he wrote again about the peace that he had been commissioned by Colin to negotiate with Pompallier, who was in Sydney at this time awaiting the arrival of the *Rhin* from New Caledonia with Father Viard aboard. (Epalle seems not to have known that Pompallier intended to make Viard his coadjutor.) 'I have just returned from my fourth meeting with Bishop Pompallier', he told Colin. Present at the last two meetings were the two Marists in charge of the mission supply centre in Sydney, he said, and they would also attend the remaining meetings until definite conclusions were reached. 'I can tell you now, however, that as yet nothing has been accomplished. Perhaps it would suffice for me to say that his obstinacy is still the same. . . .'[13]

Finally, on 11 October 1845, Epalle signed a contract which read: 'Memorandum of Agreement entered into this day between John Kettle, owner of the Schooner *Marian Watson* of 146 tons . . . , and His Lordship, Bishop Epalle, now about to proceed to various places in the North and South Pacific Ocean . . . The Former agrees to let, and the Latter agrees to charter, the said Schooner Month by Month [and] at His Lordship's option to proceed, wind and weather permitting, to such Port or Ports in the said Pacific as His Lordship or such person as may be authorised in writing to act on his behalf may require and direct, on the following terms and conditions. . . .'[14]

Epalle now had a ship at his disposal, but by 22 October he still did not know for sure where in Melanesia he wanted to go. He sent Colin a letter that day saying he would set sail 'certainly' on the following day. 'It almost looks as though we shall be settling in the Solomons.' The bulk of his letter was concerned with New Zealand, which 'made us lose two and a half months here. If only I could have foreseen the loss of so much time, and above all the scanty results[of meetings with Bishop Pompallier], we would already be on some Melanesian island today.'

Colin had asked Epalle to inform Pompallier that it would be necessary for him to contribute something to the Marists for training personnel for his mission. Pompallier balked at this, however, saying that he intended to open seminaries in New Zealand to train his own clergy. 'But I am not at all authorised to give you any definite information in this regard', Epalle told Colin. 'The bishop plans to leave for Europe soon and so is making no more decisions. . .'

Epalle had started his letter to Colin early on the day before he was to sail for Melanesia and in the course of the morning Bishop Pompallier arrived. 'Now it is midnight and I am back again at this letter', he continued. Pompallier had made numerous accusations against Colin and Epalle tried to list them, but finally gave up. 'It is now almost two hours past midnight and I shall never get finished . . . Let me go and take my rest . . . What we need now is prayers.'[15]

The *Marian Watson* sailed on schedule, moving slowly out of Sydney harbour on Thursday, 23 October 1845.[16] It was a festive occasion for the missionaries, because the shore was filled with their friends who had come to say a last farewell. The *Marian Watson* was a two-masted schooner and Father

Verguet said it looked 'like a small Noah's ark. Aboard were chickens, rabbits, goats, sheep, horses and oxen; there were even two greyhounds . . . We took along all these animals in order to have them reproduce at our settlement and in order to subsist on them before long in that wild country without being a burden to the natives.'[17]

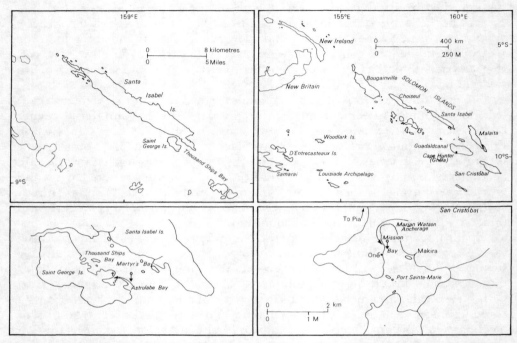

49 Frame One, lower right: The first foundation of the Vicariate Apostolic of Melanesia was made in the Solomon Islands at Makira, Port Sainte-Marie, on the southwest coast of San Cristóbal Island. Sketch based on map by C. M. Léopold Verguet, *Histoire de la première mission catholique au vicariat de Mélanésie,* opp. p. 129.

Frame Two, upper right: The first missionaries to reach the Vicariate Apostolic of Melanesia examined possible locations at San Cristóbal and Santa Isabel in the Solomon Islands and then chose Makira in San Cristóbal.

Frame Three, upper left: Bishop Epalle arrived at Thousand Ships Bay on 12 December 1845 in search of a likely location for his first foundation in Melanesia. Exactly one week later he was dead.

Frame Four, lower left: This sketch shows where the *Marian Watson* was anchored (anchor), where Bishop Epalle was mortally wounded on 16 December 1845 (Martyr's Bay), and where he was buried (cross) on 20 December. Sketch based on map by Verguet, *Vicariat de Mélanésie,* opp. p. 307. *(Chapter 20).*

At Epalle's request Captain Richards[18] made a week's stopover at New Caledonia and left again on 23 November. It was 9 A.M., Monday, 1 December 1845, when San Cristóbal (also Arossi) came into view. This was the south-easternmost island of the Solomon Archipelago, about 122 kilometres long and 37 kilometres wide.

The *Marian Watson* approached San Cristóbal on 2 December. Since navigational charts contained no entries for depth of water or suitable anchorages, Captain Richards had to proceed slowly. The schooner was still five or six leagues from land when Bishop Epalle asked one of his missionaries for a medal of the Blessed Virgin Mary and threw it into the sea. He was within the waters of his Vicariate Apostolic of Melanesia, and this was his way of consecrating the entire vicariate to the Virgin Mary. Near the coast was a tiny island which the missionaries called 'Sentinelle', since it looked as if it was keeping guard. It proved to be a natural marker for a large bay, which Captain Richards examined and found to be deep enough and highly suitable for anchorage. In honour of Bishop Jean-Baptiste Epalle the missionaries called it 'Port Saint-Jean-Baptiste' and there the *Marian Watson* anchored.

The bishop with some of the missionaries and sailors, began reconnoitring the area in a whaleboat. 'When we reached land on the first day', Father Verguet said, 'the bishop had us all kneel down to recite an Ave Maria in thanksgiving. Then he buried in the earth a medal of the Most Blessed Virgin, thus dedicating to her this land, the first of his vicariate.' The reconnoitring was successful and resulted in the discovery of four deep bays with suitable anchorages. But no native villages were found.

On the third day, however, more than 100 canoes with over 400 natives encircled the *Marian Watson*, convincing Epalle that the island was well populated. By sign language the natives indicated that more people lived at the north end of the island. But before deciding to make his first foundation at San Cristóbal, Epalle wanted to visit Santa Isabel Island. It was in the centre of the archipelago and map makers and geographers alike called it the most important of the Solomon Islands. About 3 P.M. on Saturday, 6 December, the *Marian Watson* left San Cristóbal and sailed northwest.

After three days the ship was opposite Guadalcanal Island. No landing was made, but the anchor was dropped at Cape Hunter, called Ghéla by the local people. The natives who came out in canoes and encircled the schooner looked ferocious; their faces were painted white and their lips were red with betelnut juice. Apprehensive at the sight of them Captain Richards ordered his sailors to place a barrier of rope nets several metres in height completely around the ship's deck. He feared that otherwise some natives might climb aboard and catch the crew and passengers by surprise. And when the number of natives encircling his ship became alarmingly large, he ordered his sailors to load their guns and place a small cannon on the poop deck. Apparently the natives were familiar with European ships, because at the sight of the cannon they disappeared.[19] Epalle now better understood the significance of one of the clauses in the contract which he had signed on 11 October. It had stated that the *Marian Watson* was 'tight, staunch and strong; sufficiently manned and armed for defence. . . .'[20]

The next stop was Santa Isabel Island and here there was no difficulty in finding a port. French navigational charts with great precision showed the location and soundings of Thousand Ships Bay at the southern end of the long island. The *Marian Watson* dropped anchor near Astrolabe Harbour in this bay on Friday, 12 December 1845, only to be surrounded immediately by canoes filled with natives who wanted to come aboard and barter. The canoes were in constant motion and the natives, who seemed very bold, gesticulated and shouted incessantly.

'Since we intended to settle in their midst', Verguet said, 'we did not want to repel them by a cold reception and so we invited some of them to come aboard.' Captain Richards bartered with them for yams, sugar cane and sometimes a pig. Father Verguet obtained for himself a bracelet of human teeth. What the natives wanted most of all in exchange was a hatchet. But before surrendering their goods for one, they would swing it over their heads and test it in every possible way. They rejected those that were too heavy.

By sign language the natives succeeded in making the missionaries understand that they were at war with a certain tribe on the Santa Isabel coast. Pointing to this tribe's village with one hand, and striking their head with the other, they grimaced as if they were in great pain. Verguet said that the pantomine meant, 'If you go there, they will kill you'.

But were these natives telling the truth? Perhaps their threat was nothing but a trick so that none of the highly prized trade goods of their visitors would be bartered to anyone but them! In any event Bishop Epalle had to get on with the work of founding his first mission station, so without delay he named a reconnaissance party which he himself wanted to lead. Its other members were his vicar general, Father Frémont; his secretary, Father Étienne Chaurain (1819–87); and the skilled carpenter and builder, Brother Prosper. Captain Richards sent along four oarsmen and placed Second Officer Blémy in charge. Reconnoitring was done on 13, 14 and 15 December and the schedule was identical each day. About 6 A.M., shortly after sunrise, the party would leave the *Marian Watson* aboard a whaleboat and return about 6 P.M., shortly before sunset.

After three days of reconnoitring only the coastline and uninhabited land had been examined. The natives with whom they had been bartering daily aboard the *Marian Watson* had seemed peaceful enough. Epalle therefore decided that he could now safely begin making his first contacts with people on shore. With the help of presents he hoped that one tribe or the other would allow him to settle in their midst.

On Tuesday, 16 December, after Epalle had finished a lengthy meditation, he and his party left as usual about 6 A.M. After rowing for an hour they reached the Santa Isabel shoreline, where—after rounding Maunga Point and losing sight of the *Marian Watson*—they saw a large group of men standing motionless, silent and well-armed. Thinking that this was a ceremonial way of receiving visitors, Epalle and his party disembarked. To give evidence of the peacefulness of their mission, they had decided to leave behind in the whaleboat the weapons that they had brought along for self-defence.

As the missionaries and sailors approached the silent group, the leader stepped forward to greet them. His head was decorated with feathers and he carried a most attractive shield. Later the missionaries learned that his name was Londo. He spoke to Second Officer Blémy, who did not understand a word. Blémy then offered Londo some pieces of iron, the kind that was everywhere in

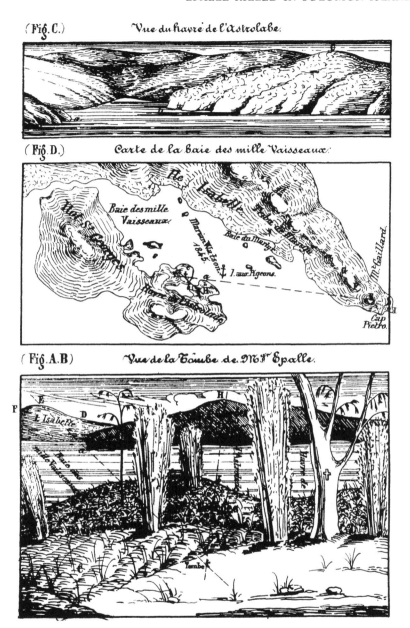

50 The Reverend C. M. Léopold Verguet, an eye-witness, made these drawings to show Astrolabe Harbour (top), Thousand Ships Bay (centre), and a close-up of the spot (bottom) where Bishop Epalle was buried on 20 December 1845 at Saint George Island in the Solomon Islands (Tombe). The centre drawing shows where the *Marian Watson* was anchored, where Epalle was attacked (Baie du Martyr), and where he was buried (cross). *Source: Verguet, Histoire de la première mission catholique au vicariat de Mélanésie, opp. p. 307. (Chapter 20).*

great demand as a trade article. Londo seemed to despise the pieces of iron as a gift below his dignity, but he nevertheless accepted them. Blémy then tried offering the chief a small hatchet, and this made him very happy and proud.

Another native then noticed Bishop Epalle's episcopal ring and offered him in exchange several pieces of half-spoiled fruit. This incident did not escape Londo, who examined the ring closely and immediately wanted to have it. Epalle simply smiled, but did not remove the ring from his finger. Londo then issued an unintelligible order to his warriors, who at once broke rank and in groups of two or three approached each of the nine Europeans. Those who encircled the bishop began jostling him as they seemingly examined his garments. Then without any warning a native standing behind him raised his hatchet high in the air and, holding it with both hands, let it come crashing down on the bishop's head. The warrior cried out at the same time, giving the signal to attack.

On seeing his bishop receive this blow Father Chaurain spun around just in time to avoid being struck by two clubs already raised over his head. He grabbed some rocks nearby and used them to fight his way through the crowd until he reached the safety of the whaleboat. Brother Prosper saved himself by jumping into the water and swimming to the whaleboat. This made Londo and his warriors change their tactics and they quickly split into three groups: one group continued to strike the bishop, another headed for the whaleboat and tried to make it sink, and the other group chased after those still on shore. But a sailor, who succeeded in reaching the whaleboat, shot off his pistol and frightened away two of the groups. He then shot in the direction of the group that was hacking away at the bishop's head and trying to tear the clothes off his back. This frightened them and they also ran away.

Seeing his bishop stretched out on the sand and alone, Father Chaurain jumped into waist-high water and hurried to him. The natives had dragged Epalle a long distance in an effort to pull off his clothes and now he was lying there motionless, apparently dead, with his face buried in the sand. Deep gashes covered his head, which was bathed in blood. His cassock had been torn to shreds and part of it, part of his trousers, his hat, handkerchief and episcopal ring were all missing. This coast was later named 'Martyr's Bay'.

Father Frémont and Brother Prosper hastened to assist Chaurain in carrying Epalle to the whaleboat, and it soon became evident that he was still alive. But he had lost so much blood that Frémont was convinced that he would die and asked if he wished to go to confession. When there was no answer, he gave his bishop conditional absolution. Frémont, too, was badly wounded. In making his escape he had seen a club lying at his feet which he could have used to defend himself. But he did not pick it up, saying later that he had preferred to let God take care of preserving his life. Second Officer Blémy, too, was seriously hurt.

It was about 10 A.M. when a lookout on the bridge of the *Marian Watson* announced that the whaleboat was returning. Because of the early hour those aboard feared that perhaps an accident had occurred. They had not been able to see what was happening on land. As the whaleboat came closer, their fears were confirmed. They could see Bishop Epalle holding his head between his hands and his hands were resting on his knees. Seated at his side was Frémont, whose hat was stained with blood.

Carefully they lifted Epalle aboard and Dr Guior examined him at once. He had five gashes in his head from which blood was still trickling. And in four places the cranium was pierced. One opening was so large that part of the brain was protruding and running onto the bishop's clothing. 'A horrible sight', Verguet said. 'I could not look at these five deep and gaping wounds without shuddering; one of them alone would have been enough to bring death.' Dr Guior announced sadly that his examination made him despair of saving the bishop's life.

Epalle then received the Last Anointing from Father Jacquet and for the remainder of that day the missionaries prayed at his side. He lingered on and they took turns keeping vigil throughout the night. Occasionally the bishop became delirious. And although he apparently never had a conscious moment, he was heard to say at times, 'Jesus, Mary, Lord'.

Captain Richards on Wednesday evening, 17 December, unceremoniously informed the Marists that he was sending out a punitive expedition on the following day to kill a dozen members of the Maunga tribe, the one to which Londo and his warriors belonged. When the missionaries objected and asked for reasons, he explained that this was a natural sequel to the murderous attack on the reconnaissance party. Besides, his crew was forcing him to take this measure, he added, 'since they refuse to go ashore again, if they are not allowed to take revenge for an offence of this kind'.

After discussing the matter among themselves the missionaries concluded that silence on their part would be interpreted as consent. Therefore Father Chaurain was delegated to tell the captain that they were opposed to his taking such action. 'It is not up to us to determine whether or not it is your duty to revenge the wounding of your second officer and the insult against your crew; you must know what obligations your office as captain imposes upon you. As for us, no matter how great our sorrow might be at the sight of our dying bishop, it is still controlled enough and Christian enough for us to detest every kind of vengeance.'

After a short while the captain returned and said that some of his sailors would in fact be going ashore on the following day. But their purpose was to barter for yams and taros, because the supply of fresh vegetables aboard ship was exhausted.

During the night the Marists began to doubt the captain's word, telling one another that his need for fresh vegetables was nothing but a subterfuge for the intended reprisal. It was 5 A.M. the next morning, 18 December, when Chaurain wrote a letter which all the priests signed. He presented it to Captain Richards while some of the sailors were preparing to go ashore in the whaleboat. The letter read: 'Mr Captain: Not aware of all the motives prompting you to send a landing party to the shore where our bishop was mortally wounded, we believe that we must protest loudly and declare that we want no act of reprisal. This is contrary to the very nature of our mission, which is completely one of sacrifice and of

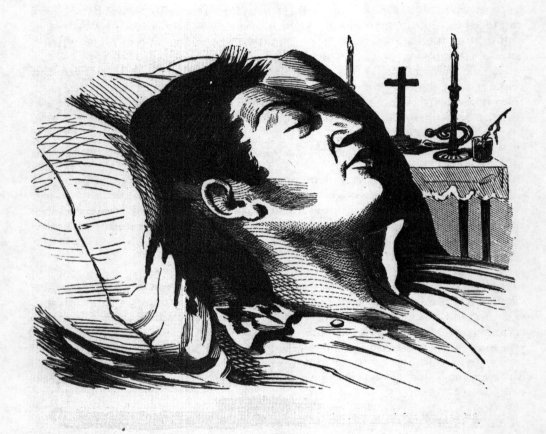

51 The Most Reverend Jean-Baptiste Epalle (1809–45), the first Vicar Apostolic of Melanesia and Micronesia, was mortally wounded on 16 December 1845 by the Maunga tribe at Thousand Ships Bay in Santa Isabel Island of the Solomon Islands. *Source: Eyewitness sketch by the Reverend C. M. Léopold Verguet, Histoire de la première mission catholique au vicariat de Mélanésie, opp. p. 112. (Chapter 20).*

peace. We beg of you, and if need be we insist, that you enter this protest in your legal journal. Respectfully . . . Frémont, Chaurain, Montrouzier, Verguet, [Joseph] Thomassin, Jacquet.'[21]

The captain read the letter and then informed the missionaries that the landing party would not go ashore. On receiving these new orders from their captain the sailors, heavily armed with guns and swords, slowly and regretfully dispersed.

On Friday morning, 19 December, Epalle was still alive. About 11 A.M. that day he half opened his eyes several times and clutched at a crucifix that was handed to him. When he began to breathe with great difficulty at 3.30 P.M., Vicar General Frémont asked Father Verguet to read the official liturgical prayers for those in their last agony. The Marists were all kneeling in a circle around Epalle's bed and Captain Richards, Dr Guior, and one of the ship's officers stood silently by. It was shortly before 4 P.M. when Bishop Epalle took his last breath and died. Simultaneously his missionaries burst into tears.

Due to a provision made by Epalle, Father Frémont at once became head of the orphaned mission and was to remain in charge until the arrival of a new bishop. One of his first responsibilities was to decide where to bury Epalle. After a discussion with his missionaries the consensus was that Epalle should be buried as close as possible to the place where he had died. But all feared that if his body were discovered by the natives, it might be exhumed and violated. They therefore decided to bury him under cover of darkness on nearby Saint George Island, which was uninhabited. This island formed the western shore of Thousand Ships Bay. Fathers Chaurain and Verguet were sent there with five sailors to dig a grave, while those aboard the *Marian Watson* vested Epalle's corpse in episcopal robes.

The next morning, Saturday, all aboard ship were awake by 3.30 A.M. On the main deck they erected a simple altar for the funeral Mass and surrounded it with curtains to hide the candlelight from possibly wakeful eyes on Santa Isabel Island. At 4.30 A.M. Father Chaurain began the Mass. 'It was the first time that I had celebrated Mass in the Vicariate of Melanesia', he said, 'and before my eyes just two steps away lay the body of my bishop.' In addition to the missionaries the entire Protestant crew was present, as well as two New Caledonians. At 5 A.M. the funeral cortege pushed away from the *Marian Watson* and forty minutes later reached the shore of Astrolabe Harbour at Saint George Island. All disembarked at a place indicated on navigational charts as Débarcadère, i.e. Landing Place, and twenty metres from there they quickly buried Bishop Epalle. No grave marker was used, but Verguet did make careful drawings of the burial place and of surrounding landmarks, which could be used to relocate the grave at a later date.[22]

After the burial Frémont consulted his missionaries again. Should they go north to New Ireland, remain at Santa Isabel, or return to San Cristóbal? It would be preferable to remain at Santa Isabel, some argued, so that the mission could begin near the place where the bishop was buried. But if no suitable place could be found in the immediate vicinity, it would be better to return to San

Cristóbal. Most wanted to remain and on Monday, 22 December, Fathers Paget, Thomassin and Verguet continued the reconnaissance at Santa Isabel that had been interrupted on 16 December. 'But this time we were on our guard', Verguet said. 'We were all well armed and did not make the mistake of leaving our weapons in the whaleboat. The captain had ordered the sailors not to leave the whaleboat and to assist us with their firearms only from a distance. . . .'

The reconnaissance party did not return to the place where the Maunga tribe had attacked Epalle and his party, but followed the coast southward from that point. Here they found fresh water, numerous inhabitants and much unoccupied land. Their contacts with the natives were peaceful and they bartered for coconuts, shells and bracelets. According to Verguet, the only hostile tribe in Thousand Ships Bay 'was the tribe which our bishop had visited first. If he had begun his visiting in the other direction, nothing would have happened.' But was Verguet correct in maintaining this? Had his reconnaissance party been unarmed, it too might have been attacked.

In spite of the numerous advantages, however, there were no suitable anchorages close to these shores. This meant that the vast amount of supplies aboard the *Marian Watson*, as well as all future supplies for the missions, would have to be transported across the wide bay by rowboat, a very difficult task. This disadvantage made Frémont decide to return to San Cristóbal to open the first mission station.

On arriving at the Solomon Islands in early December the Marists had learned that Loukou, a member of the Mahia tribe on the north end of San Cristóbal, had been a cabin boy for some years on an English ship. This meant that he would be able to serve as interpreter for the Catholic mission at San Cristóbal. Frémont therefore was most eager to win his services and had the *Marian Watson* stop first at Loukou's village. Loukou came aboard completely nude, greeted all with a handshake, accepted a small glass of brandy and, after making a toast, drank it down without wincing. 'He gravely sat down before the captain', Verguet said, 'and we were astonished at his nudity, which he did not at all mind.' Captain Richards then gave him a shirt and succeeded in disposing him favourably toward the missionaries. Loukou urged the missionaries to settle in his own village and showed them some of his property, which they could purchase, but they found it unsuitable. He then sailed with them the next morning to the southern side of the island where the *Marian Watson* anchored once again at Port Saint-Jean-Baptiste.

As had happened one month earlier, when the *Marian Watson* arrived here for the first time, numerous natives appeared in canoes as if from nowhere, and their friendliness greatly impressed the missionaries. But this time by gestures they indicated that the *Marian Watson* should follow them. Loukou assured Captain Richards and Father Frémont that the natives came from a heavily populated area nearby and that the schooner could safely go there and would find a good anchorage. But first Fathers Chaurain and Montrouzier with Brother Prosper and some sailors made a survey and on their return gave assurance that what Loukou had said was correct. On Saturday evening, 3 January 1846, the

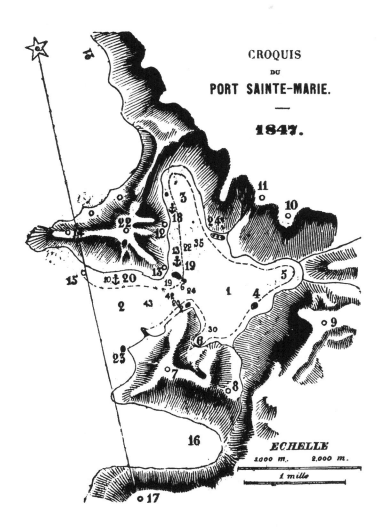

CROQUIS
DU
PORT SAINTE-MARIE.
—
1847.

Ce plan a été dressé : l'intérieur du port, par les PP. L. Verguet
et Thomassin ; le goulet et les abords, par A. Félix Sicard, officier
de l'*Arche-d'Alliance.*

52   The first foundation in the Vicariate Apostolic of Melanesia and Micronesia was made at Makira, Port Sainte-Marie, in San Cristóbal Island at the southern end of the Solomon Islands. The large numbers identify the location of Oné Village (12), the anchorage in Mission Bay used by the *Marian Wat-son* (18), the direction in which one must go to reach Pia (21), and the location of the mission station at Makira (24). *Source: C. M. Léopold Verguet, Histoire de la première mission catholique au vicariat de Mélanésie, opp. p. 129. (Chapter 20).*

344 FOUNDING OF THE ROMAN CATHOLIC CHURCH IN OCEANIA

Marian Watson followed the canoes and passed through a channel into a superb harbour, three kilometres long and two kilometres wide. It was protected from the wind by high mountains round about and had many excellent anchorages. In thanksgiving to the Virgin Mary for having brought them to the end of their journey, the missionaries called it Port Sainte-Marie, otherwise called Makira Bay.

After Captain Richards anchored his ship to the left of the harbour entrance at a spot called by the Marists Mission Bay, they were eager to purchase land as soon as possible so that they could begin building their mission station. Loukou sought out the leader of the local tribe, who would have to authorise the purchase, but he was assisting at the burial of a relative in a nearby village. Instead of waiting idly for his return, the Marists began examining the area. Some suggested that the mission station should be built at Oné, a village of 150–200 inhabitants near the anchorage used by the *Marian Watson*. But others considered it dangerous to settle so close to a native village and preferred instead Makira, an uninhabited piece of land opposite the entrance to Port Sainte-Marie, which was finally purchased.

During their first eight days at Makira, the priests and Brothers built a large shed, which was meant to serve later as a stable. The sailors did not help with the work, but instead kept watch from their whaleboat for a possible surprise attack. At the end of the day the sailors and all the priests and Brothers except three returned to the *Marian Watson* to spend the night on board.

The three left behind were Fathers Frémont and Verguet and the gardener, Brother Charles, who had to keep watch over the tools. To protect themselves at night they would go inside the shed and barricade the door. After making sure that their firearms were loaded and placing a ladder against a lookout window in the garret above the entrance, they went to sleep completely dressed. At the least strange sound their dogs would bark and the first missionary to awaken grabbed his gun and ran up the ladder to see if natives were approaching for an attack. There was an understanding with those aboard the *Marian Watson* that a shot fired into the night meant that help was needed immediately. But, as Verguet pointed out later, it would have taken a quarter of an hour for them to arrive, 'and meanwhile the natives could have massacred us 20 times'.

The three missionaries were so tired at the end of each day, however, that they slept right through the night. 'During the two months that it took to build our station', Verguet said, 'we were never disturbed at night. Whenever we were exposed to some danger, it was always before sunset.'

While the missionaries spent their days working, the idle sailors in the whaleboat turned to debauchery. A local native became indignant when his wife was raped and decided to take revenge. He hid in the rushes alongside a brook, not far from the construction site, and there waited for the first white man to come along. As Providence would have it, Father Montrouzier came to that brook to refresh himself at the end of his day's work. Stooping down to drink, he saw a native peering at him through the rushes, brandishing a spear. Being unarmed he turned and fled, but after a few steps he felt a spear crash into his back. It broke off, leaving the point imbedded in his spine, and he cried out in pain. At that moment Verguet happened to be outdoors with his pistol in hand. Hearing cries for help he fired a shot into the air to ward off possible pursuers and ran into the forest, where he found Montrouzier alone, moaning with pain. 'I have been speared and I am dying', he screamed. 'I know I shall not live . . . Do not let me die without giving me absolution.'[23]

Other missionaries arrived quickly on the scene and helped Verguet carry Montrouzier to the mission station. The spear had penetrated his cassock and waistcoat and Dr Guior's examination showed that the point was buried in the bone. It had splintered and he was unable to extract it. Being very seriously wounded and in need of much rest, Montrouzier was unable to be of further help to the San Cristóbal pioneers. Arrangements were therefore made for him to return on the *Marian Watson* as far as New Caledonia. That mission station was now two years old and so he could receive more attention there. For three months the ugly wound suppurated, ejecting throughout that time the many splinters, and only then did it heal.

The spearing of Father Montrouzier was the most serious accident suffered by the Marists while building their first mission station at San Cristóbal. Having tools stolen by the natives was a daily occurrence, but ordinarily a threat sufficed to have them returned. Finding timber suitable for constructing a house was also a problem. There was only one type of tree that was satisfactory, called nari. Because it produced excellent nuts, and because each tree had a different owner, it was difficult to obtain them. But after two months not only the shed but also a large house with a roof of palm leaves had been completed. 'It was a gigantic task for the 12 of us', Verguet admitted, 'and we never would have been able to finish the work without the help of the natives! Each day some 30 of them were at our service . . . They carried the timber from the forest on their shoulders, sometimes from places half an hour away.' Verguet himself had worked in the forest with a team of twenty sawyers.

Once the work of construction was completed, the only task that remained was to transfer to land the mission's numerous provisions, including all the animals which had not died en route. 'Although more than a year had passed since we had left France,' Verguet wrote some years later, 'surprisingly enough our grape, olive, orange and fig seedlings did not perish. This was due to the intelligent care given them by our gardener, Brother Charles. Our flower seeds and vegetable seeds were also still good and later we would have many experiences. The potatoes did not succeed at all, but gourds prospered. Tobacco grew inordinately large, each stalk reaching more than six feet and having very large leaves. The fig trees and orange trees seemed to prosper, but the grapevines did not. Maize and also sesame oil plants grew well.'

Once installed in their mission station the Marists no longer needed the *Marian Watson*, which was expensive to charter, so Captain Richards prepared to leave for Sydney via New Caledonia. At the request of the missionaries he sold them his surplus arms and salted provisions. He also took three missionaries aboard for the return trip. Father Montrouzier and also Brother Prosper, who had supervised the building at Makira, were to sail as far as New Caledonia. And Father Chaurain intended to sail all the way back to Sydney to purchase new supplies for the mission, especially food. Before leaving San Cristóbal, Captain Richards invited all the missionaries aboard his ship for a farewell dinner.[24]

The *Marian Watson* arrived back in Sydney on 23 April 1846, exactly six full months after it had sailed for Melanesia.[25] Quickly the news spread throughout the city that Captain Richards had returned safe and sound and that Bishop Epalle was dead.

21

Australia's first three dioceses: Sydney, Hobart Town, Adelaide

5 APRIL 1842

When Bishop Polding left Sydney with Vicar General Ullathorne in November 1840 for England, Ireland and Rome, he was still in charge of the Vicariate Apostolic of New Holland and Van Diemen's Land, an ecclesiastical territory embracing all of modern Australia. Officially at this time he was a vicar apostolic with the rank of titular bishop. He hoped that England and Ireland would provide him with priests for the fast growing Catholic population of Australia. And convinced en route by Ullathorne of its urgency, he hoped that Rome would name new bishops to take over parts of his vast vicariate. In the early part of their six-month journey Ullathorne had worked out a detailed plan, not only for new bishoprics, but for establishing the hierarchy in Australia as well. And although Polding intended at first not to bring up the hierarchy aspect of the plan to Rome, he later agreed that 'the sooner . . . the Hierarchy can take its proper form, the better'. His first project apparently was successful because Captain Peter Dillon, writing from London on 17 November 1842 to Superior General Colin of the Marists, said that Polding 'has left Liverpool for Sydney with 18 priests'.[1]

Captain Dillon was right about the total number in Polding's party, but he was wrong about all eighteen of them being priests. Only eight were priests! Of the others, two were studying for the priesthood, five wanted to become priests or monks, and three were Brothers of the Christian Schools of Ireland, nowadays called simply Christian Brothers (C.F.C.). The names of the teaching Brothers were Francis Larkin, Peter Scannell and Stephen Carroll.

How had Polding managed to get them after so many fruitless attempts? While in Rome he persuaded Cardinal Prefect Fransoni of the Evangelisation Congregation to write for him on 22 January 1842 to Brother Michael Paul Riordan, who had been elected to succeed Rice as superior general of the Irish teaching Brothers on 25 July 1838. Fransoni told Riordan that according to Polding 'it would be very useful for religion in his vicariate, if schools could be founded there headed by teachers chosen from the congregation in which Your Reverence fulfils the office of superior general with such great praise. However, it would be necessary', Fransoni continued, 'that at least four of your truly qualified members be designated by Your Reverence for this task and that they go with the Vicar Apostolic to New Holland where they will find everything necessary for living respectably.'

Riordan answered on 9 April 1842 from Waterford, Ireland, saying that he was 'eager to comply with whatever request might be directed to me by the Sacred Congregation or by Your Eminence'. But there were 'so many difficulties and so many obstacles' in the way, that he had had to delay in sending his reply. He did not see how he could accommodate Polding without at the same time causing 'very great inconvenience for the already established houses of our institute'. Nevertheless he hoped to be able to give Polding 'three well experienced brothers in vows'. Riordan signed himself as 'Superior General of the Society of the Brothers of the Christian Schools in Ireland and in England'.

Not wanting to force anyone to leave his home country contrary to his inclination, Riordan asked for volunteers. 'Only towards the middle of October were the names of those to go made public', Brother Stephen Carroll recalled. 'In the end of October we three met in Liverpool.' Riordan was there to see them off as they left with Polding on 2 November 1842 aboard the *Templar*. They reached Sydney on 9 March 1843 and went ashore the next day. Before the end of that year the three teaching Brothers were running three Sydney schools with large enrolments on Macquarie Street, Kent Street North and Abercrombie Place. But Polding's funds proved insufficient for their support and for the efficient administration of their schools and soon they returned to Ireland.[2]

Polding's principal task in 1842, however, had been to persuade Rome to name more bishops for Australia. After taking up lodging at the San Calisto Hospice of the Benedictines in the Trastevere section of Rome, he wrote to Cardinal Prefect Fransoni of the Evangelisation Congregation on 19 January, stating his case. 'Not only do we we need a larger number of priests, so that the work of the Church may continue to grow, but many bishops must also be sent into this vineyard, if we wish to do the job well and see everything have a happy result.'

He explained that 'this region, where we labour, is very extensive and embraces almost one-fifth of the land area of the entire world'. His territory was nearly as big as Europe itself,[3] he said, and he also had to look after Van Diemen's Land (now Tasmania) and Norfolk Island. This island, he said, was 350 leagues away from Sydney, 'our principal city'. And if a bishop wished to visit the churches and chapels of his mission stations like he should, 'very much precious time is wasted by travelling and it also costs an immense amount of money'. To overcome these difficulties, he said, it would be necessary 'to ordain three bishops and send them into our vineyard'.

Polding did not want these new bishops to be merely vicars apostolic, like himself. He maintained that the title vicar apostolic had no meaning for Protestants, who were busy with plans to found full-fledged dioceses very soon in all British colonies. And so it was necessary for the Catholic Church 'to establish episcopal sees without delay' in which bishops would enjoy 'ordinary jurisdiction'. Besides, he said, the Catholic population of Australia was constantly on the increase and was forever requesting that the hierarchy be established.

But on the other hand Polding did not want these new bishops to be deprived of 'the most ample faculties' usually granted to vicars apostolic. To make his plan juridically acceptable, he said that each new diocese could be part of a separate vicariate apostolic. In this way the same man could be diocesan bishop and vicar apostolic and so enjoy all powers deriving from each office. The titles of the new bishops, he suggested, could be taken from some city within their jurisdiction. For example, 'the first one could be called Bishop of Sydney and Vicar Apostolic of New Holland; the second one could be called Bishop of Hobart Town and Vicar Apostolic of Van Diemen's Land or Tasmania; and the third, Bishop of Adelaide and Vicar Apostolic of South Australia'.

Cardinal Fransoni had no objection to Polding's proposal, but he did need more precise information, such as suggestions for the exact boundaries that might be assigned to the new ecclesiastical territories, a list of possible candidates to head the new diocese-vicariate combinations, and a report on the qualifications of the various candidates proposed. Fransoni had Secretary Archbishop Cadolini request this information of Polding on 25 January 1842 and the bishop replied from his San Calisto address in Trastevere on 7 February. The creation of the three new dioceses and vicariates apostolic was then placed on the agenda for the next General Meeting of the Evangelisation Congregation scheduled for 28 February.

All cardinals attending this meeting received a copy of Polding's letter of 7 February. In it he had called New Holland a continent and said that England intended to colonise all of it. 'The division now being proposed for its ecclesiastical government', he said, 'is nothing but a beginning and must be followed by other divisions. It is therefore of the greatest consequence to act on the basis of some principle and to follow some plan that applies not only to the present needs of the Church, but also to the future, when more bishops will be requested as collaborators.' Polding suggested the adoption of this principle: 'Whenever the British government establishes a new state in New Holland and gives it a local government independent of other local governments, the Holy See ought to take action as quickly as circumstances of the moment may suggest and erect in that same state a mission or vicariate. . . .'

Cardinal Castracane had been chosen to report on this matter to the other cardinals at the meeting and explained to them at great length precisely what Polding meant by these words. 'He does not mean that new bishops should be assigned there with a title *in partibus*, as generally is the case with vicars apostolic,' Castracane said, 'but rather that the bishops assigned there ought to have *titles taken from some city within their jurisdiction and have in addition the authority of vicar apostolic.*'

In defence of Polding's position Castracane said that the Church most wisely adapts itself to the times, when its own good evidently requires this, and he gave some examples. 'Your Eminences are aware that very many dioceses erected recently in the United States of America have boundaries which coincide generally with the boundaries of individual states. You also know of the dioceses of Montreal, of Charlottetown, and of Kingston in Upper Canada, of Nova Scotia, and of others as well, which are limited for the most part by the boundaries of their province or civil territory. . . .' Castracane also mentioned

Polding's argument on the importance of not allowing 'heterodox Anglicans to be first in so serious a matter'. Catholics instead ought to be 'the first ones to found new episcopal sees in those regions'.

The cardinal then pointed out where the three bishops ought to reside— Hobart Town, Adelaide and Sydney—following exactly the suggestions of Polding. He also called attention to Perth, the chief city of Western Australia, since this section of the country in 1829 had also received its own civil government. According to Polding's principle, Perth should also have been among the proposed dioceses and Western Australia among the proposed vicariates apostolic. 'But this state can be considered as still in its infancy', Castracane explained, quoting Polding, and therefore a different arrangement could be adopted temporarily. The suggestion made by Polding was that Western Australia for the present should remain attached to his territory. He would then send his vicar general to Perth to look after church affairs in that part of the country. But Polding had also intimated that the Holy See might want to give him a coadjutor in view of the fact that he would have to remain in New South Wales, Castracane said. In that case Polding planned to send his coadjutor to remote areas of his vicariate such as Western Australia.

'In order to obtain a proper idea of the geography of these areas,' Castracane told the cardinals, 'it would be very useful to consult the second volume of the geographical compendium . . . published in Turin in 1840 by the celebrated and most erudite geographer Cavalier Adriano Balbi.' The full title of this book announced that it had been compiled 'according to a new plan which keeps in mind the latest peace treaties and most recent discoveries'. Castracane said the cardinals could find 'Australia or Central Oceania treated on page 798 and the pages that follow'.[4]

Here again is an example of how up to date the Evangelisation Congregation was in its geographical knowledge. Balbi's work was published in 1840 and was used for the preparation of this meeting of 28 February 1842.

After having explained the juridical and geographical aspects of Polding's proposal, Castracane mentioned the names of the candidates whom Polding proposed for the two new bishoprics. Polding himself was to remain at Sydney. For Hobart Town in Van Diemen's Land he had suggested Father Robert William Willson, a secular priest in England. In justifying the placement of a bishop there, Polding had pointed out that the British government in 1840 had chosen the province of Van Diemen's Land, or Tasmania, as the new location for its penal colony. Some 200 condemned people were being shipped there each year and at least one-third of them were Catholics, he said. And the non-Catholics could be converted.

For the bishopric of Adelaide, Polding presented four candidates, saying that their ages ranged from thirty-five to forty:

1. Father William Bernard Ullathorne, the English Benedictine who formerly had been Polding's vicar general. He had visited Rome in 1837 as Polding's

delegate to report to the Evangelisation Congregation on Catholic affairs in Australia and now resided in England.

2. Father Francis Murphy, Polding's current vicar general.

3. Father Gentili, a missionary assigned to the Central District of England and a member of the Institute of Charity founded in Italy by Father Antonio Rosmini in 1828. Polding did not know Gentili personally, but said that the Evangelisation Congregation could easily obtain information on him by contacting Rosmini and the Vicar Apostolic of the Central District in England.

4. Father Francis Appleton, a Benedictine. He had earlier been prior of the Benedictine monastery in Douai, France, and currently was serving as a missionary in Liverpool.

Polding gave no list of candidates for a possible coadjutor. But he did say that the Holy See, if it wanted to give him one, could choose the coadjutor from the above list.

After Cardinal Castracane completed his presentation, he asked the cardinals to vote on the following seven points:

1. Should the pope be asked to make Van Diemen's Land or Tasmania a bishopric or vicariate apostolic to be called Hobart Town?

2. Also South Australia, to be called Adelaide?

3. If the reply is affirmative for numbers one and two, should the pope be asked whether Bishop Polding, presently Vicar Apostolic of New Holland, may give up his titular Bishopric of Gerocesarea *in partibus* and take instead that of Sydney in New South Wales, having jurisdiction over it and over Western Australia as well, and also over the rest of what has not yet been separated from his original territory?

4. If the reply is affirmative for numbers one and two, who should be Bishop of Hobart Town?

5. Who of Adelaide?

6. Should the pope be asked to provide a coadjutor with right of succession for Sydney, and who should he be?

7. If the reply is negative for numbers one and two, what is to be done for the benefit of religion there?

The replies of the cardinals were affirmative, not negative, for numbers one, two and three. As Bishop of Hobart Town they decided to ask Pope Gregory XVI to name Father Robert William Willson (1794–1866), who 'for 15 years in the City of Nottingham has fulfilled his office as missionary remarkably well'. And as Bishop of Adelaide they decided to suggest Father William Bernard Ullathorne (1806–89), 'a man of proven outstanding talent who fulfilled his office excellently as vicar general' under Bishop Polding. They also favourably discussed giving Polding a coadjutor, but decided to postpone their decision on this particular issue until they could obtain more information about Father Francis Murphy, Polding's vicar general.[5]

Three things, however, were very strange about these decisions reached by the cardinals on 28 February 1842. First of all, point number one spoke of making 'Van Diemen's Land or Tasmania a bishopric or vicariate apostolic to be called Hobart Town', and point number two spoke of making South Australia a bishopric or vicariate to be called Adelaide. This was hardly a summary of the content of the paper read by Castracane, since he clearly supported the proposal made by Polding, namely, that both Van Diemen's Land (or Tasmania) and South Australia should become vicariates apostolic and that both Hobart Town and Adelaide should become dioceses.

Secondly, Secretary Cadolini indicated in none of the five places, where it is usually to be found, the precise date on which he presented these decisions of the Evangelisation Congregation to the pope.[6] Did he perhaps bring the matter to the pope's attention repeatedly, consulting during the intervals with Cardinal Prefect Fransoni or Bishop Polding or both?

And thirdly, there was a delay of thirty-six days before an apostolic letter of Pope Gregory XVI, dated 5 April 1842, was issued in the form of a brief and announced: ' . . . We decree that the bishop, [who is] Vicar Apostolic of the Island and Land of Van Diemen, should take the title Hobart Town from the chief city of that state . . . , and that the bishop, [who is] Vicar Apostolic of the State of South Australia, should take the title Adelaide from . . . the first city of that state. . . .' In the same apostolic letter the pope gave Polding the new title of Bishop of Sydney, leaving the Vicariate Apostolic of New Holland under his jurisdiction, but excluding from it Van Diemen's Land (Tasmania) and South Australia. The pope's apostolic letter also gave the Bishop of Hobart Town and the Bishop of Adelaide the faculties usually granted to vicars apostolic.[7]

This action by the pope meant that he had adopted in their entirety Polding's suggestions for three full-fledged dioceses[8] within three separate vicariates apostolic, with the bishop of the diocese in each case also being a vicar apostolic. And since Secretary Cadolini has left no record of the date of the papal audience at which Pope Gregory XVI approved of this novel arrangement, the date of the apostolic letter—5 April 1842—is accepted as the foundation date for the three dioceses and the corresponding vicariates apostolic.

During Secretary Cadolini's audience, the pope had also agreed that Willson and Ullathorne should be named the bishops of Hobart Town and Adelaide respectively. Although Ullathorne was well enough known in Rome, further official action on behalf of both candidates was suspended until Charles Cardinal Acton (1803–47) could be asked for his comments on Willson's qualifications. A resident of Rome since 1831, Acton was counsellor to the Holy See on English affairs. Although he would be proclaimed cardinal only on 24 June 1842, he had been named cardinal *in petto* by Pope Gregory XVI three years earlier. Willson, born in Lincoln, England, in 1794, had been in charge of Nottingham since 1825 and Acton long ago had heard about him. On 10 April 1842, therefore, Cadolini was able to tell the pope: 'Most favourable reports have been received from England by His Eminence [*sic*] Acton on the priest Reverend Robert Willson. . . .' Cadolini consequently suggested that the pope authorise the

official designation of Willson as Bishop of Hobart Town and of Ullathorne as
Bishop of Adelaide, and this the pope did.

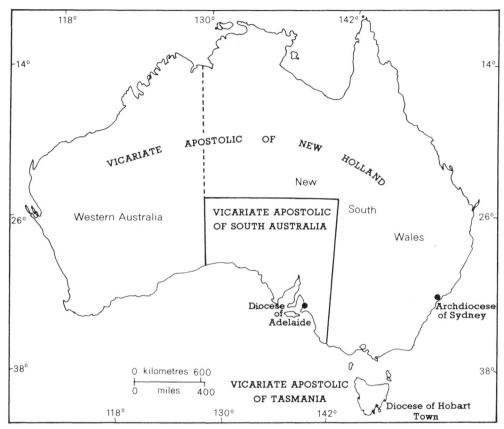

53 Pope Gregory XVI at the suggestion of Bishop
Polding founded the Australian hierarchy on 10 April
1842. The Archdiocese of Sydney and the two suffragan Dioceses of Hobart Town and Adelaide were
conceived as enclaves in the already existing
Vicariates Apostolic of New Holland, Tasmania and
South Australia, which were not abolished. The
archbishop and two bishops, although now raised to
a higher rank with regard to their archdiocese and
dioceses, continued to serve as vicars apostolic of
their respective vicariates apostolic. (Chapter 21).

In virtue of the apostolic letter of 5 April the three dioceses of Sydney, Hobart
Town and Adelaide were completely independent of one another. This meant
that Polding's request to have the hierarchy established—that is, to have a
juridical interdependence among the bishops—had been overlooked or inten-
tionally bypassed. Cadolini also referred to this matter in his audience of 10 April
1842. 'Now that these dioceses have been founded,' he said, 'New Holland
should not be deprived of the advantages which flow from uniformity of
discipline and from unity of direction. Therefore it is further proposed to Your
Holiness to constitute an ecclesiastical province by making the Bishop of Sydney

354 FOUNDING OF THE ROMAN CATHOLIC CHURCH IN OCEANIA

the archbishop metropolitan and the other bishops his suffragans.' The pope readily gave his consent.[9]

When reporting back to the cardinals of the Evangelisation Congregation on the pope's establishing the hierarchy in Australia on this day, Cadolini said: 'After His Holiness was informed of this proposal of the Sacred Congregation by the Secretary in the audience of 10 April 1842, he graciously gave his approval to all points and ordered that an Apostolic Letter in the form of a Brief should be sent to the Most Reverend John Bede Polding, who consequently shall receive the title Archbishop of Sydney. . . .'[10]

Polding was still in Rome at this time and Cadolini sent him a letter on 13 April addressing it, 'To the Bishop of Sydney and the Vicar Apostolic of New Holland'. The letter contained a copy of the 5 April 1842 apostolic letter of Pope Gregory XVI and Cadolini mentioned that its contents were already 'fully known' to Polding. He said it was a pleasure for him to inform Polding 'that the Holy Father was pleased to raise the episcopal see of Sydney to archiepiscopal rank; the bishops of Hobart Town and of Adelaide shall be dependent upon it as suffragans'. He assured Polding that another brief would be sent as soon as possible 'regarding this new honorary disposition of His Holiness'.[11]

On the following day, 14 April, Cadolini wrote to Cardinal Lambruschini, Secretary of Briefs of His Holiness, asking him to have briefs prepared announcing the elevation of Sydney to the rank of archdiocese and the designation of Hobart Town and Adelaide as its suffragan sees. Additional briefs were to be drawn up naming Willson and Ullathorne the bishops of Hobart Town and Adelaide respectively.[12]

Prior to his going to Rome, Polding had repeatedly asked Ullathorne to take the proposed Diocese of Hobart Town, but Ullathorne had constantly refused because he foresaw endless clashes with Father Therry of Van Diemen's Land, notorious for 'his want of management in temporal affairs', as Ullathorne expressed it. The result was, Ullathorne said, 'that I received a letter from the Bishop informing me that our relations were at an end'. Surprised, but also relieved, Ullathorne at once resigned his offices in Australia and took charge of Coventry in the Midlands. Nevertheless Polding had strongly recommended him to Roman authorities for the see of Adelaide, believing that submitting his name for an Australian see was 'due to his character, to his services, to his talents and piety. . . .'

By 7 May, Polding was informed that 'the people of Nottingham' and 'the Protestant magistrates' had raised such an outcry over the removal of Willson, his sole candidate for the bishopric of Hobart Town, that the pope had permitted Willson to refuse the nomination. And so Polding saw Cadolini and suggested another priest as substitute. Cadolini passed on this information to Pope Gregory XVI on 23 May, saying that the replacement suggested was Father Joseph Peter Wilson, 'the Benedictine prior of Saint Gregory the Great [Monastery at Downside, England]', upon whom Polding 'lavishes the greatest praise'. The pope then authorised the substitution.[13]

On the day after seeing the pope about naming a different priest as first

Bishop of Hobart Town, Cadolini sent Archbishop Polding (he was still in Rome at San Calisto Hospice) the news that 'the Holy Father has deigned to consent completely to your wishes'.[14]

By this time, however, Cadolini already had on hand the papal brief from Cardinal Lambruschini naming Father Robert Willson the Bishop of Hobart Town. So he sent it back on 25 May, a Wednesday, informing Lambruschini that His Holiness had authorised the substitution of 'Father Joseph Wilson of the English Congregation of Benedictines' for this office. And he asked that the necessary changes be made as quickly as possible, 'because Archbishop Polding of Sydney would like to leave Rome in the first days of next week and wishes to take along with him the Brief in question. . . .'[15]

Ullathorne, resolved as he was 'to decline the Episcopate in any shape', went to Rome to plead his own case. After giving his reasons for declining to Cardinal Prefect Fransoni, he was freed from the appointment to Adelaide. Polding then informed Cadolini that in place of Ullathorne he would like to see Father Francis Murphy, his vicar general, named Bishop of Adelaide. There was no time for Cadolini to see the pope, nor was there time for delay, since Polding was anxious to take along the brief for Murphy as well. So Cadolini, presuming that the pope would give the proper authorisation at his next audience, wrote a second letter to Lambruschini on 25 May, nearly identical to the first, and asked that Father Francis Murphy be named the first Bishop of Adelaide instead of Ullathorne. And since he already had the papal brief naming Ullathorne, he returned it to Lambruschini with his letter.[16]

It was not until four days later, Sunday, 29 May 1842, that Secretary Cadolini was able to have his next audience. He told the pope that Ullathorne had refused to accept the Diocese of Adelaide 'because of his inability to support the hot climate of New Holland'. And he added that the Archbishop of Sydney had proposed instead Father Murphy, his vicar general, for this office. The pope agreed to the substitution and named Father Francis Murphy, born in 1795 in Navan, County Meath, Ireland, in Sydney since 1838, the first Bishop of Adelaide.[17]

Like Ullathorne, Father Joseph Peter Wilson, prior of Downside, also delayed in indicating acceptance of Hobart Town. A fellow Benedictine, Bishop T. J. Brown, in a long letter had strongly advised him not to accept. In a postscript Brown said: 'The clergy and people in Australia are almost all Irish, having a strong national feeling. Dr. Ullathorne, and I think Dr. Polding, told me that the Australian Irish clergy, and their countrymen, including the Bishops in Ireland, were sore at being under an English Bishop and a Regular.' (Polding, being a Benedictine, was a 'Regular', that is, a member of a religious order.) Brown's conclusion was: 'Let Dr. Polding recommend Irishmen for Bishops, and more good will be done.' Wilson of Downside eventually declined his appointment as Bishop of Hobart Town.

Once again Polding began to think of Willson of Nottingham for the office. He was an Englishman, but not a member of a religious order, and according to Ullathorne had 'remarkable qualities and . . . singular fitness for that penal settlement'. Willson, again approached, was subsequently placed under obedience by the Holy See to accept the office. And so Cadolini found himself in the embarrassing position of having to write yet another letter to Lambruschini for a papal brief.[18]

Archbishop Polding was still in England when the papal brief arrived naming Willson the first Bishop of Hobart Town. Willson's episcopal ordination took place in Saint Chad's Cathedral in Birmingham on 28 October 1842 with Polding as the ordaining prelate. Visits to France, Rome, Ireland, as well as business matters, delayed Willson's departure for Australia until January 1844. He reached Hobart Town on 11 May 1844 and was installed as its bishop in Saint Joseph's Church the following day, Sunday.

Archbishop Polding had convoked a provincial council and Willson arrived in Sydney on 16 August 1844 to take part in it. Murphy had not yet been ordained Bishop of Adelaide by this time. With Willson present, Polding then ordained Murphy in Saint Mary's Cathedral, Sydney, on Sunday, 8 September 1844, two years and three months after his nomination by the pope. He thus became the first bishop to be ordained in Australia. Archbishop Polding with his two suffragan bishops, Willson and Murphy, then held the First Provincial Council of Australia on 10–12 September.

Not only 'the hot climate of New Holland', however, had prompted Ullathorne to refuse the Diocese of Adelaide. He had told the Evangelisation Congregation that he considered assigning a bishop to Adelaide as being premature. The poverty of the place, he maintained, was so bad that the lone priest stationed there (Father Benson) would soon be obliged to leave. He himself had visited Adelaide in 1839, learned that there were not more than fifty Catholics, and found only one Catholic family above the condition of a labourer.

One wonders, however, whether Ullathorne's 'inability to support the hot climate of New Holland', the reason given to the pope for his refusing Adelaide, had anything to do with his refusal at all. Immediately after Willson's episcopal ordination by Polding in the Birmingham cathedral, Ullathorne was assisting the new bishop with unvesting in the sacristy and said to him: 'Now that the mitre is on your head and not on mine, I have no objection to go out [to Australia] and help you.' 'Are you in earnest?' Willson asked. Ullathorne was in earnest, but he remained at Coventry. And although he refused the two Australian bishoprics of Hobart Town and Adelaide in 1841 and 1842, as well as the bishopric of Perth in 1845, he accepted an English bishopric in 1846.

Polding, oddly enough, while presenting Ullathorne to Rome as a candidate for the Adelaide bishopric, was at the same time suggesting to influential people that Ullathorne 'would be more efficient' in England 'than even in South Australia'. And again he said, 'Dr. Ullathorne (*entre nous*) would do better for the proposed Benedictine Vicariate [in England] than anyone else I am acquainted with'. When Ullathorne became a bishop in 1846, he was placed in charge of the Vicariate Apostolic of the Western District of England. In 1848 he was transferred to the Vicariate Apostolic of the Central District of England. And after going to Rome where he successfully worked for the reestablishment of the hierarchy in England, he was named first Bishop of Birmingham in 1850, an office which he held until his resignation in March 1888, one year before his death.[19]

The Prefecture Apostolic
to the Aborigines of Australia
is given to the Passionists

12 JUNE 1842

Bishop Polding wrote from Sydney on 10 January 1840 to the Association for the Propagation of the Faith, a fund-collecting agency in Lyon, France, expressing deep regret that he did not have a priest whom he could send to work among the Aborigines. These dark-skinned food gatherers and hunters were thinly scattered over vast areas of Australia. At this time Polding was Vicar Apostolic of New Holland and Van Diemen's Land, an office which made him spiritually responsible for all of what is now Australia. He left Sydney on 16 November that year in order to recruit personnel in Europe and arrived at Le Havre, France, early in May 1841.[1]

In 1842 he was in Rome and on 10 April of that year he succeeded in having Pope Gregory XVI establish the Australian hierarchy. Although Polding was placed in charge of the Archdiocese of Sydney at this time, he was left in charge of the Vicariate Apostolic of New Holland. This meant that he was still responsible for all of Australia's Aborigines except those residing in the states of Tasmania and South Australia. These two states on 5 April of that year at Polding's suggestion had been separated from his vicariate apostolic to become independent vicariates apostolic.

While in Rome for these negotiations Polding met forty-year-old Father Raimondo Vaccari. This priest had been born in Rome, enjoyed great fame as a preacher, and had many influential friends among the laity, the upper ranks of the clergy, and the cardinals at the Vatican. Polding explained how much he needed someone to dedicate himself to the conversion of the Aborigines and Vaccari volunteered. He was a member of the Passionists, a religious order officially known as the Congregation of the Passion of Jesus Christ (C.P.). Being in vows he needed the permission of his superior general to leave for Australia.[2]

Vaccari asssured Polding that he would have no trouble acquiring the necessary permission; he also had hopes of obtaining some Passionist priests to join him. But Father Superior General, Antonio di San Giacomo, knew that Vaccari had a difficult and complex character; he judged him unfit for such a mission and refused to grant the desired permission. Undaunted by this initial failure Vaccari made repeated requests, but all in vain. He then had Archbishop Polding approach the superior general and try to persuade him, but the archbishop's efforts also proved ineffectual.

Being resourceful men, Vaccari and Polding then asked others to intercede for them. Soon high ecclesiastical dignitaries, as well as men famed for sanctity, began contacting the superior general. They pointed out that he was 'opposing the will of God' and they urged him to consider 'the great good that could be accomplished in the new world', if only he were to send some priests there under Father Vaccari, 'a man of extraordinary zeal and fervour'. Among those who approached Father Antonio di San Giacomo were Cardinal Orioli, an influential member of the Franciscan Conventuals (O.F.M. Conv.) and also Father Vincenzo Pallotti, who had founded the Society of the Catholic Apostolate (S.A.C.) in Rome in 1835 and was 'considered by all Rome to be a saint'.

In spite of these exhortations, however, the superior general was still unwilling to release Father Vaccari for missionary work among the Aborigines.

But at this point high church authorities stepped in. 'I was ordered to send him', Antonio di San Giacomo later said. 'He obtained the mission by himself and would not stay here any longer. From then on I remained passive, assigning to him the three companions requested of me and I let him go.' The three companions were Fathers Giuseppe Snell, aged forty, Luigi Maria Pesciaroli, aged thirty-six and Maurizio Lencioni, aged twenty-eight. Pesciaroli and Lencioni, like Vaccari, were born in Italy; Snell was born in Lyon, France.[3]

It was almost at the end of his stay in Rome that Polding finally succeeded in getting these four Passionist priests for his mission. Pope Gregory XVI had agreed to receive him in audience on Sunday, 29 May 1842, together with Secretary Cadolini of the Evangelisation Congregation, because a day or two later Polding intended to leave Rome.[4] In his negotiations with the Evangelisation Congregation he had made it clear that he wanted the Passionists to be under his jurisdiction, just like the other priests within his territory. And when he left Rome in the first days of June, he was under the impression that the Evangelisation Congregation had agreed to this type of arrangement.[5]

But on Sunday, 12 June 1842, when Secretary Cadolini had his regular weekly audience with Pope Gregory XVI, he requested the pope's authorisation to issue letters patent to Snell, Pesciaroli and Lencioni as missionaries apostolic for Australia, and to Vaccari as prefect apostolic. The pope granted this request.[6] By doing so he not only made Vaccari a prefect apostolic, but also automatically raised Vaccari's mission to the rank of prefecture apostolic. This meant that juridically the mission to the Aborigines was removed from Archbishop Polding's jurisdiction and was placed under the jurisdiction of Vaccari.

Why this sudden turn of events without Polding's knowledge? As Vaccari would one day explain, he too had no advance knowledge of this promotion and had not sought it. All official steps had already been taken when he was informed by his influential friends that they had approached Cardinal Prefect Fransoni and had persuaded him to ask the pope to make Vaccari a prefect apostolic.[7]

Following instructions earlier received from Polding the four Passionists left Rome that summer for Liverpool. Together with Polding and the fourteen others whom he had recruited for service in Australia, they left Liverpool aboard the *Templar* on 2 November 1842, just five days after Polding had ordained Willson a bishop in Birmingham. They sailed via the Cape of Good Hope and landed at Sydney on 10 March 1843.[8] Polding, an English Benedictine, aged forty-eight, had had six years of missionary experience in Australia and was entering his see city for the first time as archbishop and as head of the newly established Australian hierarchy. Vaccari, an Italian Passionist, aged forty-one, had no foreign missionary experience at all and knew no English, the language of this British colony. Little difficulty was anticipated from this lack of English, however, because he and his companions were to work exclusively among the Aborigines. Polding gave the Passionists lodging in his own house.

Believing that the Passionists were completely under his jurisdiction, Polding decided where they should settle, what they should do, and how their needs should be supplied. The place that he chose was far up the eastern coast, at Dunwich on Stradbroke Island in Moreton Bay, opposite modern Brisbane. It was frequented at that time only by Aborigines, except for the pilot station some thirteen kilometres to the north at Amity Point where six or eight whites generally resided. He explained to the Passionists that this was meant only as a temporary location for their mission, since they needed to become acquainted with the customs of the Aborigines and learn their language. Then later a decision could be reached on where the mission should be permanently established.

As for their needs, Polding was against giving them funds to purchase supplies in nearby Brisbane Town, as Brisbane was then called, arguing that undoubtedly costs were higher there. Instead he promised to supply them regularly by ship from Sydney. He would serve as their agent, so to speak, and they needed only to send him their requests for food, clothing and other items. He would then purchase these goods and have them transported by coastal steamer about every three weeks, using for this the funds destined for their mission.

In discussing the details of location, mission methods, and supplies, Vaccari did not always see eye to eye with Polding. And at one point, when his fiery temperament got the best of him, he solemnly announced that the pope had named him prefect apostolic, and that consequently he, and not Polding, was the real head of the mission. This news alarmed Polding, who was well acquainted with the canonical implications of that title. If true, it meant that the mission to the Aborigines would be an enclave in his Vicariate Apostolic of New Holland and that consequently it would not be under his jurisdiction. This was something that Polding was not prepared to accept.

He then told Vaccari that in all of his dealings with the Evangelisation Congregation there had never been any talk of the mission to the Aborigines becoming a prefecture apostolic. Furthermore, he himself had expressed the wish that the Passionists should be placed under his jurisdiction like all other priests within his territory, and his understanding was that this condition had been agreed upon by the authorities in Rome.

Regardless of what Polding's understanding in the matter was, Vaccari insisted, the pope had in fact named him prefect apostolic.

With each man claiming that he was right, there was a deadlock until finally Polding insisted that Vaccari present him with documentary proof of his

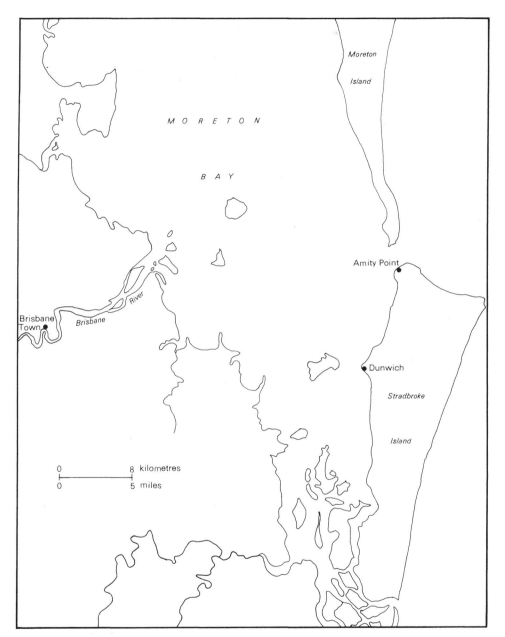

54   Dilapidated buildings at the former penal colony of Dunwich on Stradbroke Island housed the Passionist mission opened there for Aborigines on 24 May 1843. The Passionists usually referred to their location as 'Dunwich Island'. Today it is officially known as North Stradbroke Island, since the sea has meanwhile cut off a long slender portion called South Stradbroke Island. *Source: Royal Australian Survey Corps. (Chapters 22, 23).*

appointment. Vaccari then produced his official document, signed and sealed, and laid it before Polding, who was visibly shocked![9]

This clash proved most unfortunate for the Prefecture Apostolic to the Aborigines and was destined to leave its scars on these two men, who were so envious of each other's power. It seems strange that Polding, who at this time had over 6,500,000 square kilometres under his jurisdiction, should have balked at giving a bit of territory to Vaccari. Eventually Vaccari yielded to Polding.

Governor Gipps at Polding's request officially recognised the Passionists as missionaries to the Aborigines. He gave them permission to use Stradbroke Island and the dilapidated government buildings at Dunwich on the island's west coast as their base of operations for two years starting in May 1843. Polding then took Snell to the new mission, leaving Sydney aboard the coastal steamer *Sovereign* on 18 May, two months after his return from Europe. They reached Stradbroke Island in Moreton Bay District on 24 May 1843, feast of Mary, Help of Christians, foundation date of the mission. Later they were joined by Prefect Apostolic Vaccari, the two other Passionists, and Father Henry G. Gregory, the Benedictine who was Polding's secretary, all of whom left Sydney on 30 May for Stradbroke Island.

The fact that Polding considered himself to be in charge of the mission is evident when he writes from Moreton Bay District to Father Francis Murphy, his vicar general in Sydney. 'I passed upwards of a week at Dunwich', he said, 'and made considerable progress in the forming of a vocabulary.' He had gathered the children for classes and they seemed to be 'quite as apt as other children, but more giddy . . . Dunwich is in a state of great ruin. It is large, containing much capability if we had money. There is a detached building which the blacks call their own; in this they sleep; this I intend for their school and dwelling, when they choose. Then there are four rooms consecutive, in another building, enclosed and adjoining a large store, 56 feet by 30 feet; this I propose to be their church. I have made a regulation that there is to be no food without work. All have professed their readiness to labour provided that the corn and the produce be for themselves . . . They have fish in abundance . . . I cannot find on the island a piece of ground eligible for a garden; but in front of the house, about two miles off, there is an island very fit for the purpose and abounding in water. This latter element is abundant and excellent in Dunwich . . . The first Mass celebrated was on the Feast of the Ascension, the gospel of which is so appropriate.' (Ascension Thursday that year fell on 25 May, the day after Polding and Snell reached Stradbroke Island.)

The government estimate of 1843 spoke of 1,500 Aborigines within an eighty kilometre radius of Brisbane Town. By that year the agricultural settlement founded for the Aborigines a short distance to the west of Brisbane Town by the United Brethren from Herrnhut, Saxony, often called the Moravian Church, 'had completely failed', Polding said. He had therefore been in favour of establishing the Roman Catholic mission for Aborigines on Stradbroke Island, since in this way they would more effectually be kept separated from contact with white settlers. At the same time the missionaries would be near enough to

Brisbane Town for protection in case of emergency. The archbishop provided them with a boat so that they could visit the numerous islands in the bay and, if necessary, go to Brisbane Town. Polding and Gregory returned to Sydney in July, leaving the four Passionists to shift for themselves. However, Polding held the purse strings and he continued to act as if he had full jurisdiction over Vaccari, over his priests, and over his prefecture apostolic.

As early as 10 February 1838 Polding had stated that he wanted to assign priests to Port Macquarie on the coast north of Sydney, and also to Moreton Bay, to work among the white settlers. One of his reasons for going with the Passionists to their new mission was precisely to reconnoitre Moreton Bay District with Gregory, which he did, to see where a parish for whites might be founded. Actually as early as 9 December 1843 Fathers McGinnety and Hanly left Sydney aboard the *Sovereign* for Moreton Bay District. McGinnety built a stone church in Ipswich and Hanly a stone church fifteen by eight metres in Brisbane Town.

The Passionist missionaries were not at Dunwich long when they sent letters to their superior general, telling him about Vaccari's clash with Polding. They gave him a pessimistic view of their mission as well, saying that Polding had sent them to an island practically deserted except for a few Aborigines. Not only did they have much to suffer, but there was very little hope of doing any good and it seemed as if they had been sent into a kind of exile. Snell's, Pesciaroli's and Lencioni's letters also had harsh words for Vaccari, who had completely alienated them by his vexations and unreasonableness.[10]

Archbishop Polding had urged the Passionists to learn all they could about the culture of the Aborigines as a necessary condition for successful missionary work. A proof of their diligence can be found in a 29 January 1844 letter, written after they had been on Stradbroke Island eight months, which Pesciaroli sent to a friend, Gaspare Bernardo Cardinal Pianetti, Bishop of Viterbo, Italy. He said that he was writing 'from this very remote part of the world, from this wild country, from the midst of unfortunate and nude inhabitants of the forests'. Dunwich Island, his name for Stradbroke Island, was on the coast north of Sydney, he said, '45 miles before you reach the tiny village called Brisbane Town. This island is about 40 miles long, but very much less in width, and contains 150 indigenes.' He and the other three missionaries were living on the shore of a bay in a building that was falling into ruin. 'Earlier it had served as a prison for condemned Englishmen here', he said.

Dunwich on Stradbroke Island had an interesting history. After John Oxley discovered the Brisbane River in 1823 the Moreton Bay Penal Settlement was officially proclaimed on 15 August 1826. Captain Patrick Logan, soldier and commandant of the Penal Settlement, recommended its removal from the Brisbane River area to Dunwich on 19 June 1827 and he was able to report on 1 May 1828 that at Dunwich the military barracks and barracks for convicts had been completed and occupied. Almost a thousand convicts filled the Penal Settlement by 1831 but in May 1839 it began to break up and near the end of that year there were only twenty-nine prisoners left. The order which had established Moreton Bay Penal Settlement was finally revoked on 11 February 1842; this was four months before the Prefecture Apostolic to the Aborigines had been founded in Rome. By the time the first Passionist arrived at Dunwich on 24 May 1843 the buildings there had been at the mercy of the elements for four years.

Pesciaroli explained the customs of the Aborigines in great detail for Cardinal Pianetti. 'Every tribe numbers 30, 40 or at most 50 individuals', he said, and one numbering about 40 members 'often' stayed in their vicinity. He had used the word 'often', he said, 'because all of them have a fixed and distinct place where they generally reside, but they do not remain in that place more than 8 or 10 days. They leave it again and again to wander about here or there, just like those animals which often go back to a place and stay awhile where they find more pasture. They either live in the open or make themselves a kind of provisional shelter from the bark of trees. Often they abandon it the next day or now and then they set it afire.'

The Aborigines at Dunwich Island had known Europeans—the convicts—for a long time and were rather sociable and also docile. 'But we have been told not to place too much trust in their apparent docility', Pesciaroli said, 'because their nature makes them betray even those who do good to them.' In appearance they were 'not as ugly or black as the African Moors'. And in order to make themselves more beautiful, 'they daub their bodies very often with charcoal and over this they paint various stripes or spots, using red earth or some other coloured material'. He considered them to be 'rather tall' and said 'their constitution is strong and robust. But in spite of this they are cowards to the extreme, and they are gluttonous, slothful, immoral and also revengeful.'

Practically all the men took shells and cut gashes with them in their arms, shoulders, back and legs. 'The raised flesh on healing then forms decorations which please them and make them very proud, but which also cost them a good bit of pain.' Little girls have the small finger of their left hand bound in such a way as to impede circulation. 'After some days the first knuckle is torn off, so that it can be dedicated—as I was told—to the boa, the fish, and the kangaroo. We deduce that by this offering our aborigines hope to obtain success for themselves in hunting, and an abundant catch of fish, since these are practically the only two means of subsistence which they have.'

Their diet also included the tubers of a certain kind of plant. 'When these are roasted', Pesciaroli said, 'they taste something like potatoes. They also eat the iguana, an animal like the lizard, but very much larger; the flying fox, which resembles a huge bat; and the kangaroo, which is not to be found on this island, but exists in great numbers on nearby islands. Fish, however, is their most common daily food. To catch it, six or seven of them jump into the sea near the shore, each one holding his own net made from thin cords that come from tree roots. First they form a semicircle and then gradually surround the fish, murmuring all the while some words between their teeth. And when they notice that the fish is in the centre, they all rush toward this one point, shouting loudly and apparently stupefying the fish. Then they grab it, roast it while it is still palpitating, and eat it. Or, let me rather say, they devour it.'

Fire played a very important role in their lives, Pesciaroli said. 'Carrying a piece of burning wood on their person is a kind of special devotion practised by them. And when they do not have it, or when the fire goes out, they take a very porous dried out piece of wood, make a small depression in it, and then fit into this depression another piece of harder wood. This piece they handle skilfully, beginning to bore with it at once. While the piece below is being perforated, it gets hot, starts to smoke, and begins to burn.'

In witnessing burials Pesciaroli noticed that fire also played an important role. 'After the corpse has been placed in the tomb prepared for it,' he said, 'they never fail to place at one side of it one of their defensive weapons and at the other side a piece of burning wood.' Searching for some reason behind this, Pesciaroli thought they believed 'that fire, their inseparable companion in the wanderings of this life, must be even more necessary for their limbs after they have become stiff with the coldness of death.' Or perhaps fire might be their symbol of immortality, he said. 'For in the same manner as the flame rises toward heaven by freeing itself from the material, which it sucks up and consumes, they may believe that they, too, after the death of their body, shall rise above the atmosphere and shall find there the delights of eternal banquets as a compensation for the great privations which they have been forced to endure here below.'

Most important for the missionaries, of course, was learning the language, since it was indispensable for conveying the teachings of Christianity. But they found it 'very difficult'. According to Pesciaroli what made it so difficult was the ability of the Aborigines to express so much in so few words, 'something which follows necessarily from their scarcity of vocal sounds. They do not pronounce and do not have these letters of the alphabet: c, f, s, and z. As a result of this language problem we do not yet know what to say about their [possible] conversion. Nor have we made enough progress yet to be able to explain in their language the eternal truths as fittingly as their presentation demands. But God is omnipotent! And the confidence, which we have placed in his infinite mercy from the time of our arrival, shall not be betrayed.'

Pesciaroli concluded his long report by requesting Cardinal Pianetti to send his blessing. And he added: 'I also make bold to ask that you recommend me to the Lord, who sees well how much I am in need of his divine assistance.'[11]

Not infrequently the Passionists individually, in pairs, or as a group, joined the Aborigines in their wanderings through the forests. They hoped in this way to gain their confidence and to obtain a better understanding of their way of life. 'We accompanied them now to one place, now to another', Pesciaroli said. 'We slept near them under the stars and we also ate with them.'

The missionaries gradually realised that they could do little or nothing for the conversion of a people constantly on the move. But neither could they alter this nomadic character of the Aboriginal tribes. They were convinced, however, that something could be done for the children, especially the boys, and they learned that the parents were ready to cooperate. And so after they were at Dunwich for a year they drew up a plan which they presented to Archbishop Polding for approval and subsidising. 'It will be necessary for us', they told him, 'to bring about 20 of the sons of the aborigines into our midst and house them, feed them, clothe them, and conduct classes for them.' And in addition to making them Catholics, 'it would be advisable to educate them, give them instructions in agriculture, and make them civilised'. To cover the costs, Polding was invited to contribute whatever sum he considered expedient.

The same Latin letter which spelled out this plan for Polding also begged him to change immediately his method of providing for the needs of the mission. The existing system was causing the missionaries such extreme hardship that at times they did not even have a piece of bread. As artfully as they could, they asked that in the future they be allowed to administer their own funds and make their own purchases. They did not ask for a specific amount, but left it to Polding to determine what annual allotment he might wish to grant them. They would then assume responsibility for acquiring their own supplies at nearby Brisbane Town or by ordering them from Sydney. This system, they believed, would guarantee that their real needs would be provided for properly and as a result there would be no more basis for complaint.

But Archbishop Polding neither supported the plan for the conversion of the Aborigines, nor did he change his system of providing supplies for the mission. Did he disagree with the plan as such? Did he have no trust in the administrative ability of the Italians? Was he in debt himself? It is hard to say. But one can easily understand how these missionaries living among penniless Aborigines might come to resent having an archbishop a thousand kilometres away hold the purse strings for their mission.

The missionaries were deeply convinced that their plan for the conversion of the Aborigines submitted to Polding was their only hope of success. A year later they were approached by the Governor of New South Wales residing in Sydney. When he asked for their views 'on the most suitable method of fostering the welfare of the aborigines', they sent him the same plan that they had sent to Polding.[12]

Even under the best of conditions a mission so difficult as this could hardly succeed. And with Polding showing no understanding for the Passionists, and with their resentment against him always increasing, the chances for success became ever slimmer. Vaccari, in fact, had never really forgiven Polding for assuming full jurisdiction over what he considered to be legitimately his mission and his priests. In an irked mood he wrote to Cardinal Prefect Fransoni of the Evangelisation Congregation in Rome on 19 February 1844, three weeks after Pesciaroli had written to Cardinal Pianetti, and complained that he and his priests, although entrusted with an independent prefecture apostolic, were being treated in exactly the same way as if they were priests under Polding's jurisdiction.[13]

Polding, too, had complained about the Passionists in the past and would continue to complain about them in the future. As early as June 1843, just one month after they had moved into their tumble-down quarters on Stradbroke Island, he wrote to a fellow Benedictine: 'I fear that our Italian friends will be but bunglers . . . and I am determined to procure [for their mission], if I can, our own people.'[14] This eagerness of Polding to oust the Passionists might explain why he kept them so much under his thumb. For if they had succeeded in getting a foothold, and if in practice they had become jurisdictionally independent from him, he would no longer have been able to remove them. To achieve his goal he had to do everything possible to make them fail. If the Passionists were 'bunglers', then Polding contributed to their bungling, and it began to appear that he might prove to be the biggest 'bungler' of all.

23

The Diocese of Perth
and the Vicariates Apostolic of
Essington and King George Sound

4 MAY 1845

Twenty-eight-year-old Captain Charles Howe Fremantle of the frigate *Challenger* sailed under orders from England on Christmas Day 1828 and from the Cape of Good Hope on 20 March 1829. The Lords Commissioners of the Admiralty had instructed him 'to proceed immediately . . . to the Swan River on the Western Coast of New South Wales, where you will on your arrival take formal possession of that part of the Coast in the name of His Majesty [King George IV] which possession is meant to be extended to the whole of the Western Coast'. When reporting back to the Lords Commissioners of the Admiralty, Fremantle said that he had 'anchored off Garden Island . . . on the 25th April, and on the 27th proceeded through the passage into Cockburn Sound, which is most rocky and intricate . . . The weather being unsettled and boisterous, it was not till the 2nd of May that I could land at the Swan River distant 9½ Miles from Cockburn Sound; on that day formal possession was taken of the whole of the West Coast of New Holland in the name of His Britannic Majesty and the Union Jack was hoisted on the South head of the River.'

Fremantle's men on 1 June sighted a merchant ship which proved to be the *Parmelia*. Aboard were Captain James Stirling, 'Lieutenant Governor of the New Settlement at Swan River, and other Gentlemen with their families holding situations in the Colony'. On 8 June the *Sulphur* anchored in Cockburn Sound bringing a detachment of troops for Swan River. One of Captain Fremantle's instructions had been to 'employ working parties on Shore constructing Huts, or other commodious dwellings for reception of Troops which may be weekly expected after your arrival there'. He was also to 'endeavour to find Springs of Fresh water as near the river as may be', and was to instruct those under his orders on shore 'to be constantly on the alert to prevent surprise from the Natives, and especially to be very guarded with respect to the women'.

The private diary of Captain Fremantle states that he offered all possible assistance when Lieutenant Governor Stirling 'made his mind up to establish a Town up the Swan River to be called Perth, & to lay the first Stone of it on the King's birthday the 12th August 1829. . . .' But 'there being no stone contiguous for our purpose, to celebrate the commencement of the new Town, *Mrs. Dance* cut down a tree. . . .' Volleys were fired, speeches were made, some cheers were given, and they named 'the Town Perth according to the wishes of Sir George Murray', then Secretary of the Colonies. When Fremantle left on 28 August 1829 to join the Naval Commander in Chief on the East India Station at Trincomalee in Ceylon (nowadays Sri Lanka), he said there were nearly 300 persons at Swan River. And when he returned for a visit three years later (September 1832), he 'found the Settlement of Fremantle with several houses built, mostly occupied by persons keeping Stores'. And he estimated that 'the number of Settlers at present on the West Coast of Australia is about 2,000'.

But the growth of population was relatively slow in this state of Western Australia, an immense territory which covered one-third of the Australian continent. And so ecclesiastically it remained part of the Vicariate Apostolic of New Holland under the jurisdiction of Archbishop Polding of Sydney. In reply to an 1842 letter from some Roman Catholics residing in Perth requesting priests, Polding removed Father John Brady from Windsor District and named him a vicar general on 1 September 1843. 'We make, constitute and depute you our Vicar General for Western Australia and for the surrounding areas in spiritual as well as temporal matters. . . .' (This was the same Father Brady originally destined by Ullathorne for Norfolk Island. But on arriving in Sydney on 24 February 1838, Brady was assigned instead to Windsor, which Father John McEncroe said was 'about 40 miles up the country' from Sydney. McEncroe took up work on Norfolk Island in 1839 and Father Richard Walsh succeeded him in 1841.)

After a visit to Adelaide, Brady arrived on 4 November 1843 at Albany on King George Sound, the southernmost settlement in his territory. He reached Fremantle on 8 December and Perth on 13 December. Governor Hutt granted him three allotments of land for church, school and presbytery, and on 27 December that same year the foundation stone was laid for Saint John the Evangelist Church. Brady informed Polding that he planned to sail for Europe in January 1844 to recruit personnel for his mission. Father John Joostens, an elderly Dutch priest who had accompanied him from Sydney, remained behind to look after the Catholics of Western Australia.

Polding from Sydney sent Brady instructions in Europe via London on 23 March 1844. 'It seems that Belgian and French missionaries ought to be preferred under every respect', he said. Polding specifically mentioned the Oblates of Mary Immaculate (O.M.I.), a religious community founded in France in 1816 by Eugène de Mazenod, who in 1844 was Bishop of Marseille. This community 'seems filled with an excellent spirit', he said, 'and the missionaries whom it has sent to the savages of [Canada in] North America have done great good. This community, I believe, would serve our purpose . . . And it would also be much better if all [the priests recruited] were members of a single religious community, being bound likewise by the holy bonds of charity and obedience. . . .'[1]

Like so many heads of foreign missions recruiting personnel and soliciting funds in Europe, Brady soon found his way to Rome.

Less than four months after Polding sent his letter to Brady, two Spanish Benedictine priests named Rudesindo Salvado, aged thirty, and his close friend, José Serra, were wondering what apostolate they should choose for themselves.

Walking through the groves of the Cava Monastery some forty kilometres from Naples, Italy, they discussed the pros and cons of labouring for the conversion of primitives. On the following day, 12 July 1844, they decided to dedicate their lives completely to work among primitives.

Anxious to obtain the views of the Evangelisation Congregation on their project before making it known to others, they were able after some delay to leave their monastery, on the day after Christmas, and arrived in Rome on Sunday, 29 December. Father Giovanni Brunelli, secretary of the Evangelisation Congregation since 27 January 1843, received them kindly and was pleased to learn that they wished to work for the conversion of primitives anywhere in the world. He suggested eastern Australia, since it had so many Aborigines and especially since Archbishop Polding, the vicar apostolic there, was a Benedictine like themselves.

By this time Brady was in Rome. And since he was a vicar general of Polding, Brunelli suggested that the two Benedictines obtain information from him about the Aborigines of eastern Australia. Brady no doubt reported back to Brunelli what he thought about the two prospective missionaries. Then on 14 January 1845, after they had been in Rome little more than two weeks, they were officially informed by the Evangelisation Congregation that they would be sent to Sydney to work under Polding's direction. In thanksgiving for this decision they made a pilgrimage to Subiaco, east of Rome, and celebrated Mass there in the cave where Saint Benedict, the founder of their order, had lived.[2]

Like the Benedictines, Brady also had a project which he wished to discuss with the Evangelisation Congregation before making it known to others. And like Polding three years earlier, he believed that bishops as well as priests were needed, if the Catholic Church was to flourish in Western Australia. But unlike Polding he was unfamiliar with the ways of Rome and bungled, presenting his project for consideration at the weekly Particular Meetings of the Evangelisation Congregation and getting nowhere. He became discouraged and prepared to leave Rome.

But then he met thirty-four-year-old Father Jean-Félix-Onésime Luquet (1810–58), ambitious and energetic, a member of the Paris Foreign Mission Seminary. This priest had been sent to the Vicariate Apostolic of Pondicherry in India as a missionary in 1842. At the 1844 synod convoked by Bishop Clément Bonnand (1796–1861), Vicar Apostolic of Pondicherry, Luquet had been one of the most active participants, defending a plan which he had developed for establishing the hierarchy in India. Bonnand sent Luquet to Rome to present this plan personally to the Evangelisation Congregation to hasten its adoption.

Luquet, who knew well how to get his way, was busy contacting officials in Rome when he met Brady. In fact, he had written to Bishop Bonnand in India on 6 December 1844 that Rome was considering the possibility of making him a bishop. And so now he reproached Brady for his discouragement and said he should not bother with the Particular Meetings; instead he should present a detailed *Memorandum* for possible consideration at the more important General Meetings which took place only once a month. As a result of Luquet's coaxing,

Brady agreed to do this and also accepted Luquet's assistance and guidance in composing the text.[3]

Brady presented his finished *Memorandum* to the Evangelisation Congregation on Saturday, 22 February 1845; it suggested that Western Australia should be divided into three ecclesiastical territories, each eventually to have its own bishop. And on a printed map he indicated the boundaries in colour. The westernmost territory was to be called the Diocese of Perth; the one to the north, the Vicariate Apostolic of Essington; and the one to the south, the Vicariate Apostolic of King George Sound. (The founding of a military station at King George Sound in 1826 had marked the beginning of British settlement in Western Australia.) This last territory was regularly referred to in the documents of the Evangelisation Congregation as the Vicariate Apostolic of *Sonde*, an imitative Italian word for 'Sound'.

Explaining why he had chosen these three places, Brady said that Perth was 'the centre of the whole western part of New Holland and the seat of government. . . .' Essington and King George Sound were civil districts and their boundaries could well be the boundaries of the two vicariates apostolic to be named after them. Essington on the north coast was an important port on the route from Australia to China and India. And King George Sound on the south coast was 'a magnificent port visited very often by French, English and American whalers. And over 6,000 souls dwell on its shores.'

Brady thought that the Evangelisation Congregation might object to his project on the grounds that Western Australia's limited population did not warrant the immediate foundation of three distinct territories. He therefore stated in his memorandum that the population could be expected to grow at a rapid pace because of the 'prodigious speed' being made possible by the use of steam. 'This force,' he said, 'whose energy astonishes even those who work with it, is being applied each day in proportions which exceed the dreams of fantasy itself. Steamships are multiplying on the surface of the oceans and iron rails are running in all directions along the surface of the continents. And because of these fabulous means of locomotion, today one can almost say that time itself no longer exists and that distances have been suppressed. The inhabitants of the air see their speed being challenged by the inhabitants of the earth.'

To prove that his convictions were not the product of an idle dream, he informed the Evangelisation Congregation that 'the Queen of England when addressing the two Houses announced that her government has increased the number of steamships for service in the Pacific Ocean'. And not to be outdone by England, 'the King of France gave orders to Bordeaux to proceed immediately with the construction of two steamships for service in Oceania'.[4]

The carefully worked out memorandum prompted Cardinal Prefect Fransoni and Secretary Brunelli to place Brady's proposal on the agenda of the General Meeting scheduled for 10 March 1845. As usual a background report on the proposal was drawn up for the cardinal members of the Evangelisation Congregation and was distributed to them in advance. It bore Cardinal Castracane's name and he subsequently read the report at the General Meeting. He was well

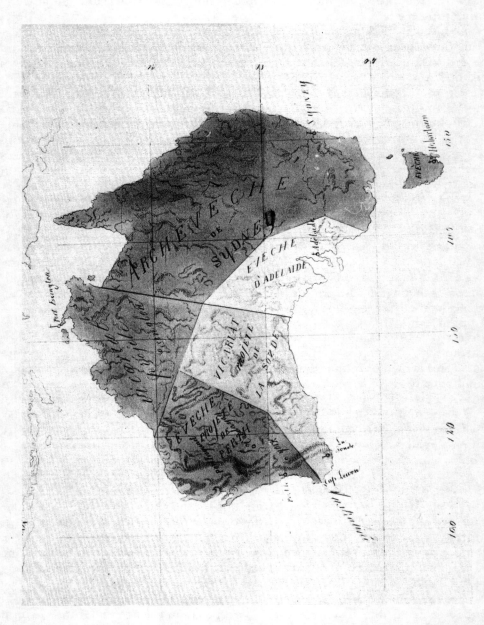

55 This map in colour was submitted to the Evangelisation Congregation by Father John Brady, vicar general of Archbishop Polding of Sydney, on 22 February 1845 while he was in Rome. It indicated the possible boundaries for dividing the western half of Australia into the Diocese of Perth, the Vicariate Apostolic of Essington, and the Vicariate Apostolic of King George Sound. *Source: PF: Acta vol. 208 (1845) f. 94r. (Chapter 23).*

acquainted with the Australian scene, since he had prepared the report for the General Meeting of 28 February 1842 which discussed Polding's proposal to create three dioceses within three vicariates apostolic.

Castracane considered Brady's proposal too grandiose, however, and modified it drastically. Instead of asking the cardinals to vote on the creation of three distinct ecclesiastical territories for Western Australia, as Brady had suggested, he said the proposal was to create a single Vicariate Apostolic of Western Australia, whose vicar apostolic was to receive episcopal rank and reside in Perth. This city, he said, was 'the centre of the entire western part of New Holland and contained 3,000 inhabitants, half of whom are Catholics. . . .' The fact that Brady had no letter from Polding suggesting that Western Australia should become a vicariate apostolic was no obstacle, he said, because Polding had stated in 1842 that it could be made a vicariate apostolic at once. But Western Australia had been left under his jurisdiction at that time, since he had described the new state as being 'in its infancy because of the calamities which it had suffered'.

There were only two candidates presented to the cardinals for the combined office of vicar apostolic and bishop. One was Father Brady himself, who was eminently qualified for such an office, Castracane said, as could be seen from Polding's letter of 1 September 1843, which was printed in the appendix of the report. This letter contained Brady's appointment as vicar general. The other candidate was Father William Bernard Ullathorne, residing in England, the only candidate suggested by Brady. Castracane reminded the cardinals, however, that Ullathorne had been offered the Diocese of Adelaide in 1842, but at that time 'was reluctant to receive the episcopal dignity and still is'.

He then asked the cardinals to vote on the following questions:

1. Should the Holy Father be asked to erect Western Australia into a separate vicariate apostolic?
2. If the answer to number one is yes, what candidate should be proposed for the office of vicar apostolic with episcopal rank?
3. If the answer to number one is no, then what is to be done instead for the benefit of religion there?

The cardinals voted in favour of creating the Vicariate Apostolic of Western Australia with Perth as the residence of the vicar apostolic with episcopal rank. This bishop, too, like those of other episcopal sees in Australia, was to be subject to the Archbishop of Sydney. And they chose Ullathorne for the office of vicar apostolic and bishop. But since it was doubtful whether he would accept, they postponed their definitive choice until hearing from him. If he declined to accept the office, he was to indicate 'what candidate in his Benedictine Order or among the secular clergy he might judge most suitable'.[5]

The General Meeting had been held on 10 March and subsequently the Evangelisation Congregation obtained tentative papal approval for the foundation of Perth Diocese and for naming Ullathorne its first bishop. Fransoni wrote to Ullathorne on 22 March, saying 'it seemed to the Sacred Congregation that nothing could be more opportune' for the benefit of religion in Western Australia than founding a diocese there with the episcopal residence at Perth. To this the pope had agreed. And in view of Ullathorne's virtue, his vast knowledge of Australia, and his being placed on a list of candidates for the episcopal office by Polding in 1842, 'the Sacred Congregation has decided, and His Holiness has been highly pleased, to confer upon you the mentioned Diocese of Perth. . . .' Fransoni hoped that Ullathorne would 'not refuse to accept the dignity', since he was 'altogether qualified' to administer the diocese to the advantage of souls. 'I await your favourable reply.'

But since Fransoni did not really believe that Ullathorne would accept, he asked him in a postscript 'to supply accurate information on the piety, knowledge, and fitness for the episcopal office' of Father Francis Appleton, an English Benedictine, and of Father John Brady, the one who had presented the *Memorandum*. It took some time for Fransoni's letter to reach England and for Ullathorne's reply to come back to Rome. When it arrived, it announced Ullathorne's refusal to accept the Diocese of Perth. Since he considered that diocese 'the most suitable for a mission to the blacks', Ullathorne recommended Father Brady 'who had had a long experience in the Island of Bourbon among the negroes, was an excellent missionary, and had a great attraction for the aboriginal population'. Brady was then presented as candidate in Ullathorne's place.[6]

It was Sunday, 4 May 1845, when Secretary Brunelli approached Pope Gregory XVI for definitive ratification of the simplified plan as approved by the cardinals. But the pope, who himself had been cardinal prefect of the Evangelisation Congregation from 1826 to 1831, overruled the decisions made by the cardinals at their General Meeting eight weeks earlier and gave his full approbation instead to the elaborate plan as originally proposed by Brady.

When reporting back to the cardinals, Brunelli phrased the matter diplomatically and said that the pope had agreed to their first decision, but in the following manner. 'The western section of New Holland with its very extensive territory is to be erected into a true diocese and into two vicariates apostolic as proposed by the Reverend Father John Brady, who until now has been Vicar General of the Archbishop of Sydney for that same region. The bishop [of the diocese] will have Perth as his see city and is therefore to be called the Bishop of Perth; he will be subject as suffragan to the Archbishop of Sydney. The Essington District will constitute one vicariate apostolic and the Sonde [King George Sound] District will constitute another; both of these will be governed by the Bishop of Perth in virtue of his [being granted the additional] title of Vicar Apostolic. Further, until these same vicariates can be erected into two distinct dioceses with the territories proper to them, they are to be administered [by the Bishop of Perth] with the help of a pro-vicar based in the principal place of each of the two districts mentioned above.'

The pope had also stated that the borders for the three new ecclesiastical territories would be those indicated on the printed map submitted by Brady. But the Holy See was retaining the right, even after all three territories had become dioceses, 'to divide them and alter their borders as time and other circumstances might require'.

Brunelli then pointed out who was to receive this threefold office. 'Reverend Father [William] Bernard Ullathorne of the English Benedictine Congregation has declared himself altogether opposed to accepting the office of bishop. Therefore His Holiness, mindful of what has been said not only by one source regarding the piety, zeal, prudence and other gifts of the Reverend Father Brady, has chosen him to be bishop of the new church of Perth and has given him as well the title and faculties of vicar apostolic, as has already been indicated, for the two districts mentioned above. He has also ordered that an Apostolic Letter in the form of a Brief should be written to cover all these points.'[7]

Brady was ordained a bishop in Rome on Trinity Sunday, 18 May 1845, two weeks after he had been named Bishop of Perth by Pope Gregory XVI. And on 5 June, when he had his private audience with the pope, he brought along the two Spanish Benedictines, whom he had persuaded to go with him to Western Australia instead of joining Polding in eastern Australia.[8] Then on the following day the pope officially named them 'Missionaries Apostolic for the Diocese of Perth in Western Australia', and he authorised Brunelli (recently raised to the rank of archbishop) to provide them with the necessary letters patent.[9]

In addition to winning the Benedictines, Brady also succeeded in winning the Passionists. Superior General Antonio di San Giacomo had become greatly dissatisfied with Polding for the way in which his priests at Dunwich were being treated. He learned that Brady was in Rome, that he was recruiting priests for Western Australia, and that he was even prepared to offer the Passionists the Vicariate Apostolic of Essington or the Vicariate Apostolic of King George Sound. This seemed like an answer from heaven to his problems and so he officially requested the Evangelisation Congregation to transfer his men from Polding's to Brady's jurisdiction.

While these negotiations were going on, Antonio di San Giacomo wrote about them to the Reverend Father Dominic of the Mother of God, superior of the Passionists in England, living at Aston Hall, near Stone, Staffordshire. After telling Dominic that 'in February 1844 our men in New Holland were still on an island with a few Aborigines, but were deprived of the funds needed to do good', he mentioned Brady's plan, but without mentioning his name. 'There is an Irish missionary here now who has come from the west coast of that great continent', he said. 'Negotiations are under way for constituting on that coast three missions with vicars apostolic. Each of these missions is to have its funds independent from those of the Archbishop of Sydney. And one of the missions is supposed to be entrusted to us. . . .' He added that Prefect Apostolic Vaccari was 'as capricious and eccentric as ever and there will be no question, therefore, of his being head of the mission just mentioned, if in fact it is founded. But do not breathe a word about this to anyone. . . .'[10]

The news that the pope actually had created the Diocese of Perth and the vicariates apostolic of Essington and King George Sound pleased Antonio di San Giacomo very much, because he was convinced that his priests, if forced to remain in eastern Australia under Polding, 'will have to suffer much and will be able to do little or nothing'.[11] Losing no time he wrote to Polding on 3 June 1845, two days before Brady and the two Benedictines were to be received in audience by the pope. Referring to his priests in Polding's territory, he said: 'I have petitioned the Sacred Congregation for the Evangelisation of Nations to send them to the western part [of Australia], where His Holiness, Pope Gregory XVI, has recently established a new see in the city of Perth.' Enclosed with his letter were sealed instructions from the Evangelisation Congregation. Polding was told that Vaccari's office as prefect apostolic, which had always remained a sore point, would be automatically dissolved by his releasing the Passionists and allowing them to go to Perth.

This official news about losing the Passionists to Brady could not possibly please Polding. As early as 10 April 1845 when writing to the Evangelisation Congregation he interrupted his letter to say: 'I had written thus far when I received a letter from Rome from Monsignor Brady to the effect that the Superior of the Passionists had some notion of removing those missionaries to the western coasts of Australia. I am convinced that such a course would be imprudent, for the language is entirely different, and all their labours for the past two years would be thrown away.' He said, too, that this would produce a bad effect on the minds of the natives who 'would lose all confidence in the missionaries, persuaded that others would forsake them in like manner', and on the minds of the Europeans who 'would be only too glad to lay hold of it as a proof that it was useless to attempt to civilise the blacks. . . .'[12]

It now seemed to the Passionist superior general that his order's work in Australia would prosper for many reasons. He was pleased with Brady; he had been assured that Polding would have nothing to say about the funds destined for his order's vicariate apostolic; he foresaw that Vaccari would insist on remaining at Dunwich; and he was convinced that the other three priests would work well together. Besides writing to his priests and formally assigning them to Western Australia, he also wrote—but somewhat later—to Dominic in England, telling him what had happened. When Bishop Brady was leaving for his new diocese in Western Australia, he said, 'it was arranged that our men should take over a mission there, which was already erected into a vicariate apostolic, but which for the present was to remain under the Bishop of Perth'.[13]

Bishop Brady had been most successful in recruiting personnel. With a party of twenty-eight, including Sisters of Mercy from the Convent of Saint Leo in Carlow, Ireland, he sailed from London aboard the *Elizabeth* on 16 September 1845 and arrived at Fremantle on 7 January 1846. But where would the funds be found to support such a large staff? Three years later the official census would show that there were 4,600 colonists in the whole of Western Australia and of these only 306 were Roman Catholics. One of the bishop's first disappointments was the realisation that he had been mistaken in presuming that the government would reimburse him for the transportation costs of his personnel. His diocesan debt began mounting at an average of 2,000 pounds a year.

Brady had brought along three French priests and two French Brothers from the Society of the Immaculate Heart of Mary founded in 1839 by Father François-Marie-Paul Libermann (1802–52), an Alsacian convert from Judaism, whose novitiate was at La Neuville near Amiens, France. This group was given charge of the numerous Aborigines near Albany and in other parts of the Vicariate Apostolic of King George Sound. But one of the priests in the group, Father Bouchet, died a few days after reaching Perth. Father Thevaux, the superior, and Father Thierse together with the two Brothers actually reached the area. But they found only a few friendly tribes constantly on the move gathering food and so they succeeded in making little impression on them. And the European settlers did not welcome them because they did not speak English. Their supplies ran out and also their ammunition for hunting. When it became evident that Bishop Brady could not help them, Father Libermann obtained permission from Rome to have his missionaries transferred to Mauritius.[14]

The two Spanish Benedictines had also been in the party of twenty-eight, along with two Benedictine novices, and they were entrusted with the Aborigines in the vicinity of Perth. A month after landing, in February 1846, Father Superior Serra and Father Salvado set out from Perth with the two novices in search of a site for their mission station. They had already begun putting up temporary buildings in a valley near a fresh water gully in the Victoria Plains when they had to move because the property had been previously claimed by someone else. Eventually they settled on a sixteen hectare plot granted to them by the government on the Moore River about 136 kilometres north of Perth. They called their foundation New Norcia in honour of the Italian town where Saint Benedict, founder of the Benedictine Order, was born.

But the Benedictines fared no better under their Irish bishop than the Passionists had fared under their English archbishop. 'When we began this mission in the beginning of 1846', Salvado said, 'I quickly realised that it was impractical to accompany the aborigines in their wanderings.' What was needed was some centre of operations, but this immediately created a problem. Who would support the venture? Bishop Brady 'said that he did not have the funds which we needed and suggested that we should abandon the site, if we could not find them ourselves'. Thirty-four years later, after spending more than half his life among the Aborigines, Salvado wrote to Cardinal Simeoni, then prefect of the Evangelisation Congregation, that 'neither the bishop, nor the clergy, nor the Catholics of the Diocese of Perth, ever contributed . . . even a cent for the benefit of this mission of New Norcia'.

At the mission's outset, in fact, when Brady said that he could give the Spaniards no more supplies, Salvado—an accomplished pianist—returned in rags to Perth. After having his tattered clothes mended on the fringe of town, he gave a three-hour concert one evening, using a piano lent for the occasion by a Protestant minister. With the proceeds he bought a dray and a team of bullocks and drove them himself back to the mission laden with supplies.

The two Spanish priests persevered and with the help of Benedictine Brothers who came from Europe they managed to build a self-sustaining mission. No real progress was made, Salvado said, 'during the 14 years when the Bishop of Perth

Diocese was its superior and had this mission under his spiritual and temporal jurisdiction. . . . But once jurisdictional separation was established, New Norcia began to prosper. And those aborigines, who on the basis of specious reasoning had been called incapable of imbibing any culture or intellectual instruction, became officials in charge of the post office and telegraph office here, were paid by the government for this work, and were praised by higher authorities for their intelligence and efficiency.'

The mission officially became known as 'The Abbacy *nullius dioeceseos* of New Norcia' and still has this name today. The two Latin words literally translated mean 'of no diocese', that is, the mission was within the jurisdiction 'of no diocese'. The jurisdictional area created for it by Rome was rather small, however, covering no more than 42 square kilometres. Salvado called this 'a little thing in itself, but the big thing that saved the mission'.[15] He meant it was 'a little thing', in comparison to the 2,537,350 square kilometres of jurisdictional area remaining for the Bishop of Perth; but it was 'a big thing', because it made the Benedictines free to develop the mission as they wished.

About the time that the Benedictines were founding their mission to the Aborigines in Western Australia, the Passionists were dissolving their mission to the Aborigines at Dunwich on Stradbroke Island. Fathers Snell, Pesciaroli and Lencioni sailed from Brisbane for Western Australia via Sydney on 25 June 1846. But they did not meet Archbishop Polding during their Sydney stopover, because he had left for a second trip to Europe on 16 February. The three Passionists sailed from Sydney without Vaccari for their new mission in Western Australia.[16]

Back in Europe their superior general, Antonio di San Giacomo, did not know whether or not the Dunwich mission had been dissolved. When he learned from Dominic in England that he had met Polding, he wrote right back on 25 September 1846. 'If he is still in England,' he said, 'I would like you to find out all you can about our men who went with him to New Holland.' He told Dominic about the clash which the Passionists had had with Polding. 'Contrary to the repeated instructions given by me to all of them,' he said, 'they were not entirely submissive to the orders of the archbishop in the beginning, because Father Raimondo [Vaccari] foolishly wanted to insist on his rights as prefect apostolic . . . What I especially want to know is whether the three have separated from Father Raimondo and whether they have gone to . . . Western Australia to join Bishop Brady of Perth.'[17]

Dominic succeeded in getting in touch with Polding and wrote back that the archbishop wanted to keep Vaccari, that he wanted to have additional Passionists, and that he was a saint. 'Polding may be a saint,' the superior general answered on 13 April 1847, 'but he did not live up to any of the promises that he made to me when he tore away from my breast four religious.' Polding had provided them with only 'scarce supplies of food, just as one would send to prisoners, and he kept them so impotent that they could not do the work for which they had undertaken such a long voyage . . . I do not know how they were able to stand up under such severe physical punishment for three years. Dr

Polding may therefore keep Father Raimondo, who wants to stay there and does not get along well with the others, but he will not get any other Passionists.'[18]

Raimondo Vaccari remained at Dunwich at least until 24 April 1847, eleven days after his superior general wrote the above letter, but on 20 July he too arrived in Sydney. When Polding returned to Sydney on 6 February 1848, however, he learned that the three Passionists had left for Perth and that Vaccari only six weeks earlier had sailed for Valparaiso with a Franciscan priest named Bassi.[19]

En route Vaccari suffered shipwreck but survived, arrived a debtor in Peru, used the pseudonym 'Wilson' to escape his creditors, and found work as a vegetable gardener at a Franciscan monastery in Lima. His piety edified the Franciscans, who discovered his identity and invited him to join their order. He was dispensed from his vows as a Passionist on 10 August 1861 at the age of fifty-nine, took vows as a Franciscan and spent the rest of his life in Lima.[20]

The three other Passionists en route from Sydney to Perth made a stopover at Adelaide, capital of South Australia. Here they learned that Bishop Murphy of Adelaide was eager to have them take up work in his diocese. Snell had become superior automatically, being older than Lencioni and Pesciaroli and also being longer in vows, and was beginning to feel the weight of his responsibilities toward them. Apprehensive about Bishop Brady's ability to support them, and thinking they might have as much to suffer in underdeveloped Western Australia as on Stradbroke Island, he decided not to go to Bishop Brady's Diocese of Perth, contrary to the orders that had been issued by Rome, and with his two priests remained in the Diocese of Adelaide.[21]

While Archbishop Polding was in Rome in 1847 he apparently informed the Evangelisation Congregation why he had become dissatisfied with the Passionists. This criticism was passed on to the Passionist superior general, who then made it known in veiled terms to the three priests in Adelaide on 7 October 1847. Pesciaroli answered with a lengthy defence on 2 November 1848, telling his superior general it was evident from his letter that accusations had been lodged against them in the offices of the Evangelisation Congregation.

In answer to the first accusation, 'That we made a serious mistake in not subjecting ourselves to Archbishop Polding', he said that no trouble would ever have arisen 'if only the Evangelisation Congregation had previously advised us not to inform Polding' that Vaccari had been named prefect apostolic.

The second charge, 'That . . . we wanted money and comforts', must have arisen from asking Polding for an annual allocation of funds to purchase supplies, he said. 'If we had been provided with food and clothing on time, as we should have been, we then would have lived there in peace. We would have thought only of our duty and there would have been no further mention of the prefecture, nor of the Evangelisation Congregation. And Your Reverence would have received no complaints from us. Polding, too, would never have had the displeasure of being asked by us for the allocation indicated above, an allocation which he himself was to determine on the basis of what he judged to be necessary.'

The third charge was, 'That we wanted to do things our own way and always in opposition to what Polding proposed to us'. Pesciaroli therefore asked: 'But in what respect were we not subject to Polding? What did we do our own way? When did we oppose what Polding suggested to us? Did he mean that we did not cultivate the land? But he told us that Dunwich would not be the permanent site of our mission. Or did he mean that we did not go out two by two, following the aborigines whenever they went here and there in the deep forest searching for food, fighting other tribes, and changing their residence for some time?' They had tried all of this, he said. 'But we gained no other advantage from this than to observe that they did not change their nature, did not live differently, nor was their deportment among themselves and with us any different then from what it was when they were in the vicinity of our residence. . . .' Polding had ordered Vaccari to baptise the children of the Aborigines. '*Perhaps* we would have baptised them', Pesciaroli said, if Polding had helped found a boarding school. But having no such school, and seeing how the Aborigines were almost constantly on the move, they had considered this order impractical and did not carry it out. Without a boarding school there was no guarantee whatsoever for a thorough Catholic training.

The final accusation was, 'That we had neither the zeal nor the interest to carry out those activities which were necessary for making the mission effective, and that we did not have a precise notion of the true nature of missionary work among infidels'. In defence Pesciaroli said that their boarding school plan, which he explained in some detail to his superior general, had been geared to make their mission effective. 'What more could we have done, in order not to be judged as having no zeal or interest in getting this mission going?' It was Polding, he charged, who 'did not want to carry out' this plan for educating, civilising and converting the Aborigines.

He pointed out further that it was also necessary to keep in mind that mission work among Aborigines was more difficult than among other peoples. In proof of this he offered the testimony of Bishop Pompallier of New Zealand. This bishop had come to Dunwich in August 1844 at the request of Polding, who thought that his experience with the Maoris of New Zealand would be helpful to the Passionists. 'When Bishop Pompallier came to visit us', Pesciaroli said, 'he told us that he noticed an extremely great difference between the indigenes of New Zealand and those of our island. When arriving in his mission he needed to do nothing else but learn its language, make friends with the [New] Zealand natives, and preach to them our holy religion. He also stressed that we would have to labour very hard before we could reap some fruit from our mission. He was knowledgeable and he judged it correctly. And here ends our short justification.'[22]

Meanwhile Father Dominic in England and Father Superior General in Rome were receiving letters from the three Passionists, telling of their difficulties in South Australia. 'Our situation is still uncertain and is beginning to become critical', Snell told Dominic on 2 April 1847. He enclosed other letters to be forwarded to the superior general.[23]

Then on 13 December 1848, just six weeks after Pesciaroli had written his apologia, another letter reached Dominic from Lencioni written in his and in Pesciaroli's name from Adelaide on 22 July of that year. 'You know, no doubt, that not even the Bishop of Adelaide needs us now', it said. 'Six years have passed and we have done nothing else but suffer uselessly. Nor have any steps been taken to give us hope that our situation will improve. I therefore entreat Your Paternity, I beseech you, I implore you to obtain for us passage to England, where I hope we can be of some use.'[24]

Dominic, whom Lencioni and Pesciaroli called their 'last refuge on this earth', sent a copy of Lencioni's letter to Antonio di San Giacomo that very same day. 'I do not know whether you need permission from the Evangelisation Congregation to recall these religious from Australia', he said. 'But if you do, I would ask you to obtain it.'[25]

Apparently there was a breakdown in communications, because Lencioni worked in Adelaide for seventeen years. He died there at the age of forty-nine on 6 April 1864, four days before he was to sail for Europe. Snell was assigned to the Morphett Vale area and died at Melbourne, capital of the adjoining state of Victoria, on 15 July 1861 at the age of fifty-nine. Pesciaroli had been assigned to Mount Barker, about forty kilometres from Adelaide, and eventually succeeded in leaving Australia for England. He happened to be there when Father Dominic died and was the only one with him at the hour of death. Subsequently he went to Rome where he died on 1 September 1874 at the age of sixty-eight.[26]

Although Bishop Brady never received the expected assistance of the Passionists, to whom he had wanted to entrust one of his vicariates, he nevertheless tried to make a start among the Aborigines in the Vicariate Apostolic of Essington. There was an Italian priest from the Tyrol named Father Angelo Confalonieri in the large party that he had brought from Europe. This priest volunteered to work among the Aborigines at Port Essington and Brady gave him full powers as vicar general. Although the bishop had managed to recruit only one Irish priest, Father Powell, whom he placed in charge of the cathedral at Perth, he had won eight Irish students of rhetoric, all over twenty years of age, who volunteered to serve as catechists. Two of these, James Fagan and Nicholas Hogan, left Perth with Confalonieri a few days after their arrival with Port Essington as their destination at the northern tip of Australia, northeast of present-day Darwin. There was no shipping service up the west coast of Australia, however, so the missionary band had to go via Sydney and the Torres Strait, circumnavigating three-quarters of Australia to reach their destination.

Confalonieri hoped to leave the coast and penetrate to tribes in the interior. But when sailing through Torres Strait surrounded by dangerous reefs his party was shipwrecked, catechists Fagan and Hogan drowned, and the only survivors were the captain and Confalonieri. He eventually reached Port Essington, opened a mission for Aborigines, began work on a dictionary, and translated some prayers and New Testament readings. In two years' time he won about 400 followers. But on 16 June 1848 Captain MacArthur at Port Essington wrote to church authorities in Sydney that Confalonieri had been 'seized with a treacherous attack of fever' on 31 May and 'calmly expired' on 9 June. Two days later he was given 'honourable burial', MacArthur said, 'his own instructions being faithfully carried out . . . His remains were accompanied to the tomb by the officers and military with all the respect that was due to a man so highly esteemed.' Polding later forwarded to Perth a copy of the letter and enclosed 'a small cross and scapular which our dear missionary with brotherly affection, dying, wished to be transmitted to his sister'.[27]

The Dioceses of
Melbourne, Port Victoria and Maitland

9 MAY 1847

Archbishop Polding of Sydney while in Rome on 1 February 1847 formally submitted to the Evangelisation Congregation for its approval the resolutions of Australia's First Provincial Council held on 10–12 September 1844.[1] While these resolutions were under study, he had occasion to bring up other matters during his conversations with Cardinal Prefect Fransoni and Secretary Brunelli. One of these was the foundation of a new diocese in Australia to be called Melbourne. Polding was invited to submit his proposal in writing and this he did on 22 February. An 'Instruction' called *Neminem profecto* issued by the Evangelisation Congregation on 23 November 1845 had urged the heads of mission territories to advise the Sacred Congregation whenever circumstances seemed to require an increase in the number of bishops. In the introductory remarks of his formal request Polding said that this 'Instruction' made him feel that it was his duty to call Fransoni's attention 'to the Church of Sydney'.

He explained that his archdiocese extended 'from 12 degrees south latitude to 38 degrees . . . and contained within its boundaries an area greater in extent than that of the combined kingdoms of France, Germany and Italy'. The population in the south was considerable. And Melbourne, 'which numbers about 10,000 inhabitants, is destined to become the capital of the State of Australia Felix, when this portion of New Holland is granted its own government distinct from that of New South Wales. . . .' This particular name was being considered for the state, he said, because of 'its singular fertility and the other natural advantages which it enjoys'. (The Latin word *felix* means fertile, fruitful, rich.) Currently the territory was being ruled by a vice-governor or lieutenant, appointed by the Minister of Colonies, under the jurisdiction of the Governor of New South Wales. 'But the lieutenant governor enjoys sufficient power in ordinary matters and for the most part it is not necessary for him to have recourse to Sydney in questions concerning church and state.'

When the new state was actually founded in 1851 the name chosen for it was Victoria instead of Australia Felix. Melbourne became its capital.

The boundaries suggested by Polding in his 1847 memorandum were identical with those 'which the civil government has proposed for the state. . . .' They were 'the Diocese of Adelaide to the west, the Murray River to the north, and an imaginary line drawn from the river itself to Cape Howe at the southeastern corner of Australia'. Having the new diocese extend over the entire

SOMMARIO ⁱ

NUMERO I.

*Pro-memoria presentato da Monsig. G. Beda Polding Arcivescovo
di Sydney nell'Australia per l'erezione di due nuovi Vescovati
in Malbourne, ed in Vittoria ossia Essington.*

Eminenza Rma

Nell'istruzione veramente apostolica pubblicata dalla S. C. a' 23.
Novembre si ammoniscono tutti quei cui è confidata la sollecitudine delle Chiese di rendere informata la medesima S. C. ogni
qual volta le circostanze sembrino esigere che si aumenti il numero de' vescovi.

Sotto l'influenza di questa si salutevole ammonizione è il mio do-
vere d'invitare l'attenzione di V. Emza alla Chiesa di Sydney.

Questa diocesi si stende dal 12. fino al 38 grado di latitudine meridionale. La sua larghezza hon è uguale in tutti i luoghi ma è
sempre vastissima. Comprende entro i suoi limiti uno spazio più
grande della estensione dei regni presi insieme di Francia, Ger-
mania ed Italia.

Verso il mezzo giorno la popolazione è considerabile. La città prin-
cipale della parte denominata l' *Australia Felice* è *Melbourne*
che contiene circa 10. 000. abitanti, ed è destinata ad essere la
capitale della Provincia dell' Australia Felice quando questa por-
zione della N. Olanda dovrà erigersi in un governo distinto da
quello di *New South Wales, Nuova Galles Meridionale,* di cui
è capitale Sydney.

Presentemente sta sotto un vice-governatore o luogotenente, il quale
benchè nominato dal Ministro delle Colonie stà pure sotto la giurisdizione del Governatore di *New South Wales.* Ciò non ostante
nelle cose ordinarie il Luogotenente Governatore gode di potere
sufficiente, e nelle relazioni che esistono tra la Chiesa ed il Governo non è necessario per lo più di avere ricorso a Sydney.

In quanto a questo capo perciò non vi è difficoltà nell' erigere *Melbourne* in Sede Vescovile con giurisdizione sopra tutto quel ter-
ritorio, che a cagione della sua singolare fertilità, e degli altri van-
taggi della natura che gode, chiamasi Australia Felice.

Dopo il mio arrivo in Europa ho saputo che gli Anglicani di New
South Wales hanno fissato uno dei loro Vescovi a Melbourne la
quale città gli dà il suo titolo. Questo fatto somministra una forte
ragione perchè vi si debba nominare un Vescovo Cattolico senza
ritardo.

Una ragguardevole Chiesa di 140. piedi in lunghezza e con ogni altra cosa in proporzione, è stata eretta in Melbourne principalmente

A

---

56   This printed copy of Archbishop Polding's letter
of 22 February 1847 to Cardinal Prefect Fransoni was
used as background material at the General Meeting
of 3 May 1847 which led to the foundation of the
Dioceses of Melbourne, Port Victoria and Maitland
on 9 May 1847. *Source: PF: Acta vol. 210 (1847) f.
170r. (Chapter 24).*

state would be most advantageous, Polding said, and he was convinced that it would be able 'to provide sufficient funds for the maintenance of a bishop. . . .' Proof of this was Melbourne's respectable church forty-two metres long which had been paid for 'principally by the contributions of the faithful'.

Besides this Polding had learned after arriving in Europe 'that the Anglicans of New South Wales have placed one of their bishops at Melbourne and he takes his title from this city. This fact is an important reason why a Catholic bishop ought to be assigned there without delay', he said.

Still another reason for assigning a Catholic bishop to Melbourne was the incentive that this would give to Catholic education. Melbourne had neither a seminary to train candidates for the priesthood, nor a school of higher learning to prepare students 'for the learned professions'. Both institutions would have a guarantee of continuance and success, he said, if a local bishop were assigned there. And if students 'destined for the learned professions' were to find in Melbourne a school of higher learning 'directed by Catholics', this would prove 'most advantageous' for the Catholic religion. He was convinced that the Diocese of Melbourne by itself could support these schools.

In Polding's own words, 'the most important duty' for a bishop in an area where clergy are scarce is 'to supervise the education of youths from whom the future clergy must come'. Consequently any candidate for the office of Bishop of Melbourne 'not only has to be discreet and zealous in his work, possessing ardent piety and a love without limits for his people, but he also must have the talent to instruct candidates for the cloister and for the sanctuary'. Polding felt, however, that there was no priest in Australia fit to run a seminary, and so he had to seek a candidate for the office of Bishop of Melbourne elsewhere. On the other hand the 'Instruction' issued by the Evangelisation Congregation had asked that special regard be given 'to those missionaries who have worked and acquired experience in that portion of the vineyard of the Lord for which a bishop is to be proposed'.[2]

Polding submitted his list of candidates on 25 February. The first three had worked in Australia and had acquired experience there, but for one reason or the other Polding excluded them. In the first place he mentioned Father John McEncroe from Ireland, about fifty years of age, Dean of Sydney District, and active in New South Wales for some fifteen years. 'He is a good theologian, speaks with great facility in public, and is rather greatly loved.' But he had little initiative, was somewhat timid and excessively cautious, 'all of which is often a great handicap in forming a diocese. . . .' Polding requested, however, that he be named 'a Doctor of Sacred Theology' by the pope.

In the second place he mentioned Father James Goold, 'an Augustinian about 35 years of age from the Diocese of Cork, who has been in the mission about eight years. He has worked with great success and has distinguished himself by introducing order, where formerly disorder prevailed, and also by erecting schools. Under his direction the people of his district have become a model community which we propose to others [for imitation] because of their frequenting the sacraments and their pious practices of devotion. He is zealous and prudent and he is loved and esteemed by all Catholics and Protestants. He is sufficiently versed in theology, but not particulary so. He is gifted with good sense and he sees clearly what is right.'

But Goold had a very active temperament and Polding believed that it would be difficult for him to adapt himself 'to the tedium connected with the formation of a seminary . . . Except for this I believe that under every other aspect he would be an excellent bishop.' To prove what confidence he had in Goold, Polding told Fransoni that, when asked by Bishop Pompallier of New Zealand to suggest a British subject who might become coadjutor in New Zealand, he had suggested Goold without hesitation 'as the most suitable'. And although Polding personally was convinced that the political situation in New Zealand seemed to require the nomination of a British subject as coadjutor for Pompallier, he would be 'greatly displeased' if Goold were to be removed from New South Wales.

Father Henry Gregory, 'now about 33 years of age', was listed in the third place. He was an English Benedictine and Polding's vicar general, whom Polding had wanted as his own coadjutor in January 1846. 'But I doubt that he would be able to govern alone a diocese so large as Melbourne and one that quickly will become so very important.' He needed nearby a guiding hand 'to moderate and direct him', Polding said, because of his very impetuous temperament.

The fourth candidate on Polding's list was Father Richard Placid Burchall, an English Benedictine. He was about thirty-four years of age and had been superior of the English Benedictine Monastery of Saint Edmond in Douai, France, for eight years or more. Currently he was training thirty candidates for the priesthood for the vicars apostolic of England, who had great confidence in him. All young priests who had completed their studies under Burchall had turned out to be 'excellent men'. Consequently he would be ideal for heading the proposed Melbourne Diocese and for supervising its seminary. He was in fact, 'the most suitable candidate', since Goold in a way was excluded, there being no one else but Goold who 'could do so much good in New Zealand'. Polding did not hide from Fransoni that the English Benedictines would be opposed to Burchall's being removed from Douai; yet he felt certain that they would release him 'for the good of the [Australian] Mission'.

Curiously enough Polding no longer said in his present proposal, as he had done five years earlier, that the bishop who was to head the diocese (to be named after the capital city) should also be named vicar apostolic with jurisdiction over the entire state. He now said simply that the Bishop of Melbourne should be given jurisdiction over the entire state. Also on the map that he eventually submitted with his various proposals, he made no mention of vicariates apostolic, but indicated his own archdiocese and the other dioceses as extending over entire states.

During one of Polding's visits to the offices of the Evangelisation Congregation, he had seen the map which Bishop Brady of Perth had submitted two years earlier when making his proposals for the foundation of his diocese and the two Vicariates Apostolic of Essington and King George Sound (or Sonde). Although Brady's proposal had been accepted in its entirety by Pope Gregory XVI, now dead, Polding found much in it worthy of criticism and he pointed out its weaknesses in a long appendix to his list of episcopal candidates for Melbourne.

He objected principally to the ecclesiastical boundaries indicated by Brady and adopted by Rome for Perth, Essington and King George Sound. He reminded Cardinal Fransoni that when the first three dioceses of Sydney, Hobart Town and Adelaide were founded in 1842, the norm applied to fix their boundaries was to adopt already existing civil boundaries, since they were so well known. This norm, he said, had been established by the Council of Chalcedon (451) and had been reiterated by Pope Saint Gregory II (715–31). He also quoted the exact text: 'After taking into consideration the extent of the areas, you should make the bishoprics coincide with the territory ruled by individual government authorities, thus delimiting what is to be included within the jurisdiction of the individual sees.'[3] Abiding by this norm would avoid future controversies over the extent of a bishop's jurisdiction, Polding stressed.

He then proceeded to show from Brady's map how this norm had been seriously violated and how Brady's boundaries 'would not provide for the actual needs of the faithful'. He called attention to the fact that in 1845 the Vicariate Apostolic of King George Sound had been formed partly from the state of Western Australia and partly from the state of South Australia. This meant that the boundaries decreed for the Diocese of Adelaide in 1842 had been changed, since originally that diocese had extended over the entire state of South Australia.

The same was true for the Vicariate Apostolic of Essington, since it was carved partly from the state of Western Australia and partly from the state of New South Wales. (At this time the state of New South Wales included what later came to be known as the state of Queensland and the Northern Territory.) Port Essington itself, the headquarters of the vicariate, was in New South Wales and not in Western Australia. This meant that Rome had also changed the boundaries of Polding's Archdiocese of Sydney in 1845, since as founded in 1842 it had embraced the entire state of New South Wales.

Polding pointed out further that it was impractical to have the Bishop of Perth administer the Vicariate Apostolic of Essington, because there was no direct contact by ship between Perth and Port Essington. He said that a person first had to go from Perth to Sydney and from there to Port Essington, which was visited by ship 'only five or six times a year'.

Polding had a simple solution for all these problems. 'To obviate future doubts', he said, 'it would be opportune to decree that the Diocese of Perth embraces the entire civil State of Western Australia.' King George Sound, the headquarters of the Vicariate Apostolic of King George Sound, would by this act be placed 'under the Diocese of Perth, with which it has direct contact'. The Vicariate Apostolic of Sonde or King George Sound would then be 'no longer opportune' and could be suppressed. And the Vicariate Apostolic of Essington in the north, formed likewise partly from the state of Western Australia, could also be suppressed 'as no longer opportune'. Thus the boundaries decreed in 1842 would be restored to the Diocese of Adelaide and it would once again

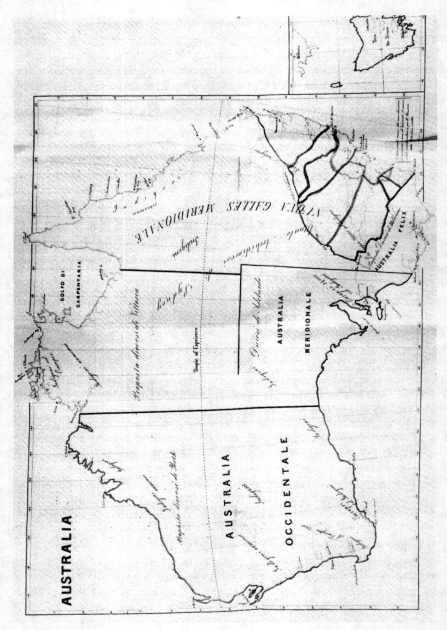

57 Archbishop Polding of Sydney submitted this map to the Evangelisation Congregation with his proposals of 22 and 25 February 1847 for reorganising the ecclesiastical divisions in Australia. He proposed the Diocese of Melbourne, new boundaries for the Diocese of Perth, the suppression of the Vicariate Apostolic of King George Sound, and new boundaries for the Vicariate Apostolic of Essington, adding that it might become instead the Diocese of Victoria. *Source: PF: Acta vol. 210 (1847) f. 169r. (Chapter 24).*

extend over the entire state of South Australia. Also the section of New South Wales to the north, removed from the Archdiocese of Sydney in 1845 to create the Vicariate Apostolic of Essington, would be restored to the Archdiocese of Sydney and so once again would be placed under Polding's jurisdiction.

This proposal, however, still left the dioceses of Australia immense. And the Archdiocese of Sydney merited particular attention, Polding said, because it extended more than 480 kilometres southward and over 2,400 kilometres northward. 'I therefore propose that another diocese be erected in this northern part having Port Essington, or Victoria [as Port Essington was more widely known in Europe], as the episcopal see. Its western boundary would be the territorial limits assigned by the government to the State of Western Australia. Its eastern boundary would be 140 degrees longitude (calculated according to the Greenwich or London system). And its southern boundary would be the [northern] territorial limits of South Australia. This boundary would be lengthened, however, by drawing a straight line along 26 degrees south latitude up to the eastern border of Western Australia.' The strip of unexplored land between the eastern boundary of Western Australia and the western boundary of South Australia, Polding suggested, could remain temporarily under his jurisdiction.

The candidate whom he proposed as first Bishop of Victoria was Father José Serra, one of the two Spanish Benedictines recruited in Rome in 1845 by Brady. Polding had never met Serra, but he had been told by the Evangelisation Congregation that it had received an excellent recommendation on Serra from the Abbot of Farfa, the head of a well-known Benedictine abbey north of Rome. Polding explained that 'extrinsic reasons' had made him propose Serra. 'We have to turn elsewhere, because there are neither men nor means available [in Australia] for the new diocese. And it seems to me that a Spanish bishop deprived of subsidies could successfully call upon the charity of his fellow countrymen in the Philippine Islands. The churches there are very rich and Christianity has done so much good among the indigenes that they now number four million Catholics.'

Added to this were the frequent and important commercial contacts between Sydney and the Philippines. Polding therefore believed that 'if the new bishop were to go there to be ordained, he could then proceed to Victoria with new missionaries and subsidies. And whereas the presence of a French bishop would make the English jealous, the naming of a bishop from another country would cause no trouble.'[4]

Polding's two memorandums of 22 and 25 February 1847 had proposed two new dioceses for Australia. Writing seven weeks later (16 April) to Cardinal Fransoni from the English College in Rome he proposed a third, the Diocese of Maitland. The English press had recently carried the news, he said, that the Anglicans in Australia were planning to increase their bishoprics from one to four. They 'are making every attempt to take possession of those very vast states, and consequently it will be necessary to oppose their plans energetically. I therefore request that another episcopal see be erected at Maitland, not far from

Morpeth, the location of one of the proposed Anglican bishoprics. But at present the boundaries should not be fixed and the new bishop should be named coadjutor to the writer.'

The candidate suggested by Polding as first Bishop of Maitland and as his coadjutor surprisingly was Burchall, the very one whom he had recommended so warmly seven weeks earlier for the Diocese of Melbourne. He indicated no reason for his choice. Perhaps he wanted Burchall to take in hand his own seminary in Sydney. In place of Burchall he suggested that Goold be appointed the first Bishop of Melbourne.[5]

All of Polding's proposals were well received by Cardinal Fransoni and on 3 May 1847 they were taken up at a General Meeting of the Evangelisation Congregation, only seventeen days after Polding's latest proposal. Cardinal Castracane, the expert on Australia and Oceania, was chosen to explain the proposals to the assembled cardinals. He gave three specific reasons why it was necessary to create new dioceses in Australia without delay: (1) 'The Anglicans are trying to establish dioceses very quickly and are furnishing them with abundant funds.' (2) 'To avoid questions of jurisdiction it is expedient to reorganise the territories by designating precisely the boundaries of the respective dioceses.' (3) 'And, as is proved by the progress being made by religion in the United States of America, benefits generally result from the presence of bishops and heavenly blessings also descend in abundance wherever they have been sent.' It was necessary to keep in mind, he said, 'that this request comes from Archbishop Polding, who has zealously laboured with admirable success in that mission from 1834 onwards, and so he has been able to form an accurate judgment of its spiritual needs'.

Castracane then explained Polding's proposals for the three new dioceses of Melbourne, Victoria or Essington, and Maitland. There was one slight change. Instead of allowing the strip of unexplored land between the two states of Western Australia and South Australia remain under Polding's jurisdiction, Castracane suggested that it should be added to the Diocese of Adelaide, thus making its western boundary coincide with the eastern boundary of the Diocese of Perth.

In presenting Polding's third proposal he said, 'It is doubtful whether Essington or Victoria will long enjoy enough importance to warrant the creation of an episcopal see there, since revisions are now being made in the deportation laws by the English Parliament. The decision might be reached not to send the condemned to the territory of Essington. In that case this place would not have the civil importance which might attract merchants and other inhabitants.' But, he added, 'a bishopric at Essington is quite important for establishing a mission there for the benefit of the aborigines. From such a mission one could learn and decide which would be the most effective methods for bringing about the conversion of the blacks, who are scattered throughout other dioceses as well.'

Only after presenting Polding's proposals for the foundation of the dioceses of Melbourne and of Essington or Victoria, did Castracane bring up Maitland. He said that no boundaries would be determined for it at the present time other than those of Maitland itself. 'This method of creating a diocese without determining its territory has already been used for the dioceses of Oregon', he said. The city of Maitland 'with 5,000 or 6,000 inhabitants has a beautiful church dedicated to Saint John the Baptist'. This third diocese had been proposed 'in view of efforts being made by Anglicans to establish four episcopal sees in Australia instead of the one already there'. The Bishop of Maitland would at the same time serve as Polding's coadjutor, he said.

Castracane then mentioned the names and qualities of the candidates proposed by Polding for the three new dioceses and asked the cardinals for their views on the following questions:

1. 'Should the Holy Father be asked to erect the new episcopal sees of Melbourne and Victoria with the boundaries indicated by Archbishop Polding, and who from the list of candidates should be proposed to His Holiness for nomination as bishop of both respective sees?'
2. 'Should the Holy Father be asked to erect Maitland into an episcopal see in the manner indicated by the archbishop, and what candidate should be proposed to His Holiness for nomination as its bishop and as coadjutor to the same archbishop?'

The cardinals voted in favour of founding all three dioceses. They chose Goold as Bishop of Melbourne, Serra as Bishop of Victoria, and Burchall for the double role of Bishop of Maitland and coadjutor to Archbishop Polding. They added, however, that provisions would have to be made in order to satisfy the obligation of residence in Maitland.

When these resolutions were presented to Pope Pius IX on 9 May 1847, he 'approved completely of the Sacred Congregation's decision to erect new episcopates in Australia and also of the choice of bishops for those sees. And he ordered that Letters Apostolic should be dispatched in the form of Briefs.'[6]

Once again Archbishop Polding had succeeded in obtaining everything from Rome that he wished. This meant that six of Australia's first seven dioceses had been suggested by him. And even the one not suggested by him, Perth, had had its boundaries altered because of Polding's suggestion. All seven still exist today under the same name, except Victoria, which is now called Darwin. This last diocese is the only one which has not been subdivided since its foundation.

Polding's chief purpose in coming to Rome, however, had been to win approval for the decisions reached by the First Provincial Council of Australia over which he had presided. The archbishop in an ecclesiastical province convenes and presides over a provincial council, which is attended by all the bishops in the ecclesiastical province. Its purpose and role are to consider and adopt measures for the increase of the faith, the regulation of morals, the correction of abuses, the settling of controversies, the establishment and maintenance of uniform discipline. The minutes and the resolutions, called decrees, must be approved by Rome. Among the specific issues discussed at the First Provincial Council of Australia were these: Proper life style for clerics; clerical dress; studies, daily prayer, spiritual retreats and theological discussions of clerics; the Sacrifice of the Mass; the sacraments in general; in particular the sacraments of Baptism, Eucharist, Penance and Matrimony; and preaching the Word of God.

The minutes and resolutions submitted by Polding to the Evangelisation Congregation on 1 February 1847 had meanwhile been scrutinised and were presented by Cardinal Castracane for discussion at the General Meeting of 7 June 1847. The cardinals withheld their approval until some changes were made. When the amended resolutions were submitted one month later at the General Meeting of 12 July, they were approved. Six days later, on 18 July, Pope Pius IX also gave his approval.[7]

Goold eventually was ordained the first Bishop of Melbourne and Serra the first Bishop of Victoria, later regularly referred to as Port Victoria. In place of Burchall, proposed by Polding as his coadjutor and first Bishop of Maitland, the one eventually named to these two offices was Father Henry Charles Davis, a thirty-three-year-old Benedictine. Bishop Davis reached Sydney at the end of 1848. He assisted Polding diligently in administering the Archdiocese of Sydney, but never reached his own Diocese of Maitland. He died prematurely in 1854.[8]

Surprisingly enough Serra, the Spanish Benedictine assigned to work among the Aborigines in Western Australia, learned of his nomination as Bishop of Port Victoria in Europe. On 13 March 1847, less than a month after Polding dated his memorandum proposing Serra for this office, the First Diocesan Synod of Perth was held at New Norcia by Bishop Brady and Fathers Serra, Salvado and Joostens. The synod decided that Serra should go to Europe to collect funds for the bankrupt diocese. Serra must have been in Europe only a short time when he was ordained Bishop of Port Victoria in Rome by Cardinal Fransoni on 15 August 1847.

When this news reached Bishop Brady in Perth, he became frantic, thinking that Serra now would surely collect funds only for his own diocese and not for the Diocese of Perth. He therefore had Father Salvado, the other Spanish Benedictine at New Norcia, leave Fremantle on 8 January 1849 for Europe to collect funds for the Diocese of Perth. At the same time Brady asked Rome to assign him a coadjutor since financial worries were beginning to affect his mind and body. This Rome did in July 1849, giving him Bishop Serra as coadjutor, making Serra administrator of the diocese's temporal goods, and relieving Serra at the same time of his Diocese of Port Victoria. Salvado by this time had reached Italy and so the Diocese of Port Victoria was given to him. Cardinal Prefect Fransoni, in exile with Pope Pius IX, ordained Salvado a bishop in Naples on 15 August 1849.

When Coadjutor Bishop Serra arrived back in Fremantle on 29 December 1849, he had with him aboard the Spanish frigate *Ferrolana* seven priests and thirty-two aspirants to the Benedictine Order. He set out for New Norcia mission with his party early in January; the future of New Norcia seemed assured. Brady, however, would not hear of relinquishing any authority in temporalities to Serra and soon was involved in litigation against him. Confusion multiplied, opinions clashed, and laymen took sides. Brady then left for Rome in February 1850; by December 1851 he was back in Fremantle. He left again in August 1852, this time never to return. After a lengthy stay in Rome he retired to France and to his home Diocese of Kilmore in Ireland. Never having formally resigned his office as Bishop of Perth, he retained the title until he died at Amelu les Bains in France on 2 December 1871.[9]

25

Pompallier leaves New Zealand to defend himself in Rome

16 APRIL 1846

After spending Christmas of 1844 with Archbishop Polding of Sydney, Bishop Pompallier arrived back at Kororareka in the Bay of Islands, New Zealand, at 2 P.M. on 19 January 1845. That day at 5 A.M. a Maori warrior named Hone Heke had cut down the flagstaff at Government House in Kororareka for the second time in two weeks. These and other Maori attacks eventually prompted the British to transfer their capital from Kororareka to Auckland.[1]

With relations between the Maoris and the British continually worsening and with British charges against him steadily mounting, Pompallier began to regret more than ever that the Friendly or Tonga Archipelago, formerly under his jurisdiction, had been removed and made part of the Vicariate Apostolic of Central Oceania in 1842. He wrote to Cardinal Prefect Fransoni once again on this subject on 3 March 1845, reminding him that the archipelago was very close to New Zealand, that he knew its language, and that it could serve as a refuge for him in case political differences should force him to leave New Zealand.[2]

Actually on 12 January 1845, seven weeks before Pompallier wrote this letter, Pope Gregory XVI at the suggestion of the Evangelisation Congregation had acceded to his earlier requests and had placed the Friendly Archipelago once again under his jurisdiction, but without separating it territorially from the Vicariate Apostolic of Central Oceania. The news was still en route.[3]

Before dawn on 11 March, eight days after Pompallier wrote to Rome, Hone Heke and Kawiti, another Maori leader, led a new attack against Kororareka. Rushing the town from three different directions, they cut down the flagstaff and occupied one of the two blockhouses, forcing the Europeans to flee to the seven ships lying at anchor in the bay. Pompallier and his two priests succeeded in getting aboard the *Russell*, which he had chartered earlier. Already stowed aboard were his church records, sacred vessels and religious goods, as well as clothing and other movable goods.[4]

A bigger threat than Hone Heke to Pompallier's remaining in New Zealand was Governor FitzRoy, head of the British colony. According to him it was Pompallier, among others, who was fomenting the anti-British demonstrations of the Maoris. When the bishop learned of this, he wrote to Captain Home of the *North Star* on 1 April, maintaining that he wished nothing else but 'peace and happiness both to the white man and the native. I spared no pains to procure peace before the war, and I am still [doing] the same . . . It is not my intention to deprive this country of the ministry which I have exercised for eight years. I fear neither robbers nor fire nor death. . . .' He asked Home to relay this letter to FitzRoy.

Several days later, on 9 April, FitzRoy wrote to Lord Stanley of the Home Office in London, charging that 'Frenchmen as well as Americans have instigated and encouraged the natives to resist the authority of Great Britain. . . .' Referring explicitly to Pompallier and his priests, he called attention to the fact that they were all Frenchmen and that they were 'in constant communication' with the French corvette, *Rhin*, which 'was at the Bay of Islands in January last and is now daily expected to return there from Akaroa on her way to Tahiti and France. . . .' It was therefore necessary, he said, to have an Aliens Bill which would authorise him to expel from New Zealand those aliens suspected of causing difficulties for the government.

FitzRoy then set to work preparing a draft and wrote to Lord Stanley on 9 September, when it was completed. The bill was needed, he said, because both Maoris and Europeans had testified that 'some of the French priests in New Zealand are intriguing or advising against British authority. . . .' And on 23 October he wrote to Bishop Pompallier and accused him of making the natives hostile towards the British.[5]

When FitzRoy wrote to Lord Stanley on 9 September 1845, Pompallier was in Sydney having conferences with Bishop Epalle, Vicar Apostolic of Melanesia and Micronesia. Pompallier was trying to resolve with Epalle's help his many problems with the Marists.[6] And on 23 October, when FitzRoy wrote to Pompallier, he was still in Sydney waiting for the arrival of the *Rhin*. Captain Bérard at his request had agreed to bring Father Viard from New Caledonia to Sydney, where he was to be ordained Pompallier's coadjutor. When the *Rhin* finally arrived with thirty-six-year-old Viard aboard on 29 October, Epalle and his missionaries had already left—only six days earlier—for New Caledonia and the Solomon Islands, to lay the foundations for the Vicariate Apostolic of Melanesia.[7]

Pompallier was still in Sydney on 19 December that year, when he wrote to Cardinal Prefect Fransoni of the Evangelisation Congregation to thank him for his letter of the previous 22 February. Together with that letter, he said, he had received 'two briefs from our Holy Father, Pope Gregory XVI. One returns to my jurisdiction the Friendly Archipelago, those islands which I earlier had evangelised, and the other authorises me to ordain one of my missionaries as my coadjutor.' His choice fell upon Father Viard, he said, who would soon be ordained a bishop. After that Pompallier would 'depart for France and Rome . . . My conscience, confirmed by the Most Reverend Polding, Archbishop of Sydney, makes it an imperious duty for me to undertake this voyage and I shall leave as soon as possible.'

Still hurt over Central Oceania having been removed from his jurisdiction and given to Bishop Bataillon, and Melanesia and Micronesia having been given to Bishop Epalle, he pleaded with Fransoni. 'I kindly ask you not to create any other vicariates apostolic, nor any other bishops in Western Oceania, at the precipitous requests of the Reverend Colin, Superior General of the Priests of the Society of Mary. The policy which he is following tends to attach clergymen to himself who are 7,000 leagues away and to detach them from the bishop where they are working . . . I shall easily be able to give proof of this in Rome, where I hope to arrive about July 1846 . . . I have laboured here so much and have borne so many afflictions caused more by members of the Society of Mary than by enemies of our Holy Faith . . . And now I have been told here that the Superior General does not want to send me any more personnel and that the Association for the Propagation of the Faith [in France], influenced by that same Superior General, will considerably lessen its allocations for my vicariate apostolic.'[8]

As the irony of history would have it, the day on which Bishop Pompallier was complaining to Rome about the foundation of new vicariates apostolic in Western Oceania was the same day on which Bishop Epalle, Vicar Apostolic of Melanesia and Micronesia, died aboard the *Marian Watson* from mortal wounds received in the Solomon Islands.

The news that Rome had returned the administration of the Friendly or Tonga Archipelago to Pompallier created a dilemma for the priests in charge of the Marist supply centre at Sydney. They wondered which bishop, Bataillon or Pompallier, would consider it his responsibility to supply the missionaries in that archipelago with food, clothing and other supplies. Since Rome had made Pompallier administrator of that part of Bataillon's territory, some thought that the responsibility therefore was his. But Pompallier maintained that the territory was still Bataillon's and that therefore Bataillon had also the responsibility of providing supplies. Father Calinon, a Marist in Sydney at this time, acquainted Superior General Colin on 24 and 27 November 1845 with this dilemma. 'We are wondering who will provide us missionaries with temporal goods', he said. And he added the very disquieting news that Archbishop Polding's feelings toward the two Marists in charge of the supply centre at Sydney had 'cooled considerably' as a result of his conversations with Bishop Pompallier.[9]

Viard was ordained a bishop on Sunday, 4 January 1846, by Archbishop Polding in Saint Mary's Cathedral in Sydney. When he and Pompallier arrived in New Zealand aboard the *Rhin* toward the end of January, they could not have known that the Under Secretary of State for the Foreign Department in London had written on the previous 10 October to the Under Secretary of Lord Stanley about the charges made by FitzRoy against Pompallier and his French priests. 'The position of our [British] missionaries with regard to the French [Government] in Tahiti', the note said, 'is similar to that of the French with regard to us in New Zealand. And it will not have failed to occur to Lord Stanley that, while we are complaining of the harsh conduct of the French authorities towards British missionaries in Tahiti on alleged grounds of suspicion, which the French maintain to be sufficient, but which we regard as inadequate, it might be hazardous to resort on our part to similar measures on similar grounds towards the French missionaries in New Zealand. . . .'

Something of great advantage for Pompallier had happened in New Zealand during his absence. FitzRoy had been replaced as governor by Sir George Grey, who had arrived in Auckland on 18 November. And when Lord Stanley forwarded the 10 October note from the Under Secretary of State for the Foreign Department to Governor Grey, he added a warning about the Aliens Bill suggested by FitzRoy. 'The law authorising the removal of aliens may need to be introduced,' he said, 'but observe the utmost caution in exercising such a power.'

Governor Grey sent a lengthy reply to Lord Stanley from Government House in Auckland on 2 June 1846. It merits being cited in its entirety, not so much because it is a vindication of Pompallier and his priests, but rather because it obliterates the grounds used by Pompallier for having the Friendly or Tonga Archipelago restored to his jurisdiction.

'I have the honour to acknowledge receipt of your Lordship's despatch of 15th October last,' Governor Grey said, 'regarding the strong terms in which my predecessor had adverted to the influence exercised by the French Roman Catholic bishop and priests in bringing about the disastrous events which had taken place at the Bay of Islands.

'I beg to state that when first I proceeded from Auckland to the Bay of Islands, immediately after my arrival in the Colony, my mind was much prejudiced against Dr. Pompallier and the Roman Catholic clergy. I have no doubt that the same individuals who made to me the reports which induced me to adopt these impressions were the persons who had influenced my predecessor. His confidential despatch to your Lordship on the 9th April shows indeed that such was the case.

'On my arrival, however, at Bay of Islands I found that a considerable portion of the forces of the loyal natives acting with our troops was composed of Roman Catholics and that Her Majesty had no more gallant and loyal subjects than these natives were. I moreover ascertained that previously to the attack upon Kororareka the leading native chiefs in the vicinity (who were Roman Catholics) had offered to the Police Magistrate their assistance in defending the town, which had been declined. These circumstances made me hesitate before I adopted any measures against the Roman Catholic bishop and his clergy.

'I have now no hesitation in stating that I have, ever since my residence in New Zealand, received every assistance from these gentlemen, and that I believe that the accusations against them originated in prejudice and were wholly unfounded, and I am perfectly satisfied that they did everything in their power to promote peace and good order.

'I see in the same series of despatches remarks which appear to indicate that Commodore Bérard of the French corvette, *Rhin*, had also fallen under the suspicion of the local government. I feel it due to that amiable officer to state my entire conviction that he was in no manner whatever directly or indirectly concerned in promoting any outrages in New Zealand; and I am sure that numerous British officers of rank would join me in this expression of opinion.

'I apprehend the real facts of the case are that the affairs of New Zealand were in the most alarming and critical state, that they were undoubtedly brought into this condition by mismanagement and injudicious proceedings, and that then, as is usual in such cases, everybody was anxious to throw the blame upon some other person. In this instance, this feeling was probably heightened by the fact of the Church of England missionaries, feeling that their large claims of lands, said to have been purchased from the natives (and which claims will yet give rise to native wars if not to disputes between the Government and the natives) made them contrast very disadvantageously in the eyes of the aborigines with the Roman Catholic missionaries and the missionaries of some other Protestant bodies.

'I am far from denying that some Europeans have instigated the natives to acts of outrage; but I believe that the persons who do this are generally individuals suffering under some imagined grievances, or those who expect to make large profits by contracts or to derive benefit from a large military and naval expenditure. I really believe that in some instances the mere desire of obtaining efficient protection from the mother country induces individuals to exaggerate the dangers with which they are threatened and thus to encourage the natives.

'With regard to Dr. Pompallier's having mistaken his position by imagining that he was entitled to maintain a perfect neutrality between the Government and those in arms against it, I have to observe that this system of neutrality was extensively recognised by the Government as regarded not only the missionaries but the natives, and was not put an end to until after my arrival in the Colony.'

Governor Grey then added this postscript:

'Since addressing the above despatch to your Lordship I have received the following letter from the gentleman who held the office of Police Magistrate of the Bay of Islands district for a considerable period of time before the destruction of Kororareka:—

Referring to a conversation held by me this morning with His Excellency the Lieutenant Governor relative to an allegation that Dr. Pompallier and the French mission under his charge in the Northern District had exercised an undue and pernicious influence upon the minds of the natives: I have the honour to state for the information of His Excellency that from an experience of five years I believe the contrary to have been the case and have always found the bishop and his subordinate clergy anxious to allay irritation, promote a good feeling and afford every information in all matters connected with the natives; and that on one occasion, a report having reached me that the French priest at Wangaroa had made use of statements of an injurious tendency, I placed myself in communication with Dr. Pompallier who immediately declared that, were the report well founded, he would visit the offence with the severest punishment; but I am happy to state that upon a strict investigation it appeared that there were no grounds whatever for the charge.

THOS BECKHAM
Police Magistrate

Your Lordship will see that this gentleman, from an experience of five years, bears the most conclusive testimony to the propriety of conduct of Dr. Pompallier and the Roman Catholic clergy.'[10]

Bishop Pompallier was on the high seas when Governor Grey wrote this glowing tribute. He had left Akaroa, New Zealand, for France on 16 April 1846 aboard the *Rhin*. It was unfortunate that news of his vindication could not immediately reach him, as well as Fransoni, Colin and Bataillon, since it would have spared each of these men much grief in the weeks and months to come. It meant, in fact, that there was no longer any danger of Pompallier's being expelled from New Zealand and he therefore did not need the Friendly or Tonga Archipelago as a possible refuge.

Viard wrote to Superior General Colin on 12 January 1846, eight days after his episcopal ordination, that his instructions from Pompallier were to visit the various New Zealand missions and then proceed to the tropical islands 'to take possession of the missions of Tonga, Wallis and Futuna'. But Bataillon, Vicar Apostolic of Central Oceania, had his headquarters on Wallis. Viard told Colin that if he succeeded in taking over these missions, as Pompallier had ordered, then Bataillon would have to transfer his headquarters elsewhere. He added, however, that he did not see how Pompallier would be able to care for even the closest of these missions, namely Tongatapu, since his New Zealand headquarters was 800 leagues away.[11]

The *Rhin* with Bishop Pompallier aboard had not yet reached France when Colin received Viard's letter of 12 January announcing that Pompallier would be sending him soon to take possession of the missions in Tonga, Wallis and Futuna. Colin by this time had known for more than a year that Rome had decided to return the Friendly or Tonga Archipelago to Pompallier; Fransoni had informed both him and Pompallier by separate letters on 22 February 1845. The cardinal at that time had assured Colin that the archipelago was being returned to Pompallier 'provisionally for administration', stated that 'the said islands or archipelago' would later be returned to Bataillon's vicariate apostolic, made no mention of Wallis and Futuna, and assured him that no other changes were involved. Bataillon would receive back the archipelago, Fransoni had said, 'as soon as' there was no longer any danger of expulsion from New Zealand for Pompallier and his missionaries, or when Pompallier took over the Vicariate Apostolic of Micronesia, 'as had been foreseen when the Vicariates of Melanesia and Micronesia were founded'.[12]

Colin had accepted this 1845 decision from Rome and did not react.

But he did react now, and strongly so, on learning from Viard that he was being sent by Pompallier to take over not only the Tonga Archipelago, but Wallis and Futuna as well. He rushed off to advise Rome of the unwarranted claims being made by Pompallier and as proof gave Viard's letter to the officials of the Evangelisation Congregation. They added it to their growing Pompallier-Colin dossier and attached this note: 'The Superior General of the Marists on 6 August 1846 takes the liberty to suggest that it would be in the best interest [of the mission] if at least the Wallis Islands [including Futuna] were reserved for Bishop Bataillon. . . .'[13]

Anxious to have Viard take over the missions of Tonga, Wallis and Futuna as soon as possible, Pompallier had chartered the 55-ton schooner *Providence* for him on 22 December 1845 while in Sydney, even before Viard's episcopal ordination.[14] By April of the following year Viard was in Wallis to discuss the entire matter with Bataillon. And on 24 April, just eight days after Pompallier had left New Zealand for Europe, Bataillon wrote Colin the results of this tête-à-tête. 'You already know', he said, 'that according to a brief of the Supreme Pontiff dated 7 February 1845 the Friendly Archipelago has been placed under the administration of New Zealand. Here we have not yet received any word from the Roman Curia, but this last February we did receive from Bishop Pompallier a copy of the brief along with a letter from His Grace.

'In his letter he declared to us that he understands as included in the Friendly Archipelago the islands of Wallis and Futuna, even though there is no mention of them in the brief. And he stated that on the basis of the letter that he has received [from Rome], he must regard us as charged with the temporalities of the mission of Tonga, Futuna and Wallis . . . , and that in spiritual matters he grants me the faculties that I shall need.' Pompallier had also said, Bataillon continued, that 'for a long time to come' it would be impossible for him 'to send missionaries to replace us in the various islands which he claims . . . And in order to reach an understanding with us on the changes that will have to be made', he said that he would be sending Coadjutor Viard.

Bataillon and his priests had studied this letter from Pompallier and had decided, as he told Colin, 'to let matters rest as they were formerly, until we receive new orders'. He would continue to consider Wallis and Futuna as belonging to himself, until such time as Pompallier presented him with an official document clearly dispossessing him of those islands. 'And as for Tonga,' he said, 'I have not yet received any official word from the Roman Curia. We have written to it, presenting our stand and asking for clarifications on the brief concerning the [Tonga] Islands. And so I shall not dispossess myself of them either, until such time as I receive from the Holy Father official orders and the clarifications on the brief in question, which I have requested from His Holiness.'

Bishop Viard did come to visit him, he said, 'and agreed all the more readily with our decision since he, like us, sees the very great inconveniences that will result from the changes which will have to be made. And besides they already have enough to do to disentangle matters in New Zealand without coming to the tropics to use up their last penny by meddling in affairs here. He will therefore return to New Zealand to occupy himself exclusively there until new orders arrive. And it is he who will be carrying this letter to pass it on to our procurator in Sydney, who in turn will be charged to have it reach you as quickly as possible.' According to Bataillon, 'all the missionaries of New Zealand and Bishop Viard himself' considered the proposed changes a catastrophe. 'And we, all of us, think that if these changes do take place, they will cause great harm to the progress of religion in the Central Vicariate.'[15]

Bataillon also gave Viard a letter for Father Dubreul, procurator in charge of the Marist supply centre at Sydney. His special reason for writing, he said, was the news that Bishop Pompallier 'has left for Europe several months ago'. (Bataillon's information was incorrect; Pompallier had left New Zealand for Europe on 16 April, the very month when Bataillon was writing to Dubreul.) 'I want you to hurry and leave [for Europe] yourself,' Bataillon said, 'so that you will arrive [there] before he has completed all his affairs. . . .' And if Dubreul could not go to Europe himself, he was to send off the enclosed letter for Colin and another for Pompallier at the very first opportunity. 'There is nothing more important than for you or our letters to arrive in Europe before the matters concerning our missions are decided', he said. 'And so lose no time. . . .' He also enclosed a letter from Father Petit-Jean of New Zealand, so that Dubreul could see what the Marists there thought of the proposed changes.

In addition to urging Dubreul to hurry to Europe, the letter gave him numerous instructions on what to do upon arrival. In Rome he was to inform the officials at the Evangelisation Congregation of the serious difficulties foreseen by Bataillon if these changes were introduced. And in France he was supposed to contact the officers of the fund-collecting Association for the Propagation of the Faith and tell them that any word which they might have heard from Pompallier about changes in Tonga, Wallis and Futuna was 'mere speculation'. He was to say that Pompallier had not yet sent any of his priests to these islands, that Bataillon was still in charge, and that most likely he would be in charge for a long time to come. Therefore until the whole matter was definitely settled the association should continue sending the allocations for these islands to Bataillon, 'since', as he said, 'I am the one who must look after the needs of the missions in question. . . .'[16]

By this time the officers of the association in France had already sensed that all was not well between Pompallier and the Marists. Baron Antoine de Jessé, president of its Central Council in Lyon, had written to Cardinal Prefect Fransoni on 17 January 1846, three months before Bataillon's letters to Colin and Dubreul. De Jessé's letter was prompted by documentation received from Pompallier, and when relaying it to Rome he said: 'Difficulties seem to have arisen between the venerable bishop in question and the respected superior general of the Congregation of Marists, responsible for supplying the New Zealand mission with missionaries. But the [Central] Council has neither the authority nor the duty to intervene in this delicate affair and until now it has remained aloof. It believes that it must continue to do so. . . .'[17]

Cardinal Fransoni answered on 7 February that he highly approved of the stand taken by the president and the council in 'not taking sides in the differences known to have arisen' between Pompallier and Colin. But he added that the financial report on the Western Oceania Vicariate prepared by Pompallier and sent to the Central Council in Lyon, and now forwarded by it to Rome, must have achieved its purpose. That purpose was to prevent the complaints submitted against Pompallier by the Marists from influencing the Central Council in its distribution of funds to the detriment of the bishop and his mission.

Fransoni, who had urged the Central Council earlier to maintain such impartiality, now asked it again to be as generous and devoted in assisting Pompallier as it was in serving other vicars apostolic.[18]

Following almost immediately upon these two letters of de Jessé and Fransoni, but having no causal relationship with them, was a 17 February 1846 decree of the Evangelisation Congregation which abolished a 16 September 1842 decree. One of the purposes of the earlier decree, as Fransoni told Pompallier as late as 22 February 1845, was to foster harmony between him and his Marist missionaries and their superior general.[19] This decree had been issued as a norm to be followed by all vicars apostolic and religious communities in Oceania, and also for those in Ava-Pegú, as Burma was then called.[20]

But at their General Meeting of 9 December 1845 the cardinals of the Evangelisation Congregation had to admit that 'many of the points' included in the decree 'do not at all contribute toward the harmony' originally intended. It was therefore decided to request Pope Gregory XVI to abrogate this decree and to prescribe instead for Oceania and Ava-Pegú 'those regulations which have been introduced and sanctioned for vicariates apostolic located elsewhere'. Secretary Brunelli brought this resolution to Pope Gregory XVI on 14 December and 'His Holiness gave his approval in all points, ordering that it be made known to those concerned'.[21] By this action Pompallier was freed of the obligation of conducting his correspondence with the Evangelisation Congregation through Colin.

When sending the new decree to Colin on 7 March, Fransoni said that it 'concerns the missions of Oceania and has been sanctioned by the Holy Father'. It was to serve as a norm for the vicars apostolic in Marist mission territory, the cardinal said, and he asked Colin kindly to forward the enclosed copies to them.[22]

Since Pompallier left New Zealand one month later, his copy of the decree never reached him there. He arrived in France at the Mediterranean port of Toulon on 28 August and then went via Marseille to Rome in order to report on the difficulties that he was experiencing in his mission and to obtain remedies for them. He arrived in Rome, as he said, 'on the feast of the Exaltation of the Holy Cross, 14 September. . . .' After listening to his complaints the officials at the Evangelisation Congregation suggested that he first go to Lyon and try to reach an understanding with Father Colin there. This he agreed to do.[23]

With Pompallier now being in Europe and a confrontation likely to take place at any time, it was necessary for Colin and his council to have in advance a clear stand on these two questions: 'Should the Society of Mary make efforts to keep New Zealand? And if so, how should it collaborate and under what conditions?' Colin and his council discussed this matter on 11 October and reached the following conclusions:

1. If Bishop Pompallier were transferred to Tongatapu in the Friendly Islands, the Society could take direct action to keep the New Zealand mission.
2. The Society could take action to have Bishop Viard become the coadjutor

of Bishop Bataillon, and it could present Bishop Douarre, currently coadjutor to Bishop Bataillon, for the office of Vicar Apostolic of New Caledonia.

3. If Bishop Pompallier should resign, then the Society could work toward the foundation of two separate vicariates in New Zealand.

4. The Society could not take action directly to have Bishop Pompallier return to New Zealand. Nor would it take action to have New Zealand divided into two vicariates under Bishop Pompallier.

At this meeting one further question was brought up: 'In case all matters are settled in such a way that Bishop Pompallier eventually returns to New Zealand, can the Society give its assistance to this mission?' The reply was: 'Yes, in the best way possible.'[24]

Colin and the Marists now had a concrete program to follow and were ready to negotiate with Pompallier and Rome.

While speaking about Pompallier on 24 November, one month later, Colin went on record as saying: 'I had nothing at all to do with his becoming vicar apostolic. The Administration of Lyon [Archdiocese] proposed him [to Rome] . . . and later the Society acquiesced.'[25]

This is not exactly correct, however, because Colin did play a decisive role in Pompallier's being considered by both Lyon and Rome as a candidate to head the first Marist mission in Western Oceania. The proof is partly in Colin's reply of 3 August 1835 to a query received from Pompallier: 'It would give me great pleasure to see you set out for this foreign mission [of Western Oceania]', he said. ' . . . And I hope that the good God will indeed strengthen you in this vocation, because at the present moment I can think of no one else but you who can fill the position [of mission superior] that is offered to you. And so do not neglect this matter. . . .'[26]

Unknown to Colin this letter was forwarded to Rome by Father Pastre of Lyon, a confidant of the Evangelisation Congregation, and was accepted there as Colin's nomination of Pompallier to head the mission. Subsequently Rome received a similar nomination from the administrator of Lyon Archdiocese. Pastre made the same proposal. On the basis of these three recommendations Rome then decided to name Pompallier head of the mission. And since it meanwhile had become a vicariate apostolic, Rome gave Pompallier immediately the rank of vicar apostolic and bishop.[27]

When Pompallier and Colin were unsuccessful in resolving their common problems in Lyon, as the officials of the Evangelisation Congregation had hoped they might do, they both came to Rome seeking arbitration from the Evangelisation Congregation and from the pope. Pompallier was in Rome on 8 December 1846 when he addressed a 5-page introductory letter and a 256-page report to the cardinals of the Evangelisation Congregation.[28] Since Colin was already in Rome when Pompallier arrived, he was presented with the third part (67 pages) of this memorandum and was asked to comment on it. This he did from Rome on 26 January 1847.[29]

Also in January a third and a fourth combatant arrived on the Roman scene to take part in this new battle between Pompallier and Colin. One was Father Dubreul from Sydney, sent by Bishop Bataillon to speak on his behalf against Pompallier's position regarding Wallis, Futuna and the Friendly or Tonga Archipelago. Dubreul did get to speak about this topic with Cardinal Prefect Fransoni that month, but no decision was taken immediately since the Pompallier-Marist question was vast and had to be studied as a whole.[30] The other combatant was Archbishop Polding of Sydney, who would side with Pompallier. He had come to Rome to present to the Evangelisation Congregation for its approval the resolutions of Australia's First Provincial Council.[31]

Undoubtedly Pompallier in leaving New Zealand had hoped to receive understanding and support in Rome from Pope Gregory XVI, who had devoted so much of his life to the development of missionary work in Oceania. It was this pope who had warmly received Pompallier in audience in 1836 prior to his departure for Western Oceania. But he had died on 1 June 1846, while Pompallier was still aboard the *Rhin* en route to France. It would be up to his successor, Pope Pius IX, to find a solution to the Pompallier-Marist conflict.

26

Plans to establish the hierarchy in Western Oceania are blocked

1 MAY 1847

The Evangelisation Congregation at its General Meeting of 3 May 1847 fully approved of the proposal of Archbishop Polding of Sydney, then in Rome, that three new dioceses should be founded in Australia. Six days later Pope Pius IX, during his audience of 9 May, ratified this decision and named as bishops the three candidates presented by Polding.[1] Also on 3 May the Evangelisation Congregation had planned to vote in favour of creating an ecclesiastical province in the vast territory originally embraced by Bishop Pompallier's Vicariate Apostolic of Western Oceania, thus establishing the hierarchy there. Had it done so, Pope Pius IX undoubtedly would have ratified that decision as well at his 9 May audience. This would have launched a new era for the Catholic Church in Western Oceania.

Before voting on this proposal, however, the Evangelisation Congregation was anxious to bring about a reconciliation between Bishop Pompallier, originator of the idea, and Father Colin, superior general of the Marists. Rome had tried repeatedly to reconcile these two men when one was in New Zealand and the other in France, but always without success. Now with both of them in Rome the cardinals decided to try again. But instead of seeing the Colin-Pompallier feud come to an end, the cardinals would see it develop into a glaring tragedy for the people and for the Church of Western Oceania. Step by step the drama unfolded in the following way.

Bishop Pompallier, writing from Rome on 8 December 1846, addressed a 5-page letter to the cardinals of the Evangelisation Congregation and a 256-page *Memorandum* in three parts. 'I have been able to compose this during my painful travels and long voyages,' he said, 'and I call your indulgent attention especially to Part Three.' Part one (175 pages) gave minute details on the historical development of his Vicariate Apostolic of Western Oceania. Part two (14 pages) contained a financial, spiritual, and personnel report from 31 December 1843 to 31 December 1846. And part three (67 pages) described for the cardinals 'a very serious difficulty which exists not only in the areas under my jurisdiction, but also in nearly all vicariates apostolic both past and present'.[2]

This 'difficulty' resulted from a lack of unity among the clergy and faithful under the jurisdiction of a bishop. And the immediate cause for this lack of unity, according to Pompallier, was to be found in the superiors of religious orders. They had a right, he said, to make provisions for the internal government of their religious communities at work within a given territory, but at times they overreached this limited area of competence. 'They become paternalistic, they govern, they pass judgment, and they even predominate over pastoral activity. . . .' All of this causes division among the missionaries and makes excellent men become dissatisfied with their vocation, he said. Endless polemics result and 'paralyse episcopal authority and episcopal activity, becoming at the same time a fruitful source of what are always schisms substantially ·and sometimes schisms formally'.

It was not his purpose, Pompallier said, to censure the personal faults of anyone. 'It is rather my intention to make known the viciousness of a situation which exposes the missions to languor, confusion, division and ruin.' If no remedy were to be found soon, the nascent Christianities in Oceania would be destroyed 'by confusion comparable to that which afflicted the builders of the Tower of Babel. . . .' It was precisely to prevent such evils that he had undertaken a voyage of 6,000 leagues 'to the Vicar of Jesus Christ, in order that I might call his attention to what concerns the salvation of a new and enormous flock of the Lord. . . .'[3]

Pompallier's *Memorandum* suggested a remedy for the evils which he had mentioned. All his problems with the Marists would be solved, he implied, if the hierarchy were to be established in the vast territory which originally belonged to his Vicariate Apostolic of Western Oceania. And he offered the Evangelisation Congregation a concrete proposal for the kind of ecclesiastical province that he had in mind. It would have one archdiocese and six suffragan dioceses. Together with his proposal he submitted a map indicating in colour the precise boundaries of the various ecclesiastical territories.

He was undecided whether the archbishop should reside at Kororareka, up to now his headquarters in the Bay of Islands at the far north end of New Zealand, or farther south at Auckland, the new capital city with 3,500 inhabitants. The boundaries of the projected archdiocese included both Kororareka and Auckland. They were drawn by Pompallier evidently with the thought in mind that he might become the archbishop, since they included the Tonga Islands, his contemplated place of refuge. But he no longer needed this archipelago as a refuge, since unknown to him the danger of his being expelled from New Zealand by the British government had passed.

From the way Pompallier drew his boundaries—all oval—it was clear that originally he envisioned only two divisions for the combined territories of New Zealand and the Tonga Islands. The archdiocese was to include the Tonga Islands and the major part of New Zealand's North Island; the proposed Diocese of Port Nicholson (now Wellington)—that city had 4,000 inhabitants—was to include the rest of New Zealand. But then as an afterthought he cut off from the oval describing the limits of the archdiocese the bottom part by drawing a horizontal line through North Island near the mouth of the Waihou or Thames River. This new division he called the Diocese of Tauranga. Perhaps it was to justify this third division that he said New Zealand itself after some years 'might have four or five suffragan dioceses making up a single ecclesiastical province'.

Also at a later date 'the numerous archipelagoes and islands in this area could

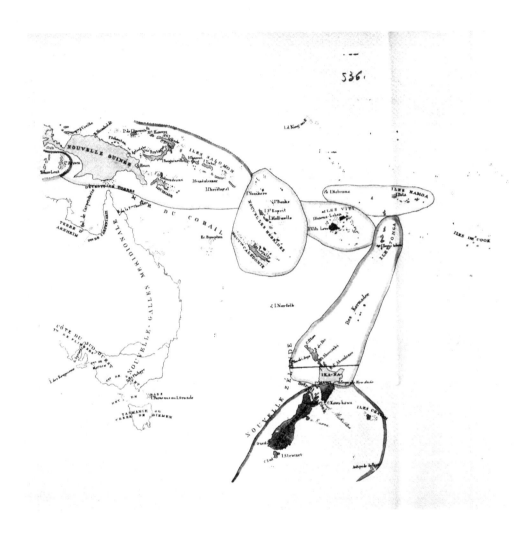

58   Bishop Pompallier, Vicar Apostolic of Western Oceania, submitted this map in colour to the Evangelisation Congregation on 8 December 1846 when presenting his plan for establishing the hierarchy in Western Oceania. The archiepiscopal see was to be located in New Zealand, but he was undecided whether the archbishop should reside at Kororareka or at Auckland. Note that Viti was another form for Fiji and that Hamoa was another spelling for Samoa. *Source: PF: SOCG vol. 969 (1847) f. 536r. (Chapter 26).*

be erected into several ecclesiastical provinces', he said, 'if God gives stability
to the churches that will be founded there'. But he thought it advisable for the
time being to unite the archipelagoes and New Zealand in a single ecclesiastical
province. The four remaining suffragan dioceses according to his plan were to
be the Samoa Islands with Wallis and Futuna, the Fiji Islands, New Caledonia
with New Hebrides, and New Guinea with its surrounding archipelagoes. This
last diocese was identical in size with the already established Vicariate Apostolic
of Melanesia.

Pompallier's closest friend and confidant in Oceania was Archbishop Polding
of Sydney. Pompallier had seen his friend's Vicariate Apostolic of New Holland
and Van Diemen's Land become an ecclesiastical province in 1842 and expand
to include another diocese in 1845. And during some four months of residence
with Polding late in 1845 he had discussed at length the advantages of an
ecclesiastical province. It therefore was no surprise that Pompallier was now
anxious to see this same development take place in his own vicariate apostolic.
Added to this was the fact that his own territory, once so vast, had dwindled so
much that it now embraced only New Zealand. But if the hierarchy were to be
established, and if he were to receive the archiepiscopal see, he would have a
stronger hand within his own jurisdictional area. Also, as metropolitan and head
of the ecclesiastical province he would regain some degree of authority over all
the territories originally belonging to him. This is what Pompallier wanted; this
is what Colin feared.

In his accompanying letter Pompallier quoted a recent 'Instruction' called
Neminem profecto from Rome dated 23 November 1845 which had encouraged
the heads of mission territories to take measures to have the hierarchy established in their districts as soon as possible. 'Therefore in proposing to Your
Eminences that the vicariates apostolic of Western Oceania be erected into an
ecclesiastical province', he said, '. . . I am fulfilling your formal directives.'[4]

Luquet, according to his biographer, assisted Pompallier in drafting the 8
December 1846 *Memorandum* on establishing the hierarchy in Oceania. The
thirty-six-year-old India missionary by this time was a bishop, coadjutor to
Bishop Bonnand of Pondicherry Vicariate. How had this come about? Nearly
all cardinals in the Evangelisation Congregation had requested that Luquet draw
up clarifications on the various issues treated by the Pondicherry Synod, which
he had attended and whose results he had brought to Rome for approval. His
Résume des éclaircissements, printed on very large sheets, ran for 207 pages with
11 pages of index. These he submitted on 9 April 1845 and they were discussed
together with the results of the synod at the following General Meeting of the
Evangelisation Congregation on 19 May. The *ponens* or relator for this item on
the agenda was Angelo Cardinal Mai, former secretary of the Evangelisation
Congregation. At the end of his presentation he suggested 'that the priest,
Reverend Luquet, be recommended to His Holiness for a bishopric *in partibus*
because of his outstanding merits in this affair'. His having that office would
make it possible for him 'to put into effect the many and very good things that
he has proposed'.

No less a dignitary than Cardinal Prefect Fransoni ordained Luquet a bishop on Sunday, 7 September 1845, in the Church of Santa Maria in Vallicella, better known as Chiesa Nuova. But Fransoni soon received an August 1845 letter from Bonnand, who was altogether unaware that Rome had decided to give him a coadjutor. Luquet did not know the local language, Bonnand said, and should return to India 'as a missionary and not as a coadjutor'. Besides, it was premature to appoint a coadjutor. The newly ordained bishop, therefore, had to find ways of busying himself in Rome, hoping that Bonnand's attitude might change with time. 'You moved so quickly', Bonnand later told him, 'that we no longer were able to follow you.' Besides, the majority of missionaries did not want him to come back, Bonnand added. The Paris Foreign Mission Seminary, to give Luquet some office at least, made him provisionally its procurator at the Holy See by letter of 26 January 1846, the office which he was holding when he collaborated with Pompallier.

Since Colin was in Rome at this time, the officials of the Evangelisation Congregation decided to give him part three of Pompallier's *Memorandum* in order to have his comments on the proposed ecclesiastical province.[5] Colin made his observations in writing and under date of 26 January 1847 presented them to Secretary Brunelli. He was not at all in favour of establishing an ecclesiastical province and the hierarchy; in fact, he opposed it. But he was in agreement that a vicariate—not a diocese—should be founded for a new ecclesiastical territory to include New Caledonia and New Hebrides, which until now were part of the Vicariate Apostolic of Central Oceania. Bataillon had very early placed these two archipelagoes under the care of his coadjutor, Douarre. As Pompallier had, Colin also suggested that Douarre be made head of this new territory, but as a vicar apostolic, not as a suffragan diocesan bishop. It was Douarre who had brought the Catholic faith to New Caledonia, Colin said, and so he ought to be placed in charge. Since he was already a bishop, no new candidate for the bishopric was needed.[6]

As early as 26 May 1842 Colin and the Marists in Lyon had envisioned in their plan for the ecclesiastical development of Western Oceania a distinct vicariate apostolic for New Caledonia and New Hebrides. The Solomon Islands, which at that time were also to be included, had been added instead to the Vicariate Apostolic of Melanesia founded in 1844. And so Colin in this letter to Brunelli was giving approval, not to Pompallier's idea in the month-old *Memorandum* of 8 December 1846, but to a Marist idea which was already five years old![7]

Colin was strongly opposed to Pompallier's proposal that Bataillon's Vicariate Apostolic of Central Oceania be immediately divided in three with the Tonga Islands becoming part of the New Zealand archdiocese, Fiji becoming a suffragan diocese, and Samoa with Wallis and Futuna also becoming a suffragan diocese. These three archipelagoes still belonged to Bataillon's vicariate apostolic territorially, even though the Tonga Islands in 1845 had been placed provisionally under the jurisdiction of Pompallier at his request.

Action should be suspended, Colin urged, so that Bataillon could be asked in advance for his opinion. Changes made by Rome without forewarning were most disconcerting for mission bishops and their missionaries, he maintained. And as proof he cited the 1845 example when Rome at the unilateral suggestion of Pompallier had removed the Tonga Islands from Bataillon's jurisdiction. Confusion was still rampant, because no one knew for certain which bishop was responsible jurisdictionally and financially for the missions of Tonga, Wallis and Futuna. He told Brunelli that Bataillon had received a letter in which Pompallier claimed that the territory restored to him included Wallis and Futuna. But this did not at all seem to be indicated by the papal brief in question.

Nor was he of the opinion that New Guinea with its surrounding archipelagoes should become a suffragan diocese. 'Circumstances do not seem to favour taking that kind of action for this mission', he said, 'since the one designated as coadjutor to [the late] Bishop Epalle, and who will now succeed him, left France only in November 1845.[8] We have not yet received any news from him and we cannot foresee what part of Melanesia he will be able to penetrate and where he will be able to plant the torch of faith. It is therefore prudent to wait.'[9]

In a word Colin did not express agreement with Pompallier's proposal on a single point. The problems that he had with Pompallier were already enormous under the present system in which individual missions were organised as separate and independent vicariates apostolic. Now if Pompallier were to become archbishop and metropolitan of the ecclesiastical province and were to have all the former Marist vicars apostolic under him as suffragan bishops, Colin was convinced that his problems with Pompallier would surely increase. On the other hand he carefully avoided making any observations whatever on the divisions suggested by Pompallier for New Zealand. Thus it appeared that Colin tended toward having New Zealand become a separate ecclesiastical province with Pompallier in charge. Although the remaining vicariates apostolic in Western Oceania were to retain their status for the present, they also could eventually become dioceses in an ecclesiastical province. But the bishops in charge would be Marists, and the ecclesiastical province would be freed from all connection with Pompallier.

Having the proposal of Pompallier and the reactions of Colin, the officials of the Evangelisation Congregation were eager to make use of one additional source of information before bringing up the matter at a General Meeting. That source was the extensive documentation contained in the archives of the Evangelisation Congregation itself.

Eight specific questions arising from Pompallier's proposal and the Pompallier-Colin conflict were presented to Olimpiade Corsi, the archivist. Three of these concerned the advisability and method of establishing the hierarchy in a territory under the jurisdiction of the Evangelisation Congregation. The archivist replied to these three questions by citing the examples of Maryland and of Oregon in the United States of America, of Canada, and of Australia. He said that in each of these four areas conditions were identical with those of Pompallier's Vicariate Apostolic of Western Oceania, except for the fact that the

PLANS FOR HIERARCHY IN WESTERN OCEANIA 411

others already had a metropolitan or archiepiscopal see with suffragan sees or
dioceses. The four areas mentioned had made great progress and had also
acquired stability through the erection of the hierarchy, he said, and he then
proceeded to give a brief history of each one's development into an ecclesiastical
province.

First he spoke of Maryland, one of the original thirteen states, which had
entered the Union in 1788. One year later Baltimore, its capital, received its first
bishop, the Most Reverend John Carroll, who 'had a very vast diocese to
govern'. Carroll in 1792 asked Rome to divide his territory, saying that he was
not able to provide properly for distant Catholic communities. When no action
was taken by Rome, he renewed his request in 1802 and asked that one
additional diocese be formed.

The Evangelisation Congregation answered on 22 June 1802, suggesting to
Carroll that not only one but four or five additional dioceses should be founded.
An ecclesiastical province could then be created with him as archbishop and
metropolitan. The archivist remarked that this recommendation of the
Evangelisation Congregation dating back to 1802 'seems to foreshadow today's
request' coming from Bishop Pompallier.

Carroll was asked 'to inform the Sacred Congregation in an orderly and clear
way in what places the episcopal sees should be located, what boundaries should
be assigned to each see, how the new bishops would be able to support
themselves, how priests could be obtained and sent there, who would make up
the diocesan clergy, who would hold office as pastors. . . .' And he was also given
the alternative of having 'several coadjutors with episcopal rank', if this
appeared more advisable to him than having new dioceses created. Carroll's
reply asked that four suffragan dioceses be founded, the archivist said, 'and so
the metropolitan see of Baltimore was erected on 4 March 1808 . . . The ones
chosen as the first bishops were those whom this first prelate of the United States
of America had proposed. . . .' He added that Pompallier in making his present
request seemed to be aware of this practice of the Evangelisation Congregation.

The archivist next gave the historical background to the foundation of the
first ecclesiastical province of Canada. He said that Bishop Joseph-Octave Plessis
(1763–1825) of Quebec 'was well aware of the preponderance of bishops over
vicars apostolic', and as early as 1818 had requested that Quebec should become
a metropolitan see within an ecclesiastical province. Plessis had said that
'independent bishops do not form an organic unity, nor can they do the same
[amount of] good. And since no single bishop has the authority to convoke the
others, it is not possible to hold a provincial council nor to take uniform
measures of discipline.' However, in 1818 there were obstacles of a political
nature stemming from the British government and the project had to be
postponed.

In 1841 Bishop Ignace Bourget (1799–1885) of Montreal was in Rome and
he repeated the request of Bishop Plessis. Rome then asked Bishop Wiseman of
London to inquire of the British government whether it had any objections. It
had none and so the hierarchy was established in Canada on 5 (read 13) May

1844, the archivist said, with Quebec becoming the metropolitan see and Montreal, Kingston and Toronto becoming suffragan sees. Lest the cardinals might fear that the British government would have objections to the hierarchy's being established in New Zealand and the rest of Western Oceania, the archivist pointed out that for overseas territories the British government would not be opposed. Proof of this was the fact that it even provided bishops there with a generous subsidy.

'In recent years', the archivist added, 'two [more] archiepiscopal churches have been erected: one in Sydney, the capital of New Holland [now Australia], and the other in Oregon City, the capital of Oregon'.[10] When erecting these two ecclesiastical provinces the Evangelisation Congregation did nothing else but conform to the wishes of Bishop John Bede Polding and Bishop Francis Norbert Blanchet (1795–1883), 'knowing that no one was better able than they to say who was suitable for the episcopal office and in what places they should be located'.

The archivist added that the suffragan dioceses of a given ecclesiastical province had not all been erected at the same time. Baltimore originally had only the suffragan dioceses of Philadelphia, Boston, New York and Bardstown (later called Louisville), 'and now there are more than four times that amount. . . .' Sydney had received only two suffragan dioceses when the ecclesiastical province was founded, the archivist said. 'But if it pleases Your Eminences, perhaps now they will be increased.' He was referring to Archbishop Polding's two recent letters from Rome of 22 and 25 February 1847 in which he had formally requested the Evangelisation Congregation to found two new suffragan dioceses for Australia, Melbourne and Victoria.[11]

Concluding this aspect of his research the archivist remarked that the founding of the hierarchy anywhere had always greatly influenced the growth of Catholicism, 'especially in the United States of America'. But this fact was so widely known, he said, 'that it seems useless to remind anyone about it'.

Pompallier's *Memorandum* had also mentioned that jurisdiction over the Mangaia or Cook Islands should be transferred from him to the Vicar Apostolic of Eastern Oceania. The transfer was particularly advisable, he said, because those islands were not only closer to the Eastern Oceania Vicariate, but their language was a dialect similar to that of Tahiti and of the other Society Islands, whose languages were known to the Picpus missionaries working in the Eastern Oceania Vicariate. The archivist supported Pompallier's view, but suggested that the cardinals first consult the Vicar Apostolic of Eastern Oceania before making the transfer.

The archivist was also asked to do research on whether the spiritual and temporal administration belonged rightfully to the bishop, a question prompted by part three of Pompallier's *Memorandum*. There was no doubt whatsoever in the archives, he said, that both the spiritual and the temporal administration belonged to the bishop and that he was also free to allow into his diocese priests other than those who were members of the particular religious community already working there.

Pompallier, eager to have more authority over those serving under him, was desirous that such priests coming into his territory, as well as catechists, should not be allowed to join the Marists or some other religious order and the archivist was asked to see whether such a prohibition was contained in the archives. But he found none. The only ones who needed a dispensation to join a religious community, he said, were priests who had made their studies while residing in one of the colleges associated with the Evangelisation Congregation and therefore had taken the prescribed oath to serve the missions,[12] or priests who were born in mission lands and who had been ordained *titulo missionis*, that is, for these same missions.

The most delicate question given to the archivist concerned the mutual relations between bishops and the religious order priests working within their dioceses. His research brought to light a document which, he said, had often been restated and left no doubt that religious order priests were dependent upon their bishops in the administration of the sacraments and in the care of souls. But with regard to discipline within their own religious community, they were dependent upon the superiors within their own religious orders. 'But in England and in China', he said, 'they depend completely upon the vicars apostolic'. This had been decreed in two apostolic constitutions, *Speculatores domus Israel* of Pope Clement IX (1667–9), and *Apostolicum Ministerium* of Pope Benedict XIV (1740–58).[13]

'If the Sacred Congregation should be pleased to apply to the Marists of Oceania what it decreed for the Jesuits of Madurai,' he said, 'it would not be out of place to mention here the decree of the Sacred Congregation dated 9 September [read December] 1845. . . .' He explained that in virtue of this decree (or decision) the Vicar Apostolic of Madurai, India, if he was a Jesuit, was also the religious order superior of the Jesuits. And it was his duty to see to it that they observed the rules of their religious community.[14]

Having so much information from Pompallier, from Colin and from the archivist, the Evangelisation Congregation was now ready to proceed to the next step in its preparations for introducing Pompallier's proposal at a General Meeting. As was customary one of the cardinal members was designated to make a special study of the material at hand and to draw up an exhaustive report. The one chosen was Luigi Cardinal Lambruschini, who had been intimately associated with the development of the Catholic Church in the Pacific ever since de Solages made his proposal in 1829 for a prefecture apostolic in the South Sea Islands; at that time Lambruschini was Archbishop of Genoa and simultaneously nuncio apostolic in Paris.

He began his report by saying that Pompallier as first Vicar Apostolic of Western Oceania could rightfully be called 'the apostle of those regions'. And he gave particular praise to part two of Pompallier's 'voluminous but very clear and orderly report'. That part could be used as a model, he said, to urge other heads of mission territories to inform the Evangelisation Congregation 'with equal diligence and exactness' about the financial status of their mission, the source of its income, how this was used, and what results were achieved, 'all of which contributes to the well-being and prosperity of the churches. . . .'

Part three of the *Memorandum* was 'most important', he said, and was meant 'to guarantee the stability and the progress of the missions in Oceania'. This section contained not only a report on the difficulties connected with missionary work as presently organised in Western Oceania, but also suggested what might be done 'to provide an efficacious remedy'.

The 'efficacious remedy' suggested by Pompallier was the immediate establishment of the hierarchy in the vast territory originally included within the boundaries of his Vicariate Apostolic of Western Oceania. The principle urging Pompallier to make this request, Lambruschini explained, was that 'the government of every mission requires unity of action both in temporal and spiritual matters. . . .' On one hand the members of religious communities engaged in missionary work considered it necessary to have some tie or special bond to keep them in close contact with their religious community and its spirit. This helped support them in their striving to acquire evangelical perfection, Pompallier said. But on the other hand, when they served as missionaries under the vigilance and guidance of a bishop, who is only a vicar apostolic, they were inclined to request from the Holy See certain concessions, such as those granted by Rome to the Marists in September 1842. Pompallier maintained that experience on the spot had shown these concessions to be impractical and also harmful to such a degree that Rome subsequently revoked them 'on 17 February of this past year'.

Complaints coming from the Jesuit mission in Madurai, India, where Superior General Roothaan had applied the 1842 decree, were under discussion at a General Meeting on 9 December 1845 when the cardinals decided to ask the pope expressly to revoke the decree. The relator that day was Cardinal Castracane and he pointed out that, in fact, the decree was not applicable to India, since 'His Holiness had wanted it restricted expressly to only the missions of Oceania and Ava-Pegú'. He mentioned by the way that as a result of the decree relations had worsened between Superior General Colin, 'who had urgently requested it', and Bishop Pompallier, whereas the decree had been intended to eliminate this friction.

At this meeting new regulations were drawn up for the Jesuit mission of Madurai, which could also be applicable to Oceania and Ava-Pegú. Therefore the cardinals decided to ask Pope Gregory XVI expressly to revoke the decree, 'so that vicars apostolic and prefects apostolic of missions in Oceania and Ava-Pegú can communicate directly with the Sacred Congregation, regardless of the society to which they belong'. In other words, it was the first point in the decree, the one introduced by Superior General Roothaan of the Jesuits, and not the other four points from Colin, which principally was responsible for the revocation of the decree.

Part of Pompallier's documentation consisted of a printed version of the 17 February 1846 decree, pasted among the pages of his handwritten report. The decree was only a few lines long. Experience had proved, it said, that the directives issued on 16 September 1842 did not contribute to concord and to the advantage of the missions. The cardinals at a General Meeting on 9 December 1845 therefore had decided to ask the pope to abrogate it, suggesting instead that the personnel and heads of the missions concerned should follow the same directives issued for all other vicariates apostolic. Secretary Brunelli then saw Pope Gregory XVI on 14 December; he approved of the proposal and ordered that all concerned should be informed.[15]

Pompallier stated his problem bluntly. 'The vicars apostolic who are bishops, and the members of religious communities who are dependent upon them, never know with precision the limits of one another's rights. This prepares the way for the most serious disputes among them, the most terrible discord and interminable polemics.' Even provincial superiors, he said, whose task it is locally to supervise religious order members and enforce the rule of their community, 'render the activity of a vicar apostolic difficult, paralyse it, and at times make it impossible. . . .'

But none of these difficulties exist, Pompallier maintained, if the vicar apostolic is instead a full-fledged bishop and heads a diocese, 'since then the common law of the Church serves as a norm for his conduct'. This section of Lambruschini's report was dedicated to the motivation offered by Pompallier for his proposal and it concluded with the statement that it was 'necessary to give the missions of Oceania the standard form [of Church government], one that is completely hierarchical'. Using documentation submitted by Pompallier as well as information gleaned from him in conversations, Lambruschini then listed the individual territories that would make up the ecclesiastical province, pointed out their boundaries, and gave the names of candidates who could be placed in charge.

Before indicating the candidates proposed by Pompallier for the various sees of this new ecclesiastical province, Lambruschini paused to praise Pompallier for his 'unlimited devotion and submission to the Holy See' and particularly for 'the great example of rare modesty' which he had given. 'In order to let the Sacred Congregation enjoy the greatest liberty in its deliberations . . .', Lambruschini said, 'and in order to remove all personal consideration on his behalf, he had stripped himself completely of the office conferred upon him, as well as of all the faculties that he had received, handing them over to the Holy See. He also excluded himself from the list of candidates whom he had suggested for the sees mentioned, so that no one could doubt even slightly the sincerity of his sentiments.' In other words Pompallier not only had resigned as Vicar Apostolic of Western Oceania, lest it look as if he wanted to become archbishop in the new ecclesiastical province, but also had excluded his own name from his list of candidates for the sees of this new ecclesiastical province.

Earlier Pompallier had been undecided about Kororareka or Auckland as the location for the archiepiscopal see, but now he favoured Kororareka because it offered 'all the advantages for that purpose'. The archdiocese as drawn on his accompanying map included the northern tip of New Zealand, the Kermadec Islands, and the Tonga Islands. And because Viard, a Marist, spoke English perfectly and was acquainted with the Tonga Islands, Pompallier proposed that he should become the Archbishop of Kororareka and that Father Antoine Garin, also a Marist, should be his coadjutor.

Tauranga Diocese, one of the suffragan sees, extended from Mercury Bay to the Terakako latitude inclusively. (Terakako, called Presqu'île Terakako on Pompallier's map, is today called Mahia Peninsula.) The candidate for the office of bishop was Father Claude-André Baty, also a Marist.

Port Nicholson (now Wellington) Diocese reached from below the Terakako latitude to the islands south of New Zealand. Pompallier suggested offering this entire diocese to any religious order willing to take it, but not to the Marists.

Wallis Diocese included Wallis, Futuna, Rotuma and the Samoa Islands, and had a total population of approximately 50,000. The candidate was Bataillon, currently Vicar Apostolic of Central Oceania.

Lakemba Diocese included the Fiji Islands. The candidate was Father Charles Mattieu, the pro-vicar of Bataillon.

Port Balade Diocese included New Caledonia, Loyalty Islands, New Hebrides, and other islands north of these. Douarre, currently coadjutor of Bataillon, was the candidate.

San Cristóbal Diocese included New Guinea, New Britain, New Ireland, the Solomon Islands, and numerous other outlying islands and archipelagoes. The candidate was Bishop-Elect Georges Collomb, currently Vicar Apostolic of Melanesia and Micronesia.

The ecclesiastical province as proposed by Pompallier therefore included an archdiocese and six suffragan dioceses. And all were to have Marists in charge except the Diocese of Port Nicholson. This ecclesiastical province could eventually be divided, Lambruschini said, 'into two or even more ecclesiastical provinces, when the Catholic population increases and when the growing prosperity of the churches already established there makes this necessary or useful'.

Pompallier had repeatedly met with Cardinal Prefect Fransoni during his months in Rome and he was told that the Holy See would not accept his resignation, but contrarily would name him the archbishop and metropolitan in charge of the new ecclesiastical province. Lambruschini therefore said in his report: 'Your Eminences might decide against depriving those missions of the work of that most respected, highly meritorious and capable prelate, who founded them. . . .' And in an amended list of candidates he put Pompallier's name in place of Viard's for the Archdiocese of Kororareka. And since no other religious community could immediately be found to take over the Diocese of Port Nicholson, Viard was presented as candidate for this diocese. All the other candidates remained the same.

But 'in order that the proposed reorganisation might have the best results', Pompallier wanted more than the establishment of the hierarchy. He very much wished that 'the Holy See might grant to the Archbishop of Western Oceania, whosoever might be chosen, ample powers and instructions meant specifically for him. Then from the very beginning he would be able to establish and maintain for the future as well that unity of doctrine, of ecclesiastical discipline and of liturgy completely in conformity with the Holy Roman Church.' With such powers and such specific instructions the archbishop, according to Pompallier, could maintain this unity 'not only within his own archdiocese, but in the suffragan dioceses as well, thus promoting concord and harmony among the individual prelates'.

Pompallier was most anxious, Lambruschini said, 'for a decree to be issued which would permit each bishop in proportion to his means and to his need for clergy to admit into his own diocese any priests whomsoever of tested character and zeal'. He wished further that the diocesan administration should be 'completely free and in the hands of the bishop, with all being directed by him and done in his name as regards both the temporal and the spiritual government of the diocese. . . .' He also considered it 'opportune', Lambruschini said, 'for the archbishop residing in New Zealand to have the same powers as the archbishops of Baltimore, Oregon and elsewhere'. And in addition he was most anxious to see 'the same regulations' applied to the ecclesiastical province of Western Oceania, 'which are already in force in the dioceses of the United States of America regarding the presentation of bishops and all other matters'.

These and similar requests coming from Pompallier had prompted the archive research which became an integral part of Lambruschini's report.

The cardinal then explained that Colin had been in Rome when Pompallier arrived with his *Memorandum* and that therefore part three containing the proposal on the hierarchy had been given to him in order to have his reaction. In general Colin had agreed with the principles stressed by Pompallier, Lambruschini said, and did not deny that a better type of organisation was needed. But Colin had also 'pointed out some facts which make it appear expedient to postpone the realisation of certain aspects of the proposed ecclesiastical province'. Lambruschini explained that Colin's reservations concerned Bataillon's Vicariate Apostolic of Central Oceania and Collomb's Vicariate Apostolic of Melanesia. Both were already organised as vicariates apostolic with specific boundaries having been laid down for them. Bataillon therefore ought to be asked in advance for his views before Rome proceeded to divide his territory, Colin said. As for Melanesia, Colin had suggested suspending all action until news arrived from Bishop Collomb on whether or not he had been able to make a foundation in Melanesia.

Lambruschini said it would be up to the cardinals to decide what action to take regarding Bataillon and his vicariate. 'But as for the New Guinea mission and the proposed Diocese of San Cristóbal, news has arrived recently that Bishop [Collomb] . . . and his collaborators are making a foundation precisely in the island already mentioned, which would give its name to the nascent diocese. The news is that they are living there undisturbed, have begun to preach the gospel, and are enjoying the confidence and affection of the people.' Although Lambruschini himself seemed to favour the immediate transformation of Melanesia from a vicariate apostolic to a diocese, he said that 'if it should appear more opportune to Your Eminences, the erection of this diocese could be deferred to a later date, when there is further development and when the results are more widespread'.

There were thirteen points in Lambruschini's report. In the last one he brought up still another difference between Colin and Pompallier. Colin had requested explicitly that the directives contained in the Evangelisation Congregation's decree of 16 September 1842,[16] 'and afterwards revoked by the Holy See by decree of 17 February 1846', should once again be put into effect. According to Colin these directives were necessary if he was to maintain the proper contact with his missionaries and have some measure of control over them. Pompallier, on the other hand, insisted that it was precisely this control or influence, that 'is prejudicial to the authority and rights of the bishop, paralyses his actions . . . , and is a source of serious trouble'. Lambruschini referred to the solution reached by the Evangelisation Congregation for the Jesuits in the Madurai Mission of India and said that the same solution could be used for Oceania.

As was customary Lambruschini then concluded his report with a series of questions for the cardinals to vote upon at the General Meeting:

1. Should the vicariates apostolic of Western Oceania be formed into an ecclesiastical province?
2. If so, should the Cook or Mangaia Islands be made part of the Eastern Oceania Vicariate?
3. Should the candidates for heading the individual territories be taken from Pompallier's written list or from his list as amended after conversations with the Evangelisation Congregation, and should these candidates be presented to the pope for nomination?
4. If the answer to question number one is negative, then should at least some of the vicariates apostolic be erected into an ecclesiastical province? And who should be the bishops?
5. Is it in place to give the archbishop of New Zealand specific faculties and instructions—what kind?—for establishing and maintaining within the province unity of doctrine, discipline, liturgy, etc.? And should the regulations established for the dioceses of the United States regarding the election of bishops and other matters be extended as well to the above-mentioned ecclesiastical province?
6. Are special provisions to be made for these prelates so that they may not only accept all priests whomsoever from abroad as needed, but also be completely free in both the temporal and the spiritual administration of their dioceses?
7. Should the pope be asked to declare that secular priests and catechists within these dioceses may not join any religious order without the formal consent of the bishop?
8. And should the regulations of Madurai, India, regarding the supervision of discipline in religious orders be adopted for the dioceses in Western Oceania?[17]

Copies of Lambruschini's report had already been printed for the cardinal members of the Evangelisation Congregation, but not yet distributed, when Colin hurriedly delivered a letter dated 9 April 1847 to Cardinal Prefect Fransoni. Apparently he had learned that Lambruschini's report—did he see a copy?—was most favourable to Pompallier's project and that it most probably would be accepted in its entirety. What disturbed Colin most of all was the news that Rome now intended to make Pompallier the archbishop and place him in charge of the ecclesiastical province. And so he presented all the arguments that he could muster against Pompallier's candidacy. His letter appeared so important that Fransoni, Lambruschini and Secretary Brunelli decided to print it as an appendix to the official report, so that the other cardinal members could individually examine its contents.

Pompallier was also given a copy of Colin's letter and was invited to make some comments on it.

Lambruschini then combined the objections of Colin and the rebuttal of Pompallier and printed this as an appendix to his report. Colin's first objection to Pompallier's candidacy was that New Zealand recently had become an exclusively English colony and therefore ought to have a British subject as bishop. And since Archbishop Polding of Sydney was currently in Rome, it would be an easy matter for the Evangelisation Congregation to learn from him the name of a British subject worthy of that office. He added that his French priests in New Zealand had also suggested that English or Irish clergy take up work in New Zealand.

In his rebuttal Pompallier agreed that such a step ought to be taken, but not at once. It would be wiser to prepare gradually for the changeover, he said. Besides it was not even feasible for a bishop and clergy from England or Ireland to step into the New Zealand mission immediately, because they would not know the language and customs of the Maoris. He and Viard and the other French missionaries already working there, however, knew not only their language and customs, but they could speak English as well and therefore were able to look after the Maori and the English linguistic groups. In addition to this they enjoyed the esteem of the British government. Consequently there was no reason to defer establishing the hierarchy, Pompallier said.

Colin's second difficulty referred to the complicated Friendly (or Tonga) Islands question. He said that the Evangelisation Congregation's 1845 decision to place these islands under Pompallier's jurisdiction had caused great difficulties for the Vicariate Apostolic of Central Oceania headed by Bataillon and that 'the resultant harm has lasted for more than a year now'. It was urgent that the Holy See determine clearly and precisely who actually had jurisdiction over the islands of Wallis and Futuna and who 'must provide for the Friendly [or Tonga] Archipelago'. His society, he said, could not prudently send new missionaries there, 'unless it first knows this. . . .'

Pompallier brushed aside this difficulty by simply agreeing with Colin that the Tonga Islands along with Wallis and Futuna should be returned to Bataillon. But as a result the Kororareka Archdiocese became ridiculously small, since it now embraced only the northern tip of North Island along with the Kermadec Islands. It was this consideration, no doubt, which made Pompallier revert to his original boundary farther south for the archdiocese; he suppressed the proposed Diocese of Tauranga and absorbed its territory into the Archdiocese of Kororareka. And so again there was no reason for deferring the establishment of the hierarchy.

Colin's third objection was that the Society of Mary was still 'in its infancy' and 'needs peace in order to catch its breath after the trials which it has undergone in the past ten years. It humbly requests the Sacred Congregation that none of its priests should be elevated now to the episcopacy, either as a vicar apostolic or as a coadjutor, since the circumstances do not at all appear favourable for these new arrangements'. It was necessary, he said, 'to hand over to time the task of calming the spirits of the missionaries and rebuilding their courage'.

By referring only to vicars apostolic and coadjutors, Colin was ignoring the entire issue at hand. Pompallier had not suggested creating new vicars apostolic, but rather new diocesan bishops, who would be needed to head the suffragan dioceses within the new ecclesiastical province, which he had proposed. According to Pompallier, Colin's objection was more imaginary than real, since no new Marists in Europe had been proposed as candidates for the episcopacy, but only those already engaged in missionary work in Western Oceania. And if, in fact, no Marists were available for these offices, then other priests could be brought in and be ordained bishops, he said. Consequently, there was no reason for deferring the establishment of the hierarchy.[18]

Colin's letter, so carefully drafted, but so cleverly dismissed by Pompallier, did not succeed in stopping the wheels of Rome. Without further delay Cardinal Prefect Fransoni placed the plan for establishing the hierarchy on the agenda of the next General Meeting scheduled for 3 May 1847. Inclusion in the agenda was already an indication that the authorities favoured the project and Colin must have realised this.

Since Rome had ignored Colin's pleas, there was no alternative for him but to plead directly with Pompallier.[19] Is that what he did? It seems so, because on 1 May, Saturday, only two days before the General Meeting was to be held, Pompallier presented Cardinal Prefect Fransoni with a new and urgent request that he be allowed to retire once and for all from the New Zealand and Western Oceania scene.

Forty-five-year-old Pompallier said that originally he had submitted his resignation in order to have more freedom in drawing up his plan for establishing the hierarchy in Western Oceania. But in addition to this there were other reasons for resigning, such as his deteriorating health and his ailing stomach. Then there was also the English policy regarding Frenchmen in Western Oceania, which made his own position rather obscure, he said, and seemed to indicate that New Zealand ought to have an English bishop at once. He suggested that Father Goold of the Sydney Archdiocese, a British subject, could be made archbishop and that Viard, until now Pompallier's coadjutor, could be

Goold's coadjutor. And if it appeared inadvisable to make Goold an archbishop at once, then Viard could become archbishop and Goold his coadjutor. Another reason for resigning, he said, was that he was meeting opposition from some of the Marists in New Zealand.

Pompallier therefore requested the Evangelisation Congregation to obtain the following three favours for him from Pope Pius IX: (1) He wished to have written testimony that the principles which he had followed in governing his mission were in conformity with those of the Evangelisation Congregation; (2) he wanted permission to retire from his office as bishop and asked to be numbered among the invalid missionaries in the homeland; and (3) he asked that he be granted an annual subsidy.

'It makes me very happy', he said, 'that after 11 years of voyages and apostolic labours I have been able with God's help to bring matters to such a point that you are being prompted to establish an ecclesiastical province in this area, which I found in a savage state.' Once founded, the ecclesiastical province would serve as a shield for his successors against polemics, 'which are inseparable from vicariates apostolic'. And the end result would be a greater growth and strengthening of 'the Kingdom of God on those far distant shores, which offer such beautiful harvests to be gathered in by Mother Church'.[20]

How strange a letter for Pompallier to write! It contradicted all the arguments which he had given less than three weeks earlier when telling the Evangelisation Congregation his reactions to Colin's letter of 9 April. His failing health and ailing stomach were no obstacles then to his accepting the offices of archbishop and metropolitan. Nor had he considered it necessary to install a British subject as bishop at once, nor even advisable, since he himself enjoyed the esteem of the British government. And besides, a new bishop would not be acquainted with the language or culture of the Maoris. It was clear that the reasons which he gave were not the real reasons.

Colin learned immediately of Pompallier's resignation and he reacted that same day, 1 May, with a letter of his own to Cardinal Altieri, a member of the Evangelisation Congregation. His letter told of his admiration and affectionate respect for Pompallier because he had handed in his resignation.[21] And he added that 'the Society of Mary will oblige itself voluntarily to give Bishop Pompallier an annual indemnity of 3,000 francs until the moment when that prelate will be provided for in some other way. . . .' The Society of Mary would also be greatly pleased, he said, if Pompallier were to be given by the Holy See as a mark of esteem the honorary title of titular archbishop.

It could be that Colin had prompted Pompallier's letter, because with his letter he now submitted a plan of his own for the establishment of the hierarchy in Western Oceania. With Pompallier out of the picture, all his previous objections to its immediate establishment had suddenly disappeared. He even said that he would be pleased to see the hierarchy established in the following way, provided that no new Marists were ordained bishops:

1. Instead of making three divisions for New Zealand, as suggested by Pompallier, there should be an archdiocese at Auckland and
2. A diocese at Port Nicholson.
3. The jurisdiction of Wallis Diocese ought to extend over the three archipelagoes of Tonga, Samoa and Fiji.
4. The Diocese of New Caledonia should include that archipelago.
5. No change should be made for the time being in the status of the Vicariate Apostolic of Melanesia.
6. And, finally, the nomination of coadjutors should be postponed. 'Only one new bishop would be needed for this arrangement', he added. 'That would be at [Port] Nicholson and he would have to be a British subject. Bishop Viard, of course, would become Archbishop of Auckland.'[22]

This unexpected about-face by both Pompallier and Colin upset the plans of the Evangelisation Congregation. Nor was it possible to print their two letters of Saturday, 1 May, and distribute them in time to the cardinal members for the General Meeting of Monday, 3 May. But since the creation of the hierarchy for Western Oceania was on the agenda, it was brought up anyhow. On learning that Pompallier had formally submitted his resignation, the cardinals decided to postpone consideration of the project. They gave orders that meanwhile Pompallier's letter as well as 'all else connected with the prelate's request' should be printed and distributed to them for study. Only then would they decide whether or not Pompallier should be allowed to resign.[23]

In the following two weeks, while Colin was confined to his room with a serious illness, the disturbing news reached him that a decision on the hierarchy question had been postponed until the June meeting and that Pompallier's resignation might not be accepted after all. Unable to contact Cardinal Prefect Fransoni personally and eager to lose no time, Colin dictated a letter on 15 May and also a *Memorandum* titled, 'Some Reflections on the Resignation of Bishop Pompallier and the Grave Inconveniences That Will Result If the Evangelisation Congregation Fails to Accept It'. He asked Fransoni to print the *Memorandum* and distribute it to all members of the Evangelisation Congregation. 'When my health improves', he said, 'I shall come to see you.'

Colin intended to show by his *Memorandum* that Pompallier was unfit to head the proposed ecclesiastical province of Western Oceania. Bluntly he said that Pompallier's 'faults of administration do not come from his heart, but from his lack of intelligence. . . .' From New Zealand he had sent glowing reports to Europe, while around him everything was collapsing. He had failed as an administrator in his vicariate apostolic and he had caused his missionaries to be filled with ennui and discouragement. And although Pompallier blamed others for the lack of unity afflicting his mission, he was equally responsible for it, if not more. What degree of obedience did he want from the Marists in New Zealand, Colin asked. 'They obeyed him to the extent of sacrificing the most essential parts of their rule, such as that which forbids them to live alone at the peril of their lives, their salvation, and their perfection.'

In answer to Pompallier's complaint that the Marists had usurped his episcopal authority, Colin answered, 'It seems to us that he has all the authority that he wanted. . . .' He had first named Colin his agent in Europe, then Epalle, and finally he chose a Benedictine in London. 'We did not object to his choice of outside personnel . . . and he now has an outsider as his agent.' And why did Colin discontinue sending missionaries to Pompallier? Because in 1843 he had received a letter from Pompallier ordering him to send no more personnel. Colin also criticised Pompallier for not giving his New Zealand mission a solid foundation, charging that he had not followed the Evangelisation Congregation's instructions promulgated by Pope Gregory XVI, which had stressed how necessary it was 'to found schools; to establish fixed points of action; to prepare with all ardour and all possible care a native clergy, since without it nothing permanent, nothing complete can exist'. And lest any of the cardinals, like so many other people, still believed that Pompallier was a Marist, Colin assured them forcefully that he was not.

Believing that he had thus eliminated Pompallier as a possible candidate for the office of archbishop and metropolitan of the new ecclesiastical province, Colin repeated what he called 'my ideas' on the proposed ecclesiastical province as they had been contained in his letter of 1 May, making these two additions. He suggested (1) that Goold be named Bishop of Port Nicholson and (2) that Douarre be called not only the Bishop of New Caledonia, but also of New Hebrides.

To lend more weight to his words, Colin said that he had taken counsel with Father Augustin Theiner (1804–74) of Rome, a German-born church historian, whom he described as an Oratorian well known for 'his wise counsel, apostolic zeal, superior intelligence and eminent knowledge'.[24]

However, it is difficult to determine for which aspect of his *Memorandum* Colin consulted with Theiner. He would hardly have needed Theiner's help to determine the boundaries or names of the new dioceses. In the case of the Vicariate Apostolic of Melanesia the name and boundaries were not to be changed at all. And ever since 26 May 1842 Colin had been planning for the separation of New Caledonia and New Hebrides from the rest of Bataillon's Vicariate Apostolic of Central Oceania, hoping to see these two archipelagoes some day become a separate mission.[25] In practice Douarre was already in charge of the two archipelagoes and now Colin, like Pompallier, wanted this mission to become a diocese. Did Colin perhaps use Theiner's 'wise counsel' for the New Zealand proposals? Pompallier, at first undecided, had eventually chosen Kororareka as the residence for the archbishop instead of Auckland, the capital city. Colin, who had seen Pompallier's proposals, chose Auckland. Both Pompallier and Colin were in agreement, however, on the choice of Port Nicholson as the episcopal residence for the diocese covering South Island.[26]

Pompallier soon learned that Colin had submitted a *Memorandum*. He then requested a copy from Cardinal Prefect Fransoni, received it on 1 June, and after examining it addressed a rejoinder on 4 June to all the cardinals of the Evangelisation Congregation. Now they had still another proof of what he had been maintaining all along, he said, namely, that Colin and not he was the one who wielded Church authority in Western Oceania. To refute Colin's charges of faulty administration and lack of intelligence, he pointed out that Western Oceania did not have a single native Christian when he went there eleven years earlier. But now even Colin himself had agreed that the area was so well developed that an ecclesiastical province could be established there. While working in Western Oceania, Pompallier added, he had had a hard life and had not spared himself. Now he was weak and feeble and wanted to retire.[27]

Colin's *Memorandum* and Pompallier's retort became the latest appendix in the ever expanding dossier on the establishment of the hierarchy in Western Oceania. The decisions to be taken by the cardinals at their next General Meeting scheduled for 7 June 1847 would not be easy. But the issue had to be resolved in some way; it could not be left pending forever.

27

The Vicariate Apostolic of New Caledonia

27 JUNE 1847

'Better Method of Organising the Missions of Western Oceania as Proposed by Bishop Pompallier' was the topic on the agenda of the Evangelisation Congregation's General Meeting of 7 June 1847. Cardinal Lambruschini, who had prepared the report originally for the General Meeting of 3 May, presented it now with some additions and changes. He reminded the cardinals that they had postponed treatment of this topic the previous month in order to be able to judge better, after receiving all available documentation, whether or not Bishop Pompallier should be allowed to resign. Two of the most important documents now included as an appendix were Bishop Pompallier's letter of 1 May 1847 containing a new and urgent request that he be allowed to resign, and Father Colin's letter of the same date, which praised Pompallier's action, offered to give him a yearly indemnity, urged that he be made an honorary archbishop, and presented a substitute plan for the establishment of the hierarchy in Western Oceania.[1]

Dropping Pompallier's plan and substituting that of Colin, Lambruschini said that it conformed 'in general' with that of Pompallier, except for the fact that New Zealand would receive two sees instead of three and that the status of the Vicariates Apostolic of Melanesia and Micronesia would not be altered. As for the candidates, Colin wanted Viard to get the Auckland Archdiocese, Bataillon to get the Wallis Diocese, Douarre to get the New Caledonia Diocese, and Collomb to remain Vicar Apostolic of Melanesia and Micronesia. According to this arrangement only Port Nicholson Diocese would need a new bishop.

Colin had suggested that a British subject should be placed over Port Nicholson Diocese, Lambruschini explained. Pompallier was of the same view and had proposed that Father Goold of Sydney should be given that office. 'However, Your Eminences might prefer to place him at Auckland instead and make Viard his coadjutor; or you might want to make him Viard's coadjutor.' It was true that Goold at the previous meeting had been named the first Bishop of Melbourne, Lambruschini said, but the apostolic brief naming him to this office had not yet been dispatched and so he could still be assigned to New Zealand. At the moment, however, there was no other candidate available for Melbourne. A further possibility was to name Father Antoine Garin, a French Marist, the first Bishop of Port Nicholson, and then later have an English priest succeed him. Or perhaps Father Charles Lovet of Sydney, who had been at

Stoneyhurst College in England, could be named for New Zealand. His name had been suggested by Polding as a second choice in case Goold might not be available for Melbourne.

At this point Lambruschini took it for granted that the thing for Rome to do was to accept Pompallier's resignation and to adopt Colin's plan for establishing the hierarchy. Drawing from a letter of Colin, Lambruschini explained that Colin now 'would be pleased with the erection and formation of an ecclesiastical province in Western Oceania. . . .' He therefore invited the cardinals to vote on the following questions:

1. Should action be taken on the common suggestion of Pompallier and Colin and should the pope be asked to establish an ecclesiastical province for the vicariates of Western Oceania?
2. If so, is Colin's plan to be preferred?
3. If so, should Father Antoine Garin be named for the Diocese of Port Nicholson?
4. Should the Mangaia or Cook Archipelago be transferred to the Mission of Eastern Oceania?
5. Should Pompallier be allowed to resign with the annual subsidy suggested? Should he be given a statement approving his government of the vicariate?
6. To which of Pompallier's requests should approval be granted?[2]

The questions at the end of a report usually are phrased in anticipation of an affirmative vote. But after discussion got under way, it became clear that the majority was averse to what the questions suggested. The cardinals then adopted these four resolutions instead:

1. If the pope is in agreement, let the erection of an ecclesiastical province in Western Oceania be postponed.
2. To improve the system of ecclesiastical government the pope should be requested to erect two episcopal sees in New Zealand, Auckland and Port Nicholson, using the boundaries suggested by Pompallier; he should likewise be requested to erect a vicariate apostolic in New Caledonia.
3. The following candidates should be presented to the pope for the two dioceses. By no means should Bishop Pompallier be allowed to resign; instead, his titular see of Maronea *in partibus* should be dropped and he should be allowed to choose either Auckland Diocese or Port Nicholson Diocese. Further, he should receive Father Charles Lovet as his coadjutor with a titular see *in partibus*. Bishop Philippe Viard's titular see of Orthosia *in partibus* should be dropped, as also his office of coadjutor, and he should be placed in charge of that diocese which Pompallier does not accept.
4. Finally, the Vicariate Apostolic of New Caledonia should be conferred upon Titular Bishop Guillaume Douarre of Amata *in partibus* and his office as coadjutor to Bishop Bataillon of the Central Oceania Vicariate Apostolic should be dropped.[3]

What had caused this complete about-face which surprised even the minor officials of the Evangelisation Congregation who had helped work out the report? According to Father Gabriel-Claude Mayet, confidant of Colin, it was action taken by Pompallier. In advance of the meeting he had 'paid a visit to all of the cardinals, begging them not to accept his resignation. He went so far as to cast himself in tears at the feet of Cardinal Lambruschini, who was the relator for this topic.'[4]

The cardinals passed still another resolution at their General Meeting that morning, clarifying further why the points presented for the vote were not accepted. It read: 'The Sacred Congregation recommends very strongly to the Cardinal Prefect and also to Cardinal Lambruschini . . . that they try to establish true concord of mind and heart between Bishop Pompallier and Father Colin, Superior of the Congregation of Marist Priests.' The two cardinals in their 'eagerness to see the cause of religion advance', were to show Pompallier and Colin 'how much the renewal of that concord and its continuance is intimately bound up with the spread of the Church'. Colin had to understand 'that the preeminence of authority belongs to the bishop'. And it was necessary to convince Pompallier 'that still a new ornament would be added to his merits, if he were carefully to remove every occasion of displeasure and adapt himself benignly and prudently' to circumstances of time and place.

'Nor is it fitting that the Superior of the Marists should deputise one of his members to preside as provincial superior over the priests of his congregation in Oceania. On the other hand it would be of benefit for religion, if the bishop were to choose some Marists as his consultors, particularly for the actual administration of temporal goods. The bishop should discuss serious matters with them and then conduct his affairs accordingly. Steps must also be taken so that eventually a seminary is founded in order to provide a clergy for the indigenes of Oceania.'

Colin was to be informed that he could not transfer elsewhere missionaries already assigned to a place by their bishop, without first asking the bishop. Nor could Colin do this if the bishop were reluctant. 'At the same time the bishop ought to be so endowed that his missionaries have no just cause for complaint, at least in so far as this is possible for him. And although the mission has indeed been entrusted to the Congregation of Marists, this is no obstacle—should serious reasons require that the bishop be provided with more help—to bringing in additional missionaries who do not belong to that congregation, but are suitable and are endowed with the required qualities.'[5]

These resolutions, still to be ratified by the pope before becoming official, were a victory for neither Colin nor Pompallier, although they did contain the instructions that each wanted the other to follow! There was only one thing that both wanted and both obtained, namely, that Port Nicholson should become a diocese. Both had also wanted the hierarchy to be established, but this was not done. Both had wanted the Vicariate Apostolic of Central Oceania to become a diocese, but it remained a vicariate apostolic. Both had asked that New Caledonia become a diocese; it was separated from the Central Vicariate, as they had requested, but it became only a vicariate apostolic. Pompallier had wanted the Vicariate Apostolic of Melanesia to become a diocese, but it remained a vicariate apostolic, as Colin had wished. Both had asked for the creation of an archdiocese, which Pompallier wanted to have called Kororareka and which Colin wanted to have called Auckland; the name chosen was Auckland, but it became only a diocese. Colin had wanted Rome to accept Pompallier's resignation, but this was not done. Pompallier had expected to see his authority extended over an entire ecclesiastical province, but instead it was restricted to an even smaller territory than ever before, the Diocese of Auckland or the Diocese of Port Nicholson, whichever he might choose.

Colin learned immediately of the decisions taken by the eleven cardinals at their 7 June meeting and, as Lambruschini later said, he was 'highly displeased over the feared return' of Pompallier to New Zealand.[6] In a final effort to keep Pompallier from returning he wrote a 'highly confidential' letter to Pope Pius IX on 8 June, the day after the General Meeting. Attached to it was 'some documentation which perhaps can show how necessary it is to accept the resignation of Bishop Pompallier for the good of the mission of New Zealand'. The documentation consisted of fourteen or fifteen letters of his missionaries describing the faults of Pompallier. He had not submitted the documentation earlier, he explained, because he had always hoped 'that this affair could end in peace. . . .'

In addition to this, he said, he now felt obliged in conscience to reveal to the pope 'a circumstance which afflicts us profoundly. Undoubtedly because of the numerous privations in the mission, Bishop Pompallier has contracted for some time the deplorable habit of drinking strong liquor and at times to some excess.' This had led to violent outbursts, reported to Colin by his missionaries who had to suffer from them. 'In order to quiet my conscience I place this secret in the bosom of Your Holiness, so that enlightened from above you can decide whether Bishop Pompallier's return to New Zealand can still be useful for this desolate mission. . . .'[7]

The doctor would not allow Colin to deliver the letter until his foot was somewhat improved. On 15 June accompanied by Bishop Luquet, Colin went by carriage to the Quirinal Apartments, residence of Pope Pius IX, and was carried up the huge staircase in an armchair. Colin, the pope insisted, was to be seated for the entire audience and the pope even had pillows brought in to support his leg in the most comfortable position. Judging Colin's age from his appearance, the pope ventured that he was already seventy-two. When Colin replied that he was only fifty-seven (Pius IX was fifty-five), the pope replied: 'Your great labours for the Church have made you old before your time.' Colin delivered and discussed his important letter of 8 June and found the pope attentive and sympathetic to his problems, promising to take up the matter of the letter with Cardinals Lambruschini and Fransoni.[8]

Meanwhile Cardinal Prefect Fransoni and Cardinal Lambruschini, carrying out the instructions issued by the nine other cardinals at the 7 June General Meeting, had invited both Colin and Pompallier to join them for an amicable discussion of their common problems. The cardinals, aware of Colin's infirmity, suggested coming to Hotel Bouisse in Piazza d'Aracoeli, where he resided. But many prelates and clerics stayed at this hotel and Colin felt that a visit from two cardinals would give rise to wild rumours. Cardinal Fransoni's office in the Evangelisation Congregation was then designated as the meeting place. The cardinals by coincidence scheduled this meeting for 15 June, the date of the papal audience, but at a different time. Colin did not attend.

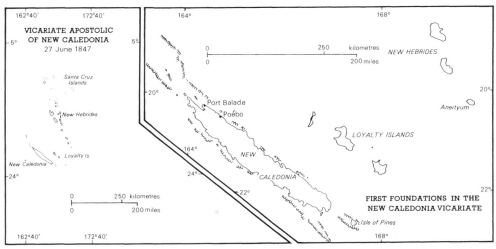

59 The foundation of the Vicariate Apostolic of New Caledonia on 27 June 1847 was the only immediate result of Bishop Pompallier's proposal to have the hierarchy established in Western Oceania. Coadjutor Bishop Douarre celebrated the first Mass on New Caledonia soil on Christmas Day 1843 in Mahamata village alongside Port Balade, where he opened a mission, followed by others at Poébo and Isle of Pines in New Caledonia and at Aneityum, the southernmost island of New Hebrides. (*Chapters 27, 30, 34, 35*).

On 16 June, however, Colin visited Fransoni at his private residence and on 17 June also Lambruschini at his private residence.[9] He excused himself for not attending the meeting and later gave Fransoni two of his reasons in writing: 'The first reason was that His Holiness had granted me for this same day the good fortune of an audience. I could not prudently go out twice in the same day without aggravating the indisposition that was hindering my walking. The second reason, and this is the principal one, was a sentiment of propriety and delicacy. It did not seem proper to me that I should have to explain in the presence of Bishop Pompallier the disagreeable state of the New Zealand Mission. . . .'[10]

Colin visited Fransoni again on 18 June, gave him a letter written that day, and also presented him with a copy of his letter to the pope of 8 June. 'In the audience which I was fortunate to obtain with our Holy Father', he said, 'His Holiness recommended that I clearly make known to you everything about the matter which I had the sorrow of discussing with you on the 16th of this month. It is this that compels me to communicate to Your Eminence officially and in writing a verbatim copy of the letter which I addressed to His Holiness. It is attached to this letter and I have added some information to it.'

The information added for Fransoni by Colin to the duplicate copy of his letter to the pope was that Bishop Luquet, Father Theiner and Princess Wolkonsky could all testify that Pompallier drank to excess. And it was known, he added, that the bishop had alcoholic beverages delivered to Hotel Minerva (in Piazza della Minerva), where he had resided from 15 to 19 September 1846, and also to Hotel Bouisse, where he had resided from 9 to 25 November. In his letter addressed to Fransoni, Colin complained about large sums of money being spent by Pompallier in France.[11]

During the two visits of 16 and 18 June, Fransoni had begged Colin in vain to continue sending missionaries to Pompallier's mission and to continue collaborating with him. Colin then left Rome for France on 18 June.[12]

Pompallier, still in Rome at this time, informed the Evangelisation Congregation on 21 June that he planned to leave for Loreto on 26 June, and that he was most eager 'to obtain before that date an audience with our Holy Father, the Pope, so that I may take leave of His Holiness and receive his apostolic blessing. . . .'[13]

Then on Sunday, 27 June 1847, the day after Pompallier's departure, the Evangelisation Congregation presented its resolutions of 7 June to Pope Pius IX for ratification. He agreed with the cardinals that the foundation of an ecclesiastical province in Western Oceania should be postponed. He also ratified their decision to detach 'the extensive island and region of New Caledonia' from the Vicariate Apostolic of Central Oceania 'and to erect it into a separate vicariate to be called by the same name of New Caledonia'. And he relieved Bishop Douarre of his office as coadjutor to Bishop Bataillon of Central Oceania and made him the first Vicar Apostolic of New Caledonia, at the same time giving him 'all the necessary and suitable faculties for the office entrusted to him'.

The resolutions passed by the cardinals on 7 June had also called for the creation of the two dioceses of Auckland and Port Nicholson, had urged that Pompallier's request to resign should be rejected, and had suggested that Pompallier be given his choice of these two dioceses and that Viard be given the other. But evidently because of the information that Pope Pius IX had received from Colin about Pompallier, he decided not to create these two dioceses. Nor did he reject Pompallier's request to resign, but merely suspended its acceptance. And at the same time he kept Pompallier and Viard in office as Vicar Apostolic of Western Oceania and coadjutor respectively.[14]

This meant that the foundation by Pope Pius IX of the Vicariate Apostolic of New Caledonia on 27 June 1847 and the choice of Douarre as its first vicar apostolic were the only immediate positive results of the General Meeting held by the Evangelisation Congregation on 7 June.

Some weeks before Pompallier's departure from Rome, he had asked Fransoni for 'a letter recommending me to the charity of the faithful. With the help of their donations I would be able to send some personnel with good vocations to New Zealand, where they are needed so badly.' He explained to the cardinal that the allocation granted him that year by the Association for the Propagation of the Faith would not cover the transportation costs of these men. Fransoni had promised to provide the requested letter, but Pompallier had left Rome without receiving it. Writing on 29 June from the Shrine of the Holy House of Loreto, Pompallier reminded Fransoni of his promise and asked him to send the letter to Loreto.[15]

It is not difficult to imagine why the letter had not been issued earlier, since it came to be taken for granted in the offices of the Evangelisation Congregation that Pompallier's resignation would be accepted. But in view of the pope's decision of 27 June, Pompallier technically was to remain in charge of the Vicariate Apostolic of Western Oceania and so Fransoni now sent him the letter, apparently even before receiving Pompallier's reminder.[16]

Fransoni's letter of recommendation was dated 1 July 1847 and read as follows: 'The Most Reverend Jean-Baptiste Pompallier, [Titular] Bishop of Maronea and Vicar Apostolic of Western Oceania, has finished the business at the Holy See for which he made a trip to Rome. Returning now to France he wishes to try and find as many priests as he can, who would like to go to New Zealand or Western Oceania to serve as missionaries there. Since such a journey is much more costly than the vicar apostolic can afford, we recommend that prelate most highly . . . to the charity of the faithful, asking that they try to assist him with money and in other ways.'[17]

From this letter of Fransoni, written after Pope Pius IX had expressed his views on the resolutions taken by the Evangelisation Congregation, it is clear that Colin had not been successful in his attempt to block Pompallier's return. The letter, in fact, referred explicitly to Pompallier as Vicar Apostolic of Western Oceania and authorised him to obtain funds and personnel for his mission, in spite of Colin's special appeal to the pope and his three visits in three days to Cardinals Fransoni and Lambruschini.

But even before this, when writing to Cardinal Fransoni on 18 June, the day on which he left Rome, Colin had already admitted defeat. Convinced that Pompallier would be returning to New Zealand, he explained why he could not fulfil Fransoni's wish and guarantee further Marist collaboration with Pompallier. 'No bond of obedience obliges the priests of our society either to go to the foreign missions or to remain there', he said. 'It is only their zeal and their devotion which make them dedicate themselves to this kind of ministry. . . .' Knowing only too well the antagonistic attitude of his men in New Zealand, he found it impossible to predict 'what might happen at the return of Bishop Pompallier', and this in spite of a most sincere desire on his part 'to contribute to the welfare of the New Zealand Mission'.[18]

Would someone else succeed where Colin had failed?

28

Pope Pius IX
is asked to make New Caledonia
a papal colony

10 AUGUST 1847

At this point in Western Oceania's history two figures who were to play decisive roles in the Pompallier-Colin affair entered the Roman scene within a week of each other. One was Alessandro Barnabò. He was successor to Archbishop Brunelli, who had been secretary of the Evangelisation Congregation since 1843 and was named Nuncio Apostolic to Spain on 12 July 1847. Barnabò succeeded him in office that very day with the title pro-secretary.

The other figure was Bishop Douarre, formerly coadjutor to Bishop Bataillon of the Vicariate Apostolic of Central Oceania and since 27 June 1847 the Vicar Apostolic of New Caledonia. Discouraged over France's loss of interest in New Caledonia as a possible French colony,[1] and eager to see the New Caledonia-New Hebrides section of Bataillon's vicariate become an independent vicariate apostolic, he had resolved to leave Oceania late in 1846 to promote these two causes in Paris and Rome. But while he was en route both Pompallier and Colin were pushing their separate plans in Rome for having the hierarchy established. These efforts without any assistance from Douarre led to the establishment of the Vicariate Apostolic of New Caledonia.

When Colin returned to France and informed Douarre, now there, that he had been named Vicar Apostolic of New Caledonia, Douarre drew up with Colin's approval some 'Particular Regulations' which were to serve as guidelines and directives for Marists working in his vicariate. Since both men thought it advisable, or even necessary, to have these norms approved by the Evangelisation Congregation, and since Douarre hoped to receive funds from this same congregation for his mission, he left France for Rome on 19 July 1847, just one week after Barnabò had taken office.

Like Colin, Douarre was greatly disappointed that Bishop Pompallier's resignation had not been accepted and that the hierarchy had not been established. Before leaving France he urged Colin to allow him to talk about Pompallier and the New Zealand Mission in Rome and Colin agreed.[2] In fact, Colin even suggested that he discuss the matter with Bishop Luquet, procurator at the Holy See of the Paris Foreign Mission Seminary, and with Father Theiner, the famous research worker and historian. Colin himself had been in frequent contact with these two men while in Rome, often asking their advice and confiding in them. In fact, he urged Douarre to be very open with them and to take whatever new steps they might suggest.[3]

Douarre visited the offices of the Evangelisation Congregation at Piazza di

Spagna in Rome on Tuesday morning, 27 July, just eight days after taking leave of Colin. The officials presented him with the papal brief announcing the creation of the Vicariate Apostolic of New Caledonia and another document naming him its first vicar apostolic.[4] He could hardly have been pleased, however, with the imprecise way in which the territory placed under his jurisdiction was indicated. The papal brief stated merely that the pope was separating 'from the Vicariate Apostolic of Central Oceania the island and region of New Caledonia' and was erecting this into a separate vicariate apostolic to be called New Caledonia.[5]

Before writing to Colin that evening, Douarre saw a copy of his 15 May 1847 *Memorandum* prepared for the Evangelisation Congregation spelling out his plan for the establishment of the hierarchy in Western Oceania. When telling Colin that he had already discussed 'our great concerns' with Luquet and Theiner, and that he had had a particularly long talk with Theiner, he pointed out that they considered it 'altogether necessary' for the good of the Marist missions in Western Oceania to have an ecclesiastical province established there as proposed by Colin in his *Memorandum*. Douarre's only other comment on the *Memorandum* was that Colin might well have presented Bataillon rather than Viard for the office of Archbishop of Auckland. Moreover, Luquet and Theiner had 'absolutely' insisted that he should submit a *Memorandum* himself on all pending Marist issues, and he urged Colin to give him the authorisation to do so.[6]

But Douarre did not wait for Colin's reply, being pressed by Theiner and Luquet, and two days later (29 July) composed his *Memorandum on New Caledonia* for Cardinal Fransoni. Strictly speaking his title was a misnomer, because only the first of the *Memorandum*'s four sections dealt specifically with New Caledonia. This first section described briefly the beginnings of missionary work, its obstacles, and the possibilities which the future offered. The climate was so mild and the air so healthy, Douarre maintained, that New Caledonia could well become a recuperation centre for other missions of Western Oceania. And the soil was so fertile that this mission would be able to provide not only its own produce but that needed by other missions as well.[7]

The second section of Douarre's *Memorandum* stressed how important it was to have the hierarchy established just as Colin had suggested on 15 May. In listing the proposed archdiocese and dioceses, he simply copied from Colin's *Memorandum*, except in the case of the proposed Diocese of New Caledonia and New Hebrides. Here he went into great detail, listing the various islands and archipelagoes which he believed should be contained within the borders of this diocese to be entrusted to him.

The third section was devoted to his 'Particular Regulations', now expanded and amended to apply to all Marist missions in Western Oceania, and no longer only to the Vicariate Apostolic of New Caledonia, as had been agreed upon with Colin. They were meant to 'regulate the rights of bishops and missionaries' and he divided them into eight articles.

The fourth and final section stressed again how important it was for the

Evangelisation Congregation to accept Pompallier's resignation. 'The most disagreeable consequences' would follow from his return to New Zealand, Douarre predicted. Not only would the British government become suspicious, but the mission itself would be ruined! Douarre maintained he was not exaggerating when he said that if the missionaries could foresee, or if they were to suspect, that Pompallier would be returning, they would not wait for 'His Excellency's arrival before leaving for other areas or before returning to Europe'. Consequently, he told Fransoni, 'if you wish to save not only the New Zealand Mission, but also all the missions entrusted to the Marists', it was 'urgent, most urgent', for the Evangelisation Congregation to carry out the plan described by Colin on 15 May, or at least one similar to it.[8]

Douarre wrote to Fransoni again on 5 August, saying he had forgotten to mention that the 'Particular Regulations', which he was requesting for all Marist missions, were 'not at all new, since the Paris Foreign Mission Seminary has had them for 200 years'. And if the Evangelisation Congregation should find difficulties at the moment in changing the vicariates apostolic of Western Oceania into dioceses, something that was urgently needed, the New Zealand problems mentioned in his own *Memorandum* could be eliminated nonetheless by naming for the time being 'one or more archbishops: Bishop Viard for New Zealand and Bishop Bataillon for Wallis. . . .' In fact, he said, the nature of the areas concerned and the difficulties of communication required that there be several ecclesiastical provinces. And in proportion as their number increased, 'the Holy See will preserve its control more evenly over these distant missions, since it will be dividing its authority among a larger number of [mission] heads. . . .'[9]

The Evangelisation Congregation took seriously the 'Particular Regulations', since they concerned Douarre's Vicariate Apostolic of New Caledonia, and made a special study of them. Barnabò then discussed them with Douarre and presented a host of objections. Apparently Douarre was unable to answer them on the spot, or did not want to do so before consulting with Luquet and with Theiner, because on 6 August he sent Barnabò four full pages of replies. He said that he had been encouraged to do so by Barnabò's 'goodness' in receiving him and his 'patience' in listening to him.[10]

There was no official reaction, however, to Douarre's other proposals, except for word reaching him that Cardinal Prefect Fransoni was suspicious and believed that he was allowing himself to be manipulated by Luquet and Theiner. 'In the presence of God, and after having taken counsel, I decided to address this humble supplication to you', he wrote Fransoni on 10 August. 'Your Eminence believes that I am being pushed by Bishop Luquet and Father Theiner in the steps that I am taking. I beg you to believe that the only motives of my actions are the glory of God, the obligation I have of making the truth known, and the fact that this can contribute to the welfare of our missions.'

Douarre then urged Fransoni to print his *Memorandum on New Caledonia* and give all the cardinals of the Evangelisation Congregation a copy, saying that he hoped to receive a letter of clearance for all its contents from Colin before the next General Meeting. As for himself, he intended to leave Rome by the end of August, because ten missionaries were sailing in September to his Vicariate Apostolic of New Caledonia aboard the *Stella del Mare*. 'I need some [financial] help from the Evangelisation Congregation', he added. 'I have not received anything from it since I became a bishop.' Transportation costs for his ten new missionaries amounted to 5,000 francs per missionary, he said, but he had no more than 27,000 francs.[11]

Mail service between Rome and Lyon in 1847 was surprisingly good. Within eight days Colin had Douarre's letter of 27 July, answered it on 4 August, and Douarre had the reply by 13 August. The letter from Colin was not at all what Douarre had hoped for! Regarding the 'Particular Regulations', Colin instructed Douarre to present to the Evangelisation Congregation only what he had prepared at Lyon for his own territory 'without the additions or changes which you feel ought to be made. . . .' Regarding the reorganisation of the missions in Western Oceania through the establishment of the hierarchy as outlined in his own *Memorandum* of 15 May, Colin said that 'good manners and a sense of delicacy would seem to forbid us to return so soon to a type of organisation which the Sacred Congregation has rejected'. Whether the Marist bishops in Oceania 'for the moment' continue to be vicars apostolic is 'of little importance', he said. 'Nor is it prudent at the present time to ask for a state of affairs different from that which now exists. . . .'[12]

Douarre was a very nervous young bishop after reading Colin's letter, since in his *Memorandum on New Caledonia* submitted to Fransoni on 29 July he had done everything that Colin now told him not to do. And not having received the expected clearance from Colin for his proposals, he would remain suspect in the eyes of Cardinal Prefect Fransoni. How could he free himself from this predicament? He sought out Father Theiner and received an answer. Douarre then wrote back to Colin on 13 August and stated that he was writing the letter in Theiner's room, thus betraying how unsure he was of himself.

'I have seen your letter of 4 August and I have admired your delicacy', Douarre said. 'But now since our affairs are moving along at a good pace, it is necessary for you to give me carte blanche. His Eminence is beginning to give in! And besides, it is impossible to turn back, or you will be the loser and our missions as well.'

He said that he had taken Colin's advice and had spoken frankly with Bishop Luquet and with Father Theiner about New Zealand. And he had lost no time and would lose no time in taking the new steps suggested by these two men. 'I shall do nothing without consulting them,' he assured Colin, 'and they ask that we allow ourselves to be helped.' He begged Colin to send him a letter approving the steps that he was taking. He also wanted extracts from letters of missionaries who had complained about Pompallier. His own reputation was at stake, he said, and Colin certainly would not want him 'to pass for an impostor'.

To help get his way Douarre reminded Colin that Archbishop Polding of Sydney was taking steps to have the Marist vicariates apostolic of Western Oceania incorporated in the ecclesiastical province of Australia and so made dependent upon him. And he repeated that 'it is necessary for you to make a collection of what has been written [against Bishop Pompallier], since you yourself said that I could take new steps, if Bishop Luquet and Father Theiner advised me to do so'. He added that recently he had sent a letter to Fransoni and that he would have sent Colin a copy, if it had not been so long. 'Father Theiner was of the opinion that I should have sent it to His Holiness. . . .' For the rest, he was simply following the advice of Luquet and Theiner, as Colin had suggested. 'Therefore, if I should happen to take some false steps, my Reverend Father, attribute them to no one but yourself.'[13]

Douarre coached by Theiner did not tell Colin the whole truth. What he did not tell Colin, for example, was that three days earlier, on 10 August, he and Bishop Luquet had submitted a highly confidential document to Pius IX with the startling proposal that he, the pope, should take over New Caledonia as a papal colony! And so if Colin were to give Douarre carte blanche, as requested, he would be giving his support unknowingly also to this document titled *Memorandum on Taking Possession of New Caledonia by the Holy See*. Nor were things 'moving along at a good pace', as Douarre led Colin to believe. Instead, a cloud of suspicion hung over Douarre's head and he was in danger of being considered by Rome a meddler or, as he himself said in his letter to Colin, 'an impostor'.

How could the Vicar Apostolic of New Caledonia suggest that the pope take over the principal island of his vicariate apostolic and make it a papal colony? It is difficult to say whether the proposal originated with Douarre, the first co-signer of the document, or with Luquet and Theiner. Both bishops signed it, however, and so both were responsible for it. Since Douarre was such a pliable tool in the hands of Luquet and Theiner, the idea could have originated with them. In fact, when presenting the document to Pope Pius IX on 10 August, it was Bishop Luquet who sent an accompanying letter of the same date to Cardinal Ferretti, secretary of state of His Holiness. The letter said that Luquet was submitting the proposal 'at your request' and he urged the cardinal 'to let me know with the greatest secrecy the name of the one who will be given the task of examining this project, so that Bishop [Douarre] of Amata and I can provide him with the explanations that he might desire. . . .' Luquet added that he had already suggested to the pope taking possession of a colony when Marziou, the founder of the religious and commercial shipping company Société française de l'Océanie, had passed through Rome.[14]

Douarre was psychologically disposed to go along with such a proposal, because originally he had hoped that France would make New Caledonia its colony. If New Caledonia were a colony, his missionary work would prosper, he believed, because he could then expect financial assistance from France, free transportation on French vessels for his missionaries, and freedom from interference by Protestant missionaries who would not be allowed into the territory.

In fact in January 1844, one month after Douarre as coadjutor to Bishop Bataillon had brought the first missionaries to New Caledonia, a representative of the French government hoisted the French flag there, thus indicating that France was claiming this island as its colony. But on 3 July 1846 the flag was taken down and France no longer considered New Caledonia as one of its possessions. While in France prior to his trip to Rome, Douarre had tried to revive the government's interest in retaking New Caledonia, but in vain. The political climate in France and abroad, officials had told him, made further colonising activities in Western Oceania impossible.[15]

It was only natural that Douarre after reaching Rome should discuss France's lack of interest with Luquet and Theiner. The practical conclusion to these conversations evidently was that perhaps the pope would be interested in making New Caledonia a papal colony. After all, there were Papal States, and so there could just as well be a papal colony.

Douarre's and Luquet's *Memorandum on Taking Possession of New Caledonia by the Holy See* was divided into four parts. Part one gave a description of New Caledonia. The island contained 'no other European inhabitants except Catholic missionaries and some persons attached to the mission', and 'it would be possible to cultivate there all tropical produce in abundance'. Maize, already introduced by the missionaries, 'thrives there as well as animals, which multiply very rapidly. . . .' And if the missionaries 'only had sufficient funds, thousands of people would already be employed under their supervision'. There were important mineral deposits; 'fishing could become very profitable, even for commerce'; and three ports had already been discovered.

Part two stressed further advantages. (1) The Papal States would be able to launch maritime commerce. This would be facilitated by the Société française de l'Océanie, which planned to have a ship operating out of the Port of Rome as soon as possible. 'Further, if so desired, the Société française will also fly the papal flag on all its other ships.' (2) The moral and political interests of the indigenous peoples would be safeguarded by the pope, and their continued existence would be guaranteed, the bishops said. On the other hand, wherever the great European powers had established themselves, the local peoples had been destroyed by violence and corruption. 'Therefore a humanitarian issue militates in favour of this project.' (3) Some truly Christian families could be brought to this island and 'would contribute tremendously to the conversion and civilisation of the indigenes under the direction of the missionaries'.

Douarre and Luquet explained in part three how simple it would be to take possession of the island. According to the practice adopted by European countries, 'the power which raises its flag in a land of savages by that very fact takes possession of it, and this possession is considered legitimate'. And according to the same practice, 'it is not necessary to guard the flag by military occupation, but only to care for it by a commissary appointed for this purpose'. One of the laymen attached to the mission 'could fulfil the function of Papal Commissary and look after the flag'. Thus there would be no expense for the Holy See once the act of taking possession had been completed.

Nor would the act of taking possession itself involve any expense for the Holy See, since Viscount Jean des Cars had promised to carry the pope's flag to

New Caledonia with him 'and hoist it there in the name of His Holiness, if he were authorised to do so'. Des Cars was an officer of the Sardinian Navy and commandant of the three-masted Genoese merchantman *Stella del Mare*. This ship had been chartered by the Société française de l'Océanie and Douarre's missionaires had booked passage on it to New Caledonia. During des Cars's recent visit to Rome his collaboration in the papal colony venture had been secured under the seal of secrecy. Douarre and Luquet were convinced that other nations would support the Holy See's action, or at least give it their consent. Since in maritime warfare the papal flag was always considered a neutral flag, the great powers had nothing to fear. In fact, they 'often take possession of a land, not so much for their own advantage, but rather out of fear of rivals. They therefore would be pleased to see the papal flag guaranteeing the independence of New Caledonia. . . .'

Part four repeated that Commander des Cars would take possession of the island and that a layman attached to the mission would be given the title of Papal Commissary and would look after the flag. No other steps would be taken 'in order to be able to remove the flag without inconvenience, if the reactions to this step should prove unfavourable. As for the task of having the natives agree to the act of taking possession, this would be left to the missionaries.' To make certain that the enterprise would be most successful, Douarre and Luquet requested authorisation from the Holy See '*secretly* to take the necessary steps in order to obtain . . . not only the consent, but also the support of the French Government, and from the British Government at least its tacit consent'.

In conclusion Douarre and Luquet requested that a decision on this matter be reached as soon as possible, so that they might profit 'from their forthcoming voyage to Genoa and to France in order to complete the negotiations'.[16]

The seven-page document marked 'Highly Confidential' quickly reached Pope Pius IX. For him to reject the proposal out of hand would have been impolite; for him to accept it out of hand would have been imprudent. Since it had been formally submitted by two bishops, one of them the Vicar Apostolic of New Caledonia himself, there was no alternative for the pope but to examine it. Instead of examining it himself, however, he asked five cardinals of the Evangelisation Congregation to do so.

It was 12 August when Pope Pius IX in his own hand wrote a message for Pro-Secretary Barnabò on the back page of the Douarre-Luquet report. 'Let a study of the *Memorandum* be made in a Particular Meeting composed of Cardinals Fransoni, Ostini, Castracane, Orioli and Altieri', he said. 'Assuming as premise [of the argumentation] that the pope is not and must not be a conquistador, one can allow the realisation of the project—up to now the pope is unacquainted with it—provided it be ascertained: (1) that religion would profit from it, and (2) that in advance both France and England would give their consent.'[17]

Cardinal Ferretti, the secretary of state, forwarded to Barnabò on 14 August the *Memorandum on Taking Possession of New Caledonia by the Holy See* with the message by the pope on the back page. 'By order of His Holiness', he told

Barnabò, 'the attached pages are being transmitted to the Most Reverend Pro-Secretary of the Evangelisation Congregation, so that the affair to which the said pages refer may be examined under papal secrecy at a Particular Meeting composed of the Most Eminent Cardinals indicated in the margin and chosen by His Holiness himself . . . Then in due time the Pro-Secretary himself shall report to His Beatitude on the results of the discussion. . . .'[18]

This special attention on the part of the pope for a proposal coming from Douarre was bound to force both Fransoni and Barnabò to give special attention themselves to any suggestions from Douarre.

But at this time Douarre was on the point of leaving Rome with nothing but unwritten promises. The mailman was good to him, however, bringing him letters from France from which he immediately made excerpts. These he sent to Barnabò on 16 August, just two days after Barnabò had received the two letters from Pope Pius IX and the cardinal secretary of state. Douarre was still deeply convinced of the necessity 'to establish ecclesiastical provinces and dioceses', he said, and he hoped that the cardinals of the Evangelisation Congregation would finally take some steps in this direction. If they failed to act promptly, he warned, they would have to answer 'before God for our New Zealand mission, not to mention all the rest of our missions'.

After this introduction Douarre quoted Colin as writing on 4 August that it was necessary, in order to save the New Zealand mission, for it to receive an English bishop who would not be merely a coadjutor. 'If by word of mouth you can come to the aid of this desolate mission of New Zealand,' Colin had written, 'you certainly will be doing a good work. . . .'

Douarre had also received a letter dated 31 July from Father Poupinel, Colin's secretary, who was also the society's mission procurator in Europe. 'Your Excellency, you will perform a great service for yourself and for our society, if you succeed in having Rome set up regulations which preserve for our bishops and for our society their respective rights. If this does not happen, we foresee that the scope of our society most probably will be altered.' Still another excerpt from Poupinel's letter read: 'Your Excellency, kindly request an official reply on the matter of the Friendly [or Tonga] Archipelago. It is necessary for our Reverend Father Superior to know to whom it belongs before he sends more missionaries to the Central Vicariate.'

A letter from Colin written on 10 August was also quoted: 'I have learned from Bishop Pompallier that New Zealand's vicar apostolic [that is, Pompallier himself] and Coadjutor Bishop Viard are to remain in office as formerly. In this hypothetical situation I find myself obliged to allow our missionaries to transfer freely to another vicariate, for it is impossible for me to permit the previous state of affairs to continue. Kindly advise the Evangelisation Congregation accordingly, and find out at the same time whether the Friendly Islands have been given to Bishop Bataillon. . . .'

Although Douarre did not receive the requested carte blanche, the quotations from these three letters were practically its equivalent, because they supported his 'Particular Regulations', his dire predictions of what would happen if

Pompallier remained in office, and his insistence that some steps must be taken immediately for the ecclesiastical reorganisation of Western Oceania. The excerpts went even further, because they called for an official statement by Rome as well on whether it was now Bataillon or perhaps still Pompallier who had jurisdiction over the Tonga or Friendly Islands.

Good cards had been dealt to Douarre and he played them well. 'I have no comments to make', he said when closing his letter to Barnabò. 'But I would ask that you give me a written reply regardless of what decisions are reached by the Sacred Evangelisation Congregation. . . .' The matter was evidently urgent, because Colin's 10 August letter as cited by Douarre said, 'We await you impatiently at the end of the current month.'[19]

The reaction to Douarre's letter of 16 August was immediate! Two days later, on 18 August, Douarre was given a private audience by Pius IX, who granted nearly everything he wished. The pope assured him that he would receive a letter from the Evangelisation Congregation on the 'Particular Regulations' which he was promoting for Marist missions. The Friendly or Tonga Archipelago would be returned to Bishop Bataillon. And the pope said that he himself would see to it that a letter would be sent to Bishop Pompallier ordering him not to leave France until he had been invited by the Holy See to do so. With Pompallier no longer in Rome, it was easy for the Holy See to act to his disadvantage.

On the following day, 19 August, Douarre posted a letter to Colin with all of this good news, promising to explain to him when they met what steps he had taken to achieve these goals. He had also received 3,000 francs from the Evangelisation Congregation, he said, 'but this is less than nothing and I do not really know where I shall find sufficient funds for my mission'.[20]

These were tremendous victories for Douarre, especially in view of the fact that all of this information had been given to him directly by Pope Pius IX even before the Evangelisation Congregation had drawn up the official documents! Was he being given treatment par excellence by the pope because of his proposal that New Caledonia become a papal colony? Or was it because Rome was beginning to fear that the Marists might otherwise desert Western Oceania entirely?

On 20 August, just two days after the papal audience, Fransoni fulfilled still another of Douarre's wishes by being more specific in an official document about the boundaries of the Vicariate Apostolic of New Caledonia. Writing on that date to Bishop Bataillon to inform him that his Central Oceania Vicariate was being reduced in size, Fransoni said that the boundaries of the newly created Vicariate Apostolic of New Caledonia would embrace 'the islands located between 160 and 170 degrees [east] longitude and those between 5 and 24 degrees [south] latitude. . . .'[21] This meant that besides 'the island and region of New Caledonia', as stated in the first official documents, the vicariate apostolic also included New Hebrides and the Santa Cruz Islands, precisely what Douarre had indicated in his *Memorandum on New Caledonia* submitted to the Evangelisation Congregation on 29 July 1847.

Fransoni's letter to Bataillon also brought up the delicate question of the Friendly or Tonga Archipelago. He had not reacted earlier to Bataillon's correspondence on this matter, he said, because he had believed that it would be easier to settle the issue once Pompallier had reached Rome. And this was exactly what had happened. Now he would present the matter to the pope as soon as possible, he said, and he would ask him to restore the Tonga Islands to Bataillon just as they were originally.[22]

That same day, 20 August, Fransoni also addressed a letter to Douarre, enclosing the above letter for Bataillon and another letter of the same date for Colin, asking that Douarre deliver both of them. The cardinal was convinced that Colin would be in agreement with the 'Particular Regulations', he said, and he informed Douarre that this acceptance by Colin would be sufficient for the Evangelisation Congregation to consider them to be in force. As for other matters, 'we have made known the mind of the Sacred Congregation and its wishes both to you and to the Reverend Colin'.[23]

In Colin's letter Fransoni said that he would receive a report from Douarre 'on all that has been granted to him, agreed upon, or concluded. . . .' He also assured Colin that Bataillon's request regarding the Tonga Islands was being attended to. And he asked Colin to submit his views on the 'Particular Regulations' drawn up by Douarre 'for the missions of Oceania. . . .'[24]

Then at the papal audience of 22 August 1847 Fransoni had Barnabò bring up the Tonga Islands question and the pope agreed that they should be placed once again under Bataillon's jurisdiction. The decree of 24 August announcing the pope's decision stated that Pompallier had been given jurisdiction over them 'only provisionally' because of peculiar circumstances in New Zealand. But meanwhile Pompallier had made proposals for the reorganisation of church government in Western Oceania and 'had declared it most opportune' to place them once again under Bataillon's jurisdiction. And since Bataillon and Colin also had 'earnestly requested' that this be done, Pope Pius IX 'wanted to grant the wishes held in common' by these three men and ordered the requested transfer.[25]

With his letter informing Colin on 24 August that the pope had returned the Tonga Islands to Bataillon's jurisdiction, Fransoni enclosed a letter of the same date which Colin was instructed to pass on to Pompallier 'after reading it and sealing it'.[26] The letter for Pompallier read: 'After the departure of Your Excellency from the City [of Rome] His Holiness seriously pondered again and again all those things which you proposed in your letter of 8 December last year for enactment at the General Meetings. But in addition to this he gave consideration to other reports about the adverse circumstances particularly of those missionaries in the vicariate entrusted to you . . . Subsequently the pope decided definitely that it would be most opportune for Your Excellency to defer your return trip to your mission. He therefore gave us the order to inform you that you are to remain in France until all these affairs have been settled and until it should appear favourable to His Holiness for you to return to the missions.' Fransoni added that in his absence his most worthy coadjutor, Viard, 'shall take

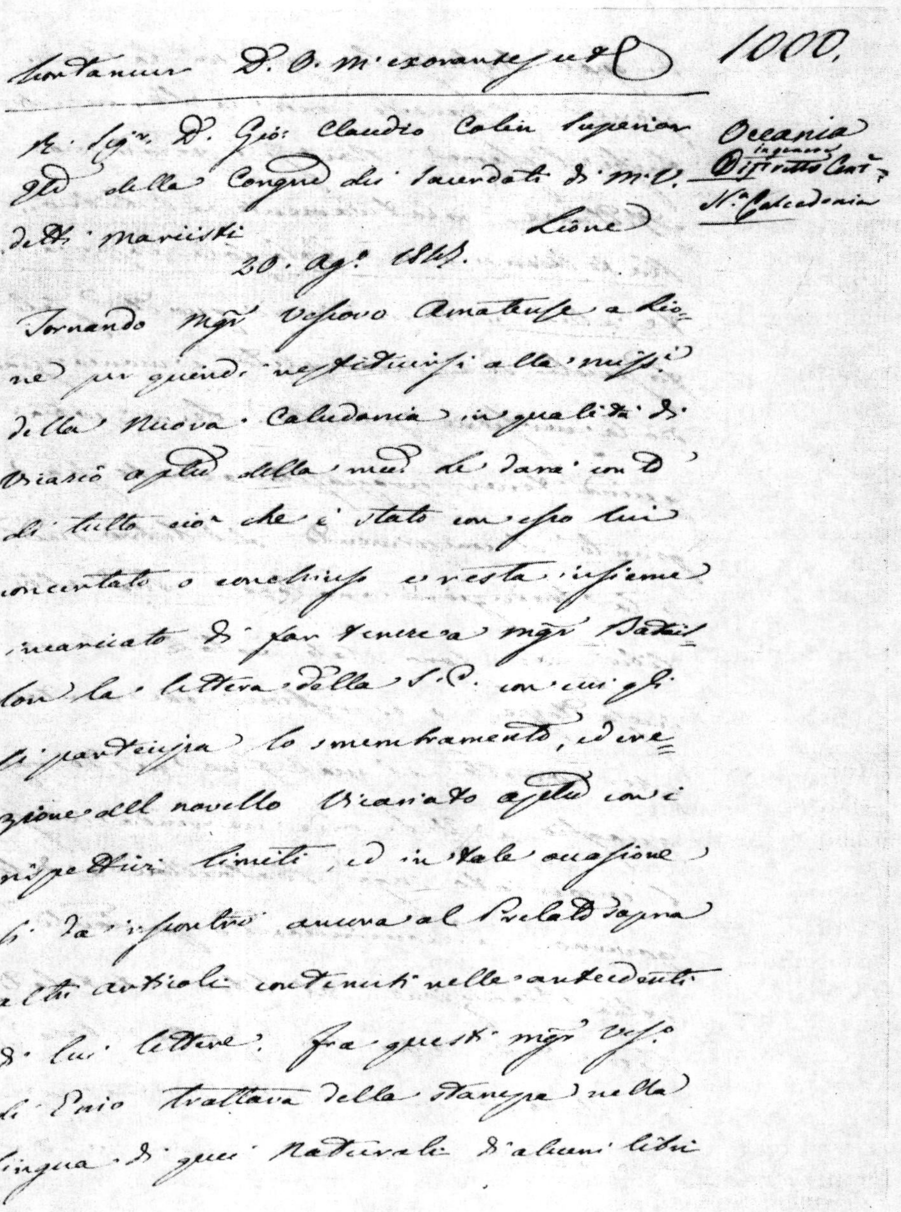

Contentur D. O. M. exorante etc. 1000.

R. Sig.r D. Giò: Claudio Colin Superiore Gen.le della Congne dei Sacerdoti di M. V. detti Maristi — Lione — Oceania / Distretto Cent.e / N.a Caledonia

20. Ag.o 1847.

Tornando Mgr Vescovo Amatense a Lione per quindi restituirsi alla miss.e della Nuova Caledonia in qualità di Vicario Ap.lico della med.a le darà con.to di tutto ciò che è stato con esso lui concertato o conchiuso e resta insieme incaricato di far tenere a Mgr Bataillon la lettera della S. C. con cui gli si partecipa lo smembramento, e la erezione del novello Vicariato Ap.lico coi rispettivi limiti, ed in tale occasione si da risposta ancora al Prelato sopra altri articoli contenuti nelle antecedenti di lui lettere: fra questi Mgr Vesc.o di Enos trattava della stampa nella lingua di quei Naturali d'alcuni libri

60 This is the first page of the Evangelisation Congregation's file copy of Cardinal Fransoni's seven-page letter of 20 August 1847 to Superior General Colin. It refers to the successful mediation of Bishop Douarre in Rome in July and August of that year and also to some requests of Bishop Bataillon. *Source: PF: LDB vol. 336 (1847) f. 1000r. (Chapter 28).*

care of the vicariate and shall conduct all pastoral functions'. And the Marists in Lyon would provide him 'with the agreed upon sum of 3,000 francs per year' for his subsistence.[27]

Fransoni's letter to Colin containing the above letter for Pompallier said that 'the Holy Father and the Sacred Evangelisation Congregation are in accord with Your Reverence that your society shall provide an annual sum of 3,000 francs for the prelate's support, as was earlier agreed upon'. This arrangement was to continue as long as Rome kept Pompallier in France 'or until he receives another appointment'.[28]

This diplomatic arrangement for keeping Pompallier out of New Zealand indefinitely was bound to please Colin immensely.

Douarre then sent Colin a most cheerful letter from Rome on 25 August, saying, 'We have finally won our famous case! You shall be receiving a letter from the Evangelisation Congregation, which will bring you up to date on everything. After posting this letter I shall be leaving [Rome] without delay, bringing with me the brief which returns the Friendly Archipelago to Bishop Bataillon. The decision taken regarding Bishop Pompallier will not appear complete enough for you; however, it seems that the Evangelisation Congregation was quite embarrassed over this matter . . . The amount which they suggested that you give him is, in effect, a contract which ties his hands as far as the Evangelisation Congregation is concerned. The letter will be passed on to you and will tell you more than I could myself . . . I must ask you to wait until my return to France in order to learn how we have obtained nearly everything that we wanted. . . .' It had been particularly toward the end of his stay in Rome, Douarre pointed out, that the Evangelisation Congregation suddenly became most agreeable and began to act toward him with all possible benevolence. 'It is to His Holiness that we owe the solution to our problems', he said.[29]

It was only in the weeks following Douarre's departure on 28 August that his and Luquet's *Memorandum on Taking Possession of New Caledonia by the Holy See* was carefully examined by the Particular Meeting ordered by Pope Pius IX.[30] Barnabò by way of introduction told the five cardinals that Douarre while in Rome had given a consoling report on his work in New Caledonia. 'And since he has found favourable dispositions everywhere, he is taking along on his return to the mission a goodly reinforcement of priests.'[31]

Barnabò then read his carefully prepared introductory remarks on the Douarre-Luquet proposal itself. It was Douarre who had conceived the project in favour of his New Caledonia mission, he said. Luquet, on learning about it from Douarre, gave it his support, since he considered it to be 'opportune'. Barnabò also explained how the document had been submitted to the pope and how the pope had then transmitted it to him through the cardinal secretary of state, 'ordering that it be presented under papal secrecy at a Particular Meeting with Your Eminences present. It pleased the Holy Father to designate you expressly for that purpose.'

After summarising the proposal of the two bishops for the five cardinals, Barnabò expressed his own views and betrayed his lack of enthusiasm for the project. 'One can easily understand that what motivated the good prelates in suggesting such an undertaking to the Holy Father', he said, 'was nothing else but their desire to guarantee for those poor Indians[32] protection from harm and from oppression. This they expected to achieve by procuring the loving protection and concern of the common father of the faithful for them in place of the tyrannical and destructive yoke of another power . . . Nevertheless it does not seem that they have kept in mind or reflected upon all the principles which have constantly been inculcated by the Supreme Pontiffs and which still hold today. . . .'

Barnabò then stated that the pope, 'in handing over this matter to be discussed and examined by Your Eminences, makes known his own mind openly and clearly. That is, in view of the principles just mentioned, and before all else, the basis to be established is *that the pope is not and must not be a conquistador.* And then, if it should be possible to exclude and separate such a notion from the proposed project, one would still have to discuss subsequently whether and in what manner it would be fitting to permit it. In this case, however, *it would first have to be ascertained*: (1) *That religion would profit from it, and* (2) *That France and England would give their prior consent to it.* These are the precise statements indicated by the Holy Father in his own hand on the back page of the *Memorandum.*'[33]

In spite of this, however, the cardinals were free to prescind from the pope's reservations, Barnabò said, and they could make 'any observation whatsoever, be it favourable to the project or against it', since the pope was most eager to have their personal opinions.

Without calling it a deterring factor, and labelling it merely 'news which must not be overlooked', Barnabò called one further item to the attention of the cardinals. Namely, when Douarre was on the point of leaving Rome on 28 August, he informed the Evangelisation Congregation that 'he had just received letters from New Caledonia announcing the arrival of some English Methodists'. Now it was possible, Barnabò added, that the Methodists might be 'the vanguard of some premeditated military occupation by Britain in some part of the island'. These words of Barnabò would seem to imply that if Britain had designs on the island, the Holy See should keep out.

'Your Eminences will kindly manifest your wise opinions in this matter', Barnabò concluded, 'so that the pro-secretary in fulfilment of the papal commands can report to His Beatitude the results of the discussion. Then this question can be resolved: *Whether, and in what way, and how, would it be proper to permit the project in question?*'[34]

What stand did the five cardinals take? From the brief report given by Barnabò after seeing Pope Pius IX it would appear that they had opposed the project, because the report said simply: 'The Holy Father in his audience of 23 September ordered the Reverend Pro-Secretary to do nothing more about this proposal and to drop the matter.'[35]

It is disappointing not to find any details on the stand taken by the cardinals in the pertinent dossier in the archives of the Evangelisation Congregation. But in a way this silence is understandable, since the cardinal secretary of state had instructed Barnabò that the entire matter was to be examined 'under papal secrecy'. The views of the five cardinals may turn up yet some day, perhaps in the archives of the cardinal secretary of state.[36]

Bishop Douarre, instead of rushing back to New Caledonia, loitered in France and tried once again to interest the French government in taking over New Caledonia as a colony. But he informed Colin from Paris on 23 December 1847 that his latest efforts were as unsuccessful as the previous ones. Finally he gave up in September of the following year.[37] There was then nothing left for him to do but return to his vicariate apostolic and try to conduct missionary work there in spite of New Caledonia's being neither a papal colony nor a French colony.

Bishop Luquet, who prior to meeting Douarre had been named coadjutor to the Vicar Apostolic of Pondicherry in India, was not wanted in India and was obliged to submit his resignation in 1851 while still in Rome. He then retired to the French Seminary there and spent the rest of his life writing pious books and mission histories. He died in Rome in 1858 at the age of forty-eight.[38]

Father Theiner in 1851 was promoted by Pope Pius IX to the office of assistant to the prefect of the Vatican archives with right of succession. But later he was deposed for releasing secret information. He died in 1874 at the age of seventy.[39]

To all appearances the Pompallier-Colin question was settled. In reality, however, the fires had not been extinguished. They were merely smouldering and would soon again burst into flame, causing Rome to make still further changes in the ecclesiastical organisation of Western Oceania.

29

Collomb is ordained bishop in New Zealand
for the Vicariates of
Melanesia and Micronesia

23 MAY 1847

Bishop Epalle's last letter to Superior General Colin from London dated 18 January 1845 expressed his 'great happiness' over Colin's proposal that twenty-eight-year-old Father Jean-Georges Collomb should receive part of his territory in Melanesia and also become a bishop and vicar apostolic there. However, Epalle did suggest that if Colin did not know where he had settled before Collomb left France, then Collomb should be named his coadjutor instead. He admitted having no illusions about being able to provide single-handed for a territory so vast as Melanesia. And therefore he begged Colin to do all in his power to influence Rome 'either to divide my mission of Melanesia or to give me a coadjutor. . . .'[1]

Five months later, on 18 June, Colin submitted his formal request to Cardinal Prefect Fransoni that Epalle be granted a coadjutor.[2] And in order to make Rome take action more quickly, he stated that Epalle had appeared so feeble after his return from Rome, 'that we are afraid he will not be able to withstand the fatigue of this long journey'. And if the hotter climate should not restore his strength, or if his weakened condition should keep him in Sydney for a long time, 'the 13 young missionaries accompanying him will find themselves in a difficult situation'. It would therefore be prudent, he said, 'to give him a coadjutor immediately'.

Without mentioning Collomb's name, he told Fransoni that Epalle's last letter from London had stated 'that he would accept with pleasure as his coadjutor a priest of our society, whom he designated for us, and who probably will be among the missionaries leaving for Oceania in September'. Colin added that 'in spite of the displeasure which we feel at seeing bishops multiplied within our society, we shall faithfully follow whatever advice Your Eminence sees fit to give us. And we intend to neglect nothing whatsoever that might contribute to the expansion of the reign of Jesus Christ among the infidels. . . .'[3]

Fransoni replied on 12 July that he would gladly give his personal support to the petition. Providing Epalle with a coadjutor was most opportune, he said, 'both because of the state of health of the esteemed bishop and because of the importance and extent of the missions entrusted to him'. Colin should indicate 'the name and qualities of the candidate whom Bishop Epalle desires', Fransoni said, and then he would bring up the matter at a General Meeting and prepare a report on it for the pope in order to obtain his approval.[4]

Because Collomb was not yet thirty years old, the canonically required age for bishops, Colin sought a letter of recommendation from Bishop Jean-François-Marcel Turinaz, head of the Tarentaise Diocese in which Collomb was born. Turinaz obliged and on 29 July stated that Collomb had constantly been 'outstanding in his observance of rules, in his exemplary conduct, in his application to work, and in his success at studies during both his college course and his university courses taken at Turin'. Collomb had doctorates in theology, canon law, and civil law, he said, and his knowledge of theological matters was beyond the average.[5]

Colin forwarded this recommendation to Cardinal Fransoni on 23 September 1845 together with his own. 'The weakened health' of Epalle and 'the need to hasten the promulgation of the gospel in the two immense Vicariates of Melanesia and Micronesia', he said, were the chief reasons for naming a coadjutor. These reasons had helped him overcome his 'repugnance at seeing too many young bishops of our society being spread throughout Oceania'.

Formality required the presentation of three names. Colin placed Collomb's name in the first place, saying that he was born on 30 April 1816 and that he had always been distinguished 'by his good character, his piety, and his talents'. He had also been professor of dogmatic theology at the major seminary of Moutiers. Colin added that Epalle on leaving London had written 'that he would agree with pleasure to having this young priest for his coadjutor'. And Colin urged Fransoni to send the papal brief as soon as possible, if the choice in fact should fall upon Collomb, since he had to leave 'with 12 other missionaries at the end of October' for Oceania.[6]

But when Colin's letter reached Rome, the autumn holidays had already begun and no further General Meetings of the Evangelisation Congregation, nor audiences with the pope, were to take place until 11 November. Sending this explanation to Colin on 29 November, Fransoni said that it therefore had not been possible for him to fulfil Colin's request and have the papal briefs in his hands by the time Collomb and the other missionaries were scheduled to leave. But he assured Colin that his request would be on the agenda of the next General Meeting scheduled for January 1846. 'I shall then inform you about the election', he said. And he added that there was no doubt in his mind that the person to be chosen would be the one whom Colin wanted.[7]

Collomb sailed from Le Havre for Western Oceania neither in September, nor in October, as Colin's two letters to Fransoni had preannounced, but on 15 November.[8] One day and one month later, on 16 December 1845, Bishop Epalle was attacked and mortally wounded in the Solomon Islands. His death on 19 December, while Collomb was on the high seas, made the naming of another bishop for Melanesia and Micronesia imperative.

Acting on the assumption that Epalle was still alive, the Evangelisation Congregation held a General Meeting on 26 January 1846 to discuss the advisability of giving him a coadjutor with right of succession. Cardinal Prefect Fransoni did far more than he had promised; not only did he give the proposal his support, but he also presented it personally and led the discussion.

He pointed out to the cardinals that at the General Meeting of 15 July 1844 they had postponed choosing a coadjutor until the new mission would be sufficiently established. But in spite of this condition not yet being fulfilled, there were now 'two very serious reasons' which made it urgent to have a coadjutor. One was the fact that 'a deadly and long illness' had attacked Epalle and had postponed his voyage to Oceania. 'And it had weakened his physical forces in such a way', that it was now 'not only useful, but altogether necessary', for him to have the assistance and support of a coadjutor. For this reason Epalle himself through Colin had submitted from London 'the most urgent request' that he be granted a coadjutor 'in case he should become unavailable, an eventuality which one fears is not far off'.

In order to press his point with the other cardinals, Fransoni had greatly exaggerated 'the weakened health' mentioned by Colin. But in doing so he manifested in an uncanny way what had actually taken place in Oceania.

The other 'very serious reason' which he gave for appointing a coadjutor was 'the great vastness of the mission'. He explained that 'according to the decree of foundation it was to be governed by only one vicar apostolic, although it was already divided into two vicariates. The actual separation and the choice of another distinguished prelate were to be left to an opportune time.' It was this consideration, Fransoni said, which had prompted Epalle to request a coadjutor, since with his help 'he hopes to obtain more rapid progress for the Catholic faith in both Melanesia and Micronesia, thus hastening the time when the already decreed division can be executed'.

Colin had been asked to submit the names of three candidates, Fransoni added, and the one whom he praised particularly was the first one, 'the youngest, who nevertheless will very soon reach the canonical age'. By this time Collomb was only three months short of his thirtieth birthday. In spite of his youth, Fransoni explained, 'he is preferable to the other two and would be more pleasing and acceptable to both Bishop Epalle . . . and Reverend Colin'. Fransoni noted that a letter of recommendation had also been received from Collomb's diocesan bishop.

The cardinals were then asked whether Epalle should be given a coadjutor and, if so, which of the three candidates should be presented to the pope. They voted in favour of Collomb and instructed the secretary to request from the pope a dispensation of some months because of the canonical age impediment. Informed of the choice of the Evangelisation Congregation, Pope Gregory XVI gave his consent on 1 February 1846 and also the requested dispensation.[9]

The official documents were sent to Colin by Fransoni on 7 March for forwarding to Collomb. In his accompanying letter Fransoni said that 'the wishes of Bishop Epalle and of Your Reverence have been fulfilled in their entirety. . . .'[10] Losing no time Colin posted the official documents to Collomb via Sydney on 24 March.[11] Collomb, who would have to present these documents personally to a bishop in order to receive episcopal ordination from him, was authorised 'to receive episcopal ordination from any Catholic bishop whomsoever, provided he enjoys communion with the Holy See'.[12]

Where would the official documents catch up with Collomb?

Arche d'Alliance, the three-masted 313-ton ship on which he was travelling with a group of Marist missionaries, belonged to the Société française de l'Océanie. This unique religious-economic enterprise was geared to be self-supporting and at the same time to benefit Catholic missionary work in Oceania. Bishop Epalle in 1844 had played an important role in the formation of this organisation, which was launched by a young French merchant from Le Havre named Marziou. Marziou dreamed of sending ships to Oceania with mission supplies paid for by interested Catholics through subscription fees, but the plan did not work and was subsequently modified under the influence of Epalle, who was convinced that the missions in Oceania could not succeed without the collaboration of a lay apostolate. Then Société française de l'Océanie was born. But postponement followed postponement and no ship was ready to take Epalle and his missionaries to Oceania when it was time for them to leave.[13]

Superior General Colin of the Marists brought the organisation once again to the attention of Cardinal Prefect Fransoni, writing on 18 June 1845 and requesting for it the blessing of Pope Gregory XVI. He believed that it would 'provide the greatest service for missionaries and for the peoples of Oceania', and he called Marziou, the founder, 'a pious merchant and a fervent Catholic'. In fact, his letter served as an introduction for Lieutenant Auguste Marceau, Knight of the Legion of Honour, who had given up an honourable position in the French Navy in order to take over command of *Arche d'Alliance*.[14]

Colin's letter was presented to Fransoni by Marceau who also submitted from Rome on 6 July 1845 a nineteen-page memorandum on the Société française de l'Océanie. The memorandum pointed out that the number of missionaries volunteering for work in Oceania was constantly increasing and that in some islands there already were such excellent results that one could 'hope for the proximate conversion of the 15 million souls spread throughout these archipelagoes. . . .' On the other hand, the missionaries were having great difficulty getting there, 'found themselves abandoned after reaching their destinations', and had to endure much suffering and danger. It was this, he said, that had prompted the late Bishop Rouchouze, first Vicar Apostolic of Eastern Oceania, to remark during his last sojourn in France: 'If Providence does not give us the means to visit our nascent churches and provide them with the help they need, I tremble for the future of our missions in Oceania.'

Marceau pointed out that 'precisely because of this preoccupation with a need for communication among the different islands', Bishop Pompallier of Western Oceania had hired a ship and Bishop Rouchouze of Eastern Oceania had come to Europe to buy one. But Pompallier's action contributed to the financial ruin of his mission and he was forced to sell the ship. And Bishop Rouchouze, who had purchased the *Marie-Joseph*, 'went aboard with some 20 priests and nuns and was lost at sea'.

These two unfortunate experiences had forced Oceania bishops to renounce whatever intentions they might have had of providing their own inter-island shipping services, Marceau said. And how long would they have to wait until commercial shipping agencies would be attracted to their islands? 'Moreover, how many souls will be lost for lack of assistance during this time?' What was needed, he said, was something that could be done by laymen who were interested in religion. They could assume responsibility for 'transporting missionaries to the midst of peoples who have no contact with Europeans', and they could also protect them and see to it that they obtained everything necessary for their subsistence.

However, if Société française de l'Océanie was to survive, it had to develop commercial relations in Oceania. Consequently it intended to place some Europeans in each mission; they were to serve as agents and as teachers of European culture and of various professions. 'These families, all of them Christian and chosen with care, will become auxiliaries for the missionaries by their good example and by introducing the natives to work. They will also assure the missionaries of a livelihood.' Marceau went on to say that his organisation 'would found in all missions agricultural, commercial and industrial establishments and would employ in these, besides the personnel of the organisation itself, also natives insofar as they are needed. . . .'[15]

Fransoni thanked Marceau on 18 July for the memorandum on his organisation with its goal of 'providing help for very important missions, particularly those in the vast archipelagoes of Oceania. . . .' The project 'appears most commendatory in all of its aspects to the Sacred Congregation', he said, and he praised it for services which it intended to provide for the spread, progress and stability of the Catholic faith in the missions of Oceania. In fact, the Sacred Congregation would in time manifest its good pleasure even further by obtaining approbation for the organisation from the Holy Father himself, he promised, 'as soon as the project is carried out by Your Excellency and experimented with for a sufficient period of time. . . .' He added that it might become necessary as time went on to change or omit some aspects of the plan.[16]

Arche d'Alliance was blessed by the Bishop of Nantes on Saturday, 30 August 1845, and on 1 September a booklet published there described the purposes and organisation of the Société. It pointed out that missionaries would have nothing at all to do with its commercial aspect, even though the organisation would transport them to their missions, provide them with inter-island transportation, and keep them in contact with their home country.[17]

It all looked so advantageous for the missionaries on paper. But in Collomb's case, at least, the route to his destination was extremely circuitous and appallingly time-consuming. There was a stop at Tahiti where Commandant Marceau purchased some seventy tons of mother-of-pearl. There was a stop at New Caledonia, where Collomb found Colin's letter of 24 March 1846 with the news that Rome had named him coadjutor to Bishop Epalle with right of succession. But the official documents accompanying the letter had been sent via the Marist supply centre in Sydney and had been kept back there.[18]

At last on Sunday, 7 February 1847, one year and three months after leaving Le Havre, *Arche d'Alliance* finally brought Collomb within the boundaries of his Vicariate Apostolic of Melanesia. Aboard ship with him were twenty-six-year-old Father Montrouzier, returning from his period of recuperation in New

Caledonia, and twenty-three-year-old Father Cyprien Crey and twenty-five-year-old Brother Optat Bergillon, both arriving in Melanesia like their bishop-elect for the first time. From Montrouzier, who fourteen months earlier had helped bury Bishop Epalle at Saint George Island and who himself some weeks later had been speared in the back at San Cristóbal, Collomb received first-hand reports on his new mission territory.

'We crossed over the boundary of the Melanesia Vicariate at approximately 10.30 in the evening', he wrote in his diary, 'and in that same instant we heard a thunderclap and saw lightning flash across the entire horizon.' A terrible storm broke loose and the crew busied itself battening down the hatches and drawing in the sails. Collomb and his three missionaries nevertheless went to the four corners of the ship and threw into the churning sea Immaculate Conception and Saint Benedict medals blessed by the bishop. Montrouzier asked whether he could also throw into the waves a silver-chained rosary. 'We recited the Exurgat Deus; seven Our Father's, Hail Mary's and Glory be's of the Blue Scapular for the souls in Purgatory; some prayers to the Blessed Virgin and the Angelus. All this we did by way of blessing our arrival in the mission.'

The following day, 8 February, Collomb offered Mass aboard ship for God's blessing on his mission and about 5.15 that afternoon San Cristóbal came into view. The next morning they sailed toward shore and many canoes filled with natives came out to greet them. But Marceau was unable to find the passage leading into Port Sainte-Marie and Montrouzier did not remember where it was. Finally a whaleboat was sent to find it. Then on 10 February the three-masted sailing vessel was trapped in a calm and stood practically motionless all day.

Finally about midday on Thursday, 11 February, a canoe arrived with a native aboard who recognised Montrouzier and mentioned the names of all the priests and Brothers based at San Cristóbal. Collomb exclaimed: 'Then they all are alive; thanks be to God!' Two hours later another canoe arrived with thirty-year-old Father Paget aboard. 'How pale, how weak he is', Collomb wrote in his diary. 'He could not get on deck without having himself hoisted aboard. Then he fell to our knees and asked for a blessing from Europe.'

That afternoon a wind brought *Arche d'Alliance* as far as the passage, but not into it. By whaleboat Collomb and his missionaries went ashore where they embraced their colleagues. 'But they are so wasted away', Collomb noted, 'and all of them either have had fever or still have it. We went immediately to chapel to visit the Blessed Sacrament. And that evening I announced that I had been named to succeed Bishop Epalle and that I intended to depart with *Arche d'Alliance* to have myself ordained a bishop wherever possible.'[19]

All the San Cristóbal missionaries were living in the large house built at Makira in the Oné tribal area at Port Sainte-Marie. And here they were trying to follow as closely as possible the daily order of the central Marist house in Lyon.[20]

From his weakened staff Collomb learned of their efforts to found a second residential station at Pia Bay north of Port Sainte-Marie in the Pia tribal area, where Fathers Verguet and Thomassin had been appointed to do the recon-

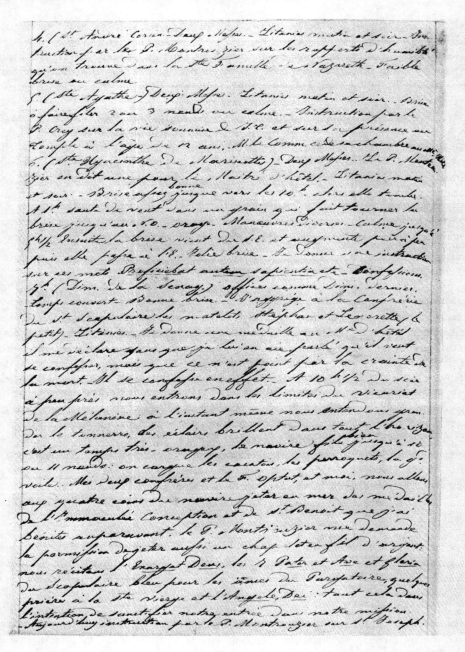

61   In the lower half of this page from the diary of Bishop Collomb dated 7 February 1847 he describes the reaction of himself and his missionaries as he entered for the first time within the boundaries of his Vicariate Apostolic of Melanesia. *Source: SM: 'Journal de Mgr. Jean Georges Collomb' (November 1845 to March 1847), p. 177. (Chapter 29).*

noitring. When the Oné natives saw them preparing to leave, they gave fearful warnings about the ferociousness of the Pia tribe. Convinced that the warnings sprang from self-interest, the missionaries said that nothing would stop them from going. Then an Oné native volunteered to serve as their guide; he was married to a Pia woman and consequently was assured of a welcome by the Pia tribe.

Their native canoe was paddled by four oarsmen and on arriving at Pia Bay, Verguet fired a shot in the air, frightening the natives. 'This solemn beginning was necessary in a land where we were arriving for the first time', he later explained. 'We were nothing but two men, weakened by fatigue and fever, and fear of our firearms was the only thing capable of making us respected.'

Once on shore the missionaries explained that with their guns they killed only birds, not men. The natives then took them to the forest, pointed out a bird, and asked them to shoot it. The test was easy, but decisive, since on this first shot their entire reputation would depend. Verguet carefully took aim and fired. The bird toppled from branch to branch and finally to the ground. As the natives passed it around, each one examined the wound and remarked on the terrible weapon.

Usually Verguet averaged one bird for two shots, but when hunting on this particular day he managed to get five birds with five shots. 'This made the natives think that the gun never missed', he said, 'and it gave me the reputation in the entire tribe of being a great warrior. . . .' The natives were also astonished to see the bullets of his small pistol pierce a coconut, perforate the trunk of a palm tree, and skip endlessly over the calm waters of the bay. Their spears, tomahawks, and arrows without feathers were no match.

While Verguet was busy with his ballistic feats, Thomassin had been trying to find a suitable place for a foundation and had also been giving catechism lessons. Older men with him soon heard about Verguet's marksmanship and wanted to see him in action. 'And so I planted an old worm-eaten board in the sand on the beach', he said. 'I loaded my gun, walked 20 paces away, and took aim. My intention was only to knock it down, but the result was far beyond my expectations. The board split in two lengthwise, making them think that the gun could also cut a man in half.'

That evening the natives danced for the missionaries and the missionaries sang for them. After several delightful hours with the village folk, the two priests spread out their mat of palm leaves on the ground and went to sleep alongside the families of their guide and his brother-in-law. They had a wooden pillow and were kept warm by a nearby fire. Several times Verguet awoke with the thought that he and his partner might be attacked and eaten alive. Feeling with his hand in the dark to make sure that his gun was still next to his hard pillow, he dismissed the idea and went back to sleep.

On the following day the missionaries announced that they would like to come and settle in the village and they promised to give the natives as much iron as they wanted in exchange for a completed house. After much betelnut chewing the village council agreed to their request and said that they could pick out whichever building they wanted. 'They brought us to one of the nicest ones in the village, which measured 10 by 25 metres and had a roof supported by 12 sculptured columns. We offered them 12 small axes, very highly prized in these islands. . . .' After reaching an agreement the two priests returned to Oné and reported their success.

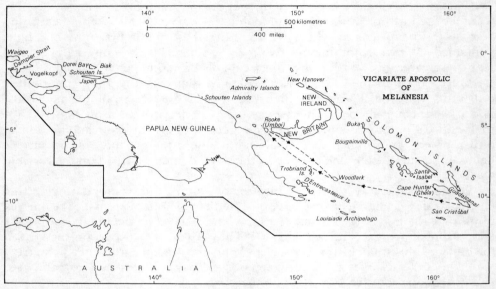

62 The Marist missionaries abandoned San Cristóbal Mission after twenty months on 3 September 1847 in favour of Woodlark Island. From there they expanded in 1848 to Rooke (now Umboi) Island, which they also abandoned on 17 May 1849 in order to rejoin the personnel at Woodlark Island. (*Chapters 20, 29, 30, 31, 35*).

But Makira Mission was hit so hard by fever and it lingered so long that there were no missionaries available to open the contemplated mission prior to Collomb's arrival. Verguet may have been exaggerating a bit when he reported that in his own case he had been attacked by fever every two days for eight months and had to lie down habitually. 'My stomach could digest no food', he said. 'I vomited several times after each meal . . . and gradually became weaker.'[21]

Collomb spent much of his time at San Cristóbal poring over the papers left behind by Bishop Epalle. On Ash Wednesday, 17 February, he went by whaleboat with Fathers Paget and Jacquet to a village situated on a hilltop about one hour southeast of Makira. 'I found it beautiful and well ventilated', Collomb said. 'And, as I mentioned to our Fathers, I am inclined more and more to go along with the doctor's views and have Fathers Frémont and Crey and Brothers Aristide and Optat go and stay there provisionally for some months, so we can learn whether the fever is caused by the island's climate or by Makira's location.' He also asked his missionaries on 18 February to try to explore the island, but without risking their lives. 'Not having the [papal] bulls at hand', he noted in his diary that day, 'I did not want to exercise my authority, although I knew that they had arrived in Sydney. I am satisfied with making my views and my wishes known.'

Then on Friday, 19 February, a light breeze blowing from shore pushed *Arche d'Alliance* out to sea. Aboard with Collomb was twenty-nine-year-old Father Verguet, who on 12 February, the day after Collomb's arrival in San Cristóbal, had confided to him that he had no missionary vocation and wanted to return to France.[22]

Commandant Marceau had informed Cardinal Prefect Fransoni while in Rome that there had been talk of making Société française de l'Océanie 'a maritime religious order'.[23] In fact, Verguet while en route from San Cristóbal to Sydney was prompted to remark that Marceau's ship was 'like a religious house'. Marceau served Mass daily on his knees in the presence of his sailors, received Holy Communion daily, and also made an hour's meditation each day. For all aboard his ship there was an hour of morning and evening prayer. After sunset he regularly went on deck and sang the Litany of the Blessed Virgin Mary with the entire crew responding, 'ora pro nobis!' And each day before evening prayer Bishop-Elect Collomb gave the sailors religious instruction.[24]

It was fifteen minutes past midday on Saturday, 6 March 1847, when *Arche d'Alliance* entered the passage at Sydney. And by about three o'clock Collomb was already at the Marist centre where he at once received the papal bulls naming him Titular Bishop of Antiphellus and Epalle's coadjutor with right of succession. But he could not be ordained a bishop in Sydney, because Archbishop Polding was in Rome at the moment asking Cardinal Prefect Fransoni to create three new Australian dioceses: Melbourne, Victoria and Maitland. Nor could Collomb be ordained by Bishop Pompallier, since he, too, was currently in Rome trying to have the hierarchy established in Western Oceania. Collomb then wrote on 8 March to Pompallier's coadjutor at Kororareka in New Zealand, Bishop Viard, giving advance notice that he intended to come there to be ordained a bishop by him.[25]

Commandant Marceau on arriving in Sydney received a papal brief naming him a Knight of Saint Gregory the Great. But the expected letter of credit from Marziou, director at Le Havre of the Société française, was not there and he found himself in great financial embarrassment. He had left Le Havre nearly sixteen months earlier and now had no more funds. In order to get some he sold the seventy tons of mother-of-pearl which he had purchased in Tahiti. And he decided to return to Tahiti, where the Société had an agent, hoping to find some news there from France and also the indispensable funds.

Writing to Superior General Colin on 6 May after being in Sydney for two full months, Collomb reported that Marceau was sailing with *Arche d'Alliance* to Tahiti with 100 head of cattle and 500 or 600 sheep. 'I must therefore take passage on a different ship . . . and I can find none that will bring me as far as San Cristóbal. . . .' He had succeeded, however, in making a contract with the owner and captain of the 175-ton English schooner *Spec* (short for *Speculator*), which was scheduled to sail either to Batavia (now Jakarta) in the Dutch East Indies or to Manila in the Philippines. The ship would go somewhat off course, taking him as far as New Caledonia via New Zealand, where he had to go in order to be ordained a bishop. Marceau had assured him that at Port Balade in New Caledonia he would meet the 74-ton brig *Anonyme*, also owned by the Société, and that he could charter it month by month.

Collomb knew that Colin would be particularly interested in his efforts to track down reliable information on locations which could serve as residential mission stations. After all, Port Sainte-Marie at San Cristóbal was far too small to hold all his missionaries and they would only become dissatisfied there. And if it seemed definite by his return that the climate was causing the sickness of his missionaries, and if they meanwhile had not found a more healthful location on the island, he believed that it might be necessary to abandon San Cristóbal temporarily, even though he regretted doing so. Nor did he know exactly where he might make his new foundations, 'because the circumstances in which we find ourselves make us rely on our plans less than ever'.

After the *Anonyme* brought him to San Cristóbal, and after he had made all necessary arrangements with his missionaries, he intended 'to depart with nine of them and go to Saint George Island, if we feel that we shall be able to exhume the remains of Bishop Epalle at that time and take them with us. Otherwise we shall head directly for Woodlark Island situated at 9° south latitude and 151° east longitude.[26] I have complete confidence that we shall be able to make a safe and important foundation there. Then I shall go with some Fathers and Brothers to Buka Island, north of Bougainville [Island].' Many maps showed them united, he said, 'but in reality they are two different lands'.

After leaving missionaries behind at both Woodlark Island and Buka Island, Collomb planned 'to visit the northern coast of New Ireland and the southern coast of New Britain', even though he had no missionaries to assign there. 'It is also possible that I may go and see some other lands, for example, the eastern coast of New Guinea. It seems to me most opportune that I take advantage of this ship, which God is placing at my disposal, to seek out immediately the places where I could assign to greater advantage the personnel that you in your charity shall be able to obtain for me.'

He added that Captain Auguste Marceau and another gentleman named Joubert had run around Sydney for two days seeking all possible data on Melanesia. 'M. Marceau and I as a result of this information have drawn up my campaign plan as I have described it to you.' Collomb also told Colin that a rendezvous with Marceau was to take place at Woodlark Island in March 1848, since Marceau believed that *Arche d'Alliance* could be there by that time.

One of the Sydney informants was Captain Grimes of the *Woodlark*, now retired. He had discovered Woodlark Island in the 1830s and named it after his ship.[27] Grimes, however, had only seen the island from a distance and did not go ashore. But he had been on Buka Island and said that its inhabitants were 'a very beautiful race'. The island also had numerous fields and abundant food supplies.

Another Sydney informant was Captain Cayle of the *Scamander*. He had visited Woodlark Island three times and reported on it most favourably. If he himself had to live on some island, he would choose Woodlark, he said. And if he had to counsel a friend who wanted to make a foundation somewhere, he would tell him to go to Woodlark. According to Collomb's information the island was '31 miles long, quite close to New Guinea, about 80 leagues from New Ireland, closer than that to both New Britain and the Solomon Islands, and very close to the Louisiade Islands'. The population was approximately 3,000 and the people were 'all Polynesians manifesting great goodness of character'.[28]

Cayle said that the island was quite high, could be seen from a distance, and was almost entirely flat. A map showed two mountains and Collomb was told that a delightful river provided sweet water. In addition there were chickens, yams and an abundance of food in general. 'For this reason whalers go there to renew their supplies, although as yet no anchorage has been discovered except at a nearly island to the west.' Collomb pointed out that Cayle's information on Woodlark dovetailed perfectly with that supplied by the captain of *Protheus*, another whaler, who had also visited Woodlark.

Both captains had supplied information on New Ireland as well. Cayle said that the northern coast was wooded, flat, furnished with an abundance of food, and well-populated with very good-natured natives. The *Protheus* captain, however, did not agree that they were very good-natured. Nothing more than the southeast point of the island was known to date and Collomb feared they might contract fever there.

There were numerous smaller islands scattered around the principal islands of Melanesia, according to Cayle, 'and all of these are heavily populated and have abundant foodstuffs. There are also villages on the south coast of New Britain and on the north coast of New Guinea.' Numerous whales and also many sperm whales were to be found on those shores. And there were also oysters and turtles, notably in the northern islands of the Solomon Archipelago. 'But the captains whom we were able to consult', Collomb said, 'had nothing to say about these places, except that they would not dare entrust themselves to the natives of those islands.'

Collomb had not been idle during his two months in Sydney. Besides getting information, he had busied himself buying foodstuffs for a year: dried biscuits, wine, salted beef, salted pork, etc. And if more food were needed, Marceau promised to bring it 'when he comes to visit us in the beginning of February 1848. . . .' Collomb had also purchased various medicines, including sulfate of quinine, and 'a certain quantity of objects for bartering with the natives, like iron, small beads, red calico, etc.' Another major item on his expense account was 'the lumber needed to build the walls, doors, windows and roofing for two houses about 25 feet long, 21 feet wide and 11 feet high'. Nearly all of it had been specially treated for the tropics.[29]

The *Spec* finally left Sydney on the morning of 9 May with Collomb, Verguet and all their supplies and reached Kororareka in New Zealand on 20 May after midday. The two travellers were received with open arms by Bishop Viard and the other two priests and two Brothers stationed there. On the following day the *Spec* sailed on to Auckland; on its return it would pick up Collomb and Verguet and take them to New Caledonia.

In the interval Collomb was ordained a bishop. He described the ceremony briefly and simply when writing to Colin: 'My episcopal ordination took place in the beautiful wooden chapel of the Apostles Saints Peter and Paul on 23 May, the Feast of Pentecost. . . .'[30]

While waiting for the *Spec* to return, Collomb wrote letters to Pope Pius IX, Cardinal Prefect Fransoni and Father Superior General Colin. On 31 May he informed the pope of the time and place of his episcopal ordination. And he asked for the pope's blessing for himself and his missionaries, that they might grow in holiness and that 'the many islands and almost innumerable tribes to which they will be sent' could pass more quickly 'from the shadow of death to the admirable light of Christ'. He himself was overjoyed that now, as bishop, it was his task 'to seek out the sheep who do not yet belong to the fold of Christ Jesus and to expand the holy Church of God' in those most remote islands 'and among peoples notorious for their barbarity'. He intended 'to fight the good fight' so that he might gain his own salvation and that of the infidels, 'relying solely upon the omnipotent grace of Christ' and 'remaining faithful unto death'.[31]

On the same day he also informed Fransoni of his episcopal ordination and mentioned his plans for opening new foundations in Melanesia. He had good reason to hope, he said, that after some months he would be able to place missionaries at Woodlark Island and others at Buka Island, because he had heard such good reports on their climate and people. 'I also intend to inspect several other areas in this same year with the help of God, especially New Ireland, New Britain, and perhaps the northern coast of New Guinea. Then, when other missionaries are sent to us, they can be assigned more quickly and more safely. Further, it shall be our particular aim to provide suitable education for youths, insofar as this is possible. And so there will be schools for training catechists and, if it should so please the Lord, the initial steps at least will also be taken as well for preparing an indigenous clergy.'[32]

Collomb's letter contained three urgent and specific requests. He asked the Holy See (1) to separate the Vicariate of Micronesia from the Vicariate of Melanesia 'as soon as possible', and (2) to divide the Vicariate of Melanesia 'into several other vicariates, so that the empire of Satan may everywhere collapse more quickly. . . .' But even prior to taking these two steps the Holy See ought (3) to send him a coadjutor, since he absolutely needed the assistance of another bishop 'because of the vastness of the territories entrusted to us, because of the many dangers threatening our life, and because of the very serious difficulties connected with the pastoral office'.[33]

On the following day, 1 June, Collomb wrote to Colin, again telling him about Woodlark and Buka, 'where I hope we shall be able to establish ourselves very advantageously. . . .' He and Verguet were waiting for the *Spec* to return any day from Auckland and his next move would be to go with it to New

Caledonia, where he hoped to find the *Anonyme*, which would take him to Melanesia and the islands that he wanted to visit there.[34]

Eight months later Cardinal Prefect Fransoni contacted Superior General Colin and informed him that Pope Pius IX and the Evangelisation Congregation had received letters from Collomb with news about his episcopal ordination and his plans for the development of his mission. After mentioning his urgent requests Fransoni said that all three were worthy of consideration and the Evangelisation Congregation was 'well disposed to go along with these wishes, especially by providing him quickly with the assistance of a coadjutor. . . .' But before asking the Holy Father to give Collomb faculties to choose for himself 'a candidate from among the most suitable of his missionaries', and before dividing and subdividing his mission, Fransoni wished 'to know the wise views that Your Reverence will kindly make known to me regarding this matter. I shall therefore postpone replying until immediately after hearing from you. . . .'[35]

Fransoni had hoped that Collomb's proposal would stir up Colin's zeal 'so that he would increase considerably the number of missionaries to be sent to work in Micronesia in view of the division to follow'.[36]

Colin answered Fransoni's letter of 31 January 1848 on 12 February. He definitely was in favour of having the two vicariates of Melanesia and Micronesia separated, he said. But what Fransoni did not expect was Colin's remark that it would give him the greatest pleasure if the Holy See were then to give the Vicariate of Micronesia 'to some other religious community and also provide it with a vicar apostolic'. He called this 'an efficacious means of hastening the spread of the gospel and of saving more quickly so many souls which are perishing'.

This reaction by Colin should have been expected, because from the very beginning he had been averse to accepting responsibility for the Micronesian part of the double vicariate. In fact, he had accepted it only temporarily, being forced to do so by Rome, but with the understanding that he would soon be relieved of it. The understanding was that, should Pompallier be expelled from New Zealand by the British, he would be free to choose one or the other of the two vicariates, Melanesia or Micronesia, as a place of refuge. But by January 1848 this was no longer a threat. In fact, currently Pompallier—although still Vicar Apostolic of Western Oceania—was confined to Europe until he should be invited by Rome to return to his mission. Therefore Colin's request at this time to have Micronesia entrusted to another religious community was no retreat by the Marists in the Pacific. That would come later.[37]

As for Collomb's other request to have his Vicariate Apostolic of Melanesia subdivided, Colin hesitated to give his consent. 'It is difficult to foresee in which part of his vicariate Bishop Collomb will be able to establish himself', he said. 'Also, what basis would be used for this subdivision? We do know that unhealthful conditions in San Cristóbal Island and in the Solomon Islands have made the vicar apostolic think of transporting his missionaries elsewhere.' This information had been in Collomb's letter to Colin about his Woodlark and Buka plans.

Nor did Colin think that Collomb should receive a coadjutor at this time. 'The latest news that we have received from San Cristóbal informs us that all the missionaries have been afflicted by a malignant fever in that place and they say it is extremely bad.' In fact, he would be little surprised to learn, he said, 'that they have become victims either of this malady or of the ferocity of the islanders. In this case there will be no alternative for Bishop Collomb but to withdraw and retire to our other vicariates.' These circumstances 'would seem to me to make the nomination of a coadjutor premature'.

In Colin's mind there was no great advantage for a bishop to have a coadjutor when launching a vicariate deprived of all human resources. 'As I see it,' he said, 'the office of coadjutor would simply compound difficulties insofar as it destroys in a way the unity of government in a mission, becoming at the same time a possible occasion for divisions and complaints. It would therefore appear prudent to us, especially in these circumstances, to postpone the nomination of a coadjutor, since all of our missions are suffering from a kind of confusion and discouragement as a result of what has happened.' (Here Colin was referring to the turmoil caused by the clash with Bishop Pompallier.) 'For this very same reason I already requested the Sacred Congregation last August [1847] graciously not to elevate any priests of the Society of Mary to the episcopacy at this time.'[38]

Without indicating approval or disapproval of Colin's reasoning, Fransoni on 4 March replied that he would present his views to the other cardinals of the Evangelisation Congregation. However, he did find it 'very hard' to proceed with separating the two missions of Melanesia and Micronesia as Colin wished, 'because of the difficulty at this time in finding a religious community to which Micronesia might be entrusted'. On the other hand the division could have been made easily and quickly, he said, 'if your admirable society had assumed the obligation of remaining there and subsequently providing a certain number of missionaries as needed'.

As for the coadjutor issue, Fransoni clearly disagreed with Colin. 'I think we could grant him a coadjutor', he said, 'but we would limit the faculty in such a way that the prelate could choose one for himself only if some urgency should arise.' Fransoni said that he would await Colin's reply and that it would make him happy 'if you were to indicate to me whether your society could make efforts of some kind on behalf of Micronesia, since this would facilitate the desired division. . . .'[39]

When twelve weeks passed and no reply came from Colin, Fransoni had the matter brought up at a General Meeting on 29 May 1848. Cardinal Lambruschini explained the issue to the other cardinals, acquainting them with the urgent petitions in Collomb's letter of 31 May 1847, with Colin's reaction of 12 February 1848, and with the counterproposals contained in the Sacred Congregation's reply of 4 March. But Colin 'has not yet replied on these proposals', he said.

Lambruschini then led the discussion and invited the cardinals to vote on this question: 'If for the present the requested division of Melanesia and Micronesia is to be postponed because of insufficient personnel, should the Holy Father nevertheless be asked to grant opportune faculties so that Bishop [Collomb] of Antiphellus may go ahead and choose a coadjutor, if either the welfare of his mission or the circumstances might require it?'[40] The cardinals, however, decided to postpone taking action on all three points, suggesting only that for the moment 'a letter be sent to the Reverend Colin urging him to send some missionaries temporarily [to Micronesia] in order to provide some assistance'. At the same time Cardinal Prefect Fransoni was instructed 'to begin negotiations with some religious community which might like to be placed in charge of this mission'.

Pro-Secretary Barnabò on 4 June brought these decisions to Pope Pius IX for approbation. The pope agreed that the division of the two vicariates of Melanesia and Micronesia should be postponed, but he considered it 'expedient that the designation of a coadjutor should not be delayed'. He therefore gave orders to have Bishop Collomb informed 'that he should designate for the Sacred Congregation a suitable person for that office as soon as possible'.[41]

The Evangelisation Congregation's decree of 13 June stated that His Holiness had granted Collomb's wishes and had authorised him 'to choose for himself—provided it be opportune or necessary—a coadjutor with episcopal rank, with a title *in partibus*, and with right of succession, picking from among his own missionaries one whom he judges most suitable for that office'.[42] According to a papal brief dated 23 June, Collomb's coadjutor was to be given the Titular See of Claudiopolis.[43]

With all official documents at hand Fransoni wrote Collomb on 30 June 1848, five months after receiving his two letters of 31 May 1847 addressed to himself and to the pope, and said: 'We were most happy to receive letters from Your Excellency a short while ago . . . and we cannot but highly commend Your Excellency's circumspect zeal . . .We also exhort you in the Lord to continue with vigour in making every effort at cultivating the vineyard entrusted to you.' This statement, he explained, had been dictated by Pope Pius IX himself, who had wanted it sent to Collomb in his own name 'along with testimony of his paternal benevolence toward Your Excellency'.

Fransoni explained also that the Sacred Congregation had first obtained Colin's views and then had maturely considered all the various aspects of Collomb's proposals. It had decided to postpone separating Micronesia from Melanesia temporarily, 'especially since . . . it is very difficult for your society to be able to take charge of the new Vicariate of Micronesia; nor do we have . . . another society of missionaries available to send there'. But after seeking and finding this kind of help, Fransoni promised, he would 'take action on the proposed division as soon as possible'. And in order that Micronesia might be prepared for this division, 'and that at least the light of faith may be brought to it, the Sacred Congregation has asked the president of your meritorious society to increase the number of Your Excellency's missionaries as much as he can'.

As for his wish to have a coadjutor, Fransoni strangely enough told Collomb that the cardinals had 'very gladly' supported his request 'and decided to refer this matter to the Holy Father and His Holiness gave his approval. . . .' Actually, the cardinals had voted to postpone granting Collomb a coadjutor and the pope had reversed their decision! With his letter Fransoni enclosed the pertinent papal brief.[44]

That same day, 30 June, Fransoni also wrote to Superior General Colin, repeating much the same information. The cardinals had postponed separating the Vicariates of Melanesia and Micronesia, he said, because of the difficulty at this time in finding a religious community to take over the Vicariate of Micronesia. But they would continue taking all necessary steps to make the division possible. 'If I should succeed in finding such a community for Micronesia,' he said, 'this community could not become capable of assuming charge of it and caring for it without the help and cooperation of Marist priests at least for some time.'

He asked Colin therefore to increase the number of missionaries assigned to Melanesia and to provide Collomb temporarily with some missionaries for Micronesia so that preparations could begin there 'for the requested division'. He also urged Colin to assure Collomb 'that the Sacred Congregation will make every effort to fulfil his wishes for the requested division as soon as it can'.

Explaining why Collomb was being given a coadjutor contrary to Colin's wishes, Fransoni said that Collomb's reasons 'appeared so strong that the Holy Father did not believe it possible to deny him in his circumstances the requested assistance'. He requested Colin to forward to Collomb the enclosed papal brief and letter, which he left open 'so that you can learn its contents'.[45]

After a lengthy absence Colin returned to his Lyon office and found Fransoni's letter of 30 June waiting for him. Hastily he acknowledged its receipt on 11 August 1848, assuring the cardinal that he was forwarding the enclosed letter and papal brief to Collomb at once.[46] But Collomb would never receive them, because by this date he was already dead.

30

New Caledonians put the Marists to flight

18 JULY 1847

When the *Spec* arrived at the Port Balade rendezvous in New Caledonia on 29 June 1847 with Bishop Collomb and Father Verguet aboard, the *Anonyme* of the Société française de l'Océanie was not there waiting for them. It had left Port Balade for Sydney on 26 May to purchase supplies for the New Caledonia Mission and there was no telling when it would return. Originally Collomb had intended to transfer all his food stores, lumber, equipment and other supplies to the *Anonyme* and then proceed without delay to San Cristóbal in his own Vicariate Apostolic of Melanesia.[1]

Unwilling to wait indefinitely for the *Anonyme* to return, Collomb urged Captain Burns of the *Spec* to name his price and take him and his cargo all the way to San Cristóbal in the southern Solomons. But the bishop's entreaties were to no avail because previous shipping engagements obliged the *Spec* to sail west to Batavia in the Dutch East Indies, instead of north to the Solomons. Collomb had no alternative but to unload his cargo and store it at Balade (or Baïaoup) Mission while waiting for the *Anonyme* to return. Over and above his own supplies he had brought along numerous items for the New Caledonia Mission and also packages for various individuals and trade goods for the Société française.[2]

In a whaleboat Collomb and Verguet went up the Baïaoup River a short distance to where Balade Mission was located. The bishop was impressed with the friendliness of the natives, especially when they spontaneously offered their services to unload the cargo from the *Spec* and transfer it to the mission station. Since the church was the largest building on the property, most of the goods were stored there.

Father Jérôme Grange (1807–52) was in charge of Balade Mission and when welcoming Collomb and Verguet warned them that they were arriving 'at a very critical time'. The surrounding natives had been short of food because of drought, had gone in search of it, and had returned very hostile to the mission. Grange explained that on 15 April a new mission had been founded at Poébo and Father Pierre Rougeyron (1817–1902) had gone there to supervise the construction of a new house. 'But I have reason to fear that by this time the savages there have pillaged us and perhaps massacred us', Grange said. Nor would his eight years of experience in Western Oceania allow him to interpret the slapping of their thighs by Baïaoup natives as an unadulterated expression of joy over the bishop's arrival. Again and again he warned Collomb and Verguet not to trust them. 'There is no doubt that they are joyful at seeing the bishop's provisions deposited on their island', he told Verguet. 'But they will not permit His Grace to take them away again to San Cristóbal.'

Poébo Mission, where Rougeyron was located, was being built on the flat top of a lone hill almost a league from the sea. Plans called for two small buildings with a large one in between. At this time one of the small ones was finished and Rougeyron was working on the large one. Learning of the arrival of Collomb and Verguet, he visited them at Balade Mission on 30 June. Rougeyron was in charge of missionary work in New Caledonia during Bishop Douarre's absence and planned to abandon Balade Mission in favour of Poébo Mission. Since this could be done only gradually, he instructed Father Grange to send all the livestock to Poébo, move into the warehouse the goods which at present were stored in the chapel, and then dismantle the chapel.

Brother Prosper, a carpenter by trade, and Brother Auguste, also based at Poébo, came to Balade Mission for a visit on 3 July. They reported that in their local tribal area someone had been killed and eaten on the previous day. Collomb noted this in his diary.

Then on 14 July, Aumérand, one of three crew members of the shipwrecked *Seine* employed at Poébo Mission, arrived with the youth Augustin to get the livestock. Angered at seeing their area gradually deserted, the Pouma natives that evening set fire to the grass and trees next to the mission gardens. What 'undoubtedly' prompted this, Collomb said, 'was their hearing about Father Rougeyron announcing in Poébo that he planned to abandon Balade soon'.

Rougeyron had sent along an invitation for Verguet to come for a visit and so he accompanied Aumérand and Augustin the next day, 15 July. Together they led the horses, cows and she-goats through the winding jungle paths to Poébo, where there were extensive fields suitable for grazing. In view of the unrest among the natives, and the forebodings of Father Grange, Bishop Collomb had feared that Verguet and the others might be maltreated en route by natives eager to steal the livestock. But after a four-hour walk the party reached Poébo without a mishap. 'The grass was so high', Verguet said, 'that we could see only the tips of the horns of our cows . . . And on meeting natives we could see only their heads above the grass. . . .' When Rougeyron heard about Grange's fears from Verguet, he attached no importance to them, saying that there were frequent rumours about attacks. Captain Raballand, for example, had informed the Fathers at Balade Mission on 23 May that he was told the natives were planning to pillage their mission and kill them as soon as his ship sailed out of port. But when his *Anonyme* set sail for Sydney on 26 May, nothing happened. Rougeyron said that according to a recent rumour the entire Pouma tribe at Port Balade would attack the mission immediately after the departure of the *Spec*. But he placed no faith in it whatsoever. If he had, Verguet said, 'we would have gone to Balade in order to unite all our forces there and so be able better to defend this principal establishment, which contained all our provisions. . . .'

In order to calm Collomb, Verguet sent him a message on 16 July, the day after his arrival in Poébo, reporting that they had run into no trouble en route.

He also asked whether he could stay there for a week. At the same time he passed on the rumour about the planned attack by the Pouma natives against Balade Mission, adding that Rougeyron gave it no credence whatever. Collomb answered on the same day, allowing Verguet to remain there a week, but urging him to be careful and to take no chances. He added that Captain Burns of the *Spec* would be coming ashore that evening to get their mail for posting in Batavia.[3]

Collomb's and Grange's fears were warranted because at 6 P.M. on 10 July some natives had stolen about 300 francs' worth of merchandise belonging to the Société française. And so it was with misgivings that they saw the *Spec* disappear over the horizon before noon on 17 July. That evening by way of precaution some items that could be stolen more easily were transferred from the church to the warehouse.

Also that same evening Antoine and Marie, a boy and a girl who helped the missionaries with chores around the house, warned them that they would be attacked on the following day. At this time there were seven Europeans residing at Balade Mission: Bishop Collomb, Father Grange, Brothers Blaise and Bertrand, Doctor Baudry, engaged in scientific research on the island and likewise serving as representative for the Société française de l'Océanie, a carpenter named Marie-Julien from *Arche d'Alliance*, and a Scotsman named George Taylor. 'We did not pay much attention to the words of these children', the missionaries said later in an official report. But Collomb did consider their warning important enough to mention in his diary.

The next day was Sunday, 18 July, and around 8 A.M. a sub-chief named Gomène visited the mission. He insisted that he wanted to be a friend and promised to come back that afternoon with all the goods stolen on 10 July, if the missionaries would enter friendship with him. They agreed and at one o'clock he returned armed with tomahawks. With him was the head chief Bouéone armed with a spear. They were accompanied by two children each carrying a package of stolen goods. Bouéone explained that the goods had been stolen without his knowledge and he invited the missionaries to come and get them. The missionaries were locked inside their house, which was built on high posts; the ground floor had not yet been enclosed.

Brother Blaise Marmoiton opened the trap door and went downstairs in spite of Father Grange's repeated warnings that it was a plot. Grange then followed, not wanting Blaise to be alone when exposing himself to danger. Gradually others also came out of the house. The parley was under way when suddenly a dozen natives armed with spears and tomahawks appeared as if from nowhere and came rushing headlong at the group through the ground floor area of the house. Although unarmed the Europeans shouted wildly and rushed the natives while Brother Bertrand dashed to the kitchen, where some guns were stored. He was so excited when loading his double-barrelled shotgun that he put two charges of gunpowder into one barrel. The gun went off like a cannon, putting the natives to flight, but seriously wounding his left hand. The missionaries and other Europeans scurried back upstairs into their house and locked the trap door. In the melee a spear had been driven into the lower left portion of Brother Blaise's chest, but he managed in spite of it to get back into the house.

When little Marie appeared on the scene, Father Grange quickly scribbled a note for Father Rougeyron about the attack and asked her to take it quickly to him at Poébo. On the way she was stopped by Chief Bouéone, who forced her to return to her village under pain of death. At three o'clock that afternoon she managed to get word to Father Grange about what had happened and warned him that the church filled with supplies would be set on fire. 'Almost immediately afterwards we noticed fire at the top of the thatched roof,' Bishop Collomb said, 'but it was impossible to save anything.' In his diary he noted simply: 'All my provisions were sacrificed!' That same evening both Antoine and Marie brought word to Father Grange that on the following day the head chief would pillage the mission and massacre its personnel assisted by warriors from all villages within his tribe.

On Monday, 19 July, no one dared to leave the house, not even for food. At daybreak all had noticed that their whaleboats in the harbour, salvaged from the shipwrecked *Seine*, were burning. 'Thinking this was the last day of our lives,' they wrote in their official report, 'we all made our confessions. . . .' They also received Holy Communion and Bishop Collomb consumed the remaining particles. Taylor, the Scotsman, had been taking religious instructions from Father Grange and made his confession after being baptised conditionally.

'Numbers of natives arrived from every side totalling about 250,' Collomb said, 'and the attack began at about one o'clock [in the afternoon].' There was a high fence around the house and the natives, who were daubed in black and crying out ferociously, hid behind it or behind nearby boulders. They began throwing rocks at the house trying to pierce the wooden walls. No one in the house could reach them, however, because they did not dare enter the yard.

It was 2.30 and the natives were getting tired from their stubborn fighting when one of their chiefs from the other side of Baïaoup River cried out that someone should set the house on fire. Two natives holding flaming torches scaled the fence and ran toward the house; a gunshot in their direction failed to put them to flight. They ran directly to the carpenter shop below the house and in a moment the heaps of woodshavings scattered over the floor were ablaze. Underneath his feet Bishop Collomb could see the flames licking the posts supporting the house.

The dilemma was frightening! 'To remain inside would be to perish in the flames; to go outside would be to fall under the blows of the savages.' All assembled in the house chapel once again and even Brother Blaise left his bed and dragged himself there as best he could. Although smoke was now pouring into the tiny chapel, he was calm and had a smile on his face. 'I come here to await the final blow', he said. Father Grange gave Bishop Collomb general absolution and the plenary indulgence at the hour of death; then all got down on their knees before the bishop and he did the same for them. Collomb and Grange each vowed to celebrate 100 Masses in thanksgiving to Almighty God, if they should be delivered from this predicament. 'All of us then embraced one another and said our adieus till heaven, where we expected to meet after a few moments.'

Then someone in the besieged group suggested that they might still have a chance of saving their lives, if they abandoned their property and house for pillaging. Grange went to a window and addressed the furious mob, saying that the key to the storehouse would be handed over on condition that the fire be extinguished and their lives be spared. Chiefs Oundo and Gomène both agreed to this and had the fire underneath the house extinguished. Oundo then made a sign for Grange to come down. He was still by the window talking with the chief when a spear grazed his skin and left an ugly wound. Doctor Baudry, the agent for Société française, then tossed the key through the window. The crowd fought for it and dashed off toward the warehouse.

Since the natives were momentarily distracted, Grange opened the trap door and went down first. While he was talking with Chief Oundo, Bishop Collomb and Brother Bertrand ran toward the woods and were quickly followed by Doctor Baudry, Marie-Julien and George Taylor. Two natives, having seen Collomb and Bertrand escape, advanced toward them menacingly with drawn spears. At that moment Baudry came on the scene and pointed his gun at them while Marie-Julien and Taylor both fired a shot, scaring them off. Grange followed on the run, chased by natives throwing rocks. His spear wound caused him severe pain, making him fall twice, but he was able to get up again.

When the fleeing party stopped to take a count, they noticed that Brother Blaise was missing. Collomb wondered what to do and all said that it would be impossible for Blaise to follow them to Poébo. And carrying him would certainly expose everyone to danger of death. Besides, all were convinced that the natives would be satisfied with the booty and would spare Blaise's life, especially since Grange had bargained for this and had recommended him to Chief Oundo's special care. With all haste the six continued on their way to Poébo. Collomb complained of dizziness and cramps and both he and Grange repeatedly fell exhausted to the ground. They had not eaten for two days.

On their way they passed through Diréoné and learned from Michel, the catechist there, that the Baïaoup natives had spread orders everywhere to massacre them. While the group rested, Michel sent word to Father Rougeyron at Poébo about the catastrophe and he in turn immediately sent Louis, another catechist, who with Moeaou served as guide for the remainder of the journey. On learning how famished all were, Louis suggested that they hide in the grass while he go off to find some food. But they were fearful and insisted that he must not leave them for a single moment. At eight o'clock that evening they finally reached Poébo and were so weak that they could hardly stand. Both Collomb and Baudry had lost their shoes in the mud.

Early the next day, 20 July, Louis, the catechist, and another mission friend, Augustin, went to Balade Mission to learn how Brother Blaise had fared. When Louis returned, he sadly reported that Brother Blaise had been killed. With the point of the lance still in his breast, he had tried to follow the others to Poébo, but fell to the ground some steps from the house. Antoine and Marie, the two ever faithful children, seeing him lying there, rushed to comfort him and prayed at his side. When the pillaging at the warehouse was finished, some natives came across the dying Brother. With their clubs they beat him unconscious, stripped him of his clothing, and proudly walked off with this new booty. On regaining consciousness and finding himself stark naked, Blaise plucked handfuls of grass and sprinkled it over himself. Then two other warriors came by with a hatchet and cut off his head. Blaise's dead body was treated heinously while the two children prayed nearby. That evening Marie prepared a shallow grave and silently buried the thirty-five-year-old Brother.

Poébo Mission had nearly doubled in size with the arrival of the six refugees from Balade Mission on 19 July. Already living at Poébo were Fathers Rougeyron and Verguet and Brothers Prosper and Auguste, besides three crew members of the *Seine* now employed by the mission. On 20 July the missionaries held a conference and unanimously agreed that their position in New Caledonia was untenable. But how leave the island? Thinking that they could be saved by one of the English ships that periodically came to Ienguène to barter for sandalwood, they sent Brother Auguste and Aumérand to see if a ship happened to be there. But they found none.

Meanwhile the Poébo area natives, envious of the Pouma tribe's recently acquired wealth, began planning an attack on Poébo Mission. The thirteen Europeans on the premises could not help but notice the warlike preparations and began keeping watch day and night, in order not to be caught off guard. They had food enough for a month and expected the *Anonyme* to arrive within a matter of days.[4]

'We encircled ourselves with embankments made of rocks and the natives were not to go beyond that limit', Verguet said. 'We also placed wooden sentry boxes at the four corners and mounted guards there, each one taking his turn. And we converted the two houses into fortresses as best we could . . . Our extreme danger forced us to lead a soldier's life and we never appeared at the threshold without being heavily armed. . . .'

In spite of all this 'the natives became bolder day by day and we could see them holding meetings at the foot of the hill on which we were located . . . To break up their meetings we ordinarily had to do nothing else but let our two large dogs from Newfoundland attack the natives. Since New Caledonians fear only what can hurt them, they dreaded these dogs more than all the missionaries combined . . . And the male dog was so big that he could knock down a man by jumping at him. When we released the dogs, the natives climbed to safety in the trees.'[5]

Father Rougeyron had his own ideas about missionary work and told Bishop Collomb that he would gladly remain in New Caledonia after the others had left. In order to succeed among the natives, he said, it was necessary to go native, 'adopting their manner of life entirely, sleeping like they do, eating like they do, and wearing no clothing except the most indispensable'. Rougeyron spoke 'with great conviction', Verguet said, 'and we did not doubt his sincerity. But we found his ideas more beautiful in theory than in practice, and we could not agree with him.'[6]

Three full weeks of anxious waiting passed and the *Anonyme* still did not appear. Meanwhile the provisions at Poébo Mission were diminishing and the natives were becoming more hostile and more prone to attack each day. Then on Monday morning, 9 August 1847, as everyone was having breakfast, there were excited shouts that a ship was coming. All looked out, but saw nothing, and believed they were being deceived by the natives once again. But catechist Louis ran to the top of a high hill and returned bubbling with glee, assuring the missionaries that a ship was in sight and that it was coming toward shore. They quickly set to work penning letters in both French and English, not knowing whether the ship was French or English. They wanted the captain to receive word as surely and quickly as possible about their precarious situation. As the ship came closer they could see that it was a three-masted vessel, but it sailed right by Poébo and headed for Port Balade.

That evening under cover of darkness Aumérand and Bocherel, two sailors from the shipwrecked *Seine*, and Marie-Julien, the *Arche d'Alliance* carpenter, worked their way to the coast and on a rickety whaleboat belonging to a friendly chief rowed with him to Port Balade to deliver the urgent letters and ask for help. At 11 P.M. they reached the vessel and were overjoyed to learn that it was the *Brillante*, a French sloop of war under Commandant (or Captain) Eugène Dubouzet, who had received orders from the French government to accompany Bishop Collomb as far as San Cristóbal and, if he so wished, even farther north to Santa Isabel Island.

The missionaries at Poébo on the morning of 10 August saw three boats filled with men coming toward them from the direction of Port Balade; they were also able to distinguish the French flag. But a strong contrary wind was blowing and it was nightfall by the time the three boats reached Poébo River. Lieutenant Le Fer de la Motte was in command and, as instructed by Dubouzet, sent ashore thirty well-armed men led by Officer Fournier and two pupils of the mission school. With them was Father Gilbert Roudaire (1813–52), who had come aboard the *Brillante* to take up work at the New Caledonia mission. Their torchlight procession began winding its way from the coast toward Poébo Mission, while others stayed behind to man the heavily armed boats.

Fournier gave Collomb a letter from Dubouzet, inviting the bishop to come aboard his ship at once to decide on what measures should be taken to save those on shore. Bishop Collomb and Father Grange almost immediately left with Fournier and his men for the coast and the three armed boats brought them to Port Balade. 'It was four o'clock in the morning when we arrived aboard the corvette', Collomb said. 'Monsieur Commandant du Bouzet [read Dubouzet] received us very cordially and, after taking some light refreshments, we told him our experiences. It was decided that the corvette should go to Poébo at once and we set sail at eight o'clock.'

But there was little wind that day and it was evening before the *Brillante* was opposite Poébo. And so not until nine o'clock the next morning, 12 August, was the vessel able to enter the roadstead. Dubouzet immediately sent ashore a company of about thirty men led by Lieutenant Le Fer de la Motte, with orders to go to the mission station; Bishop Collomb and Father Grange were in this landing party. The whaleboats that took them ashore were again armed for war and some fifteen additional men stayed behind and guarded them. On arriving at Poébo Mission, Collomb immediately held a conference with the four Marist priests (Rougeyron, Grange, Verguet and Roudaire) and once again all agreed that their position in New Caledonia was untenable, at least for the moment. They decided not to burn down their house, believing that the natives would then pillage it immediately after their departure and thus be distracted from attacking them. And they decided to take aboard all their domestic animals as well as the many sacred vessels and other goods that had been salvaged.

Losing no time Brother Auguste prepared the livestock for immediate embarkation and he with the help of some local boys friendly to the mission led the animals to the coast. En route they were guarded and there was no opposition from natives in the vicinity. At Collomb's request, however, Le Fer de la Motte had left behind seven of his men to keep watch at the mission station, since the boys had reported that the mission would be attacked that night. This left the missionaries and others free to pack their belongings for embarking on the following day.

It began to rain that night and this turned out to be a mixed blessing. It dispelled the natives, who never fought in the rain, and at the same time it made the paths slippery along which the cargo had to be carried the next morning. It was still raining at dawn and no one departed from the *Brillante*. 'But finally we saw many men leaving the corvette', Verguet said, 'and one hour later the disembarking party arrived at the mission. . . .' It was Friday, 13 August, and Collomb noted in his diary that the rescued and rescuers numbered ninety men, of whom eighty-four were armed.

The arduous trek to the coast and to freedom had hardly begun, 'when a group of savages scaled the barrier and began to pillage the house', Verguet said. Others were in hiding en route, waiting to ambush the long column of marching men. Catechist Louis suspected this and suggested an alternative route. It was taken, but the natives attacked nevertheless and five sailors were wounded. One native was shot in the foot and another died from a bayonet wound in the chest. The *Brillante*'s twenty-four cannon 'had trouble enough protecting our retreat and bringing us aboard safe and sound', Verguet said. Once aboard the missionaries found the officers most generous and ready to share their cabins and their possessions.

On the following day, Saturday, Dubouzet sent a punitive expedition ashore to search out and punish the responsible Poébo natives, but they had all fled. In retaliation the sailors burned down some grass houses and cut down some coconut trees near shore. On Sunday, 15 August, Feast of the Assumption of the Blessed Virgin Mary, Collomb and the rest officially gave their thanks to Commandant Dubouzet and his crew for having rescued them and were treated to a festive meal. On Monday about eleven o'clock 'we had the consolation of seeing the brig *Anonyme* arrive . . .', Collomb said. 'Thanks to a strong wind it needed only 12 days to make the voyage from Sydney.' On Tuesday, 17 August, with the help of Dr Baudry and Fathers Rougeyron, Grange and Verguet, Collomb wrote an official report on what had taken place at Port Balade and Poébo.[7]

Collomb now had two ships at his disposal, the *Brillante* and the *Anonyme*, and had to decide whether to accept the offer of the French Navy or of the Société française. 'After consulting with the Fathers', he wrote in his diary on 18 August, 'I decided to be satisfied with the *Anonyme* and let the *Brillante* go to Sydney via Aneityum.' Aneityum, the southernmost island in New Hebrides, was a centre for whalers and ships engaged in the sandalwood trade. Collomb indicated the reasons for his decision: 'On the one hand I am obliged to transfer at least part of our personnel to another island as soon as possible, in view of the climate at Makira and in view of the state of health of the Fathers and Brothers at the time I left San Cristóbal. And because of the good reports given to me about Woodlark and also because of arrangements made with M. Marceau [to meet me there], it is there that I must hasten to go.' Dubouzet, however, had told Collomb that it was impossible for him to go as far as Woodlark, so this ruled out his ship.

'On the other hand', Collomb added, 'it is necessary that either the brig [*Anonyme*] or the corvette [*Brillante*] should bring news to Aneityum about what has happened to us for the information of captains who may want to come to Balade. . . .' (Collomb was thinking in particular of Auguste Marceau, captain of *Arche d'Alliance*, who had written Father Rougeyron from Sydney that he planned to visit Balade on his return trip from the islands of Central Oceania.) 'Therefore it is necessary that I take the brig placed at my disposal by M. Marceau, by which our mission is able to make very great advances. I informed M. Commandant du Bouzet [read Dubouzet] in writing about the decision which I had made and I also dispensed him from going to San Cristóbal or even as far as [Santa] Isabel, if I should so require, an order that he had received from the government.'

On 19 August both the *Brillante* and the *Anonyme* sailed to Port Balade. That evening Catechist Michel came aboard and shed so many tears that he was hardly able to speak. He was 'pained at seeing the missionaries leave', Collomb said, 'and promised that he himself would baptise babies in danger of death and also other people who might be well disposed. . . .'

The missionaries heard rumours aboard ship on 20 August that a punitive expedition against the Pouma natives at Port Balade was to take place on the following day, Saturday. 'I wrote a letter which was signed also by Fathers Rougeyron, Grange and Verguet,' Collomb said, 'in which we declared ourselves completely dissociated from every aspect of this act of vengeance against the people who did us evil either at Baino [also Baïaoup] or at Poébo.' Dubouzet answered officially that it was not at all the interests of the Catholic mission that were prompting him to be severe with the guilty. It was rather a question of meting out punishment for violating sacred promises made to a ship of war, for violating human rights in the case of French subjects, for violating the interests of the Société française, and for stealing property belonging to the French government. The punitive expedition did go ashore on Saturday and was led by Dubouzet himself. The natives kept out of range and Dubouzet gave orders that none were to be killed. Their gardens were destroyed, however, eighteen coconut trees were cut down, and some thirty houses were burned.[8]

Bishop Collomb had been detained in New Caledonia seven full weeks waiting for the *Anonyme* to return. Writing to Superior General Colin from the *Brillante*, he said that 'the extraordinary delays in entering the mission entrusted to my care' were not the only tests given him by God. 'In addition I have all of a sudden lost all my provisions, the lumber and other supplies which I had bought in Sydney for my dear colleagues in San Cristóbal and for the two foundations which I had intended to start. . . .' He enclosed both his diary and his official report on what had happened in New Caledonia for both Colin and the presidents of the two Central Councils of the Association for the Propagation of the Faith in Lyon and Paris. From these two documents, he said, they would be able to see why the New Caledonia missionaries were being forced to withdraw, 'at least temporarily', and they would also see what enormous losses his own mission of Melanesia had suffered.

After praising Commandant Dubouzet highly for his rescue operation, Collomb told Colin that he would be leaving for San Cristóbal in a day or two. And should the missionaries based there want to remain, he would take away some of them nevertheless and open a second mission at Woodlark or elsewhere. Further, experience had shown that he could not rely upon the ships of the Société française for the necessary transportation and protection; he had therefore written to the French consul at Sydney, to Governor Charles-François Lavaud at Tahiti and to Admiral Tromelin at Valparaíso, informing each of them where he could be found, in case they might wish to have a warship visit him and his missionaries. (Lavaud, formerly captain of the *Aube*, had been named on 6 September 1846 governor of the so-called Etablissements français de l'Océanie and Commissioner of the King for the Society Islands.) 'Above all else', Collomb explained to Colin, 'it is the dangers to which we shall be exposed that have prompted me—in spite of my earlier repugnance to do so—to request a visit by a ship of state.'[9]

Collomb also wrote that same day, 21 August, to Father Victor Poupinel, Marist procurator general in Lyon: 'My estimate of the actual losses that we suffered last 18 and 19 July is 20,000 francs. . . .'[10]

To help the *Anonyme* prepare for its long voyage, the *Brillante* surrendered an anchor, a chain, a piece of sail, and other nautical supplies, and food enough for twelve persons aboard for six months. Collomb believed the staff in his mission, including himself, totalled thirteen, and so he also purchased food enough for that number of people for six months. And from Father Rougeyron he bought various supplies that had just arrived with the *Anonyme* for the New Caledonia Mission, now being abandoned.[11]

As for personnel, the New Caledonia missionaries had decided to return with the *Brillante* to Sydney, its destination, and there await further orders from Bishop Douarre, expected back from Europe soon. Father Verguet, who had changed his mind many times and was still with Bishop Collomb, informed the bishop on 21 August that he would not be travelling with him to San Cristóbal, but would go to Sydney with the others. He had had his fill of Melanesia and was determined to return to France, quit the Marists, and become a diocesan priest. Father Roudaire, who had just arrived aboard the *Brillante* for the New Caledonia Mission, also went to Sydney.

Collomb as newly ordained bishop would be entering his Vicariate Apostolic of Melanesia alone.[12]

On Sunday, 22 August, after bidding adieu to the *Brillante*'s five sailors wounded in the rescue effort, Collomb transferred to the *Anonyme*, accompanied by Commandant Dubouzet and Fathers Rougeyron, Grange and Verguet, who then took leave of him. Two hours later—it was about three o'clock in the afternoon—first the *Brillante* and then the *Anonyme* left Port Balade under a favourable wind, the one sailing east and the other north-northeast.[13]

Seven years later in the safety and comfort of his residence at Carcassonne in southern France, Father Verguet spelled out the dilemma in which a missionary coming to a primitive area finds himself. 'If he arrives in the mission without bringing supplies, he will die from hunger and misery', he wrote. 'But if he should come with provisions, these arouse the cupidity of the natives, who then will attack him, steal these goods from him and kill him . . . Mission work, therefore, is very difficult and perilous in these barbaric countries.'[14]

31

Collomb dies on Rooke Island

16 JULY 1848

It was Sunday, 22 August 1847, when Bishop Collomb left Port Balade in New Caledonia aboard the *Anonyme* and sailed north-northeast toward San Cristóbal in the Solomon Islands, the only island with missionaries in his vast double vicariate. He arrived there at noon on Saturday, 28 August, after an absence of six full months. A contrary wind made it impossible for Captain Raballand to enter Port Sainte-Marie and so he dropped anchor offshore. When large numbers of native canoes did not immediately come out to greet the ship, as was customary in these islands, Raballand and the bishop both became alarmed. Eventually two or three light canoes did come toward the ship and Collomb gave the occupants a letter or two for the priests at Makira Mission. But later he learned that the letters were never delivered.

After dusk a lone canoe made its way to the *Anonyme*. The occupant had a letter for Collomb filled with bad news from Father Jean-Pierre Frémont. It told how three missionaries had suffered violent deaths at the hands of the natives and how a fourth had died peacefully in bed. 'We cannot come out to you', the letter said, 'because our whaleboats are no longer in serviceable condition.'

That night Collomb asked the *Anonyme* sailors one by one to accompany him ashore the next day to rescue the remaining missionaries. The five who volunteered went to confession, fearing that they might be killed.

On Sunday, 29 August, the *Anonyme* was able to enter Port Sainte-Marie and around noon Collomb and the five sailors went ashore. There was no glorious reception for the new bishop. 'I gave my blessing to my dear surviving missionaries,' he said, 'visited the Blessed Sacrament, said a prayer before the images of the Blessed Virgin and Saint Joseph, and prayed the De Profundis at the grave of Father Crey. This was the extent of my welcome ceremony.' Father Cyprien Crey had come from France with Collomb aboard *Arche d'Alliance* and had been assigned to San Cristóbal in mid-February 1847. On 15 March, a month after reaching his mission and a month before his twenty-fourth birthday, he had died from fever.

The three missionaries who suffered violent deaths were Father Jean-Marie Paget, Father Claude Jacquet and Brother Hyacinthe Chatelet. About a month after Crey's death they had set out for Wango Village on San Cristóbal's north coast to investigate the advisability of opening a residential station there. En route they passed through the territory of the Toro tribe, where they were given a friendly reception on 20 April. But on reaching a tiny cluster of huts they were quickly surrounded by warriors and could neither flee nor defend themselves. There was a loud cry and the attack began. A spear was driven through thirty-year-old Father Paget's breast, killing him on the spot. Father Jacquet was killed by a hatchet blow on the head. It was he who sixteen months earlier had conducted the obsequies aboard the *Marian Watson* for Bishop Epalle, who had also been killed by hatchet blows to the head. A spear was thrown at Brother Hyacinthe, but only grazed his skin; then he was killed with the same hatchet used to kill Jacquet. All three bodies were left lying in pools of their own blood, were then carted away and were never seen again. According to a rumour that reached Makira Mission, their flesh was eaten at a cannibalistic feast.

Collomb recounted for the San Cristóbal missionaries what had happened in New Caledonia and this greatly disturbed them. 'But it seemed to me', he said, 'that the losses which I suffered in New Caledonia and the dangers which I encountered, were nothing but simple tests that God wanted to use to prepare me for the much greater sacrifices to be encountered on my arrival in Melanesia.'

From the very day of his arrival at San Cristóbal, Collomb said, 'we deliberated whether we should stay there. Since the matter was so important, we reflected on it for three or four days and prayed God to enlighten us.'[1] The San Cristóbal missionaries told him that their lives were in constant danger ever since their three colleagues had been killed on 20 April. No place on the island seemed safe and they had to keep vigil day and night against possible attacks. They had been a target for arrows and once the roof of their house had been set on fire.[2] 'Our conclusion was that we could not remain on the island any longer', Collomb said, 'without exposing ourselves to almost certain massacre.'

His decision to leave San Cristóbal saddened him and he wondered whether this was equivalent to pronouncing 'a sentence of eternal damnation' against the inhabitants of that island. 'However, we do hope that this retreat will be only momentary,' he said, 'and that our unfortunately large number of victims, who have been sacrificed in the Solomons, will draw down upon that archipelago after a short while the grace of salvation.'[3]

By this time Collomb's staff was reduced to three priests and three Brothers. Before leaving San Cristóbal he provisionally gave the title 'Pro-Vicar of Melanesia and Micronesia' on 1 September to thirty-seven-year-old Father Jean-Pierre Frémont and to twenty-six-old Father Jean-Xavier Montrouzier. Usually a bishop names only one pro-vicar; then should the bishop die or become incapacitated, the pro-vicar immediately takes charge of the mission until further notice. In view of the deadly climate and the murderous natives, Collomb may have wanted two pro-vicars in order to be doubly sure that at least one of them would survive him.

The next day, 2 September, Collomb wrote in his diary that the decision was definitive: they would give up San Cristóbal (after being there twenty months) and leave for Woodlark (or Murua) Island. About eight o'clock on Friday morning, 3 September 1847, the *Anonyme* with the entire mission staff and all supplies aboard left Port Sainte-Marie.[4] 'We sailed toward the west in search of the Woodlark Islands,' Collomb wrote back to France, 'about which I had been given favourable reports in Sydney.'[5]

By this time Collomb had heard a disquieting rumor, which he apparently discounted. It said that Woodlark natives within the past two years had massacred a shipwrecked crew of fifteen.[6] A news story on this incident was carried in the 9 May 1846 issue of the *Salem Observer* of Salem, Massachusetts. The author, who said he was the sole survivor, maintained that twenty-eight (not only fifteen) of the crew of the British ship *Mary* 'were horribly massacred by the natives of Woodlark islands'.[7]

Collomb said it was 15 September, 'the Octave of the Nativity of Mary, [when] we entered a beautiful and excellent port'. It was on the southern coast of Woodlark and was called Guasopa by the local people. In gratitude to the Virgin Mary and in honour of her recent feast the missionaries called it Port of the Nativity. They spent the first few days examining the coast and discovered four main villages as well as many others of less importance. He chose Dabalouaou Village for his residence since it was the largest and 'in the midst of all the others'.

After the bishop gave presents to the chief on Saturday, 18 September, in exchange for a piece of land, the villagers built two houses on them in their own style, finishing each in less than a day. According to Collomb, the two huts were 'the most miserable that you can imagine. Never have I seen houses anywhere that were poorer than these of Woodlark. They are simply shelters made of leaves and are so badly constructed that they protect you against nothing but the heat of the sun.' The missionaries called their two huts Our Lady of Seven Sorrows Mission.

Writing three months later (21 December 1847) Collomb had to admit that fever was troubling them as much in Woodlark as it had at San Cristóbal. Frémont had fever habitually, Montrouzier suffered from it very often, and all the others had had attacks of fever, but they were not very serious. 'I, too, pay my tribute to the climate', Collomb said.

Reporting on these matters to the directors of the Association for the Propagation of the Faith in France, Collomb said that he hoped 'this picture of annihilation, to which our mission has been reduced after two years of effort', would not discourage them, especially in view of the fact that so many funds and so many men had been poured into the mission. There must be no let up of zeal anywhere, he said, because now his missionaries were becoming acclimatised and the Melanesians were becoming more gentle. 'I have resolved with the grace of God to sacrifice myself, if necessary, for the salvation of the innumerable peoples entrusted to me', he said. 'The more unworthy they seem of the happiness that we have come to bring them, the greater must be our solicitude for them and the livelier our zeal. . . .'[8]

To make sure that he gave his missionaries a good example in studying the local language, Collomb learned ten new words a day and each day reviewed with one of his priests what he had already learned. And so that no child would die without baptism, he divided the island into districts and assigned one to each

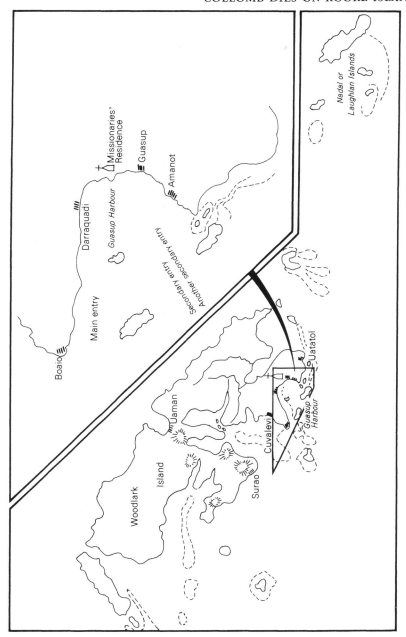

63   The Marist missionaries arrived at Woodlark (or Murua) Island on 15 September 1847 and chose Guasup (nowadays Guasopa) Harbour for their headquarters. They named the harbour Port of the Nativity, because they arrived on the octave of the feast of the Nativity of the Blessed Virgin Mary. The original maps with Italian inscriptions were drawn by Reverend Angelo Ambrosoli of the Seminary for Foreign Missions of Lombardy. *Source: Fig. opp. p. 304 in: Beatificationis ... Ioannis Baptistae Mazzucconi ... positio.... (Chapters 29, 30, 31, 35).*

of his priests. 'My principal devotion will be to follow the holy canons, to observe the rubrics, and to give to worship that dignity which the Church requests', he said. 'We shall do everything, absolutely everything, as in Rome.'[9]

Collomb, who had three priests, needed one more to open a second main station, because a Marist rule called for a minimum of two priests at a mission. That priest was thirty-five-year-old Father Gregoire Villien, who was en route to Collomb's mission aboard *Arche d'Alliance*. The ship left Rotuma Island north of Fiji on 6 January 1848 and headed for San Cristóbal, since Commandant Marceau thought that Collomb was still there. On arrival he learned of the transfer to Woodlark, so he set sail for that island with Villien. But en route a tropical cyclone severely damaged his ship and almost sank it. Marceau gave up trying to reach Woodlark and sailed to Sydney instead, arriving there on 6 March. Here Villien found the *Anonyme*, which had returned to Sydney after transferring Collomb and his missionaries from San Cristóbal to Woodlark.[10]

Advising Superior General Colin of his movements on 2 April 1848, Villien said that he would be leaving Sydney aboard the *Anonyme* on 11 April, if at that time the winds were satisfactory. By the end of April he expected to be in Woodlark. 'The brig will remain in the service of Bishop Collomb for some months yet', he said. 'With its help he will then be able to visit some of those islands in his vast vicariate, which seem to him more advantageous for the mission. . . .'[11]

Father Villien landed at Woodlark (called Moin by the missionaries) on 25 April 1848, the Tuesday after Easter. That same day Bishop Collomb and Father Frémont discussed the qualities of all mission personnel and decided to open a second mission station. Calling the four priests and three Brothers to his room, Collomb announced that Frémont would be in charge of the new mission as prefect apostolic. His two companions were to be Villien and twenty-seven-year-old Brother Optat Bergillon, a gardener by trade. The others would continue at Woodlark Misison: Montrouzier as prefect apostolic, Father Thomassin as treasurer, and Brothers Genade and Aristide.

Before the day was over Collomb wrote in his diary: 'I also have each Father's approval for a plan, which I have conceived.' His plan was to visit first of all the shores of Woodlark Island, 'then to have a look at the Mussim Islands, and after that to search for Rooke [now Umboi] Island or some other island near New Guinea in order to make our new foundation there'. He wanted to follow this up with 'a look at the coasts of New Britain, New Ireland, etc., then pay a visit to Fathers Frémont and Villien, and return finally to Moin [i.e., Woodlark], or at least to send the brig back there'. Collomb and his men also wanted to pick out en route the best place for founding a third mission station, since they expected the *Stella del Mare*, chartered by the Société française de l'Océanie, to arrive soon with new personnel.[12] (It had sailed from Marseille with fourteen Marist missionaries aboard, most of them for Bishop Douarre's mission, on 23 October 1847.)

Before Villien's arrival the Woodlark missionaries had already done intensive language study, had begun work on a catechism, and had baptised many infants and adults in danger of death.[13]

Numerous supplies had to be brought aboard the *Anonyme* for founding the new mission. Finally on 9 May a favourable wind pushed the *Anonyme* away from Woodlark. Much tacking was necessary in order to reach the Mussim Islands, where the ship arrived on the following day. During this first day at sea Frémont, Villien and Optat were all seasick and Collomb was sick with fever. On 11 May they saw very high mountains, which they thought were the D'Entrecasteaux Islands or the Louisiade Archipelago. And lying before them were the Trobriand Islands.

Then on 12 May, Collomb was sick again all day with fever and stomach trouble.

A magnificent view greeted the missionaries at five o'clock in the morning on Saturday, 13 May. Directly ahead of them was Rooke (or Umboi) Island with an active volcano to the east of it on Ritter (or Kulkul) Island and the larger Tupinier (or Sakar) Island behind the volcano. To the right was New Britain, clearly discernible, and to the left the towering white mountains of New Guinea. After sailing past the small Siassi Islands surrounded by dangerous reefs, the *Anonyme* at midday reached the east coast of Rooke and sailed along it. Collomb noted in his diary that the nearby mountains of New Britain, 'the gigantic mountains and imposing aspect of New Guinea' to the southwest, and sloping Rooke Island with its columns of smoke were 'a magnificent sight to behold'.[14]

The *Anonyme* reached Cape King on the northwestern coast of Rooke Island on Monday, 15 May. Here Captain Raballand found a small port which appeared ideal. And very close to the anchorage was a large village called Nurua[15] with 400 or 500 people. Captain Raballand and Bishop Collomb along with two sailors boarded a whaleboat to examine the anchorage more closely and found it ideal under every aspect. As they paddled about, nearly a hundred men curiously watched their every move from shore. Collomb noted that no women or children were among them, and no young men under twenty.

Since Raballand and Collomb judged the place ideal for anchorage and for a mission station, they rowed toward the men on shore. At first the men seemed filled with distrust and anxiety and tried to make their visitors understand that there was no need for them to come ashore. But when Raballand reached out pieces of iron as presents, the men tried en masse to jump into the whaleboat, Collomb said, 'giving us coconuts, yams and taros'. The bishop told the villagers that, after sailing completely around their island, he would like to return and make a settlement in their midst. This seemed to please them. 'We gave the name Saint Isidore to both the village and the port', Collomb wrote in his diary that day. Father Villien later explained to his cousin in Europe that the name 'Saint Isidore' was used 'because he was the saint whose feast we celebrated on the day of our arrival, 15 May 1848'.[16] Nowadays Port Saint Isidore is known as Luther Anchorage.

Sailing counter-clockwise around Rooke Island the *Anonyme* on 16 May approached within eleven kilometres of the New Guinea coast. 'It is a very

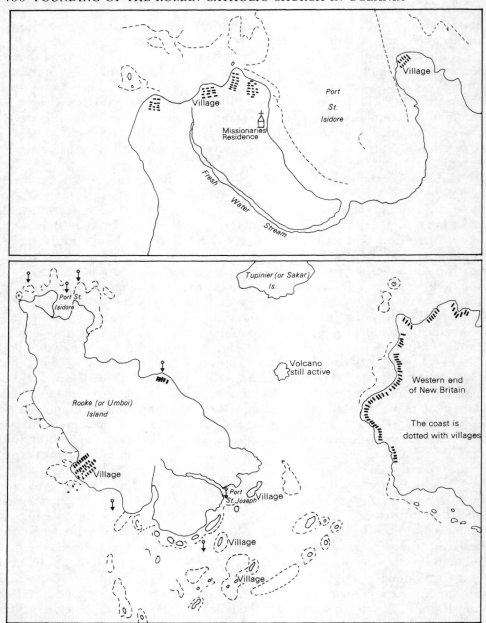

64 The Marist missionaries on 13 May 1848 sighted Rooke (or Umboi) Island situated between New Guinea and New Britain. On 15 May they reached an excellent harbour at the northwest corner of the island, which they called Port Saint Isidore. They decided to establish their headquarters there in the immediate vicinity of Nurua village just as at Woodlark they had made their foundation in the immediate vicinity of Dabalouaou village. The original maps with Italian inscriptions were drawn by Reverend Angelo Ambrosoli of the Seminary for Foreign Missions of Lombardy. *Source: Fig. opp. p. 176 in: Beatificationis ... Ioannis ... Baptistae Mazzucconi ... positio. ... (Chapter 31).*

beautiful land', Collomb noted, 'and the tops of its mountains are hidden in clouds.'

Collomb's choice of Port Saint Isidore was not final. On Thursday, 18 May, he asked Fathers Frémont and Villien what their wishes were regarding a location. Frémont preferred Port Saint Isidore, but Villien, 'because of what he had read in Malte-Brun', Collomb said, preferred the Schouten Islands.[17] When Collomb asked Raballand what he thought about the Schouten Islands as a location, the captain said that he would go anywhere the bishop wanted him to go. But his 74-ton brig would be badly swamped by strong winds making that voyage, he said.

When Collomb asked about the New Britain mainland, Raballand hesitated, stating that his ship was not armed well enough for sending his crew to the mainland where they would be 'in the midst of a thousand savages'. His own suggestion was that Collomb would do best by making his foundation on a small island. 'You can learn the language there', he said, 'and you will be able to train your catechists there. In two years' time a ship can transport your house to the mainland, and meanwhile you can easily make excursions there.'

By 22 May a decision had not yet been reached, so Captain Raballand told the missionaries that they could hardly find a better place than Port Saint Isidore. Collomb waited until Sunday, 28 May, and then told Frémont and Villien that he considered Port Saint Isidore a suitable spot for founding their mission station. That same day he engaged some members of the crew to make preparations for going ashore to build a house.

Bishop Collomb went ashore on 30 May with Captain Raballand and Father Villien to begin negotiating with the people of Nurua Village. Father Frémont was sick again that day and stayed aboard ship. 'I took neither pistol nor sabre', Collomb said, 'but the captain hid some weapons under his shirt in case of attack . . . It was his own idea. I carried no arms, fearing that if I did, the natives would not let us remain . . . They received us in a friendly manner and gave us hot sweet potatoes . . . and also water in bamboo containers. We believe that Alukam is the chief.'

Construction work on the house stretched over the entire month of June. Collomb went ashore each day with the three or four sailors who were doing the building. He noted in his diary on 2 July that work on the house was still under way and that he himself was suffering from 'very great fatigue'. It was the last entry that he made in his diary.[18] Finally on Thursday, 6 July, the missionaries were able to move into their new house. But by this time Collomb's condition had worsened, and he was suffering very much from fever contracted in Woodlark and from a very severe stomach disorder. 'These continual and acute sufferings together with the solicitude inherent in his new office have exhausted him', Villien wrote on 10 July, 'and we fear that very soon we shall likely be deprived of his wisdom and charity.' Frémont was also suffering from constant fever, Villien said, 'and he considers it a companion that the good God has given him'. Brother Optat, however, was bursting with energy. And Villien himself was able to say: 'I feel at least as well as I did in Europe'.

Describing Rooke Island for his cousin in France, he said: 'It is oval in shape, runs from southeast to northwest, is of moderate size, and has a circumference of perhaps 20 to 25 leagues . . . And its position could not be more advantageous for the mission! Lying in the Dampier Strait between the two mainlands, it has New Britain to the east only four leagues away and New Guinea to the west only seven leagues away, not to mention the 16 islets encompassing it to the south. A short distance away there are three islands which are quite large and populous. Through the communications that the natives have with one another, it will be an easy matter for us missionaries to learn how we can penetrate into these areas. And if Rooke by the mercy of God should become Catholic, the route to these large islands will be opened for us, or at least will become greatly simplified. . . .'

As for Rooke, Villien said, 'we are not only the first missionaries who have set foot on this island, but also the first whites'. He called it a lovely island and said that its south side would have been ideal for a settlement, except for the fact that it was so swampy. Volcanic rock on the shores and mountainsides and the decapitated form of Rooke convinced him that the island was of volcanic origin. The volcanic soil was also responsible for the lush vegetation on every side. 'And hardly one league away from Rooke there is a very active volcano,' he said, 'emitting thick and numerous columns of smoke from several craters located in the conic peak of that island.'

Describing the habits of the people, he said that they built their houses on posts along the shore, and used spears, bows and slings for arms. 'But we have not yet been able to learn whether they are like their famous New Guinea neighbours, who use human flesh for food.' And like the natives of San Cristóbal, he noted, those of Rooke were also avid chewers of betelnut. 'When I see myself so close to New Guinea and New Britain, where the Gospel has not yet been preached, the thought comes to me that I shall indeed be moved to make the necessary sacrifices to go and plant religion in those vast lands.' He asked for prayers to hasten the arrival of 'this happy day'. And if 'this good fortune' of launching mission work in New Guinea or New Britain should not be granted to him, he said, the prayers of his readers would then obtain this favour 'at least for others'.[19]

Frémont, who had lived in San Cristóbal for twenty months, wrote from his new home at Nurua on 11 July to Superior General Colin. 'I am like the knights errant', he said. 'I do nothing but go from one island to another. If this kind of life continues, I shall end up knowing a multitude of languages, because they are different on every island with which we have become acquainted so far.' Like Villien the day before, he also mentioned in his letter that from Rooke 'we can see New Guinea and New Britain. I wish we could transport ourselves there bodily as easily as we can do so in spirit! If we but knew their language, and if they but wanted to listen to us, we would soon be spread out over this immense territory. In fact, you may even be hearing this good news some day, because we have learned that our islanders are in touch with those of [New] Guinea. And God, who directs all, will undoubtedly provide us with the means [of getting there], if this is one of the plans in his Providence.'[20]

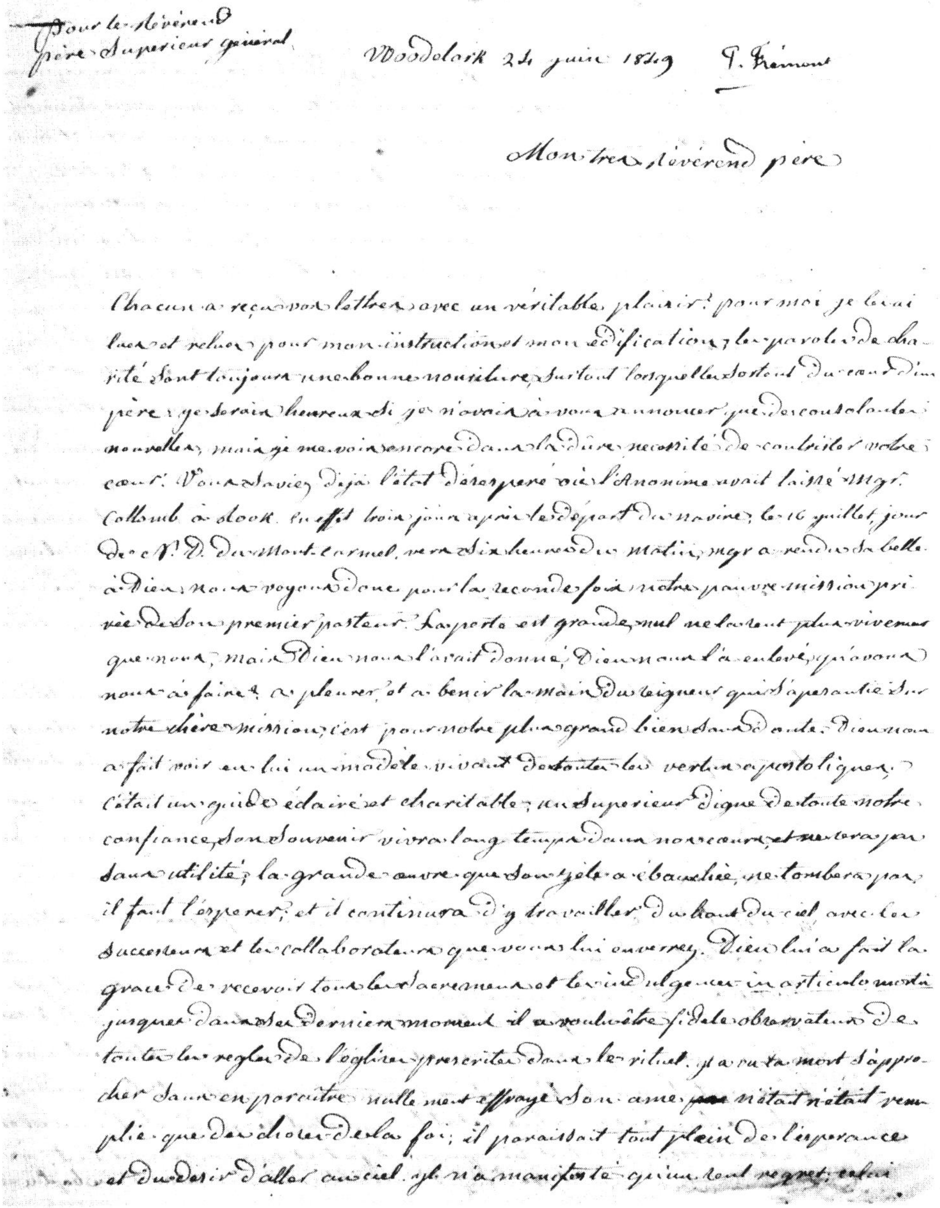

Pour le Révérend père Supérieur général

Woodlark 24 juin 1849 P. Frémont

Mon très révérend père

Chacun a reçu vos lettres avec un véritable plaisir; pour moi je les ai lues et relues pour mon instruction et mon édification, les paroles de charité sont toujours une bonne nourriture, surtout lorsqu'elles sortent du cœur d'un père; je serais heureux si je n'avais à vous annoncer que des consolantes nouvelles, mais je me vois encore dans la dure nécessité de contrister votre cœur. Vous savez déjà l'état désespéré où l'Anonime avait laissé Mgr. Collomb à Rook. En effet trois jours après le départ du navire, le 16 juillet, jour de N. D. du Mont Carmel, vers six heures du matin, mgr a rendu sa belle âme à Dieu. Nous voyons donc pour la seconde fois notre pauvre mission privée de son premier pasteur. La perte est grande, nul ne la sent plus vivement que nous, mais Dieu nous l'avait donné, Dieu nous l'a enlevé, n'avons nous à faire qu'à pleurer et à benir la main du seigneur qui s'appesantit sur notre chère mission, c'est pour notre plus grand bien sans doute. Dieu nous a fait voir en lui un modèle vivant de toutes les vertus apostoliques. C'était un guide éclairé et charitable, un supérieur digne de toute notre confiance, son souvenir vivra longtemps dans nos cœurs, et ne sera pas sans utilité; la grande œuvre que son zèle a ébauchée, ne tombera pas, il faut l'espérer, et il continuera d'y travailler du haut du ciel, avec les successeurs et les collaborateurs que vous lui enverrez. Dieu lui a fait la grace de recevoir tous les sacremens et l'indulgence in articulo mortis jusques dans ses derniers moments il a voulu être fidèle observateur de toutes les règles de l'église prescrites dans le rituel. Il a vu la mort s'approcher sans en paraître nullement effrayé, son ame n'était n'était remplie que des choses de la foi; il paraissait tout plein de l'espérance et du désir d'aller au ciel. Il n'a manifesté qu'un seul regret, celui

65 Letter from Pro-Vicar Frémont from Woodlark, New Guinea, dated 24 June 1849, describing for Superior General Colin the death of Bishop Collomb at Rooke Island in New Guinea on 16 July 1848. *Source: SM: OSM/208, f. 1r. (Chapter 31).*

Meanwhile supplies aboard the *Anonyme* were constantly diminishing and Captain Raballand had to think of returning to Sydney, since his voyage to Woodlark and Rooke had taken longer than he had anticipated. Collomb originally had planned to leave Rooke for further reconnoitring, but his health was so bad that all judged a sea voyage impossible for him, and so he stayed behind. The *Anonyme* then left Port Saint Isidore for Sydney via Woodlark on Thursday, 13 July 1848. That day happened to be Father Villien's thirty-sixth birthday.[21]

Raballand, after reaching Woodlark, explained all that had happened in Rooke to Father Montrouzier, who in turn on 13 August passed on this information to Procurator General Poupinel at the Marist headquarters in Lyon. The missionaries at Rooke had been so concerned about their bishop's poor health, he wrote, that they completely forgot about giving Raballand the letters written by Collomb for Rome, for Superior General Colin, and for the Association for the Propagation of the Faith in Lyon. And by the time Raballand took leave, Collomb was so sick that he 'was barely conscious and could speak only with difficulty. Alas, shall we so soon again be orphans a second time!'

As for Woodlark, Montrouzier assured Poupinel that this mission was making good progress. 'We are always satisfied with our natives here in Woodlark', he said. 'And in our house we have two children, one of whom is starting to read.' But for the past two months 'the rains have been more frequent and fever is making itself felt more intensely'.[22]

There was another letter written by Collomb, not mentioned by Montrouzier, which the worried Rooke missionaries had forgotten to send with Captain Raballand. It was a letter of five pages, unfinished, and addressed to Commandant Marceau of *Arche d'Alliance*. Father Frémont added the following lines to it on 28 July 1848: 'I am having forwarded to you all that Bishop Collomb wrote to you. And at the same time I must announce to you the sorrowful news of his death. He was not able to finish the letter that he wanted to send you via the *Anonyme*. He had come to Rooke to help Father Villien and me get established here and intended then to return by that same ship to Woodlark. But by the time the ship had to leave, he had already become so weak, that everyone agreed it would be impossible for him to embark. In fact, on the third day after the ship's departure, that is, on 16 July, in the morning, the Feast of Our Lady of Mount Carmel, he died in my arms after being fortified with all the helps of the Church. His death, like his life, was both edifying and holy. We may well believe that from heaven he will protect his mission, and that he will be a devout intercessor for all his friends. . . .'[23]

Collomb had remained conscious to his dying breath, Frémont said, 'and his soul had been completely filled with the desire and the hope of going to heaven'. Convinced that Collomb was a saint, Frémont made a novena at his grave.[24]

The Rooke Mission now consisted of Fathers Frémont and Villien and Brother Optat. But Villien, from the time of his arrival in Melanesia, had been obsessed with the notion that he would meet an early death. Seeing Bishop Collomb die so quickly, his former classmate and close friend, he was deeply disturbed. He became even more dejected after contracting fever and his melancholy spirit—according to Frémont—made the fever worse.[25] Then on 13 November 1848, four months after Collomb's death, Villien also died and was buried in the sand at the seashore alongside Collomb.[26] By this time the letter that he had written to France about Rooke Island on 10 July, six days before Collomb's death, could not have reached its destination. In it he had this to say about Port Saint Isidore: 'It is here that we made our foundation on the beach very close to a large village of 400 or 500 souls. And in all probability it is here, where I shall definitely be stationed, where I shall end my days, and where my last remains shall be laid to rest. . . .'[27]

With the death of its second bishop and its fourth priest, the double Vicariate Apostolic of Melanesia and Micronesia was reduced to one priest and one Brother at Rooke and two priests and one Brother at Woodlark. But for lack of communications neither the missionaries at Woodlark nor the Marists at the supply centre in Sydney knew that Collomb and Villien had died at Rooke. Father Rocher, head of the Sydney supply centre, chartered the 58-ton English schooner *Mary Ann* to bring personnel and supplies to Woodlark and Rooke.[28] The ship had a four-man crew and reached Woodlark on Sunday, 29 April 1849. Aboard were two new priests for Melanesia, thirty-six-year-old Father Pierre Trapenard and twenty-nine-year-old Father Eugène-Joseph Ducrettet. There was also some mail for Bishop Collomb.

Montrouzier, in virtue of authorisation received from Collomb at the time of his departure from Woodlark, opened all the mail addressed to Collomb. And pending Collomb's decision—no one at Woodlark knew he was dead—Montrouzier provisionally assigned Trapenard to Woodlark and Ducrettet to Rooke. Montrouzier decided to accompany Ducrettet to Rooke, since there were some official matters that he wished to discuss with Collomb.

The *Mary Ann* with Captain Wilson at the helm left Woodlark on 5 May and reached the vicinity of Port Saint Isidore early on Sunday morning, 13 May 1849.[29] This was the first anniversary of the arrival of Bishop Collomb and his missionaries in the waters of Rooke Island. Captain Wilson did not know, however, which beach area to choose, since there were seven different ones. After being perplexed all morning, he finally saw a distant canoe approaching. Father Frémont was aboard and soon was telling the others the sad news that Bishop Collomb had died ten months ago and that Father Villien had died six months ago. During all that time he and Brother Optat had been waiting for additional personnel.[30]

Since Frémont and Montrouzier had each been named pro-vicar by Collomb, both were now technically in charge of the Vicariate Apostolic of Melanesia and Micronesia. 'For the sake of greater unity', Montrouzier said, an agreement was reached with Frémont 'that I alone should take care of the external affairs connected with the office of pro-vicar, with the understanding that nothing was to be done without mutual consent'.[31]

The first thing that the two new heads of the mission had to decide was whether the mission station at Rooke Island should be continued and, if so, who should be assigned to it. Frémont did not want to have the 'young and impressionable' Ducrettet. He was from Savoy and therefore would be, according to Frémont, just as melancholy as all Savoyards. Frémont knew only too well what melancholy had done to Villien. Nor was Montrouzier an alternative, because he was suffering from fever and, as Frémont said, 'could not have remained at Rooke without risking his life'. In fact, Montrouzier had explicitly told Frémont that he could give him no other priest but Ducrettet. As for Brother Optat, some disease had attacked his feet, making him suffer almost continually.[32]

By the following day, 14 May, Frémont and Montrouzier had made up their minds to abandon Rooke temporarily and concentrate their forces on Woodlark. 'Father Ducrettet was somewhat angry at seeing us take this decision', Montrouzier said, but he and Frémont believed that their decision conformed with written instructions received from Superior General Colin. He had insisted on having at least two priests at a mission station.[33] Writing to Cardinal Prefect Fransoni in Rome, Montrouzier listed the following reasons for abandoning Rooke: the character of the natives; the unhealthiness of Rooke (two missionaries had died there in six months); the impossibility of immediately obtaining as many priests as required by positive instructions from Superior General Colin for maintaining a mission station; and the fear that Europe's political turmoil would postpone indefinitely the arrival of new personnel.[34]

They had abandoned Rooke Island, Montrouzier told Superior General Colin, but this did not mean that they had no hope of ever returning there. Conditions would surely become favourable some day and at such time they could profit from the many advantages to be gained from 'the magnificent position' of Rooke Island, lying as it did between New Guinea and New Britain and having a rather large population of its own.[35]

It took some time for Father Frémont and Brother Optat to pack all the things that they wished to bring to Woodlark. When the work was done and the ship was ready to leave, Frémont locked the house carefully and begged the people of Nurua not to touch it. He told them that some day missionaries would surely return.[36] The *Mary Ann* then sailed out of Port Saint Isidore with Fathers Frémont, Montrouzier and Ducrettet and Brother Optat aboard. It was Ascension Thursday, 17 May 1849. On 30 May they reached Port of the Nativity (now Guasopa Harbour) and Our Lady of Seven Sorrows Mission in Woodlark.[37]

The retreat from Rooke to Woodlark meant that the Vicariate Apostolic of Melanesia and Micronesia was beginning to collapse. Would it ever regain vigour enough to expand again? The five priests and two Brothers now at Woodlark manned two different mission stations. 'We apply all our time to the salvation of the indigenes', Montrouzier wrote Cardinal Prefect Fransoni on 22 June 1849. 'And they give us much hope! We have already baptised 91 inhabitants; we have made 14 infants angels and we hope that 12 adults are already enjoying eternal bliss.'[38]

The Société française de l'Océanie had been founded to serve, among other missions, the Vicariate Apostolic of Melanesia and Micronesia. And like that vicariate it, too, was beginning to collapse. In fact, between the deaths of Bishop Collomb and Father Villien, the board of directors of Société française in Le Havre wrote to the nuncio apostolic in Paris, Archbishop Raffaele Fornari, advising him that conditions in Europe were such that their organisation was being forced into bankruptcy. They therefore requested him to issue a letter in the name of the Evangelisation Congregation addressed to either the bishops or the laity of France, urging them to provide the required financial assistance. Fornari replied to the board that he had no authority to issue such a letter. Then on 9 October 1848 he forwarded their request to the Evangelisation Congregation in Rome.[39]

Cardinal Prefect Fransoni answered Fornari on 27 November, two weeks after Father Villien's death on Rooke Island. He told Fornari that the Evangelisation Congregation greatly appreciated the contributions being made by the Société française to missionary work. It was greatly displeased, however, over the news that the organisation was in imminent danger of bankruptcy. 'Therefore this same Sacred Congregation most gladly would hasten to the assistance of this well-merited Société,' he said, 'if only it were not likewise suffering from these very same conditions . . . Because of them it is difficult to meet even current expenses. However, the Sacred Congregation is confident that the exhortation mentioned by you, and to be directed to the various zealous bishops of those dioceses, asking that they urge the faithful to help the said Société, could have a favourable result . . . I therefore leave it up to your prudent judgment to decide whether you wish to issue such an invitation, or recommendation, in the name of the Sacred Congregation, and you may use whatever wording you judge fit. . . .'[40]

Melanesia had proved a much greater challenge for zealous French missionaries and idealistic French businessmen than they had anticipated. In the face of this challenge could one or the other, or perhaps both together, survive? Only time could tell!

32

The Vicariates Apostolic of Marquesas Islands and Tahiti Islands

9 APRIL 1848

Pope Gregory XVI on 12 November 1845 gave his approval to an 'Instruction' called *Neminem profecto* prepared by the Evangelisation Congregation. This document stressed that 'the two principal and so to say necessary means for propagating the Catholic Faith and giving it a firm foundation' were 'the sending of bishops, whom the Holy Spirit has assigned to rule the Church of God, and the diligent formation of an indigenous clergy'. The 'Instruction' was published on 23 November that year and was sent to those in charge of mission territories, and also to heads of mission-sending societies. Archbishop Bonamie, superior general of the Picpus missionaries, was among those who received a copy.

The 'Instruction' made many citations from the Bible and from Church documents to prove that the Apostles as well as the popes had always named bishops and ordained an indigenous clergy. These citations were followed by eight concrete directives. 'In the first place,' it read, 'each and every mission head, no matter under what title he governs his missions, must see to it that the Catholic Faith is promoted and strengthened. This means that in territories where bishops are still lacking, they are to be placed in charge as quickly as possible. And if the vastness of the areas should require it or allow it, then the number of bishops there could be increased by dividing these areas, so that eventually the churches may be organised according to the perfect form of hierarchical rule.'[1]

By the time this 'Instruction' was issued the Marist missionaries, who had arrived in Oceania in 1837, had three vicariates apostolic with bishops in charge, and one of these was a double vicariate. The Picpus missionaries, however, had only two vicariates apostolic with bishops in charge, despite their having been in Oceania ten years earlier than the Marists.[2] The 'Instruction', therefore, was bound to have some effect on the Picpus superior general. Bishop Pompallier, incidentally, would later cite this 'Instruction' when presenting his 8 December 1846 plan for establishing the hierarchy in Western Oceania.[3] And Archbishop Polding would cite it on 22 February 1847, when proposing the new Diocese of Melbourne.[4]

Bonamie wrote from Paris to Cardinal Prefect Fransoni on 11 February 1846, thanking him for the 'Instruction'. 'It has given me the idea that perhaps it would be well to have a vicar apostolic named for the Gambier, or Mangareva, Archipelago', he said. 'All of the islanders in this archipelago are Catholics, but

COLLECTANEA

S. CONGREGATIONIS DE PROPAGANDA FIDE

SEU

DECRETA INSTRUCTIONES RESCRIPTA

PRO APOSTOLICIS MISSIONIBUS

VOL. I.

Ann. 1622–1866. NN. 1–1299.

ROMAE
EX TYPOGRAPHIA POLYGLOTTA
S. C. DE PROPAGANDA FIDE
MCMVII.

66   Title page of a collection of Decrees, Instructions and Rescripts issued from 1622 to 1866 by the Evangelisation Congregation for missionaries. The collection was published in 1907. *(Chapters 24, 26, 32).*

opus properandum evangelica illa verba quodammodo impellant : *levate oculos vestros, et videte regiones, quia albae sunt iam ad messem* (Ioan. cap. 4, v. 25).

Istiusmodi igitur causae fuerunt cur Sacra haec Congregatio opportunissimum duxerit singulos Missionum praesides iterum iterumque hortari, et monere, ut tantum negotium coniunctis viribus impensius persequantur. Quare in generalibus comitiis diei 19 Maii praesentis anni de Pudicheriani conventus deliberationibus agens, ut eximium Episcopum Drusiparensem, aliosque probatissimos praesules in sancto, de quo sermo est, proposito magis magisque confirmaret, ceteros autem, ubi opus sit, ad lata toties de hac ipsa re decreta pro suo munere revocaret, per hanc instructionem ad omnes Archiepiscopos, Episcopos, Vicarios Apostolicos, aliosque Missionum praesides mittendam, ea quae sequuntur, statuere omnino, ac mandare in Domino existimavit.

1. Et primo quidem omnes ac singuli Missionum praesides, quovis titulo earum regimen gerant, ita rei catholicae promovendae, et firmandae operam navent, ut ubi adhuc desiderantur Episcopi, praefici quantocius possint ; ubi vero regionum amplitudo postulat aut sinit, ipsorum Episcoporum numerus, territoriis divisis, augeri, Ecclesiaeque ad perfectam hierarchici regiminis formam constitui tandem aliquando queant.

2. Illud insuper aeque studiosissime curent, quod etiam praecipui illorum muneris est, ut ex christianis indigenis, seu incolis earum partium, probati clerici instituantur, ac sacerdotes initientur ; quo scilicet crescente fide, fideliumque numero, disciplinae ecclesiasticae usus paulatim invalescat, ac religionis catholicae stabilitati prospiciatur. Huius rei causa maxime proderit, immo necessarium erit, seminaria condere, in quibus adolescentes, qui a Deo ad sacerdotium vocati fuerint, bene diuque educentur, sacrisque doctrinis imbuantur.

3. Ad omnem vero scientiam, ac pietatem levitae indigenae informandi et in sacro ministerio sedulo exercendi sunt; ita quidem, ut, quod iamdudum Apostolica Sedes in votis habet, ad ecclesiastica quaevis munia, atque ad ipsum Missionum regimen idonei fiant, et episcopali etiam charactere digni existant. Quae tamen

maximi sane momenti res, ut tutior evadat, et non sine religionis emolumento perfici suo tempore possit, qui ad tantum onus designantur, illi ferendo assuescant oportet. Quapropter, quos ex indigenis clericis Missionum praesides praestantiores censuerint, eos gradatim ad potiora implenda munera instituant, ac suos quoque Vicarios pro opportunitate deputare non renuant.

4. Hinc reiiciendus, ac omnino abrogandus erit mos indigenas presbyteros ad cleri tantum auxiliaris conditionem eis merito molestam deprimendi. Quin potius paulatim, et, cum fieri prudenter poterit, ea regula inducenda, ut inter evangelicos operarios, sive indigenae ii sint, sive europaei, ceteris paribus, praelationis ordo ex antiquiori Missionis exercitio servetur, atque adeo honores, officia, et gradus illis tribuantur, qui diutius sacro munere perfuncti sint (1).

5. Ad haec compluribus in locis factum est, ut, neglecta et posthabita indigenae cleri institutione, evangelici iidem operarii laicos catechistas adiutores sibi in ministerio adsciscere consueverint ; et forsan eorum operam plerumque fidei dilatationi perutilem experti sint. At cum non satis consentanee Apostolicae Sedis menti, atque ecclesiastici ministerii rationi id egerint, et graves etiam hac in re abusus ex praedictorum catechistarum seu imperitia, seu licentia praevaluisse innotuerit, Sacra haec Congregatio singulis Missionum praesidibus mandare non praetermittit, ut donec eiusmodi laicorum auxilium, ob cleri indigenae defectum, vel paucitatem necessarium fuerit, viros morum integritate, et fide omnino conspicuos ad id muneris eligi ac erudiri rectissime satagant. Ceterum hac etiam de causa omnem per eos operam in cleri indigenae institutionem dari iubet, ut nempe progressu temporis, iuvenes potius levitae, et novus idem clerus catechistarum officia pedetentim occupent, et diligentius impleant.

6. Quia alicubi in Indiarum etiam regionibus christiani ritus orientalis, ac praesertim syro-chaldaicus, subsistunt: ideo missionarii, si quando de iis inter catholicos agetur, observent omnino Benedicti XIV P. M. sapientissimam Constitutionem, quae incipit *Allatae sunt,* editam die 26 Iulii anno 1755.

7. Quod in praedicta Constitutione *Sacrosancti Apostolatus Officii* Alexander VII olim monuit Indorum parochos, ut *caverent*

De ritibus orientalibus in Indiis.

In rebus publicis ne se ingerant missionarii.

(1) In Litt. S. C. de Prop. F. 12 Iunii 1858 ad Vic. Ap. Pondicher. haec declarantur : « Statuto proinde missionariorum europaeanorum, ex Apostolici Missionarii titulo ac dignitate qua ditantur, praeeminentiae quodam veluti iure, alia quaelibet superaddatur distinctio, seu decanatus gradus, ut presbyteros indigenas in choro aliisque conventibus praecedere debeant, supervacuum esse intelliges, quemadmodum habita ac servata inter apostolicos ipsos missionarios, pro ministerii evangelici exercitio, ratione et ordine, in usu iugiter fuisse doces. Interim tamen, firma hac missionariorum apostolicorum, indigenarum presbyterorum

respectu, praestantia, nil obstare percipies, quominus naturalis idem clerus ita curetur ac foveatur, ut, cum tempus advenerit, prout laudata Instructio et allatae pariter Seminarii (Parisien.) regulae commendant, par esse valeat ad quaevis Ecclesia munia obeunda, quin europaeanorum operariorum ulterius egeat moderamine. Inter haec vero, ac salva missionariorum apostolicorum praeeminentia, nil item impedire videtur, quominus quaedam , ut ad maiora paretur et erigatur naturalis idem clerus, indigenis quoque presbyteris inter ipsos praestantia ac decus aliquod tribuatur, habita meritorum sive laborum in vinea Domini ratione ».

67   As figure 66, p. 544. This page contains the substance of the 'Instruction' called *Neminem profecto* issued by the Evangelisation Congregation with the approval of Pope Gregory XVI on 23 November 1845 urging subdivisions of existing jurisdictional areas, when feasible, the training of an indigenous clergy, the naming of indigenous bishops to head vicariates apostolic and dioceses, etc. This document was quoted by Archbishop Polding of Sydney, by Archbishop Bonamie, superior general of the Picpus Fathers, and by Bishop Pompallier when suggesting to Rome that new vicariates or dioceses be created in territory entrusted to them. *(Chapters 24, 26, 32).*

they total only about 4,000.[5] Since this archipelago is very distant from both the Sandwich and the Marquesas Islands, however, I believe that the presence of a bishop there would be most advantageous and likewise would free the vicar apostolic in the Marquesas Islands from making long, expensive and difficult voyages.' And if 4,000 people were not enough to create a new vicariate apostolic, Bonamie added, then 'some nearby archipelagoes, which will be evangelised as time goes on, could be joined to the Gambier, or Mangareva, Vicariate'.

In the same letter Bonamie informed Fransoni that he had sent twenty-two missionaries to Oceania in July of the previous year and that more priests and two more Brothers would be going there in the coming month. 'Catholicism continues to make great progress in the Sandwich [now Hawaii] Archipelago,' he said, 'where we already have more than 14,000 Catholics.'[6]

In view of the directives given in the 'Instruction' and in view of the large number of men being provided for Picpus missions in Oceania, Fransoni could hardly refuse Bonamie's request. But in order to make the Gambier Archipelago an independent vicariate, Fransoni said in his reply of 7 March, 'it would be fitting, because of the restricted number of the faithful, to include—as you yourself suggested—some other nearby islands'. If such islands were not included, 'it would then appear to be sufficient to have the assistance perhaps of a prefect or pro-vicar', who would depend upon the Vicariate Apostolic of Eastern Oceania or upon the Vicariate Apostolic of the Sandwich Islands.

'Now in order for me to make the proposal to my Eminent Colleagues,' the cardinal said, 'it is necessary for me to have an exact and detailed plan, which Your Grace can send me for this purpose. In it you will indicate for me at the same time some candidates who in your judgment would be fit to rule the new vicariate. From their number the Sacred Congregation could then choose the one who is most capable and who is worthy of the episcopal office.'

Fransoni had still another request. 'I would be pleased, if on that occasion you were to include for me with the above plan an exact report on the size, area, boundaries, population, etc., of the Oceania missions entrusted to your well-merited society. Also add some words on the number of missionaries now living in each mission and whatever else may contribute to a complete and comprehensive report on these same missions . . . I shall be waiting for your reply.'[7]

That year and also the next, Fransoni waited in vain for a reply. It is impossible to say for certain what made Bonamie drop this idea. Was the preparation of a complete and comprehensive report on all Picpus missions in Oceania too big a job for him? Or was he preoccupied with the Marquesas Islands? This archipelago consisted of a northwest group of six islands and a southeast group of five islands, all of which had been annexed by France in August 1842. Like the Gambier Islands, they were within the boundaries of the Vicariate Apostolic of Eastern Oceania. Bonamie had made a contract with the French government on 3 March 1843, pledging that he would keep the Marquesas Islands staffed with eight priests. And in virtue of the same contract the French government had agreed to pay their salaries, build their churches, and provide additional help. But when the government failed to live up to its part of the contract, Bonamie protested on 20 April 1846.[8] This was just a few weeks after Fransoni had written to Bonamie about the Gambier Islands.

Now Bonamie was optimistic and had every hope that the French government would eventually provide the promised funds, and so the Marquesas Islands financially could become an independent administrative unit. And since 'one of the kings there had already embraced the faith', as Bonamie later told Fransoni,[9] the islands could also become an independent jurisdictional unit. It was therefore more apropos to make these islands instead of the Gambier Islands an independent vicariate apostolic. Therefore it is not surprising that Bonamie from Paris on 1 February 1848 answered Fransoni's letter without even mentioning the Gambier Islands.

Acting as if he had only lately received the cardinal's letter of 7 March 1846, Bonamie said: 'I had the honour of proposing to Your Eminence some time ago the formation of a third vicariate apostolic in Eastern Oceania because of great distances separating the various archipelagoes and because of difficulties in communication. Your Eminence replied that you wished to know which islands would depend upon this vicariate and what precisely was their location. The enclosed note will indicate this for you. In the supposition that this third vicariate apostolic were to be created, the two other vicars apostolic would be restricted, one to the Marquesas Archipelago and the other to the Sandwich Archipelago. And since these [two] archipelagoes are composed of many islands which are very distant from one another, each of the vicars apostolic would still have enough to do to occupy his zeal. . . .'[10]

Bonamie was confused here, or at least made a remark that succeeded in confusing even Pro-Secretary Barnabò of the Evangelisation Congregation. Reading his text one gets the impression that the Vicariate Apostolic of the Sandwich Islands up to this time extended beyond the archipelago itself, but this was not the case. When the Vicariate Apostolic of the Sandwich Islands was created on 18 July 1844, Pope Gregory XVI approved the decision of the Evangelisation Congregation which said that 'a new and distinct Vicariate Apostolic of the Sandwich Islands' should be erected 'by separating these from the other islands contained in the Eastern [Oceania] Mission. . . .'[11] Presumably Bonamie was well aware of this. If so, he was then simply reaffirming this fact here, using it as a precedent for making the Marquesas Islands by themselves an independent vicariate apostolic.

Eager to keep Fransoni posted on the expanding missionary activity of his order, he said: 'No doubt Your Eminence has learned through the newspapers that last [23] October [1847] four priests and four Brothers of our community departed for Oceania aboard the ship *Stella del Mare*. I also have the pleasure of informing Your Eminence that in the Sandwich Archipelago, where six years ago there were no more than 300 or 400 Catholics, we now have over 18,000. Thanks be to God, this mission is very flourishing. . . .'[12]

Bonamie suggested in his enclosed note that the following archipelagoes be included in the new vicariate apostolic: Tahiti Islands, with Tahiti as principal island; Cook Islands, with Mangaia as principal island; Low (or Tuamotu) Islands; Gambier Archipelago, with Gambier as principal island; Easter Island; and Roggewein Archipelago.[13] Sailors who had visited these islands, he said, estimated their population at 45,000 to 50,000.[14]

According to Bonamie's way of thinking, this collection of archipelagoes made up the 'new' or 'third' vicariate apostolic, whereas the Vicariate Apostolic of Marquesas Islands was the previously existing Vicariate Apostolic of Eastern Oceania under a new name. But how explain his way of thinking, when it would seem much simpler and at first glance more logical to separate the Marquesas Islands from the already existing Vicariate Apostolic of Eastern Oceania and make them the 'new' or 'third' vicariate apostolic?

It would seem that Bonamie's manner of presentation was determined by the fact that Bishop Baudichon, coadjutor to the Vicar Apostolic of Eastern Oceania (lost at sea), had the right of succession and had been residing in the Marquesas Islands since 1839. He was therefore well acquainted with these islands, their language and their culture, and would be the logical choice to head the Vicariate Apostolic of Marquesas Islands. So instead of transferring him to a 'new' vicariate apostolic, Bonamie conceived of reducing in size the existing Vicariate Apostolic of Eastern Oceania so as to include only the Marquesas Islands, then changing the name to Vicariate Apostolic of Marquesas Islands and making Baudichon the vicar apostolic. This would mean that technically Baudichon would advance from the office of coadjutor to that of vicar apostolic within the same vicariate apostolic.

Another important consideration making Bonamie call his collection of archipelagoes the 'new' vicariate apostolic was the fact that he wanted included the Cook Islands, with Mangaia as principal island. This archipelago had never been part of the Vicariate Apostolic of Eastern Oceania and so there was more than a simple division in question here. In effect, and without explicitly saying so, Bonamie was asking to have the Cook Islands removed from the jurisdiction of the Marists and transferred to the jurisdiction of the Picpus missionaries. Or, more specifically, he wanted to have the Cook Islands removed from the Vicariate Apostolic of Central Oceania and attached to the third vicariate which he was proposing.[15]

It was strange that Bonamie should list the Cook Islands with all the other archipelagoes and not explain that they belonged to the Marists and were part of the Vicariate Apostolic of Central Oceania. Was he perhaps not aware of this? Or did he purposely keep silent about it in order not to complicate the situation and cause delay? Protocol would have required Rome to approach the Marist superior general and the Vicar Apostolic of Central Oceania to ask if they were agreeable to the transfer.

Actually Bishop Pompallier one year earlier, when making his proposals for establishing the hierarchy in Western Oceania, had suggested to the Evangelisation Congregation that the Cook or Mangaia Archipelago be transferred to the Picpus Fathers in Eastern Oceania. Being under the false impression that these islands were part of his own Vicariate Apostolic of Western Oceania, he felt free to suggest this. The transfer was called for, he said, because of the geographical position of these islands; they touched the western frontier of Eastern Oceania, but lay a great distance away from the rest of the archipelagoes in Western Oceania. Further, the Mangaia people spoke a dialect similar to that of Tahiti and other Society Islands and the Picpus Fathers knew those languages. Pompallier's proposal was presented to the cardinal members of the Evangelisation Congregation for a vote at the General Meeting of 7 June 1847. But no vote was actually taken because the cardinals had wanted first to resolve the pending Pompallier-Colin conflict.[16]

Possibly Bonamie was aware of Pompallier's proposal. And since Pompallier had given the above information to the Evangelisation Congregation, incorrect though it was, Cardinal Prefect Fransoni may not have realised that a Central Oceania territory was in question. Although there is no documentation to support this view, there is also none to contradict it, and it does explain why Bonamie and the Evangelisation Congregation acted the way they did.

Fransoni answered Bonamie immediately on 19 February 1848, saying that he would be happy to create a new vicariate apostolic, the third in Eastern Oceania. He invited Bonamie to submit the name of the candidate whom he would like to have placed in charge.[17]

Bonamie replied without delay on 7 March, saying that he and his council proposed Father Florentin-Étienne Jaussen as their first choice. This Picpus priest was born on 12 April 1815 and was currently based in Valparaíso. Bonamie also pointed out seven reasons why Jaussen ought to have a coadjutor; why the coadjutor should be Father Antoine Doumer, born on 13 February 1806 and superior of the Picpus house in Valparaíso; and why it would be well to keep the coadjutor at Valparaíso where he could serve Picpus missions in Chile as well as those in Oceania. And since a ship was scheduled to leave France for Valparaíso toward the end of April, Bonamie asked Fransoni kindly to have the papal bulls in his hands by that time.[18]

Obligingly Cardinal Fransoni brought up the matter of founding a third vicariate in Eastern Oceania at the following General Meeting of 3 April 1848. In fact, he himself presented the proposal and explained it as follows. First of all, the existing Vicariate Apostolic of Eastern Oceania was to be reduced in size so as to contain only the Marquesas Islands. Baudichon, coadjutor of the vicariate with right of succession, would be named vicar apostolic. But the name, Vicariate Apostolic of Eastern Oceania, would be dropped in favour of a new name, Vicariate Apostolic of Marquesas Islands.

He then pointed out the archipelagoes which were to constitute the third or new vicariate apostolic. And since the name 'Vicariate Apostolic of Eastern Oceania' had been dropped when renaming the existing Picpus vicariate apostolic, it could now be reused to name this new vicariate apostolic. Fransoni likewise proposed Jaussen as candidate for the office of vicar apostolic and suggested that he be given Doumer as coadjutor. In order that the cardinal members might see Bonamie's reasons for this and at the same time know precisely which archipelagoes were to belong to the new vicariate apostolic,

Fransoni had given each of them before the meeting a copy of Bonamie's 1 February 1848 letter with the appended note.

In the ensuing discussion the cardinals agreed to all proposals except one. They were not in favour of the name proposed for the new vicariate. Instead of calling it the Vicariate Apostolic of Eastern Oceania, they voted in favour of naming it after its principal island and therefore chose the name 'Vicariate Apostolic of Tahiti Islands'.

When Pro-Secretary Barnabó presented the Sacred Congregation's resolutions to Pius IX on 9 April 1848 (it was the second Sunday before Easter), the pope 'approved and confirmed' all of them.[19]

It was not until 17 May that Fransoni forwarded to Bonamie the official documents. He explained that he had used all possible haste in bringing up the proposal for founding a third vicariate apostolic and that in fact it was discussed at the General Meeting of 3 April. 'However, because of concurrence with other no less important business and also because of the Easter holidays and some present difficulties, it was not possible for me to send you the papal briefs on these matters before today. . . .' (The briefs were dated 9 May 1848.) Bonamie could see from them, Fransoni said, that the decisions taken by the Holy See 'conform fully with your wishes. . . .'[20]

Bonamie must have been pleased that his every wish had been fulfilled. And he probably thought that the new arrangement would also please Baudichon, who had sent a castigating letter on 1 April 1847, when he was still coadjutor of the Vicariate Apostolic of Eastern Oceania. Bishop Baudichon accused Archbishop Bonamie of using vicariate money for Picpus activities.[21] Since Baudichon would now be responsible only for the Marquesas Islands, and since Bonamie expected him to receive a steady stream of financial aid in virtue of the contract with the French government, there was at least some hope that the financial misunderstandings between the two men would be resolved.

On 17 May, the same day that he wrote to Bonamie, Fransoni also informed Baudichon that he had been made Vicar Apostolic of Marquesas Islands at Bonamie's suggestion. The remainder of his territory, Fransoni added, had become the Vicariate Apostolic of Tahiti Islands with Bishop-Elect Jaussen in charge.[22]

Would this news please Baudichon as much as it pleased Bonamie? Hardly! In no instance had a bishop of Oceania ever accepted gracefully the division of his territory, even when asked for views in advance. Baudichon had not been asked either by Bonamie or by Fransoni. It could hardly be expected that he would be an exception to the rule. For the time being, however, a decision had been reached and there now were three vicariates apostolic in Picpus territory instead of only two. But meanwhile the Marist vicariates in Oceania had increased to four.[23]

33

New Zealand is divided into
Auckland and Port Nicholson Dioceses

4 JUNE 1848

Cardinal Prefect Fransoni of the Evangelisation Congregation wrote to Superior General Colin of the Marists on 20 August 1847, asking for his views on the 'Particular Regulations' drawn up for the missions of Western Oceania by Bishop Douarre, Vicar Apostolic of New Caledonia. On 24 August he wrote again, saying that the pope had returned the Tonga or Friendly Islands to Bishop Bataillon, something that both Bataillon and Colin had asked for a long time. Fransoni's chief purpose in writing, however, was to bring to Colin's knowledge the contents of his enclosed 24 August letter addressed to Bishop Pompallier. It ordered the bishop by authority of the pope not to return to New Zealand until further notice. Colin was told to read the letter, seal it, and then transmit it safely to Pompallier.[1]

Colin answered on 27 September that he was well pleased with the 'Particular Regulations' and that he would like to receive authority from Rome to publish them under his own name and as part of the Marist Rule. Then, after they had been used provisionally, he would submit them along with amendments drawn up by himself and vicars apostolic in Western Oceania, so that they might be definitively approved by the Holy See. He also expressed his great pleasure over the news that the Tonga or Friendly Islands had been returned to Bishop Bataillon.

Referring to Pompallier's reaction to Fransoni's letter of 24 August, he said: 'It did not seem to us, however, that His Grace looked upon the invitation to remain in France as definitive.' Instead he had counteracted the directives contained in the letter by referring to other documents received from the Evangelisation Congregation. These authorised him 'to travel to various dioceses in Europe in order to recruit either personnel or funds for the New Zealand missions'. Pompallier had also answered 'in an altogether evasive manner' when Colin had offered to send his coadjutor, Bishop Viard, 'some priests for the relief of that desolate mission'. Consequently Colin did 'not yet dare believe that this question has been completely settled'. While waiting, he told Fransoni, he would send no more priests to New Zealand.[2]

Six weeks later, on 8 November, Bishop Douarre also wrote to Rome from Lyon about Bishop Pompallier. But he wrote directly to Pope Pius IX. After thanking the pope once again for being so good to him while in Rome, he spoke at length about Pompallier, saying that the bishop seemed to have misunderstood his orders from the pope. In fact, he was not leaving the government of his vicariate in the hands of his coadjutor. For example, Colin had offered to send priests to Viard, but he received an evasive answer from Pompallier, who would have had to supply funds for their voyage. As a result Colin could not send them. But he was giving Douarre ten or twelve missionaries and recently had sent fourteen to other parts of Western Oceania. Then, too, Pompallier was wasting money received from the Association for the Propagation of the Faith in Lyon and he was also telling tales about the Marists during his travels.[3]

Pope Pius IX immediately handed over Douarre's letter to Cardinal Prefect Fransoni and he, prompted by this letter and by the earlier one from Colin,[4] wrote at once (19 November 1847) to Pompallier in a very severe tone. Fransoni knew, from what Colin and Douarre had said, that it was his 1 July 1847 letter of recommendation[5] which Pompallier was using to justify his continued recruiting and fund collecting, while ignoring the later directives sent by Fransoni on 24 August in the name of Pope Pius IX.[6]

'In our letter of 24 August', Fransoni said, 'we made known to Your Grace the mind of our Holy Father, namely, that you were to extend your stay in France, that Bishop [Viard] of Orthosia had been given complete charge over your mission, and that for the duration you were to enjoy proper support, since the Superior General of the Society of the Blessed Virgin Mary[7] would be paying you an annual sum in cash of 3,000 francs.'

But news from the Marist Superior General—there was no mention of Douarre—and from Pompallier himself had made him aware, he said, 'that you instead are making use of a permission to recruit missionaries and to collect funds, that you received from the Sacred Congregation in advance of the above letter. As a result you are causing difficulties when the matter comes up of sending members of the [Marist] Society to New Zealand and of providing for the needs of that same mission.' Now it was self-understood, Fransoni insisted, 'that whatever had been granted earlier must be considered as suspended in view of the most recent wishes of our Most Holy Father. Nevertheless we believe that Your Grace must be informed once again in a special way that you have been released from your responsibility of caring for this mission, until it appears advisable to His Holiness either to make some other arrangement, or to give you the faculty of taking up once again the government of that vicariate.'[8]

Following his earlier practice, Fransoni sent this letter of 19 November to Colin so that he could see its contents and then pass it on sealed to Pompallier.[9]

Fransoni's letter was still en route to Colin, however, when Pompallier wrote from Paris on 23 November to Fransoni, reminding the cardinal that around mid-September he had requested 'that the Sacred Congregation should not take a definitive stand on the affairs of my mission before it receives the important documents that I want to present to you'. But time had passed so quickly, he said, that 'these documents are not yet ready, but they are making progress'. He said that Fransoni would receive them through the nuncio apostolic in Paris, 'who has kindly been so good as to protect me in the circumstances in which I find myself, giving me his counsel and his advice and offering me his services in order to facilitate my correspondence with the Holy See and particularly with Your Eminence'.

Pompallier told Fransoni that his recruiting and fund collecting were making good progress. He already had fifteen to eighteen clerics from various dioceses and the head of the Holy Ghost Seminary had promised him seven more. As for funds, the faithful had given him 10,000 francs and he expected the total to reach 200,000 or even 300,000. His preparations for returning to New Zealand were also progressing day by day.[10] This letter of Pompallier had no effect in Rome.

On receiving the 19 November letter for Pompallier, then in Paris, Colin must have been reassured that Rome was on his side. When he forwarded the letter, he renewed his offer to send missionaries to Bishop Viard in New Zealand. But Pompallier still had all New Zealand funds in his hands and did not reply.[11]

There was no longer any misunderstanding on Pompallier's part when he received Fransoni's 19 November letter in Paris. Realising that his hands were now tied, he took the only further action possible: he left France for Rome and was there by 22 December 1847. He would try to plead his case once again in person.[12]

Unaware that Pompallier was back in Rome, Cardinal Fransoni on Christmas Eve wrote to Archbishop Fornari, nuncio apostolic in Paris, so that he would know the facts about Pompallier. Ever since receiving Pompallier's letter of 23 November, in which he said the nuncio was 'so good as to protect me in the circumstances in which I find myself', Fransoni had been wanting to write. 'Although His Holiness has not yet accepted the resignation submitted by the Most Reverend Pompallier . . .', he said, the pope had ordered him to remain in France until new arrangements were made and had exonerated him from all responsibility for New Zealand, handing it over instead to Coadjutor Viard. His Holiness had also arranged for the bishop to get an annual pension of 3,000 francs from the Marists, an obligation which they had 'graciously' assumed. Fransoni said the nuncio would find this information useful in dealing with Pompallier, and he was free to make whatever use of it he wished.[13]

Colin also was not aware that Pompallier was in Rome and wrote to Fransoni from Lyon on 28 December, announcing that 'Bishop Pompallier has been in Paris since the beginning of October'. He told the cardinal that he had forwarded to Pompallier the 19 November letter, had again offered him Marists for Bishop Viard in New Zealand, but had received no reply. 'I have learned that the good bishop has become more and more embittered. And in Paris he prejudiced the Most Reverend Nuncio to such an extent that Bishop [Douarre] of Amata was very badly received when he paid the nuncio a visit in November.' Pompallier had also given false information to the Archbishop of Paris, had been showing others the memorandums printed by the Evangelisation Congregation, and had continued his criticism of missionaries who were members of religious orders. At this point, Colin said, it made little difference whether he or Pompallier was to blame, since in either case it appeared impossible for him to collaborate with Pompallier for the good of the mission. 'It would therefore seem necessary', he said, 'either that our missionaries should leave New Zealand, or that we be permitted to receive the allocations of the Association for the Propagation of the Faith [in Lyon], so that we can send some missionaries to Bishop Viard. . . .'[14]

Colin did not tell Fransoni that a month earlier he had, in fact, made an appeal directly to the Lyon fund-collecting agency, causing its president to write to Fransoni on 27 November. According to President Antoine de Jessé, Colin had asked that a part of the 1847 funds, which were destined for New Zealand, 'should be designated specifically for the needs of the missionaries of his community, among whom he includes the Most Reverend Coadjutor Viard, who are located in this vicariate. He also asks that the sum thus appropriated should be placed either in his hands or in those of the coadjutor just named.' The president wanted to know from Fransoni 'whether, in fact, we are to divide the New Zealand allocation into two parts, one of which is to be sent to the vicar apostolic [Bishop Pompallier] and the other to the Marist Missionaries? Or should we rather assign the entire allocation to Bishop Viard by virtue of his being coadjutor?' He added that Colin strongly insisted that, should the allocation be assigned in name to Pompallier, 'at least something ought to be designated for the needs of the Marist Missionaries and this sum should then be transmitted directly to him or to Bishop Viard. . . .'[15]

Replying to Colin's letter of 28 December, Fransoni assured him on 14 January 1848 that all was well and that there was nothing to fear. He had, in fact, already written 'categorically' to the nuncio apostolic in Paris, he said, clarifying for him any doubts that might have arisen in his mind concerning Bishop Douarre. And he had also informed the nuncio of the regulations 'adopted by the Holy Father' with regard to Pompallier, as these were expressed in the letter 'which Your Reverence transmitted to him'. In the meantime, Fransoni said, Colin must have learned that Pompallier 'recently has again presented himself in Rome. I can assure you in all sincerity, however, that his unexpected arrival has resulted in no sinister consequences for the welfare of the missions, nor for the society of which you have charge.'

Fransoni also wished Colin to know that when the Sacred Congregation was asked by President de Jessé about the funds needed to send Marist missionaries to New Zealand, 'the Sacred Congregation answered him that Your Reverence's petition was in conformity with arrangements made by the Holy Father, and that therefore it was in order for him to assign the subsidies to Bishop Viard. No doubt he has meanwhile contacted you on the use of these funds and their remittance. As a result I believe that every obstacle which may have kept you from sending new missionaries to New Zealand, as Your Reverence proposed, has now been removed. . . .'[16]

On 15 January, the day after Fransoni had written so convincingly to Colin, Pompallier wrote to Fransoni and to all the other cardinals of the Evangelisation Congregation. The letter sent to Pompallier dated 19 November 1847, forbidding him to manage New Zealand funds and personnel, had prompted him to come to Rome, he said. 'Persons in high places in the Church as well as my own conscience persuaded me to make this journey.'

He began his defence by saying that he had recruited about twenty-five clerics for his mission, thanks to authority received from the Evangelisation Congregation. But all of these would foresake him now, if Rome's prohibition were to last a long time. He therefore wished to go with them very soon to New Zealand. 'But then someone might say that if I go back to New Zealand with numerous members of the secular clergy, the Marists will want to leave the country. That in turn would make their Christian communities suffer . . . , because on arrival my new personnel would not know the local language like those whom they are replacing.'

For these objections, however, Pompallier had several answers: '(1) In general the ones already there do not want to leave; it is the Reverend Colin who wants this, not they themselves. As proof of this take Bishop Viard, who is in charge of them in my absence. He never stops writing to me that they are impatiently waiting for my return and for the many new men that I shall be bringing with me . . . (2) The New Zealand Archipelago is vast and there is sufficient work for legions of missionaries. The Marists could stay with the Marists in one section of the archipelago and in another section the secular clergy could stay with the secular clergy. All would do their work, each group in its own section, under the immediate authority of the bishop and his coadjutors designated for this entire archipelago.' (3) Should all or some of the Marists at the Reverend Colin's instigation want to leave New Zealand, then let them go, Pompallier suggested. His secular clergy and his three seminarians would then take charge. 'In this case the veteran missionaries in New Zealand could go to the Ascension [or Ponape] Archipelago in Micronesia, which has been asking for the benefits of salvation for many years.'[17]

During the whole month of January and on into February, Bishop Pompallier bombarded Cardinal Prefect Fransoni and Pro-Secretary Barnabò with endless reasons why he should be allowed to return to New Zealand. Finally on Monday, 7 February 1848, Barnabò gave Pope Pius IX a comprehensive report covering nine pages on the sad state of affairs still existing between Pompallier and Colin to the detriment of the Church in New Zealand. He also explained how the latest decision was reached to let Coadjutor Viard run the New Zealand mission, give him its funds, and keep Bishop Pompallier in France. All believed that 'this prudent interim measure' had tempered the situation and restored peace to the New Zealand mission, he said, until Bishop Pompallier 'appeared in Rome again unexpectedly at the beginning of the current year determined to protest against the great wrong which he says was done to him by that arrangement'.

Pompallier had presented 'voluminous memoranda, reports and expositions', Barnabò said, all aimed at showing how harshly he had been treated to the dishonour of the episcopal office. 'And he busies himself with the reports of the Reverend Colin and of the Vicar Apostolic of New Caledonia and tries to confute them. He also tries to show that his honour will be compromised, if he should not be allowed to return to New Zealand, where he says that he is expected and will be welcomed by the representatives of Britain and by the governors of the colony.'

In his documents Pompallier had indicated his own solutions for the problem, repeating to a large extent the substance of the proposals already contained in the *Memorandum* presented to the cardinals at their General Meeting of 7 June 1847. Pompallier admitted, however, that he could hardly work directly with the Marists. He therefore suggested, to avoid sending away all the Marists, that as before he should be placed in charge of all of New Zealand, but that he ought to be given two coadjutors instead of one. 'He would then divide his missionaries, putting the Marists in one part of the mission with Bishop Viard, the present coadjutor, whereas Pompallier would go to the other part with the other coadjutor—still to be chosen from outside the [Marist] Society—and with the secular priests whom he had recruited.' In the Marist section he would limit himself to exercising the pastoral ministry.

Pompallier was also certain that he could get enough funds, Barnabò said. As for personnel, he had recruited enough to staff his section of the mission and more had been promised to him by the superior of the Holy Ghost Seminary and by other institutes. Since New Zealand was ruled by Britain, he would leave it up to the Holy See to decide whether it would be expedient to exclude the French Marists from New Zealand altogether and replace them with British priests.

'Therefore it will be incumbent upon Your Holiness', Barnabò said, 'to decide whether it would be fitting for the Congregation to give consideration exclusively to these new appeals and requests. Or would it perhaps be more opportune to have the Sacred Congregation study the entire question once again, summarising all previous facts and information and taking into consideration at the same time the new memoranda of the prelate. Then the Congregation could propose to Your Holiness some solution which it would consider very prudent and just. . . .'

The pope decided to have the entire matter reexamined at a General Meeting. He wanted the cardinals to find a solution which would remove the obstacles hindering the propagation of the faith in New Zealand, and which at the same time would benefit the Christian communities there.[18]

On 7 February, the same day on which Barnabò discussed New Zealand with Pius IX, Colin wrote to Fransoni that he was sending some missionaries to New Zealand in March. He was answering Fransoni's comforting letter of 14 January, which had assured him that all New Zealand funds would henceforth be made payable to Coadjutor Viard.[19]

Colin's letter of 7 February was hardly in Rome when Pompallier on 17 February wrote to all the cardinals of the Evangelisation Congregation, requesting authorisation from them to return to New Zealand, since he now had all the priests and funds that he needed. And if they should feel that they might not want to grant his request, he said, then he would be bound in conscience to request that he be allowed to take legal action in order to prove that his petition to return to New Zealand was just.[20] There were depositions enough for a case, it seemed, since by this time he had submitted over a hundred pages of self-justification written in his own hand.[21]

Fransoni had no alternative; he had to inform Colin that the pope wanted the Pompallier-New Zealand question brought up once again at a General Meeting. But he waited until 4 March 1848, seven weeks after having emphatically assured Colin that Pompallier's arrival in Rome had had 'no sinister consequences' for either the New Zealand mission or the Marist missionaries. 'Once again I need to ask you', Fransoni began, 'for your opinion on a project that was presented not long ago to the Holy Father by the Most Reverend Pompallier, who insists on receiving some definite word regarding his own uncertain situation.'

Not mincing words the cardinal said that Pompallier had requested permission to return to New Zealand in a governing capacity. 'He suggests that New Zealand be divided into two vicariates apostolic, one to be left in the care of Bishop Viard and his Marist Priests, whereas the government of the other vicariate would be retained by himself and by the priests whom he allegedly has recruited outside of your society.'

Pompallier also had a second proposal, Fransoni said. Namely, he 'would remain in charge of the entire undivided vicariate and have the assistance of two coadjutors. He would let the Marist priests be completely dependent upon Bishop Viard and they would cultivate one section of the island [of New Zealand]. He himself would remain in the opposite section of the same vicariate with his own priests and his other coadjutor.' Colin was also assured that 'the Holy Father and the Sacred Congregation are aware of the observations and remarks made by Your Reverence in this matter. . . .' But since Fransoni was anxious to find a permanent solution for Pompallier's case, he now had to decide 'whether or not it is fitting on every count to exclude his return to the mission'. Colin's views were therefore needed on Pompallier's two proposals.

At the same time Fransoni wanted to know whether he could actually rely on what Pompallier had said about Coadjutor Viard and the other missionaries wanting him to hurry back. 'I remember your telling me about receiving various letters from these good missionaries, and also some from Bishop Viard, which expressed quite different sentiments on this point. . . .' Fransoni needed this information now, he said, 'in order to be able to give the Holy Father a report on the true state of affairs. . . .' And by no means was Colin to hold back his New Zealand missionaries, who were nearly ready to depart, simply because of Pompallier's proposals. 'The decisions taken provisionally' on sending subsidies to Bishop Viard 'still hold', he said.[22]

Rome might well have guessed that Colin by no means would accept the second proposal. What he had been fighting for all these years was to have himself and his priests cut off completely from any association whatsoever with Pompallier. The other alternative, placed first by Fransoni probably because he considered it the more acceptable, was something like Colin's own proposal of 1 May 1847. At that time he had suggested a twofold jurisdictional division of New Zealand in place of the threefold one proposed by Pompallier. He had also insisted vehemently that Pompallier must not be considered a candidate for either ecclesiastical territory and that 'Bishop Viard, of course', should receive the northern jurisdiction to be called Auckland.[23] The alternatives placed before him now, however, considered Pompallier a candidate in both cases.

In Colin's reply of 29 March there was not a single word of comment on either of Pompallier's proposals. 'Very humbly we beg the Sacred Congregation kindly to permit us henceforth not to intervene in any way . . .', Colin said. 'For more than seven years our silence with the Most Reverend [Bishop Pompallier of] Maronea has been our only means of having peace and we prefer this peace to the honour itself of collaborating in the foreign missions. . . .' Colin was confident, however, that Fransoni's zeal for the salvation of souls and his kind interest in missionaries would make him find the right solution for this problem which, if left unsolved, would destroy the missions. As for remarks made by missionaries about Pompallier, the cardinal could find all that he needed in the fourteen or fifteen letters given by Colin to Pope Pius IX in June 1847 and in those brought to Rome by Bishop Epalle in 1843.

Colin had learned in the previous month that Pompallier had written from Rome to the Association for the Propagation of the Faith in Lyon 'requesting a very considerable sum in order to send numerous missionaries to New Zealand'. He explained to Fransoni that the 1847 allocation being made by the Lyon agency 'in favour of the Vicariate of New Zealand is not more than 40,000 francs. Of this amount, 25,000 francs are reserved for the livelihood of the 25 missionaries stationed there. The remaining 15,000 could not suffice for sending out two new groups of missionaries. Therefore I find myself forced to suspend our preparations and to assign these missionaries elsewhere.'[24]

Three months passed and still Colin received no news from Rome about New Zealand. He waited one more week and then wrote to Fransoni on 6 July 1848 as follows: 'As for New Zealand, which has been a land of inconceivable confusion for all, we abandon ourselves completely to the wisdom of the Holy See. For the greater glory of God and in the interest of peace, we shall—if necessary—leave this mission without regret. And we shall reserve for ourselves no other duty but that of praying with greater fervour so that the Lord in his mercy may bless the pious efforts of those missionaries whom the Holy See will call upon to succeed us.'[25] Unknown to Colin the New Zealand question by this time had been settled and the resolutions of the Evangelisation Congregation as approved by the pope were en route to him. In view of what he had stood for, he could hardly be pleased with the outcome!

Back in Rome on 9 March 1848 Pompallier had submitted still another long report, this one running for ninety-nine handwritten pages. It increased to over two hundred pages the depositions that he had made against Superior General Colin and the Marists. In this new report he intended to show the opposition that he as vicar apostolic had been forced to endure from June 1836, when he was ordained a bishop in Rome, until his recent visit to Rome in December 1847.[26]

Briefly, he accused Colin of intervening between Rome and the lawfully constituted vicar apostolic. For example, according to him it was Colin who had promoted the foundation of the Central Oceania Vicariate in 1842 and thus had

had removed 'from my jurisdiction all the principal archipelagoes in the Torrid Zone'. Not long after that Colin had Pompallier's pro-vicar, Father Epalle, 'named and ordained a bishop in Rome in 1844 in order to take away from me two other considerable parts of my jurisdictional territory and to have them conferred upon him as the two Vicariates Apostolic of Melanesia and Micronesia'. Pompallier himself had been unaware of all these new creations, he said, and 'there remained for me nothing more than New Zealand, where political circumstances hardly allowed me to remain any longer'.

Then in December 1846, when Pompallier had come to Rome with his plan for establishing the hierarchy in Western Oceania, he had found the Evangelisation Congregation well pleased with his proposal. But it 'displeased too much the Reverend Colin and those who shared his plans and designs. Therefore he made every effort, not only to leave me in charge of not even half of New Zealand, but also to have me excluded from all of Western Oceania, where I had founded almost all the missions in existence, had put them on a sure footing and had directed them.' Colin's wishes and efforts had all been caused 'by false reports, by subreption and by intrigue. And they were on the point of being realised completely—how unjust and disgraceful this would have been for the episcopacy!—when the Sacred Congregation's experience and wisdom prevented this from happening.'

It was clear from all this, Pompallier said, that 'the Reverend Colin knew only too well how to divide in order to rule and exterminate'. For although each bishop in Oceania had received from the Holy See 'the title and the right' to govern his own territory, he governed it 'in fact under the direction of the superior general of the order'.[27]

When the General Meeting ordered by Pope Pius IX was finally held on Monday, 29 May 1848, the relator once again was Cardinal Lambruschini and the topic to be discussed was called 'Remonstrances of the Vicar Apostolic of New Zealand'. Officially Pompallier was still the Vicar Apostolic of Western Oceania, and that is how he always signed himself.[28] But the Marists regularly, and at times also the Evangelisation Congregation, as in the case just mentioned, referred to him as the Vicar Apostolic of New Zealand. This was practically all that remained of his once vast vicariate.[29]

Relator Lambruschini informed the cardinals at the General Meeting that it was His Holiness himself who had ordered the New Zealand question to be treated once again. After summarising the long sad story of the unhappy working relationship existing between Pompallier and Colin, Lambruschini reported briefly on the latest correspondence received from both men. The Evangelisation Congregation had tried 'with loving exhortations, advice and incentives to reestablish the harmony that had been destroyed . . . , to bring them together and to restore their interrupted contacts. But each time new causes of discord arose. . . .' The business of the present meeting, therefore, was to find a solution 'which once and for all will end these quarrels . . . that are paralysing the propagation of the faith' in New Zealand.

Lambruschini said that the cardinals would have to take into consideration the solutions proposed by Pompallier and also his urgent and repeated requests for authorisation to return to New Zealand with the priests whom he had recruited. But did the cardinals want him to go back there 'with the refuse that he has picked up in the dioceses'? Or would they rather prefer to leave the mission in the hands of Coadjutor Viard, who was ruling it well? The twenty-five Marists in New Zealand were already acquainted with the language there, he said. And it seemed very strange that the many Marists in Western Oceania had no problems with other vicars apostolic, nor with Coadjutor Viard, nor with Superior General Colin, but only with Bishop Pompallier. Lambruschini then asked: 'What suitable arrangement can be suggested to His Holiness for this affair now under study, so that definitive action can be taken for the benefit of the New Zealand Mission?'

In the discussion that followed it was pointed out that the cardinals one year earlier at their General Meeting of 7 June 1847 had already resolved to found the two Dioceses of Auckland and Port Nicholson, with Bishop Pompallier—he was to have first choice—and Bishop Viard in charge. But Colin's visit to the pope and the failure of Fransoni and Lambruschini to bring about a reconciliation between Pompallier and Colin had suspended this resolution indefinitely. By vote the cardinals now adopted the same resolution in this modified form.

'Bishop Pompallier must be sent back to the New Zealand Mission, but in the following way: Once the two Dioceses of Auckland and Port Nicholson are established, the first is to be assigned to the Most Reverend Pompallier, who as soon as possible must present to the Sacred Congregation an English candidate for the office of his coadjutor with right of succession. He will give up his other coadjutor, the Most Reverend Viard, who will become an independent vicar apostolic as follows: Those Marists who have protested that they cannot live in harmony with the Most Reverend Pompallier, will be allowed to leave [him] and go to the Diocese of Port Nicholson in order to exercise the sacred ministry under their colleague Viard. Further, the Most Reverend Pompallier is to be urged to reach a true reconciliation of mind with the head of the Society [of Mary], which is so highly deserving of merit because of those distant missions. He should also be informed that it is the wish of the Sacred Congregation that he remember to provide himself with a goodly number of English personnel when assembling his new clergy. Until such time as these are able to exercise their ministry perfectly, he ought not to be deprived of the Marists already skilled in this work.'[30]

Auckland and Port Nicholson were to be 'dioceses properly so called', the cardinals decided, but Pompallier and Viard were to administer them provisionally as vicars apostolic. The Evangelisation Congregation also decided 'that it would be very good and proper, after discussing the matter with His Holiness, to open its mind and to issue opportune instructions' to Bishops Pompallier and Viard and Superior General Colin 'on the missions of Oceania'.[31]

On Sunday, 4 June 1848, Pro-Secretary Barnabò presented these resolutions to Pope Pius IX and he approved and confirmed all of them.[32]

By this act the pope created the Dioceses of Auckland and Port Nicholson (later Wellington) and placed Pompallier and Viard respectively in charge. Had they been advanced to the rank of residential bishops, as had been proposed in the suspended resolution of 7 June 1847, the decision taken by the Sacred Congregation and by the pope would have been definitive. But by giving each diocesan head merely the rank of 'vicar apostolic or administrator apostolic'[33] the Holy See made it clear, without saying so explicitly, that it was sending Pompallier back to New Zealand on probation.

Pompallier could be only partially pleased with Rome's decision. Although it did send him back to New Zealand, something that he had wanted more than anything else, it also cut away half of his previous territory and placed him on a par with Viard. Nor would Colin be very well pleased either, since Viard did not get the Auckland Diocese, where most of the mission stations were located. And for him Pompallier's return to New Zealand in any capacity was an omen of unrest and ultimate ruin for the mission.

Pope Pius IX on Trinity Sunday, 18 June, granted to both Pompallier and Viard for their new dioceses all the ordinary and extraordinary faculties which formerly had been granted to Pompallier as Vicar Apostolic of Western Oceania.[34] Then two days later Cardinal Fransoni wrote a new letter of recommendation for Bishop Pompallier authorising him to recruit priests and to collect funds for the Diocese of Auckland.[35] Except for the date and his new title, the letter was identical with the one issued by Fransoni the previous year.[36]

At this point only one step remained on Cardinal Fransoni's agenda. He still had to write the three difficult letters to Pompallier, Viard and Colin, advising them of the decisions that had been taken and urging them to collaborate at long last for the welfare of the New Zealand Missions. He dated all three letters 30 June 1848.

After addressing Pompallier as 'Bishop of Maronea and Vicar Apostolic or Administrator Apostolic of the Diocese of Auckland in Western Oceania', Fransoni said: 'You will learn from the attached apostolic brief what we have told Your Grace already by word of mouth.' The cardinal pointed out explicitly, however, that Auckland and Port Nicholson were 'dioceses properly so called', that they were 'to be subject immediately to the Apostolic See', that Pompallier would govern Auckland Diocese 'with the title of vicar or administrator apostolic', that Viard would no longer be his coadjutor, that instead he would administer Port Nicholson Diocese with the title of 'vicar apostolic or administrator', and that in addition he would do this 'independently'.

Fransoni went on to say that there were 'certain other things which were sanctioned at the General Meeting of 29 May, which were likewise approved by His Holiness, and which by order of His Holiness are to be made known and recommended to you via this letter'. In view of the 'affection' which the Marists had for Bishop Viard, also a Marist, the pope had judged it 'most opportune' that they be allowed to transfer from Auckland Diocese to the Diocese of Port Nicholson 'and that you at the same time be granted the power of acquiring elsewhere, especially from England, as many suitable and tested priests as you can. These will then practise the sacred ministry under your jurisdiction in the

Diocese of Auckland. It is the mind of His Holiness, however, that as long as the new priests just mentioned are not capable of bearing the burden, you are to make use of the help and work of the missionaries of the Blessed Virgin Mary Society.'[37]

Further, the pope wanted Pompallier to present to the Evangelisation Congregation as quickly as possible a candidate from among his English priests, one 'who you truly think in the Lord and know is altogether suitable, more so than others, for the office of being your coadjutor and for ruling the diocese, a man worthy of the espiscopal character, whose election could then be considered by the Sacred Congregation'. It was also 'the mind of the Sacred Congregation and of His Holiness', Fransoni added, 'that Your Grace approach the President of the same Society [of Mary]—you are not unaware of his excellent merits because of the missions in Oceania—and that, having laid aside every contention of mind, you begin using all means to reestablish with him true and sincere accord.'

In conclusion the cardinal stressed once again that he had been obliged to mention all of these things 'by order of His Holiness'. For his own part he advocated earnestly 'that you always show yourself to be a good shepherd toward the flock entrusted to you and also a benevolent father toward your priests. For it is more by charity and by example, than by authority and severity, that you will attract them and spur them on toward promoting the propagation of the faith and adhering to the road of virtue.'[38]

The letter for Bishop Viard, dated 30 June 1848, was addressed to 'The Bishop of Orthosia,[39] Vicar or Administrator Apostolic of the Diocese of Port Nicholson in Western Oceania'. At Pompallier's request, Fransoni said, the Sacred Congregation at its General Meeting of 29 May had taken up the business of settling affairs touching upon the Vicariate Apostolic of Western Oceania. He then told Viard what he had already told Pompallier about the new ecclesiastical organisation of New Zealand and his role in it. And he explained that 'for now' both he and Pompallier would govern their dioceses 'as vicars of the apostolic see. . . .'

The pope had also given orders, Fransoni went on to explain, that 'his mind be made known' to Viard and that 'opportune instructions' be given to him. 'For His Holiness knows well that those otherwise excellent priests of your well-merited Society perhaps would not work so eagerly under Bishop [Pompallier] of Maronea as under your jurisdiction.' For that reason His Holiness had authorised Pompallier to recruit priests elsewhere and had allowed the Marists in Auckland Diocese 'to transfer to Port Nicholson Diocese to be under Your Grace and so help you in your pastoral duties'. But not all were to make the transfer at the same time, Fransoni said. 'You realise, of course, that this transfer or crossing over must be done gradually, lest by one blow the other diocese be deprived of giving spiritual assistance to the faithful before the new personnel . . . are equal to the evangelical task.'

Fransoni was convinced, however, that 'in the future, no less than in the past', Viard would continue to foster the best of relations with Bishop Pompallier. 'We also trust that the said bishop will always maintain the same regard toward you, so that everything may be done in charity and in the bond of peace. . . .'[40]

The letter to Superior General Colin was also dated 30 June 1848. It had been the task of the General Meeting of 29 May, Fransoni said, 'to propose as ordered by His Holiness a definitive and efficacious measure to bring to an end the displeasing pending affair of the Vicariate of Western Oceania'. And although the cardinals had kept in mind Colin's remarks of 29 March, they also believed it 'fitting to give some consideration to the Bishop of Maronea'. After a most mature examination 'they believed that the controversy could be reconciled in the following manner, which carries the sanction of the Holy Father'.

Fransoni then repeated the essential points mentioned in his letters to Pompallier and Viard, expanding certain aspects which referred more directly to Colin and the Marists. Once the new priests recruited by Pompallier were acquainted with the local language and had begun practising the ministry in Auckland Diocese, Fransoni said, 'the Marist priests still in that diocese will be at liberty to pass over to the Bishop of Port Nicholson and remain there under the jurisdiction of their colleague, the Most Reverend Viard. His Holiness wished to have this made known by letter to the two bishops and also to Your Reverence', Fransoni said. 'He also exhorts you to inculcate again in your missionaries that they should not abandon the spiritual assistance of the faithful of Auckland so long as these people are not provided with other priests.'

It was also the wish of the pope, Fransoni said, that Bishop Pompallier should be 'urged on efficaciously, as was done, to realise a true and sincere reconciliation of mind with Your Reverence and with your society which is so well merited because of the Oceania missions. And I feel certain that Your Reverence, in view of the excellent spirit with which you are animated, will also fulfil in good measure the wishes of our Holy Father. You will receive the bishop with similar affection and will forgive in the Lord every motive for past differences, according to the teaching of the Apostle to the Gentiles (Col. 3:13). . . .' Fransoni expressed the hope that these arrangements would be 'completely satisfactory' to Colin and that they would 'succeed in obtaining the desired goal, which is likewise in Your Reverence's heart, namely, the true welfare, tranquillity and progress of those missions. . . .'[41]

Colin answered Fransoni's New Zealand letter on 11 August 1848. 'We experienced deep pleasure, Your Eminence, on learning that the Sacred Congregation has taken a definite stand on the New Zealand affair.' As Colin saw it, however, the decision reached was not completely devoid of unpleasantness, since it did contain and perpetuate the germ of division and recrimination. 'But the issue had to come to an end eventually and the Sacred Congregation has taken the stand which it has considered the most suitable; we applaud it without reserve. However, in spite of our being fully aware of the good spirit of our missionaries, we do not dare predict that they shall agree to remain in this mission.'

In reference to Fransoni's suggestion that the Marists work in Viard's diocese, Colin pointed out that 'a prudent article' in the Marist Rule automatically ended membership in his society for those—and in this case for Viard—who were elevated to the episcopacy, 'because otherwise we would be over-burdened with too many bishops'.[42] Colin nevertheless would initiate contacts with Viard, thus 'conforming to the desires of the Sacred Congregation until such a time when His Grace should deign to let us know his true intentions'.

Referring to his relationship with Pompallier, Colin promised that in spite of what had happened in the past, and with the help of God in the future, he would harbour in his heart no other sentiments toward the bishop 'but the most sincere charity and the most affectionate compassion. In this way we hope to put into practice the paternal wishes of His Holiness, which for us shall always be orders. . . .'[43]

Four days later, on 15 August 1848, Colin wrote in quite a different tone to Father Theiner, his Oratorian priest friend in Rome. Apologising for his long silence, he explained that after returning to France he had noticed that Pompallier had become weaker and more sensitive. 'I did not want to give him occasion to say (he will do it anyhow) that I busied myself about him and that I was bribing someone in Rome to calumniate and betray him. For almost 12 years he played the comedian in New Zealand; then he switched to burlesque. And now the scene would have turned into a tragedy, if the Sacred Congregation had not finally lowered the curtain and sent him back to the antipodes as principal actor with his new title of Administrator Apostolic for the Diocese of Auckland. God knows well that I applaud the measure. . . .'

Colin also had a request to make of his friend in Rome. He would be highly pleased, he said, 'if you could obtain for me confidentially the new documentation on the latest steps taken in Rome by the Most Reverend [Bishop Pompallier] of Maronea. . . .' He also passed on to Theiner news of Bishop Douarre, saying that he had not been able to leave for New Caledonia in March, as expected. But now he was 'planning to leave very soon on a ship of state'. As for Bishop Viard, he would have enough priests if the Marists in New Zealand were willing to transfer with him to Port Nicholson Diocese. This, Colin said, would also exempt him from sending any new missionaries there.[44]

To all appearances Colin was happier to have Pompallier in New Zealand than in France, an attitude contrary to the one that he had in Rome in 1847. As he himself later explained, he had begun to alter the aims of the Society of Mary after his return from Rome in 1847. Instead of putting the chief emphasis on foreign missions, he began stressing more the apostolate in France. A foundation made there could endure and in France there was also peace, at least in comparison with the conflicts that he had always known in New Zealand.[45] But Colin's new apostolate was being harmed by Pompallier who was spreading stories everywhere about the Marists. In view of the shift in goals, it was now better to have Pompallier in far-off New Zealand.

Did Pompallier realise his dream of bringing back to New Zealand large numbers of priests from the secular clergy to staff his new Diocese of Auckland? He had left New Zealand on 16 April 1846 and arrived back in Auckland on

8 April 1850. A recapitulation of what had happened during those four years would have to begin with Pompallier's voyage from New Zealand to Toulon, Marseille and Rome, where he arrived in mid-September 1846. The business, delays and conflicts connected with his proposal to have the hierarchy established in Western Oceania kept him in Rome until late June 1847 when he left for Loreto, Italy, and then for France where he collected funds and recruited personnel. When this activity was forbidden by Rome a second time in November 1847, he returned to Rome in December to plead his case. At his insistence his cause came up repeatedly in meetings until he was entrusted with the newly founded Diocese of Auckland on 4 June 1848; later that month he was again authorised to recruit personnel and collect funds. He also made a trip to the Holy Land in 1848.

Then in April 1849 he visited the Sisters of Mercy at Carlow, Ireland. He was in England in May, in Belgium in June, and back in Carlow in August to accompany eight Sisters of Mercy via Dublin, Liverpool and London to Antwerp. Here Pompallier and the nuns boarded the 533-ton *Océanie* under Captain Radou on 27 August 1849 and sailed that same day for New Zealand. The late Lillian G. Keys, Pompallier's biographer, says that he also had in his party twelve clerics (six French, two English, two Irish, one Flemish, one German), but that many of them had not yet completed their studies for the priesthood. After an extended stopover in Sydney, *Océanie* finally disembarked its passengers at Auckland on 8 April 1850. By that time the two Englishmen were no longer in the party.[46]

Bishop Viard described Pompallier's return for Father Colin and he in turn described it for Cardinal Fransoni. On returning to New Zealand, Colin said, Pompallier 'did not bring there from Europe but a single priest and some young clerics. And these, not yet being elevated to the priesthood, shall not be able to exercise the sacred ministry for a long time'. Pompallier consequently needed for his Auckland Diocese the Marist priests in New Zealand meant for Viard, who now wanted Colin to send Marists from France for his own Diocese of Port Nicholson. But Colin turned a deaf ear to Viard's request for more priests. 'It is painful for us not to be able to supply them for him,' Colin told Fransoni, 'and even more painful to learn that several of his missionaries are asking to return to Europe.'[47]

Superior General Colin in this 1850 letter was sounding the retreat of his society from New Zealand. From 1848 to 1850 he had told Rome repeatedly that he wanted to give up not only Micronesia, but Melanesia as well. Would he eventually abandon Oceania altogether?

34

The Vicariate Apostolic of the
Samoa or Navigators Archipelago

11 AUGUST 1850

Bishop Guillaume Douarre, Coadjutor of Bishop Bataillon, Vicar Apostolic of Central Oceania, had hardly arrived in France in mid-1847 when Pope Pius IX on 27 June created the Vicariate Apostolic of New Caledonia, made him its first vicar apostolic, and relieved him of his previous office of coadjutor.[1] Seven months later Douarre was still in France when news arrived in Lyon about the attack of 18 July 1847 on Balade Mission in New Caledonia, forcing his missionaries to flee to Australia.[2]

Since Douarre was not in Lyon at the time, Superior General Colin on 7 February 1848 sent a copy of the letter containing the news to Cardinal Prefect Fransoni of the Evangelisation Congregation.[3] Colin wrote again on 12 February assuring the cardinal that he would give Douarre sufficient personnel to make a new attempt. And since the bishop had promised 'not to found any station without eight missionaries, priests and brothers', Colin had promised 'to do the impossible for him'.[4]

On Douarre's return to Lyon he, too, sent news of the calamity to Rome, first on 16 February and again on 18 February.[5] He and Colin also sent Fransoni a copy of the procès-verbal, composed and signed by the missionaries before they left New Caledonia, in which they described all phases of the attack and its sequel.[6]

Fransoni told Colin on 4 March 1848 that he hoped Douarre's zeal would find a way to remedy the disaster. And he expressed the wish that the young bishop, now thirty-seven, would hasten back to Oceania so that he could be of assistance to his banished missionaries.[7] (Douarre had left Oceania in late 1846.) Three days later Fransoni acknowledged Douarre's two letters and consoled and encouraged him.[8]

Originally the contingent of missionaries for New Caledonia was scheduled to leave in March. But Douarre was still in France by the middle of August 1848, hoping to receive passage on a ship of state.[9] When eventually he reached New Caledonia, he decided to launch the mission once again at Balade on the northeast coast, since it had such a fine harbour and since the tribesmen seemed repentant of their 1847 attack. But on hearing soon afterwards that there were plans afoot to massacre him and his entire staff, Douarre decided to flee. They went to the tiny Isle of Pines located about forty-eight kilometres southeast of New Caledonia. Here Douarre remained with ten of his missionaries, sending the other nine to Sydney.[10]

Since Bishop Douarre believed that it was impossible for him to achieve anything in New Caledonia, he decided to send Pro-Vicar Claude-Marie Bernin to Lyon and Rome in order to acquaint Colin and Fransoni with what had happened and to request new orders. He gave Bernin a letter for Colin written on the Isle of Pines on 6 January 1850. 'The Reverend Bernin, who is leaving for Sydney in order to depart for Europe, will bring you up to date on the sad circumstances which have obliged us to leave New Caledonia a second time', he said. 'We have also been forced to withdraw our missionaries from Aneityum and before long we shall be obliged to abandon the entire vicariate. . . .' Aneityum was the southernmost island of New Hebrides Archipelago, which also was part of his vicariate apostolic.

'I would beg you to ask Rome for another vicariate', Douarre urged Colin. 'You know there are difficulties of every kind in the missions of Melanesia, Micronesia and the Fiji Islands, and so I do not feel I have the courage to begin a mission in any of those lands. Nor would there be anything for me in New Zealand. For as you know, my Very Reverend Father, something there prompts me not to accept! But if someone were to suggest that you ought to solicit for me the Navigators Islands in Central Oceania, and that therefore you should also request that this archipelago be erected into a vicariate apostolic, I would not accept it, unless I were formally commanded to do so by Rome. The reason for this is my conviction that such a division would cause pain for the Most Reverend Bataillon.'[11]

What Douarre meant by his euphemism was that Bataillon would be offended, would be incensed.[12] And rightly so! Bataillon's residence was on tiny Wallis Island at the centre of a semicircle formed by the Fiji, Friendly or Tonga, and Navigators archipelagoes, all of which were under his jurisdiction. The archipelago known as Navigators Islands, nowadays called Samoa, was the closest to his residence of the three, and this was precisely the one that Douarre wanted. Further, Douarre's New Caledonia Vicariate, created in 1847, had absorbed the far western portion of Bataillon's vicariate; Douarre's present proposal would absorb the eastern portion. These considerations might well be calculated to anger Bataillon. But if Rome formally commanded Douarre to accept the Navigators Islands, he could always tell Bataillon that he had been forced to take them. He would not mention, of course, that he himself had insisted upon getting the formal command!

In his letter Douarre also explained to Colin why the nineteen priests, expelled from his vicariate, were not giving a helping hand in other hard-pressed missions. He had in fact urged them to go to nearby Marist vicariates—these were Central Oceania and Melanesia—and had even assured them that this would please him. 'But up to now all have refused to separate themselves from me', he said, 'and have declared that they will follow me wherever the Holy See might wish to send me, unless you should give them other orders. So it is up to you, now, to make a decision. If you judge it opportune for us to receive another mission, then let it be one that is less difficult and less costly than the one which has already been entrusted to us. And if you think that no missions ought to be accepted other than those which you already have, then my missionaries will wait for you to tell them where to go. As for me, my Very Reverend Father, I can always find a very small corner in one of your houses where I can live and die forgotten. . . .'

Meanwhile, however, it was urgent for him and his men to receive a decision, he said, and he begged Colin to lose no time in soliciting that decision from Rome conjointly with his pro-vicar.[13]

Five months later Pro-Vicar Bernin was in Lyon and delivered Bishop Douarre's letter to Superior General Colin, who at once wrote to Cardinal Fransoni on 12 June 1850. He told the cardinal that news about the death of Bishop Collomb, second Vicar Apostolic of Melanesia and Micronesia, had hardly arrived, 'when other letters came from New Caledonia informing us that the second attempt to get this mission established had completely failed. God, whose designs are always adorable, has been satisfied with the good will of the vicars apostolic and their missionaries in both of these missions. He has let them see the infidel land which they went to evangelise, but in his Providence he has refused them success. We submit ourselves with complete resignation to his Divine Will, no matter how painful we find this new sacrifice.'

Fransoni would learn from Bernin, Colin said, 'of the insurmountable obstacles encountered by the vicar apostolic and his missionaries. Kindly receive him with your usual goodness and benevolence.' Bernin's purpose in going to Rome was to present Douarre's proposals 'to which we adhere', Colin said; 'but we leave it up to the wisdom of the Sacred Congregation to indicate for us the most suitable action to take in this sorry situation.'

But before it acted on Douarre's proposal, Colin wanted the Evangelisation Congregation to give some consideration to a proposal of his own. 'We would be pleased with a mission in America', he said. 'Many requests have already come to us from various places in that part of the world, but we have held off because we were completely absorbed with the missions of Oceania. On the other hand, it is costly for us to bring back so many missionaries who have been transported to Oceania.'

Colin knew that the handful of sick Marists at Woodlark, the only mission station with personnel in the vast Vicariates of Melanesia and Micronesia, would appreciate receiving additional personnel. 'If we were not afraid of offending our conscience by exposing uselessly the lives of our colleagues,' he said, 'we would suggest that Your Eminence name one or two prefects apostolic for Woodlark and the surrounding islands, including New Guinea. Then we would try to engage some of the missionaries of the Most Reverend [Douarre] of Amata to go to this new mission. However, I doubt that this proposal would please them, since they all have informed me of their desire to follow the Most Reverend [Douarre] of Amata. . . .'[14]

This was the extent of Colin's token gesture on behalf of Melanesia and Micronesia.

On 14 June 1850, two days after Colin wrote his letter to Fransoni, Bernin drew up for the cardinal an extensive report on the New Caledonia calamity.

To all appearances there was some coaching by Colin, at least in the section where Bernin suggested new fields of activity for the banished bishop and his personnel. Douarre, Bernin said, 'would accept with gratitude a vicariate in Paraguay, or in Colombia where missionaries have already been requested from the Society of Mary, or also in Oregon [in North America], if this were possible'. Colin, he said, joined his petitions to those of Douarre 'in asking for another vicariate and in requesting that it be, as far as possible, in America'. However, 'in order not to abandon immediately the three vicariates of New Caledonia, Melanesia and Micronesia', Bernin suggested that provisionally some prefectures apostolic could be established with Marists in charge.[15]

By 'America' Douarre and Colin meant both North and South America. And when Colin told Fransoni that 'many requests' had come 'from various places in that part of the world', he meant in addition to the bishops of the three areas mentioned by Bernin also the bishops of Saint Louis and Dubuque in the United States and of Toronto in Canada.[16]

Pro-Vicar Bernin, bearer of a certified copy of Douarre's letter to Colin,[17] Colin's letter to Fransoni, and his own lengthy report, was well received at the Evangelisation Congregation in Rome. He was told by Cardinal Fransoni, however, that a transfer of Bishop Douarre and his priests to America was out of the question. In fact, the only territory that could be offered to Douarre as a substitute for the Vicariate Apostolic of New Caledonia was what the bishop himself had proposed, the Navigators Archipelago.

Fransoni's unequivocal stand made it clear that he was not at all agreeable that the Marists should shake the dust of Western Oceania from their feet and seek mission fields elsewhere. If they did so, it would be his job to find someone else to take their place. And who would want it?

As a result of Bernin's conferences with Cardinal Prefect Fransoni and Barnabò (who had been made secretary on 13 August 1848), it was agreed that (1) the Vicariate Apostolic of the Navigators Archipelago would be created and given to Bishop Douarre who would go there with some of his priests; (2) other priests would be sent to the missions of Melanesia and Micronesia under the direction of one or two prefects apostolic; and (3) another prefect apostolic with some priests would be left on the Isle of Pines, if possible, 'to keep an eye on New Caledonia and not abandon it completely, in case it should please the Lord to revive this mission'.

According to Cardinal Fransoni one obstacle blocked the realisation of this threefold proposal, namely that it was only fitting that Bishop Bataillon should be consulted before the division took place, since the Vicariate of the Navigators Archipelago would be carved from his Vicariate of Central Oceania. Bernin objected, however, saying that getting a reply from Bataillon would take two years, whereas the plight of Douarre and his missionaries could brook no delay. 'A prompt remedy' was needed, he said. Either Douarre should be given some new territory in Oceania or he should be recalled to Europe.

Since the Evangelisation Congregation was definitely opposed to having Douarre and his missionaries return to Europe, some substitute measure had to be found for consulting Bataillon. The solution, Fransoni suggested, was for Colin formally to petition the creation of the new vicariate, which implied a division of the Central Vicariate. He could be considered as having a title to do so, since the missions of Western Oceania in a general way were entrusted to his society. In fact, the cardinal said, other vicariates had been founded at Colin's request without waiting for the consent of the respective vicars apostolic. Examples of this were the vicariates of Central Oceania, Melanesia and Micronesia, and New Caledonia.

Colin in his letter of 12 June 1850 to Fransoni had said that he 'adhered' to Douarre's proposals; thereby he agreed implicitly to the division of Bataillon's vicariate and to the creation of a new one. But Fransoni wanted an explicit request for the Navigators Archipelago and so asked Bernin to write in his name and invite Colin to present such a request. This Bernin did after being assured by Fransoni that Bataillon subsequently would be informed by Rome of the division in a fitting and diplomatic way, as had been done in previous similar cases.[18]

Answering Bernin on 26 July, Colin said that he could not persuade himself to ask for the division of Bataillon's vicariate as requested by Fransoni. This would be overstepping his rights, since vicars apostolic by their elevation to the episcopacy had ceased to be his subordinates and were instead dependent directly upon the Holy See and the Evangelisation Congregation.

Bernin sent Colin's remarks to Fransoni, incorporating them in a letter of his own on 5 August 1850. Apparently in exasperation he added: 'Therefore, in the name of the Most Reverend [Douarre] of Amata, and because you have told me that you are not able to give him anything else, I ask Your Eminence for the Navigators Archipelago.' Bernin indicated that Douarre took it for granted that he would be placed in full charge of the new vicariate and that consequently he would be 'completely independent' of Bishop Bataillon. 'His Grace also requests that Your Eminence give him a written command to accept it. I am obliged to say this by my instructions; it was also mentioned in the letter to the Very Reverend Colin of which you have an extract.'

Colin was eager for Rome to take action immediately on behalf of his priests originally assigned to New Caledonia, Bernin said, because they 'have been compelled to inactivity for such a long time', causing him to be deeply concerned over their spiritual welfare. Bernin then issued what appeared to be a threat: 'If you should not be able to give him a clear and precise reply before the end of the month of August, be it for reasons which he could not but respect, he then would see himself obliged to have Bishop [Douarre] of Amata return to Europe. He would also feel obliged to grant his missionaries the freedom of following him [Bishop Douarre] to Europe, or of going to America to place themselves at the service of bishops there, who are asking him for personnel. And should this be the case, he would further see himself forced, though with regret, to request that you consider the proposal regarding prefectures, which he made to you, as not having been made. Although he does not care for Oceania at all, he does have a large number of missionaries at various places there. He would consider this

516 FOUNDING OF THE ROMAN CATHOLIC CHURCH IN OCEANIA

a fortunate circumstance facilitating negotiations for the Evangelisation Congregation in finding another religious community for Melanesia.' Colin's thinking was that another missionary group would take over Melanesia more readily if it knew that there were experienced missionaries on the spot to train its incoming priests.

Cardinal Fransoni, however, had told Bernin that it would be possible to divide the Central Oceania Vicariate immediately and give a part to Bishop Douarre. In that event, Bernin said, Colin had five specific points which concerned the Marist missionaries at Woodlark in Melanesia, and these Bernin listed. He concluded his letter by saying that he had been instructed to submit all the above views. 'Kindly take them into consideration', he urged Fransoni, 'and give me a prompt reply.' In a nota bene at the end of this letter of 5 August he said: 'I shall be leaving Rome on the 14th at the latest; probably on the 10th.'[19]

Bernin had requested the Navigators Archipelago in Douarre's name; but neither he nor Douarre had any authority over these islands. Colin did have some kind of authority over them according to Fransoni, but he did not dare to use it. This threw back into the lap of the Evangelisation Congregation the problem of offending Bataillon, an inevitable sequel to dividing his vicariate without previously consulting him. Consequently, when Cardinal Prefect Fransoni and Secretary Barnabò held a Particular Meeting on Thursday, 8 August 1850,[20] in order to study the Douarre-Bernin-Colin proposals, their discussion centred around Bataillon. Fransoni was convinced, however, that 'what could be adduced as contrary arguments did not seem able to counterbalance the advantages foreseen from the proposed expedient'. He therefore 'expressed his view in favour of the request in all of its parts'.[21]

On Friday morning, 9 August, Bernin had a conference with Barnabò, who was authorised by Fransoni to advise him—since he was leaving Rome—that there was every reason to hope that Douarre would receive the Navigators Archipelago, as requested.

At five o'clock on Saturday afternoon, 10 August, Bernin wrote his personal observations for Barnabò on their conference of the previous day, not realising how quickly Rome was acting on this matter. 'As Your Excellency knows,' he said, 'neither Bishop [Douarre] of Amata nor the Reverend Father Colin have the Navigators [Islands] in mind. The desires of both of them would take them to America or to any other civilised spot, which the Evangelisation Congregation would be able to offer us. . . .'[22]

But time was running out for Bernin! Earlier that same day Fransoni had written a letter which Bernin was to take to Superior General Colin. 'The requests made in the name of Your Reverence in a letter received from the Reverend C[laude-Marie] Bernin, Pro-Vicar Apostolic of New Caledonia,' he said, 'have been favourably received by the Sacred Congregation. To wit: the designation of two prefects apostolic for the mission of Melanesia and Micronesia as well as the proposed separation of the Navigators Archipelago from the Central Vicariate, in order to erect it as a distinct vicariate for the Most

Reverend Bishop [Douarre] of Amata.[23] The request to designate another prefect apostolic, should circumstances warrant this for those places of the New Caledonia Mission where perhaps there are still some members of the staff of the honoured Bishop [Douarre] of Amata, has also been granted.'

Fransoni enclosed letters patent and also faculties for the new prefects apostolic, leaving them blank as Colin had requested, but asking that he later send in the names of the candidates chosen so that the Sacred Congregation could complete its records. In order to erect the proposed Vicariate Apostolic of the Navigators Archipelago, however, 'superior sanction' of the pope was needed. 'I shall not fail to present the matter in question to His Holiness at the next audience tomorrow', he said, 'and I am convinced that it will meet with no obstacles. Then I shall inform you of the result in the coming week.'[24]

On the following day, Sunday, 11 August 1850, Secretary Barnabò had the audience for the Sacred Congregation referred to by Cardinal Fransoni and he read to Pope Pius IX a detailed eleven-page 'Report on Western Oceania'. It emphasised the difficulties which the Marists were having in the Vicariate of Melanesia and Micronesia and in the Vicariate of New Caledonia. In the former vicariate, the first vicar apostolic had been killed at the outset and the second had died soon after from fever; only a remnant of their missionaries survived on a small unhealthy island where they were awaiting reinforcements or new orders. These 'repeated disasters', in fact, had persuaded Superior General Colin to ask the Evangelisation Congregation to exonerate his society of responsibility for this mission.

'And in New Caledonia almost the same disaster occurred as in Melanesia and Micronesia because . . . of the ferocious character of these islanders. . . .' He described for the pope how one missionary had been killed and the rest put to flight, how a second attempt had been made under the new vicar apostolic, Douarre, and how this group also had to flee when the bishop learned 'that it had been decided to massacre all of them'. Since Douarre had fled with ten of his missionaries to the Isle of Pines and had sent nine other missionaries to Sydney, he now wanted new orders and had sent Pro-Vicar Apostolic Bernin to Lyon and to Rome to get them.

As an alternative to recalling such a large number of missionaries and their bishop to Europe, Barnabò said, it had been suggested that the Navigators Archipelago be separated from the Central Oceania Vicariate and be erected into an independent vicariate apostolic with Douarre in charge as vicar apostolic. This would provide a new mission field for him and he could take along some of his missionaries. A further proposal was 'to send other missionaries [of his] to the missions of Melanesia and Micronesia, but under the direction of one or two prefects [apostolic]. The choice of vicars apostolic with the rank of bishop [for those missions] would be postponed until the efforts of the missionaries there should prove to be more fortunate, or when the Sacred Congregation should succeed in finding other personnel to send there.' If practicable, he added, another prefect apostolic would be sent to the Isle of Pines 'in order to keep an eye on New Caledonia and not abandon it completely. . . .'

Not a word was said by Barnabò of Colin's desire to send the New Caledonia missionaries to America and of Douarre's similar desire to obtain a vicariate apostolic there.

Barnabò then explained in great detail why it was impossible to contact Vicar Apostolic Bataillon in advance, as called for by protocol, and why Superior General Colin had refused, when the Sacred Congregation had asked him to request formally the division of the Central Oceania Vicariate and the foundation of the desired vicariate. Pro-Vicar Bernin had then made the request, he said, since a decision on behalf of the missionaries had to be taken by the end of August 'on either changing their location or recalling them to Europe'.

Describing the conference that he and Cardinal Prefect Fransoni had held on this matter three days earlier (8 August), he told the pope that the cardinal was 'in favour of the request in all of its parts', in spite of the counter arguments proposed. Of these the chief one was that 'in the past, when divisions and foundations of new vicariates were made without previous official consultation of the prelates, they had shown themselves displeased'. This had been the case, Barnabò said, 'with Bishop Pompallier when the Central Vicariate was erected and again afterwards when the Vicariate of Melanesia and Micronesia was erected'. Also Bishop Bataillon had been displeased when New Caledonia was separated from his vicariate and again when the Friendly or Tonga Archipelago was removed in order to be attached to Bishop Pompallier's Western Vicariate, 'although this was only a provisional measure. . . .' He pointed out further for the pope's information that both Bishop Douarre and Superior General Colin 'are convinced that a division will displease' Bishop Bataillon. For this reason 'it is desired that Bishop [Douarre] of Amata in his brief should be commanded to take charge'.

Barnabò also pointed out some positive observations made by Colin. He had stated that both Bataillon and Douarre were dependent upon the Evangelisation Congregation, that they held office as vicars of the Holy See, and that they would easily recognise the great good that would accrue to religion from founding the new vicariate.

Additional motives 'which His Eminence appreciated so highly and would make him favour the request, if this should seem well to Your Holiness', Barnabò said, were 'the circumstances in which such a large number of experienced and well-merited priests together with their zealous prelate find themselves; the abandonment of the missions of Melanesia and Micronesia, where some of the missionaries in question would go; and the vastness of the Central Vicariate. . . .' Here Barnabò proceeded to list for the pope the main islands and archipelagoes in Bataillon's vicariate.[25] If Bishop Douarre were also active in this vast expanse of islands, he said, the propagation of the Catholic faith would be expedited. Besides, Douarre had formerly been Bataillon's coadjutor.[26] And finally, Barnabò pointed out, there were also 'the advantages that would flow from dividing large missions and making them smaller, from increasing activity there, and from multiplying centres with bishops'.

Because Pro-Vicar Bernin meanwhile had had to leave Rome, Barnabò added, Cardinal Fransoni had given him hope 'that the proposed reorganisation on behalf of Bishop [Douarre] of Amata would be graciously accepted. Nor did His Eminence believe that he had to delay in sending the necessary letters patent and documents for the designation of the prefects apostolic in the missions of Melanesia and Micronesia and also for the Isle of Pines, if feasible, to facilitate taking up work again in New Caledonia. However, he did postpone replying to the Superior of the Society [of Mary] on the creation of the Vicariate Apostolic of the Navigators Archipelago, in order to await whether Your Holiness in your wisdom would judge it opportune to give your approval. And this was the purpose of my presenting this present report.'

After hearing it Pope Pius IX confirmed the nomination of the prefects apostolic and he gave orders that the Vicariate Apostolic of the Navigators Archipelago should be created. 'He also pointed out', Barnabò said, 'that a letter should be sent contemporaneously to Bishop Bataillon explaining the motives which had induced the Holy See without further delay to take these measures which are required for the welfare of the faithful and that of so many missionaries, who would otherwise have had to be recalled from those places at great expense.'[27]

By this action Pope Pius IX on 11 August 1850 founded the Vicariate Apostolic of the Navigators Archipelago.

Fransoni wrote to Colin on Wednesday, 14 August, saying that he had made the report to the Holy Father, mentioned in his previous letter, and that His Holiness 'has deigned to approve and sanction the changes suggested on behalf of Bishop [Douarre] of Amata and his collaborators'. Pius IX had ordered as well the preparation of special briefs to announce the foundation of the new vicariate apostolic and to name the new vicar apostolic, 'and I myself shall transmit them to Your Reverence as soon as they are ready'.

With his letter of 14 August to Colin he enclosed additional letters of the same date for Bataillon and Douarre, adding to them 'an authentic copy of the decree of the Sacred Congregation'.[28] It would take some time before the papal briefs would be ready, Fransoni told Colin, and by receiving the decrees the two bishops would have official word as soon as possible of the decisions reached. The letters had purposely been left open so that Colin could read them and also the enclosed decree and, if he wished, make copies of them. 'You will then kindly transmit them to the respective prelates, so that the provision in question may take effect. . . .'[29]

In the letter to Douarre the cardinal said that Colin and Bernin had sent him word on what had happened in New Caledonia and had informed him how the bishop and his companions had been forced to abandon that area against their will. Wanting to assist him, and yet not being able to allow the missions of Oceania 'to be deprived of so many priests and of your ministry', Fransoni said, 'we presented the matter to His Holiness for a solution. What His Holiness thought should be done—in accord with the wish of the Sacred Congregation—you will learn from the enclosed decree of the Sacred Congregation itself. And we have no doubt that you will carry out, as is proper, the wishes of the Holy See without delay, and with that complete respect and devotion which you manifest toward the Holy See.' The cardinal assured him that the papal brief ordered by His Holiness would be forwarded as soon as possible. He also promised to acquaint Bataillon with the contents of the enclosed decree and with all else concerning the new vicariate. And he told Douarre that when in God's plan the time should come to reestablish the mission of New Caledonia, the Sacred Congregation would do all in its power to achieve this. 'Meanwhile we commend to you very highly the government of the new vicariate which has been entrusted to Your Grace. . . .'[30]

The most difficult letter of all for Fransoni to write was the one addressed to Bishop Bataillon, Vicar Apostolic of Central Oceania. He began by saying that Bataillon must have learned of the tragedy which had struck the New Caledonia mission. 'The Most Excellent Bishop [Douarre] of Amata, namely, was forced together with all his priests to desert completely the vineyard entrusted to him. This happened after long efforts and tireless labours, after taking all kinds of care—but in vain—for promoting the eternal salvation of these peoples, and after being placed in extreme danger of death by their ferocity. As a result almost 20 priests of the Society of Mary and their bishop would have had to return to Europe unless the Holy See had provided otherwise.'

Another consideration, he pointed out, was the fact that in Melanesia and Micronesia 'the missions had hardly begun when their first and their second bishop and also many priests were snatched away by death. This almost utterly ruined the missions.' At the time this news arrived, he said, the Sacred Congregation had been planning to get more priests and even bishops for that double vicariate; it was also planning to divide it so that there would be more activity in that vast territory.

In fact, Fransoni said, the Evangelisation Congregation was also thinking of approaching Bataillon about a similar division for his Central Vicariate, 'when we heard of the two sorrowful calamities and learned of the straits in which our beloved Bishop [Douarre] of Amata and his priests found themselves. Their plight was such that they needed help without delay; nor did it allow us the opportunity to ask for and learn your view, as we would have liked to do. Therefore this Sacred Congregation, after maturely considering all aspects, and not wanting to lose the ministry of so many priests and their excellent bishop, which it could use in such extensive regions, easily persuaded itself in these circumstances and in view of the advantages that would accrue to religion, that Your Grace would not be offended, but would be most happy, if some part of the Central Mission should be given over to the above-mentioned bishop, a former coadjutor in that same mission, to be ruled by him and to be cared for by his companions. The result would be', Fransoni continued, 'that your own burden would be lessened and that you would more easily be able to care for your vicariate and provide for its needs, since it would be reduced in size.

'The decision was therefore reached that some of the priests of New Caledonia should be sent to evangelise the peoples of Melanesia and Micronesia. It was also decided to entreat our Holy Father kindly to entrust the government of the archipelago called Samoa or Navigators, after separating it from the Central Mission and erecting it into a vicariate apostolic, to Bishop [Douarre] of Amata and to the rest of his missionaries. We make no delay in informing Your Grace that His Holiness approved and sanctioned this. Later on we shall send you the Apostolic Letter in the form of a brief, which His Holiness ordered to be issued on this matter and to be communicated to Bishop [Douarre] of Amata and to you.' Fransoni also told Bataillon that the Sacred Congregation at a later date and at a time determined by God would give thought to reviving the New Caledonia mission. And he earnestly recommended Douarre and his missionaries to Bataillon, saying that he knew they were all very closely bound together, since they were members of one and the same society.[31]

This was Fransoni's way of trying to keep Bataillon from being offended.

The name 'Samoa' came up for the first time in official usage by Rome in this 14 August 1850 letter to Bataillon and was mentioned also in the Evangelisation Congregation's decree of that date. The papal brief that Fransoni had promised to send also referred to the 'Vicariate Apostolic of the Samoa or Navigators Archipelago'. This brief in duplicate and also another announcing the choice of Douarre as the first vicar apostolic were dated 20 August 1850.[32] Fransoni sent them to Colin on 7 September and asked him kindly to forward them to Bishops Douarre and Bataillon.[33] Colin replied on 25 September that he had received the 14 August letters and decrees near the end of August, and recently the papal briefs as well, all of which he had forwarded to Bishops Douarre and Bataillon without delay.[34]

Rome's work was done. It had fulfilled to the letter the wishes of Douarre, Bernin and Colin, with the sole exception of not allowing Douarre and his priests to go to America. Douarre's transfer from the office of Vicar Apostolic of New Caledonia to that of Vicar Apostolic of the Samoa or Navigators Archipelago did not mean, of course, that the New Caledonia Vicariate was dissolved. But it did mean that three huge vicariates—Melanesia, Micronesia and New Caledonia—no longer had Marist bishops in charge. Was this a premonition of a massive Marist retreat from Oceania? If so, would Rome succeed in finding other missionaries to take their place?

35

The Marists ask to be discharged of Micronesia and Melanesia Vicariates

1848-50

The Society of Mary was not founded as a foreign mission society. Its involvement in this area began on 10 February 1836 with its acceptance of responsibility for conducting missionary work in Western Oceania.[1] But the constant strife which Superior General Colin had with Bishop Pompallier and the impossibility of giving what he considered due spiritual direction and guidance to his members on the other side of the world, as well as their physical suffering and mental anguish, led him gradually to lose interest in Oceania. The turning point came during his six-month stay in Rome, from 4 December 1846 to 18 June 1847, when he tried in vain to have Roman authorities accept Pompallier's resignation as Vicar Apostolic of Western Oceania.

Ten weeks after Colin left Rome for France, his Oratorian priest friend and confidant, Father Theiner, wrote to him on 28 August 1847, reproving him for losing interest in Oceania. 'Only one thought afflicts me,' he said, 'and it is that Your Paternity apparently still wishes to abandon missionary work and to dedicate yourself completely to France. But I adjure you for the love of Jesus Christ to banish this thought from your noble and holy heart. If you do not, you shall deprive your society of numerous heavenly blessings. And as I see it your society appears to be particularly revitalised by the Lord in our days for reanimating the dying faith in France and also for lighting the flame of faith among idolatrous peoples. Can anyone have a more holy, a more heavenly mission! And finally, you and your sons fight under the banner of the Holy Virgin Mary and is not she the Mother of all men, infidels as well as Christians? Then cast aside the efforts which you are making in order to acquire a comfortable future. . . .'[2]

Eventually Pompallier was ordered by Rome to remain in France indefinitely and the funds which he formerly had received were directed to Coadjutor Viard, a Marist, through Colin's hands. This settlement made Colin feel that New Zealand could now be developed in peace by him and his society and he wrote to Cardinal Prefect Fransoni in a happy frame of mind. 'I cannot thank the Sacred Congregation enough', he said, 'for at last putting an end to a state of affairs which could not last much longer. In fact, as our New Zealand missionaries wrote in 1846, it would be difficult to find in the whole of Church history a situation analogous to that which has troubled this mission for 11 years.'[3]

This letter from Colin dated 7 February 1848 crossed a letter that Fransoni wrote to him on 31 January for his views on a proposal dated 31 May 1847 that had just arrived from Bishop Collomb, Vicar Apostolic of Melanesia and Micronesia. Collomb proposed that the Vicariate of Micronesia be separated from the Vicariate of Melanesia 'as soon as possible' and that the Vicariate of Melanesia then be subdivided 'into several other vicariates'. Colin replied on 12 February 1848 that he was in favour of having the two vicariates separated and that it would give him the greatest pleasure if the Holy See were then to entrust Micronesia 'to some other religious community and also provide it with a vicar apostolic' of its own. But a subdivision of the Vicariate of Melanesia, he said, was premature.

This reply from Colin disillusioned Fransoni, since he had thought that the suggested division would stir up Colin's zeal on behalf of Micronesia and prompt him to send a rather large number of missionaries there. Nor was he aware that this request to be relieved of responsibility for Micronesia fitted into Colin's plan for giving his society a predominantly French-oriented apostolate. Fransoni informed Colin on 4 March that his proposal for immediately separating the Melanesia-Micronesia Vicariates would be presented to the other cardinals at a General Meeting. But this would be 'very hard' to realise, he pointed out, 'because of the difficulty at this time in finding a religious community to which Micronesia might be entrusted. . . .' Fransoni hinted strongly that if Colin kept some men there, it would be easier for the Evangelisation Congregation to find another order willing to take over. The superiors of the new group would want someone there on the spot to train their men. He asked Colin to let him know whether his society 'could make efforts of some kind on behalf of Micronesia, since this would facilitate the desired division. . . .'

Meanwhile Bishop Pompallier, who was in Rome, had asked all the cardinals of the Evangelisation Congregation on 15 January 1848 and again on 17 February to allow him to return to New Zealand because he now had personnel and funds. He had also presented to the pope, in an effort to have his uncertain status clarified, some concrete proposals for dividing New Zealand between the Marists and himself. Fransoni indicated these concrete proposals in his letter to Colin of 4 March and asked him to express his views on them.[4] Fransoni did not inform Colin, however, that Pompallier had suggested sending the New Zealand Marists to Ascension or Ponape in Micronesia, if they did not want to remain in New Zealand with him, since that archipelago 'has been asking for the benefits of salvation for many years'.[5]

Colin's reply of 29 March 1848 made no mention of Micronesia and took no stand on Pompallier's concrete proposals. He was evidently disillusioned by the Roman authorities who once again, after giving him such assurances, were wavering on the question of keeping Pompallier in Europe. It would be best for him to keep silent, he said, and he ended his letter on a sombre note with a reference to the French Revolution which had made Louis-Philippe lose his throne the previous month. 'The grave events taking place in France', he said, 'leave us uncertain about our future and by the same token about the collaboration that henceforth we shall be able to give to the foreign missions. . . .'[6]

Barnabites

Whereas Colin considered uprisings and revolutions in France a restricting factor for missionary work, forty-two-year-old Father Luigi Agostino Cornaggia of Milan, son of Marchese Carlo Cornaggia, believed that a revolution in Italy might make missionary work possible for him. He was professor of mathematics, natural history and other subjects at Collegio di Santa Maria degli Angeli conducted by the Clerics Regular of Saint Paul, Barnabites, at Monza, near Milan. He wrote to Cardinal Fransoni and asked to be assigned to a foreign mission in case his religious community should be suppressed by some uprising. His letter was dated 2 March 1848, just two days before Fransoni had written to Colin stating that it would be difficult for him to find a religious community to take over Micronesia.

'Eighteen years ago, when I was on the point of taking vows after a three-year probation,' Cornaggia wrote, 'I said that I would serve the [Evangelisation] Congregation in any office that might be given to me and, in case of suppression, that I would dedicate myself to the missions. The recent turbulence in Italy has made us fear that this moment has arrived. And the revolution which has now exploded in Paris hardly leaves me any reason to doubt it. I therefore humbly submit this petition of mine in order now to obtain letters patent which would be valid, only in case of suppression, for that part of the world to which the Sacred Evangelisation Congregation would be pleased to destine me, even though it be the frozen regions of the Eskimos. . . .' He added that he enjoyed excellent health and knew already or was studying Latin, Greek, French, German, English and Spanish languages which he might need where he would be sent. His brothers in Milan would give him 2,000 Milan lire a year, if suppression did take place, and this 'would be enough', he said, 'so that I would not be a burden to the Sacred Congregation. . . .'[7]

The problem of possible suppression of the Barnabites was discussed in Rome by Superior General Francesco Maria Caccia and his four assistants that month on 26 March. 'It has been asked whether it might be expedient, in view of the peculiar circumstances endangering religious orders in Italy today, to ask the Sacred Congregation for the Evangelisation of Nations to grant us some sacred mission in infidel lands, so that if our members should be forced to leave the colleges which we now have, they could—if they so wished—flee to the foreign regions. . . .' The vote was affirmative.[8] Superior General Caccia that same day prepared a request for such a mission, so that 'if we should be forced to desert our colleges, we could legitimately flee to these foreign nations'.[9]

The Barnabites were reading the signs of the times well. At Montevideo, Uruguay, Giuseppe Garibaldi, the Italian patriot and general, was preparing to embark with some fifty soldiers to fight and work for unity. He set sail for Italy three weeks later, 15 April.

With Father Cornaggia's letter in hand Pro-Secretary Barnabò wrote to the Barnabite superior general on 20 April 1848, calling him Father Paolo Picconi, because he was unaware that this office had changed hands on 1 May the previous year. He enclosed Cornaggia's letter and said that Cardinal Prefect Fransoni had charged him 'to request the view of Your Most Reverend Paternity' on the offer made.[10]

Caccia answered on 25 April that all of the information in Cornaggia's letter about himself was correct and he praised the priest highly. In fact the Barnabite Order, if suppressed, would appreciate 'having some mission in infidel lands assigned to it by the authority of the Holy See', he said, 'to which not only one or the other, but many religious of the same community could go and, in view of their way of life, also carry out in a united way the task of evangelisation. . . .'[11]

Barnabò on 6 May asked Superior General Caccia to inform Father Cornaggia that Cardinal Prefect Fransoni would keep his offer in mind in case the order were suppressed. 'And although we hope it will not take place', Barnabò added, Fransoni would try to see whether there was some mission where Cornaggia and other Barnabites could work together if suppression did take place. He added, however, that it would be necessary for the Barnabites to supply sufficient funds 'to cover the expenses of the voyages, etc., because circumstances at the present time make it impossible for the Sacred Congregation to provide for such costs. . . .'[12]

Negotiations with the Barnabites about a possible mission had proceeded thus far when the Evangelisation Congregation held a General Meeting on 29 May 1848 at which the principal business under discussion was whether or not Bishop Pompallier should be sent back to New Zealand. Since this problem involved the Marists, another Marist problem was brought up, namely, Collomb's proposed separation of the Vicariate of Micronesia from that of Melanesia, and the cardinals were advised of Colin's views on the matter. They decided to postpone the separation and instructed Fransoni to write to Colin once again, urging him to supply some missionaries for Micronesia temporarily. Meanwhile the cardinal prefect was 'to begin negotiations with some religious community which might like to be placed in charge of this mission'. These decisions, as well as those regarding New Zealand, were approved and ratified by Pope Pius IX on 4 June 1848.[13]

One need not page through the minutes of the Evangelisation Congregation meetings very long to learn that one of its most ready solutions for problems is to use two problems as solutions for one another. And that is what happened here: since the Barnabites wanted a mission, and since the Marists wanted to get rid of one, the Marist mission was offered to the Barnabites. But instead of writing to Superior General Caccia this time, Barnabò wrote to Procurator General Benedetto Grampini, with whom he had more direct contact, referring in this new letter of 23 June 1848 to his previous letter of 6 May to Caccia.

'A most opportune circumstance now makes it possible for the Sacred Congregation to utilise the activity of various members of your institute,' he said, 'since the proposal has been made to separate the mission of Melanesia from that of Micronesia in the western part of Oceania. The second of these would be entrusted to the Barnabite Fathers and the first would remain entrusted to the

Society of Marist priests of Lyon, now residing there. They would also offer to remain there and give assistance until the Barnabite Fathers are in a position to manage this mission by themselves.'

The Barnabite mission in Micronesia would be headed by 'a vicar apostolic with the rank of bishop', chosen from among the Barnabites. 'And as the Catholic faith spreads throughout those vast archipelagoes', the Barnabites would provide the reinforcements as needed. For a start, Barnabò said, eight or ten priests would be sufficient. And he stressed particularly for Procurator General Grampini that the situation in Europe made finances still a problem for the Evangelisation Congregation, as he had already pointed out in his letter of 6 May to Superior General Caccia. It therefore was necessary for the Barnabites 'to try to provide either entirely or at least for the most part the funds needed for the expedition in question', just as Cornaggia's relatives had pledged to do, thus 'exonerating the Sacred Congregation completely from such expenses'.

Barnabò asked Grampini to take up the matter with Superior General Caccia. And if his reply should be positive, and if the Barnabites could accept the mission at once, 'the Most Eminent Prefect would then make further arrangements with you to put the desired plan into effect. I therefore ask you to give me a reply, since in the negative case I would have to turn to another religious community. . . .'[14]

Grampini answered Barnabò on 30 June 1848, explaining that the delay was due to his having to get Caccia's views, as Barnabò had instructed him to do, and that Caccia in turn had wanted to get the views of his four assistants. Grampini, who said that now he knew his superior general's sentiments 'precisely', pointed out that Caccia's 'desire to have a mission . . . was—if I may express it in this way—limited by various conditions'. The first of these was the suppression of the order, which had not taken place and which would make it 'easier to provide the personnel needed for the mission'. In this event the assistance from missionaries there on the spot would be needed until the Barnabites could manage by themselves.

'Another condition and wish expressed', Grampini said, 'was that the personnel to be assigned to the mission could still remain united in some way in practising their apostolic ministry. This would be the case if they had a mission field for themselves, or a portion of a continent, or at least an island of some extent, not excluding other minor ones not too far distant. But this condition cannot be verified in the proposed mission of Micronesia, it seems, since it would contain exclusively the smallest of the many islands of Oceania. In them of necessity the missionaries would be so far apart from one another as not to be able as the need arises to visit and consult with one another without exposing themselves to inconvenience, to dangers, and—I might also add—to the expense of sea voyages that would not be very short.'

The third and last condition for acceptance was that the Barnabite Congregation 'would not have to bear by itself the cost of transportation and of successive maintenance of personnel', but would receive financial assistance 'as is practised toward other religious orders'. This aid was all the more needed because Caccia's supplying of men would be caused by suppression of the order, which meant that its funds 'either would be totally lacking or at least would have dwindled very much'. This in turn would cause an insuperable difficulty, Grampini noted, 'since the cost of sending and providing for the new missionaries would be so enormous, in view of the immense distance of these archipelagoes from us, that such an expense could not be borne by the Congregation of Barnabites, neither in its entirety nor in notable part'.

Notwithstanding, Grampini concluded, the Barnabites would always be ready to accept a mission proportionate to their needs and resources.[15]

Grampini's reply, which most likely was delivered that day by hand, left no doubt in Barnabò's mind; the Evangelisation Congregation would have to offer Micronesia to someone else!

It would appear that Fransoni and Barnabò had been suspending other business pending the reply from Grampini, because they waited until 30 June 1848, the date of Grampini's letter, before writing to Superior General Colin about the decisions taken by the Evangelisation Congregation on 29 May and approved by Pope Pius IX as early as 4 June. 'The difficulty that I earlier mentioned to Your Reverence about finding at this time a religious community to which the Micronesia Mission could be entrusted', Cardinal Prefect Fransoni wrote, 'has caused the Eminent Fathers to postpone for the time being' the division of the Vicariates of Melanesia and Micronesia, but meanwhile efforts would still be made 'to obtain the desired result'. In an apparent reference to one of the points mentioned by Grampini, Fransoni told Colin that if he did succeed 'in finding . . . a [religious] community for Micronesia, this community could not become capable of assuming charge of it and caring for it without the help and cooperation of Marist priests at least for some time'.

It was therefore necessary as a preparation for such a transfer that Colin should send 'some new missionaries temporarily' to Bishop Collomb, especially 'in view of the extensive size of Melanesia itself'. Fransoni asked Colin to assure Bishop Collomb 'at the same time that the Sacred Congregation will make every effort to fulfil his wishes for the requested division as soon as it can'.[16]

This letter was still en route to Colin when he wrote to Fransoni from Belley on 6 July 1848, saying that in his last letter he had expressed fears for the success of the San Cristóbal Mission in Melanesia. 'My fears were founded on the unhealthy climate . . . and above all on the cannibalistic nature of the islanders. Alas, my apprehensions have been realised most unfortunately!'

He then explained how Bishop Collomb had escaped with his life at New Caledonia and how he had arrived at San Cristóbal on 28 August 1847 only to learn 'that one of his missionaries had died from exhaustion, that three others had been massacred and beaten by the savages, and that six others—three priests and three Brothers whom he still had—were consumed with fever. During the four months just passed they had been besieged in their cabin by the islanders, who wanted to take their lives. . . .' Bishop Collomb then took the surviving missionaries aboard and abandoned San Cristóbal, going with them to Woodlark, Colin said, 'an island which is a short distance from the Louisiades. But it appears equally unhealthy since the missionaries are affected there by fever like they were at San Cristóbal.'

Colin then pleaded with Rome. 'Your Eminence, behold a mission that has been almost annihilated. It has cost the Society of Mary 18 missionaries. . . .' Five of these had lost their lives—Bishop Epalle at Santa Isabel Island and four others at San Cristóbal—and 'many have been forced to withdraw for reasons of health'. As a result there were only three priests and three Brother-Catechists now with Bishop Collomb and their health 'is practically ruined because of privations and sickness'. New Caledonia, where a lay Brother had been killed, and now San Cristóbal, Colin said, distresses us but does not discourage us. 'For we know that the blood of martyrs is a glory for the Church and the seed of Christians. And yet these sorrowful events give us an opportunity to propose that the Sacred Congregation should kindly give the two important missions of Melanesia and Micronesia—for the sake of the salvation of souls—to other societies which have more abundant resources and which are more solidly established. This proposal, which has been on our mind for some time, has been caused by grave difficulties of the times and has been counselled by wise bishops and other grave personages. It will be a pleasure for us if the Sacred Congregation deigns to receive favourably our proposal. In this hypothesis we do not at all doubt that Bishop Collomb would gratefully accept the nomination as coadjutor of Bishop Bataillon, Vicar Apostolic of Central Oceania.'[17]

Fransoni sent Colin his sympathy on 7 August 1848, saying that in spite of the calamity in Melanesia, 'I would not know how I could approve and follow Your Reverence's suggestions, namely, to declare your excellent society exonerated from the care of those missions, to entrust them to another religious community, and to transfer Bishop Collomb to the office of coadjutor to the Vicar Apostolic of Central Oceania. Let me say first that it would be impossible for me now to find another religious community to take your place, one which would be in a position to take on such a task, since I have no funds at this time to cover the exorbitant costs of the voyages. Nor do I consider it prudent to adopt any decision before we obtain further information from Bishop [Collomb] of Antiphellus on the arrangements that he may have made after abandoning San Cristóbal.

'In fact, what happened in New Caledonia did not crush the zeal of the excellent Bishop [Douarre] of Amata, but only animated it all the more, prompting him to make attempts in several places to reestablish his destroyed mission. In the same way we must not be quick to despair that Bishop [Collomb] of Antiphellus will not find another place in so great an expanse of archipelagoes and islands as are contained in his double vicariate; I mean a place that is safe and has at the same time a healthful climate, where he can revive the nascent mission. With this in mind and trusting in divine assistance, which I do not cease to implore incessantly from the most loving God, I suspend for now every measure whatsoever while awaiting further news, which I hope will be most reassuring. . . .'[18]

Colin did not yet have this 7 August 1848 letter from Fransoni when he wrote to Fransoni again on 11 August, the day after receiving further news about the San Cristóbal missionaries now on Woodlark Island with Bishop Collomb. When the ship had left them, Colin told Fransoni, they were all sick with a severe fever. Colin pleaded that 'withdrawing them from such a position as promptly as possible would seem to be an act both of charity and of justice. The relatives of the missionaries keep clamouring insistently that this should be done; certainly the Sacred Congregation will not fail to give its approval. Consequently we are taking immediate steps to help them. Nevertheless I shall not fail to engage them earnestly to remain at their posts—at least until the Evangelisation Congregation has replaced them with other priests taken from some other community that is more solidly established—on condition that their health has improved by the time my letters arrive and that the mission offers some chances of success.'[19]

Colin then wrote to his missionaries along these lines, instructing them, if necessary, to retire to Sydney in order to regain their health and then to proceed from there to other Marist vicariates.[20]

Meanwhile Bishop Collomb had died on 16 July 1848, but the news did not reach Cardinal Fransoni until early March 1850. He wrote to Colin on 9 March, saying that he had just received from Pro-Vicar Montrouzier in Melanesia 'the very sad news of the death of the Most Reverend Collomb'. It was precisely to prevent such an unfortunate 'interruption in the pastoral ministry' that Collomb in June 1848 had been granted 'the faculty of choosing a coadjutor with right of succession. . . .' But his death in the following month, Fransoni said, meant that 'the brief in question did not reach the deceased bishop in time for him to make use of it before he passed on to eternal rest'. The Sacred Congregation was eager 'to have a successor as soon as possible', and Fransoni therefore asked Colin 'to indicate for me what priests from among those excellent missionaries, or what other individuals in your well-merited society, could in your judgment be kept in mind by the Holy See as most capable candidates for the above-mentioned office, men worthy of the episcopal dignity. This information would expedite the papal decisions that need to be made.'[21]

Colin, however, wanted no successor named for Bishop Collomb. In fact, he wanted to renew his previous requests to have his society exonerated completely of responsibility for Melanesia and Micronesia. He addressed his reply to Barnabò, although he was answering a letter from Fransoni, and pleaded for his intercession with the Sacred Congregation. Barnabò at this time was no longer pro-secretary, but secretary, having advanced to that office on 13 August 1848. In fact, later that year he became for all practical purposes the acting prefect of the Evangelisation Congregation, because Cardinal Prefect Fransoni fled to Naples on 24 November 1848, the same day that Pope Pius IX fled to Gaeta on the coast north of Naples. Since this exile lasted until 12 April 1850, it is not surprising that Colin on 23 April 1850 should address his plea to Barnabò.

'In the Vicariate of Melanesia', he said, 'our two bishops, the Most Reverend Epalle and the Most Reverend Collomb, as well as four priests and one Brother-

Catechist, met sudden deaths, some by hatchets of the infidels and others because of the rigours of an unhealthy climate. Six additional missionaries have been obliged to abandon this mission because their health wasted away completely. Out of 20 missionaries furnished for this vicariate there remain at Woodlark no more than seven: five priests and two Brother-Catechists. Further, these men have been remarkably weakened by the privations and fevers which are customarily to be found in these lands.'

Colin explained how the news of the killings at San Cristóbal and the sickness of the survivors had prompted him to invite the missionaries to go to Sydney to recuperate and then go to another Marist vicariate, unless there was hope of success in their mission. But the missionaries had replied to him in 1849, he said, that they did not dare to make the decision to abandon the mission by themselves and that they were waiting impatiently for additional personnel or for unequivocal orders to leave. 'These being the circumstances,' Colin said, 'it would not appear prudent for us to designate one of the missionaries still at Woodlark for the episcopacy, because we would be exposing ourselves to the unpleasantness, probably, of learning either that he had died or that he had retired to Sydney even before receiving his bulls.'

Nor did Colin 'dare to believe that it enters into the designs of Providence that a society or association simply of priests, such as ours, should intervene in the designation of vicars apostolic. Your Excellency will understand readily the wisdom of the motives that seem to command this abstention for us. We could well furnish some missionaries for those vicars apostolic who would appear willing to give us guarantees of peace and security. But the experience that we have acquired in the past 14 years, during which time we have been occupied with foreign missions, has convinced us that it was neither wise, nor expedient, for a simple religious community to bring together so many of its missionaries in an area like Oceania, above all in view of the measures that have been used and imposed until now. Therefore, Monsignor, we dare to call your attention to our letter', dated 11 August 1848,[22] 'and to renew to you the request that we made to the Sacred Congregation at that time, namely, that it entrust to other religious communities the two Vicariates of Melanesia and Micronesia. It would seem that the salvation of souls and the need to hasten the promulgation of the Gospel in these numerous islands would require that the Holy See take this measure.

'We do not refuse to keep at Woodlark the missionaries now there,' he said, 'and even to increase their number, should they become firmly established there. But we do believe that such a vast mission as Melanesia is beyond our forces alone and our means alone. Our New Zealand missionaries in their letters [when referring to the Port Nicholson Diocese which has been assigned to our society] state that nothing has been left over for them but a vast wilderness to be cleared away. If we could be certain that a number of them would agree to transfer to Melanesia in order to join their colleagues at Woodlark, we would gladly assign them there. But we are not aware of their sentiments, nor of the stand that they ultimately will take.'

Colin summed up his letter by begging Barnabò 'kindly to explain to the Sacred Congregation the motives which compel us to discharge ourselves of the Vicariates of Melanesia and Micronesia. Also make known the respect that we have for it and present our very humble excuses. . . .'[23]

Picpus Fathers

Barnabò was moved by Colin's letter and at the end of it he appended this brief note: 'Reply that efforts will be made to find other missionaries and then write to Most Reverend Bonamie and offer him the mission. . . .'[24]

Bonamie in Paris was superior general of the Picpus Fathers, who at this time were in charge of the three vicariates of Sandwich Islands, Marquesas Islands and Tahiti Islands in Eastern Oceania. Bonamie, however, had been informed earlier that Rome was thinking of offering Melanesia to his religious community. He had learned this from Bishop Baudichon, Vicar Apostolic of Marquesas Islands, who was in Rome when Barnabò received Colin's letter of 23 April 1850.

Baudichon, as coadjutor for Bishop Rouchouze, the Vicar Apostolic of Eastern Oceania who perished at sea, was in charge of the very extensive Eastern Oceania Vicariate for several years. But on 9 April 1848, due to Bonamie's proposal, Rome reduced the size of this vicariate, restricting it to the Marquesas Islands, placing Baudichon in charge (or allowing him to succeed in virtue of his right of succession as coadjutor), and renaming it the Vicariate Apostolic of Marquesas Islands. The much larger remnant of the previous Eastern Oceania Vicariate was called the Vicariate Apostolic of Tahiti Islands and another Picpus member was placed in charge.[25]

Baudichon was at Papeete in Tahiti on 13 December 1848 when he received news of this division; he was incensed and wrote into his diary that letters from Valparaíso had announced 'the division of my diocese into two parts, of which the better has been given to the Most Reverend Jaussen, newly elected and ordained a bishop. . . .'[26] Without even going to the Marquesas Islands, Baudichon left Tahiti on 28 January for France, arriving there on 13 July 1849. He was resolved that if he could not succeed in persuading Superior General Bonamie to ask Rome to reunite the two vicariates as they were originally with himself in charge, he would go to Rome to plead his case. On 21 October he did leave Paris for Rome and remained there seven months, serving all the while as Bonamie's intermediary with the Holy See for matters concerning the Picpus Fathers. Of course, his principal concern was to provide for his own case.

When Baudichon arrived in Rome, Cardinal Prefect Fransoni was in Naples, since Pope Pius IX was still in exile, but the pope had meanwhile transferred his residence from Gaeta to Portici. Baudichon visited Fransoni in Naples on 22 November and the cardinal promised to ask the pope personally for an audience for Baudichon. After waiting several days for word and getting no reply, Baudichon simply went to Portici on the morning of 26 November, was received at once by Pope Pius IX, and spoke to him about his Marquesas Islands problem. The pope said that he could not at all decide the issue, since first it would be necessary for Baudichon to write a report on the matter for the Evangelisation Congregation.

After a second audience with the pope about other matters on 1 December, Baudichon returned to Naples and went to see Cardinal Fransoni, telling him how graciously he had been received by the pope and mentioning what he had said about the Marquesas Islands. Describing his audience with Fransoni for Bonamie on 2 December 1849, Baudichon said the cardinal intended to reconsider what was done and 'to give me back my diocese in the way it was before this last division'. But Baudichon did not know if his religious community would like this, so he asked Bonamie if he objected. He also asked how he should draw up his report and what he should ask for.[27]

Baudichon then returned to Rome, apparently visited Secretary Barnabò, and wrote to Bonamie on 10 December that the Evangelisation Congregation 'seems disposed to increase the size of my vicariate by adding that of Tahiti or, if this new arrangement is not practicable, to give me another. If this other vicariate were to be Baja [or Lower] California, I would be delighted! But perhaps His Eminence, Cardinal Fransoni, will suggest New Guinea and a part of Micronesia. In this case I would ask Your Grace not to accept, because this mission would not have been abandoned by the Marists but for the fact that it is very unhealthy and unapproachable because of the ferocity of its inhabitants. The Reverend Colin has lost many missionaries there as victims of fever.'[28]

Why did Baudichon think that Rome might offer him a vicariate apostolic in Lower or Baja California? Before he left Paris on 21 October 1849 for Rome, he must have learned from Superior General Bonamie about his most recent exchange of letters regarding California with Cardinal Prefect Fransoni. Earlier that year Bonamie had suggested that California be entrusted exclusively to his religious community as a vicariate apostolic. (The Diocese of Upper and Lower California had been founded in 1840, its first bishop had died in 1846, and no successor had been appointed.)

Fransoni replied from Naples in June 1849 that he had forwarded the letter about the Vicariate Apostolic of California to Pope Pius IX in Gaeta at once and shortly thereafter had personally discussed it there with the pope. 'After my report I found the pope well disposed to accept your offer, that is, to place the congregation presided over by you in charge of that mission by erecting it at least provisorily into a vicariate apostolic and naming as superior someone from this same congregation to be designated by Your Reverence.' The cardinal then explained that extraordinary faculties for California had been given some months back to the Bishop of Galveston, Texas. But he did not know whether a reply had come to Rome from the Bishop of Galveston. In order to prevent entanglements, Fransoni had informed Secretary Barnabò in Rome of Bonamie's proposal and of the pope's favourable attitude toward it. With battles raging in Rome, however, no reply from Barnabò had yet reached Fransoni, but he hoped to have word soon.

Fransoni wrote from Naples again on 10 August, saying that while the Evangelisation Congregation was considering Bonamie's proposal and deciding what to do ecclesiastically for California, word had arrived that the Seventh Provincial Council of Baltimore had proposed candidates for the office of bishop in California and the pope had chosen one of these candidates.

Bonamie wrote back very disturbed on 27 August, saying that Fransoni's letter of June had formally promised to give the California mission to his religious community exclusively. Nor did he accept Fransoni's 10 August offer of a prefecture apostolic in California to be staffed exclusively by his own religious community, but under the jurisdiction of the new bishop. Fransoni answered on 26 September that the expressions used in his June letter 'were not understood in their genuine sense and significance', since in this letter he had restricted himself to stating 'that His Holiness had *favourably accepted* your proposal. . . .' Fransoni reemphasised his point: 'Although I was altogether desirous of seeing the good priests of your congregation dedicate themselves to the sacred ministry in California, still I never made you a formal promise to give that mission to them exclusively.'

The Seventh Provincial Council of Baltimore held on 6–13 May 1849 and attended by twenty-five bishops, had submitted three names of candidates 'for the vacant see of Monterey in Upper California', since its goods were being despoiled and since the area had passed from Mexican into American hands. By the Treaty of Guadalupe Hidalgo on 2 February 1848, Upper or Alta California with other vast territories had been ceded by Mexico to the United States. Lower or Baja California remained part of Mexico; with Upper California it had previously constituted one diocese. If the new bishop was to have jurisdiction only over Upper California (which joined the Union on 9 September 1850 as the state of California), then Lower or Baja California could become a new vicariate apostolic to be entrusted to the Picpus Fathers.

This is what Bishop Baudichon's letter of 10 December 1849 to Bonamie implied, and Bonamie took up the idea in a new letter to Fransoni on 19 January 1850. For eleven years, he said, the inhabitants of the Marquesas Islands had resisted the efforts of his missionaries. In view of this, 'and assuming that in its wisdom the Sacred Evangelisation Congregation might perhaps consider the Vicariate Apostolic of Marquesas Islands insufficient to occupy usefully a bishop, I boldly present Your Eminence with an idea which to me seems capable of producing a much greater good. My idea would be not to leave the vicar apostolic in this archipelago at all as long as the inhabitants persist in their resistance to grace. This vicariate apostolic could then be joined to the last one created for Tahiti, Mangareva and the other islands of Eastern Oceania. Thus there would be for the moment only two vicariates apostolic in this part of Oceania, that of Tahiti and that of Sandwich. This of course would not prevent leaving some missionaries in the Marquesas Islands in order to continue there the good work already begun and to give it, by the grace of God, the greatest possible development.

'The Tahiti Vicariate could then remain in charge of Most Reverend Jaussen,' Bonamie said, 'or it could be entrusted to Most Reverend Baudichon. This latter bishop, who knows the places well, does not believe that it would be advantageous to maintain the two Vicariates Apostolic of Marquesas and Tahiti. Your Eminence is free to make inquiries [of him] on this point, if you should consider it appropriate.'

Bonamie felt obliged to give some word of explanation why he now was asking to have the two vicariates reunited, when they had been established as separate vicariates less than two years ago on 9 April 1848 at his request. There was at that time 'reason to hope for the proximate conversion of the inhabitants' of the Marquesas Islands, he said, 'because one of the kings had already embraced the faith'. A further reason for the division was the fact that the Marquesas Islands were 'very distant' from Tahiti, Mangareva and the other islands.

'But to get back to the idea which I began to present to you above,' he said, 'I would propose to Your Eminence's wisdom that you send the vicar apostolic who becomes free, either the Most Reverend Jaussen or the Most Reverend Baudichon, to Baja California. It would seem to me that the creation of a vicariate apostolic there would prove most advantageous, not only for this part of California, which is very abandoned, but also for many of our Oceania missions, which would find there some material resources to fill their pressing needs. In this event we would do everything possible to supply the new vicar apostolic with some missionaries and some catechists. . . .'

The Baja California question did not admit of an easy solution, because it was not clear to the Evangelisation Congregation to which ecclesiastical province of the United States the Diocese of Monterey in Upper California ought to belong. Nor had this been indicated in the Acts of the Seventh Provincial Council of Baltimore which came up for discussion at the General Meeting of 10 June 1850. Rome's decision in this matter was simply to wait and see how things developed. Meanwhile the Diocese of Monterey was to remain a suffragan diocese of Mexico City having under its jurisdiction both Baja California—as Mexico continued to call it—and Upper California. This made it impossible to give Baja California to the Picpus Fathers and as a result Bonamie's letter went unanswered.[29]

But on 22 April 1850, ten days after Pope Pius IX and Cardinal Fransoni returned from exile to Rome, the cardinals of the Evangelisation Congregation took up Baudichon's case and decided that Marquesas Islands Vicariate and Tahiti Islands Vicariate could be reunited. 'No difficulty stands in the way of realising this project', Baudichon wrote Bonamie three days later. 'They only want to know whether you want them to proceed at once. The Cardinal Prefect will be writing to you on this matter and then shall await your reply before taking the next step. If you should like to know my frank opinion on this matter, I must confess that I earnestly desire to have my diocese returned to me in the way it was before and also as soon as possible. . . .'[30] (Baudichon curiously always referred to his vicariate apostolic as a diocese.)

By coincidence Colin's pleading letter to Barnabò, in which he begged more insistently than ever to be relieved of responsiblity for Melanesia and Micronesia, had been written on 23 April 1850, the very day after the cardinals had decided that the Vicariates of Marquesas Islands and Tahiti Islands could be reunited. Since no letter had yet been written about this to Bonamie when Colin's letter reached Rome, Fransoni and Barnabò decided to offer Melanesia and Micronesia to Bonamie, thus letting the Picpus and Marist problems resolve one another.

It was 14 May 1850 when Fransoni told Bonamie that the information received on 'New California' (a term widely used for Upper California) along with other reports seemed as a whole 'to paralyse and exclude the project presented to me by Your Excellency through the mediation of the Most Reverend Baudichon and with which I have been busy for some time already'. But since it was 'expedient to reunite provisionally' the Marquesas Islands and Tahiti Islands Vicariates in such a way, he said, 'that the Most Reverend Baudichon could remain in charge of governing it, you would then be able to dispose of the activity of the Most Reverend Jaussen for some other undertaking. Therefore I come to you with the proposal that you take charge of a mission in Oceania, no less important [than Baja California], and certainly one that would be much easier for your well-merited society to accept and look after along with the others already entrusted to you in those regions.'

Fransoni told Bonamie that he was referring to 'the double and at present united Mission of Melanesia and Micronesia which up to now has been entrusted to the respectable Society of Marists'. He explained that Colin from the beginning had taken charge of this area 'against his will, since he did not have a large number of priests at his disposal and he was also already obligated by contract to care for other missions'. Some attempts had been made to found missions in those areas, but in some of those islands the results were unfortunate 'because of the unhealthy air which made various missionaries die, or because of the ferocity of the inhabitants by whom some were killed. These factors have made the superior in question decide to petition the Sacred Congregation kindly to exonerate his society from the charge in question and to give the mission mentioned above to another religious order.'

Colin had also wished 'that his seven surviving missionaries living at present on Woodlark Island might transfer to some other vicariate to be with their colleagues'. However, Fransoni said, he would inform Colin that he was trying to find another religious community to take over the area and would ask him not to pull out his missionaries, if at all possible, until the new ones arrived.

'Before turning to some other society, I come to offer the mission first to Your Excellency, asking the courtesy of a reply as soon as possible. And if it is in the affirmative, as I hope it will be, also let me know whether you would like to have the Most Reverend Jaussen placed in charge of the group and have him given pastoral rule over the vicariate. In order to provide for every contingency, it will be possible also to provide him with faculties for the choice of a coadjutor. Meanwhile we look forward to your reply so that we can propose this matter at a General Meeting. . . .'[31]

That same day Fransoni wrote to Colin, saying that his letter of 23 April with its declaration that he was 'not in a position' to continue providing for Melanesia

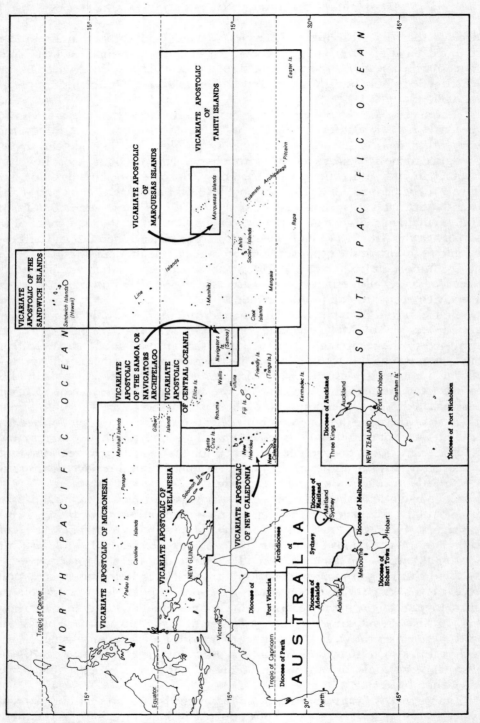

68   In the period from 1825 to 1850 ecclesiastical organisation in Oceania expanded from one prefecture apostolic to eight vicariates apostolic in Melanesia, Micronesia and Polynesia; two dioceses in New Zealand; and one archdiocese and six dioceses in Australia constituting an ecclesiastical province. *(Chapters 18, 32, 33, 34, 35).*

and Micronesia had caused him deep displeasure. 'In spite of this, however, I shall begin making suitable inquiries in order to procure another group of missionary priests, so as not to leave that mission completely abandoned. Then in due time I shall inform you of the results of my efforts in this matter and shall send further instructions for you and for your missionaries at Woodlark. Meanwhile I hope that your excellent priests will not be forced to leave this station until the new priests arrive. Some temporary assistance and direction for them from your priests would be more than helpful. . . .'[32]

Bonamie did not see Fransoni's letter of 14 May when it arrived, because he was travelling. Then further delays were caused when the superior general of the Sisters of the Sacred Hearts of Jesus and Mary died, the community affiliated with the Picpus Fathers.

Meanwhile in Rome at Bonamie's suggestion Baudichon had contacted the officials at the Evangelisation Congregation to see whether any action had been taken regarding Baja California and the reunification of the two vicariates. 'I went to the Evangelisation Congregation after the receipt of your letter of the 5th of this month,' Baudichon wrote on 24 May, 'hoping to receive a definitive reply on our affairs. But I was disappointed once again. I was told that they are waiting for a reply from Your Grace regarding the new proposal that His Eminence, the Cardinal Prefect, has made to you: to take charge of that part of Oceania which the Marists wish to abandon. In an earlier letter I took the liberty of stating simply what I thought about this mission. The time that has passed away since then has not at all changed my ideas on this point. Hence I have nothing to add to what I said then. . . .'[33] A disappointed man, Baudichon left Rome for Paris at the end of May.

When Bonamie answered Fransoni on 4 June, he said: 'We could ask for nothing better than to accept the mission which Your Eminence offers us, if only we had the means to do so. But the same reasons which oblige the Marists to abandon it, hinder us from taking charge of it. We do not have the personnel that would be needed there. . . .' With these few words, having been warned in advance by Baudichon, Bonamie dismissed both Melanesia and Micronesia.

As for reuniting the two Picpus vicariates, he had changed his mind and was now opposed to such a move. 'I would prefer in view of the circumstances that they continue to remain separated,' he said, 'since I am convinced that two vicars apostolic would do more good than only one. In fact, by his zeal and energy the Most Reverend Jaussen has already obtained such success, that it gives us high hopes for the propagation of the faith among the Tuamotus. . . .'[34] Bonamie added that there was talk about France possibly making the Marquesas Islands a penal colony. If this happened, there would be no lack of work there for Baudichon. And besides, his health was so delicate, Bonamie said, 'that I do not think he would have strength enough to do all the work that would be required, if the two vicariates apostolic were united. . . .'[35]

Matters worsened between Baudichon and Bonamie as the months went on, the one saying that the Marquesas Islands were not large enough a field of activity for a bishop, and the other maintaining they were. Baudichon submitted his resignation which was finally accepted by Pope Pius IX in March 1854. By that time Bonamie was no longer superior general.

Oblates of Mary Immaculate

On the back of Bonamie's letter of 4 June 1850, which had turned down the Melanesia-Micronesia offer, Secretary Barnabò added a brief note: 'The Bishop of Marseille can now be contacted about sending there the Oblates of the Conception.'[36] The Bishop of Marseille was Eugène de Mazenod, born on 10 August 1782. (He was declared 'Blessed' by Pope Paul VI on 19 October 1975.) In 1816 before becoming a bishop he had founded a community known today as the Oblates of Mary Immaculate (O.M.I.). By 1850 his community had eleven houses in France, six in England, others in Canada and in the United States of America, and still others in Ceylon. Rome had recently asked him to take over a vicariate in Natal in South Africa, and he agreed.

'In spite of the obligations already assumed by your edifying Congregation of the Immaculate,' Fransoni wrote him on 25 June 1850, 'as well as others which you are contemplating, I could not restrain myself from offering to your congregation a new area for practising the evangelical ministry. And although it may be difficult for you, I hope that you will be able to assign some personnel for that purpose. It is not fitting, I believe, to leave untried all possible inquiries to find someone to come to the help of a most important mission which otherwise will be completely abandoned. I mean the double and at present united Vicariate Apostolic of Melanesia and Micronesia in Western Oceania. Formerly entrusted to the well-merited Society of Marists, it has now been refused by their superior general because of the loss of the first two vicars apostolic together with some missionaries, because of scarcity of personnel, and because of difficulty in sending personnel in sufficient numbers.'

Fransoni did not conceal from de Mazenod that the second vicar apostolic and also some priests had died because of the unhealthy climate, whereas the first vicar apostolic and some of his missionaries had been killed.[37] He also explained that the missionaries still there were on an island which seemed to be less harmful to their health. The Marist superior general had therefore been advised 'not to have them return until replacements have been provided, and also not before the arrival of the new missionaries, so that the ones who are there can lend very necessary assistance and direction, at least for a short time'.

In case de Mazenod's community of Oblates 'dared' to take on the mission in spite of the news about it, which was not very reassuring, Fransoni suggested that 'at least seven or eight zealous and excellent priests' should be sent there, while others could follow later. No news would be more welcome to him, he said, than to hear that de Mazenod was ready to accept this new mission. And if that were the case, he asked him to indicate the names of those most worthy of being chosen for the office of vicar apostolic with the rank of bishop.[38]

De Mazenod replied from London on 25 July 1850, giving Fransoni a two-page description of the activities of his religious community around the world, and reminding him that recently he had agreed to accept a vicariate in

Natal. From all this, he said, 'it will appear evident to Your Eminence that sufficient proof exists for attesting to the good will of our congregation, the last and the least of those to be born in the Church of God. To do something else now, or something more, would be beyond its powers. I therefore find myself forced to refuse the offered Vicariate of Melanesia in Oceania, because I do not have enough personnel. And even if I did have enough, I would still refuse, not being able to flatter myself that I would succeed where the Marists had not succeeded. Certainly they are lacking neither in zeal nor in personnel, since I have already heard that they wish to make a foundation in England.'[39]

Fransoni wrote back briefly on 16 August: 'The observations which you make do not permit me to insist upon your acceptance of the Vicariate of Melanesia and Micronesia.'[40]

New Caledonia missionaries

By the time de Mazenod's refusal arrived in Rome, Cardinal Prefect Fransoni had a solution for his problem. He could send to Melanesia and Micronesia some of the missionaries who had been expelled from New Caledonia and were now idly awaiting new appointments. Pro-Vicar Bernin of New Caledonia, the spokesman of Bishop Douarre, Vicar Apostolic of New Caledonia, had actually been in Rome at the time when Fransoni had written his letter to de Mazenod on 25 June 1850. It was Superior General Colin himself who had suggested using these men, when it became clear that no personnel for Melanesia and Micronesia would be available from New Zealand. In fact, Colin had had the idea that instead of discharging Douarre of the New Caledonia Vicariate, as the young bishop was insisting, it would be preferable for him to be named vicar apostolic of the combined Vicariates of New Caledonia, Melanesia and Micronesia. Then he would be able to pick out and use for foundations whatever suitable locations he might find, wherever they were, and send his missionaries there.[41]

Bernin had brought with him to Rome Colin's 12 June reply to Cardinal Fransoni's letter of 14 May 1850, in which the cardinal had stated that he was taking action to provide priests 'for the two Vicariates of Melanesia and Micronesia as promptly as possible. . . .' Fransoni had urged Colin to do everything possible to keep his priests at Woodlark Island, since they would be able to help train the new missionaries when they arrived. Colin now suggested in reply that 'one or two prefects apostolic for Woodlark and the surrounding islands, including New Guinea,' should be named. He would then try to persuade some of Bishop Douarre's missionaries to cross over into this new area, although he was doubtful that it would please them to do so. And although Melanesia and Micronesia as a whole were much too large for the Marists, he was prepared to have his men do missionary work there, in someone else's vicariate apostolic, if health conditions allowed it. He therefore stated that 'this new measure' of naming prefects apostolic 'would not at all be contrary to the nomination of a vicar apostolic to be taken from outside our society'.[42]

Since Fransoni and Barnabò had been unsuccessful in obtaining personnel from the Barnabites, Picpus Fathers, and Oblates of Mary Immaculate, they were now only too happy to go along with Colin's proposal of prefectures apostolic in Melanesia, especially since he said there was hope of persuading some of the banished New Caledonia priests to go there. This was still another reason, besides the element of cost, why the Evangelisation Congregation did not want Bishop Douarre and his priests to go to America. Through Pro-Vicar Bernin they advised Colin of their agreement with his proposal for Melanesia and said that they did want him to send New Caledonia missionaries there. Bernin remained in Rome to complete the negotiations and Colin sent his reply for the Evangelisation Congregation to Bernin on 26 July 1850, laying down five rather lengthy conditions for the naming of such prefects apostolic. Bernin rewrote them in a letter which he submitted to Cardinal Fransoni on 5 August 1850.[43]

On the back of his own copy of this letter Bernin called it 'an ultimatum' for Cardinal Fransoni, since he had already submitted other summaries of his lengthy 14 June 1850 report on New Caledonia on 2 July and again on 25 July, but without any reaction whatever. Bernin explained in this new letter that the naming of prefects apostolic was being suggested by Colin only on condition that Rome by the end of August would come to a decision about Bishop Douarre and his missionaries. If Rome took no action, Bernin said, then Colin would be obliged to instruct Douarre to return to Europe and to allow his missionaries to follow him there or go to America and work there for other bishops who had been asking Colin for personnel. This would automatically cancel out the request for naming one or two prefects apostolic in Melanesia, although Colin personally felt that having them would prove helpful for Fransoni in obtaining another religious order to take charge. And if Douarre and his missionaries left Oceania, and if the Marists at Woodlark were not forced to leave by the unhealthiness of the island or for other reasons, Colin would then also allow them to remain there provisionally, but would not consider himself obliged 'to replace any who might die there'.

Bernin told Fransoni in his 'ultimatum' that if Rome by the end of August reached a decision on what Douarre should do, and if the prefectures in Melanesia were to be established, then Colin still had five observations to make.

'Firstly, in case the Woodlark missionaries actually did become firmly established there, he [Colin] would not be able to support them nor send them the superfluous missionaries from New Caledonia and New Zealand, unless the Roman Curia provisionally would grant to one or two of them the title of prefect apostolic together with all powers attached to that title.

'Secondly, the Reverend Father Colin calls attention, Your Eminence, to the fact that in this matter we are dealing with uncertainties and the Woodlark missionaries, endangered as they are, either may no longer be alive or may have already removed to Sydney by the time the decisions of the Holy See arrive. It therefore would seem prudent that Your Eminence should leave blank the formularies with the powers to be granted to the prefects and that you should also include the faculty for the surviving missionaries to choose from among themselves him, or them, whom they should consider most capable.'

Thirdly, if circumstances should allow it, he said, the Marists at Woodlark would remain dependent for the rest of their lives upon the new vicar apostolic to be chosen from outside the Society of Mary, provided that this bishop 'would leave them free to follow the rule of our society and that he would not be able to remove them without their consent from the islands pioneered by them, except in case of misconduct.

'Fourthly, it is necessary to advise Your Eminence that this nomination of prefects, should you deign to accept it, will be completely null and void if unforeseeable circumstances should have obliged the Woodlark missionaries to leave their post before learning about the decisions taken by the Evangelisation Congregation.

'Fifthly, in order to prevent any later painful discussion and to avoid every embarrassment, the Reverend Father Colin makes bold to request that Your Eminence announce yourself by letter to the Woodlark missionaries that, once they depend pastorally upon their [new] vicar apostolic, they will have both the right to follow their rule and also the right not to be removed without their consent from the islands pioneered by them, except in case of misconduct.'

Bernin ended his 'ultimatum' of 5 August by asking Fransoni for a prompt reply, adding that he would be leaving Rome 'on the 14th at the latest; probably on the 10th'.[44]

Bernin's ultimatum had its effect! Fransoni on 8 August decided to issue the letters patent and other necessary documents 'for designating prefects apostolic in the Missions of Melanesia and Micronesia', and also for the Isle of Pines, should it prove feasible to have a prefect apostolic there, in order to favour taking up work again in New Caledonia. He also took action at the same time on the more basic issue of Douarre, deciding that the Navigators Archipelago should become a new vicariate apostolic with Douarre in charge.[45]

Fransoni informed Colin two days later, on 10 August, that all of his requests received through Pro-Vicar Apostolic Bernin had been favourably accepted and he enclosed the corresponding letters patent and faculties. He also expressed agreement regarding the conditions requested by Colin, should the vicar apostolic come from another missionary order. 'And although such a circumstance might well be quite remote, I nevertheless assure you that, if it should come to pass, those measures will be taken which you desire to have adopted in favour of your missionaries. . . .'[46]

Meanwhile Colin's plan of giving the Society of Mary a new direction and reducing its foreign missionary thrust had made much progress. In fact, to bring up to date his friend and confidant in Rome, Father Theiner, the Oratorian priest, Colin had sent along a letter for him with pro-Vicar Bernin written on 12 June 1850. 'Since my return from Rome in 1847,' he said, 'we have gradually and more immediately directed the little Society of Mary toward establishments in this country, where they are more calm and more durable than in the foreign missions. We have accepted the direction of many houses of theology or of major seminaries and of many secondary schools. These establishments, as also our houses for [those preaching parish] missions, which we shall multiply proportionately as the society gets stronger, give us consolation. They also provide us an occasion to train our young personnel. And the sympathetic good will of our Lord Bishops lets us enjoy that peace which compensates amply for the numberless difficulties that we have encountered until now in the foreign missions. Perhaps we are called to collaborate in the foreign missions only slightly.'[47]

After Bernin's return to France, Colin received a second letter from Cardinal Prefect Fransoni dated 14 August, stating that Pope Pius IX on 11 August 1850 had approved and sanctioned the changes suggested on behalf of Bishop Douarre and his missionaries and had also approved the steps taken by Fransoni himself on behalf of Melanesia and Micronesia, already mentioned in his earlier letter of 10 August.

Besides sending Colin the letter meant for himself, Fransoni enclosed unsealed the letters meant for Bishops Douarre and Bataillon as well as the Evangelisation Congregation's decree. All of these official papers mentioned the foundation of Bishop Douarre's new Vicariate Apostolic of the Samoa or Navigators Archipelago, the naming of prefects apostolic for Melanesia, Micronesia and New Caledonia, and the sending of the banished New Caledonia missionaries to the new prefectures apostolic and to the new vicariate.

When reading carefully all of this documentation, Superior General Colin was greatly disturbed at seeing what Cardinal Fransoni (and Secretary Barnabò) evidently had in mind. Colin could read between the lines that Fransoni felt he now no longer needed to look for another religious community to take over Melanesia, Micronesia and New Caledonia. Since these areas would have prefects apostolic and would be furnished with personnel drawn from the former New Caledonia staff of Bishop Douarre, they were now provided for. Fransoni had betrayed his thinking in his letter to Colin when he said that the 'circumstance might well be quite remote' in which Marists would be working under a non-Marist vicar apostolic in Melanesia. Colin did not at all want such an arrangement to be 'quite remote'. The enclosed decree of the Evangelisation Congregation had also hinted at this 'remoteness' when it said that the pope had been asked to create the new vicariate apostolic, because then some of the New Caledonia priests 'could be sent to evangelise the tribes of Melanesia and Micronesia'.[48]

It seemed clear to Colin that all his proposals had miscarried, because instead of being relieved in the immediate future of responsibility for Melanesia, Micronesia and New Caledonia, he was now saddled with them indefinitely. Distressed and disturbed, he decided that the hour had come to inform the Evangelisation Congregation that he was giving the Society of Mary a new direction, diminishing its missionary thrust. Briefly, and almost coldly, he acknowledged the receipt of the decree and various letters on 25 September 1850 and then launched into this exposé for Cardinal Fransoni.

'In the beginning the missions of Oceania held a kind of attraction for us,' he said, 'precisely because of the dangers to which they would expose the lives of our missionaries and because of the privations of every kind to which our missionaries would be subjected. But for some years now, and above all since

1847 and 1848, we have come to understand gradually that a community could not, with prudence, scatter its missionaries throughout the islands of Oceania without giving them guidance and that it was also necessary for a society to have fitting guarantees.' The 'expulsion' of his missionaries from their New Zealand mission stations had been a striking proof, he said, that such guarantees did not yet exist for his missionaries. 'These foundations, which had cost them 10 years of heroic patience, were all in the Auckland Diocese [of Bishop Pompallier]; only one missionary for some years now has been in that part [of New Zealand] which forms the Diocese of Port Nicholson.'

These 'grave inconveniences' disturbed him, he said, 'and in 1848 and 1849 we hastened to advise the Most Reverend Bataillon, Bishop of Enos, to provide himself with other missionaries for the numerous islands of the Fiji or Viti Archipelago. Similarly, we informed the Most Reverend Viard, Bishop of Orthosia, that we would be pleased to see his priests follow him to Wellington . . .[49] From then on we would not be able to supply him with new missionaries, we said, and we told him that we were giving another direction to our society.'

Colin added that meanwhile he had learned that Bishop Pompallier, on arriving in New Zealand in April 1850, had brought with him only one priest and also some young clerics, 'who would not be able to practise the sacred ministry for a long time'. This meant that very many of the Marists, due to Rome's previous instructions, had to remain at their posts in Pompallier's Diocese of Auckland. Bishop Viard had tried to facilitate this for Bishop Pompallier, but then had to request Colin for more Marist priests from France for himself. 'It is painful for us not to be able to supply them for him', Colin told Fransoni, 'and even more painful to learn that several of his missionaries are asking to return to Europe.'

Colin also clarified for Fransoni precisely what he had had in mind when suggesting the nomination of prefects apostolic. 'When the first news arrived [here] about the latest abandonment of New Caledonia by the vicar apostolic and his priests,' he said, 'we recognised how regrettable it was that so many missionaries transported to that place should be obliged to abandon these unfortunate populations completely. How advantageous it would be, if they could hold on somewhere for awhile, either in the Melanesia Vicariate or in the New Caledonia Vicariate. And how profitable this in turn would be for the new missionaries whom the Holy See is seeking and will assign to the task of reviving and firmly establishing these difficult and important missions. For upon their arrival they would then find a sure foothold and also some inhabitants of these islands who have already been made somewhat tractable.'

Because of 'these weighty considerations' and his concern 'for the glory of God and the salvation of souls', Colin was convinced that the missionaries of New Caledonia and of Melanesia ought to be free and ought to have the opportunity of applying themselves where and as required in these grave circumstances. And they ought 'to apply themselves zealously on behalf of these peoples, if they should find the occasion to do so, even at the peril of their lives'.

Colin stressed for Fransoni that it was 'with this purpose in mind' that he had considered it his duty on Pro-Vicar Bernin's departure for Rome 'to suggest to Your Eminence the creation of some prefectures apostolic'. And although it was impossible to foresee what the results might be, 'by making this proposal we in no way had the intention of taking charge anew—and above all not exclusively—of these grave and difficult missions. And so we hasten to repeat to Your Eminence our humble entreaties that other missionaries should be sent there as promptly as possible.'[50]

All of this coincided with what Superior General Colin much earlier had told Bishop Douarre and Father Rocher, the Marist in charge of the mission office at Sydney. Writing to Rocher on 13 June 1850, the day before Pro-Vicar Bernin left Lyon for Rome, Colin said, 'Do not forget the missionaries at Woodlark. It is possible that we shall engage some of the missionaries of New Caledonia to go and join them, but as yet nothing has been decided. . . .'[51]

Colin developed the same idea in a letter to Bishop Douarre on the following day, 14 June 1850. He said that Bernin, who left for Rome that day, would negotiate with the Evangelisation Congregation 'in favour of a location in America according to your desires. But if he is unable to obtain from the Holy See a suitable place in that country, I have instructed him to request conditionally that they make you Vicar Apostolic of New Caledonia, Melanesia and Micronesia. You will then be free to take over those places which prove to be more suitable. Your Grace will readily understand how disagreeable it would be for the society to abandon these three vicariates in Oceania at once with everybody right there on the spot.'[52]

Part of Colin's proposal pleased Douarre. But nothing that Fransoni had done pleased Douarre, although it was all done at his own bidding and that of his pro-vicar. He wrote to Fransoni from Sydney on 16 January 1851, signing himself Vicar Apostolic of the Navigators Islands. ('Navigators Archipelago' had appeared in official correspondence and decrees.) He said that he had arrived in Sydney to make preparations for returning to New Caledonia, 'when the bulls reached me by which His Holiness named me Vicar Apostolic of the Navigators Islands. I would have preferred to have been left free to choose between the former and the new vicariate. The terms of the letter informing me of the Evangelisation Congregation's decision were so very formal that I bowed my head in sign of acceptance. But I did so with a repugnance that Your Eminence will find hard to imagine. All my affection centres on New Caledonia; and although its inhabitants are extremely cruel, I love them. . . .'

He explained to Fransoni that approximately sixty New Caledonians had been transported in two ships to Futuna and among them were the troublemakers responsible for his banishment and that of his missionaries. So it would now be possible for them all to return safely to Balade.

He said further that he was especially averse to the Navigators Islands 'because I know that the Most Reverend Bataillon must establish himself there. . . .' He was also convinced that he himself was not the man to be placed in charge of them and, since he was now forty, he was too old to learn the language of those islands. He was particularly desolate because he would be leaving New Caledonia 'at the moment when it is menaced with being invaded by Anglican ministers'. He said that six Anglican bishops recently had held a meeting in Sydney 'and they decided that two of them, one from New Zealand and the other from New Holland [now Australia], should be placed in charge of the Solomon Islands, New Hebrides, Loyalty Islands and New Caledonia, and that they should begin with the place last mentioned'. They had appealed to the generosity of all Anglicans in Sydney, he said, and had obtained sufficient funds to purchase a ship. Because of his orders from Rome, however, Douarre had decided to move on to the Navigators Islands, 'but with extreme repugnance'. First, however, he intended to establish the new prefect apostolic in New Caledonia.

Douarre ended his letter to Fransoni with a plea for a successor. 'I would be very happy', he said, 'if another were to carry out these projects . . . I have written to Very Reverend Father Colin many times on this subject . . . and have acquainted him with my motives. These make me wish to have a replacement, not because of any ennui that I experience with the missions, but rather because I have reason to believe that another vicar apostolic would do better than I.'[53]

Colin had not personally replied to Bishop Viard of Port Nicholson Diocese regarding his request for more personnel, but had Procurator General Poupinel do so in his name. 'Enlightened by the trials which it has had to endure in its members,' Poupinel wrote on 7 September 1850, 'our society wishes to take suitable measures in order to guarantee their religious future and the stability of their missions, before it sends any new personnel to Oceania.'[54]

After Cardinal Prefect Fransoni received Superior General Colin's letter of 25 September 1850, explaining the new direction that he was giving to his society and insisting that another community be given responsibility for Melanesia, Micronesia and New Caledonia, he did not approach any other religious community. He simply decided to wait and see how things might develop in those three areas.[55]

Lombardy's Seminary for Foreign Missions

But the year 1850 had not yet run its course when a letter arrived in the offices of the Evangelisation Congregation dated 5 December 1850 from Bishop Angiolo Ramazzotti of Pavia in the province of Lombardy, Italy. Much earlier he had suggested to the Bishops of Lombardy that they found within their ecclesiastical province a seminary to train young men from Lombardy for foreign missionary work. They agreed, the proposal was approved by Pope Pius IX on 21 February 1850, and on 1 December that year Archbishop Bartolomeo Romilli of Milan and seven other Bishops of Lombardy signed and sealed a document formally erecting the seminary. As originator of the idea, Ramazzotti with his letter of 5 December now presented the formal document of foundation to Cardinal Prefect Fransoni. Ramazzotti himself had donated his residence at Saronno, some twenty kilometres northwest of Milan, to house the seminary.

With his letter the Bishop of Pavia also submitted several requests in the name of the Archbishop of Milan and the Bishops of Lombardy. One of these dealt with a possible mission for the newly founded seminary, so that the candidates could already begin reading about it and preparing themselves for it. 'If in this matter it is permitted to express the wish of the students already enrolled in the new seminary . . . ,' he said, 'they would like to have some virgin territory, a people that has not yet heard the name of Christ . . . The Archipelagoes of Micronesia, to which the venerable Congregation of Marists has not been able to dedicate itself except in part, is a very vast field for new missions and would be the land which the said students would like to water with their sweat and also—should need be—with their blood. . . .'[56]

Cardinal Fransoni replied to Bishop Ramazzotti on 16 January 1851, acknowledging receipt of his letter. He considered it proper, however, to address his formal reply to Archbishop Romilli of Milan, but still he wanted Ramazzotti to know its contents. 'And so I am sending it to you with the request that after reading it you have it sealed and give it to the prelate. . . .'[57]

In his letter to Archbishop Romilli, also dated 16 January, Fransoni said that he had lost no time in speaking of the contents of the letter to Pope Pius IX, who was very pleased to learn that the project of the Bishops of Lombardy was now a reality and that the seminary was already open. As for the wish of the students, he said, 'I would like to assure Your Excellencies that their great desires will be completely fulfilled. In fact, circumstances at the present time make it possible to designate at this moment already, and for them exclusively, the desirable and vast Missions of Melanesia and Micronesia. For lack of personnel the Marists of Lyon are asking to be exonerated of them. Therefore as soon as your seminary is able to furnish a small group of tried and tested priests, they will be sent quickly to the coveted regions mentioned. And in addition to these, there will always be available for the zeal of these same students other vast regions that have been lying abandoned up to now. No matter how large the number of sacred ministers that the seminary is able to supply, there will never be lacking a field to be cultivated by them.'

Fransoni concluded by assuring Archbishop Romilli 'and all your respectable colleagues of my deep concern and my readiness to cooperate in every way that is possible for me. . . .'[58]

Without even searching, Fransoni had finally found someone to take over responsibility for the Vicariates Apostolic of Melanesia and Micronesia. But since the seminary at Saronno—it was transferred to Milan in June 1851—had been open for such a short time, he waited until 21 August 1851, when the first priests were ready to leave for Oceania, before informing Superior General Colin that he had found another missionary group to take over Melanesia and Micronesia.[59] The Milan seminary was at first referred to by its founders and members as Lombardy's Seminary for Foreign Missions, but Rome referred to it as the College of Saint Calocero of Milan because it was located in the immediate vicinity of a well-known shrine (destroyed during World War II) in honour of this saint. The seminary eventually became known as the Institute for Foreign Missions of Milan (I.M.E.), a name which it kept until 1926 when it merged with the Pontifical Seminary of the Apostles Saints Peter and Paul of Rome to become the Pontifical Institute for Foreign Missions (P.I.M.E.). This is still its name today.

To all appearances Fransoni's problem of finding personnel for Melanesia and Micronesia had been solved. As for New Caledonia, a third attempt was to be made there, this time under the leadership of a prefect apostolic. Bishop Viard in the Diocese of Port Nicholson, New Zealand, had been told he would get no more personnel until the Society of Mary had received certain guarantees from Rome for mission areas. And Bishop Bataillon had been instructed to obtain non-Marists for Fiji. Colin, in fact, sent no more missionaries to Oceania for the balance of his term of office. He resigned as superior general on 9 May 1854.

His attitude, however, was not shared by all members in the Society of Mary, and one of those was Bishop Bataillon, Vicar Apostolic of Central Oceania. Writing from Sydney to Cardinal Prefect Fransoni on 15 June 1852 he said: 'It is to be regretted that our good Father Superior sends us no more colleagues because of the difficulties which we have in these distant missions and, above all, because of misunderstandings and inexact reports. He seems to dislike these missions. Or at any rate he has fears, he mistrusts, and he suspends sending missionaries.'

Colin had recently written to him, he said, that it would be necessary for him to approach the Evangelisation Congregation 'for new priests for the Fiji Islands, which he intended to give up. In my reply I begged him to continue sending us help for the entire vicariate. But he seems determined to furnish personnel no longer, except for the Navigators Islands and the Friendly Islands, which are a very small part of my vicariate. Further, it is his intention little by little to remove all his subjects from Oceania. This news shocked me all the more, because I did not know to whom to ascribe the cause. And I am greatly afflicted when I see our colleagues discouraged and our missions suffering so much harm, since these latter are already so difficult and so troublesome by themselves.'

Priests from France, according to Bataillon, 'and above all those from our small society are better suited than any others to do good among the natives of Oceania. How desirable it would be, Your Eminence, if you by your influence could make our Very Reverend Superior decide to continue providing help, at least for our Central Mission. It has been entrusted to him and to the society, rather than to us personally. For the present needs of the vicariate ten or twelve more priests would suffice. If we were to receive this help, we could go on for a long time without making new requests for missionaries.'

Bataillon's letter was a plea for Oceania. 'How good it would be, Your Eminence, if you were to write and encourage him, to exhort him, to recommend that he continue the work which has been entrusted to him. I have no doubt that abandoning it would be contrary to the will of God. Our missions here in Oceania are difficult, but also possible, and much good has already been done. We also have reason to believe that with time and with patience more good will still be done.'[60]

Time has proved that Bataillon was correct. His Society of Mary went on to become one of the greatest missionary orders of the Roman Catholic Church, with Oceania as its field of specialisation. In spite of beginning to falter at this time in history under Father Colin's direction, the Society of Mary had earlier contributed mightily, along with many others, to the founding of the Roman Catholic Church in Oceania in the quarter century just past.

Oceania had only one prefecture apostolic in 1825; by 1850 it contained one archdiocese, eight dioceses and eight vicariates apostolic. The archdiocese was Sydney. The dioceses were Hobart Town, Adelaide, Perth, Melbourne, Port Victoria and Maitland in Australia, and Auckland and Port Nicholson in New Zealand. The vicariates apostolic were Sandwich Islands, Marquesas Islands and Tahiti Islands in Eastern Oceania, and Central Oceania, Melanesia, Micronesia, New Caledonia and the Samoa or Navigators Archipelago in Western Oceania. There had been remarkable growth indeed and much good had been done. And 'with time and with patience', as Bishop Bataillon had foretold, more good would still be done.

Symbols used for the archives consulted

To designate the archives at the international headquarters of a religious order, the official Latin abbreviation of the order is used, but without periods.

B   Generalate Archives of the Clerics Regular of Saint Paul, usually referred to as Barnabites. Via Giacomo Medici, 15; 00153 Rome, Italy.

CP   Generalate Archives of the Congregation of the Passion of Jesus Christ, usually referred to as Passionists. Piazza SS. Giovanni e Paolo, 14; 00184 Rome, Italy.
CP(SS): A subdivision titled 'Provincia Spiritus Sancti, Documenta Fundationis Primaevae, 1842, etc.'

CSI   Archives of Saint Isidore College (C.S.I.: Collegii Sancti Isidori). Via degli Artisti, 41; 00187 Rome, Italy.

PF   Archives of the Sacred Congregation for the Evangelisation of Nations (PF: 'de Propaganda Fide', the traditional and often still used title of the Sacred Congregation). Palazzo di Propaganda Fide; Piazza di Spagna, 48; 00187 Rome, Italy.

PF: Acta: *Acta Sacrae Congregationis*, i.e. the minutes of General Meetings attended by the cardinal members, giving a full report on the issue up for discussion, the decisions reached, and the position taken later by the pope.

PF: CP: *Congregazioni Particolari*, i.e. the minutes and the documentation used at Particular Meetings, those at which a committee of cardinals studies a particular question.

PF: LDB: *Lettere e Decreti della Sacra Congregazione e Biglietti di Monsignor Segretario*, i.e. a verbatim record of practically all letters written by the cardinal prefect and the secretary as well as copies of numerous decrees issued by the Sacred Congregation.

PF: SC: *Scritture riferite nei Congressi*, i.e. documents of secondary importance discussed at weekly meetings not attended by the full membership of cardinals.

PF: SOCG: *Scritture originali riferite nelle Congregazioni Generali*, i.e. incoming letters and reports from bishops, missionaries, royalty, government officials, nuncios, minutes of synods, etc., used as a basis for discussion at General Meetings.

PF: Udienze: *Udienze di Nostro Signore*, i.e. requests of a personal or private nature for faculties, indulgences, matrimonial dispensations, etc., brought to the pope's attention by the secretary because granting them exceeded the powers of the cardinal prefect or of the Evangelisation Congregation.

PIME   Generalate Archives of the Pontifical Institute for Foreign Missions (P.I.M.E.: Pontificium Institutum pro Missionibus Exteris). Via F. D. Guerrazzi, 11; 00152 Rome, Italy.

SAC   Generalate Archives of the Society of the Catholic Apostolate, called also Pallottines. Piazza Vincenzo Pallotti, 204; 00186 Rome, Italy.

SM   Generalate Archives of the Society of Mary, usually referred to as Marists. Via Alessandro Poerio, 63; 00152 Rome, Italy.

SSCC   Generalate Archives of the Congregation of the Sacred Hearts of Jesus and Mary, often referred to as the Picpus Fathers (SS.CC.: Congregatio Sacrorum Cordium Iesu et Mariae). Via Rivarone, 85; 00166 Rome, Italy.
+This symbol is used in SSCC. It is a substitute for 271.788, the Universal Decimal Classification number for the Congregation of the Sacred Hearts of Jesus and Mary (SS.CC.).

Other abbreviations used are:

AMO   Société de Marie, *Annales des missions d'Océanie*, vol. 1. See the listing in the Bibliography.

OM   *Origines maristes (1786–1836)*. See the listing in the Bibliography.

Notes to text

Chapter 1   The Prefecture Apostolic of the Sandwich Islands

1   Honoré Laval, *Mémoires pour servir à l'histoire de Mangareva*, p. xv; Reginald Yzendoorn, *History of the Catholic Mission in the Hawaiian Islands*, p. 34; Léonce Jore, *L'océan Pacifique au temps de la restauration et de la monarchie de Juillet (1815–1848)*, 1:31, 125f; Gavan Daws, *Shoal of Time*, pp. 71, 73, 426. Jore gives 27 September (p. 125) as the embarkation date and Daws gives 27 November (p. 71). Since Daws presumably had better source material, the author has used his date.

2   PF: SC Oceania vol. 1 (1816–41) f. 29r–30v.

3   William E. Strong, *The Story of the American Board*, pp. 3f, 56f, 63. Bradford was about ten kilometres from Andover. Young men from the Sandwich Islands often found their way to New England with friendly sea captains.

4   PF: SC Oceania vol. 1 (1816–41) f. 25r–30v, 43v, 60r. The Constitution *Inscrutabili*, subsequently prepared and formally announcing the establishment of the Sacred Congregation for the Evangelisation of Nations, is dated 22 June 1622. In the Sacred Congregation's title, 'of Peoples' is also correctly used in place of 'of Nations'.

5   PF: LDB vol. 306 (1825) f. 287 rv; PF: Udienze vol. 65 (1825) f. 753r.

6   The complete official title was Congregation of the Sacred Hearts of Jesus and Mary and of Perpetual Adoration of the Most Blessed Sacrament of the Altar. On entering the novitiate the Picpus Fathers and Brothers took a new name and were regularly called by this new name and not by their family name. The priests like the Brothers were called 'Brother'. This latter practice, not being followed by the author because it may cause confusion for the reader, was officially discontinued in 1840. The practice of all receiving a new name was discontinued in 1953. In the case of Coudrin, for example, his civil name was Pierre, and his new name was Marie-Joseph. In signing circular letters he used Marie-Joseph-Pierre Coudrin.

7   SSCC: 271.788–91 (093.2)–3, pp. 205f, no.

315; +911–18 f. 56r, 57r. The cross (+) is used at times in SSCC designations as a substitute for 271.788, the Universal Decimal Classification number used for the SSCC religious community.

8   PF: Udienze vol. 65 (1825) f. 753r.

9   SSCC: +911–18 f. 57r, 58r; PF: LDB vol. 306 (1825) f. 299r.

10   Ibid., f. 499rv.

11   Ibid., f. 500r.

12   SSCC: +911–18 f. 58r; PF: SC Oceania vol. 1 (1816–41) f. 33r; PF: Udienze vol. 65 (1825, Part II) f. 753r.

13   Reiner Jaspers, *Die Missionarische Erschliessung Ozeaniens*, p. 150f.

14   The September date is also on a duplicate of this letter sent to Caprano and on a personal letter accompanying it. The date 6 September 1825 is clearly an error since the letter to which Coudrin is replying was not written in Rome until 10 September. In his letter to the cardinal, Coudrin says that the ship will be sailing 'about the middle of next November', and in his letter to Caprano he says that the same ship will be leaving 'in about five weeks'. Not 6 September, but 6 October, would be 'about five weeks' before the middle of November. See PF: SC Oceania vol. 1 (1816–41) f. 33r–35v. The Picpus diary covering this correspondence gives the date as 6 October. See SSCC: +911–18 f. 58r.

15   PF: SC Oceania vol. 1 (1816–41) f. 33rv. A professed member is one who has taken vows of poverty, chastity and obedience.

16   SSCC: +911–18 f. 58r; Antoine Lestra, *Le père Coudrin*, 3:352.

17   Lestra, *Père Coudrin*, 3:352f; SSCC: +911–18 f. 58r; Jaspers, *Erschliessung Ozeaniens*, pp. 152f.

18   PF: Udienze vol. 65 (1825) f. 601r. As far as the pope was concerned, the new mission was hereby formally established. The Evangelisation Congregation needed only to draw up the documents and forward them to Coudrin. The single official date recognised today for a present or past decision of the Holy See, according to the Reverend Josef Metzler, O.M.I., archivist of the Sacred Congregation for the Evangelisation of

Nations, is the date on which the pope during an audience gives his approval.

19 PF: Udienze vol. 65 (1825) f. 754r; Josef Metzler, 'Das Apostolische Vikariat der Kopten unter Massimo Giuaid (1821–1831)', *Euntes Docete* 14 (1961): 45–54; Josef Metzler, 'Bemühungen der S.C. "de Propaganda Fide" um die Wiedervereinigung der Koptischen Kirche mit Rom', ibid. 17 (1964): 100-7; PF: LDB vol. 306 (1825) f. 551rv. After an imprisonment of twenty-nine years Chasciur was pardoned and continued to live in Rome.

20 PF: LDB vol. 306 (1825) f. 550v–551r.

21 PF: Udienze vol. 65 (1825) f. 753r–754v. This includes a copy of Father Coudrin's letter. The original is in PF: SC Oceania vol. 1 (1816–41) f. 39r.

22 PF: Udienze vol. 65 (1825) f. 692rv.

23 PF: LDB vol. 306 (1825) f. 636r–637r.

24 Ibid., f. 637r–638v.

25 Troyes is about 160 kilometres southeast of Paris.

26 PF: SC Oceania vol. 1 (1816–41) f. 43r–44r.

27 PF: LDB vol. 306 (1825) f. 660v–661v.

28 SSCC: +911–18 f. 59r. This influence of Coudrin upon Macchi seems apparent from the speed with which Macchi subsequently wrote to Rome and from the fact that his letter contains much argumentation previously used by Coudrin and the Picpus Fathers.

29 PF: SC Oceania vol. 1 (1816–41) f. 47r–48r.

30 PF: LDB vol. 307 (1826) f. 20r.

31 PF: SC Oceania vol. 1 (1816–41) f. 49r.

32 Lestra, *Père Coudrin*, 3:353f; SSCC: +911–18 f. 60r.

33 SSCC: +911–18 f. 60r.

34 SSCC: +911–6 f. 274–282.

35 Ibid., +911–18 f. 62r–64r; Lestra, *Père Coudrin*, 3:356.

36 PF: SC Oceania vol. 1 (1816–41) f. 53r.

37 SSCC: +911–18 f. 65r.

38 Ibid., +95(044)–2, Tom 1.

39 Ibid., +911–18 f. 66r.

40 PF: SC Oceania vol. 1 (1816–41) f. 59r–60r.

41 Ibid., f. 61r, Coudrin to Caprano, 21 March 1828.

42 PF: LDB vol. 309 (1828) f. 366v–367r.

43 Yzendoorn, *Catholic Mission in the Hawaiian Islands*, p. 34.

Chapter 2   The Prefecture Apostolic of the South Sea Islands

1 Some Catholics of this period used the word 'Methodist' as a generic term for all non-Catholic missionary groups, as Dillon may be using it here. In the South Sea Islands visited by him there was a Methodist group, the Wesleyan Missionary Society, but also two other non-Methodist groups, the Church Missionary Society and the London Missionary Society.

2 PF: SOCG vol. 944 (1829) f. 566rv.

3 Ibid., f. 566v; SSCC: +95(044)–9 p. 17; Georges Goyau, *Les grands desseins missionnaires d'Henri de Solages (1786–1832)*, pp. 47f. Goyau here spells the name of the rector incorrectly, writing MacSweeney. Cf. Patrick Boyle, *The Irish College in Paris from 1578 to 1901*, pp. 78, 79, 87. The Holy Ghost Fathers, also called 'Spiritans' in the United States of America and in Canada, have as their full title Congregation of the Holy Ghost under the Protection of the Immaculate Heart of Mary. See Letter, Gerald W. Fitzgerald, C.S.Sp., to Wiltgen, 20 February 1978.

4 PF: SOCG vol. 944 (1829) f. 565r; ibid., vol. 948 (1833) f. 30r; Lestra, *Père Coudrin*, 3:366.

5 Lestra, *Père Coudrin*, 3:365-7, 377; SSCC: +95(044)–9 p. 19. Historians of another age for some reason did not give complete names in their writings for persons of secondary importance. Nor did important persons all have the practice of signing their full names to letters. Pieau, for example, signed official letters simply 'Pieau, Secretary General to the Grand Almonry'.

6 SSCC: +95(044)–9 pp. 16f; Lestra, *Père Coudrin*, 3:377; Adrien Boudou, *Les jésuites à Madagascar au XIXe siècle*, 1:9; Goyau, *Les grands desseins*, p. 28; PF: SOCG vol. 948 (1833) f. 31r.

7 PF: SOCG vol. 944 (1829) f. 566v; SSCC: +95(044)–9 p. 17.

8 L. G. Keys of New Zealand has identified the Schoracaï River for me as the Waihou (or Thames) River which empties into the Hauraki Gulf at the Firth of Thames in northern New Zealand. Letter, Keys to Wiltgen, 6 December 1969. Dillon's word Schoracaï seems very closely related to Pompallier's word, Bay of Shouraki, which in turn is closely related to Hauraki Gulf, the modern name for the bay into which Dillon's river emptied. Brian Boru (941–1014) was king of Ireland (1002–14).

9 PF: SOCG vol. 944 (1829) f. 566v–567v.

10 Ibid., vol. 948 (1833) f. 31v; Lestra, *Père Coudrin*, 3:365, 377.

11 PF: SOCG vol. 944 (1829) f. 571r–573v.

12 Lestra, *Père Coudrin*, 3:365, 377; SSCC: +911–18 f. 62r.

13 SSCC: +911–18 f. 72r, 73r; PF: SOCG vol. 948 (1833) f. 33r; Lestra, *Père Coudrin*, 1:83, 3:366f.

14 Goyau, *Les grands desseins*, pp. 61–3.

15 SSCC: +95(044)–9 p. 17.

16 Ibid., p. 20; PF: SOCG vol. 944 (1829) f. 579v–580r; Lestra, *Père Coudrin*, 3:365. Lestra on page 371 mistakenly says 16 November for 16 October.

17 Adams, the last of the mutineers, died in 1829, the same year that de Solages wrote this letter.

18 PF: SOCG vol. 944 (1829) f. 581r–582r.

19 SSCC: +95(044)–9 p. 21f.
20 PF: Acta vol. 192 (1829) f. 126r–127v; PF: SOCG vol. 948 (1833) f. 31r.
21 SSCC: +95(044)–9 p. 32f.
22 Lestra, *Père Coudrin*, 3:367. Coudrin's quotation here shows that he believed the letter was sent to de Solages, and Lestra leaves the reader under this impression. But since Perreau had written, de Solages would hardly get the answer. In PF: SOCG vol. 944 (1829) f. 561v, Cardinal Pacca says that Cappellari sent the letter to Perreau, not to de Solages. A copy of the letter, however, was not kept on file in PF: LDB vol. 310 (1829), although copies of other letters for this period were kept on file.
23 De Solages on 5 May 1831 accused Coudrin of keeping him in suspense 'pendant plusieurs mois', which is certainly an exaggeration. One should read 'weeks' for 'months'. Coudrin himself said that he first learned of the plan in October 1829 after his return to France from Rome. This was the month in which he was approached by de Solages and Dillon. Cf. PF: SOCG vol. 948 (1833) f. 33r; SSCC: +911–18 f. 73r; Lestra, *Père Coudrin*, 3:373.
24 Lestra, *Père Coudrin*, 3:378.
25 Ibid., p. 367.
26 Ibid.
27 SSCC: +91(093.2)–3 no. 315.
28 Lestra, *Père Coudrin*, 3:371f. Lestra says on page 368 that de Solages came to them. But Hilarion says that they went to de Solages, and de Solages also says that they called on him. Cf. SSCC: +911–18 f. 74r; PF: SOCG vol. 948 (1833) f. 33r.
29 Lestra, *Père Coudrin*, 3:368, 371; PF: SOCG vol. 948 (1833) f. 33r.
30 SSCC: +95(044)–9 p. 48f.
31 PF: SOCG vol. 948 (1833) f. 33r; ibid., vol. 944 (1829) f. 567r.
32 Lestra, *Père Coudrin*, 3:373.
33 Ibid., p. 374; SSCC: +95(044)–9 pp. 20, 22; Goyau, *Les grands desseins*, pp. 68f, 72, 74f, 109f, 115.
34 Goyau, *Les grands desseins*, pp. 82f.
35 Lestra, *Père Coudrin*, 3:368, 370.
36 Ibid., p. 368.
37 Goyau, *Les grands desseins*, p. 77.
38 Ibid., pp. 29f.
39 Ibid., pp. 83–6; Lestra, *Père Coudrin*, 3:370.
40 Lestra, *Père Coudrin*, 3:370. Lestra on page 369 says 'la lettre fut envoyée . . . le 5 décembre 1829'. Although the letter may have been *sent* on 5 December, because the next day was Sunday, the actual date on the original letter is 6 December 1829. See PF: SC Oceania vol. 1 (1816–41) f. 87r–88r; and also Hilarion's record in SSCC: +91(093.2)–3 no. 425.
41 SSCC: +91(093.2)–3 nos 426f, 429, 434f;

Lestra, *Père Coudrin*, 3:371f; SSCC: +911–18 f. 74r.
42 SSCC: +911–18 f. 74r; PF: LDB vol. 310 (1829) f. 734r, 813v.
43 Lestra, *Père Coudrin*, 3:375.
44 PF: SOCG vol. 944 (1829) f. 584v.
45 Ibid., f. 575r–585r.
46 Since most of the sources in this period use 'Oceania' or the now outdated 'Oceanica' and relatively few use 'Polynesia', the author uses 'Oceania' throughout to avoid confusion. Oceania is a world of more than ten thousand islands in the Pacific Ocean bordered by and including New Guinea, Palau and the Marianas on the west, Hawaii (formerly Sandwich Islands) on the north, Easter Island on the east, and New Zealand on the south. Australia is generally also included. With time Oceania came to be divided into (1) Australia, (2) Melanesia (New Guinea eastward to Fiji), (3) Micronesia (Marianas, Carolines, Marshalls and Gilberts), and (4) Polynesia (a triangle of many islands, including Hawaii, New Zealand and Easter Island).
47 The author is particularly indebted to the Belgian ambassador to the Holy See and to Mrs Liliane Wellens-De Donder, scientific attachée to the Centre national d'histoire des sciences at the Bibliothèque royale in Brussels, for tracking down this *Atlas*. Subsequently a complete copy was discovered in the library of the Evangelisation Congregation, a first edition, which must be the one used by Cardinal Pacca.
48 PF: Acta vol. 192 (1829) f. 462r–473v; see also PF: SOCG vol. 944 (1829) f. 463r, 560r–563r, 566v, 569r–570r.
49 PF: LDB vol. 311 (1830) f. 76v.
50 Ibid., f. 73v–75r.
51 Ibid., f. 76rv. In addition to the name 'South Sea Islands', that is, 'Insulae Maris vulgo dicti del Sud', this prefecture in correspondence and in the course of discussion was variously referred to as 'Polinesia Australe ossia Isole del Mar Pacifico' [see PF: Acta vol. 192 (1829) f. 462r], 'Insulae Oceani Australis', 'Insulae magni Oceani', and 'Insulae in Mari Pacifico seu Australi' [see PF: LDB vol. 311 (1830) f. 73v, 76r].
52 PF: LDB vol. 311 (1830) f. 75rv.
53 Ibid., f. 31v–32v.
54 Lestra, *Père Coudrin*, 3:375.

Chapter 3   De Solages arrives in Bourbon

1   A league is approximately three miles (five kilometres). The Low Archipelago, today called the Tuamotu Archipelago, was divided into three sections by M. De Krusenstern, author of the first atlas on Oceania. The central section included the islands that Bougainville had designated as the Dangerous Archipelago and the northwest section included the islands that Fleurieu had designated as the Bad Sea Archi-

pelago of Le Maire and Schouten. See 'Note sur l'Archipel des îles Basses', in Philippe Vandermaelen, *Atlas universel*, vol. 5 (Oceania), plate 43. Other authors (Dumont d'Urville, Domeny de Rienzi, etc.) say that Bad Sea and Dangerous were synonyms for the entire Tuamotu Archipelago. But it is clear that Coudrin is here using the names in Vandermaelen's sense, because he explicitly says 'four archipelagoes'.

2 PF: SC Oceania vol. 1 (1816–41) f. 87r–88r.
3 Lestra, *Père Coudrin*, 3:373.
4 Ibid., pp. 376f; Goyau, *Les grands desseins*, p. 77.
5 PF: SC Oceania vol. 1 (1816–41) f. 95rv; PF: LDB vol. 310 (1829) f. 685r and vol. 316 (1835) f. 217r–218v; OM 4:322. Here OM says that Pastre became prefect apostolic in 1822. Bertout, however, wrote to Pro-Prefect Ercole Consalvi on 15 January 1823 asking for a duplicate set of faculties and letters patent for Pastre, saying: 'Eighteen months ago I already sent him the letters [patent] as prefect, but either because of shipwreck of the vessel that carried them, or for other reasons, they never reached him.' Therefore the original appointment was made in 1821. Secretary Pedicini presented the matter to Pope Pius VII on 2 March 1823, Pastre's appointment was confirmed, and Pro-Prefect Consalvi forwarded the new set of documents to Bertout for Pastre on 8 March 1823. See PF: Udienze vol. 61 (1823) f. 194r, 206r; PF: LDB vol. 304 (1823) f. 142rv.
6 PF: LDB vol. 311 (1830) f. 116r, 597r.
7 Ibid., f. 119r–120r; Lestra, *Père Coudrin*, 3:376.
8 Lestra, *Père Coudrin*, 3:376; PF: LDB vol. 311 (1830) f. 116v–118v; PF: Acta vol. 198 (1835) f. 370r.
9 Lestra, *Père Coudrin*, 3:377.
10 Ibid., p. 376.
11 Ibid., p. 370; SSCC: +95(044)–9 p. 18, Memorandum, de Solages to the Grand Admiral of France, 10 May 1830.
12 SSCC: +95(044)–9 pp. 18, 20.
13 Kamchatka is an easterly peninsula of Siberia between the Okhotsk and Bering seas.
14 This last quotation is from Lestra, *Père Coudrin*, 3:375.
15 Goyau, *Les grands desseins*, pp. 92–103, 110.
16 SSCC: +95(044)–9 f. 18.
17 PF: SOCG vol. 948 f. 33v–34r.
18 SSCC: +95(044)–9 f. 29.
19 Lestra, *Père Coudrin*, 3:377f.
20 Goyau, *Les grands desseins*, p. 108.
21 Ibid., pp. 109f, 115; Boudou, *Les jésuites à Madagascar*, 1:11; Lestra, *Père Coudrin*, 3:377; SSCC: +95(044)–9 f. 20f.
22 SSCC: +95(044)–9 f. 20f.
23 PF: LDB vol. 311 (1830) f. 321rv; Lestra, *Père Coudrin*, 3:376.
24 See the text following note 38 of chapter 2.

25 Boudou, *Les jésuites à Madagascar*, 1:11f; Goyau, *Les grands desseins*, p. 113.
26 Goyau, *Les grands desseins*, pp. 116f.
27 Lestra, *Père Coudrin*, 1:378f. Nine adults were baptised on 2 February 1829 in the Sandwich Islands and made their First Communion on 19 April.
28 Ibid., p. 396; SSCC: +95(044)–9 f. 24.
29 SSCC: +95(044)–9 f. 18f, 22f.
30 Ibid., f. 21f.
31 Goyau, *Les grands desseins*, pp. 120f.
32 SSCC: +95(044)–9 f. 29.
33 Ibid., f. 21, 25–27; Goyau, *Les grands desseins*, pp. 121, 123.
34 Goyau, *Les grands desseins*, p. 122.
35 PF: SC Oceania vol. 1 (1816–41) f. 97r–98v.
36 Lestra, *Père Coudrin*, 3:380.
37 PF: LDB vol. 311 (1830) f. 595v–600r.
38 Goyau, *Les grands desseins*, p. 124.
39 Ibid., p. 125.
40 Ibid., p. 127; SSCC: +95(044)–9 f. 30; PF: SOCG vol. 948 (1833) f. 34r.
41 PF: LDB vol. 311 (1830) f. 887v–888v, 1002r–1003v. Cappellari's letter was dated 27 November 1830.
42 Lestra, *Père Coudrin*, 3:396; Goyau, *Les grands desseins*, pp. 127, 129.

Chapter 4 The Vicariate Apostolic of Eastern Oceania

1 Lestra, *Père Coudrin*, 3:380f.
2 For identification of the Bad Sea and Dangerous archipelagoes see chapter 3, note 1.
3 SSCC: +91(093.2)–3, no. 429.
4 See chapter 2.
5 Lestra, *Père Coudrin*, 3:381.
6 PF: SOCG vol. 948 (1833) f. 30r–34v.
7 Goyau, *Les grands desseins*, p. 99; Lillian G. Keys, *The Life and Times of Bishop Pompallier*, pp. 88f.
8 Keys incorrectly calls de Solages a bishop. *Life of Pompallier*, p. 38.
9 Lestra, *Père Coudrin*, 3:383; Goyau, *Les grands desseins*, p. 186.
10 Goyau, *Les grands desseins*, p. 187; PF: LDB vol. 313 (1832) f. 146v–147v.
11 Lestra, *Père Coudrin*, 3:396; SSCC: +95(044)–9 f. 34–50.
12 Boudou, *Les jésuites à Madagascar*, 1:14.
13 Lestra, *Père Coudrin*, 3:397.
14 Goyau, *Les grands desseins*, pp. 188–90.
15 Boudou, *Les jésuites à Madagascar*, 1:22f. The Sisters of Saint Joseph of Cluny had been founded in France in 1807 by Blessed Anne-Marie Javouhey, whose youngest sister Claudine (along with two others) joined the congregation and received the name Sister Rosalie. She was sent to Bourbon in 1824 and remained there until 1839. Eventually she became the

16 Ibid., pp. 16f; Goyau, *Les grands desseins*, pp. 192, 195, 209f.

17 Goyau, *Les grands desseins*, pp. 209, 211, 214, 230; Boudou, *Les jésuites à Madagascar*, 1:20, 22.

18 Boudou, *Les jésuites à Madagascar*, 1:18, 23.

19 Ibid., pp. 17, 21, 23.

20 PF: Acta vol. 196 (1833) f. 20v; SSCC: +911–18 f. 79r–80r.

21 SSCC: +911–18 f. 73r, 77r, 79r; PF: SC Oceania vol. 1 (1816–41) f. 119r, 125v, 212r.

22 SSCC: +911–18 f. 80r, 81r. Monsignor Garibaldi was the chargé d'affaires. Lambruschini, the former nuncio, had been named a cardinal by Gregory XVI on 30 September 1831.

23 Ibid., f. 81r, 82r.

24 Boudou, *Les jésuites à Madagascar*, 1:24–6.

25 Goyau, *Les grands desseins*, p. 190.

26 Ibid., p. 187; Lestra, *Père Coudrin*, 1:383.

27 Goyau, *Les grands desseins*, p. 203; Boudou, *Les jésuites à Madagascar*, 1:32f.

28 PF: SC Oceania vol. 1 (1816–41) f. 119r, 125v; PF: Acta vol. 196 (1833) f. 26r–27v, 151r. Rouchouze appears in the sources with three different first names: Étienne (baptismal name), Jérôme (religious name), and Stephen (English form of Étienne).

29 PF: Acta vol. 196 (1833) f. 21v, 27v.

30 Cardinal Pacca died in Rome at the age of eighty-seven. By coincidence Via Cardinal Pacca, the street in Rome named after him, runs past the international headquarters of the Daughters of Our Lady of the Sacred Heart, a congregation of Sisters founded to collaborate with the Missionaries of the Sacred Heart (M.S.C.) and active today in many places in the Pacific. For this religious community many authors use the abbreviation O.L.S.H., based on their above title in English, instead of F.D.N.S.C., the official abbreviation based on their Latin title.

31 PF: Acta vol. 196 (1833) f. 20r–23v; PF: SOCG vol. 948 (1833) f. 30r–35r.

32 SSCC: +911–18 f. 82r; PF: Acta vol. 196 (1833) f. 151r–153r.

33 Since the prime meridian of Paris is 2°19′ east of the prime meridian of Greenwich, Hilarion's border line of 159° west of Paris was equivalent to 156°41′ west of Greenwich.

34 PF: Acta vol. 196 (1833) f. 145r–146v, 149r–150v; PF: LDB vol. 314 (1833) f. 545v.

35 PF: LDB vol. 314 (1833) f. 544r–545v.

36 *Ius Pontificium de Propaganda Fide*, Pars Prima, 5:78–80.

37 PF: LDB vol. 314 (1833) f. 608v, Letter, Pedicini to Coudrin, 27 July 1833.

38 Ibid., f. 544r. See chapter 3, note 1. The 16 January 1830 decree giving the limits of the Prefecture Apostolic of the South Sea Islands used the Tropic of Capricorn as the southern boundary only in a qualified sense, since it said that the mission extended from Easter Island inclusive to New Zealand inclusive, both of which are below the Tropic of Capricorn. The 8 June 1833 decree giving the boundaries of the Vicariate Apostolic of Eastern Oceania incorporated the eastern half of the earlier prefecture, and stated that the vicariate stretched from Easter Island inclusive to Roggewein Archipelago inclusive, etc. The missionaries of Eastern Oceania nevertheless had doubts and approached the Sacred Congregation, and it confirmed by a new decree of 10 January 1834 that Easter Island, Pitcairn and Rapa Islands belonged to the vicariate, even though they were below the Tropic of Capricorn. See SSCC: +(093.2)–3, no. 606.

39 Goyau, *Les grands desseins*, pp. 249f, 259f; Boudou, *Les jésuites à Madagascar* 1:31–5; Lestra, *Père Coudrin*, 3:397; PF: SOCG vol. 950 (1835) f. 418r–422v.

40 PF: SC Oceania vol. 1 (1816–41) f. 145r–146r; SSCC: +911–18 f. 83r; SSCC: 1–70–3J.1779.

41 SSCC: +911–18 f. 83r; PF: LDB vol. 314 (1833) f. 505v, 607r, 608v, 611v.

42 Boudou, *Les jésuites à Madagascar*, 1:71.

43 Goyau, *Les grands desseins*, p. 282; Letter, Bishop Puset of Tamatave to Wiltgen, 4 December 1969.

Chapter 5 The Picpus missionaries reach the Gambier Islands

1 SSCC: +911–18 f. 85r; Lestra, *Père Coudrin*, 3:402.

2 Lestra, *Père Coudrin*, 3:402; SSCC: +911–18 f. 85r–87r.

3 SSCC: +911–18 f. 86r–88r.

4 Ibid., f. 87r, 88r; Laval, *L'histoire de Mangareva*, pp. xxiif. Although Irish, Murphy always used the French form 'Colomban' and it is also in all official records.

5 Letter, Reverend Amerigo Cools, SSCC archivist, to Wiltgen, 6 March 1971; Letter, Liausu to Coudrin, 24 May 1834, in *Annales des sacrés-coeurs* (1934), pp. 527f.

6 Letter, Liausu to Coudrin, 19 July 1834, in *Annales des sacrés-coeurs* (1934), pp. 530f, 534–7.

7 Letter, Caro to Coudrin, 15 July 1834, ibid., pp. 528f.

8 SSCC:+911–18 f. 90r; PF: SC Oceania vol. 1 (1816–41) f. 216r.

9 Diemen Island, now Tasmania, was discovered by A. J. Tasman and was generally called Van Diemen's Land.

10 PF: Acta vol. 200 (1837) f. 211r; PF: LDB vol. 315 (1834) f. 302v–303r. Downside Monastery became Downside Abbey in 1900.

11 Letter, Abbot Wilfrid Passmore of Downside Abbey to Wiltgen, 26 November 1969.
12 Lestra, *Père Coudrin*, 3:410, Letter of 17 July 1834. Another form of 'Hierocaesarea' is 'Gerocesarea'.
13 SSCC: +911–18 f. 90r; PF: SC Oceania vol. 1 (1816–41) f. 220r–223v. The Chatham Islands are to the east of central New Zealand and the Kermadec Islands are to the north.
14 PF: SC Oceania vol. 1 (1816–41) f. 229rv; Lestra, *Père Coudrin*, 3:411. Laval, also there, said their two assistants came from Rapa and New Zealand. See Laval, *L'histoire de Mangareva*, p. 18.
15 Lestra, *Père Coudrin*, 3:411. Darling's letter was translated from the French. It is impossible to say whether the original was in English.
16 Letter, Caro to Bishop of Santiago, 23 February 1835, in *Annales des sacrés-coeurs* (1934), pp. 528f.
17 Ibid., p. 532.
18 Lestra, *Père Coudrin*, 3:412, Letter, Rouchouze to Coudrin, 26 May 1835.
19 Ibid.; Laval, *L'histoire de Mangareva*, map 2.
20 Letter, Cools to Wiltgen, 6 March 1971. Fransoni, a former nuncio to Portugal, became cardinal prefect on 21 November 1834.
21 PF: SC Oceania vol. 1 (1816-41) f. 229rv.

Chapter 6 The Vicariate Apostolic of Western Oceania

1 . PF: LDB vol. 314 (1833) f. 603v–604r, 612r; PF: Udienze vol. 61 (1823) f. 206r; OM 4:322.
2 PF: LDB vol. 314 (1833), f. 607v.
3 PF: Acta vol. 198 (1835) f. 361v.
4 PF: SC Oceania vol. 1 (1816–41) f. 220r–223v.
5 PF: LDB vol. 315 (1834) f. 444rv.
6 Ibid., vol. 316 (1835) f. 550r–551v; see also PF: Acta vol. 198 (1835) f. 182v for the 4 December 1829 letter of Pastre on obtaining priests for Madagascar. The archive copy of Fransoni's letter mentions New Ireland ('Nova Irlanda') in place of New Zealand ('Nova Zelanda') when listing the major archipelagoes in the proposed mission, but this is evidently a copyist's error and definitely was not in the original letter sent to Pastre. See also J. Coste and G. Lessard, eds, *Origines maristes (1786–1836)*, 1:770. The Archives of the Catholic Diocese of Auckland under POM 1-1/3 have a copy of Fransoni's letter to Pastre of 4 July 1835, presumably given to Pompallier by Pastre and brought by him to New Zealand, which mentions 'Nova Zelanda' and not 'Nova Irlanda'. If this is a true copy, and not a corrected copy, it is further proof that 'Nova Zelanda'—which was undoubtedly intended—actually was in the original letter. See Letter, Bishop Delargey of Auckland and archivist R. M. Ross to Wiltgen, 26 January 1972.

7 PF: Acta vol. 198 (1835) f. 370rv. Undoubtedly OM 4:321 is correct in giving Pastre's birth as 4 January 1779. Pastre was therefore fifty-six years of age and not, as he says, fifty-five.
8 PF: SC Oceania vol. 1 (1816–41) f. 285r–286v.
9 PF: LDB vol. 316 (1835) f. 622rv.
10 Note that Pastre in an evident reference to Fransoni's letter of 4 July 1835 says 'New Zealand' and not 'New Ireland'. See note 6.
11 PF: Acta vol. 198 (1835) f. 371v.
12 OM 2:489f.
13 Ibid., 4:230–3, 337–9.
14 PF: Acta vol. 198 (1835) f. 371v–372r; PF: SOCG vol. 950 (1835) f. 649rv.
15 PF: LDB vol. 316 (1835) f. 673r.
16 Léon Buffet, *Vie du P. Mermier*, pp. 20f, 43, 45, 108, 234f.
17 PF: Acta vol. 198 (1835) f. 370v–371v; PF: SOCG vol. 950 (1835) f. 646r–647r.
18 PF: LDB vol. 316 (1835) f. 697rv.
19 OM 1:791; PF: Acta vol. 198 (1835) f. 372v; PF: SOCG vol. 950 (1835) f. 651r.
20 PF: SOCG vol. 950 (1835) f. 605r, 639r. An anonymous and therefore unreliable note on f. 605r says that Fesch was the relator, but on the same page he is not mentioned in the list of cardinals present. And on f. 639r Castracane in his own hand says he was 'Ponens' at the meeting. See also OM 1:796–8 for a long study on the authorship and relator of this report, and also OM 4:278–80 for additional data on Fesch. Although it is practically certain that Fesch did not author this report, neither did Castracane, according to OM, but rather a consultor. Castracane on 2 January 1836 said the report was 'delivered by me' and on 11 March 1836 called it 'my report'. See OM 1:817, 856.
21 There is no mention here of New Ireland but only of New Zealand. The other four archipelagoes are the very same and are listed in the same order as those in Fransoni's letter to Pastre of 4 July 1835. See notes 6 and 10.
22 PF: Acta vol. 198 (1835) f. 360r–364r.
23 PF: SC Oceania vol. 1 (1816–41) f. 99r–108v.
24 PF: Acta vol. 198 (1835) f. 364r–366r.
25 OM 1:796, 820.
26 OM 1:646, 675–86, 700, 731–8, 753–8, 833–5; ibid., 4:214–6. The Brothers of the Christian Schools (F.S.C.) were founded by Saint Jean-Baptiste de La Salle at Reims, France, in 1680. They are also called the De La Salle Brothers after their founder and in the United States are known as the Christian Brothers.
27 PF: Acta vol. 198 (1835) f. 366r–369r; PF: SOCG vol. 950 (1835) f. 639r, 653r.

Chapter 7 The Marists accept responsibility for Western Oceania

1 PF: LDB vol. 317 (1836) f. 34v–35r.
2 Ibid., f. 37rv.

3   OM 1:843f; PF: SC Oceania vol. 1 (1816–41) f. 327rv.
4   PF: SC Oceania vol. 1 (1816–41), f. 325r.
5   OM 1:839–41.
6   PF: SOCG vol. 950 (1835) f. 653r.
7   Ibid., f. 654r.
8   PF: SC Oceania vol. 1 (1816–41) f. 305rv.
9   Ibid., f. 306r–307r.
10 OM 1:846, Pompallier to Champagnat, 17 February 1836.
11 Ibid., pp. 850–3.
12 Ibid., pp. 857f.
13 Ibid., pp. 858–61.
14 *Acta Gregorii Papae XVI*, 2 (Pars Prima Canonica):106f. See also Psalm 112(113): 3, and Hebrews 11: 6.

Chapter 8   Pompallier is named Vicar Apostolic of Western Oceania

1   PF: SC Oceania vol. 1 (1816–41) f. 325r.
2   Ibid., f. 329r, 333r.
3   PF: SOCG vol. 950 (1835) f. 649rv.
4   Fransoni had learned from Pastre's letter that the anonymous candidate mentioned in Colin's letter was Pompallier. See OM 1:774, 809, 844; ibid., 2:726, note 5.
5   PF: Udienze vol. 85 (1836, Part I) f. 365r, 370v. Pastre's words in italics were underlined in the script used by the secretary and must have been particularly stressed. 'Bishop-elect' is the title used for designating a bishop not yet ordained.
6   See OM 1:882f.
7   Ibid., pp. 861f, 869–71.
8   Ibid., p. 884, de Pins to Fransoni, 9 May 1836; ibid., p. 908, Pompallier to Colin, 16 July 1836.
9   Ibid., pp. 870, 899f, Pompallier to Colin, 9 June 1836.
10 OM 1:909, Pompallier to Colin, 16 July 1836. In calling it the Church of the *Immaculate* Conception, Pompallier was anticipating a dogma to be defined in 1854. The feast of 'The Conception of the Blessed Virgin Mary', after which the church was named, was placed on the Roman calendar of feasts in 1476. This was changed to the feast of 'The Immaculate Conception' after the dogma was defined.
11 Ibid., pp. 909f.
12 PF: Udienze vol. 86 (1836, Part II) f. 13r.
13 PF: Acta vol. 210 (1847) f. 212r.
14 Ibid., vol. 198 (1835) f. 368r–369r.
15 This decree mistakenly has 7 April for 17 April as the day on which Pope Gregory XVI named Pompallier a bishop and vicar apostolic.
16 OM 1:808, 819, 881, 886. The Roggewein Archipelago (now the northern Cook Islands) was somewhat to the west of the Mangaia Archipelago (now the southern Cook Islands), but was excluded from Pompallier's jurisdiction by the wording of the decree, since there the authority of Bishop Rouchouze of Eastern Oceania had 'already been legitimately established'.
17 PF: SC Oceania vol. 1 (1816–41) f. 486v; SAC: Archivum Pallottianum, Capsula 10, Pompallier to Pallotti, 8 November 1836; Heinrich Schulte, *Gestalt und Geschichte des 'Katholischen Apostolats' Vinzenz Pallottis, Erster Teil*, pp. 64f, 162. Pallotti was added to the list of canonised saints by Pope John XXIII on 20 January 1963.
18 PF: Acta vol. 210 (1847) f. 212r.
19 PF: SC Oceania vol. 1 (1816–41) f. 357r, Letter of 10 September 1836.
20 *L'ami de la religion* 90, no. 2696 (1836): 343.
21 PF: LDB vol. 317 (1836) f. 671v, 701v, 778rv. Letters: Fransoni to Pompallier, 18 August and 1 October 1836; Mai to the secretary of the Association for the Propagation of the Faith, 18 August 1836.
22 PF: SC Oceania vol. 1 (1816–41) f. 358v; PF: Acta vol. 211 (1848) f. 197r.
23 OM 1:920–32, passim.
24 OM 2:491f.
25 PF: LDB vol. 317 (1836) f. 777r–778v.
26 PF: SC Oceania vol. 1 (1816–41) f. 365r, Pompallier to Fransoni, 7 November 1836; f. 398v, Colin to Fransoni, 25 May 1837; f. 389v, Pompallier to Fransoni, 22 February 1837; PF: LDB vol. 317 (1836) f. 778rv, Fransoni to Pompallier, 1 October 1836; PF: SOCG vol. 969 (1847) f. 493rv, Pompallier to Fransoni and all other cardinals of the Evangelisation Congregation, 8 December 1846. In this last letter Pompallier first wrote and then struck out 'pro-vicar', and said instead that at Le Havre on 23 November 1836 he had designated Colin a 'representative' of the mission for France. In his above contemporary letter of 22 February 1837, however, Pompallier tells Fransoni explicitly: 'I offered to the superior general of the congregation the office of pro-vicar.' And Colin in his above letter of 25 May 1837 told Fransoni that Pompallier 'had had letters made for me as vicar general for Western Oceania', in addition to making him 'his correspondent and his chargé d'affaires in France'. Often a man, as Pompallier in this case, later misrepresents an earlier action which he has come to regret.
27 PF: SC Oceania vol. 1 (1816–41) f. 389v, Pompallier to Fransoni, 22 February 1837.

Chapter 9   Pompallier sets sail from Le Havre

1   PF: SC Oceania vol. 1 (1816–41) f. 366v, Pompallier to Fransoni, 7 November 1836.
2   OM 2:491; 4:321f.
3   Ibid., 4:223, 401.
4   Ibid., 4:223; Lestra, *Père Coudrin*, 3:425; Jaspers, *Erschliessung Ozeaniens*, p. 192; PF: SC Oceania vol. 1 (1816–41) f. 366v.
5   PF: SC Oceania vol. 1 (1816–41) f. 358v, Pompallier to Fransoni, 10 September 1836;

ibid., f. 365r–366v, Pompallier to Fransoni, 7 November 1836; PF: LDB vol. 331 (1844) f. 777rv, Fransoni to Pompallier, 1 October 1836.

6 Keys, *Life of Pompallier*, pp. 48f.

7 Ibid., pp. 49, 83f, 99; PF: SC Oceania vol. 1 (1816–41) f. 424r, Pompallier to Fransoni, 22 February 1837. See also Jaspers, *Erschliessung Ozeaniens*, pp. 130, 151; Jore, *L'océan Pacifique*, 1:31, 152.

8 PF: SC Oceania vol. 1 (1816–41) f. 398r, Colin to Fransoni, 25 May 1837. Champagnat was beatified by Pope Pius XII on 29 May 1955.

9 Ibid., f. 365r–366v.

10 Ibid., f. 367rv.

11 PF: Udienze vol. 86 (1836, Part II) f. 409v.

12 Keys, *Life of Pompallier*, p. 50; SM: OG 031, Bret's Journal of 1836–7. The four Picpus missionaries were Father Emmanuel Costes and Brother Bessarion Delon, both of whom remained at Valparaíso, and Fathers Louis de Gonzague Borgella, first to reach the Marquesas Islands, and Potentien Guilmard, missionary in the Marquesas Islands and Mangareva.

13 SM: OG 031, Bret's Journal of 1836–7, also Bataillon's Journal of 1837.

14 SM: OG 031, Bret's Journal of 1836–7, also Bataillon's Journal of 1837; PF: SC Oceania vol. 1 (1816–41) f. 389r.

15 SM: OG 031, Bataillon's Journal of 1837; Pierre Chanel, *Écrits du Père Pierre Chanel*, pp. 167f.

16 Keys, *Life of Pompallier*, p. 51; OM 4:208.

17 Laval, *L'histoire de Mangareva*, p. xv.

18 *L'ami de la religion* 90, no. 2696 (1836): 343.

19 SM: OG 031, Bataillon's Journal of 1837; Chanel, *Écrits de Chanel*, pp. 163f, 167f; PF: SC Oceania vol. 1 (1816–41) f. 366v; PF: Acta vol. 210 (1847) f. 213v.

20 It is difficult to see how Pompallier could say that Ponape (or Ascension Island) on the far northern edge of his mission was centrally located.

21 The Panama Canal was not in existence at this time, being completed only in 1914.

22 PF: SC Oceania vol. 1 (1816-41) f. 424r–425r.

23 Chanel, *Écrits de Chanel*, p. 163; Jaspers, *Erschliessung Ozeaniens*, p. 205.

24 Lestra, *Père Coudrin*, 3:411.

25 Patrick O'Reilly, *Tahitian Catholic Church*, pp. 3, 6; PF: SC Oceania vol. 7 (1861–4) f. 1063v, and vol. 1 (1816–41) 436rv, Laval to his parents, 22 June 1837. Pritchard was named English consul on 14 February 1837; he received the news near the end of 1837, and then handed in his resignation to the London Missionary Society.

26 Yzendoorn, *Catholic Mission in the Hawaiian Islands*, p. 113; Chanel, *Écrits de Chanel*, p. 163.

27 PF: SC Oceania vol. 1 (1816–41) f. 424r–425v.

28 SM: OOC/418/1.

29 SM: OG 031, Bataillon to Séon, 30 July 1837.

30 Chanel, *Écrits de Chanel*, p. 179, Chanel to Bourdin, 8–9 August 1837. Chanel gave Ponape's longitude east of Paris as given on a contemporary map. The island lies 158° 14′ east of Greenwich and today is considered part of the Caroline Archipelago.

31 PF: SC Oceania vol. 1 (1816–41) f. 424r–425v, Letter of 23 July 1837.

Chapter 10 The Vicar Apostolic of Eastern Oceania is given authority over New Zealand and the Archipelagoes of Tonga, Samoa and Fiji

1 Caret regularly uses 'Southeast Oceania' in this title when signing his name. But Secretary Mai uses 'Southern Oceania' as the title for this Prefecture Apostolic and so do Bishop Rouchouze and the minutes of the Evangelisation Congregation. The author has found no basis in any document for using 'Southeast Oceania'. Cf. PF: Acta vol. 198 (1835) f. 362r; PF: SC Oceania vol. 1 (1816–41) f. 223r, 459r; PF: LDB vol. 318 (1837) f. 918r.

2 Letter, Cools to Wiltgen, 19 September 1973.

3 PF: SC Oceania vol. 1 (1816–41) f. 452rv; PF: Udienze vol. 88 (1837) f. 338r.

4 PF: SC Oceania vol. 1 (1816–41) f. 442r–449r; PF: LDB vol. 318 (1837) f. 918rv. Cf. also L. van de Berg, *De infidelium polygamorum conversione*, pp. 36ff.

5 SSCC: +95(044)–5, no. 111. Here Pagès incorrectly gives the longitude as 95° west.

6 PF: SC Oceania vol. 1 (1816–41) f. 467r–468r.

7 See chapter 6.

8 PF: SC Oceania vol. 1 (1816–41) f. 456r.

9 PF: Udienze vol. 89 (1838) f. 60r.

10 PF: LDB vol. 318 (1837) f. 955r–956r. Cf. SSCC: +95(96)–2, p. 206.

11 PF: SC Oceania vol. 1 (1816–41) f. 467r–468r. Caret here uses 'Nukuhiva', actually the main island in the northwest group of the Marquesas Islands; he identifies it in a later letter with the 'Marquesas Islands'. Cf. ibid., f. 497v. Jaspers, reporting on this document in *Erschliessung Ozeaniens*, p. 207, reads far more into the text than it contains, when he says that Caret here takes the Evangelisation Congregation to task for having used nothing but a map to determine the limits of the Vicariate Apostolic of Eastern Oceania. He forgets that it was the Picpus community itself which suggested the limits for the vicariate and that subsequently these limits were approved by the Evangelisation Congregation and the pope. Caret in this memorandum is merely stating that the Picpus missionaries in Eastern Oceania and in Paris—for he came to Rome with the approval of Rouchouze and Bonamie—are no longer satisfied with the extent of their original request.

12 For details on the border line between the Vicariate Apostolic of Eastern Oceania and the

Prefecture Apostolic of the South Sea Islands, see chapter 4. This border line was retained when the Vicariate Apostolic of Western Oceania was created.

13 PF: Udienze vol. 89 (1838) f. 54r–55r.
14 PF: LDB vol. 319 (1838) f. 92v–95r. In this source Rouchouze is incorrectly designated as the Vicar Apostolic of *Western* Oceania.
15 Ibid., f. 91v–92r.
16 PF: SC Oceania vol. 1 (1816–41) f. 458r-459r.
17 PF: LDB vol. 319 (1838) f. 90r–91r.
18 Ibid., f. 92v.
19 PF: SC Oceania vol. 1(1816–41) f. 477r, 497r.
20 *An Ordinance Rejecting the Catholic Religion* (Lahaina, Maui, 1837), pp. 3, 5, 7. The *Ordinance* covers three pages and is printed in both Hawaiian and English. In Hawaiian the title reads: *Ke Kanawai, No ka hoole ana i ka Pope.*

Chapter 11 Pompallier leaves Valparaíso for Ponape in Micronesia

1 Lestra, *Père Coudrin*, 3:437, Chanel to Pagès, 3 October 1837; ibid., p. 433, Pompallier to Colin, 2 October 1837. Chanel tells Pagès that the crossing took thirty-three days, but in English usage we would reckon 10 August to 13 September as thirty-four days.
2 Ibid., pp. 398, 412, 431; ibid., pp. 433–6, Pompallier to Colin, 2 October 1837; ibid., pp. 437–9, Chanel to Pagès, 3 October 1837.
3 Ibid., p. 436.
4 This arrangement between the two bishops in no way altered the border lines of their vicariates. If changes should eventually prove feasible, the Evangelisation Congregation could be petitioned to make them.
5 PF: SC Oceania vol. 1(1816–41) f. 485r, Pompallier to Fransoni, 21 May 1838.
6 Yzendoorn, *Catholic Mission in the Hawaiian Islands*, p. 114.
7 Ibid., pp. 113f; Lestra, *Père Coudrin*, 3:439. Lestra on page 431 mistakenly says that Murphy was secretly ordained when Rouchouze reached the Gambier Islands in 1835.
8 PF: SC Oceania vol. 1(1816–41) f. 432r.
9 Lestra, *Père Coudrin*, 3:439, Chanel to Pagès, 3 October 1837.
10 Patrick O'Reilly and Raoul Teissier, *Tahitiens*, pp. 321f.
11 PF: SC Oceania vol. 1(1816–41) f. 429r, extract from a government dispatch from Paris, 29 September 1837; ibid., f. 428r, Lambruschini to Fransoni, 31 October 1837.
12 Lestra, *Père Coudrin*, 3:439, Chanel to Pagès, 3 October 1837.
13 Ibid., p. 437, Pompallier to Colin, 2 October 1837.
14 PF: SC Oceania vol. 1 (1816-41) f. 485r, Pompallier to Fransoni, 21 May 1838.

15 Yzendoorn, *Catholic Mission in the Hawaiian Islands*, p. 114.
16 Pompallier on 22 December 1837 gave 5 October as the date for leaving Tahiti. In his letter of 21 May 1838 to Fransoni he said, 'We left Tahiti on 4 or 5 October 1837'. And in his report for the Evangelisation Congregation written ten years after the event occurred, he said that he left Tahiti 'on 4 October 1837'. Cf. SM: OOC/418/1, Pompallier to the Commander of the French Base at Valparaiso, 22 December 1837; PF: SC Oceania vol. 1 (1816–41) f. 485r, Pompallier to Fransoni, 21 May 1838; PF: Acta vol. 210 (1847) f. 215r. But Maigret was there and wrote in his diary 'Wednesday, 4 October 1837 . . . about 10 A.M.'. Cf. SSCC: +92 Maigret p. 88r.
17 Keys, *Life of Pompallier*, pp. 61f.
18 PF: SC Oceania vol. 1 (1816–41) f. 485v, Pompallier to Fransoni, 21 May 1838.
19 Keys, *Life of Pompallier*, p. 62.
20 Jaspers, *Erschliessung Ozeaniens*, pp. 133f.
21 Keys, *Life of Pompallier*, pp. 62f.
22 Jaspers, *Erschliessung Ozeaniens*, p. 133.
23 PF: SC Oceania vol. 1 (1816-41) f. 485v.
24 SM: OOC/418/1, Pompallier to the Commander of the French Base at Valparaiso, 22 December 1837.
25 Keys, *Life of Pompallier*, p. 63.
26 Ibid., pp. 63–9.
27 Ibid., p. 69; SM: OOC/418/1, Pompallier to the Commander of the French Base at Valparaíso, 22 December 1837.
28 SM: OOC/418/1, Pompallier to the Commander of the French Base at Valparaiso, 22 December 1837.
29 PF: SC Oceania vol. 1 (1816–41) f. 485v; OM 4:223.
30 Keys, *Life of Pompallier*, pp. 70–2; OM 4:222f. Sam's name appears in many forms but is correctly written Keletaona. See Letter, Cools to Wiltgen, 23 February 1978.
31 PF: SC Oceania vol. 1 (1816–41) f. 485v-486r.
32 PF: Acta vol. 210 (1847) f. 223v; Keys, *Life of Pompallier*, p. 73; SM: OOC/418/1, Pompallier to the Commander of the French Base at Valparaíso, 22 December 1837.
33 SM: OOC/418/1, Pompallier to the Commander of the French Base at Valparaíso, 22 December 1837; PF: Acta vol. 210 (1847) f. 217v, 233r–234r; PF: SC Oceania vol. 1 (1816–41) f. 485r–486r, Pompallier to Fransoni, 21 May 1838.
34 PF: SOCG vol. 944 (1829) f. 568v.
35 PF: Acta vol. 210 (1847) f. 234r; PF: SC Oceania vol. 1 (1816–41) f. 454rv.
36 Yzendoorn, *Catholic Mission in the Hawaiian Islands*, pp. 115–7.
37 Strong, *American Board*, p. 236 (illustration).
38 PF: LDB vol. 318 (1837) f. 866v–867v.

39 Jaspers, *Erschliessung Ozeaniens*, p. 209.
40 Yzendoorn, *Catholic Mission in the Hawaiian Islands*, pp. 117f.
41 SSCC: +95(044)–3, Maigret to Bonamie, 16 January 1839.
42 Letter, Cools to Wiltgen, 5 May 1972.
43 Keys, *Life of Pompallier*, pp. 73, 77.

Chapter 12 Pompallier arrives in Sydney and meets Polding

1 Erwin Feeken, 'First Charting of the Northern Shores of Australia', p. 12; 'Historic Shipwreck'.
2 PF: Acta vol. 3 (1622–5) f. lr–5v; PF: SC Africa, Isole dell'Oceano Australe, Capo Buona Speranza vol. 1 (1643–1826), f. lr, 6r–7r. Further Jesuit interest in this part of the world up to 1750 has been catalogued by Ernest J. Burrus in 'Jesuits and Terra Australis'.
3 For the General Meetings see PF: Acta vol. 35 (1666) f. 39r, 45v–46r, 246r, 263r–265r; for Paulmier's *Mémoires* see Patrick O'Reilly, 'Le chanoine Paulmier de Courtonne et son projet d'évangélisation des terres australes (1663)'; for the correspondence of Paulmier and of Alméras see F. Combaluzier, 'Le chanoine Paulmier de Courtonne et ses rêves apostoliques vers les Terres australes (1659–1667)'. For other details see Robert Streit and Johannes Didinger, *Bibliotheca Missionum*, 21:36, and Jaspers, *Erschliessung Ozeaniens*, pp. 88–96.

Combaluzier, who did not see PF: Acta, incorrectly states in 'Le chanoine Paulmier de Courtonne et ses rêves apostoliques vers les Terres australes (1659–1667)', that Pope Alexander VII absolutely refused to go along with Paulmier's proposals (p. 113). Jaspers, who also did not see PF: Acta, makes incorrect deductions from undated correspondence of the era presented by Combaluzier. For example, Jaspers states that the Evangelisation Congregation as early as 1662 had resolved 'to erect a vicariate apostolic which was to include both Madagascar and also the Australian Lands with Paulmier de Courtonne destined to be its first vicar apostolic' (p. 92). He also incorrectly deduces from a note by Joseph Schmidlin that 'the Propaganda Congregation decided on 20 September 1666 to erect a vicariate apostolic which again was to include Madagascar and the Australian Lands' (p. 94). What Schmidlin says in the body of his text is that Paulmier in his 1666 proposal 'for a new Australian mission' suggested that 'Madagascar be the seat of its vicar apostolic'. In his note Schmidlin says that 'the erection of the new mission was decided on 20 September [1666]' and he gives as his source PF: Acta. The 'new mission' proposed by Paulmier truly was founded on that date, as Schmidlin says, but not as a vicariate apostolic

embracing both Madagascar and the Australian Lands, as Jaspers says. Cf. Joseph Schmidlin, 'Die ersten Madagaskarmissionen im Lichte der Propagandamaterialien', p. 204; Jaspers, *Erschliessung Ozeaniens*, p. 94; and PF: Acta vol. 35 (1666) f. 265r.

4 PF: SOCG vol. 193 (Indie), f. 281r, Riccio to the cardinals of the Evangelisation Congregation, 22 June 1651; PF: SOCG vol. 493 (1681) f. 235r–243v, Riccio to the cardinals of the Evangelisation Congregation, 4 June 1676; PF: Acta vol. 51 (1681) f. 205rv, General Meeting of 15 July 1681. See also: José María González, *Un Misionero diplomático*, pp. 7–19 passim, 74, 79f; Gregorio F. Zaide, *Philippine Political and Cultural History* 1: 270, 277f, 281f; Alberto Santamaria, 'The Chinese Parian (El Parian de los Sangleyes)', pp. 109f. In this latter work edited by Felix immediately before page 1 there is a map of Manila and the *Parian* as drawn by Ignacio Muñoz, O.P., in 1671. In the same book Rafael Bernal in 'The Chinese Colony in Manila, 1570–1770', mistakenly calls Riccio a Jesuit (p. 56).

Riccio's family name was actually Ricci and he was closely related to Father Matteo Ricci (1552–1610), China's foremost Jesuit missionary. In December 1603 Matteo Ricci as Jesuit superior in China had prescribed the observance of two ritual customs of the Chinese as a licit and even indispensable aid in the Christian apostolate. This resulted in the Chinese rites controversy with Jesuits and Dominicans taking opposite camps. Now Juan Bautista de Morales, who had recruited Victorio Riccio for the Far East, was the leading antagonist among the Dominicans. From the time Victorio Riccio began working among the Chinese he dropped the name 'Ricci' and always signed himself 'Riccio', or in Latin 'Riccius'. He also called himself 'Riccio' in his own history of his order's Chinese missions because, it was said, he did not want to be mistaken for a member of the Matteo Ricci camp in the rites controversy.

Riccio writing on 4 June 1676 told the Evangelisation Congregation's cardinals that he was fifty-eight years old. [See the Italian translation and Spanish original of his letter in PF: SOCG vol. 493 (1681) f. 236r, 237v.] But the baptismal register gives Riccio's birthday as 18 January 1621. (See González, *Un Misionero diplomático*, p. 8.) Riccio therefore must have been fifty-five years of age when writing to the cardinals and not fifty-eight.

González in *Un Misionero diplomático*, apparently quoting Salazar (note, p. 74), says that Riccio was 'Prefect [Apostolic] of the Missions of the Island of Formosa and of the Terra Australis of China' (p. 80). Riccio himself, however, when signing his letter of 4 June 1676 to the cardinals, said that he was prefect apostolic only of 'the Island of Formosa' and that he was 'Missionary for the same see to the Great Empire of China'. [See PF: SOCG vol. 493 (1681) f. 243r.]

5 Paul Dillon, 'A Sailor in Search of a Star', p. 11.

6 Merval Hoare, 'King of Norfolk Island', pp. 27f; Merval Hoare, 'The Discovery of Norfolk Island', p. 8.

7 PF: SC Africa, Isole dell'Oceano Australe, Capo Buona Speranza vol. 1 (1643–1826) f. 267r; Nicola Kowalsky, *Serie dei Cardinali Prefetti e dei Segretari della Sacra Congregazione 'de Propaganda Fide'*, pp. 8–10, 15, 24f, 34. Some current documents use the spelling 'Brancadoro'. For data on Paccanari and his society see: Gaetano Moroni, *Dizionario di Erudizione Storio-Ecclesiastica*, 50:89–91; Max Heimbucher, *Die Orden und Kongregationen der katholischen Kirche*, 3:88–91; John Francis Broderick, 'Paccanarists'.

8 PF: Udienze vol. 42 (1804) f. 50r-51v; PF: SC Oceania vol. 1 (1816–41) f. 7rv; Patrick Francis Cardinal Moran, *History of the Catholic Church in Australasia*, pp. 27, 36–8, 42; Patrick O'Farrell, *The Catholic Church in Australia*, pp. 4f; CSI: *Liber Discretorius (1741–1878)*. The contents of *Liber Discretorius* are in chronological order; there are no page references. This document gives the guardian's name as MacCormick, and not McCormack as Moran spells it in *Catholic Church in Australasia*, p. 39.

9 PF: LDB vol. 287 (1804) f. 74v–76r. Keys incorrectly gives the year of Dixon's appointment as 1803 in *Life of Pompallier*, p. 74.

10 PF: SC Oceania vol. 1 (1816–41) f. 7rv; O'Farrell, *Catholic Church in Australia*, p. 4; Moran, *Catholic Church in Australasia*, pp. 33, 45, 47, 51.

11 Cathaldus Giblin, 'Daniel O'Connell and the Irish Franciscans', pp. 72–5; M. J. Brenan, *An Ecclesiastical History of Ireland from the Introduction of Christianty into That Country to the Year 1829*, pp. 605–21, 680–2; CSI: *Liber Discretorius (1741–1878)*. Brenan says that Father Hayes was born on 20 January 1788. But the date given in *Liber Discretorius (1741–1878)* is 6 February 1787 and ought to be reliable, this being the contemporary record kept on candidates at Saint Isidore College. Hayes—his religious name was Joachim—died in Paris on 25 January 1824.

12 PF: SC Oceania vol. 1 (1816–41) f. 7r–8r.

13 PF: Udienze vol. 54 (1816) f. 469r–470v, 490r, 492r–493r, 503v, 505v; Moran, *Catholic Church in Australasia*, pp. 54, 56. Moran in this work quotes numerous letters (pp. 55, 59, 61 and 63) in which the Cistercian priest signed himself Flynn.

14 PF: SC Oceania vol. 1 (1816–41) f. 9r, 11r–15v.

15 PF: Udienze vol. 54 (1816) f. 590r.

16 PF: LDB vol. 297 (1816) f. 256r–257r.

17 Moran, *Catholic Church in Australasia*, pp. 54–8, 72, 75; W. T. Southerwood, *Planting a Faith: Hobart's Catholic Story in Word and Picture*, p. 5.

18 Moran, *Catholic Church in Australasia*, pp. 59–63; J. G. Murtagh, 'Australia', p. 1086; PF: SC Oceania vol. 1 (1816–41) f. 16r.

19 PF: SC Oceania vol. 1 (1816–41) f. 16r–18v. The Jesuit's name is not Grosse, nor did he write on 12 April, as given by Moran, *Catholic Church in Australasia*, p. 121.

20 PF: SC Africa, Isole dell'Oceano Australe, Capo Buona Speranza vol. 1 (1643–1826) f. 479rv; PF: LDB vol. 299 (1818) f. 308r–309r; PF: Udienze vol. 57 (1819) f. 339r; Moran, *Catholic Church in Australasia*, p. 73.

21 PF: Acta vol. 192 (1829) f. 430r–448v; ibid., vol. 200 (1837) f. 212r; Moran, *Catholic Church in Australasia*, pp. 148f; O'Farrell, *Catholic Church in Australia*, pp. 16–20; W. T. Southerwood, *Planting a Faith: Launceston's Catholic Story in Word and Picture*, p. 1.

22 Southerwood, *Hobart's Catholic Story*, p. 10; O'Farrell, *Catholic Church in Australia*, pp. 24f, 29f; Moran, *Catholic Church in Australasia*, pp. 131f, 142f.

23 Moran, *Catholic Church in Australasia*, pp. 178f; PF: Acta vol. 200 (1837) f. 211r; PF: SC Oceania vol. 1 (1816–41) f. 196r–197v.

24 PF: LDB vol. 315 (1834) f. 302v–303r. Although Rome's documents spoke of 'Van Diemen Island', Polding at once adopted the form being used in New Holland and England and in August 1834 already called himself in the press the Vicar Apostolic of New Holland and Van Diemen's Land. See Moran, *Catholic Church in Australasia*, pp. 180f, and also pp. 198f.

25 Letter, Abbot Wilfrid Passmore of Downside Abbey to Wiltgen, 26 November 1969.

26 Van Diemen's Land (68,162 square kilometres) was in fact nearly three times larger than Sicily (25,561 square kilometres).

27 PF: SC Oceania vol. 1 (1816–41) f. 225r–226r; Moran, *Catholic Church in Australasia*, p. 187.

28 PF: SC Oceania vol. 1 (1816–41) f. 339r–340r; Letter, Passmore to Wiltgen, 26 November 1969; Southerwood, *Hobart's Catholic Story*, p. 13; Moran, *Catholic Church in Australasia*, pp. 186f, 1000.

29 Moran, *Catholic Church in Australasia*, pp. 142, 149, 152–64 passim, 168, 170, 203; M. C. Normoyle, *A Tree Is Planted*, pp. 22–5, 141, 261–3, 414. Cardinal Castracane's Italian report in PF: Acta vol. 200 (1837) f. 213r, 215r, when giving the scope of Ullathorne's visit to Europe, uses the term 'Brothers of Christian Doctrine', a misnomer for Rice's religious

community, carried over from French usage. As early as 2 December 1803 in official French government documents this misnomer was being used for the Brothers of the Christian Schools (F.S.C.) founded in Reims, France, in 1680. See Georges Rigault, *Histoire générale de l'Institut des frères des écoles chrétiennes*, 3:533. That the misnomer was long and widely used is evident from copies of a papal document of 23 November 1819, a French government document of 16 May 1849, a 'Comune di Roma' government document of 21 December 1850, all sent to me by Brother John Hazell, F.S.C., archivist of the Brothers of the Christian Schools, with his letter of 16 February 1978. Since Rice's religious community in this period was called Brothers of the Christian Schools of Ireland (this title was on Rice's tombstone; see Normoyle, *A Tree Is Planted*, p. 414, and the plate following), it is easy to understand how the misnomer was applied as well to the Irish group.

30 PF: SC Oceania vol. 1 (1816–41) f. 343rv.
31 'Norfolk Island', p. 11.
32 PF: SC Oceania vol. 1 (1816–41) f. 343v, 351rv, 481v.
33 PF: SOCG vol. 952 (1837) f. 487r–488v, 507r–508r, 510v.
34 Port Arthur, founded in Van Diemen's Land in 1830 as a penal colony, was located on Tasman Peninsula, a natural prison. See Coultman Smith, *Shadow over Tasmania*, pp. 46–69.
35 PF: Acta vol. 200 (1837) f. 212r–215v. For the origin of the misnomer, Brothers of Christian Doctrine, see note 29.
36 PF: SC Oceania vol. 1 (1816–41) f. 469rv; Moran, *Catholic Church in Australasia*, pp. 203, 239, 554. Moran mistakenly says (p. 554) that Ullathorne and Brady met in Rome in 1838; it was 1837. The other priest who sailed with Brady to Australia was Father James Alipius Goold of the Order of Saint Augustine (O.S.A.), known also as Augustinians. Goold later became the first Bishop of Melbourne.
37 PF: SC Oceania vol. 1 (1816–41) f. 400r.
38 Ibid., f. 471r, 481v; PF: LDB vol. 319 (1838) f. 169rv.
39 SM: OOC/418/1, Pompallier to the Commander of the French Base at Valparaíso, 22 December 1837; Keys, *Life of Pompallier*, pp. 73, 77.
40 Keys, *Life of Pompallier*, p. 78; Moran, *Catholic Church in Australasia*, p. 895.
41 Moran, *Catholic Church in Australasia*, pp. 890–2, 895, opp. p. 896 (facsimile of Polding's 29 October 1835 letter to Poynton); Keys, *Life of Pompallier*, pp. 75–7.
42 SM: OOC/418/1, Pompallier to the Commander of the French Base at Valparaíso, 22 December 1837.
43 Ibid., Pompallier to Colin, 23 December 1837.

44 Ibid., Pompallier to the Commander of the French Base at Valparaíso, 22 December 1837; PF: SC Oceania vol. 1 (1816–41) f. 486r, Pompallier to Fransoni, 21 May 1838, and f. 505v, Pompallier to Colin, 14 May 1838.
45 Moran, *Catholic Church in Australasia*, pp. 170, 172, 205, 959; Normoyle, *A Tree Is Planted*, pp. 314, 405.

Chapter 13 Pompallier makes New Zealand his headquarters

1 SM: OOC/418/1, postscript of Pompallier to the Commander of the French Base at Valparaíso, 17 January 1838; Keys, *Life of Pompallier*, pp. 91f, opp. p. 97; PF: SC Oceania vol. 2 (1842–5, Part II) f. 557r, Pompallier to the Colonial Secretary of New Zealand, 12 September 1843; Moran, *Catholic Church in Australasia*, p. 894. Moran, who gives the extract from Pompallier's letter, says neither to whom it was written nor when. Pompallier wrote 'Tortero' (17 January 1838), but I have used 'Totara Point' (modern spelling?) as given by Keys. OM 4:338 is evidently in error, saying that Pompallier 'disembarked at the Bay of Islands in New Zealand on 10 January 1838'.
2 Keys, *Life of Pompallier*, p. 80.
3 Ibid., pp. 49, 99f; Jaspers, *Erschliessung Ozeaniens*, pp. 193f; Jore, *L'océan Pacifique*, 1:189; 2:83.
4 SM: 511.422, Dillon to Colin, 18 February 1839 and 25 January 1840; Jore, *L'océan Pacifique*, 1:187–8.
5 Keys, *Life of Pompallier*, pp. 101f; PF: SC Oceania vol. 1 (1816–41) f. 502r.
6 PF: SC Oceania vol. 1 (1816–41) f. 502r–505v.
7 Ibid., f. 485r–486v; SAC: Archivum Pallottianum, Capsula 10, Pompallier to Pallotti, 8 November 1836 and 22 May 1838; Heinrich Schulte, *Gestalt und Geschichte*, pp. 158f, 162, 164–6, 169. Referring in his 22 May 1838 letter from New Zealand to his letter from Paris, Pompallier mistakenly gives the date as 9 November instead of 8 November 1836.
8 PF: SC Oceania vol. 1 (1816–41) f. 501rv, 503r.
9 PF: LDB vol. 320 (1838, Part II) f. 1210rv.
10 Keys, *Life of Pompallier*, p. 109.
11 Ibid., pp. 110f; Yzendoorn, *Catholic Mission in the Hawaiian Islands*, p. 119. Keys mistakenly refers to this ship as *Reine de Paix*, as Father Baty did when informing Colin of the purchase on 15 April 1839, but contemporary Picpus documents all use *Notre Dame de Paix*.
12 AMO, p. 19, Baty to Colin, 15 April 1839.
13 SSCC: 116–18, Liausu to Bonamie, no date.
14 SSCC: +92 Maigret f. 104r, 105v, 106r; SSCC: +95(044)–5, no. 137, Rouchouze to Bonamie, 19 August 1838; ibid., Rouchouze to Lucas, 16 April 1839. See also Société de Marie, *Annales des missions d'Océanie*, 1:21.

15   Keys, *Life of Pompallier*, pp. 110–2, 181f.

16   Ibid., pp. 110, 114f; Laval, *L'histoire de Mangareva*, p. 184. Keys says (p. 110) that the ship arrived on 16 June 1839. But Pompallier's own letter says the new missionaries reached Bay of Islands on 14 June. See SM: OOC/418/1, Pompallier to Colin, 14 August 1839.

17   Keys, *Life of Pompallier*, pp. 113f; SM: OOC/418/1.
.

18   SM: OOC/418/1. The population indicated by Pompallier is, of course, a gross exaggeration. The late Lillian G. Keys in reporting on this Pompallier letter in *Life of Pompallier* (pp. 112f) unfortunately became a victim of the pious but altogether unreliable editorial staff of *Annales de la propagation de la foi*, whose copy of the Pompallier letter in vol. 12 (Lyon 1840) p. 400 she translates most faithfully in her book. But this is not the letter that Pompallier wrote, as a comparison with the original in the Marist Archives shows. The editorial staff took great liberty with the text. Pompallier, already exaggerating, wrote 'twelve or fifteen million souls'; the editorial staff changed that to read 'fifteen or twenty million' (Keys, p. 113). The editorial staff's version of Pompallier's letter, reproduced by Keys, says this about Pompallier meeting his new missionaries: 'On entering the dwelling of the English merchant who had had the generosity to entertain them, I searched with my eyes for these friends, these brothers. Where are they? I see them at my feet, weeping for joy. What a sweet moment! Our tears alone said how happy we were. "Come, blessed of my Father, enter into possession of the kingdom which is prepared for you!" These were my first words. What a consolation it was for me to embrace our children of Mary, new apostles for these poor souls for the salvation of whom I was so far from being adequate. . . .' (Keys, p. 112). These saccharine lines, typical of the liberties taken by the editorial staff of *Annales de la propagation de la foi*, are nothing but fiction and should serve as a warning for anyone interested in writing factual history.

19   PF: LDB vol. 319 (1838, Part I) f. 92v–95r.

20   PF: Udienze vol. 89 (1838, Part I) f. 55r.

21   PF: SC Oceania vol. 1 (1816–41) f. 498v.

22   Ibid., f. 497v; ibid., vol. 7 (1861–4) f. 1063v.

23   Jaspers, *Erschliessung Ozeaniens*, pp. 207–12.

24   PF: SC Oceania vol. 1 (1816–41) f. 544rv.

25   Ibid., f. 503r.

26   SM: 511.422.

27   Ibid., Dillon to Colin, 24 April 1840; Keys, *Life of Pompallier*, p. 117.

28   PF: SC Oceania vol. 2 (1842–5, Part I) f. 489r.

29   Keys, *Life of Pompallier*, p. 88; Jaspers, *Erschliessung Ozeaniens*, pp. 194, 197.

30   SM: Epistolae Variae Generalium, vol. 1, p. 2, no. 6.

31   SM: 511.411.

32   SM: Epistolae Variae Generalium, vol. 1, pp. 3–6, no. 8.

33   Ibid., p. 7, no. 11.

34   Ibid., p. 8, nos 13 and 14.

35   Ibid., pp. 6f, no. 9.

36   Jore, *L'océan Pacifique*, 1:196, 279, 325. Jore writes 'Compagnie Nanto-Bordelaise' (p. 196) and 'Société Nanto-Bordelaise' (p. 325).

37   SM: 511.24.

38   SM: Epistolae Variae Generalium, vol. 1, pp. 11f, no. 17.

39   Ibid., p. 12, no. 18.

40   Keys, *Life of Pompallier*, p. 117.

41   SM: 511.422.

42   Keys, *Life of Pompallier*, pp. 148–53, 377.

43   Ibid., pp. 139f.

44   Ibid., pp. 151, 168; PF: SC Oceania vol. 2 (1842–5, Part I) f. 489r, 494r, Colin to Fransoni, 17 June 1843, and Part II, f. 571r, Pompallier to the Central Council in Lyon, 6 November 1842. When writing to the Central Council, Pompallier did not indicate the same costs. 'It cost me a bit more than 23,000 francs (925 pounds sterling) . . .', he said. 'The needed repairs cost me 10,000 francs. . . .'

45   Keys, *Life of Pompallier*, p. 156.

46   PF: LDB vol. 324 (1840, Part II) f. 1080rv.

Chapter 14   The Vicariate Apostolic of Central Oceania

1   SM: OOC/418.

2   PF: SC Oceania vol. 2 (1842–5, Part I) f. 102rv, Colin to Fransoni, 18 March 1842.

3   SM: 511.422.

4   PF: SC Oceania vol. 2 (1842–5, Part I) f. 102r, Colin to Fransoni, 18 March 1842.

5   SM: 503/11.

6   SM: 511.422.

7   Ibid.

8   PF: SOCG vol. 962 (1842) f. 130r–131r.

9   SM: Epistolae Variae Generalium, vol. 1, p. 21, no. 46.

10   PF: LDB vol. 325 (1841) f. 567v–568v.

11   Ibid., f. 565v–567r.

12   SM: 511.422

13   Keys, *Life of Pompallier*, pp. 165, 168, 172; PF: SC Oceania vol. 1 (1816–41) f. 692r, and vol. 2 (1842–5, Part II) f. 566r, 572r, Pompallier to the Association for the Propagation of the Faith in Lyon, 6 November 1842. The fourteen mission stations (often with outstations also indicated) were spelled as follows and were listed in this order: Hokianga, Bay of Islands, Wangaroa, Kaipara, Auckland, Tauranga, Matamata and Waikato, Maketa, Opotiki, Terakako, Port Nicklson, Akaroa, Wallis, and Futuna.

14   PF: SC Oceania vol. 2 (1842–5, Part II) f. 572rv.

15   Ibid., Part I, f. 432r, Pompallier to Fransoni, 19 October 1842.

16 Keys, *Life of Pompallier*, pp. 175f.
17 Ibid., pp. 177, 183; PF: SC Oceania vol. 2 (1842–5, Part II) f. 572v, Pompallier to the Association for the Propagation of the Faith in Lyon, 6 November 1842.
18 PF: SOCG vol. 962 (1842) f. 123r–124r. Father Chanel was declared Blessed on 17 November 1889 and a Saint on 12 June 1954.
19 Keys, *Life of Pompallier*, pp. 178–81, 184. The name of the captain of the *Allier* is spelled 'Dubouzet' and not 'Du Bouzet', a form found in many sources. See *Annales maritimes et coloniales*, partie non-officielle, 1:5–61, for Dubouzet's report to Lavaud on his expedition to Vava'u, Wallis and Futuna.
20 OM 4:283.
21 PF: SC Oceania vol. 2 (1842–5, Part I) f. 102r–103r, Colin to Fransoni, 18 March 1842.
22 PF: SOCG vol. 962 (1842) f. 127r–128r.
23 Ibid.; SM: Epistolae Variae Generalium, vol. 1, p. 21, no. 46, Colin to Pompallier, 6 June 1841.
24 This letter has 'southwest', a mistake copied from Colin's letter of 28 December 1841 to Fransoni, which is an evident slip of the pen for 'northwest'. And Fransoni's letter mistakenly gives the date of Colin's letter of 28 December 1841 as 18 December. See PF: LDB vol. 327 (1842, Part I) f. 78rv; PF: SOCG vol. 962 (1842) f. 127r–128r.
25 PF: LDB vol. 327 (1842, Part I) f. 78r–79r.
26 Keys, *Life of Pompallier*, pp. 184f.
27 PF: SC Oceania vol. 2 (1842–5, Part I) f. 102r–103r.
28 PF: LDB vol. 327 (1852, Part I) f. 314rv.
29 Ibid., f. 314v–316r.
30 PF: SC Oceania vol. 2 (1842–5, Part I) f. 388rv, Colin to Fransoni, 27 October 1842. Colin here mistakenly gives 16 March as the date for his own letter of 18 March 1842. Here Colin also speaks of being forced to postpone his trip to Rome 'until the beginning of the month of June [1842]'. It may have been the beginning of June by the time he had completed some errands in France, but he actually left Lyon for Rome on 28 May. See Kevin Roach, 'Venerable John Claude Colin and the Mission in New Zealand', p. 160.
31 SM: 410 SCPF. The 'Overall View' lists Father Chanel among the missionaries active in Wallis and Futuna. An insertion in the margin states: 'Father Chanel was martyred on 28 April 1841'.
32 PF: SOCG vol. 970 (1848) f. 437r, Colin to Epalle, 25 July 1843; PF: SC Oceania vol. 2 (1842–5, Part I) f. 388v, Colin to Fransoni, 27 October 1842.
33 PF: SOCG vol. 962 (1842) f. 119r–122r.
34 PF: SC Oceania vol. 2 (1842–5, Part I) f. 442r–443r.
35 PF: Acta vol. 205 (1842) f. 352r–361v.
36 Keys, *Life of Pompallier*, pp. 185–90; PF: SC

Oceania vol. 2 (1842–5, Part II) f. 566r–567v, 573r, Pompallier to the Association for the Propagation of the Faith, 6 November 1842. For the details regarding Dubouzet and Keletaona, drawn from sources far too numerous to mention here, the author is indebted to the exhaustive research of Father Amerigo Cools. See Letter, Cools to Wiltgen, 23 February 1978.
37 PF: LDB vol. 325 (1841) f. 567v–568r.
38 Pompallier answered Fransoni's letter of 12 June 1841 on 19 October 1842. See PF: SC Oceania vol. 2 (1842–5, Part I) f. 432r–434v. He waited, however, until 26 November 1843 before telling the cardinal where he had received the 1841 letter and why he had not been able to answer it promptly. See PF: SOCG vol. 966 (1844) f. 281r.

Chapter 15 Tension mounts between the Marists and Pompallier

1 PF: SC Oceania vol. 2 (1842–5, Part I) f. 106r–108v.
2 PF: LDB vol. 327 (1852, Part I) f. 341v–344r.
3 Ibid., f. 315v.
4 PF: Acta vol. 202 (1839) f. 394rv.
5 Roach, 'Venerable John Claude Colin', pp. 160–2.
6 PF: LDB vol. 327 (1842, Part I) f. 510rv.
7 PF: SC Oceania vol. 2 (1842–5, Part I) f. 432r–434v. Pompallier in this letter of 19 October 1842 to Cardinal Fransoni says that Wallis had '2,800 souls'. Writing on the same day to Captain Lavaud he says its population was '2,700'. See Keys, *Life of Pompallier*, p. 187. And in both cases he says that all were baptised. He told Fransoni that the 2,800 were also confirmed, as well as an additional 120 on Futuna. Then on 6 November 1842 he wrote the president and members of the Central Council of the Association for the Propagation of the Faith in Lyon that with his priests he was able to baptise and confirm 2,780 persons on the islands of Wallis and Futuna. See PF: SC Oceania vol. 2 (1842–5, Part II) f. 566r. And Bataillon writing to Fransoni on 8 December 1843 said that Wallis had 3,600 souls, 'all converted and baptised with few exceptions', and Futuna had 'about 700 souls'. See PF: SC Oceania vol. 2 (1842–5, Part II) f. 599r.
8 Keys, *Life of Pompallier*, p. 193; SM: OMM/ 411, Epalle to Petit, 18 August 1845.
9 PF: SC Oceania vol. 2 (1842–5, Part I) f. 403v–405v.
10 Ibid., f. 388v, Colin to Fransoni, 27 October 1842.
11 Ibid., f. 390r–391v.
12 Ibid., f. 389v.
13 Ibid., f. 388rv, 393r; Roach, 'Venerable John Claude Colin', pp. 160–2, 171–9; SM: Gabriel-Claude Mayet, *Mémoires*, 7:168f; SM:

Decreta et Instructiones 1842; Joseph Albert Otto, *Gründung der Neuen Jesuitenmission durch General Pater Johann Philipp Roothaan,* pp. 517f; PF: SOCG vol. 969 (1847) f. 458rv.

14   PF: LDB vol. 328 (1842, Part II) f. 990v–993r.

15   PF: SC Oceania vol. 2 (1842–5, Part I) f. 445r–446r.

16   Ibid., f. 451rv.

17   Ibid., f. 447rv, 450rv.

18   Ibid., f. 492rv.

19   Ibid., Part II, f. 566r–576r.

20   Keys, *Life of Pompallier*, pp. 195f.

21   PF: SOCG vol. 970 (1848) f. 423r, Colin to Fransoni, 14 January 1843; SM: OMM/411, Epalle to Petit, 18 August 1845.

22   PF: SC Oceania vol. 2 (1842–5, Part I) f. 441rv.

23   PF: LDB vol. 329 (1843, Part I) f. 193v–194r.

24   Epalle was referring to Bishop George Selwyn, named and ordained Bishop of New Zealand in 1841.

25   PF: SC Oceania vol. 2 (1842–5, Part I) f. 468rv.

26   Ibid., f. 490r–491r.

Chapter 16 A French Carthusian in Rome proposes a Northern Oceania Vicariate

1   PF: LDB vol. 327 (1842, Part I) f. 316v–317r. The author could not find the early 1842 letter of Supriès, but only a reference to it in this letter of 14 April 1842 of Cardinal Fransoni.

2   PF: SC Oceania vol. 2 (1842–5, Part I) f. 464r–465v.

3   PF: LDB vol. 329 (1843, Part I) f. 303v–304r.

4   The ship canal extending sixty–four kilometres across the Isthmus of Panama and connecting the Atlantic and the Pacific was completed seventy-one years later in 1914.

5   PF: SC Oceania vol. 2 (1842–5, Part II) f. 668v–675v.

6   Ibid., Part I, f. 483r–484v. 'Malabar Rites' was the name given to a method of adapting Christianity to a particular foreign civilisation by the adoption of indigenous rites and customs as far as possible, but without conceding any fundamental Christian truth or principle.

7   Ibid., f. 504v, Supriès to Fransoni, 18 July 1843; PF: LDB vol. 330 (1843, Part II) f. 560r, 565v, Fransoni to Supriès, 20 July 1843.

8   PF: LDB vol. 330 (1843, Part II) f. 543v–544r.

9   In his text Epalle here says that Pompallier 'had not ceased thinking' of founding a mission in Ponape 'since his departure from Rome'. This seems to be incorrect, because the correspondence of Pompallier and his missionaries shows interest in Ponape only during and after their visit to Valparaíso in 1837. See chapter 9.

10   PF: SC Oceania vol. 2 (1842–5, Part I) f. 501r–502r; SM: OMM/411, Epalle to Petit, 18 August 1845.

11   PF: SC Oceania vol. 2 (1842–5, Part I) f. 500rv.

12   Ibid., f. 503v.

13   Ibid., f. 504rv.

14   PF: LDB vol. 330 (1843, Part II) f. 565v–566r.

15   PF: SOCG vol. 970 (1848) f. 439rv.

16   PF: SC Oceania vol. 2 (1842–5, Part II) f. 680rv.

17   Ibid., f. 677r–678v. See also Adriano Balbi, *Compendio di geografia*, l:v.

18   PF: SC Oceania vol. 2 (1842–5, Part II) f. 680rv.

19   PF: LDB vol. 330 (1843, Part II) f. 797v, 798r.

Chapter 17   The Vicariates Apostolic of Melanesia and Micronesia

1   PF: SC Oceania vol. 2 (1842–5, Part I) f. 487r, 489rv, 494r, 495r; ibid., Part II, f. 566r–576r.

2   PF: SOCG vol. 970 (1848) f. 439rv, Epalle to Brunelli, 24 July 1843; SM: OOC/418/1, Epalle to Colin, 13 July 1843.

3   Fransoni's report of 15 July 1844 says that Colin commissioned Epalle to negotiate in Rome at this time for the erection of 'a new third vicariate'. See PF: Acta vol. 207 (1844) f. 182r.

4   PF: SC Oceania vol. 2 (1842–5, Part I) f. 490v.

5   Ibid., f. 450rv.

6   Ibid., f. 500r–503v.

7   Ibid., f. 504rv; PF: LDB vol. 330 (1843, Part II) f. 560r, 565v.

8   PF: SOCG vol. 970 (1848) f. 439r–440v.

9   See Conrad Malte-Brun, *Précis de la géographie universelle*, 4:381, or 6:498. Book 203, pages 482–500, in vol. 6, ed. 1843, was devoted to a 'Description of New Caledonia and adjacent islands, up to and including New Guinea'. Some writers lead one to believe that Epalle and his missionaries were little concerned about the land where they were going. For example, Hugh Laracy, *Marists and Melanesians*, p. 15, says: 'The whole operation was viewed in narrow religious terms'; 'their excursion to Melanesia was made with scant reference to the environment in which they were going to work'; their 'correspondence is silent' on 'the journals of the navigators'; and as for interviews with navigators, Joseph du Bouzet is 'the only one mentioned'. However, a note by Epalle stating that he took along to Oceania a copy of Malte-Brun's book was seen by Marist researcher, Father Claude Rozier, S.M., editor of *Écrits du Père Pierre Chanel*. See Letter, Jean Coste, S.M., to Wiltgen, 4 February 1965. Epalle informed Fransoni that he had consulted with a large number of men who had visited those islands. But he mentions only one of them by name, du Bouzet, probably because of this man's renown.

10   PF: SOCG vol. 965 (1844) f. 453r–456v. Tobie, also written contemporaneously Jobie or Djobie, and nowadays Jobi, was a village name used to designate its island, nowadays called Japen, at the entrance to Geelvink Bay in northwest New Guinea. The name, Willem Schouten, who was discoverer of the Schouten Islands immediately to the north of Japen, was used either for

all Schouten Islands together, or more likely for Biak, the largest of them.

11 SM: OOC/418/1.
12 Ibid.
13 PF: SOCG vol. 970 (1848) f. 431r–432r, 437r.
14 SM: OOC/418/1.
15 Ibid.
16 SM: OMM/411, Epalle to Petit, 18 August 1845.
17 PF: LDB vol. 330 (1843, Part II) f. 797v–799r.
18 PF: SC Oceania vol. 2 (1842–5, Part II) f. 548r–549r.
19 Ibid., Part I, f. 432r–434v.
20 PF: LDB vol. 330 (1843, Part II) f. 1003r–1004r.
21 Ibid., vol. 328 (1842) f. 846r.
22 Ibid., vol. 330 (1843, Part II) f. 1003r–1004r.
23 PF: SC Oceania vol. 2 (1842–5, Part II) f. 628r.
24 PF: SOCG vol. 965 (1844) f. 467v.
25 PF: LDB vol. 331 (1844) f. 159rv.
26 Jaspers in *Erschliessung Ozeaniens*, p. 250, incorrectly states that here Fransoni is offering Pompallier only Micronesia.
27 PF: LDB vol. 331 (1844) f. 164rv.
28 Here Colin has stretched seven or eight months to a year.
29 Fransoni actually had told Colin that the vicar apostolic would get a coadjutor, *if Colin felt there was need for one.*
30 SM: OMM/000.
31 PF: SC Oceania vol. 2 (1842–5, Part II) f. 666rv.
32 PF: Acta vol. 207 (1844) f. 190r–191r.
33 PF: LDB vol. 331 (1844) f. 331rv.
34 Ibid., f. 331v.
35 PF:SOCG vol. 965 (1844) f. 464rv.
36 SM: OOC/418/1.
37 Ibid.
38 PF: SC Oceania vol. 2 (1842–5, Part II) f. 749rv. See also ibid., Colin to Fransoni, 18 June 1845, f. 975r–976r; ibid., Marceau to Fransoni, 6 July 1845, f. 981r–982r.
39 SM: OOC /418/1.
40 Ibid.
41 Nearly all of Fransoni's arguments, like this one, came from Colin's letter to him (28 October 1843) and from the letters of Epalle to him (1 August 1843) and to Brunelli (24 July 1843). But it is impossible to see how Pompallier, without New Zealand, Melanesia, Micronesia and Central Oceania (Tonga, Fiji, Samoa, New Caledonia, New Hebrides), would still have within his jurisdiction 'many other islands' and 'a very vast vicariate'. Except for a few small and insignificant islands, his vicariate would have contained only water!
42 The original text reads: 'Se debasi approvare, e decretare, la divisata erezione del nuovo vicariato di Melanesia, e Micronesia, per ora riunite, da formar poscia due distinti Vicariati?'
43 PF: Acta vol. 207 (1844) f. 182r–183v, 186r.
44 The amended version of the proposal is not given

in the minutes of the meeting, but it is clearly indicated elsewhere by Secretary Brunelli. See PF: LDB vol. 331 (1844) f. 558v–559v, Decree of 16 July 1844.
45 Ibid.
46 Ibid. See, for example, the apostolic letter of Gregory XVI, 19 July 1844, in *Ius Pontificium*, 5:342f.
47 Ibid.
48 For the full text see PF: SC Oceania vol. 2 (1842–5, Part II) f. 758r–761v.
49 Epalle said his Latin title was 'Episcopus Sionnensis, Vicarius apostolicus duorum Vicariatuum provisorie unitorum Melanesiae et Micronesiae'. See SM: OMM/411, Epalle to Petit, 18 August 1845. Keys mistakenly gives the date of episcopal ordination as 2 July in *Life of Pompallier*, p. 205. See also PF: LDB vol. 331 (1844) f. 548r, Fransoni to Colin, 25 July 1844.
50 SM: OMM/000/Noms.
51 PF: Udienze vol. 101 (1844, Part II) f. 1111rv. In spite of this division Pompallier retained the title 'Vicar Apostolic of Western Oceania', even though nothing more remained under his jurisdiction than New Zealand and a few unimportant islands. The usage of Brunelli on this occasion, identifying Epalle for the pope as 'the Vicar Apostolic of Western Oceania, that is, of the two districts of Melanesia and Micronesia', and Epalle's calling Pompallier 'the Vicar Apostolic of New Zealand', are therefore neither official nor correct. See also ibid., f. 1137r.
52 C.M. Léopold Verguet, *Histoire de la première mission catholique au vicariat de Mélanésie*, pp. 12–4.
53 PF: LDB vol. 331 (1844) f. 546r–547v.
54 Ibid., f. 548rv. The date given on the archive copy of this letter is 25 July 1844. Colin, referring to this same letter, says that it was dated 26 July. See PF: SC Oceania vol. 2 (1842–5, Part II) f. 769r, Colin to Fransoni, 9 August 1844.
55 PF: SC Oceania vol. 2 (1842–5, Part II) f. 769rv.
56 SM: OMM/411, Epalle to Petit, 18 August 1845; Société française de l'Océanie, *Extrait de l'acte de Société*, pp. 8f.
57 PF: SOCG vol. 970 (1848) f. 429rv.
58 SM: OMM/411.
59 SM: 511.422 (London).
60 PF: SC Oceania vol. 2 (1842–5, Part II), f. 860 rv.
61 SM: OMM/411.
62 Société française, *Extrait de l'acte*, p. 12; SM: OMM/411.
63 SM: Epistolae Variae Generalium, vol. 1, p. 26f, no. 59.
64 PF: SC Oceania vol. 2 (1842-5, Part II) f. 975v, Colin to Fransoni, 18 June 1845; Verguet, *Vicariat de Mélanésie*, pp. 3, 11f; SM: OMM/411, Epalle to Colin, 12 July 1845.

Chapter 18   The Vicariate Apostolic of the Sandwich Islands

1   Yzendoorn, *Catholic Mission in the Hawaiian Islands*, pp. 141–52.

2   PF: Acta vol. 207 (1844) f. 191r. Here the total of missionaries recruited by Bishop Rouchouze is given incorrectly as seven clerics, seven lay Brothers, and twelve Sisters; these figures come from Nuncio Fornari's letter of 18 April 1844 (ibid.) to Cardinal Fransoni. Authors give still other totals (e.g. seven, seven, ten; or six, eight, ten). The figures and other details used in the text come from Bonamie's Circular Letter no. 27 of 14 December 1842 in SSCC: A 22–7.

3   PF: Acta vol. 207 (1844) f. 191r–192r. Rouchouze sailed from Saint-Malo on 15 December 1842, or sixteen months before Bonamie saw Fornari, not eighteen months as they told Rome.

4   PF: LDB vol. 331 (1844) f. 298r–299r.

5   PF: Acta vol 207 (1844) f. 192rv. This source incorrectly gives the name as 'Symphorien Duboise'. See Letter, Reverend Amerigo Cools, SS.CC., to Wiltgen, 23 February 1978. Bonamie here used Caret's civilian name (François-Toussaint) and not his religious name (François-d'Assise).

6   PF: LDB vol. 331 (1844) f. 345r–346r.

7   PF: Acta vol. 207 (1844) f. 191r.

8   PF: LDB vol. 331 (1844) f. 345v–346r.

9   PF: Acta vol. 207 (1844) f. 191v–192r.

10 PF: LDB vol. 331 (1844) f. 345r–346r.

11 PF: SC Oceania vol. 2 (1842–5) f. 747r–748r.

12 Ibid., f. 747r; PF: LDB vol. 331 (1844) f. 345v.

13 PF: Acta vol. 207 (1844) f. 181r, 182r, 184r–186r. Fransoni told the cardinals at the 15 July 1844 meeting that 'almost two years' had passed since Rouchouze's departure, etc. But he had sailed from Saint–Malo on 15 December 1842, only one year and seven months earlier. See note 3 for another example of this tendency to exaggerate the length of Rouchouze's disappearance.

14 PF: Udienze vol. 101 (1844, Part II) f. 1162r, 1162r (bis).

15 Ibid., f. 1162rv. See also Letter, Reverend Amerigo Cools, SS.CC., to Wiltgen, 23 February 1978. The date is incorrectly given as 28 July 1844 in PF: LDB vol. 331 (1844) f. 561v–562r.

16 PF: LDB vol. 334 (1846, Part II) f. 960v–961v. The Proper name of the titular see is Arad, not Arathie, the form which has been used in publications to date. See Letter, Reverend Amerigo Cools, SS.CC., to Wiltgen, 23 February 1978.

17 Livro de Obitos de São Miguel, fls 43v (1832–59).

18 *Annales de la propagation de la foi*, p. 152.

Chapter 19   Tonga is returned to Pompallier

1   OM 4:316.

2   PF: SC Oceania vol. 2 (1842–5, Part II) f. 602r.

3   Ibid., f. 599rv.

4   PF: SOCG vol. 965 (1844) f. 454v, Epalle to Fransoni, 1 August 1843.

5   PF: SC Oceania vol. 2(1842–5, Part II) f. 599v, Bataillon to Fransoni, 8 December 1843; ibid., f. 600r, Douarre to Lambruschini, 16 January 1844. Here Douarre mistakenly calls Lambruschini the cardinal prefect of the Evangelisation Congregation. Fransoni was cardinal prefect from 1834 to 1856.

6   Ibid., f. 600rv; Yves Person, *La Nouvelle Calédonie et l'Europe*, pp. 94–8.

7   PF: SC Oceania vol. 2 (1842–5, Part II) f. 600r–601r. Although Colin had told Fransoni that Douarre would be leaving with five priests and four Brothers (see chapter 15), plans were not always fully realised, as in this case.

8   Keys, *Life of Pompallier*, p. 211.

9   PF: SOCG vol. 970 (1848) f. 366v–367r.

10 PF: SC Oceania vol. 2 (1842–5, Part II) f. 923v–924r.

11 PF: Acta vol. 207 (1844) f. 182v–183r.

12 PF: SOCG vol. 966 (1844) f. 284v, 286v. Since the mail was carried by sailing vessels travelling different routes, it was not surprising to have letters written so far apart arrive at the same time.

13 Ibid., f. 281r–282r.

14 PF: Acta vol. 207 (1844) f. 367r–369v. Jaspers incorrectly states that the views of Colin were not requested on this matter of returning the Friendly Archipelago to Pompallier 'because the Evangelisation Congregation believed that it had to act without delay for political reasons'. Fransoni's above words, however, show that he did not consider the matter urgent at all. And if it had been urgent, he would not have waited from 28 August 1844, when Pompallier's two letters arrived, until 23 December before taking up the matter in a General Meeting. In this interval of four months there was time enough for him to write to Colin, if he had wanted to. See Jaspers, *Erschliessung Ozeaniens*, p. 263. For confirmation that the Pompallier letter referred to was dated February 1843, see the minutes of the 15 July 1844 meeting in PF: Acta vol. 207 (1844) f. 182v.

15 PF: LDB vol. 328 (1842) f. 846r.

16 PF: SOCG vol. 966 (1844) f. 283rv.

17 Father Epalle, pro-vicar of Pompallier, was in Rome reporting on Pompallier's financial difficulties when Fransoni's letter was written.

18 PF: SOCG vol. 966 (1844) f. 285r–286r.

19 PF: Acta here mistakenly gives the date of the second letter as 15 February 1844, but it should

be 16 February. Cf. PF: Acta vol. 207 (1844) f.
369v, and PF: SOCG vol. 966 (1844) f. 285r.

20 The Latin words '*in partibus*' were used to
designate a titular see.

21 PF: Acta vol. 207 (1844) f. 369v–371r. The
Italian words in the proposal originally
presented to the cardinals for their vote were:
'ritornare', 'smembrandolo', and 'derogando al
Breve Pontificio di dimarcazione'. See ibid. For
the revised text, see PF: LDB vol. 332 (1845) f.
64v–65r, Decree of 20 January 1845.

22 PF: LDB vol. 332 (1845) f. 114r–116r.

**Chapter 20 Bishop Epalle is killed in the Solomon
Islands**

1 SM: OMM/411, Epalle to Colin, 12 July 1845;
Epalle to Petit, 18 August 1845.

2 Epalle wrote Colin on 2 May 1845 that the ship
was scheduled to leave on the following day, 3
May. But sailing vessels were dependent upon
unpredictable winds and Verguet says the ship
sailed on 4 May. Cf. ibid., Epalle to Colin, 2 May
1845; Verguet, *Vicariat de Mélanésie*, pp. 11,
21.

3 Verguet, *Vicariat de Mélanésie*, pp. 23–6, 36.

4 SM: OMM/411. Here Epalle says, 'We arrived
at Sydney on 22 June'. But in view of the many
details given by Verguet in connection with the
hour of arrival, his date of 21 June has been
chosen as the more reliable.

5 Polding became an archbishop on 10 April
1842, when Sydney was raised to the rank of
archdiocese.

6 Waigeo was situated in the far northwest corner
of the Vicariate of Melanesia. When reporting
this same population figure to Rome on 1 August
1843, Epalle had said that it came from seafarers
and that he considered it exaggerated. See
chapter 17; also PF: Acta vol. 207 (1844) f.
188v.

7 SM: OMM/411. Jaspers misreads this letter
when he says that Waigeo was Polding's suggestion. See Jaspers, *Erschliessung Ozeaniens*, p.
254.

8 SM: OMM/411.

9 Ibid. Jaspers also misreads this letter to Fransoni, stating that in it Epalle 'asks the Evangelisation Congregation either to divide his
Vicariate Apostolic of Melanesia into two
vicariates or to give him a coadjutor'. See
Jaspers, *Erschliessung Ozeaniens*, p. 254.

10 The author has not found this letter of Colin to
Epalle, but the content is clear from Epalle's
reply of 18 January 1845.

11 SM: OMM/411.

12 Verguet, *Vicariat de Mélanésie*, p. 53.

13 SM: OMM/411.

14 Ibid.

15 Ibid.

16 John Hosie, 'The French Mission', p. 414.

17 Verguet, *Vicariat de Mélanésie*, p. 53.

18 Verguet regularly says 'Richard', but his name
was 'Richards'. See Dorothy Shineberg, *They
Came for Sandalwood*, p. 72.

19 Verguet, *Vicariat de Mélanésie*, pp. 75–83.

20 SM: OMM/411.

21 A typographical error may be responsible for the
omission of Father Paget's name in this list by
Verguet. Maunga, as given by Laracy, has been
used instead of Mangha or Manga, both used by
Verguet. See Laracy, *Marists and Melanesians*,
pp. 17f.

22 Epalle's body was found on 18 October 1900.
See L. M. Raucaz, *Vingt-cinq années d'apostolat
aux Iles Salomon meridionales (1898–1923)*,
pp. 77f, 258.

23 Absolution is the Sacrament of Penance.

24 Verguet, *Vicariat de Mélanésie*, pp. 85–100,
103–26. See also the map and sketches opposite
p. 307.

25 Hosie, 'French Mission', p. 414.

**Chapter 21 Australia's first three dioceses: Sydney,
Hobart Town, Adelaide**

1 Osmund Thorpe, *First Catholic Mission to the
Australian Aborigines 1843–1847*, pp. 20f;
Henry Norbert Birt, *Benedictine Pioneers in
Australia*, 2:1–3, 9. Thorpe gives 16 November
(p. 20) as the sailing date and Birt gives 17
November (p. 1). Thorpe says Polding reached
Le Havre, France, in early May 1841 (p. 21); Birt
quotes Ullathorne as saying 'towards the end of
May' (p. 3). They had sailed via New Zealand
and South America. For Dillon's letter see SM:
511.422 (London).

2 PF: LDB vol. 327 (1842, Part I) f. 56v–57r.
Fransoni to Riordan, 22 January 1842; PF: SC
Irlanda vol. 27 (1839–42) f. 608rv, Riordan to
Fransoni, 9 April 1842; Normoyle, *A Tree Is
Planted*, pp. 314f, 376, 405f; Moran, *Catholic
Church in Australasia*, pp. 227, 310, 426, 432.
Moran incorrectly says Larkins (p. 426) for
Larkin and is inconsistent in listing the members
of Polding's party (pp. 227 and 426) in spite of
quoting Polding's own list drawn up on the day
of departure (p. 310).

3 Polding exaggerated the size of Australia.
Europe with 9,945,000 square kilometres and
Australia with 7,716,561 makes Australia
three-fourths (77.6 per cent) the size of Europe,
according to modern statistics. Birt in *Benedictine Pioneers*, 2:6, gratuitously states that
Polding sent his plan for new vicariates apostolic
and dioceses to Rome for consideration prior to
his going there. Birt was misled by the first
sentence in Polding's letter of 17 November
1841 addressed to the Reverend Dr. W. H.
Coombes of Shepton Mallet, Somerset, in which
Polding says: 'My letter to the Holy See with the
allocution, will be, I trust, on their way to their

destination by the time you receive this' (p. 7). Polding here is evidently referring to his letter of 21 November 1841 (pp. 10–11), which does nothing but announce his forthcoming visit to Rome; apparently it was accompanied by some allocution delivered by Polding that he wished Roman authorities to see. The balance of the letter to Coombes is devoted to specific proposals by Polding for obtaining more bishoprics for Australia (pp. 7–9). As early as 3 July 1841 Polding had pontificated at the golden jubilee of Coombes's ordination to the priesthood. And since Coombes was an old friend of Polding and an excellent classical scholar, he may well have vounteered to put into Latin Polding's important petition to Rome. This would explain why Polding described in great detail for Coombes his plan on 17 November 1841 and why these same details were all reflected in the Latin letter of 19 January 1842 which Polding presented to Fransoni in Rome. It would have been most unwise for Polding to send such a complicated and important plan to Rome in advance of his coming and unattended.

4 Adriano Balbi, *Compendio di geografia*, vol. 2. This book is the second Italian edition and is based on the third French edition (see chapter 16 of this book). It treats of 'Australia or Central Oceania' on pages 798–811, and is still in the library of the Evangelisation Congregation.

5 PF: Acta vol. 205 (1842) f. 25r–30r.

6 The date is missing in all of these sources: ibid., f. 30r; PF: SOCG vol. 961 (1842) f. 37v; PF: LDB vol. 327 (1842) f. 375r–377r; PF: Udienze vol. 96 (1842) f. 510r; and *Ius Pontificium*, 5:293f.

7 *Ius Pontificium*, 5:294.

8 The heads of these dioceses are said to be 'bishops properly so called' in a decree of the Evangelisation Congregation dated 14 April 1842. See PF: LDB vol. 327 (1842) f. 375r.

9 PF: Udienze vol. 96 (1842) f. 510rv. From the minutes of this audience as well as from the Evangelisation Congregation's decree of 14 April 1842 referring back to this audience, it is clear that Polding is mistaken when he says that the pope named him archbishop on the day before 10 April. ' . . . His Holiness was pleased to constitute me Archbishop yesterday evening', Polding wrote on 10 April to his cousin, Father Thomas Heptonstall, O.S.B., procurator of the Benedictines in London. (For the full text see Birt, *Benedictine Pioneers*, 2:32.) If the date on his letter to Heptonstall is correct, then Polding either received incorrect information or reported incorrectly the information that he had received. In any case, he ascribed to the pope anticipatorily a decision which was reached by the Evangelisation Congregation prior to 10 April. This decision of the Evangelisation Congrega-

tion—possibly reached as late as 9 April—to establish the hierarchy in Australia and to name Polding the archbishop, was presented to the pope for sanction on Sunday, 10 April, the usual day of the week for the secretary's audience with the pope. The minutes of the papal audience do not mention Ullathorne's name, but the Evangelisation Congregation's decree of 14 April 1842 states explicitly that Secretary Cadolini presented Ullathorne as candidate for Bishop of Adelaide in this audience of 10 April 1842 and His Holiness gave his approval and ordered briefs sent to him and also to Willson. See PF: LDB vol. 327 (1842) f. 375r–376r.

10 PF: LDB vol. 327 (1842) f. 376r–377r, Decree of 14 April 1842 .

11 Ibid., f. 385rv. Pope Gregory XVI's apostolic letter, which made public the elevation of Sydney to archiepiscopal rank and also the establishment of the hierarchy in Australia, was dated 22 April 1842. See *Ius Pontificium*, 5:294. Cadolini's calling Polding on 13 April 'the Bishop of Sydney and the Vicar Apostolic of New Holland' shows that Polding had been in charge simultaneously of a diocese and a vicariate apostolic. Polding also understood it in this way, because in the month after his return to Australia as archbishop he called himself 'Archbishop of Sydney and Vicar–Apostolic of New Holland' in a circular letter addressed to the clergy and faithful of Sydney on 23 April 1843 . See Moran, *Catholic Church in Australasia*, p. 431.

12 PF: LDB vol. 327 (1842) f. 385v.

13 Birt, *Benedictine Pioneers*, 2:6, 14, 34, 119. Birt, who was from Downside, gives Wilson's names as 'Joseph Peter' (p. 14); Cadolini gives them as 'Peter Joseph'. PF: Udienze vol. 96 (1842) f. 670r, 671v. Moran in *Catholic Church in Australasia*, p. 261, mistakenly says that the Benedictine, the Reverend Wilson, was Polding's first choice.

14 PF: LDB vol. 327 (1842) f. 461r.

15 Ibid., f. 461rv.

16 Ibid., f. 461v; Birt, *Benedictine Pioneers*, 2:37.

17 PF: Udienze vol. 96 (1842) f. 755v, 756v. Cadolini here incorrectly calls the vicar general Father *John* Murphy. Everywhere else he uses his correct name, Francis.

18 Birt, *Benedictine Pioneers*, 2:38, 41.

19 Keys, *Life of Pompallier*, pp. 217f; Southerwood, *Hobart's Catholic Story*, p. 22; Moran, *Catholic Church in Australasia*, pp. 261–7, 499–502; Birt, *Benedictine Pioneers*, 2:14, 33, 39, 119–21.

Chapter 22   The Prefecture Apostolic to the Aborigines of Australia is given to the Passionists

1 Thorpe, *Australian Aborigines*, pp. 20f, 187.

2 Vaccari's baptismal name was Salvatore; his

name in religion was Raimondo della Passione (Raymond of the Passion). He was born in Rome on 16 November 1801, was baptised that same day, took his first vows on 29 June 1822, and was ordained a priest on 27 September 1827. See CP: General Catalogue, no. 431.

3 Ibid., nos 474, 557, 647; CP(SS): Document no. 2, Antonio di San Giacomo to Dominic, 25 September 1846, and Document no. 3, Antonio di San Giacomo to Dominic, 13 April 1847, and 'Cenni e memorie istoriche sulla missione di Australia e California' (no author). Moran says that Snell was Swiss (so does Thorpe who may be using Moran as his source) 'and a convert, the son of a rich banker in Switzerland . . . He spoke fluently the German, French, Italian, English and Turkish languages. The Turkish he had acquired in Bulgaria, where he was for some years stationed as a missionary before he came to Australia.' See Moran, *Catholic Church in Australasia*, p. 418; Thorpe, *Australian Aborigines*, p. 28. But CP: General Catalogue, which gives vital statistics for each of the order's members, says under no. 474, devoted to Snell, that he was born in Lyon, France, in 1802, was baptised and confirmed on 20 March 1825, and took vows as a Passionist on 18 September 1826, at the monastery of Monte Argentaro.

4 PF: LDB vol. 327 (1842) f. 461rv.

5 CP(SS): Document no. 6, Pesciaroli to Antonio di San Giacomo, 2 November 1848.

6 PF: Udienze vol. 96 (1842) f. 811r.

7 CP(SS): Document no. 6, Pesciaroli to Antonio di San Giacomo, 2 November 1848; ibid., 'Cenni e memorie istoriche sulla missione di Australia e California'.

8 CP(SS): 'Cenni e memorie istoriche sulla missione di Australia e California'; O'Farrell, *Catholic Church in Australia*, p. 57; Moran, *Catholic Church in Australasia*, pp. 310, 426.

9 CP(SS): 'Cenni e memorie istoriche sulla missione di Australia e California'; ibid., Document no. 6, Pesciaroli to Antonio di San Giacomo, 2 November 1848; ibid., Document no. 2, Antonio di San Giacomo to Dominic, 25 September 1846.

10 CP(SS): Document no. 2, Antonio di San Giacomo to Dominic, 25 September 1846; Thorpe, *Australian Aborigines*, p. 192; Moran, *Catholic Church in Australasia*, pp. 407, 409f, 414–6, 424, 593f, 596.

11 CP(SS): Printed letter, Pesciaroli to Pianetti, 21 January 1844, 5 pp. The paragraph of data on the Moreton Bay Penal Settlement was kindly supplied by Allan Tredenick, Honorary Research Officer of the Royal Historical Society of Queensland, Brisbane. Letter, Tredenick to Wiltgen, 4 July 1976. In the 1840s Stradbroke Island was not yet divided into north and south sections, as it is today. Ships taking the South

Passage between Moreton Island and Stradbroke Island on their way to Brisbane river had to pass Dunwich. See *Baker's Map of Moreton Bay and Part of the Darling Downs, Clarence Districts, Shewing the Stations of the Squatters in the Northern Districts of N.S.W.*, Sydney, November 1846. Today Dunwich is an industrial town in the centre of the sand mining industry.

12 CP(SS): Document no. 6, Pesciaroli to Antonio di San Giacomo, 2 November 1848.

13 Thorpe, *Australian Aborigines*, p. 217.

14 Ibid., p. 191.

Chapter 23 The Diocese of Perth and the Vicariates Apostolic of Essington and King George Sound

1 C. H. Fremantle, *Diary and Letters of Admiral Sir C. H. Fremantle, G.C.B.*, pp. 9, 15, 20–5, 67–9, 94; PF: Acta vol. 208 (1845) f. 81v, 85rv. De Mazenod, beatified in 1975, sent missionaries to Canada in 1841, the first foreign mission of his order. See also Moran, *Catholic Church in Australasia*, pp. 135, 142, 203, 229f, 238, 554–6, 715.

2 Rudesindo Salvado, *Memorie storiche dell' Australia particolarmente della missione Benedettina di Nuova Norcia e degli usi e costumi degli Australiani*, pp. 140–3.

3 René Roussel, *Un précurseur*, pp. 34, 35, 80.

4 PF: Acta vol. 208 (1845) f. 87r–95r.

5 Ibid., f. 80r–83r. At the beginning of his report (f. 81r) Castracane refers to the General Meeting of 28 February 1842 and says that new ecclesiastical divisions for Australia or New Holland were discussed at that meeting. In the next sentence he says: 'Then were erected the Archdiocese of Sydney . . ., the Diocese of Hobart Town . . ., and the Diocese of Adelaide . . .', a clear reference to the establishment of the hierarchy. His words, however, must be understood simply in a chronological sense; he is not saying that the establishment of the hierarchy was discussed at the General Meeting of 28 February 1842. For details on that General Meeting, see chapter 21.

6 PF: LDB vol. 332 (1845) f. 172v, 173r. For Ullathorne's quotation see Birt, *Benedictine Pioneers*, 2:38.

7 PF: Acta vol. 208 (1845) f. 83rv.

8 Salvado, *Missione Benedettina*, p. 144.

9 PF: Udienze vol. 102 (1845) f. 626r.

10 CP(SS): Document no. 1. The date is given as '1844 or 1845'. The year 1844 cannot be correct; the letter was probably written in February, March or April 1845.

11 Ibid.

12 Thorpe, *Australian Aborigines*, pp. 110, 184; Moran, *Catholic Church in Australasia*, pp. 415–7.

13 CP(SS): Document no. 1, Antonio di San Gia-

como to Dominic; 1844 or 1845; ibid., Document no. 2, Antonio di San Giacomo to Dominic, 25 September 1846.

14 Moran, *Catholic Church in Australasia*, pp. 557–62.

15 Ibid., pp. 561f; PF: SC Oceania vol. 14 (1882–4) f. 10v–13r. 'Norcia' is the Italian spelling and is used in the official title of the mission. In English the town is often spelled 'Nursia'.

16 Thorpe, *Australian Aborigines*, pp. 110, 114.

17 CP(SS): Document no. 2.

18 Ibid., Document no. 3.

19 Ibid., Document no. 6, Pesciaroli to Antonio di San Giacomo, 2 November 1848; Thorpe, *Australian Aborigines*, pp. 115f, 119. Father Pietro di San Giuseppe, a Passionist, arrived in Sydney with Polding. He had been refused permission at least once by his superior general to go to Australia. See CP(SS): Document no. 3, Antonio di San Giacomo to Dominic, 13 April 1847; ibid., Document no. 6, Pesciaroli to Antonio di San Giacomo, 2 November 1848.

20 *Bollettino della Congregazione della SS. Croce e Passione di N.S.G.C.*, pp. 54f, 111; CP: General Catalogue, no. 431.

21 CP(SS): Document no. 8, Pietro to Dominic, 15 November 1848; ibid., Document no. 6, Pesciaroli to Antonio di San Giacomo, 2 November 1848.

22 CP(SS): Document no. 6, Pesciaroli to Antonio di San Giacomo, 2 November 1848.

23 CP(SS): Document no. 5.

24 Ibid., Document no. 4.

25 Ibid.

26 *Bollettino della Congregazione*, pp. 54f; CP: General Catalogue, nos. 474, 557, 647.

27 Eugénie and Hugh Laracy, *The Italians in New Zealand and Other Studies*, pp. 11f; Moran, *Catholic Church in Australasia*, pp. 313, 559f. Moran says here that Confalonieri died 'at Victoria, in Melville Island, not far from the spot now known as Cambridge Gulf'.

Chapter 24 The Dioceses of Melbourne, Port Victoria and Maitland

1 PF: SOCG vol. 969 (1847) f. 293r.

2 PF: Acta vol. 210 (1847) f. 170rv. For the complete 'Instruction', see *Collectanea Sacrae Congregationis de Propaganda Fide seu Decreta instructiones rescripta pro apostolicis missionibus*, no. 1002, pp. 541–5.

3 Polding quotes the instruction of Pope Saint Gregory II as follows: 'Ut consideratis locorum spatiis juxta gubernationem uniuscujusque ducis episcopia disponatis et subjacentia singulis Sedibus terminetis.'

4 PF: Acta vol. 210 (1847) f. 170v–173r.

5 Ibid., f. 173rv.

6 Ibid., f. 164r–167r.

7 Ibid., f. 371r–377v, 393r; *National Catholic Almanac 1963*, p. 320.

8 O'Farrell, *Catholic Church in Australia*, pp. 67f, 75. O'Farrell writes 'Henry Charles Davis' (p. 67); Moran, *Catholic Church in Australasia*, writes 'Charles Henry Davis' (p.334).

9 Moran, *Catholic Church in Australasia*, pp. 562–4.

Chapter 25 Pompallier leaves New Zealand to defend himself in Rome

1 Keys, *Life of Pompallier*, pp. 219f.

2 PF: SC Oceania vol. 2 (1842–5, Part II) f. 923v–924r.

3 PF: LDB vol. 332 (1845) f. 64v–65r; PF: Acta vol. 207 (1844) f. 371r.

4 Keys, *Life of Pompallier*, pp. 224, 226.

5 Ibid., pp. 229–32, 237f. FitzRoy's letter of 9 April mistakenly calls the *Rhin* a frigate. Technically it was a 'corvette de charge' of 800 tons, the kind of ship used for transport. See *Annales maritimes et coloniales*, partie officielle, February 1843, p. 176; March 1843, p. 338.

6 SM: OMM/411, Epalle to Colin, 6 September 1845.

7 Keys, *Life of Pompallier*, p. 205.

8 PF: SC Oceania vol. 2 (1842–5, Part II) f. 1062r–1063r.

9 Ibid., f. 1028r–1029r.

10 Keys, *Life of Pompallier*, pp. 205, 243–5, 248.

11 PF: Acta vol. 210 (1847) f. 208v; PF: SC Oceania vol. 2 (1842–5, Part II) f. 1029rv. An approximate equivalent of 800 leagues is 2,400 miles or 4,000 kilometres. O'Reilly and Teissier in *Tahitiens*, p. 261, incorrectly say that Lavaud took his good friend Pompallier aboard the *Allier*, leaving the Bay of Islands in January 1843 and bringing him to France via Tahiti and Cape Horn.

12 PF: LDB vol. 332 (1845) f. 114r–116r.

13 PF: SC Oceania vol. 2 (1842–5, Part II) f. 1029v.

14 Hosie, 'French Mission', p. 414.

15 SM: OC/418/1. Jaspers, who seems to be unaware of Viard's letter to Colin, says without giving proof that it was this letter of Bataillon which prompted Colin to rush off to Rome. See Jaspers, *Erschliessung Ozeaniens*, p. 264. But Bataillon's 24 April 1846 letter had to travel from Wallis via New Zealand and Sydney to France, and this would not have allowed enough time for it to catch up with Colin, who was in Rome with Viard's letter by 6 August.

16 SM: OC/418/1. The letter is not dated.

17 PF: SC Oceania vol. 3 (1846–7) f. 41rv.

18 PF: LDB vol. 333 (1846, Part I) f. 97v–98r.

19 Ibid., vol. 332 (1845) f. 116v.

20 The roles of Bishop Rouchouze (Eastern Oceania Vicariate) and Father Colin in the origin of this 1842 decree are explained in detail in chapter 15.

21 PF: LDB vol. 333 (1846, Part I) f. 141rv.
22 Ibid., f. 176rv; PF: Acta vol. 208 (1845) f. 502rv.
23 PF: Acta vol. 210 (1847) f. 208v; ibid., vol. 211 (1848) f. 197v; PF: SOCG vol. 970 (1848) f. 367v; Keys, *Life of Pompallier*, p. 250. Pompallier travelled aboard the *Rhin* free of charge.
24 SM: OOC/201. Jaspers misrepresents this meeting when he says, 'The Society of Mary decided officially on 11 October 1846 to give no further support at all to the New Zealand mission and particularly not to Pompallier.' See Jaspers, *Erschliessung Ozeaniens*, p. 264.
25 OM 2:474.
26 PF: SOCG vol. 950 (1835) f. 649rv.
27 See chapters 6, 7 and 8 for more details on Pompallier's appointment.
28 PF: Acta vol. 211 (1848) f. 197v; PF: SOCG vol. 969 (1847) f. 309r–491r.
29 PF: Acta vol. 210 (1847) f. 193r, 339r–340v.
30 PF: SC Oceania vol. 3 (1846–7) f. 776rv, Dubreul to Fransoni, 31 August 1847.
31 PF: SOCG vol. 969 (1847) f. 293r.

Chapter 26 Plans to establish the hierarchy in Western Oceania are blocked
1 See chapter 24.
2 PF: SOCG vol. 969 (1847) f. 309r–491r.
3 PF: Acta vol. 210 (1847) f. 208r–209v.
4 Ibid., f. 318r–321v. Pompallier incorrectly gives 28 (for 23) November 1845 as the date. See ibid., f. 318r; PF: SOCG vol. 969 (1847) f. 473r. See also chapter 24, note 2.
5 Roussel, *Un précurseur*, pp. 35–40, 82; PF: Acta vol. 208 (1845) f. 110r–114v, 130r–240r; ibid., vol. 210 (1847) f. 193r; PF: SOCG vol. 967 (1845) f. 111r–114v.
6 PF: Acta vol. 210 (1847) f. 339r.
7 SM: 410/26 May 1842, Colin to Fransoni.
8 The coadjutor was Bishop-Elect Georges Collomb. He was ordained a bishop by Coadjutor Viard at Kororareka, New Zealand, on 23 May 1847.
9 PF: Acta vol. 210 (1847) f. 339v–340v.
10 Today this archdiocese of the United States is officially called 'Portland in Oregon'. The Evangelisation Congregation decided to establish the hierarchy in Canada on 13 May 1844 and its decision was sanctioned by Pope Gregory XVI on 9 June 1844. See PF: Acta vol. 207 (1844) f. 92r.
11 Depending upon when the archivist wrote his report, he may also have been referring to Polding's later request of 16 April 1847 that Maitland, too, should become a suffragan diocese (see chapter 24). The archivist strangely made no reference to Perth, which had become the third suffragan diocese of Australia in 1845 (see chapter 23).
12 The origin of this oath goes back to 1624. For

details on its origin, as well as its evolution and application during the 1600s, see Ralph M. Wiltgen, 'Propaganda Is Placed in Charge of the Pontifical Colleges', pp. 488–504.
13 *Bullarium Pontificium S. Congregationis de Propaganda Fide*, 1:170 (*Speculatores domus Israel*), and 3:303 (*Apostolorum Ministerium*).
14 PF: Acta vol. 210 (1847) f. 198r–202r. The text of the resolution referred to here was written in longhand at the end of the minutes of the 9 December 1845 General Meeting. See PF: Acta vol. 208 (1845) f. 502r. This same resolution or decree is repeated verbatim in the archivist's printed report of 1847, making it clear that 9 September 1845 is a misprint for 9 December 1845. See PF: Acta vol. 210 (1847) f. 202r.
15 PF: SOCG vol. 969 (1847) f. 459v; PF: Acta vol. 208 (1845) f. 501r–502v.
16 See chapter 15. Keys in *Life of Pompallier*, p. 399, writes Terekeko for Pompallier's Terakako.
17 PF: Acta vol. 210 (1847) f. 189r–194v.
18 Ibid., f. 204r–206r.
19 Colin told Cardinal Fransoni in his letter of 9 April 1847 that 'here in Rome' he had often spoken with Pompallier. See ibid., f. 206rv.
20 Ibid., f. 352rv.
21 Ibid., f. 354r.
22 Ibid., f. 196[2] bis rv.
23 Ibid., f. 350r.
24 Ibid., f. 353v–358v. Theiner, born in Breslau, Germany (today Wrocław, Poland), had a German father and a Polish mother. He soon became a confidant of Pope Pius IX (1846–78), who placed him in charge of secret archives.
25 SM: 410/26 May 1842, Colin to Fransoni.
26 Jaspers gives rather large roles to Father Theiner and to Bishop Luquet in the Pompallier-Colin proposals for establishing the hierarchy. See *Erschliessung Ozeaniens*, pp. 265–71. Roussel indicates the same for Bishop Luquet. See Roussel, *Un Précurseur*, p. 82. But neither of these authors makes mention of the influence of Polding, of the nearby Australian scene where the same process was going on, and of the already established practice of the Evangelisation Congregation as indicated by its archivist. Theiner's and Luquet's roles were significant, but not exclusive.
27 PF: Acta vol. 210 (1847) f. 359r.

Chapter 27 The Vicariate Apostolic of New Caledonia
1 The two letters of Pompallier and Colin are treated in detail in chapter 26. Lambruschini says Colin's letter was sent to Fransoni; it reached Fransoni eventually but was addressed to Cardinal Altieri, a member of the Evangelisation Congregation. See PF: Acta vol. 210 (1847) f. 196[2] bis r.

2 Ibid., f. 350r–351r. This printed text erroneously has 'Pierre Garin' for 'Antoine Garin'.

3 Ibid., f. 195rv.

4 SM: Mayet, *Mémoires*, 7:159.

5 PF: Acta vol. 210 (1847) f. 195rv.

6 Lambruschini said this at the General Meeting of 29 May 1848. See PF: Acta vol. 211 (1848) f. 198r.

7 Ibid., f. 199v; PF: SC Oceania vol. 3 (1846–7) f. 571rv. Lambruschini's report, quoting from Colin's letter, speaks of fourteen or fifteen pages of documentation given by Colin to the pope. See PF: Acta vol. 211 (1848) f. 199v. But Colin's letter actually speaks of fourteen or fifteen letters from the missions. See PF: SOCG vol. 970 (1848) f. 291v.

8 SM: Mayet, *Mémoires*, 7:159f.

9 Ibid., pp. 160f.

10 PF: SC Oceania vol. 3 (1846–7) f. 848r.

11 Ibid., f. 570rv, 571v.

12 SM: Mayet, *Mémoires*, 7:161.

13 PF: SC Oceania vol. 3 (1846–7) f. 574r.

14 PF: LDB vol. 336 (1847, Part II) f. 874v–875r; PF: Acta vol. 211 (1848) f. 198r.

15 PF: SC Oceania vol. 3 (1846–7) f. 649rv.

16 In 1847 a letter written in Loreto on 29 June could hardly have arrived in Rome in time for answering two days later.

17 PF: LDB vol. 336 (1847, Part II) f. 760r. This source and also PF: Acta vol. 211 (1848) f. 198rv give the date as 1 July 1847. Keys gives the date as 30 June 1847 in *Life of Pompallier*, p. 253.

18 PF: SC Oceania vol. 3 (1846–7) f. 570v.

Chapter 28   Pope Pius IX is asked to make New Caledonia a papal colony

1 Jaspers, *Erschliessung Ozeaniens*, p. 257.

2 SM: Mayet, *Mémoires*, 7:161.

3 SM: ONC/418/1, Douarre to Colin, 13 August 1847.

4 Ibid., 27 July 1847.

5 *Ius Pontificium*, 6:39.

6 SM: ONC/418/1.

7 Jaspers goes too far when he reports Douarre as saying 'that New Caledonia would be able to provide for the needs of all mission stations in Western Oceania'. See Jaspers, *Erschliessung Ozeaniens*, p. 259. Douarre says merely that the island could supply 'the produce needed by other missions'.

8 PF: SC Oceania vol. 3 (1846–7) f. 692r–699v.

9 Ibid., f. 706rv.

10 Ibid., f. 683r.

11 Ibid., f. 689r–690r. Marists and Marist sources of this period incorrectly call this ship the *Stella Maris*, using a Latin title for the proper Italian title.

12 SM: ONC/418/1.

13 Ibid.

14 PF: CP vol. 157 (1847–51) f. 32r.

15 Jaspers, *Erschliessung Ozeaniens*, pp. 243, 257, 259. The date 3 July 1847 on page 257 is a typographical error for 3 July 1846.

16 PF: CP vol. 157 (1847–51) f. 33r–36r.

17 Ibid., f. 40v.

18 Ibid., f. 22r.

19 PF: SC Oceania vol. 3 (1846–7) f. 685r–686v.

20 SM: ONC/418/1.

21 These general boundaries would have included San Cristóbal at the southern end of the Solomon Archipelago, except for the fact that this archipelago had already been placed explicitly under the jurisdiction of the Vicar Apostolic of Melanesia.

22 PF: LDB vol. 336 (1847, Part II) f. 998v–999v.

23 Ibid., f. 997v–998r.

24 Ibid., f. 1000r, 1003r.

25 Ibid., f. 1042v–1043v.

26 Ibid., f. 1019r.

27 Ibid., f. 1019v–1020r.

28 Ibid., f. 1019rv.

29 SM: ONC/418/1.

30 The exact date of the meeting is not indicated.

31 PF: CP vol. 157 (1847–51) f. 28v.

32 The Evangelisation Congregation at this time used the name 'Indians' not only for the aboriginal peoples of North and South America and East and West Indies, but also for those of Oceania.

33 When reporting this episode Jaspers makes unwarranted and false deductions from his source material, stating that Pope Pius IX 'seriously thought of implementing the plan' and that Barnabò 'acted on the premise that Pius IX wanted to carry out this plan and his presentation was therefore favourable'. See Jaspers, *Erschliessung Ozeaniens*, pp. 260f. It is difficult to imagine what it was in the source material that prompted these statements by Jaspers and one might best challenge his three erroneous deductions in reverse order.

Was Barnabò in favour of the project? Nowhere does Barnabò say or show that he favoured it. As pro-secretary he had to present the state of the question as given by Douarre and Luquet and in doing so he was objective. Further, over and above the conditions laid down by the pope, Barnabò called two points to the special attention of the cardinals, thereby showing that he believed caution was necessary: (1) The two bishops believed that their project would be good for the New Caledonians, he said, but it did not conform to the broader principles governing the activity of the popes; and (2) the British seemed to be contemplating a military occupation of New Caledonia. These were additional barriers set up by Barnabò to acceptance of the project.

Did Barnabò act on the premise that Pius IX

wanted to carry out this plan? Jaspers in affirming this may have been misled by Barnabò's report which says—if one makes a literal translation—that the pope 'makes known his own mind in a positive way'. But 'positive' in this case does not mean 'affirmative', as is evident from Barnabò's own explanation of the word, which he gives immediately: 'That is, in view of the principles just mentioned,' etc. It is clear from the context that the phrase, 'in a positive way', means that he positively, that is, explicitly and unequivocally, or openly and clearly, wanted the cardinals to know his own reservations in the matter. There is nothing in Barnabò's report which indicates that he may have 'acted on the premise that Pius IX wanted to carry out this plan. . . .'

Did Pius IX seriously think of implementing the plan? As proof that he did Jaspers quotes in his note the words of the pope written on the last page of the Douarre-Luquet proposal, namely, 'Assuming as premise that the pope is not and must not be a conquistador, one can allow the realisation of the project' etc. Out of context the words, 'One can allow the realisation of the project', could indicate that the pope was ready to permit it. But in context the words are only a statement of the issue to be discussed as qualified in three ways by the pope, who in the same breath says about the project and about himself: 'up to now the pope is unacquainted with it'. He certainly did not seriously think of implementing a plan with which he was not even acquainted.

34 PF: CP vol. 157 (1847–51) f. 23r–24v.
35 Ibid., f. 41v.
36 From the mere absence of the results of the cardinals' discussion in the archives of the Evangelisation Congregation, one cannot deduce categorically, as Jaspers does, that no discussion took place. See Jaspers, *Erschliessung Ozeaniens*, p. 261. Since the five cardinals and Barnabò had received an order directly from the pope that a discussion should take place, and since the matter subsequently came up in an audience granted by the pope to Barnabò, one can assume without rashness that the discussion did take place and that a report was made.
37 Jaspers, *Erschliessung Ozeaniens*, p. 261.
38 Antonio Anoge, 'Jean-Félix-Onésime Luquet', in *Enciclopedia Cattolica*, vol. 7, col. 1703.
39 Silvio Furlani, 'Augustin Theiner', ibid., vol. 12, col. 45f.

Chapter 29 Collomb is ordained bishop in New Zealand for the Vicariates of Melanesia and Micronesia

1 SM: OMM/411. Epalle refers to Colin's proposal in his letter; there seems to be no copy of Colin's letter in existence. For more details see chapter 20.
2 Epalle at this time was still en route to Melanesia; he landed at Sydney on 21 June.
3 PF: SC Oceania vol. 2 (1842–5, Part II) f. 975v–976r.
4 PF: LDB vol. 332 (1845) f. 476v–477r.
5 PF: Acta vol. 209 (1846) f. 45v.
6 Ibid., f. 45rv.
7 PF: LDB vol. 332 (1845) f. 784v–785r.
8 SM: OMM/000/Noms.
9 PF: Acta vol. 209 (1846) f. 42r–43r. See also the decree of 9 February 1846 in PF: LDB vol. 333 (1846, Part I) f. 139r–140r.
10 PF: LDB vol. 333 (1846, Part I) f. 176r.
11 SM: OMM/411. Collomb mentions the date in his letter to Colin of 6 May 1847.
12 PF: LDB vol. 333 (1846, Part I) f. 139v–140r, Decree of 9 February 1846.
13 PF: SC Oceania vol. 2 (1842–5, Part II) f. 982r, Marceau to Fransoni, 6 July 1845.
14 Ibid., f. 975rv.
15 Ibid., f. 981r–988v.
16 PF: LDB vol. 332 (1845) f. 485r–486r.
17 PF: SC Oceania vol. 2 (1842–5, Part I) f. 525r–527r.
18 SM: OMM/411, Collomb to Colin, 6 May 1847.
19 SM: 'Journal de Mgr. Jean Georges Collomb'.
20 Verguet, *Vicariat de Mélanésie*, p. 125. The daily order is given here in great detail: rising at five o'clock, prayers, Mass, breakfast at nine, catechetics, spiritual reading at three, dinner at four, recitation of the divine office, recreation or study until sunset etc.
21 Ibid., pp. 189–99, 201f. Verguet on page 198 calls betelnut chewing, still widely practised in Melanesia today, a stimulant influencing the native's temperament and rendering him more fit to tolerate the arduous climate and go without food for a long time. Betelnut is to a native, he said, what a cigarette is to a Spaniard. San Cristóbal men always had betelnut in their mouths.
22 SM: 'Journal de Collomb'.
23 PF: SC Oceania vol. 2 (1842–5, Part II) f. 987r–988v, Marceau to Fransoni, 6 July 1845.
24 Verguet, *Vicariat de Mélanésie*, pp. 205f.
25 SM: 'Journal de Collomb'.
26 Note that Collomb is using longitude measurements based on the meridian of Paris. Woodlark is approximately 153° east of Greenwich.
27 *Pacific Islands Yearbook* (1963), p. 383, says Woodlark was discovered 'about 1836'. Father Carlo Salerio, writing from Woodlark on 4 December 1852, says it was discovered 'in 1832'. See PF: SC Oceania vol. 4 (1848–52) f. 737r–738r.
28 In 1967 there were 'about 2,500 people' living

'on Woodlark Island and 31 other small islands nearby'. See *Our News*, p. 9.

29 SM: OMM/411.

30 SM: OMM/411, Collomb to Colin, 1 June 1847.

31 PF: SOCG vol. 970 (1848) f. 421rv.

32 '... ut juvenilis aetas apprime informetur, utque in scholis educentur catechistae et, si etiam Domino placuerit, praeparentur saltem a longe elementa cleri indigenae'.

33 PF: SOCG vol. 970 (1848) f. 295rv.

34 SM: OMM/411.

35 PF: LDB vol. 337 (1848) f. 46v–47r, Fransoni to Colin, 31 January 1848.

36 PF: Acta vol. 211 (1848) f. 200r.

37 For further details on conditions affecting the creation of the Vicariate Apostolic of Micronesia, see chapter 20.

38 PF: Acta vol. 211 (1848) f. 223rv.

39 PF: LDB vol. 337 (1848) f. 159v–161r.

40 The text actually refers to Collomb here as Bishop 'Antiphellensis', which was the adjective form for 'Antiphellus', the titular see of Bishop Collomb. The Roman Curia catalogued the world's residential and titular bishops under the Latin form of their residential or titular sees and often referred to them simply by using the adjective form of those sees, as in this case.

41 PF: Acta vol. 211 (1848) f. 201r.

42 PF: LDB vol. 337 (1848) f. 479r. This 13 June decree mistakenly has 7 June instead of 4 June as the date of the papal audience.

43 *Prospetto della gerarchia episcopale in ogni rito e i vicariati, delegazioni e prefetture nei luoghi di missione della S. Chiesa cattolica, apostolica Romana in tutto l'orbe al primo gennaio 1850*, p. 92.

44 PF: LDB vol. 337 (1848) f. 476r–477r.

45 Ibid., f. 472v–473v.

46 PF: SC Oceania vol. 4 (1848–52) f. 106r.

Chapter 30 New Caledonians put the Marists to flight

1 SM: 'Journal de Collomb'; SM: OMM/411, Collomb to Poupinel, 21 August 1847.

2 PF: SC Oceania vol. 4 (1848–52) f. 49v, Procès-Verbal by Collomb and others to Colin, 17 August 1847; ibid., f. 460r, Montrouzier to Fransoni, 22 June 1849. The procès-verbal, or official report, was published in Verguet, *Vicariat de Mélanésie*, pp. 235–48.

3 SM: 'Journal de Collomb'; Verguet, *Vicariat de Mélanésie*, pp. 231–5, 237. The procès-verbal says that Raballand informed the Balade Mission personnel of the planned attack on 25 May, but Collomb quoting in his diary on 5 July from Grange's diary gives the date as 23 May.

4 SM: 'Journal de Collomb'; PF: SC Oceania vol. 4 (1848–52) f. 49r–51v, Procès-Verbal by Col-

lomb and others to Colin, 17 August 1847; Verguet, *Vicariat de Mélanésie*, pp. 235–48.

5 Verguet, *Vicariat de Mélanésie*, pp. 249f.

6 Ibid., p. 252.

7 SM: 'Journal de Collomb'; Verguet, *Vicariat de Mélanésie*, pp. 248, 255–65. Verguet says (p. 265) that the *Anonyme* arrived at Poébo on 15 August, but Collomb's 'Journal' has 16 August.

8 SM: 'Journal de Collomb'.

9 SM: OMM/411, Collomb to Colin, 21 August 1847.

10 SM: OMM/411, Collomb to Poupinel, 21 August 1847.

11 SM: 'Journal de Collomb'.

12 Ibid.; Verguet, *Vicariat de Mélanésie*, p. 266. Verguet here mistakenly gives the departure date as 21 August.

13 SM: 'Journal de Collomb'.

14 Verguet, *Vicariat de Mélanésie*, p. 252.

Chapter 31 Collomb dies on Rooke Island

1 SM: OMM/411, Collomb to the Association for the Propagation of the Faith, 21 December 1847; Verguet, *Vicariat de Mélanésie*, pp. 281f. The version of Collomb's letter in the SM files is a copy; the letter was published by Verguet, ibid., pp. 282–8. Laracy's Wango and Toro have been used for Verguet's Ouango and Toros. Verguet says Ouango (or Wango) was on the east coast; Laracy says it was on the north coast and his location has been used. See Laracy, *Marists and Melanesians*, p. 20.

2 PF: SC Oceania vol. 4 (1848–52) f. 460v, Montrouzier to Fransoni, 22 June 1849.

3 Collomb to the Association for the Propagation of the Faith, 21 December 1847, in Verguet, *Vicariat de Mélanésie*, p. 286.

4 SM: 'Journal de Collomb'.

5 Collomb to the Association for the Propagation of the Faith, 21 December 1847, in Verguet, *Vicariat de Mélanésie*, p. 286.

6 Ibid., p. 288.

7 *American Activities in the Central Pacific 1790–1870*, p. 8.

8 Collomb to the Association for the Propagation of the Faith, 21 December 1847, in Verguet, *Vicariat de Mélanésie*, pp. 286–8.

9 Ibid., p. 289.

10 SM: OSM/208, Villien to Villien, 10 July 1848; Hosie, 'French Mission', p. 415.

11 SM: OSM/208. Hosie in 'French Mission', p. 415, says that the *Anonyme* actually sailed from Sydney on 7 April.

12 SM: 'Journal de Collomb'.

13 PF: SC Oceania vol. 4 (1848–52) f. 460v, Montrouzier to Fransoni, 22 June 1849.

14 SM: 'Journal de Collomb'.

15 Nurua Village was not mentioned by name by Marist missionaries stationed at Port Saint Isidore, as far as the author has been able to

ascertain, but it was mentioned repeatedly by the Italian missionaries who succeeded them there, e.g. by Prefect Apostolic Reina on 18 March 1855 [See PIME: vol. 11 (Oceania) p. 143.] Some years later Nurua was obliterated by a tidal wave. Recounting Rooke folklore, Luluai Malakor-Gerard of Aupwel Village, Siassi, who was interviewed for the author on 7 March 1965 by Father W. Sasse of the Congregation of the Missionaries of Mariannhill (C.M.M.), said— and correctly so—that the first Catholic missionaries to Rooke Island landed at Nurua: 'Orait nau ol dispela mission katolik ol kamap. Na kamap nambawan long Nuru.' (Nuru is the pronunciation used by Koai—or Kowai— tribesmen, who are different from those who inhabited Nurua.) Folklore errs, however, when it states that the two missionaries who died at Nurua were killed by stoning. The Reverend Con Eckermann, a Lutheran missionary on Rooke Island since 1947, informed the author, through Dr Willard Burce on 12 January 1966, that the tradition has remained alive among the Rooke Island people that there were early missionaries who lived for a brief period on the island. According to Eckermann the tidal wave that destroyed Nurua was caused by the 1872 explosion of volcanic Ritter Island located in the Dampier Strait between Tupinier (or Sakar) Island and Kumbalup on the Rooke Island coast. The name Port Saint Isidore has not survived, no Rooke Islanders know it, and none have that Christian name.

16 SM: 'Journal de Collomb'; SM: OSM/208, Villien to Villien, 10 July 1848. This Saint Isidore, different from the one listed under 4 April in today's *Roman Calendar*, is the patron of Madrid. He lived about 1080–1130 and was canonised by Pope Gregory XV on 12 March 1622.

17 The book by Conrad Malte-Brun read by Villien was *Précis de la géographie universelle*, probably the copy brought to Oceania by Bishop Epalle. But by consulting this work it is not possible to tell whether Villien meant the collection of tiny volcanic islands far out to sea opposite the mouth of the Sepik River, or rather the much larger and better known islands at the entrance to Geelvink Bay north of Japen, since both groups then already were called Schouten Islands. Epalle, however, had indicated the Schouten Islands near Geelvink Bay as a vast mission territory in his letter of 1 August 1843, when pointing out the major islands to be included in his proposed Vicariate Apostolic of Melanesia (see chapter 17). It therefore seems more probable that Villien meant the Schouten Islands near Geelvink Bay. See Malte-Brun, *Précis de la géographie universelle*, 4:231, 377 and 6:390, 495, 498.

18 SM: 'Journal de Collomb'.
19 SM: OSM/208, Villien to Villien, 10 July 1848.
20 SM: OSM/208.
21 SM: OSM/208, Frémont to Marceau, 28 July 1848; ibid., Montrouzier to Poupinel, 13 August 1848.
22 Ibid., Montrouzier to Poupinel, 13 August 1848.
23 SM: OSM/208, Frémont to Marceau, 28 July 1848.
24 Ibid., Frémont to Rocher, 24 June 1849. A novena is nine days of special prayer.
25 Ibid.
26 Reina to no name, 31 October 1852, in Verguet, *Vicariat de Mélanésie*, p. 295.
27 SM: OSM/208, Villien to Villien, 10 July 1848.
28 Hosie, 'French Mission', p. 415.
29 SM: OSM/208, Montrouzier to Colin, 14 May 1849.
30 Ibid., Ducrettet to no name (extract), 15 June 1849.
31 PF: SC Oceania vol. 4 (1848–52) f. 460r, Montrouzier to Fransoni, 22 June 1849.
32 SM: OSM/208, Frémont to Rocher, 24 June 1849.
33 Ibid., Montrouzier to Colin, 14 May 1849. The letter was completed on 22 June.
34 PF: SC Oceania vol. 4 (1848–52) f. 460v, Montrouzier to Fransoni, 22 June 1849.
35 SM: OSM/208, Montrouzier to Colin, 14 May 1849. The letter was completed on 22 June.
36 PIME: vol. 11 (Oceania), p. 92, Reina to Marinoni, 31 October 1852. Actually Frémont himself returned on 23 October 1852, three and a half years later, with an Italian missionary group from Lombardy's Seminary for Foreign Missions, founded in 1850, located first in Saronno and then in Milan, and known today as the Pontifical Institute for Foreign Missions (P.I.M.E.). To their surprise, the house in all this time had not been touched and they were able to move into it two days later.
37 SM: OSM/208, Ducrettet to no name, 15 June 1849.
38 PF: SC Oceania vol. 4 (1848–52) f. 460v. Baptised infants who died were called angels.
39 PF: SC Oceania vol. 4 (1848–52) f. 266r.
40 PF: LDB vol. 337 (1848) f. 828v–829r.

Chapter 32 The Vicariates Apostolic of Marquesas Islands and Tahiti Islands

1 *Collectanea Sacrae Congregationis de Propaganda Fide seu Decreta instructiones rescripta pro apostolicis missionibus*, no. 1002, pp. 541–5. According to the same 'Instruction' (p. 544) young men were to be trained for the indigenous clergy 'in such a way that they may become fit for every ecclesiastical office, including that of governing the missions, and also in such a way that they may become worthy even

of the episcopal character, something that the Apostolic See has desired for a long time'.

2 The Marist vicariates were: Western Oceania (1836), Central Oceania (1842) and Melanesia-Micronesia (1844). The Picpus vicariates were: Eastern Oceania (1833) and the Sandwich Islands (1844).

3 See chapter 26.

4 See chapter 24.

5 The Picpus Fathers arrived in the Gambier Islands on 7 August 1834. It was their first mission in the south Pacific. See chapter 5. Bonamie's 1846 total of 'about 4,000' is exaggerated. In 1839 the neophytes numbered 2,121 (Caret); in 1845 the total population was 2,270 (Laval).

6 PF: Udienze vol. 105 (1846, Part II) f. 1129v, 1132r. The twenty-two missionaries left aboard the *Creisquer* on 20 July 1845.

7 PF: LDB vol. 333 (1846, Part I) f. 175rv. Jaspers misreads this source when he says that the proposal for a Gambier Islands Vicariate originated with the Evangelisation Congregation. See Jaspers, *Erschliessung Ozeaniens*, p. 223.

8 Ibid., pp. 215f.

9 PF: SC Oceania vol. 4 (1848–52) f. 510v, Bonamie to Fransoni, 19 January 1850.

10 PF: SOCG vol. 970 (1848) f. 210v.

11 See chapter 18. See also note 19 below.

12 PF: SOCG vol. 970 (1848) f. 210v–211r. Actually the jump in statistics was not from so low a figure, and consequently not so great, as Bonamie made it appear in this letter of 1 February 1848. Prefect Apostolic Maigret had informed him on 22 August 1843 that there were then 10,000 Catholics in the Sandwich Islands. In 1848 Maigret informed the Evangelisation Congregation that the number of Catholics had increased to 18,031. See Jaspers, *Erschliessung Ozeaniens*, p. 223, note 13. This was an actual increase of 8,000 Catholics in the previous *five* years according to Maigret, whereas Bonamie purports an increase of some 17,600 for the same period plus one year. Sailing from Marseille aboard *Stella del Mare* with Bonamie's eight missionaries were fourteen Marists (Bishop Douarre was at the pier to see them off), four members of the Congregation of the Mission of Saint Vincent de Paul (C.M.), called also Vincentians or Lazarists, and twelve Daughters of Charity of Saint Vincent de Paul (D.C.).

13 Bonamie gave the location of the Roggewein Archipelago as 9°–12° south latitude and 157°–164° west longitude (from Paris).

14 PF: Acta vol. 211 (1848) f. 157v. Bonamie lacks the precision of Coudrin, founder of the order, who had proposed the Vicariate Apostolic of Eastern Oceania in 1833. The Tahiti Islands, for example, were generally referred to as the Society Islands; and Mangareva, not Gambier,

was the largest island in the Gambier Archipelago.

15 The boundaries for the Vicariate Apostolic of Eastern Oceania created on 2 June 1833 excluded the Cook or Mangaia Archipelago, leaving them remain part of the Prefecture Apostolic of the South Sea Islands (see chapter 4). The Vicariate Apostolic of Western Oceania, founded on 10 January 1836, absorbed the Prefecture Apostolic of the South Sea Islands and consequently also the Cook or Mangaia Archipelago (see chapter 6). The Vicariate Apostolic of Central Oceania, separated from the Western Oceania Vicariate on 8 August 1842, included the Mangaia or Cook Archipelago (see chapter 14).

16 PF: Acta vol. 210 (1847) f. 192r, 351r.

17 PF: LDB vol. 337 (1848) f. 115r.

18 PF: SOCG vol. 970 (1848) f. 213r–214v.

19 PF: Acta vol. 211 (1848) f. 151r–155r. A decree dated 15 April 1848 and signed by Barnabò, which served as a private record of business, states that the Evangelisation Congregation on 3 April had 'decided and decreed that the Holy Father should be asked to approve the erection of the above three proposed vicariates', namely, Sandwich Islands, Marquesas Islands and Eastern Oceania. [See PF: LDB vol. 337 (1848) f. 300r.] But the Sandwich Islands Vicariate had been in existence since 1844. This confusion apparently stems from Bonamie's letter of 1 February 1848, as mentioned earlier in this chapter. Also, Thomas Francis Grannell ('Vicariate Apostolic of Tahiti') says incorrectly that 'in 1848 the Prefecture Apostolic of Southeast Oceania was divided to create this vicariate [of Tahiti] and that of the Marquesas Islands to the north'.

20 PF: LDB vol. 337 (1848) f. 355v–356r; SSCC: 1–1–4J1.

21 Jaspers, *Erschliessung Ozeaniens*, p. 221, note 8.

22 PF: LDB vol. 337 (1848) f. 353v–354r.

23 The Vicariate Apostolic of New Caledonia was founded on 27 June 1847.

Chapter 33 New Zealand is divided into Auckland and Port Nicholson Dioceses

1 For more details on these letters to Colin and Pompallier see chapter 28.

2 PF: SOCG vol. 970 (1848) f. 416r, 417r.

3 Ibid., f. 419r–420r.

4 Ibid., f. 444v.

5 See chapter 27 for more details of this letter.

6 See chapter 28 for more details of this letter. The report prepared for the General Meeting of 29 May 1848 confuses these two letters, mistakenly calling Fransoni's letter of 24 August the letter of recommendation. See PF: Acta vol. 211 (1848) f. 198v.

7 Italians automatically use 'Blessed Virgin Mary' when speaking of Mary. The official title was and is Society of Mary.

8 PF: LDB vol. 336 (1847, Part II) f. 1319v–1320r.

9 PF: SC Oceania vol. 3 (1846–7) f. 847r, Colin to Fransoni, 28 December 1847.

10 Ibid., f. 841r.

11 Ibid., f. 847r, Colin to Fransoni, 28 December 1847.

12 PF: SOCG vol. 970 (1848) f. 336r, Pompallier to Fransoni and other cardinals, 15 January 1848; ibid., f. 283r.

13 PF: LDB vol. 336 (1847) f. 1434rv.

14 PF: SC Oceania vol. 3 (1846–7) f. 847r–848r.

15 Ibid., f. 843rv. The name of the Association for the Propagation of the Faith in French, as printed on its stationery at this time, was *Oeuvre de la Propagation de la Foi en faveur des Missions Étrangères des Deux-Mondes*.

16 PF: LDB vol. 337 (1848) f. 17rv.

17 PF: SOCG vol. 970 (1848) f. 336r–337r.

18 Ibid., f. 444v–447v.

19 Ibid., f. 293rv.

20 Ibid., f. 281r–282v.

21 Ibid., f. 278r–399r.

22 PF: LDB vol. 337 (1848) f. 160r–161r.

23 See chapter 26.

24 PF: SOCG vol. 970 (1848) f. 291r–292r. Here Colin says that he placed the fourteen or fifteen letters in the hands of Pope Pius IX 'on 8 or 9 June 1847'. Actually, he wrote the pope a letter on 8 June 1847, but presented it to the pope personally only on 15 June together with the fourteen or fifteen letters. Cf. SM: Mayet, *Mémoires*, 7:159f. See also chapter 27.

25 PF: SC Oceania vol. 4 (1848–52) f. 94v–95r.

26 For the original depositions made by Pompallier, see PF: SOCG vol. 970 (1848) f. 271r–447v.

27 Ibid., f. 348r, 366r–368r.

28 For example, see his signature, ibid., f. 282r, Pompallier to the Evangelisation Congregation, 17 February 1848.

29 Keys incorrectly says that New Zealand was erected into a distinct vicariate under Pompallier's administration in 1842. See Keys, *Life of Pompallier*, p. 204.

30 PF: Acta vol. 211 (1848) f. 197r–201r.

31 PF: LDB vol. 337 (1848) f. 479v–480v.

32 PF: Acta vol. 211 (1848) f. 201r.

33 These titles are used and explained in the official letters sent to Pompallier and Viard on 30 June 1848. See PF: LDB vol. 337 (1848) f. 468r, 469v.

34 PF: Udienze vol. 108 (1848, Part I) f. 486r.

35 PF: LDB vol. 337 (1848) f. 445v.

36 See chapter 27 for the contents of the earlier letter dated 1 July 1847.

37 See note 7.

38 PF: LDB vol. 337 (1848) f. 469v–471r.

39 The titular see written here mistakenly by the scribe reads 'Orthodosia' for 'Orthosia'. (See ibid., f. 468r.) The same mistake appears elsewhere in this series of handwritten file copies of Fransoni's letters to Pompallier, Viard and Colin as well as in the related decrees. At times the scribe uses 'Orthodosia' and at other times the correct 'Orthosia', even in the same document. Cf. ibid., f. 469v, 472r, 480rv.

40 Ibid., f. 468r–469r.

41 Ibid., f. 471r–473v.

42 Colin did not indicate here for Fransoni the precise reason why he considered Viard a non-Marist. Speaking to Marists a year earlier, on 22 August 1847, Colin described the new article in the Marist Rule as follows: 'If the society has agreed [to the Holy See's appointment of a Marist as a bishop], it will continue to regard him as one of its members and will undertake to look after his affairs and send him missionaries. If the Holy See designates a Marist as a bishop and he accepts without the agreement or consent of the society, the society ceases to recognise him, as it were, except perhaps as an honorary member, and will not provide him with any subjects. Otherwise, very soon we should have 30 or 40 bishops. . . .' See Jean-Claude Colin, *A Founder Speaks*, p. 403.

After making Viard a bishop at Pompallier's suggestion on 12 January 1845 and giving him right of succession, Rome informed Colin on 22 February of the fait accompli (see chapter 19). When Viard later that year in far-off Oceania learned of his appointment (see chapter 25), he could hardly have suspected that Colin had had no role in it and that he would be penalised by Colin for accepting this appointment made by the pope. Again, when it came time for Viard to receive a territory of his own, Colin was most insistent that he receive the proposed Auckland Archdiocese (see chapter 26). But when Viard received instead the undeveloped Diocese of Port Nicholson, Colin informed Rome that Viard was no longer a member. In view of all this and in view of Colin's altogether unrealistic fear that '30 or 40' Marists would be made bishops, it appears to this author that the application of Colin's ruling to Viard was unfair, that it was more a reprimand to the Holy See for its conduct, and that it was a deus ex machina excusing Colin from sending personnel to undeveloped Port Nicholson Diocese.

43 PF: SC Oceania vol. 4 (1848–52) f. 106rv.

44 The author consulted the copy in SM, taken from Carte Theiner in the Vatican archives, made by Father Jean Coste, S.M.

45 SM: Colin to Theiner, 12 June 1850. The author consulted the copy, taken from Carte Theiner in the Vatican archives, made by Father Jean Coste, S.M.

46   These details are taken from this book and from Keys, *Life of Pompallier*, pp. 249–68 passim.

47   PF: SC Oceania vol. 4 (1848–52) f. 526r, Colin to Fransoni, 25 September 1850.

Chapter 34   The Vicariate Apostolic of the Samoa or Navigators Archipelago

1   See chapter 27.

2   See chapter 30 for details of the attack.

3   PF: SOCG vol. 970 (1848) f. 293rv.

4   PF: Acta vol. 211 (1848) f. 223v.

5   PF: LDB vol. 337 (1848) f. 162r, Fransoni to Douarre, 7 March 1858; PF: SC Oceania vol. 4 (1848–52) f. 53r.

6   PF: SC Oceania vol. 4 (1848–52) f. 49r–51v. See also ibid., f. 53r, Rougeyron to Colin, 13 August 1847.

7   PF: LDB vol. 337 (1848) f. 159v.

8   Ibid., f. 162r.

9   SM: Colin to Theiner, 15 August 1848. The author consulted the copy, taken from Carte Theiner in the Vatican archives, made by Father Jean Coste, S.M.

10   PF: Udienze vol. 112 (1850, Part II) f. 762 (4f). This information is contained in Secretary Barnabò's eleven-page report to Pope Pius IX of 11 August 1850. Since only the initial page is numbered, the author has made up his own page numbers for the report as indicated in parentheses.

11   Ibid., f. 763r.

12   On learning of Douarre's suggestion, Colin also was convinced that Bataillon would react in this way. See ibid., f. 762 (9), Barnabò to Pius IX, 11 August 1850.

13   Ibid., f. 763rv.

14   Ibid., f. 764rv.

15   PF: SC Oceania vol. 4 (1848–52) f. 423r. Bernin's report begins on f. 418r.

16   See SM: Mayet, *Mémoires*, 6:77f; also the 1850 Circular Letter of Bishop de Charbonnel of Toronto, in Candide Causse, *Evêque d'or, crosse de bois*, p. 60.

17   The copy was certified by Colin at Lyon on 12 June 1850. See PF: Udienze vol. 112 (1850, Part II) f. 763v.

18   Ibid., f. 762 (5–7).

19   Ibid., f. 765r–766r. The date of Bernin's letter to the cardinal, 5 August 1850, is not on the original copy given to the cardinal, but is on Bernin's file copy in SM: 410 SCPF, 26 July 1850.

20   Barnabò was present and called it a 'meeting'. See ibid., f. 762 (8). This was not a General Meeting, because the only ones held about that time were on 8 July and 26 August. See PF: Acta vol. 212 (1849–50) f. 295r, 465r, 491r.

21   PF: Udienze vol. 112 (1850, Part II) f. 762 (8f).

22   PF: SC Oceania vol. 4 (1848–52) f. 521rv; PF: Udienze vol. 112 (1850, Part II) f. 762 (10), Barnabò to Pius IX, 11 August 1850.

23   Colin and Bernin must have been surprised to see Fransoni write here that the request for the Navigators Archipelago Vicariate had been made by Bernin in Colin's name. It was Bernin who had made the request, it is true, but in Douarre's name, after Colin had refused to make it. See PF: Udienze vol. 112 (1850, Part II) f. 765r, Bernin to Fransoni, August 1850.

24   PF: LDB vol. 339 (1850) f. 702rv.

25   He listed Wallis (saying it was the bishop's residence), Futuna, Tonga, Samoa or Navigators Archipelago, Fiji, and also—but mistakenly—New Hebrides. This last archipelago was part of the Vicariate Apostolic of New Caledonia (see chapter 28).

26   In this connection Barnabò told the pope that Douarre 'has knowledge of the Navigators Archipelago, where he exercised the ministry'. This statement, however, must be incorrect. If Douarre visited the Navigators Archipelago as coadjutor of Bataillon, he could hardly have done more than set foot on the islands! The same ship which had brought him from France to Wallis, where he ordained Bataillon a bishop on 3 December 1843, brought him via Futuna (9 December) to New Caledonia, which was sighted on 19 December. This island and New Hebrides had been entrusted by Bataillon to Douarre. See chapter 19.

27   PF: Udienze vol. 112 (1850, Part II) f. 762r, 762 (1–10), 767r.

28   Naturally the enclosed decree of the Evangelisation Congregation would not be dated later than the letters. A note appended to the report given to the pope indicates that the three letters 'with the decree' were to be dated '14 August 1850'. See ibid., f. 767rv. The Evangelisation Congregation's copy of this decree, however, is dated 24 August 1850. See PF: LDB vol. 339 (1850) f. 743v–744v. SM has no copy of this decree, nor is the original to be found in its collection of original Rome correspondence received by Bataillon. Missing also in this collection, however, is the 14 August 1850 letter from Fransoni to Bataillon, who said himself that he had received it. The date on the decree sent to the two bishops, therefore, could not be compared with that in LDB. But a comparison of the decree as contained in LDB (dated 24 August 1850) with the letter of 14 August 1850 sent to Bataillon as contained in LDB, shows that they are for the most part nearly identical in content, phrase for phrase, a proof that the decree was copied from the Bataillon letter, or—more likely—that the letter was copied from the decree. And so the decree in substance was already drawn up on 14 August 1850, even though the LDB copy is dated 24 August 1850.

29 PF: LDB vol. 339 (1850) f. 709v–710r.
30 Ibid., f. 710rv.
31 Ibid., f. 711r–712r.
32 *Ius Pontificium*, 6:102f.; see also note 1 on page 102. This printed text has 'Hamon', a misreading or misprint for 'Hamoa', which appeared on many contemporary maps in place of 'Samoa'. 'Hamoa' was also the spelling in the Evangelisation Congregation's decree. See PF: LDB vol. 339 (1850) f. 743r–744v.
33 PF: LDB vol. 339 (1850) f. 785rv.
34 PF: SC Oceania vol. 4 (1848–52) f. 524r.

Chapter 35 The Marists ask to be discharged of Micronesia and Melanesia Vicariates

1 See chapter 7.
2 SM: 511/461.
3 PF: SOCG vol. 970 (1848) f. 293v.
4 PF: LDB vol. 337 (1848) f. 159v–161r; PF: Acta vol. 211 (1848) f. 200rv.
5 PF: SOCG vol. 970 (1848) f. 337r.
6 Ibid., f. 291r–292r. Widespread popular discontent with his rule had made King Louis-Philippe abdicate on 24 February 1848. He withdrew to Claremont, Surrey, England, and died there on 26 August 1850.
7 B: Vc no. 17, Trattato per le Missioni in partibus infidelium nel 1848.
8 B: Acta in Consultationibus Praepositi Generalis, no. 40, p. 198.
9 B: Acta Praepositi Generalis, Liber XVI (1847–53), p. 81.
10 B: Vc no. 17, Trattato per le Missioni in partibus infidelium nel 1848.
11 Ibid.
12 Ibid.
13 PF: Acta vol. 211 (1848) f. 200r–201r.
14 B: Vc no. 17, Trattato per le Missioni in partibus infidelium nel 1848.
15 Ibid.
16 PF: LDB vol. 337 (1848) f. 472v–473r. The primary function of the procurator general of a religious order is to serve as the liaison with members of the Roman Curia, and so one can presume that Grampini delivered his letter on the day that he wrote it. And Barnabò, as pro-secretary, would have been the one to compose the letter for Fransoni to sign. Contrary to popular belief, once Rome had the necessary information, it acted swiftly. Delays were caused by officials having to wait for others—in this case for Grampini—to supply the requested information.
17 PF: SC Oceania vol. 4 (1848–52) f. 94r–95r.
18 PF: LDB vol. 337 (1848) f. 603rv.
19 PF: SC Oceania vol. 4 (1848–52) f. 106r.
20 Ibid., f. 462r, Colin to Barnabò, 23 April 1850.
21 PF: LDB vol. 339 (1850) f. 188rv.
22 Colin says here that his letter was dated 12 August 1848. But the original letter sent to Rome and the copy in his own archives were both dated 11 August. See PF: SC Oceania vol. 4 (1848–52) f. 106r; SM: APM/410.
23 PF: SC Oceania vol. 4 (1848–52) f. 462r–463r.
24 Ibid., f. 463v.
25 See chapter 32.
26 SSCC: +92 Baudichon p. 383.
27 SSCC: A 20–3.
28 Ibid.
29 PF: Acta vol. 212 (1849 and 1850) f. 436r–438r, 456v, 458v; PF: LDB vol. 338 (1849) f. 167v, 170v–171r, Fransoni to Bonamie, June (day of month is not given) 1849; PF: SC Oceania vol. 4 (1848–52) f. 510r–511r, Bonamie to Fransoni, 19 January 1850; SSCC: 1–1–11E4, Fransoni to Bonamie, 10 August 1849; SSCC: 1–1–11E5, Fransoni to Bonamie, 26 September 1849. Father Joseph Sadoc Alemany, O.P. (1814–88), provincial superior of the Dominicans in the United States, was named Bishop of Monterey after his predecessor in office, Father Charles Montgomery, O.P., turned down the bishopric on grounds of ill health. Sadoc learned of his nomination in Rome, having come there to attend the General Chapter of his order, and was ordained a bishop there in San Carlo Church on the Corso on 30 June 1850. Baja California remained under his jurisdiction until 1853.
30 SSCC: A 20–3.
31 PF: LDB vol. 339 (1850) f. 383v–384v.
32 Ibid., f. 383rv.
33 SSCC: A 20–3.
34 The Tuamotu (or Low) Archipelago is an island chain extending south of the Marquesas Islands.
35 PF: SC Oceania vol. 4 (1848–52) f. 509rv.
36 Ibid., f. 512v.
37 This letter says incorrectly that the natives of San Cristóbal killed the first bishop. He was killed at Santa Isabel Island. See chapter 20.
38 PF: LDB vol. 339 (1850) f. 488v–489r.
39 PF: SC Anglia vol. 12 (1848–51) f. 545r–546v.
40 PF: LDB vol. 339 (1850) f. 712rv.
41 SM: Lettres du Procureur de Lyon (1845–56), Colin to Douarre, 14 June 1850.
42 PF: Udienze vol. 112 (1850, Part II) f. 764rv, Colin to Fransoni, 12 June 1850.
43 The date is on his own file copy (SM: 410/SCPF, 26 July 1850), but not on the original copy given to the cardinal. See PF: Udienze vol. 112 (1850, Part II) f. 766v.
44 PF: Udienze vol. 112 (1850, Part II) f. 766r.
45 See chapter 34.
46 PF: LDB vol. 339 (1850) f. 702r–703r.
47 The author consulted the copy in SM, taken from Carte Theiner in the Vatican archives, made by Father Jean Coste, S.M.
48 PF: LDB vol. 339 (1850) f. 709v–712r, 743r–744v.
49 Here Colin explained that Port Nicholson, the

name given to the diocese, was the name of a
port or bay with Wellington on its shoreline.

50 PF: SC Oceania vol. 4 (1848–52) f. 524r–526r.
51 SM: Lettres du Procureur de Lyon (1845–56),
    p. 104f.
52 Ibid., p. 105.
53 PF: SC Oceania vol. 4 (1848–52) f. 584r–585v.
54 SM: Lettres du Procureur de Lyon (1845–56),
    pp. 116f.
55 After Fransoni's letter to Bishop de Mazenod on
    25 June 1850, there are no further letters in PF:
    LDB seeking personnel prior to 16 January

1851. See PF: LDB vol. 339 (1850) and vol. 340
(1851).

56 PF: Udienze vol. 111 (1850, Part I), f. 93r–94r;
    PF: SC Collegi Vari, vol. S. Calocero di Milano,
    f. 153rv, 157r–158v. Printed sources often
    speak of Bishop *Angelo* Ramazzotti, but at this
    time he called himself *Angiolo*. Later he indis-
    criminately used both forms.
57 PF: LDB vol. 340 (1851) f. 40r.
58 PIME: vol. 11 (Oceania) pp. 25–7.
59 PF: LDB vol. 340 (1851) f. 608v–610v.
60 PF: SC Oceania vol. 4 (1848–52) f. 924r–926v.

Bibliography

Acta Gregorii Papae XVI. Vol. 2, Pars Prima Canonica. Edited by Antonius Maria Bernasconus. Rome, 1901.

American Activities in the Central Pacific 1790–1870: A History, Geography and Ethnography Pertaining to American Involvement and Americans in the Pacific Taken from Contemporary Newspapers, etc. Vol. 4. Edited by R. Gerard Ward. Ridgewood, N.J., 1967.

L'ami de la religion: journal ecclésiastique, politique et littéraire. Vol. 90. Paris, 1836.

Annales de la propagation de la foi. Vol. 17. Lyon, 1845.

Annales des missions d'Océanie. See Société de Marie.

Annales des sacrés-coeurs. No. 391. Paris, 1934.

Annales maritimes et coloniales. Paris, 1843.

Annuario Pontificio 1974. Vatican City, 1974. xciv + 1950 pp.

Australia, Land of Contrast. N.p., n.d. 52 pp.

Balbi, Adriano. *Compendio di geografia compilato su di un nuovo disegno conforme agli ultimi trattati di pace e alle più recenti scoperte . . .* 2nd Italian ed., based on the 3rd French ed. Turin, 1840. Vol. 1, 1094 pp., vol. 2, 982 pp.

Balbi, Adrien. *Abrégé de géographie rédigé sur un nouveau plan d'après les derniers traités de paix et les découvertes les plus récentes . . .* 1st ed. Paris, 1833. 1392 pp.

Beatificationis seu Declarationis Martyrii Servi Dei Ioannis Baptistae Mazzucconi sacerdotis Pontificii Instituti pro Missionibus Exteris in odium fidei, uti fertur, anno 1855 interfecti positio super introductione causae et super martyrio ex officio concinnata. Rome, 1969. xci + 677 pp.

Berg, O.F.M., L. van de. *De infidelium polygamorum conversione.* Maastrict, 1951. 67 pp.

Birt, O.S.B., Henry Norbert. *Benedictine Pioneers in Australia.* Vol. 2. London, 1911. 516 pp.

Bollettino della Congregazione della SS. Croce e Passione di N.S.G.C. Vol. 4. Rome, 1923.

Boudou, S. J., Adrien. *Les jésuites à Madagascar au XIXe siècle.* Paris, 1940. Vol. 1, 543 pp., vol. 2, 569 pp.

Boyle, C.M., Patrick. *The Irish College in Paris from 1578 to 1901.* London, 1901. 236 pp.

Brenan, O.S.F., M. J. *An Ecclesiastical History of Ireland from the Introduction of Christianity into That Country to the Year 1829.* Dublin, 1864. 682 pp.

Broderick, S. J., John Francis. 'Paccanarists', in *New Catholic Encyclopedia.* New York, 1967. 10:849f.

Buffet, Léon. *Vie du P. Mermier: fondateur des missionnaires de Saint-François de Sales d'Annecy et des soeurs de la croix.* Paris, 1927. 286 pp.

Bullarium Pontificium S. Congregationis de Propaganda Fide. Rome, 1839–40. Vol. 1, 361 pp., vol. 3, 467 pp.

Burrus, S. J., Ernest J. 'Jesuits and Terra Australis'. *Neue Zeitschrift für Missionswissenschaft*, Beckenried, 1966, 22:89–97.

Causse, O.M.C., Candide. *Evêque d'or, crosse de bois: vie de Monseigneur de Charbonnel, evêque de Toronto.* Gembloux, 1931. 309 pp.

Chanel, Pierre. *Écrits du Père Pierre Chanel, missionnaire mariste à Futuna 1803–1841.* Edited by Claude Rozier, S.M. Paris, 1960. 539 pp.

Colin, Jean-Claude. *A Founder Speaks: Spiritual Talks of Jean-Claude Colin.* Edited by Jean Coste, S.M., translated by Anthony Ward, S.M. Rome, 1975. 602 pp.

Collectanea Sacrae Congregationis de Propaganda Fide seu Decreta instructiones rescripta pro apostolicis missionibus. Vol. 1, 1622–1866. Rome, 1907. 732 pp.

Combaluzier, F. 'Le chanoine Paulmier de Courtonne et ses rêves apostoliques vers les Terres australes (1659–1667)'. *Revue d'histoire des missions*, Paris, 1935, 12:108–45.

Daws, Gavan. *Shoal of Time: A History of the Hawaiian Islands.* New York, 1968. xv + 494 pp.

Dillon, Paul. 'A Sailor in Search of a Star'. *The Word*, Roscommon, April 1970, pp. 11–3.

Feeken, Erwin. 'First Charting of the Northern Shores of Australia'. *Australian Territories*, Canberra, February 1968, pp. 12–8.

Fremantle, C. H. *Diary and Letters of Admiral Sir C. H. Fremantle, G.C.B.; Relating to the Founding of the*

Colony of Western Australia 1829. Edited by Lord Cottesloe. London, 1928, private circulation. 94 pp.

Giblin, O.F.M., Cathaldus. 'Daniel O'Connell and the Irish Franciscans'. In *Franciscan College Annual*. Multyfarnham, June 1950. 144 pp.

González, O.P., José María. *Un misionero diplomático: Vida del padre Victorio Riccio*. Madrid, 1955. 87 pp.

Goyau, Georges. *Les grands desseins missionnaires d'Henri de Solages (1786–1832)*. Paris, 1933. 295 pp.

Grannell, SS.CC., Thomas Francis. 'Vicariate Apostolic of Tahiti'. In *New Catholic Encyclopedia*. New York, 1967. 13:913.

Heimbucher, Max. *Die Orden und Kongregationen der katholischen Kirche*. Vol. 3. 2nd rev. ed. Paderborn, 1908. 635 pp.

'Historic Shipwreck'. *Australian News*, London, 1 July 1971, p. 3.

Hoare, Merval. 'King of Norfolk Island'. *Australian External Territories*, Canberra, February 1969, pp. 27-31.

———. 'The Discovery of Norfolk Island'. *Australian External Territories*, Canberra, May 1970, pp. 8–11.

Hosie, S.M., John. 'The French Mission: An Australian Base for the Marists in the Pacific to 1874'. Master of Arts thesis, Sydney, 1971. 446 pp.

Ius Pontificium de Propaganda Fide. Pars Prima. Vol. 5 (Rome, 1893), vol. 6 (Rome, 1894).

Jaspers, M.S.C., Reiner. *Die Missionarische Erschliessung Ozeaniens: Ein quellengeschichtlicher und missionsgeographischer Versuch zur kirchlichen Gebietsaufteilung in Ozeanien bis 1855*. Münster, 1972 xxiv + 288 pp. and 4 maps.

Jore, Léonce. *L'océan Pacifique au temps de la restauration et de la monarchie de juillet (1815–1848)*. Paris, 1959. Vol. 1, 418 pp., vol. 2, 442 pp.

Keys, Lillian G. *The Life and Times of Bishop Pompallier*. Christchurch, 1957. 415 pp.

Kowalsky, O.M.I., Nicola. *Serie dei cardinali prefetti e dei segretari della Sacra Congregazione 'de Propaganda Fide'*. Rome, 1962. 39 pp.

Laracy, Eugénie, and Laracy, Hugh. *The Italians in New Zealand and Other Studies*. Auckland, 1973. 23 pp.

Laracy, Hugh. *Marists and Melanesians: A History of Catholic Missions in the Solomon Islands*. Canberra, 1976. xi + 211 pp.

Laval, SS.CC., Honoré. *Mémoires pour servir à l'histoire de Mangareva: ère chrétienne 1834–1871*. Edited by C. W. Newbury and P. O'Reilly. Paris, 1968. cxlii + 672 pp.

Lestra, Antoine. *Le père Coudrin: fondateur de la*

congrégation des sacrés-coeurs. Vol. 3. Rome, 1968. 488 pp.

———. *Le père Coudrin: fondateur de picpus*. Vol. 1. Lyon, 1952. 449 pp.

Malte-Brun, Conrad. *Précis de la géographie universelle*. Vol. 4 (Paris, 1813), vol. 6 (5th ed., Paris, 1843).

Metzler, O.M.I., Josef. 'Bemühungen der S.C. 'de Propaganda Fide' um die Wiedervereinigung der Koptischen Kirche mit Rom'. *Euntes Docete*, Rome, 1964, 17:94-108.

———. 'Das Apostolische Vikariat der Kopten unter Massimo Giuaid (1821–1831)'. *Euntes Docete*, Rome, 1961, 14:36–62.

Michelis, Eduard. *Die Völker der Südsee und die Geschichte der protestantischen und katholischen Missionen unter denselben*. Münster, 1847. xviii + 539 pp. The author of the present work has not used this book as a source because it relies heavily on *Annales de la propagation de la foi*, a publication which is unreliable as an historical source for the reason illustrated in chapter 13, note 18.

Moran, Patrick Francis Cardinal. *History of the Catholic Church in Australasia*. Sydney, 1895. xix + 1003 pp.

Moroni, Gaetano. *Dizionario di Erudizione Storio-Ecclesiastica*. Vol. 50. Venice, 1851.

Murtagh, J. G. 'Australia'. In *New Catholic Encyclopedia*. New York, 1967. 1:1083–92.

National Catholic Almanac 1963. Edited by Felician A. Foy, O.F.M. Paterson, 1963. 696 pp.

'Norfolk Island'. *Australian Territories*, Canberra, July–December 1967, pp. 9–13.

Normoyle, M. C. *A Tree Is Planted: The Life and Times of Edmund Rice*. 2nd ed. Rome, 1976, private circulation. xvi + 502 pp.

O'Farrell, Patrick. *The Catholic Church in Australia—A Short History: 1788–1967*. Melbourne, 1968. x + 294 pp.

An Ordinance Rejecting the Catholic Religion. Lahaina, Maui, 1837. 7 pp.

O'Reilly, S. M., Patrick. 'Le chanoine Paulmier de Courtonne et son projet d'évangélisation des terres australes (1663)'. *Revue d'histoire des missions*, Paris, 1932, 9:321–39.

———. *Tahitian Catholic Church: History of the Mission*. Paris, 1969. 31 pp.

O'Reilly, S. M., Patrick and Teissier, Raoul. *Tahitiens: répertoire bio-bibliographique de la Polynésie française*. Paris, 1962. xiv + 355 pp.

Origines maristes (1786–1836). Edited by J. Coste, S.M., and G. Lessard, S.M. Vol. 1, 'Documents contemporains' (Rome, 1960), 964 pp. Vol. 2, 'Donées narratives' (Rome, 1961), 990 pp. Vol. 4, 'Compléments et index' (Rome, 1967), 851 pp. This excellent four-volume documentary work, available for consultation in all Marist houses in the Pacific and in numerous scientific libraries in Australia, New

Zealand, etc., contains critical editions of practically all letters and other documents mentioned in chapters 6 and 7. The dates in the text provide a ready point of reference to *Origines maristes*, which lists all letters and documents in chronological sequence. OM (as this work has been abbreviated) is given as a source in the notes only for those letters which the author did not see in the original.

Otto, S. J., Joseph Albert. *Gründung der Neuen Jesuitenmission durch General Pater Johann Philipp Roothaan.* Freiburg im Breisgau, 1939. 551 pp.

Our News. Bomana, Papua New Guinea, 30 May 1967.

Pacific Islands Yearbook. 9th ed. Sydney, 1963. 496 pp.

Person, Yves. *La Nouvelle Calédonie et l'Europe: de la découverte, 1774 à la fondation de Nouméa 1854.* Paris, 1953. 217 pp.

Prospetto della gerarchia episcopale in ogni rito e i vicariati, delegazioni e prefetture nei luoghi di missione della S. Chiesa cattolica, apostolica Romana in tutto l'orbe al primo gennaio 1850. Rome, 1850. xliii + 140 pp.

Raucaz, L. M. *Vingt-cinq années d'apostolat aux Iles Salomon méridionales (1898-1923).* Paris-Lyon, 1925. 261 pp.

Rigault, Georges. *Histoire générale de l'Institut des frères des écoles chrétiennes.* Vol. 3, *La révolution française.* Paris, 1940. viii + 650 pp.

Roach, S. M., Kevin. 'Venerable John Claude Colin and the Mission in New Zealand: 1838-1848'. Doctoral dissertation, Rome, 1963. 600 pp.

Roussel, René. *Un précurseur: Monseigneur Luquet (1810–1858) des missions étrangères de Paris.* Langres, 1960. 121 pp.

Salvado, O.S.B., Rudesindo. *Memorie storiche dell' Australia particolarmente della missione Benedettina di Nuova Norcia e degli usi e costumi degli Australiani.* Naples, 1852. 371 pp.

Santamaria, O.P., Alberto. 'The Chinese Parian (El Parian de los Sangleyes)'. Pp. 67-118 in *The Chinese in the Philippines 1570–1770*, vol. 1. Edited by Alfonso Felix, Jr. Manila, 1966. viii + 286 pp.

Schmidlin, Joseph. 'Die ersten Madagaskarmissionen im Lichte der Propagandamaterialien'. *Zeitschrift für Missionswissenschaft*, Münster, 1922, 12:193–205.

Schulte, S. A. C., Heinrich. *Gestalt und Geschichte des 'Katholischen Apostolats' Vinzenz Pallottis, Erster Teil: Die Zeit von 1835–1850.* Limburg an der Lahn, 1971. 763 pp.

Shineberg, Dorothy. *They Came for Sandalwood: A Study of the Sandalwood Trade in the South-West Pacific 1830–1865.* Melbourne, 1967. 299 pp.

Smith, Coultman. *Shadow over Tasmania: The Whole Story of the Convicts.* 16th ed. Moonah, Tasmania, 1972. 150 pp.

Société de Marie. *Annales des missions d'Océanie: correspondance des premiers missionnaires.* Vol. 1. Lyon, 1895. 644 pp.

Société française de l'Océanie. *Extrait de l'acte de Société.* N.p., n.d. 32 pp.

Southerwood, W. T. *Planting a Faith: Hobart's Catholic Story in Word and Picture.* Hobart, n.d. 161 pp.

———. *Planting a Faith: Launceston's Catholic Story in Word and Picture.* Hobart, n.d. 101 pp.

Streit, O.M.I., Robert, and Didinger, O.M.I., Johannes. *Bibliotheca Missionum.* Vol. 21. Freiburg, 1955. 796 pp.

Strong, William E. *The Story of the American Board: An Account of the First Hundred Years of the American Board of Commissioners for Foreign Missions.* Boston, 1910. 523 pp.

Thorpe, C. P., Osmund. *First Catholic Mission to the Australian Aborigines 1843–1847.* Sydney, 1950. xv + 271 pp.

Vandermaelen, Philippe. *Atlas universel de géographie physique, politique, statistique et minéralogique sur l'échelle de 1/1641836 ou d'une ligne par 1900 toises. Dressé par Ph. Vandermaelen, membre de la Société de géographie de Paris, d'après les meilleures cartes, observations astronomiques et voyages dans les divers pays de la terre.* Vol. 5, Oceania. Brussels, 1827.

Verguet, C. M. Léopold. *Histoire de la première mission catholique au vicariat de Mélanésie: 1844–1848.* Carcassonne, 1854. 320 pp. and 20 engravings.

Wiltgen, Ralph M. 'Propaganda Is Placed in Charge of the Pontifical Colleges'. In *Sacrae Congregationis de Propaganda Fide Memoria Rerum 1622–1972.* Freiburg, 1971. 1(1) 1622–1700, pp. 483–505.

Yzendoorn, SS.CC., Reginald. *History of the Catholic Mission in the Hawaiian Islands.* Honolulu, 1927. xiv + 254 pp.

Zaide, Gregorio F. *Philippine Political and Cultural History.* Vol. 1, *The Philippines since Pre-Spanish Times.* Rev. ed. Manila, 1957. 407 pp.

Index

Montrouzier, Father Jean-Xavier, 341, 475, 476, 529; at (Rooke) 485-6, (San Cristóbal) 342, 344-5, 450-1, (Woodlark) 478, 484
Monza, 524
Moorea, 154
Moore River, 377
Moravian Church, 362
Moreton Bay Penal Settlement, 198, 360-4 passim, 569 n.11
Morozzo, Giuseppe Cardinal, 6
Morpeth, 390
Morphett Vale, 381
Morris, Bishop William, 190, 197
Mortlock Islands, 127
Moulmain, 273, 275
Mount Barker, 381
Moutiers, 447
Mulgrave Islands, 268, 270, 271, 279, 280
Murphy, Bishop Francis, 351, 355, 356, 362, 379-81, 568 n.17
Murphy, Father Colomban, 90, 92, 139, 151, 554 n.4; and Sandwich Islands, 152, 156, 161, 558 n.7
Murray, Archbishop Daniel, 190, 197
Murray, Sir George, 368
Murray River, 383
Murua, see Woodlark Island
Mussabini, Archbishop Antonio, 306
Mussim Islands, 478, 479

Naha, 163
names, 151, 551 n.5
Nantes, 101, 450
Naples, 370, 392, 529, 531-2
Napoleon Bonaparte, 2, 42, 109
nari (tree), 345
Narrative and Successful Result of a Voyage in the South Seas . . . to Ascertain the Actual Fate of La Pérouse's Expedition, 23
Natal, 538-9
native clergy, see indigenous clergy
Navan, 355
Navigators Archipelago, see Samoa Archipelago
Neminem profecto, 489-90, 570 n.2, 575 n.1; and (Bonamie) 488, (Colin) 423, (Polding) 383, 385, (Pompallier) 408, 571 n.4
Netherlands, 182, 290, 307
New Britain, 118, 127, 301, 308, 334, 454, 481, 482, 486; and Collomb, 456-8 passim, 478-81 passim; diocese, 407-8, 416; prefecture, 228, 232-4 passim, 564 n.9 (ch.17); vicariate, 307-9 passim, 331-2, (of Melanesia) 287, 290, 295, (of New Guinea) 237-8
New Caledonia, 118, 127, 153, 160, 243, 323, 333, 429, 544; in Central Oceania vicariate, 241, 243; diocese, 407, 416, 422; French colony, 290, 320-1, 432, 436-7, 445; missions to (first) 320-1, (second) 511-13, (third) 544-5; and New Britain as prefecture, 228, 232-4 passim, 240, 564 n.9 (ch.17); and New Hebrides as (diocese) 407-8, 409, 423, 425, 433, (vicariate) 403, 409; produce, 433, 437, 572 n.7 (ch.28); protection for, 437, 438, 444, 572

n.33; and Solomon Islands as vicariate, 238, 243, 409; and (Collomb) 450, 456, 458-9, 463-73, (Dillon) 308, (Epalle) 331, 334, 341, (Viard) 395; see also papal colony
New Caledonia, Vicariate Apostolic of, 429, 463, 464, 518; initiated by (Colin) 238, 321, 515, (Douarre) 321, (Pompallier) 323; foundation and extent, 425-7, 429, 430, 432, 433, 440, 511, 512, 536, 572 n.21, 576 n.23; funds, 432, 435, 440; Marists for, 435, 443, 478, 511; attacks, 465-73, 475, 513, 528, (official report) 471, 472, 511, 574 n.2, 574 n.3; abandonment, 468, 470, 472-3, 511, 574 n.12; Colin seeks release from, 513-17; prefect apostolic, 514, 519, 545, 547; see also Douarre, Bishop Guillaume
'New California', 535
New England, 181, 200
New Guinea, 23, 118, 153, 200, 269, 301, 310, 454, 486; diocese, 407-8, 410, (part of) 407, 416; division into vicariates, 307-9 passim, 331-2; and Europeans, 287, 290, 307; and Marists, 219, 261, 286; penal colony, 218, 220; prefect apostolic, 513, 516, 539; starting point, 330-1; vicariate, 237-8; in vicariate of (Melanesia) 287, 290, 295, (Western Oceania) 127; and (Baudichon) 532, (Collomb) 417-18, 456-8 passim, 478-82 passim, (Dillon) 308, (Jackson) 307, (Pompallier) 128, 138, 139, 141, (Riccio) 176-8 passim, (Villien) 482; see also Melanesia, Vicariate Apostolic of
New Hanover, 290, 301, 407-8
New Hebrides, 118, 153, 243, 471; in New Caledonia diocese, 407-9 passim, 416; in vicariate of (Central Oceania) 241, 243, (New Caledonia) 238, 403, 429, 440, 512, 578 n.25, (Western Oceania) 116, 127; and (Dillon) 308, (Douarre) 320-1, (Jackson) 307, (Pompallier) 323; see also New Caledonia, Vicariate Apostolic of
New Holland, 97, 153, 181, 189, 300, 555 n.14; description, 71, 184, 185, 191, 196-201 passim, 355, 356, 552 n.46; norm for ecclesiastical divisions, 349-50; and (Flynn) 186, (Fremantle) 368, (Pastre) 103, 108, (Pompallier) 155, (Poynter) 188-9, (Ullathorne) 190; and (British) 349, (Dutch) 164, (French) 31, (Irish) 31, 182; see also Australia
New Holland, Prefecture Apostolic of the Missions of, 153, 183-4, 186; see also Australia
New Holland, Vicariate Apostolic of, 348-54 passim, 358, 568 n.11 New Holland and Van Diemen's Land, Vicariate Apostolic of, 153, 267, 347, 560 n.24; initiated by Bramston, 191, 194; foundation and extent, 94-5, 190-4 passim, 196, 197, 200-2; becomes ecclesiastical province, 353, 408
New India, 164
New Ireland, 118, 290, 301, 334, 454; in diocese of (New Guinea) 407-8, (San Cristóbal) 407, 416; independent vicariate, 307-9 passim, 331-2; misnomer for New Zealand, 555 n.6, 555 n.10, 555 n.21 (ch.6); in vicariate of (Melanesia) 287, 290, 292, 341, (New Guinea) 237-8, (Western Oceania)

608 INDEX

Trapenard, Father Pierre, 485
Trappists, 186, 220
Trésor des cartes géographiques des principaux estats de l'univers, 169
Trichinopoly, 273, 274
Trinchant, Father Paul, 106, 113, 115
Trincomalee, 369
Trobriand Islands, 118, 127, 454, 479
Tromelin, Admiral, 472
tropical islands, 225, 260-2 *passim; see also* Central Oceania, Vicariate Apostolic of
Tropic of Capricorn: as boundary of (prefecture) 50, 554 n.38, (vicariates) 81, 102, 225, 235, 238, 241
Troy, Archbishop John Thomas, 188
Troyes, 14, 16, 551 n.25
Truk Islands, 61, 118, 127
Tuamotu Archipelago, 46, 86, 214, 493, 537, 552 n.1, 579 n.34 (ch.35); contains Bad Sea and Dangerous Islands, 36, 62, 85
Tubuai Islands, 85-6
Tupinier, Baron, 59
Tupinier Island, 479-80
Turin, 189, 255, 350, 447
Turinaz, Bishop Jean-François-Marcel, 447
Turkey, 142, 306

Ualam (Oulea) Island, 271, 272
Ullathorne, Bishop William Bernard: activity in Europe, 191, 197-205 *passim;* life, 190, 197, 217, 356-7; refuses bishoprics of (Adelaide) 350-6 *passim,* 568 n.9, (Hobart Town) 354, 356, (Perth) 356, 373-4; and (Brady) 201-2, 374, 561 n.36, (Polding) 197, 347, 354
Umboi, *see* Rooke Island
uniformity of practice, 53, 138, 148, 247, 262, 353
United Brethren, 362
United States of America, 151, 514; Bishop of Monterey, 533-4, 579 n.29; and commerce, 31, 200, 214, 268, 271; government, 35, 154, 161, 276; hierarchy, 349, 390, 410-12 *passim,* 417; and (Bruté de Rémur) 189, (FitzRoy) 395, (Harold) 184, (McEncroe) 190, (O'Sullivan) 311
unity, 247, 280, 353; *see also* decrees (on fostering unity)
University School of Mende, 100
Unknown Land, *see* Terra Australis
Upper California, 137, 534, 535; diocese, 532-3; and Sandwich Islands missionaries, 74, 139, 162
Uvea, *see* Wallis

Vaccari, Father Raimondo: birth and death, 379, 568 n.2; criticised by Passionists, 363, 375; and Fransoni, 366; named prefect apostolic, 358-62 *passim,* 379, (discharged) 376, 378, 379; qualities, 358-9, 363; *see also* Aborigines of Australia, Prefecture Apostolic to the
Vaincus tribe, 230
Vaitahu, 97
Valparaíso, 20-1, 31, 61, 137; and French navy, 25, 133, 472; and Marists, 212, 216-17; as Picpus

base, 90, 92-3, 97, 100, 112, 494; and Sisters, 311; and (Baudichon) 531, (Coudrin) 136, (Maigret) 162, 212, 214, (Pompallier) 135-40 *passim,* 209, 229, 263, (Rouchouze) 311, 312
Valsugana, 181
Vancouver Island, 42, 61
Vandermaelen, Philippe, 46, 291, 552 n.47
van Diemen, Governor-General Anthony, 164
Van Diemen's Land, 153, 164, 184, 188, 330, 554 n.9, 560 n.26; and convicts, 197-200 *passim,* 350; *see also* Hobart Town, Diocese of; New Holland and Van Diemen's Land, Vicariate Apostolic of
Van Diemen's Land, Vicariate Apostolic of, 348-53 *passim,* 358; *see also* Hobart Town, Diocese of; New Holland and Van Diemen's Land, Vicariate Apostolic of
Van Everbroeck, Father Cornelius, 142-3
Vanikoro Island, 23
Vava'u, 32, 153, 160, 243, 563 n.19; and Pompallier, 156-8, 224, 233, 245, 250, 262
Verguet, Father C. M. Léopold, 305; voyage to Melanesia, 330, 332-4 *passim,* 336, 341, 342; sketches, 300, 334, 337, 340, 343; at San Cristóbal, 344-5, 451, 453-4; at New Caledonia, 463-5 *passim,* 468, 470, 471, 473; leaves Marists, 455, 457-8, 473
Viard, Bishop Philippe-Joseph: as (archbishop) 415-16, 421, 422, 425, 434, (bishop) 416, 426, (coadjutor) 402-3, 420-1, 425, 430, 439, (coadjutor of Pompallier) 322-3, 326-8 *passim,* 333, 395, 396, 399, 426, (vicar apostolic) 250, 265, 295-6; in charge of (Tonga, Wallis, Futuna) 326, 399, 400, 401, 570 n.15 (ch.25), (Pompallier's vicariate) 441, 443, 497-500 *passim;* Colin's attitude toward, 509, 510, 577 n.42; misnomers for, 327-8, 577 n.39; priests for, 497-502 *passim,* 543, 545, 547; and (Chanel) 231, 233, (Collomb) 455, 457, (Fransoni) 507-8
vicar apostolic, xxi, 103, 246, 258, 272, 348, 411; correspondence with Rome, 249, 254, 255, 402; diocesan bishop, 349, 352-4 *passim,* 568 n.8, 568 n.11; and French government, 312-14 *passim,* 316; and religious communities, 413, 415; rights of, 239, 248; *see also* decrees (on fostering unity)
vicar general, 14, 190, 197, 355; of (Lyon) 104, 117, (Pamiers) 24, 27, 39, 73, (Perth) 381-2, (Rouen) 20, 27, 30, (Sydney) 369, 372, 386, (Western Oceania) 130, 556 n.26
vicariates apostolic, xxi, 255, 322, 421; containing dioceses, 349-50, 386, 388; proposed by (Marists) 235-8, (Pompallier) 262-3
Victoria (Melville Island), 570 n.27
Victoria, *see* Port Victoria, Diocese of
Victoria, state, 383
Victoria Plains, 377
Vienna fund, 199, 201-3 *passim*
Villien, Father Gregoire, 478-82 *passim,* 484-5, 487
Vincennes, Bishop of, 189
Vincentians, 167, 169, 576 n.12
Virgin Islands, 186

Ralph M. Wiltgen is a Divine Word Missionary and Roman Catholic priest from Chicago, with a doctorate in Missiology from the Pontifical Gregorian University in Rome, and since 1960 based in Rome. He has published *The Rhine Flows into the Tiber: A History of Vatican II* (American edition 1967, French 1973, British 1978), *Gold Coast Mission History 1471-1880* in 1956, and *The Religious Life Defined* in 1970.